Exploring
Development
THROUGH
CHILDHOOD

RICHARD FABES
Arizona State University

CAROL LYNN MARTIN
Arizona State University

ALLYN AND BACON

Boston   London   Toronto   Sydney   Tokyo   Singapore

To

OUR PARENTS

Executive Editor: *Carolyn O. Merrill*

Editorial Assistant: *Lara Zeises*

Managing Editor: *Tom Pauken*

Vice President, Marketing: *Joyce Nilsen*

Editorial-Production Administrator: *Susan Brown*

Prepress Buyer: *Linda Cox*

Manufacturing Buyer: *Suzanne Lareau*

Cover Administrator: *Linda Knowles*

Cover Designer: *Susan Paradise*

Text Designer: *The Davis Group, Inc.*

Editorial-Production Services: *Lifland et al., Bookmakers*

Photo Researcher: *Helane Prottas*

Illustrations: *Jay Alexander, Susan Avishai, and LMY Studio, Inc.*

Composition: *Omegatype Typography, Inc.*

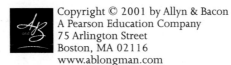Copyright © 2001 by Allyn & Bacon
A Pearson Education Company
75 Arlington Street
Boston, MA 02116
www.ablongman.com

Between the time Website information is gathered and then published, it is not unusual for some sites to have closed. Also, the transcription of URLs can result in unintended typographical errors. The publisher would appreciate notification where these errors occur so that they may be corrected in subsequent editions.

ISBN: 0-205-34212-4

Printed in the United States of America
10 9 8 7 6 5 4 3 2 1   WEB 05 04 03 02 01

Brief CONTENTS

CONTENTS

PART 2   Prenatal & Neonatal DEVELOPMENT   62

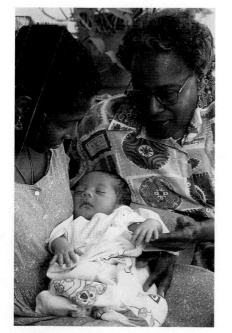

4. BIRTH AND NEONATAL DEVELOPMENT   98

PART 3 Infant&Toddler DEVELOPMENT 138

8. SOCIAL AND EMOTIONAL DEVELOPMENT IN EARLY CHILDHOOD

10. SOCIAL AND EMOTIONAL DEVELOPMENT IN LATE CHILDHOOD   342

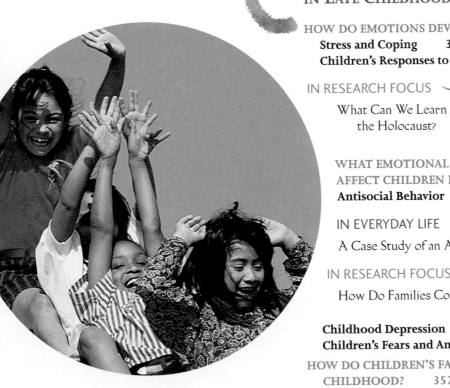

To the STUDENT

The goal of this book is to help you become familiar with the complexities and mysteries of child development from conception through late childhood. In addition to describing developmental changes, we emphasize the processes that underlie them. We consider the dynamic and diverse factors that influence infants and children and how they come to be the way they are.

The dynamics of development are reflected in the words and behaviors of infants, children, and the significant adults in their lives. By using personal stories, an informal style, and a warm tone, we tried to make the material engaging and meaningful. You may even find that the stories remind you of yourself, your siblings and friends, your children, or children you know. Children's words and actions illustrate the themes of the text and provide vivid and memorable evidence of developmental processes.

THEMES OF THIS TEXTBOOK

Every aspect of development, as well as every change in behavior and thinking, can be understood only within the context in which it is embedded. These contexts are complex, dynamic, and diverse. We place particular emphasis on *human relationships* as a context for development, because it is through relationships with others that individuals derive meaning and purpose from their lives.

DEVELOPMENT IN THE CONTEXT OF HUMAN RELATIONSHIPS
Individual development is affected by relationships, and these relationships, in turn, are affected by development. The story of each child's development is partially written by the other people in his or her life. In this way, development and relationships are mutually dependent, and helping you to understand the significance of this mutual interdependence is the principal goal of this textbook. Understanding the central role of relationships in development may lead you to new insights into your own childhood as well as the lives of infants or children who may be in your care.

DEVELOPMENT AND DIVERSITY
Children come in all shapes, sizes, and colors and vary in their abilities, personalities, and traits. They come from different cultures, have different histories and family backgrounds, and hold different values, expectations, and preferences. Identifying and understanding the major dimensions of *diversity* in children is a way to broaden and enrich the study of development.

One of the major themes of this book is that development stems from the interplay among the many qualities that children bring to their environments and the variety of environments in which they live their lives. The dynamic interplay

In the Research Focus

Can a Breathing Bear Help Preterm Infants?

Premature infants have difficulty with many tasks that full-term babies do not; they have difficulty breathing, sucking, and maintaining normal body temperature. Some interventions with premature babies have been designed to mimic life in the womb, which is assumed to be ideal for healthy development. One clever strategy is to use breathing bears—teddy bears that make audible breathing sounds. If premature infants have a breathing partner, as they would have if they had stayed longer in the womb, do they develop more quickly? Thoman and colleagues (1995) tested this idea with infants who were 35 gestational weeks old. Half these premature infants were given breathing bears, and the other half were not. After two weeks, the premature infants with the breathing bears were awake less often, slept quietly more often, and cried less than the infants in the control group. These findings suggest that a simple intervention—the introduction of an audible breathing partner—can help premature infants develop (Thoman, Hammond, Affleck, & Desilva, 1995).

Thinking It Through:
1. Do you think a breathing bear would benefit full-term babies as well? Why or why not?
2. In what other ways could a preterm baby's environment be made more like the prenatal environment?

NEONATAL INTENSIVE CARE
Like Donald, whose case was highlighted at the beginning of this section, most preterm newborns with developmental problems are put in a neonatal intensive care unit. The first step is to stabilize the newborn's body temperature and place her or him in an incubator to prevent loss of warmth. If respiratory problems are evident, the new-

Notice that this infant is in an incubator, which helps keep him warm. How has technology improved the survival chances of newborns needing intensive care? What ethical issues does this technology raise?

128

TO THE STUDENT XIX

among diverse and changing individual and environmental characteristics means that children's developmental outcomes (such as their physical and psychological health) are influenced by many factors. Development is complex, and no single factor's presence or absence will always determine a specific course of development.

Our focus on diversity is evident in our emphasis on understanding development in children with various biological, familial, social, and cultural backgrounds—children who differ, for example, in the dimensions of gender, race, ethnicity, and socioeconomic class. The focus on diversity also is seen in the variety of topics and issues covered in this textbook. A diversity logo in the text margin identifies a discussion where the theme of diversity is interwoven into the text narrative.

SCIENTIFIC INQUIRY

The main source of information for this book is the body of research on child development. Knowing how developmental scientists conduct research is essential for understanding infants, children, and the environments and people with whom they interact. This *research-based* text introduces you to the scientific method, which involves using objective, replicable procedures to reduce subjective and biased assumptions. The scientific method provides a framework through which issues concerning development can be tested and verified, sometimes revealing evidence that is contrary to popular belief.

In this book, you will be encouraged to think critically so that you can become a better consumer of scientific information. *Critical thinking* involves the ability to judge the validity, authenticity, accuracy, and value of information.

Identifying biases, distinguishing statements of fact from value judgments, and recognizing inconsistencies are hallmarks of critical thinking. Critical thinking mandates a certain frame of mind and set of attitudes, as well as a set of skills. This text aims to promote critical thinking by

▶ fostering a willingness to question assertions and claims about development

▶ encouraging consideration of a variety of viewpoints in thinking about child development

▶ pointing out meaningful applications of scientific knowledge to everyday life

▶ providing structured opportunities to respond to critical thinking questions within the text

ORGANIZATION OF THE TEXTBOOK

This textbook is divided into five parts, based on the sequence of developmental changes from conception through late childhood.

THE PARTS

Part 1 introduces the key themes and terminology in the study of child development, including the conceptual, historical, and scientific foundations of the field. A basic orientation to the major issues concerning development, research methods in the study of development, and general theories of development is presented. Part 1 also outlines the *transactional approach* to understanding human development, which serves as the conceptual foundation for this book. According to this approach, the process of human development is shaped by a continuous interplay between individuals and their ever-changing environments. Woven into the transactional approach are the important influences of human relationships. ▾

Part 2 discusses the origins of development, including heredity and genetics; how life begins; the course of prenatal development; and childbirth. Part 3 focuses on the astonishing changes and accomplishments of infants and toddlers. Special attention is given to understanding these accomplishments as they occur within the context of early relationships, especially caregiving relationships.

Part 4 focuses on early childhood and includes perspectives on physical, cognitive, social, and emotional development during the preschool years. Part 5 covers the period of childhood from the time children enter school until they begin puberty. The chapters in Parts 4 and 5 highlight the abilities that expand and develop during childhood and their links to the broadening scope of relationships found in peer and school environments.

INTEGRATION AND APPLICATION

Each of the five parts weaves the themes of the book into a visual and personal synthesis of developmental trends that illustrates the continuity of development. A part begins with a brief personal story, which introduces the main issues and orients readers to the topics taken up in the accompanying chapters. The part opener includes a list of specific learning objectives. Each part ends with "Grasping the Whole," which synthesizes and integrates the information through a "Benchmarks" chart and other learning aids. Child development involves complex changes in related processes and behaviors; it is not a product of isolated transformations. Physical, cognitive, social, and emotional development are intimately interrelated. "Grasping the Whole" brings together the different aspects of development presented in separate chapters and helps to personalize them. In each "Grasping the Whole," a Status Report figure identifies critical issues and presents statistics regarding the current status of the age group discussed in that part.

"Grasping the Whole" ends with suggestions for obtaining more information about the issues discussed in the chapters. Included are suggested readings and addresses of Websites that contain valuable information for students of development.

CHAPTER ORGANIZATION

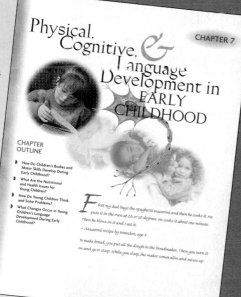

Each chapter starts with an introductory vignette and chapter outline. Main chapter headings are framed as key questions, which are then answered in the subsections that follow.

Important terms and concepts are boldfaced in the narrative where they appear and then are defined in the margin. These key terms are also listed at the end of the chapter with page references and included in an end-of-book Glossary. Figures, tables, and photos are designed to increase comprehension. End-of-chapter summary points provide meaningful ways to analyze and synthesize the information presented in the chapter.

To enhance your appreciation of how the science of child development relates to everyday life, we present many examples of practical applications of the information as it is discussed. Chapter closing activities provide meaningful opportunities for relating to chapter content. These applications and activities are designed to make the material more personally and professionally relevant.

FEATURES

Along with the pedagogical elements embedded in the chapter, each chapter includes three kinds of text features that support the themes of the book.

▶ IN EVERYDAY LIFE suggests ways of applying research findings on development to decision making and problem solving in real-life contexts.

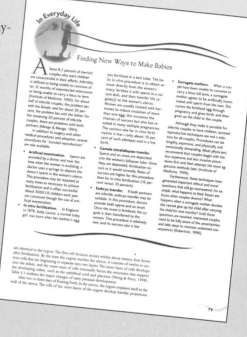

▶ IN RESEARCH FOCUS presents findings from current scientific research. The features highlight how scientists tackle issues relating to infants and children. The research is presented in an engaging and informative style and followed by "Thinking It Through" questions that call for critical thinking.

▶ AT ISSUE focuses on contemporary social and research debates concerning child development. The issues represent critical points of controversy in the field. "Thinking It Through" questions encourage you to analyze and express opinions on these issues. By answering these questions, you will gain a better understanding of the issues and develop the skills needed to evaluate research, policy, and media issues related to child development.

Supplements for STUDENTS

The Study Guide, written by Denise Bodman, Richard Fabes, and Carol Lynn Martin, all of Arizona State University, contains a mix of activities, including writing exercises, fill-in-the-blank quizzes, and matching activities, designed to take you from recitation to understanding, application, and synthesis of the material. Chapters contain learning objectives, "1 Minute Quiz" boxes, "Memory Jog" hints, a "Sage Advice" box, a crossword puzzle, and a "Study Questions" section consisting of multiple-choice and true/false questions.

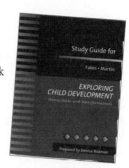

Practice Tests, written by Richard Fabes and Carol Lynn Martin, are available for you to utilize while studying for tests. Each chapter contains twenty test questions with answers. A few actual test questions from the Test Bank are included to help you prepare to take the real exam.

Companion Website at

http://www.abacon.com/fabes

offers a variety of exercises to enhance your total learning experience. The online study guide includes practice tests, learning objectives, chapter summaries, and links to relevant Internet sites on infant, child, and adolescent development.

To the
INSTRUCTOR

EXPLORING DEVELOPMENT THROUGH CHILDHOOD uses a transactional approach to explore development from conception through late childhood. The conceptual foundation of the text is that development is shaped by the continuous interplay between individuals and their ever-changing environments. Infants and children are influenced by the people with whom they interact and by their environment. Also, they influence their own development: their characteristics and actions cause others to react in certain ways, which then influence their development. This text focuses on the influences these intertwined interactions have on the physical, cognitive, social, and emotional development of infants and children. Diversity of culture and social status are emphasized to reflect current demographic trends.

Although the text is research-based and draws its information from child development research, it is written on a personal level to be accessible to students. Students are introduced to the scientific method, and their thinking skills may be enhanced through the critical thinking that is modeled within the text and through the use of probing and analytical questions throughout the text.

The text is divided into five parts, each with a part opener and closer designed to provide unity between the chapters. Each part closer contains a section entitled "Grasping the Whole," which emphasizes how all of the aspects of development are interrelated.

Part 1 introduces the transactional approach to development. Part 2 discusses the origins of development, including heredity and genetics; how life begins; prenatal development; and childbirth. Part 3 focuses on the changes that occur during infancy and toddlerhood. Parts 4–5 cover the physical, cognitive, social, and emotional development that occurs during childhood.

Supplements for INSTRUCTORS

Supplemental material designed to enhance classroom lectures and discussions accompanies *Exploring Development Through Childhood*. The ancillary material has been created to offer students and instructors information based on the transactional approach to child development.

The Instructor's Manual, written by Carol Lynn Martin, Richard Fabes, and Denise Bodman, all of Arizona State University, is an important resource for instructors. For each chapter, it contains a detailed chapter outline; learning objectives; interesting lecture topics; clearly written class activities; suggested videos, readings, and Websites; and supplemental overheads. The Instructor's Manual also contains a "Careers in Child Development" section so that you can share with your students the types of job opportunities and careers that are available in the field.

The Test Bank, written by Richard Fabes and Carol Lynn Martin, contains "Tips on Testing and Grading" to facilitate the testing and grading process. For each chapter, there are multiple-choice questions with chapter page references. The range of difficulty (easy, medium, and difficult) is indicated for each multiple-choice question, as well as whether the question is factual, conceptual, or applied. The Test Bank also includes true/false questions, fill-in questions, and essay questions.

Transparencies have been designed to enhance your classroom presentations. The transparency package contains seventy color acetate transparencies drawn from the text and other exciting sources.

The PowerPoint™ Presentation was developed by Gary Levy of the University of Wyoming–Laramie. The comprehensive lecture outline provided by the PowerPoint™ Presentation can be displayed to the entire class using a computer and an overhead projector with an LCD panel, can be printed and made into overhead transparencies, or can be printed and distributed individually to students.

Companion Website at

http://www.abacon.com/fabes

offers a variety of exercises to enhance both your teaching experience and the students' learning experience. The online study guide includes practice tests, learning objectives, chapter summaries, and links to relevant Internet sites on infant and child development.

The Allyn and Bacon Interactive Video and Video User's Guide with on-screen critical thinking questions, illustrates real-life applications of the textbook topics and provides a springboard from which to start classroom discussions. Allyn and Bacon also makes available to instructors an extensive videotape library.

Acknowledgments

For over three years, this book consumed much of our time and energy. This type of project requires the contributions and efforts of many individuals. First, we thank our families—particularly our parents—for providing us with prototypes of nurturance, love, strength, and support. This book is dedicated to them, with our love and thanks. We especially acknowledge Carol's mother, Carolyn Ivey Martin, who did not survive her battle with cancer to see the final product. We miss her, but part of her is contained in the pages and words of this book.

We owe special thanks to Carolyn Merrill, Acquisitions Editor, whose competence in monitoring the progress of this book was exceptional and encouraging. We also thank Mary Ellen Lepionka, Developmental Editor, who helped mold, rearrange, and guide the form and structure of the book. Without their help, the book would not be what it is. Thanks also to Jodi Devine for her help with the supplemental materials and to all the members of the production team (listed on the copyright page) who did such a fine job editing and designing the book. We also are grateful to other past and present Allyn & Bacon team members—Laura Pearson and Susan Badger, for talking us into this project; Sean Wakely, for his keen wisdom and advice on various aspects of the book; and Joyce Nilsen, for her tremendous assistance in marketing this text.

Many people helped us develop the content and materials for the book. Denise Bodman not only was a co-author on some of the supplemental materials but also provided us with early feedback and enthusiasm, as did Barb and Bob Weigand. Stacie Leonard and Kristina Kupanoff worked hard on the supplemental materials and gave us encouragement. We also wish to thank our colleagues in the Department of Family and Human Development at Arizona State University for providing us with a supportive and stimulating environment in which to work.

We also have benefited greatly from the ideas, insights, and issues brought up by the many people who reviewed our text while it was in the developmental stage. We would like to thank the following individuals for their feedback:

Sharon Antonelli, *San Jose City College*
Harry Avis, *Sierra Community College*
Phoebe Baker, *Tulsa Community College*
Daniel Bellack, *Trident Technical College*
Michael Bergmire, *Jefferson College*
Linda Dersheid, *Northern Illinois University*
Martha M. Ellis, *Collin County Community College*
Linda Estes, *St. Charles Community College*
Linda E. Flickinger, *St. Clair County Community College*
Tom Frangicetto, *Northampton Community College*
Janet Fuller, *Mansfield University*
Thomas Gerry, *Columbia Greene Community College*
Debra L. Hollister, *Valencia Community College*
Kevin Keating, *Broward Community College*

John S. Klein, *Castelton State College*
Kevin MacDonald, *California State University—Long Beach*
Barbara Matthews, *Palm Beach Community College*
Mary Ann McLaughlin, *Clarion University of Pennsylvania*
Shana Pack, *Kentucky Wesleyan College*
Rob Palkovitz, *University of Delaware*
Maribeth Palmer-King, *Broome Community College*
Richard Passman, *University of Wisconsin—Milwaukee*
Peggy Perkins, *University of Nevada, Las Vegas*
Randall J. Russac, *University of North Florida*
Marcia Rysztak, *Lansing Community College*
Michael F. Shaughnessy, *Eastern New Mexico University*
Patricia D. Stanley, *Louisiana State University—Shreveport*
Susan Troy, *Northeast Iowa Community College*
James Turcott, *Kalamazoo Valley Community College*
Patty Wilhite, *Northeast Louisiana University*
Peggy Wroten, *Northeast Mississippi Community College*

A final note of thanks is expressed from each of us to the other—without the love, patience, and companionship we get from each other, taking on this kind of project would have been almost unthinkable. Without each other, the job would have been much lonelier—and much less fun!

About the
AUTHORS

Richard A. Fabes, Ph.D., is professor of child development at Arizona State University, where he has been for more than 15 years. He is the Chair of the Department of Family and Human Development and is a member of the Society for Research in Child Development, National Council on Family Relations, American Psychological Association, and American Psychological Society. Fabes is or has been a member of the editorial boards of several widely known scientific journals, including *Developmental Psychology* and *Psychological Bulletin*. He has written over 100 articles, book chapters, and edited books, including a co-authored chapter in the new edition of the *Handbook of Child Psychology*. Most of these publications are in the areas of socio-emotional development of young children. He is married to Carol Martin, and away from work he enjoys tennis, traveling, and music.

Carol Lynn Martin, Ph.D., is professor of child development at Arizona State University, where she has been for more than 10 years. She is a member of the Society for Research in Child Development, National Council on Family Relations, and American Psychological Society and a fellow of the American Psychological Association. Martin is or has been a member of the editorial boards of several widely known scientific journals, including *Developmental Psychology* and *Child Development*. She has written over 50 articles and book chapters, including a co-authored chapter in the new edition of the *Handbook of Child Psychology*. Most of these publications are in the areas of gender-role development and the cognitive processes underlying it. She is married to Richard Fabes, whom she met at a professional conference when they were at separate universities, and away from work she enjoys tennis, traveling, reading, and swimming.

Exploring Development THROUGH CHILDHOOD

Introduction to Child DEVELOPMENT

My father arrived in America as an infant cradled in his mother's arms aboard a steamship packed with Italian peasants. . . . My father's childhood was shaped both by the travails of the Great Depression and by the traditional closeness of the family. Although the children spoke English with their friends at school, Italian was always spoken at home. . . . My childhood idols were cowboys. . . . But to visit my grandparents, who lived a few blocks away, was to enter an Italian village. . . . My grandmothers, who never learned much English, would cook up the best spaghetti, and my grandfather would ask me and my cousins to bring him a pitcher filled with homemade wine from wooden barrels in the basement. . . . Whatever his shortcomings, the greatest gift my grandfather gave his children was the encouragement to excel in school and achieve the education that he was denied in the mountains of Italy. A skilled craftsman who knew only sacrifice and hardship, he instilled in his sons a fierce pride in their work. Years later, my father applied these values when he became part of a history-making team . . . who helped to send the first astronauts to the moon.

—AL SANTOLI (1988, pp. 294–295)

The story of how children grow and
develop from conception through adolescence is as riveting and exciting as any
story ever told. How does life begin?
How do growth and change occur? What
factors determine who and what children
are and what they become? For example,
what factors influenced Al Santoli's development in the opening story? These questions
are central to the quest to understand child
development. Ultimately, they are central to
the quest to understand ourselves.

One of the most fascinating aspects
of children's development is that it occurs so
quickly. Relatives and friends who do not see a
child for a few months often remark on how different the child looks and acts when they see him or
her again. Parents marvel at the changes that take place
in their own child just from day to day. This book looks at
the nature of these changes, how they occur, and how families,
teachers, and other significant people respond to these changes.

Relationships are integral to development—they give context, sup-
port, meaning, and value to children's lives (and to the lives of those who work with and rear them). As
described in the opening story, families represent the central relationships in most children's lives. Additionally, children and families are influenced by the larger social and cultural environments in which
they find themselves. In his story, Al Santoli acknowledges the two cultures that shaped his life: the culture of his elders, which reflected their Italian heritage, and that of his present, which reflects US values
and customs. Al's story reveals how adaptive children are and how significant relationships help create an
environment in which they can thrive and make important contributions to society. Of course, not all
children thrive or make such contributions, and the study of development also must reflect their stories.

To grasp the whole story of development, it is important to understand the basic principles and
methods of the study of how children grow and change.

IN PART 1, YOU WILL LEARN ABOUT

- how child development is defined and the guiding
  principles that characterize the study of children and
  their development
- the issues central to an understanding of how
  development proceeds
- the historical roots of the study of child development
  and contemporary changes that influence that study
- the conceptual basis of this text and the complexity
  of the characteristics children and their families bring

- to the diversity of contexts in which they find
  themselves
- the difference between theories and facts and the
  significant issues underlying theories of child
  development
- the major theories of child development
- the scientific methods used to study children and their
  development

CHAPTER 1

Introduction to the Study of CHILDREN'S DEVELOPMENT

A child, about eleven or twelve years of age, who had been seen some time before in the woods of Caune, in France, looking after acorns and roots, upon which he subsisted, was met in the same place, towards the close of the year 1798, by three sportsmen, who seized upon him at the instant he was climbing a tree to evade their pursuit.... The most brilliant but unreasonable expectations were formed by the people of Paris respecting the Savage of Aveyron ... many persons ... thought that the education of this individual would be the business of only a few months, and that they should very soon hear him make the most striking observations concerning his past manner of life. Instead of this, what did they see?—a disgusting, slovenly boy, affected with spasmodic, and frequently convulsive motions, continually balancing himself like some of the animals in the menagerie, biting and scratching those who contradicted him, expressing no kind of affection for those who attended upon him; and, in short, indifferent to every body, and paying no regard to any thing.

—Jean Itard (1801, pp. 95–96); photo from the 1970 movie "L'Enfant Sauvage"

Jean Itard's fascinating account of the history of the Wild Boy of Aveyron, a boy who was abandoned at a young age and spent most of his early life in the wild without human contact, highlights some critical questions in the study of children and how they develop. What effects do people's environments have on them? How important are early experiences in determining children's behavior? Can children's development and behavior be changed?

WHAT IS CHILD DEVELOPMENT?

Child development involves changes in physical, social, emotional, and intellectual functioning over time, from conception through adolescence. Changes include alterations in size, shape, and function, and these alterations can be either progressive or regressive (Magnusson, 1995). Time and change work in concert to shape who we are.

In this book, child development is presented in terms of functionally defined age-related stages: prenatal, infancy and toddlerhood, early and late childhood, and early and late adolescence. These stages reflect a contemporary view of development and are helpful in conceptualizing the complex interdependent changes that take place across childhood.

In each stage of development, **developmental domains** provide a basis for focusing on specific areas of development. **Physical development** involves growth and change in a person's body and body functions. Included in this developmental domain is the study of physiological and motor development, as well as the impacts of illness, nutrition, and health. **Cognitive development** involves mental processes used to process information, become aware, solve problems, and gain knowledge. This developmental domain encompasses the study of brain functioning, perception, memory, learning, thinking, and language. **Social-emotional development** involves processes related to one's interactions with others. Included in this domain is the study of relationships, emotions, personality, and moral development. Each domain is important at all stages of development; this book examines each stage in terms of these three broad developmental domains and the interrelationships among them. For example, the Wild Boy of Aveyron's lack of human contact not only affected his ability to form social relationships but also hindered his intellectual and language development (Itard, 1801). Thus, development is multifaceted and complex, with domains and processes operating simultaneously.

child development changes in physical, social, emotional, and intellectual functioning over time, from conception through adolescence

developmental domains the three categories established to provide a basis for focusing on the specific areas of physical, cognitive, and social-emotional development

physical development involves growth and change in a person's body and bodily functions

cognitive development involves development of mental processes used to process information, become aware, solve problems, and gain knowledge

social-emotional development involves development of processes related to one's interactions with others

WHAT ARE SOME CRITICAL ISSUES IN THE STUDY OF CHILD DEVELOPMENT?

The study of child development is filled with issues that are central to a complete understanding of how children change and become who they are. Scientists agree on the need to address these critical issues but disagree about the answers to the questions they raise. These issues also capture the attention of the general public and media. For example, in a series of tragic events that occurred between December 1997 and April 1999, young students in Kentucky, Arkansas, Oregon, and Colorado opened fire on classmates. In the worst of these cases—the tragedy in Littleton, Colorado in the spring of 1999—thirteen people were killed, booby traps and bombs were planted, and the teens took their own lives. Immediately, local and national media gathered the experts to discuss the events. Laypeople also tried to make sense of the tragedy. The questions were the same as they had been before: "How could this happen?" "What caused these kids to do these terrible deeds?" "Was it something in their upbringing or something within them?" The answers to these questions are elusive, but to begin to answer them we must understand children and adolescents and the influences that affect their development.

INFLUENCES ON CHILD DEVELOPMENT

Developmental changes are brought about by a variety of different mechanisms. Some changes occur largely as a result of the unfolding of one's genetic code. These changes are referred to as **maturation,** and they involve a series of preprogrammed transformations in the form, structure, or function of an individual. One vivid example of maturation is the physical changes associated with puberty; these changes result from genetically inherited instructions that guide development of the adolescent's nervous system. Associated with maturational changes are changes in other domains of development (such as social and intellectual changes) and in other aspects of life such as diet, exercise, or stress.

Environmental factors also influence human development (Harris, 1995). Because environmental stimuli bombard children every moment of every day, their potential for influencing development is great. The influence of the environment begins very early: some aspects of the environment to which a pregnant woman is exposed (such as toxins or radiation) can affect her unborn child and influence the child's development. The effects of these early environmental exposures can be devastating and permanent.

The environment also influences behavior through **learning,** which occurs as the result of observation, experience, instruction, or practice. Learning affects a wide range of activities, behaviors, and attitudes—sports, attitudes toward people of different races, achievement in school, and aggressiveness, to name only a few. Learning also influences the process by which children become members of a social group, a family, a community, a tribe, or a team. The process by which children learn social roles and become members of groups is referred to as **socialization.** By teaching them the values, beliefs, customs, and expectations of their society, socialization helps most children to get along cooperatively in the social and cultural contexts in which they find themselves.

Some developmental changes are relatively permanent, such as the development of the skeletal system, whereas other changes may be more fleeting, such as the use of a particular cognitive strategy to add numbers. Many people make the mistake of assuming that changes caused by biological agents (such as drugs or hormones) are irreversible, whereas those caused by social agents (such as family interactions or schooling) can be modified. However, some changes brought about by biological agents can be reversed. For example, the very serious brain damage caused by the genetic disease phenylketonuria (PKU) can be prevented by altering the child's diet. On the other hand, a child may never overcome the intellectual deficits caused by parents who are too de-

maturation changes brought about largely as a result of the unfolding of one's genetic code

learning changes that occur as the result of observation, experience, instruction, or practice

socialization the process by which children learn social roles and become members of groups

TABLE 1.1
Thinking About Developmental Change

LOCUS OF CHANGE	CAUSE OF CHANGE	EXAMPLES OF CHANGE
A. Change occurs within the individual	1. Individual characteristics	Brain development Puberty
	2. Environmental factors	Prenatal exposure to X rays causes physical deformities Exposure to tennis instructor improves tennis skills
B. Change occurs outside the individual	1. Individual characteristics	Parents express more emotion when infant begins to walk Adolescent's relationship with parents changes because of the onset of puberty
	2. Environmental factors	Child's relationship with parents changes because of divorce Child becomes withdrawn because of peer rejection

pressed to interact with her or him. Table 1.1 lists some helpful ways to think about developmental change.

The extent to which biological/genetic and environmental factors influence development has been, and continues to be, hotly debated in the field of child development. This controversy is often referred to as the **nature versus nurture debate.** The nature side of the debate emphasizes the role of biological/genetic factors, whereas the nurture side emphasizes the role of the environment.

The Wild Boy of Aveyron: A Case for Nurture?

One way to examine the effects of biology and the environment on development is to study children who are deprived of human contact. Do these children develop like children who have contact with others? If so, then genetic inheritance is the major factor in their development and the role of the social environment in producing normal behavior is small. Or, does their behavior become more human after contact with other humans? Of course, conducting such an experiment by design is out of the question. But, as you learned in the chapter opening, there are rare instances in which children are abandoned early in development and left to survive on their own.

The Wild Boy of Aveyron stands out as one of the most famous and well-documented cases of a child abandoned in the wild. After the Wild Boy was captured by hunters, he was placed in a hospital in Aveyron (in the countryside outside Paris), where he was diagnosed as a "congenital idiot." At the time of his capture, the boy was about 12 years old and probably had been living alone in the wild since the age of 3 or 4.

Initial descriptions of the boy's behavior aroused much curiosity: he was described as a savage, subject to fits of anger, nervous spasms, and convulsions. He slept according to the sun; was restless, shy, and wild; sought escape at every opportunity; did not talk but growled and grunted; bit and scratched; and showed little affection. He disliked sleeping in a bed; was not bothered by cold temperatures or foul smells; ate berries, roots, and raw chestnuts; and disliked sweets. In short, the Wild Boy, who came to be known as Victor, lacked all elements of "civilized" human behavior (Malson, 1972).

Eventually Victor was brought under the care of Jean Itard, a French physician. Itard argued that Victor's retardation was the result of lack of experience and contact with humans. He believed that if Victor was given proper remedial experience he would become

nature versus nurture debate controversy over the extent to which biological/genetic and environmental factors influence development normal and civilized. Itard set out to provide educational experiences for Victor and show that the environment is the major influence on development.

Under Itard's care, Victor's behavior did change. He lost some of his wildness and made important intellectual strides. He learned to dress himself, to use table utensils to eat, and to express basic emotions. Although he never learned to speak, he learned to identify various letters. Interestingly, he learned to express simple wants and needs through writing. By the end of five years with Itard, however, Victor's behavior was by no means "normal." Compared to children his own age, Victor was still severely intellectually and socially retarded. Itard stopped the experiment because he felt that not enough progress had been made (Itard, 1801, 1806). Victor lived out his life with the woman who had been caring for him at the hospital, and he died in 1828.

Scientifically, there is little we can conclude about Itard's natural experiment. Certainly, Victor's condition improved, but the best we can say is that the results are inconclusive. We do not know enough about Victor prior to the time he was captured to answer the nature versus nurture question: perhaps Victor had some biological condition that impaired his ability to learn and become socialized. His tendency toward "fits of convulsions and spasms" may have been the reason he was abandoned in the first place (Frith, 1989).

Medical Wonders: A Case for Nature?

Itard tried to use the unusual case of Victor to study the extent to which environmental influences contribute to development. Other cases of unusual circumstances have been used to explore the degree to which biological processes contribute to development. Such is the case of Brandi Bender, who, when she was 6 years old, had the entire right side of her cortex (the outer layer of the brain) removed because of severe epileptic seizures. Because the right side of the cortex controls the muscles on the left side of the body, she lost motor control over half of her body. After seven years of intensive therapy in motor skills, math, and music, however, Brandi became talented in skills that ordinarily are associated with the right cortex of the brain. Thus, Brandi's brain was plastic enough to compensate for the loss of half of her cortex. Brandi's brain rearranged many of its connections to allow her to be skilled in areas normally controlled by the right brain. Unfortunately, not all areas regained function—she still cannot use her left arm (Nash, 1997).

Cases like Brandi's tell us that if there is a way to compensate for severe damage, the brain will find it and attempt to restore things to normal. But, like the case of Victor, Brandi's case provides only limited help in answering the nature versus nurture question. Brandi's recovery proves that biology and physiology are not the sole or dominant influences on early development. Without such environmental factors as the experiences provided by her intense therapy (ranging from leg lifts to musical drills), Brandi would never have recovered to the extent that she did. The environmental experiences she had may have determined how her brain rewired itself (Jacobs, 1997).

TEASING OUT THE ROLES OF NATURE AND NURTURE

Modern child development researchers use sophisticated techniques and strategies, such as adoption and twin studies, to address questions of nature and nurture. Additionally, the essence of the nature versus nurture debate has changed somewhat: now the debate is not over whether nature or nurture has an influence—we know that both do—but over how nature and nurture work together to influence development (Gottlieb, 1997; Rutter et al., 1997).

Determining the genetic and environmental bases for characteristics and behaviors is challenging, particularly for complex human characteristics such as intelligence, mental illness, or **personality** (a person's unique behavioral, motivational, and mental styles of responding). Much of our knowledge about the genetic transmission of physical characteristics has been acquired by studying insects and animals, but they provide poor

personality a person's unique behavioral, motivational, and mental styles of responding

What Conclusions Can We Draw from Stories About Wild Children?

The Wild Boy of Aveyron is only one of about thirty documented cases of a child growing up in the wild. One of the oldest cases is the wolf-child of Hesse, who was found in 1344 running wild in the woods. According to the story, wolves raised and protected him, and after four years in the wild he showed signs of a sudden human awakening (Malson, 1972). Another account exists of an abandoned boy named Peter of Hamburg (1724). On capture he refused the food that was offered, preferring instead to eat roots and bark. He hated captivity and escaped many times but gradually came to accept clothing and appreciate music. Although Peter never learned to talk, he did learn to imitate the gestures of others.

One of the most striking accounts (Squires, 1927) tells of the discovery in India of a lair hiding three adult wolves, two cubs, and two young children. The children had tangled hair and walked on all fours like the wolves they lived with. Their tongues hung out, and they panted and frequently bared their teeth. Amala—1 ½ years old—and Kamala— 8½ years old—spent their days in cap-tivity avoiding sunlight, groaning, howl-ing, and trying to escape. They lapped up liquids and ate food in a crouching position. When anyone approached, they arched their backs and shook their heads to show wariness.

Amala lived in captivity for only a year, but Kamala survived for eight years. During that time, she learned to use her hands to feed herself, walk up-right, drink from a cup, nod her head to say "yes," and understand simple verbal instructions. By the end of her life, Ka-mala had acquired the use of about fifty words and could carry on a rudimentary conversation.

What can we make of these stories of wild children? The evidence must be looked at carefully because hoaxes, fabri-cations, and exaggerations in these re-ports are common (Malson, 1972). Some stories, like that of the wild girl of Sogny (1731) who was reportedly visited by the Queen of Poland and became a distin-guished visitor to her house, seem more like fairy tales than scientific accounts. There also is some question about the ability of young children to survive on their own in the wild without human company. Nevertheless, to reject all the stories because of doubts about authen-ticity also seems unwise.

In any event, the cases of wild chil-dren provide only limited evidence about the roles of nature and nurture in influ-encing development. For some of the children, their behavior improved after living among humans but did not become "normal." Not surprisingly, the duration of their isolation made a difference in the children's ability to change their behavior. Thus, the "savage" nature of these wild children is not entirely due to some in-nate defect, but the degree to which na-ture or nurture is involved remains unclear.

Thinking It Through:

1. Why must we be skeptical of reports of individuals who have experienced exceptional circumstances?
2. How can very young children survive on their own? Do you think they have the capacity to fend for themselves?
3. To what extent do these cases shed light on the nature versus nurture debate?

models for studying complex behaviors and characteristics in humans. Another problem is that the environment is difficult to assess or control. Despite the difficulties, behavioral genetics researchers use a variety of techniques to assess the roles that genetics and the environment play in human behavior.

Adoption Studies

An adopted child carries the genetic inheritance of his or her biological parents but is raised by parents who are genetically unrelated to him or her. This situation provides a natural opportunity to study genetic influences. If an adopted child behaves more sim-ilarly to the parents who raised him or her, this suggests that the family environment

Identical twins share the same genetic structure. Even so, they often are very different from each other. What does this tell us about nature versus nurture?

plays a strong role in the behavior being studied. In contrast, if an adopted child behaves more similarly to the biological parents, this suggests that genetic factors play a strong role in that behavior (Plomin, Fulker, Corley, & DeFries, 1997).

Twin Studies

Another way to tease out the roles that nature and nurture play in development is to study twins. **Monozygotic (MZ) twins,** often called *identical twins,* share the same genetic code because they developed from one fertilized egg, which divided into two separate individuals. **Dizygotic (DZ) twins,** often called *fraternal twins,* develop from two separate eggs fertilized by two separate sperm cells. DZ twins may be very similar or very different genetically, just like any two siblings. On average, about 50 percent of their genetic code is shared. Both kinds of twins experience the same prenatal environment, are born at the same time, and usually live in the same family, so they share many similarities in environmental factors. Because MZ and DZ twins differ in the degree to which they share genetic codes but tend to have similar environments, they provide a way to estimate how genes and environment interact to influence development (Wachs, 1992).

If a characteristic has a strong environmental component and a weak genetic component, MZ twins should be no more alike than DZ twins on that characteristic. If a characteristic has a strong genetic component, then MZ twins should be more alike on that characteristic than DZ twins. Geneticists determine **heritability**—an estimate of the degree to which variation of a characteritic in a population is influenced by genetic factors—by comparing the degrees of similarity of MZ and DZ twins (Plomin, 1994).

Studies of twins have shown that height, for example, is largely genetically determined. MZ twins are quite similar in height, usually differing by only about ⅓ inch. DZ twins are less similar in height, usually differing by about 1½ inches (Mange & Mange, 1994). The heritability estimate suggests that 90 percent of the variation in height is due to genetic factors. Twins' weights vary much more than their heights do, suggesting that environmental factors play a larger role in determining one's weight.

Such findings suggest that the correspondence of certain physical traits increases as the degree of genetic relatedness increases. But does this relationship apply to complex human characteristics? The answer seems to be yes. For example, the risk of a person's developing schizophrenia—a serious mental illness—increases when close family members have the disorder (Gottesman, 1991). The closer the relative, the greater the risk. The risk of developing schizophrenia is greatest when an MZ twin has developed the disorder, but this risk does not reach 100 percent. This finding suggests that, although genetic factors may predispose someone to schizophrenia, nongenetic factors (such as family experiences or stress-related factors) may need to be present for the illness to occur (Gottesman, 1991). Findings such as these reinforce the importance of exploring how genes and the environment work together to influence development.

Sometimes researchers combine the twin and adoption methods, looking at the similarity or dissimilarity of twins who are reared apart. From these studies, researchers have concluded that many aspects of personality have a sizable genetic component, with roughly 50 percent of the variability in personality accounted for by heredity (Tellegen, 1988). The remaining 50 percent of the variability in personality is attributable to environmental factors, including shared experiences (such as experience in the same family) and nonshared experiences (such as influences of different teachers or friends). MZ twins raised together tend to be no more alike than MZ twins reared apart, suggesting that nonshared environments influence personality development to a greater extent than do shared experiences.

Shared environments, however, play a greater role in the development of intelligence (Plomin et al., 1997). Studies conducted on twins raised together and apart have

monozygotic (MZ) twins twins who share the same genetic code because they developed from one fertilized egg, which divided into two separate individuals; identical twins

dizygotic (DZ) twins twins who develop from two separate eggs fertilized by two separate sperm cells; fraternal twins

heritability an estimate of the degree to which variation of a characteristic in a population is influenced by genetic factors shown that intelligence test scores are most closely related for MZ twins who are raised together. About 50 percent of the variability in intelligence can be attributed to genetic inheritance and 50 percent to environmental influences. Even the shared prenatal environment of twins contributes to their similarities and may partly explain why DZ twins have higher resemblance in intelligence than do ordinary siblings (Devlin, Daniels, & Roeder, 1997).

Twin and adoption studies help us understand that genes and the environment are complexly interwoven. For instance, genes may influence exposure and susceptibility to different kinds of environments. Children who are genetically predisposed to be active will search out peers who are active, thereby affecting their development by changing the quality of their environment (Rutter et al., 1997).

Continuity versus Discontinuity

Another major issue in child development concerns the course of development: does it occur gradually and smoothly or in a series of abrupt and separate changes? Some developmental scientists focus on gradual changes and view development as *continuous*—like the development of vocabulary (see Figure 1.1a). Other scientists view development as *discontinuous* and focus on the acquisition of qualitatively new patterns of behavior—such as the transition from crawling to walking (see Figure 1.1b). These qualitatively different patterns in development are called *stages*, and, as you will see, many theories of development (such as Piaget's) are stage theories.

The advantage of using stages to represent development is that they help organize information in a meaningful way. The disadvantage of stage theories is that they gloss over the inconsistencies, complexities, and irregularities of development (Aylward, 1997; Flavell, 1982). Changes that seem abrupt, such as a child's first step, may actually be the culmination of a long gradual process rather than a sudden shift (Thelen, 1989). For instance, infants increasingly kick their legs in rhythm until they begin to crawl and walk. These early leg kicks reveal a continuity in development, setting the stage for what appears to be a rather abrupt change in the infant's development—namely, the beginning of upright self-movement (Thelen & Smith, 1998). When viewed in this manner, development is best conceived of as a dynamic and complex pattern of both gradual and abrupt changes (see Figure 1.1c).

FIGURE 1.1
Views on the Nature of Developmental Change

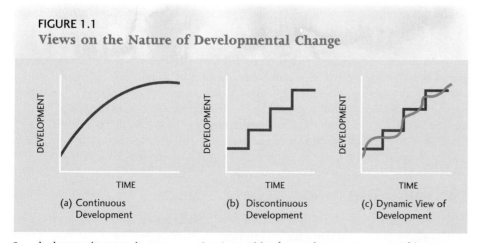

(a) Continuous Development   (b) Discontinuous Development   (c) Dynamic View of Development

Some developmentalists view change as a smooth trajectory (a), whereas others view it as a series of discrete stages (b). Still others believe that change consists of both discrete stages and smooth trajectories (c). Which of these models best fits your view of developmental change?

Ducklings follow the first moving object they see. Here, they follow Konrad Lorenz, who used ethological theory to explain development. What role do critical and sensitive periods play in human development?

CRITICAL AND SENSITIVE PERIODS

Another important issue is whether there exist **critical periods** of development—periods during which specific biological or environmental events must occur if development is to proceed normally. According to the critical period view, individuals are unusually sensitive to specific types of stimulation at certain times during development. If the stimulation is received during the critical time period, development proceeds normally; if the stimulation is not received, normal development is altered. If the needed stimulation is received at the wrong time, it is not likely to have the same impact it would have had if it had occurred during the critical period (Wachs, 1992).

Evidence for critical periods has been well documented in many animals. For example, a critical period immediately after birth has been established for imprinting in ducklings—they follow the first moving object they see right after birth, which usually is the mother duck. The strongest evidence for critical periods in child development comes from studies of language development. Children who do not have sufficient exposure to language before the age of 6 or 7 years, like Victor, may never acquire a language (Newport, 1991).

For most aspects of development, however, the concept of critical periods appears to be too narrow (Bornstein, 1989). Brandi Bender's case shows that children are remarkably resilient and can compensate for inadequate or inappropriate stimulation during important times in development. Many developmentalists use the term **sensitive period** to refer to a time that is optimal for the development of certain behaviors or functions but, unlike critical periods, is not necessary (Shavinina, 1997). The concept of sensitive periods acknowledges that it is possible for development to occur later, although it is more difficult for it to do so and recovery may be incomplete (Wachs, 1992).

INDIVIDUAL DIFFERENCES IN DEVELOPMENT

Another vital issue in the field of child development is sorting out universal versus individual developmental characteristics and events. Because children are all members of the same species, they are alike in many ways—they have similar basic forms, functions, and abilities. However, as soon as children are born (and even before), differences among them are noticeable. Also, although children share biological and cultural characteristics,

critical periods periods during which specific biological or environmental events must occur if development is to proceed normally

sensitive periods periods of time that are optimal for the development of certain behaviors or functions every child is unique. Even identical twins, who share identical genetic information, are different in many respects. The question is, are individual differences stable and permanent? Do fussy children grow up to be fussy adolescents and adults? Do shy children grow up to be shy adolescents and adults? As you will learn, individual differences tend to be consistent, but human behavior is amazingly flexible and subject to change over time and situations.

WHAT ARE THE HISTORICAL ROOTS OF THE STUDY OF CHILD DEVELOPMENT?

The desire to understand children is not new, but the science of child development is. It is only about 100 years old. Cultural and social factors in Western civilization limited scientific inquiry into child development. In addition, the study of child development has been influenced by views concerning the nature, role, and status of children in society. Historically, conceptualizations of children and developmental stages were affected by these views.

CHILDREN OF ANTIQUITY

During the millennium preceding the Common Era, many cultures of the eastern Mediterranean viewed children as helpless and incapable of caring for themselves. Because children were considered to be lacking in self-control and prone to disobedience, a heavy emphasis was placed on discipline (Borstelmann, 1983). Children were meant to serve the interests of the gods through their families and society; they had no status independent of such considerations.

Children also were viewed as naive and easily susceptible to corruption. In ancient Greece, Plato's (808 BC) concerns about this susceptibility led him to propose drastic measures. Plato was convinced that the citizens of Athens had succumbed to the decadence of the society and were unfit to rear children. He proposed that children be separated from their parents early in life and reared under state control. Selective screening would ensure that only those individuals of the highest moral character were allowed to rear and train children. Plato believed that socialization and the environment are critical factors in influencing development and that development is a continuous process. Although his contention that children should be reared by professional caregivers rather than parents seems undesirable by today's standards, it reflects the belief that children are important to the future of a society—a view held by most people today.

CHILDREN AS MINIATURE ADULTS: MEDIEVAL CHILDREN

During the European Middle Ages, children were not recognized as distinct from adults. As soon as a child could live without the constant attention and help of her or his caregiver (about the age of 6 or 7), she or he belonged to adult society (Aries, 1962). Evidence of this lack of distinction between children and adults is seen often in the art of the times, in which children were depicted as miniature adults. Medieval artists did not represent physical differences other than size in the bodies and dress of adults and children.

This lack of a distinction between children and adults did not mean that children were neglected or forsaken. It simply reflected the historical context of the Middle Ages: children's labor was considered a necessity, and because infant mortality was so high— one-half to two-thirds of all children died during infancy—adults were reluctant to recognize children as special individuals (Jaffe, 1997). Children worked liked adults, dressed like adults, and could legally be married, crowned, or hanged like adults. Distinctions

Notice how the children in this painting are depicted as if they were miniature adults. What differences would you expect to see if they were accurately portrayed? What does this tell us about the conceptualization of children during this period?

were not made between activities appropriate for children and for adults, because it was believed that children generally did not have needs beyond those of adults.

EARLY PHILOSOPHICAL ROOTS OF CHILDHOOD

A more enlightened view of childhood began to appear during the Renaissance (late fourteenth and early fifteenth century) and the Reformation (fifteenth and sixteenth centuries). More children were living to adulthood, and helping them acquire knowledge and skills at an early age became more important. Between the sixteenth and eighteenth centuries, a new conception of childhood emerged, based on the philosophy of humanism. In particular, two philosophers, writing about 100 years apart, took an interest in the welfare of children and recognized that children have needs that are different from those of adults. The two philosophers, John Locke and Jean-Jacques Rousseau, argued that childhood is a period of importance and that early development sets the stage for what one becomes later in life. But at the same time, Locke's and Rousseau's views on the primary influence and process of development differed, reflecting the nature versus nurture debate.

John Locke: *Tabula Rasa*

John Locke (1632–1704) proposed that a child is like a blank slate, or *tabula rasa*, upon which experiences in life write their story. Through interactions with people and objects in the environment, each child develops his or her unique character and abilities. Locke emphasized the long-term impact of early experiences and the responsibility parents bear for their children's character formation.

> *The great mistake I have observed in people's breeding their children . . . is that the mind has not been made obedient to discipline and pliant to reason when it was most tender, most easy to be bowed.*
>
> —JOHN LOCKE (1690/1964)

This quote reflects Locke's belief that the environment is the driving force in development. By promoting children's obedience and curiosity, parents encourage their children to develop into rational, attentive, and affectionate people. Through the experiences provided by parents, children are socialized into their culture.

Jean-Jacques Rousseau: Innate Morality

Jean-Jacques Rousseau (1712–1778) also challenged the notion that children are merely miniature and inferior adults. In contrast to Locke, however, Rousseau emphasized the importance of internal, or innate, forces. He believed that, from the time they are born, children possess an intrinsic character that is perfect and good. The role of adults, in Rousseau's view, is to let the natural positive forces in children emerge without restraint:

God makes all things good; man meddles with them and they become evil.

—JEAN-JACQUES ROUSSEAU (1762/1911)

Because of his emphasis on letting the natural qualities of the child dictate his or her development, Rousseau is humorously referred to as the "grandfather of permissive parenting." Children should be allowed to naturally unfold, with little pressure from adults (although he did sometimes advocate that parents carefully regulate their children's experiences). In emphasizing the inborn, natural qualities of development, Rousseau placed greater importance on internal (nature) rather than external (nurture) processes (Synnott, 1988).

Locke and Rousseau set the stage for the modern scientific study of child development. They assigned children a special status and argued that experiences early in development shape later development.

CHARLES DARWIN: EVOLUTION AND CHILD DEVELOPMENT

With his theory of evolution, Charles Darwin (1809–1882) radically changed the way scientists thought about child development. In his *Origin of Species* (published in 1859), Darwin proposed the revolutionary ideas that various species had a common ancestor and that species either die out or change to meet the demands of their changing environments. Darwin's views challenged the ingrained theological view that child behavior is created in a fixed and perfect form. Instead, Darwin believed that human behavior evolved slowly over time.

Darwin's theory is based on the concept of **natural selection**—the idea that, in nature, individuals who are best adapted to their surroundings survive and reproduce, and the adaptive characteristics of those individuals are passed on to the next generation. After many generations, the traits of these individuals become increasingly prevalent in the population (Darwin, 1859).

The impact of Darwin's work continues to be dramatic and pervasive. The possibility that human behavior reflects evolutionary adaptation and selection is a part of many theories of development. Theories such as ethology and sociobiology have been developed based specifically on Darwin's propositions (Wilson, 1978). Furthermore, Darwin's emphasis on common ancestors has led to comparisons between the development of human behavior and the development of similar behaviors in other species (Berman, Rasmussen, & Suomi, 1994).

G. STANLEY HALL: PIONEER IN THE STUDY OF DEVELOPMENT

Up to 100 years ago, most studies of child development consisted of philosophical treatises (such as those written by Locke and Rousseau) and biographical diaries written by parents about their infant children (Darwin, 1877). Then, at the beginning of the twentieth century, G. Stanley Hall (1844–1924) pioneered the application of scientific procedures to the study of child development. For example, he was the first to use questionnaires with children. Although his early attempts were somewhat haphazard, his research illustrated how scientific methods can be used to understand children.

natural selection the process, in nature, whereby individuals who are best adapted to their surroundings survive and reproduce, and the adaptive characteristics of those individuals are passed on to the next generation

Locke, Rousseau, Darwin, and Hall all had important influences on the early study and conceptualization of child development. Can you identify their contributions? Can you discuss their views on nature versus nurture?

Hall was the first scientist to focus attention on adolescent development and was the first to define adolescence as a separate period of life. He also wrote one of the first developmental textbooks. Thus, Hall's work directly stimulated significant areas of contemporary developmental study—scientific aspects of the study of development, adolescence, and early childhood education (Cairns, 1998).

WHAT CHANGES IN CONTEMPORARY AMERICAN LIFE INFLUENCE THE STUDY OF CHILD DEVELOPMENT?

Just as historical changes affected the study of children, contemporary changes in American population and culture have an impact on the study of child development. This impact reminds us that the study of child development is influenced by the contexts in which researchers work. Changes in family composition and increasing cultural diversity, for example, are influences that have stimulated new research.

CHANGES IN FAMILY STRUCTURE

Family life in the United States has been changing dramatically. Even the concept of "family" is changing. The prevalence of the traditional **nuclear family,** in which the biological mother and father and their children live together, has been declining for some years. In 1960, 73 percent of all children lived with their biological parents who had been married only once; by 1990, this figure had dropped to 56 percent (Popenoe, 1993).

The fastest growing family type in the United States in recent years is the **single-parent family,** in which children live with only their mother or their father. The primary cause of single-parent families is divorce, and 90 percent of single-parent families are headed by women. In 1960, only 9 percent of children under the age of 18 lived with a single parent. By 1995, the proportion of single-parent children had jumped to nearly one-quarter of all US children (US Census Bureau, 1996a), and the proportion was even larger for minority children (see Figure 1.2). As you can see from Figure 1.2, the percentage of minority children living in single-parent families is especially high for African American children. This is due primarily to the higher rate of African American children living with mothers who were never married.

nuclear family family structure in which the biological mother and father and their children live together

single-parent family family structure in which children live with only their mother or their father

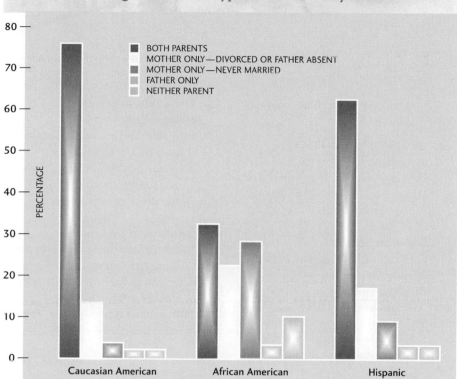

FIGURE 1.2
Children Living in Different Types of Families, by Race: 1995

SOURCE: US Census Bureau, 1996a.
Notice the dramatic differences between the graphs for African American children and those for Caucasian American and Hispanic children. What are the major differences, and what factors might account for these differences?

Another family type that has become increasingly common is the **blended family**—formed when a widowed or divorced person remarries. If the remarried husband or wife or both have children from a former marriage, a **stepfamily** is formed. About 32 percent of African American children, 16 percent of Hispanic children, and 15 percent of Caucasian American children live in stepfamilies; almost all of these children live with their biological mother (US Census Bureau, 1996a). It is estimated that about one-third of all children can expect to live with a biological parent and a stepparent for at least one year before the age of 18 (Dainton, 1993).

An **extended family** consists of one or more parents, one or more of the parents' children, and one or more other relatives (grandparents, aunts, uncles, etc.) living together in one household. This type of family is more common among certain ethnic groups. For example, sharing a residence with extended family members has long been a characteristic of African American families (Garcia Coll, 1990). Similarly, many Mexican American families include aunts and uncles, grandparents, cousins, in-laws, and sometimes even close friends. Extended family members exchange a wide range of goods and services, including child care, nursing, and emotional support (Muller & Espenshade, 1985).

Table 1.2 identifies some of the important changes that have taken place in US households since 1970. Fewer households are headed by a married couple, the average household consists of fewer people, and there are more families without children under the age of 18.

blended family family structure formed when a widowed or divorced person remarries

stepfamily family structure formed when a person who has children from a former marriage remarries

extended family family structure consisting of one or more parents, one or more of the parents' children, and one or more other relatives living together in one household

Trends in US Family Values in the Past Fifty Years

The last half of the twentieth century has seen important changes in US family values. These changes, which influence children's development by affecting the customs, values, and environments they are exposed to, can be described in terms of three patterns (Whitehead, 1993):

1. **1950 to mid-1960s:**
   Traditional familism
   The nuclear family dominated.
   Birth rates were high.
   Divorce rates were low.
   The economy was strong; the standard of living was high.
   Relatively low numbers of women were in the work force.

   Men and women had traditional gender roles.

2. **Mid-1960s to mid-1980s:**
   Individualism
   The population became more diverse.
   Marriage was more often postponed, and increased attention was paid to the single lifestyle.
   Birth rates declined.
   Birth control became more available.
   Divorce rates increased.
   Participation of women in the work force increased.
   Self-expression was emphasized.
   Feminism developed, and gender role stereotypes declined.

3. **Mid-1980s to present:**
   New familism
   Birth rates and the incidence of multiple births increased.
   Advances occurred in biotechnology and fertility treatment.
   Family structure became more diverse.
   Divorce rates leveled off.
   Increased attention was paid to the aging population.
   The discrepancy between the poor and the affluent increased.
   With Internet communication came increased globalism.

These changes in US households reflect changes in values, technology, and demographics that have occurred since 1970. Together, these trends have important effects on the environments in which children find themselves. Scientists interested in the study of child development must be attentive to these changes in order to understand the complex factors that influence the course of development.

TABLE 1.2
Household Comparisons: 1970 versus 1995

	1970	1995
Percent of households made up of married couples with children	40%	25%
People per household	3.14	2.65
Families headed by women with no husband present	5.6 million	12.2 million
Families headed by men with no wife present	1.2 million	3.2 million
Families with no children under 18 at home	44%	51%

SOURCE: US Census Bureau, 1996a.

What Is the Impact of Immigration on American Life?

Since 1987, almost 350,000 foreign-born children have come to the United States each year. In fact, first- and second-generation immigrant children are the fastest growing segment of the US population (Zhou, 1997). Most immigrant children come from Central and South America, the Caribbean, and Asia (US Census Bureau, 1997). These children come to the United States with or to join other family members.

It is not surprising that immigrants and their impact on US society have caught the attention of the public, as well as that of government officials (National Research Council, 1998). In a 1993 poll, 75 percent of American citizens supported some kind of limitation on immigration (*Time*, 1993). Their concerns may be based on public anxiety about the high cost of providing services to new immigrants. But is this concern justified?

Although legal immigrants and refugees may receive benefits such as food stamps and health care, the average household incomes of legal immigrants and refugees who enter the United States generally are *higher* than those of US-born Americans (Fix & Passel, 1994). Considering the taxes that an immigrant and his or her dependents are likely to pay over a lifetime, the United States actually gains revenue from immigrants (Glastris, 1997). However, the economic status of *undocumented* immigrants is so poor that when the immigrant population in the United States is examined as a whole, the immigrants are less well off than US-born Americans. Thus, many beliefs about immigrant children and their families are based on those immigrants who are in the United States *illegally*.

Another misconception about immigrants is that they are at risk for poor educational outcomes because of their limited proficiency in English. Research shows that immigrant children do well in school and often stay in school longer than their US-born peers with similar backgrounds (McDonnell & Hill, 1993). The academic performance of many immigrant children exceeds that of the average US-born child, despite the fact that immigrant children often come from disadvantaged or war-torn backgrounds.

In the future, the United States will be even more racially, ethnically, and culturally diverse (Castex, 1997). With increased research, other negative beliefs and stereotypes about immigrants may be dispelled. Far from being a fringe element of the American population, immigrant children and their families are an increasingly large core of US society (Future of Children, 1995).

Thinking It Through:

1. What factors contribute to negative views about the impact of immigrants on US society?
2. What do you think US immigration policy should be? Should the United States accept many immigrants into the country? Why or why not?
3. How does immigration influence theory and research about child and adolescent development?

ETHNIC AND RACIAL DIVERSITY

In addition to paying more attention to the changing family structure, researchers have become more sensitive to cultural and ethnic influences on child development. This adjustment in part reflects the fact that the US population is more diverse than ever before. According to current and projected data collected by the US Census Bureau (1996b), Caucasian Americans are the slowest growing segment of the US population and their contribution to the total population growth in this country is becoming smaller. From 1990 to 2030, the percentage of total population growth accounted for by Caucasian Americans is expected to decrease. By the year 2050, Caucasian Americans will represent only a slight majority. The Hispanic population is the fastest growing group and by the year 2025 will be the largest minority group in the United States. Similarly, the Asian population in the United States is expected to increase at a considerable pace through the year 2050.

Is Development Different for Children of Color?

The lack of attention to issues of race, ethnicity, and culture in the science of child development has resulted in studies that concentrate on explaining the differences between minority and Caucasian middle-class populations. Some scientists argue that what is lacking is an examination of the developmental processes and outcomes that are unique to children of color (Barbarin, 1993). Cynthia Garcia Coll and colleagues (1996) developed a model of development relevant to children of color. A schematic representation of this framework is presented in the figure.

Of primary concern in this model of development for minority children is the influence of social position variables—the characteristics that societies use to place individuals in a social hierarchy. These variables include (but are not limited to) race, social class, ethnicity, and gender. Inspection of the figure shows that social position does not directly influence developmental outcomes for children of color. Rather, the effect of social position on development is seen through the effects of racism, which include prejudice, discrimination, and oppression—leading, in turn, to segregation. The interplay of social position, racism, and segregation creates unique conditions that affect the development of children of color. These conditions rarely are experienced by majority populations and define the alternative pathways of development for children of color (Garcia Coll et al., 1996).

The effect of all these factors is diverse and complex. For example, *discrimination*—defined as behaviors that deny individuals or groups of individuals equality of treatment—often leads to environments that maintain the social hierarchy.

Discrimination not only limits the quantity of resources available to children of a particular group but also limits their access to those resources that are available. Because of discrimination, children of color often face situations that majority children do not, such as restricted educational, housing, or recreational opportunities (Garcia Coll et al., 1996). Placing social position, racism, and segregation at the core rather than the periphery of development will lead to a better understanding of children of color.

Thinking It Through:

1. What aspects of development are likely to be similar for all children? What aspects are likely to be different for children of color?
2. How do discrimination and prejudice influence children's development?

Although birth rates generally are higher for minority groups than for Caucasian Americans, almost one-third of the current growth in minority groups is caused by immigration. By the year 2000, the US population will be as much as 8 million larger because of immigration. By 2050, the net increase in population due to immigration is projected to be 82 million (US Census Bureau, 1996b).

Increased diversity in the US population demands greater sensitivity to human variety and the culturally diverse environments in which children are raised. However, relatively few studies have been conducted on minority children, adults, and families (Arms, Davidson, & Moore, 1992).

The task of researching the impact of diversity is complicated by the considerable variation that exists within, as well as between, minority groups (McAdoo, 1993). For example, Hispanics from Puerto Rico reside primarily in cities of the Northeast, are a relatively young group (median age is 23.3 years), and have not done well economically in the United States. In contrast, Hispanics from Cuba reside primarily in urban areas of the Southeast, particularly Florida, are relatively older (median age is 39.1 years), and generally have done well economically, particularly those who immigrated prior to 1980

Developmental Model for Minority Children

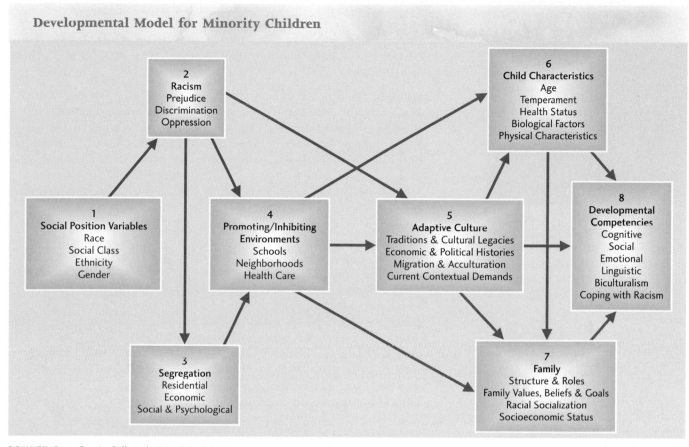

SOURCE: From Garcia Coll et al., 1996 (p. 1896).
Notice how complex this integrative model is and the important roles that social position (box 1), racism (box 2), and segregation (box 3) play. These factors are less likely to play a prominent role in the development of nonminority children. How might these factors influence minority children's development?

(Ortiz, 1995). As a result, the development of individuals in these two Hispanic groups is influenced in different ways by the backgrounds, experiences, values, and beliefs of their different subcultures.

A further complication in researching the role of diversity in development is the lack of agreement on the terminology used to identify groups. For example, in one poll 30 percent of respondents indicated that they wished their race to be identified as "African American," whereas the majority listed "black" as their choice (Roper Organization, 1993). These findings reflect a difference not only in label preference but also in the meanings of *race* and *ethnicity*. Although there are no clear, unambiguous definitions of these terms, **race** primarily refers to a group whose members share a genetic heritage (Curran & Renzetti, 1996). **Ethnicity** primarily refers to a group whose members share a common cultural heritage and a sense of belonging (Yetman, 1991). Although there is some overlap in the two terms, ethnicity is considered to be a social construct whereas race is considered to be relatively less so. For example, most (but not all) Americans of African descent are grouped racially as black; however, the term *African American* refers to an ethnic group, most often to people whose ancestors experienced slavery in the United

race a group whose members share a genetic heritage

ethnicity a group whose members share a common cultural heritage and a sense of belonging

Tiger Woods created a controversy when he declined to identify himself as being of one race or another. Many individuals are, like Tiger, multiracial, and their increasing numbers reflect the fact that the population of the United States is becoming more diverse.

States (Soberon, 1996). Thus, not all blacks in the United States are African American (for example, some are from Haiti and others from the Caribbean).

Similar confusion exists over the terminology used to refer to people of Mexican or Spanish descent. Consider the following terms (Campos, 1996; Office of Management and Budget, 1995; Soberon, 1996):

✦ **Spanish.** Used to refer indiscriminately to any person who speaks Spanish. This term is imprecise because it includes people from many different countries and continents (America, the Caribbean, Europe).

✦ **Latino/Latina.** Used to refer to people in the United States originating from or having a heritage related to Latin America (Central or South American). Because *Latin* refers to the fact that a romance language (Spanish, Portuguese, French) is the native tongue of the majority of Latin Americans, this term may not be appropriate for people from that region who do not speak a romance language (such as native Indians).

✦ **Mexican.** Used to refer to the inhabitants of Mexico. The term may be appropriate for Mexican citizens working in or visiting the United States, but it is not appropriate for people of Mexican descent who are citizens of the United States.

✦ **Mexican American.** Commonly used to recognize US citizens who are descendants of Mexicans. The term may be inappropriate for those who identify themselves as having a Spanish rather than a Mexican heritage or for those who do not view themselves as Americans by choice.

✦ **Chicano/Chicana.** Relatively recent term, used to refer to descendants of inhabitants of Mexico. Preferred by political activists and those who seek to create a new identity, it is reflective of a unique culture.

✦ **Hispanic.** Used to refer to people of Mexican, Puerto Rican, Cuban, Central and South American, and other Spanish culture or origin, regardless of race. This term is used by the US Census Bureau as an encompassing ethnic classification with many subgroups. Because of its broadness, this is the term used most often in this book.

A recent controversy concerns how to classify persons who identify with more than one race. Consider, for example, the case of Tiger Woods, who, in 1997, became the youngest golfer ever (at age 21) to win the Masters golf tournament. Tiger's father is African American (but also part Native American and Caucasian), and his mother is Asian American (from Thailand). Tiger caused a stir when he refused to identify himself as a black. Instead, he coined a term, saying he was "Cablinasian"—a mixture of Caucasian, African American, Native American, and Asian (Padilla, 1997).

Tiger's situation points out an increasing dilemma for many: what do people of mixed races call themselves? For the most part, the term **multiracial** has been used to refer to people like Tiger who are of two or more races. And there are more multiracial individuals today than in the past. In 1960, there were about 150,000 interracial marriages, compared with 1.5 million in 1990 (OMB, 1995). Today, about 2 percent of the US population (about 7 million people) can be considered multiracial. For these individuals, a single category often does not reflect how they think of themselves.

The amazing diversity of people has only just begun to be recognized in theories and research on child development (Spencer, 1990). Although many developmental processes (such as motor or language development) probably emerge in similar fashion across racially and ethnically diverse populations, our understanding of child development needs to be expanded to consider factors and situations that may be unique to a particular group (such as lifestyle or food choices). For instance, for children of color, more explicit attention needs to be paid to the unique circumstances they face (such as racism and stereotyping). Identifying and integrating these experiences and circumstances that are not shared by the majority population will provide the basis for a fuller and more inclusive understanding of child development (Garcia Coll et al., 1996).

multiracial a term used to describe people who are of two or more races

CHILDREN OF LESBIAN AND GAY PARENTS

Historically, people in Western cultures believed that the most favorable home environments are those provided by traditional two-parent families. Although rarely stated explicitly, it is most often assumed that both parents in such families are heterosexual (Patterson, 1992). In the contemporary United States, this is not always the case—many children grow up in homes where the parent or parents are gay or lesbian.

Estimates of the number of gay and lesbian parents in the United States range from 2 to 8 million, and estimates of the number of children of gay and lesbian parents range from 4 to 14 million (Patterson, 1995). The exact figures are difficult to determine because many gay and lesbian parents conceal their sexual orientation out of fear of discrimination and prejudice (Saffron, 1996). In most cases, children are born as a result of a heterosexual relationship between biological parents. After one parent acknowledges her or his sexual orientation, separation or divorce may occur, and the children are then raised in a gay or lesbian home (Falk, 1989). However, an increasing number of children, conceived through donor insemination, are now being born into lesbian homes (Chan, Raboy, & Patterson, 1998). Whatever the precise figures and contexts of conception, it is clear that the number of children of gay and lesbian parents has increased and is substantial.

Much of the research on children reared in homosexual households has been generated in the last twenty years, often because of custody disputes. Concerns about children's sexual development, the quality of the parenting provided by gay and lesbian parents, and the stress and ridicule these children might face have been raised by those who believe that children in these families are at risk and that homosexuals should be denied the rights and privileges of having a family (Focus on the Family, 1992). The scientific evidence presents a different picture, however.

Research on children from gay and lesbian homes suggests that they are no different from children reared by heterosexual parents (Flaks, Ficher, Masterpasqua, & Joseph, 1995; Golombok & Tasker, 1996; Patterson, 1995). Children's performance on standard developmental and psychological tests gives no indication as to whether they have a homosexual parent or a heterosexual parent. Thus, children raised by gay and lesbian parents appear to be just as healthy and well adjusted as those raised by heterosexual couples (Tasker & Golombok, 1997); there is no evidence to suggest that the development of children of gay men or lesbians is compromised in any respect (Patterson, 1992). The evidence to date indicates that the home environments provided by gay and lesbian parents are as likely as those provided by heterosexual parents to support and enable children's growth and development.

Of course, lesbian and gay families, parents, and children are as diverse in their backgrounds, personalities, structures, and values as their heterosexual peers. Having addressed the negative assumptions and popular prejudices that underlie the concerns about gay and lesbian parenting, researchers now are exploring issues raised by the emergence of different kinds of lesbian and gay families with children (Patterson, 1995).

WHAT IS THE CONCEPTUAL BASIS FOR THIS BOOK?

Given the diversity and variability that exist in children, families, and their environments, we believe that the best way to study and understand children and their development is to focus specifically on this diversity. Thus, we view development from a **transactional perspective,** which holds that development occurs as the result of the interplay between the diversity of qualities individuals bring to their environments and the diversity of environments individuals experience. The conceptual basis for this book

transactional perspective the view that development occurs as the result of the interplay between the diversity of qualities individuals bring to their environments and the diversity of environments individuals experience

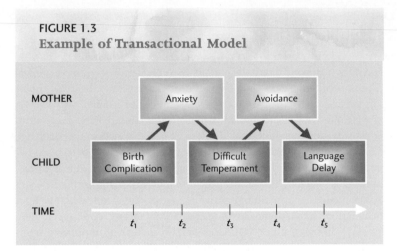

FIGURE 1.3
Example of Transactional Model

SOURCE: Sameroff, 1987 (p. 278). Copyright © 1987. Reprinted by permission of John Wiley & Sons, Inc.

By considering this transactional model, you can see that the relationship between birth complications and language delay is more complex than it appears. The model depicts different transactions that may occur between birth and the subsequent delay of language.

is the belief that development is a product of the continuous interactions between the child and his or her social context (Sameroff, 1989). Although it has long been recognized that children's environments significantly affect their development, equal emphasis must be given to the effects of children on their environments.

An example of dynamic transactions between children and their environments is provided in Figure 1.3 (Sameroff, 1987). According to this model, a complicated childbirth may make a mother anxious and nervous about her fragile newborn child. The mother's anxiety during the first months of the infant's life may cause her to be uncertain and inappropriate in her interactions with the infant. In response to such inconsistency, the infant may develop some irregularities in feeding and sleeping patterns. These irregularities might decrease the pleasure the mother obtains from the relationship and, as a result, cause her to spend less time with her infant. One outcome of her withdrawal may be that the infant is exposed to less language, which hinders the acquisition of language. In this example, the developmental outcome (delayed language of the child) is not caused by the complicated birth or by the mother's subsequent anxiety; the most direct cause is the mother's avoidance. But you can see from this example that such a conclusion would be a serious oversimplification of a complex sequence of transactions that occurred over time.

Our understanding of the complex interaction of individuals and their environments is still rudimentary (Bronfenbrenner & Ceci, 1994), but the diversity of individual and environmental factors makes it likely that development is multiply determined. No single influence determines the outcomes of development, and similar developmental outcomes can be produced in a variety of ways. Additionally, individual and environmental factors, and their interaction, change as children mature. For example, the interactions of infants and their environments are qualitatively different depending on whether or not the infant has developed the ability to crawl or walk (Campos, Kermoian, & Zumbahlen, 1992). The ability to crawl or walk creates a sense of control, as well as increasing the risk of falling and getting hurt. Thus, infants who can move about their environments have different experiences than those who cannot.

The transactional model encourages us to understand the complexity of influences on development. Particular emphasis is placed on the environment as an active force in shaping development, although the environments children are exposed to are influenced by their personal characteristics. Children tend to select environments and experiences that "fit" their general characteristics and dispositions (Rutter et al., 1997). For example, a child who likes sports will likely seek out more opportunities for sports activities than will a child who prefers to be sedentary. Children who engage in sports activities are influenced differently than those who do not have such experiences.

Because the transactional model emphasizes the divergent nature of development and the dynamic aspects of the transactions between the child and her or his environment, sensitivity to diversity is critical (Sameroff, Seifer, & Bartko, 1997). Transactional models lead us to expect that parents belonging to a particular ethnic or cultural group share beliefs and practices that overlap with, but differ in some respects from, those of parents from other cultures. Thus, children in minority families might be exposed to caregiving environments characterized by unique cultural beliefs and caregiving practices that differ from those of the Caucasian American culture. For example, Hispanic mothers engage in predominantly nonverbal interactions with their infants, whereas Caucasian American mothers engage in more verbally oriented interactions (Hurtado, 1995). Whereas, Caucasian American mothers are likely to emphasize parenting goals that relate to the development of children's confidence and independence, Hispanic mothers are more likely to value parenting goals that emphasize respectful, obedient behavior (Harwood et al., 1996). These differences reflect the fact that parental belief systems are influenced by cultural values regarding what constitutes desirable behavior (Lightfoot & Valsiner, 1992).

Differences in parental beliefs also are found in other cultures. For example, the Digo and Kikuyu are two East African cultures that have different beliefs about infant capacities (DeVries & Sameroff, 1984). The Digo believe that infants can learn within a few months after birth, and they begin to teach their infants at that time. The Kikuyu, in contrast, believe that serious education is not possible before the second year of life, and they delay education until that time. Thus, caregivers from different cultures and subcultures have different beliefs, goals, reactions, and expectations about their children, and these beliefs uniquely influence children's development.

The impact of different environments also depends on unique characteristics of the child. Some children may be more vulnerable and less able to withstand a challenging environment. For instance, Bradley et al. (1994) found that the percentage of low-birthweight children (children who weigh less than 5½ pounds at birth) living in poverty who adapt to the changing demands of their environments is exceptionally low (about 10 percent). This is significantly lower than the 40 percent incidence of adaptiveness in low-birthweight children born into more affluent, nonimpoverished homes. These findings are particularly noteworthy given that Bradley et al. did not include children with serious medical problems. Findings such as these provide evidence that certain environmental conditions can increase the vulnerability of already vulnerable children.

In this book, you will learn about the complex mechanisms, patterns, and issues related to child and adolescent development. We focus on the diversity of individual characteristics and environments that influences development and how these relate to one another. For organizational and presentational effectiveness, the chapters are broken into the domains of physical, cognitive, and social-emotional development. These developmental domains are, however, intimately interrelated; that is, children's development consists of a process of continuous interaction among all three domains.

Throughout the book, we focus on the transactions that children have with their environments. We include a wide variety of transactions, ranging from close interactions with other people (such as parent-child or peer interactions) to the impact of broad influences such as schools, neighborhoods, and culture. Implicit in these discussions is our emphasis on the role that human relationships play in influencing development. It is through their relationships—their transactions and interactions with family members, peers, teachers, and others—that children develop and learn about themselves.

Finally, although we emphasize the scientific study of child development, the study of how children develop also is influenced by values and goals. Researchers, caregivers, communities, and societies observe, interpret, and respond to developmental processes according to their values and goals (Fabes, Martin, & Smith, 1994). You are encouraged to analyze the facts and issues of child and adolescent development in terms of your own life and values. By doing so, you will find the study of child development more meaningful. The information in this book will help you make better-informed decisions about issues related to children and their development.

CHAPTER SUMMARY

What is child development?

- Child development involves changes in characteristics and behavior, from conception through adolescence.

- Child development is a continuous, complex process influenced by a variety of mechanisms. The extent to which these mechanisms reflect biological versus environmental effects is the subject of a debate central to the study of development.

- Adoption, twin, and case studies have been used to examine influences on child development. Although fascinating, these cases point out the difficulty of separating biological and environmental influences on development.

- Development may be seen as a continuous process or as a succession of qualitatively different and discontinuous patterns or stages. Recent evidence suggests that development consists of both gradual and sudden changes over time.

- The notion of critical periods implies that a specific event must occur at a specific point if development is to proceed normally. The concept of sensitive periods provides a more flexible view of development.

- The study of child development includes investigating how individuals come to be different from one another and the stability of these differences.

What are the historical roots of the study of child development?

- The science of child development is only about 100 years old. Ideas about development were once very different from what they are today.

- Children of antiquity were viewed as helpless and incapable of caring for themselves. Plato believed that most parents were too corrupt to care for their children and advocated state control of child rearing.

- In the Middle Ages, there was no concept of childhood separate from adulthood. Children were viewed as miniature adults.

- John Locke and Jean-Jacques Rousseau described how early experiences influence later development. Their views differed as to whether nature (Locke's *tabula rasa*) or nurture (Rousseau's "innate morality") was the more important influence on development.

- By tying development to the evolution of the species, Charles Darwin changed the way scientists thought about development.

- G. Stanley Hall was a pioneer in the scientific study of development and adolescence.

What changes in American life influence the study of child development?

- Family life in the United States has changed dramatically. The percentage of people living in traditional nuclear families has decreased, whereas the number of people living in alternative types of families (stepfamilies, extended families) has increased.

- The US population is more racially and ethnically diverse than ever before, and this trend will continue. By 2050, Caucasian Americans will represent only a slight majority.

- Much of the increase in ethnic and racial diversity is due to immigration.

- The increased diversity of the US population is only beginning to be recognized in the study of child development. Understanding the role of diversity is complicated by changing terminology, variation among and within ethnic and racial groups, and the lack of theories relevant to minority groups.

- The number of children growing up in gay and lesbian households has increased. Research finds no differences between these children and those raised in heterosexual households.

What is the conceptual basis for this book?

- Development is viewed from a transactional perspective, emphasizing the interplay between the qualities children bring to their environments and the environments they experience.

- The transactional perspective stresses the diverse and interdependent nature of development.

- The emphasis on understanding development in the context of human relationships reflects the belief that children learn about themselves through their relationships with others.

- Recognizing one's goals and values makes the study of child development and its application more meaningful.

KEY TERMS & CONCEPTS

blended family *(17)*

child development *(5)*

cognitive development *(5)*

critical periods *(12)*

developmental domains *(5)*

dizygotic twins *(10)*

ethnicity *(21)*

extended family *(17)*

heritability *(10)*

learning *(6)*

maturation *(6)*

monozygotic twins *(10)*

multiracial *(22)*

natural selection *(15)*

nature versus nurture debate *(7)*

nuclear family *(16)*

personality *(8)*

physical development *(5)*

race *(21)*

sensitive periods *(12)*

single-parent family *(16)*

social-emotional development *(5)*

socialization *(6)*

stepfamily *(17)*

transactional perspective *(23)*

ACTIVITIES & APPLICATIONS
Relating to Child Development

1. Interview your parents, uncles, aunts, or grandparents about their childhoods. Compare their development to your own, and identify differences and similarities in the factors, environments, and relationships that likely influenced their and your development. What historical, social, cultural, and individual factors might account for some of the differences?

2. Which do you believe is the more important influence on children's development—nature or nurture? Why? What might be some developmental examples of the interplay between genes and environment?

3. Gather information on children and families in another historical era or country or in a religious or ethnic group different from your own. Identify differences in values, customs, and beliefs about children and childrearing. How might these differences influence the children's development?

Understanding DEVELOPMENT

CHAPTER OUTLINE

Three teachers are discussing the problems of Tamika, a 9-year-old girl in the third grade at their school. Tamika is easily frustrated when interacting with others and hits other children when she gets upset. Tamika's third-grade teacher, Rob, her second-grade teacher, Cathy, and the special education teacher, Mary, all have different theories about the reasons behind it.

"She wasn't like that last year," Cathy points out. "She was fairly impulsive and never sat still for very long, but she wasn't especially aggressive toward the other children. Something must have changed."

"I know there's stress at home," Rob replies. "Her parents are divorcing."

"That's it, then," notes Cathy. "Tamika's acting out her repressed feelings about the impending divorce. That would explain why she lashes out and why she cries so easily. We should refer her for counseling."

"I don't know," says Rob. "That's a troubled family. Tamika gets exposed to a lot of anger and abusive language at home on a daily basis. Maybe she sees abuse between her parents and thinks that's the way people are supposed to act toward each other. I think we should refer the family to the social worker."

"But plenty of kids experience far worse than Tamika and don't turn aggressive," Mary states. "I think we need to look at the causes of her impulsivity and aggressiveness. She might have some problem with her health or with the way her nervous system is functioning. We really ought to refer her to a neurologist for testing."

"This is confusing," Cathy says. "Which way should we go?"

"Maybe it's 'all of the above,'" Rob suggests. "But where should we start?"

Like these three teachers, you may wonder about the causes of your own and others' behavior. As you learned in Chapter 1, questions about the origins of behavior have long fascinated developmental scientists. To what extent is our behavior due to biological factors or to the ways we are raised in our families? Can a poor family environment be overcome by positive experiences with friends and in school? Just as Tamika's teachers developed ideas about the causes of her behavior, developmental scientists formulate theories about the causes of behavior and use these to design studies about development.

HOW DO THEORIES EXPLAIN CHILD DEVELOPMENT?

Recall from Chapter 1 the story of Victor, the Wild Boy of Aveyron. Faced with the challenge of explaining and treating the Wild Boy's behavior, Itard relied on a theory for guidance. Itard believed that development is shaped by the environment and that Victor's savage behavior was due to the savage environment he grew up in. Without a theory, Itard would have had no way to explain what caused Victor's behavior, nor would he have been able to plan ways to help Victor become civilized. Theories are important because they provide the tools researchers need to organize and understand the complexities of development.

Theories are not just for researchers. In everyday life, people develop implicit theories to help them understand and explain other people's behavior. For instance, people all over the United States have tried to understand why school children murder other children. These personal theories influence interactions with others and guide major decisions that people make in their everyday lives.

SCIENTIFIC THEORIES

The implicit theories that we use every day are simply smaller versions of the formal theories that scientists use. Some people believe that scientific theories are elaborate ideas developed with little relevance to the real world. But this belief is wrong—theories are the backbone of developmental research and are very much connected to the real world. A scientific **theory** is a structured set of ideas that attempts to organize and explain facts. In contrast, a **fact** is a statement, based on observation, with which many people would agree (Miller, 1993). Facts may be single observations or summaries of many observations. For instance, your height is a fact with which any physician would agree.

Theories organize and give meaning to facts by describing how they fit together. Theories also guide future research by suggesting which investigative leads scientists should pursue. For instance, that many unborn children are exposed to crack cocaine is a fact. Should scientists focus their research on the effects of the drug on the child or on the child's later experiences in a drug-abusing family? Research based on biological theories might assess how biochemical changes associated with drugs influence development (Holzman & Paneth, 1994). Research based on environmental theories might focus on the stressful conditions associated with living in drug-addicted families (Black et al., 1994). Both kinds of theories—biological and environmental—have proved important in understanding that early drug exposure does not necessarily cause permanent, irreversible damage. We now know that family environments can buffer children from the devastating effects of early drug exposure (Leventhal et al., 1997).

Different theories provide different frames of reference for interpreting facts, and there is a tendency to interpret facts in ways that fit the theory. As you will soon learn, there are many theories of human development, each of which presents a unique perspective on development. Because human behavior is so complex, it is unlikely that any single theory will be able to explain all behavior (Miller, 1993).

EVALUATING THEORIES OF DEVELOPMENT

Developmental scientists consider whether a theory explains the available facts about the real world of child development. The more facts it explains, the better the theory is. A good theory also is understandable, predicts future events, provides practical guidance, and stimulates new knowledge. Finally, a good theory is testable—researchers must be able to determine whether its propositions are correct. If a theory is untestable, its usefulness and accuracy cannot be determined (Thomas, 1996).

Theories of development can be distinguished from one another in terms of their perspective on the developmental issues discussed in Chapter 1 (such as nature versus nurture and continuity versus discontinuity). The major theories and approaches used to study child development are categorized in terms of these issues in Table 2.1 and in the following sections.

WHAT ARE THE MAJOR BIOLOGY-BASED THEORIES OF CHILD DEVELOPMENT?

theory a structured set of ideas that attempts to organize and explain facts

fact a statement, based on observation, with which many people would agree

Many theories focus on the biological factors that underlie development—including both evolutionary processes and physiological development, such as the functioning of the brain. In the opening vignette, the idea that health factors were causing Tamika's behavior is biology-based. Biology-based theories assume that powerful organic or inherited forces influence behavior.

TABLE 2.1

Categorization of Theories of Human Development

CATEGORY	DESCRIPTION	THEORIES INCLUDED
Biology-based theories	Emphasis on inherited biological factors and processes	Evolutionary theories Ethological theories Attachment theory Neurodevelopmental theories
Psychoanalytic theories	Emphasis on unconscious internal drives and interactions with others	Freud's psychosexual theory Erikson's psychosocial theory
Environment-based theories	Emphasis on the role of the external world	Classical conditioning Operant conditioning Social learning theory
Cognition-based theories	Emphasis on the role of cognition and processing of information	Piaget's theory Vygotsky's theory Information processing theory
Contextual theories	Emphasis on the interaction between individuals and their environments	Ecological theory Dynamic systems theory

EVOLUTIONARY THEORIES

As you learned in Chapter 1, Darwin's theory of evolution is based on the idea that individuals who have characteristics that promote survival and reproduction are more likely to pass these characteristics on to future generations. For instance, early primates who had physical characteristics such as opposable thumbs and an upright stance had increased chances of surviving because they were better able to adapt to their environment and gather food than individuals without those characteristics. Likewise, the ability to communicate, reason, and cooperate increased their chances for survival. Thus, the capacities for social behavior and reasoning, along with physical characteristics, underwent natural selection (Darwin, 1877). Today, **evolutionary theories** influence many areas of research on development, including studies of social behavior and mate selection (Buss, 1998). In these studies, researchers focus on the behaviors they believe promote the survival of the species.

ETHOLOGICAL THEORY

Ethological theory, derived from Darwin's ideas about evolution, focuses on the causes and adaptive value of behavior, considering both the evolutionary history of the species and the social context. Ethologists have been influential in proposing that there are critical periods in development during which a specific type of learning occurs rapidly. For example, as you learned in Chapter 1, newborn ducklings have a critical period during which they learn to follow the first moving object they see. Because this object usually is their mother, this inherited tendency (called imprinting) increases their chances of survival.

Ethological research has focused on questions such as how adults become attached to infants, why infants prefer to look at human faces, and how facial expressions communicate emotions and intentions. For instance, developmental ethologists are concerned

evolutionary theories explanations of development that focus on how behaviors promote the survival of the individual and the species

ethological theory explanation of development that focuses on the causes and adaptive value of behavior, considering both the evolutionary history of the species and the social context

FIGURE 2.1
Infant and Adult Faces

Notice how infants of many different species have similar facial features, such as a small nose, a large forehead, and big eyes. Ethologists believe that these features are cues that evolved to elicit caregiving behavior from parents. These facial features make infants appear lovable and attractive to caregivers.

attachment theory explanation of development that focuses on the quality of the early emotional relationships developed between children and their caregivers

neurodevelopmental approaches explanations of development that focus on the relationship of brain development to behavior and thinking

with why infants of many different species have similar facial features, such as a small nose, a large forehead, and big eyes (see Figure 2.1). Ethologists proposed that these features are visual cues that have evolved to elicit caregiving behavior from parents. Research has confirmed this idea with respect to human infants (Zebrowitz, Kendall-Tackett, & Fafel, 1991); even adults who have a "baby face" are perceived by others as being more childlike in their behavior (Zebrowitz & Montepare, 1992).

ATTACHMENT THEORY

Based on ethological principles, John Bowlby (1907–1990) developed an influential theory about the importance of early relationships for the developing child. According to Bowlby's **attachment theory,** all children become emotionally attached to their caregivers, regardless of the treatment they receive from them. Attachments form as infants give cues to which caregivers respond, increasing the likelihood of infant survival.

Research today focuses on the quality of the attachment that forms. Over the first few years of life, children develop inner working models about themselves and others, based on the kind of care they have received. For example, a child who receives sensitive and consistent caregiving comes to view himself or herself as worthy. Children's inner working models become internalized views or expectations about relationships with others and provide a basic roadmap for subsequent interactions with people (Sroufe, 1989).

Recent research on attachment theory supports the idea that inner working models are influential in later development. Infants who have strong emotional ties with their caregivers are more likely than other children to explore their environments readily, to maintain contact with their caregivers, to become independent, and to have good self-esteem (Thompson, 1998). Researchers also are exploring how these early attachments influence dating, marriage, friendships, and parenting later in life (van Ijzendoorn, 1995).

NEURODEVELOPMENTAL APPROACHES

Neurodevelopmental approaches to the study of development focus on the relationship of brain development to behavior and thinking. How the brain develops and how the different parts of the brain function provide a broad basis for understanding how biology and environment both contribute to development. Studies of brain development point to the importance of the early years of children's lives (MacLean, 1985). For instance, early in development, the brain depends on environmental input to fine-tune itself so that it is maximally sensitive to its environment (Jacobs, 1997). Early ex-

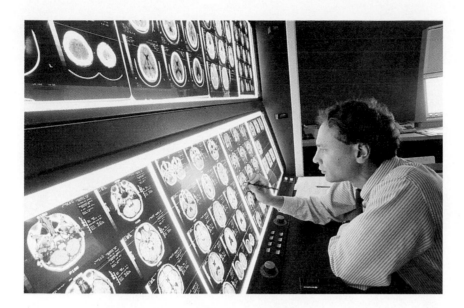

Neurodevelopmental theories focus on how the brain influences behavior and development. These theories also emphasize the importance of early experience and how early experiences influence the organization and functioning of the brain.

periences, then, have a crucial role in determining how the brain wires itself, which in turn influences how the individual later responds to stimuli.

WHAT ARE THE MAJOR PSYCHOANALYTIC THEORIES OF CHILD DEVELOPMENT?

Psychoanalytic theories of development have their origins in the belief that the most important causes of behavior are rooted in the unconscious drives and forces that develop within the mind of an individual. Although today psychoanalytic theories are not often used to guide research, they continue to influence the ways people think about human behavior. Freudian notions underlie much of the thinking about developmental issues.

FREUD'S PSYCHOSEXUAL THEORY

Sigmund Freud (1856–1939) was a physician whose training stressed biological determinism—the view that all human activity has biological or neurological causes. Freud also was influenced by Darwin's theory of evolution and Newton's law of physics (that energy cannot be created or destroyed). These influences led Freud to postulate that human behavior arises from the dynamic, internal energy that is the result of our evolutionary heritage (Green, 1989). Freud called this fixed pool of energy the **libido**—the source of action and sexual desire.

According to Freud, the human personality, or psyche, consists of three structures: the id, the ego, and the superego. The **id** represents the primitive and instinctual components of the psyche that are unconscious, irrational, and uncontrolled. The id is driven by the pleasure principle—it seeks immediate gratification and avoids pain and distress (Freud, 1923/1960). Because the demands of the id are irrational, they often do not match what the environment provides. For example, because infants cannot feed themselves when they become hungry, immediate gratification may not be available. Infants may seek gratification by crying, sucking, and maybe even hallucinating. However, the reality of the world eventually forces changes in the id. It transforms a portion of itself into a new personality structure—the ego.

psychoanalytic theories explanations of development that focus on the unconscious drives and forces that develop within the mind

libido the source of action and sexual desire

id the part of the psyche that is primitive and instinctual

TABLE 2.2
Freud's Theory of Psychosexual Development

STAGE	AGES	PSYCHIC DEVELOPMENT
Oral	Birth–1 year	Id is the only psychic structure operating. Pleasure principle operates unconsciously. Erogenous zone is the mouth—gratification and exploration occur through eating and sucking.
Anal	1–3 years	Ego develops as the result of conflicts with the social world. Reality principle operates. Erogenous zone is the anus—gratification occurs through the elimination of body wastes.
Phallic	3–6 years	Superego develops as the result of the conflict over the sexual desire for the opposite-sex parent and the rivalry of the same-sex parent. Erogenous zone is the genital region—gratification is focused on individual's own genitals.
Latency	6 years–puberty	Libido becomes dormant. Focus is on the development of skills necessary for adult functioning. There is no particular erogenous zone.
Genital	Puberty–adulthood	Focus is on mature sexual functioning and reproduction. Erogenous zone is the genital area.

The **ego** is the source of reason and operates according to the reality principle, which is based on the conditions and demands of the real world. The ego seeks to fulfill the demands of the id in ways that are acceptable to society. The ego does not, however, represent an internalized set of social rules. This aspect of the psyche develops out of the ego and becomes the superego.

The **superego,** which represents one's conscience and morals and social conventions, demands strict adherence with cultural expectations. When its demands are disobeyed, the superego punishes the individual by producing guilt, shame, and fear.

An individual's behavior depends on the dynamic interactions of these three structures. The ego continually negotiates settlements between the demands of the id and the constraints of the superego.

Freud's theory of **psychosexual development** is a stage theory of development, based on how the libido is transformed into different structures and modes of expression (see Table 2.2). During each stage, the increased sensitivity of a particular area of the body makes it an erogenous zone where libidinal energy is invested and pleasure is experienced (Freud, 1920/1965). Different erogenous zones are activated over the course of development as the child's genetic blueprint unfolds.

The ideas put forth by Freud on the importance of early development and the role that parents play in influencing children's personalities have become ingrained in our culture. One of his most enduring contributions is his concept of the unconscious—the idea that there are influences on our behavior of which we generally are not aware. His notion that there are defense mechanisms—such as repression and projection—that protect individuals from anxiety and fear also has become widely accepted. His belief that early experiences and patterns of social interactions can produce mental illness led him

ego the part of the psyche that is the source of reason and operates within the conditions and demands of the real world

superego the part of the psyche that represents one's conscience and morals and social conventions

psychosexual development Freud's stage theory of development, based on how the libido is transformed into different structures and modes of expression to develop psychoanalysis—a form of therapy designed to help individuals recover their memories of the early interactions that have influenced their behavior.

Notwithstanding the contributions, there are serious problems with Freud's theory. The most important criticism is that the theory is not based on solid scientific evidence. In fact, although Freud proposed a developmental theory, he never really studied children; he obtained his evidence from his patients' recollections, during psychoanalysis, of their childhoods. Furthermore, many aspects of Freud's theory are unmeasurable and therefore untestable—how does one measure libidinal energy or identify the source of the superego? Inherent in Freud's discussion of the libido and its source of gratification is the notion that infants and young children are sexual beings and derive erotic pleasure from their interactions. This notion was (and still is) very controversial. Freud developed his theory during a period in history when society was very restrictive in its views about sexuality. Other Freudian concepts reflect cultural biases, such as the implication that male sexuality has a superiority that makes it a source of envy and jealousy for females (Horney, 1967).

ERIKSON'S PSYCHOSOCIAL THEORY

Erik Erikson (1902–1994) was a German-born psychoanalyst who extended and refined Freud's theory of development. Erikson accepted Freud's theory of psychosexual development but believed that, for several reasons, it was incomplete:

+ It gave too little recognition to social and cultural influences.
+ It failed to recognize developmental changes beyond adolescence.
+ It did not give enough emphasis to ego development.
+ It focused primarily on the development of neurotic and maladaptive behavior and did not give enough consideration to *healthy* development.

Erikson argued that, during development, individuals go through a series of eight **psychosocial crises** that reflect a struggle between two conflicting personality characteristics. These crises represent critical periods in personality development (Erikson, 1968). The sequence and type of crisis at each stage are fixed; individuals can do nothing to prevent a crisis from occurring or to change or speed up the sequence of crises. Erikson believed, however, that these crises manifest themselves differently from person to person. For example, although all infants experience the natural conflict between Trust and Mistrust during the first year of life, individual circumstances—such as the mother's responses to the infant's crying and her weaning practices—affect the outcome of the crisis. Thus, different levels of attention given to infants may affect their development of basic trust (Wallerstein & Goldberger, 1998).

Erikson's major contribution was the detailed definitions he provided of psychosocial stages and the crisis associated with each stage, shown in Table 2.3. In addition, Erikson recognized cultural differences (Erikson, 1963) and contributed significantly to the study of adolescence, especially the process by which adolescents form personal identities (Erikson, 1968). Unfortunately, though, apart from research on adolescent identity, there is little research on childhood and adult psychosocial crises. Moreover, many of Erikson's theoretical propositions, like other psychoanalytic ideas, are difficult, if not impossible, to test (Green, 1989).

WHAT ARE THE MAJOR ENVIRONMENT-BASED THEORIES OF CHILD DEVELOPMENT?

Environment-based theories maintain that the environment in which people live and the experiences they have are major determinants of behavior. According to this view, people are relatively passive in responding to the environments they are exposed

psychosocial crises In Erikson's lifespan theory, the struggles that occur at the various stages of development between two conflicting personality characteristics

TABLE 2.3

Erikson's Psychosocial Theory of Development

STAGE	RESULTS OF POSITIVE RESOLUTION OF CRISIS	AGES
Trust vs. Mistrust	Ability to predict and depend on one's own behavior and the behavior of others	0–1 year
Autonomy vs. Shame/Doubt	Ability to do things for oneself	2–3 years
Initiative vs. Guilt	High and realistic sense of ambition and independence	3–6 years
Industry vs. Inferiority	Active and satisfying involvement in activities	7–12 years
Identity vs. Identity Diffusion	Determination of one's identity	12–18 years
Intimacy vs. Isolation	Ability to commit to another and establish a close, loving relationship	20s
Generativity vs. Stagnation	Incorporation of the needs of others into one's personal life	20s–50s
Integrity vs. Despair	Healthy adjustment to aging and mortality	50s and beyond

SOURCE: Adapted from Erikson, 1959.

to during their lives. Behavioral changes occur only when the environment is changed. Environment-based studies focus on factors that determine how behavior changes in response to everyday events. In the opening vignette, the idea that exposure to domestic violence caused Tamika's behavior is an example of an environment-based view.

CLASSICAL CONDITIONING

Ivan Pavlov (1849–1936), a Russian physiologist, was the founder of modern learning theory. While studying dogs' digestive systems, he made an important accidental discovery. When food was placed on a dog's tongue, the dog salivated as a reflex response to the food. Pavlov noticed that, after a while, dogs also salivated when they saw the food coming. For this to happen, the dogs must have learned to associate the sight of food with the taste of the food. Thus, they learned a conditioned response to a previously neutral stimulus. Many people have noticed a similar pattern of conditioning in their pets—cats often come running at the sound of a can opener because they have associated the sound of the can opener with food (Crain, 1992).

In Pavlov's studies, the typical **classical conditioning** procedure was to present, over several trials, a *conditioned stimulus*—for example, a bright light—paired with an unconditioned stimulus, such as food. The food is an *unconditioned stimulus* because it automatically elicits a response, the *unconditioned response* of salivation. The light begins as a neutral stimulus, but with repeated pairings the dog learns to associate it with the food, thereby producing a *conditioned response*—salivating at the sight of the light. (Kehoe & Macrae, 1998).

The principles of classical conditioning were first applied to humans by John Watson (1878–1958). Watson argued that infants naturally respond with fear to only two events: suddenly losing support (fear of falling) and sudden loud noises. How, then, do children develop fear of snakes or dogs or the dark? Freud would have argued that a child's fear of snakes reflects his or her repressed, unconscious drives and instincts. For Watson, the answer was that children learn to be fearful through classical conditioning.

To test this idea, Watson and colleagues conditioned an 11-month-old boy named Albert to fear a white rat (Watson & Raynor, 1920). At first, Albert was not afraid of the rat. But then Albert was shown the rat while a loud noise was made. After four pairings, Albert was shown the rat by itself, and he whimpered and withdrew from it. A few days later,

classical conditioning Pavlov's theory of how responses to neutral stimuli become conditioned

FIGURE 2.2
An Example of Classical Conditioning

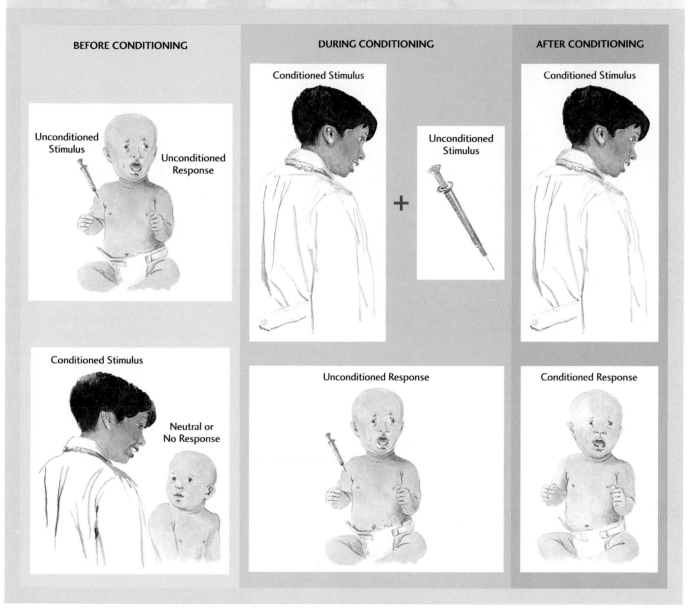

At first, the pain of the vaccination the child receives naturally elicits crying, but the sight of the doctor does not. After the child associates the doctor with the vaccination, the sight of the doctor elicits fear and crying. Thus, the child is classically conditioned to fear the doctor. Using classical conditioning principles, how might you recondition and eliminate the child's fear of the doctor?

Albert was tested to see whether he had generalized his fear to other objects or animals. He had indeed become fearful of all kinds of furry animals and objects such as rabbits and fur coats (Crain, 1992). Classical conditioning can thus be used to explain children's development of common fears such as that of going to visit the doctor (see Figure 2.2).

Watson also found a method to decondition fears. He used *systematic desensitization* to decondition the fears of a young child named Peter. Peter was afraid of many animals,

B. F. Skinner theorized that behaviors are conditioned as the result of the consequences associated
with a particular behavior. His model of operant
conditioning was extremely influential in identifying the environmental factors that control and
modify behavior. Can you describe the operant
processes through which such environmental factors influence behavior and development?

operant conditioning learning based
on the principle that the consequences
of a behavior affect the likelihood that
the behavior will be repeated

positive reinforcement presentation
of stimuli that increase the likelihood
that a behavior will recur

negative reinforcement removal of a
negative or aversive stimulus that
increases the likelihood that a
behavior will recur

punishment application of
unpleasant consequences to decrease
the likelihood that a behavior will be
repeated

extinction reducing unwanted
behavior by withholding all positive
consequences

shaping the process of rewarding
behaviors that approximate the
desired behavior

furry things, and mechanical objects. When Peter was relaxed and eating in his highchair,
Watson would bring in a caged animal and leave it visible in the distance. The animal was
gradually brought closer, allowing Peter to associate the pleasant feelings of eating with
the presence of the animal. Over repeated and gradual exposures, Peter eventually lost
his fear of the animal.

OPERANT CONDITIONING

B. F. Skinner (1905–1990) was concerned with how the environment shapes people's behaviors. **Operant conditioning** focuses on how the consequences of a behavior
affect the likelihood that the behavior will be repeated. For instance, if an infant is praised
when he or she takes a first step, the infant will be more motivated to take another step.

The principles of operant conditioning have been studied extensively and applied
effectively to many kinds of human behavior. Presenting **positive reinforcement** (such
as food or praise) increases the likelihood that a behavior will recur. Behavior also is
more likely to occur with **negative reinforcement,** which consists of removing a negative, or aversive, condition. Seat belt alarms are an example of an effective negative reinforcer: Once the seat belt is hooked, the annoying buzzing stops, thereby increasing
the chances that one will use seat belts in the future.

In contrast, **punishment** is the application of unpleasant consequences to decrease
the likelihood that a behavior will be repeated. Some parents use scolding or spanking
as punishment, in the hope that these consequences will reduce undesirable behaviors.
Punishment also may take the form of extra work, revoking privileges, or disapproval.
Studies show, however, that punishment often is effective for only a short time and may
have unintended negative side effects (such as increasing anxiety and timidity). A more
effective strategy for reducing unwanted behavior may be **extinction,** in which all positive consequences are withheld (Crain, 1992).

Complex strings of behaviors are learned through **shaping**—a process of rewarding behaviors that approximate the desired behavior. A small step toward a larger goal
is rewarded a few times, and then the next step is rewarded. For example, getting children to put their toys away can be shaped by rewarding them first when they approach
the toys, then when they pick them up, and then when they attempt to put them away
(Green, 1989).

SOCIAL LEARNING THEORY

*Four-year-old Todd watches as his friend Ian puts on high heels and a fancy dress. Several children
begin to comment about Ian's appearance, telling him he shouldn't dress up in girls' clothes. They
tease him and won't play with him for the rest of the day.*

In this story, Ian may have learned a hard lesson; the consequences of dressing in
girls' clothing can be severe, and he may be unlikely to do it again in the future. But what
does Todd learn from observing Ian? Does Todd need to experience the teasing to recognize that putting on "girls' clothes" might lead to negative consequences? According
to Albert Bandura (1925–present), much of children's learning occurs by watching the
consequences that occur to others for their behaviors, through a process called **vicarious reinforcement.** From his observation of Ian, Todd learns that boys shouldn't dress
up in girls' clothes. Knowledge of response consequences guides children's and adults'
future behavioral choices (Bandura, 1977).

Bandura's **social learning theory** is based on his idea that individuals are greatly
influenced by other people. In addition to being influenced by vicarious reinforcement,
Bandura believes that children and adults imitate, or model, the behavior of other people. Through *modeling*, individuals learn new behaviors, the contexts appropriate for those
behaviors, and their consequences.

Four processes are involved in modeling:

+ **Attention.** A person must pay attention to models to be able to imitate their behavior. The models most likely to capture one's attention are those with power, prestige, or charisma.
+ **Retention.** To imitate another person's behavior later on, a person must have a way to represent the behavior in her or his memory so that it can be retrieved when necessary.
+ **Motor reproduction.** To successfully reproduce another's behavior, a person must have the motor control or abilities to carry out the action. Imitation provides the pattern for a behavior but not the actual skill to accomplish it.
+ **Reinforcement and motivation.** Successful imitation requires that the behavior have the desired consequences, causing the person to want to repeat it.

Social learning theory often has been used to explain the impact of television on children's behavior. Popular television characters attract children's attention, and children may learn to act inappropriately by observing the behaviors of these powerful models (American Medical Association, 1996).

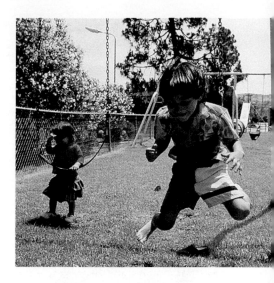

Imitation and modeling are powerful ways to learn or alter behavior. In this picture, the young sibling is trying to imitate the behavior of her older brother. What factors contribute to whether or not a child imitates or models someone else's behavior?

WHAT ARE THE MAJOR COGNITION-BASED THEORIES OF CHILD DEVELOPMENT?

Cognition-based theories emphasize the role of mental processes such as memory, decision making, and information processing in influencing development. Studies of cognitive development focus on how thinking and reasoning change over time and the effects of these changes on development. Cognition-based theories assume that an essential feature of development is that individuals strive for greater understanding of the world around them.

PIAGET'S COGNITIVE DEVELOPMENTAL THEORY

Jean Piaget (1896–1980) was a Swiss scientist who became interested in the question of how we come to know and understand the world around us. While administering intelligence tests to French school children, Piaget noticed a pattern in the reasons children gave for correct and incorrect answers on the tests. He speculated that children of different ages use different kinds of thought processes. Piaget also observed the development of his own children and became convinced that children's thinking is very different from that of adolescents and adults (Crain, 1992; Miller, 1993). This idea became the central tenet of his theory.

Piaget's View of Intelligence

Piaget defined intelligence as an active process in which people acquire information by interacting with objects, ideas, and other people. From these interactions, individuals develop better ways of adapting to life's challenges. According to Piaget, cognitive development is a process of developing the intellectual means to adapt to the environment (Langer & Killen, 1998).

Piaget believed that intelligence undergoes dramatic changes over time. These changes are so clear-cut that Piaget referred to them as stages of cognitive development (see Table 2.4). Each stage is marked by specific types of thinking and problem solving that differ qualitatively from those of other stages. Furthermore, the stages are sequential and nonreversible—children do not return to earlier stages of thinking (Zigler & Gilman, 1998).

vicarious reinforcement learning by watching the consequences to others of their behaviors

social learning theory Bandura's theory that individuals are greatly influenced by observing and imitating other people

TABLE 2.4

Piaget's Stages of Cognitive Development

STAGE TITLE	APPROXIMATE AGES (IN YEARS)	MAJOR FEATURES
Sensorimotor stage	0–2	Motoric knowledge Lack of understanding that objects continue to exist when not in view Present orientation
Preoperational stage	2–7	Symbolic representation Planning Thinking and problem solving guided by perception and appearances Egocentric thinking
Concrete operational stage	7–11	Logic used in problem solving Logic applied only to concrete objects and events
Formal operational stage	11 and beyond	Logic applied to hypothetical and abstract problems Concern with concepts like justice, equality, and fairness

Piaget's Stages of Cognitive Development

Piaget's first stage, the **sensorimotor stage,** begins at birth and lasts until about 2 years of age. The sensorimotor child relates to objects and people through his or her senses and motor skills, hence the name of the stage. The means for interacting with objects are innate reflexive behaviors, such as sucking and grasping, that change as children gain experience. Give an infant a small block, for example, and he or she will try to suck it. For infants, sucking is a **scheme;** that is, it is a cognitive guide or blueprint for processing information about the world. Infants have sensorimotor schemes that allow them to learn about the qualities of objects—their shapes, textures, and tastes. As children grow older, they develop more complex and abstract schemes. For instance, a high school student may have a scheme for solving algebraic equations.

A major accomplishment of the child's first two years is coming to understand that objects continue to exist even when she or he cannot see them—the concept of *object permanence*. During the first two years of life, children also begin to show signs of purposeful behavior, and by the end of this time, they understand how to use symbols (such as language) to represent their thoughts.

Children develop their problem-solving abilities through two continually occurring processes of adaptation: **assimilation,** or directly processing information that fits a scheme, and **accommodation,** or changing the scheme to fit the new information from the environment. For example, an infant may assimilate a new toy rattle into an existing scheme for smooth, round objects by sucking on it. He or she may then accommodate and develop a scheme for "rattle" after shaking it and realizing that some things make sounds when shaken. The interplay of assimilation and accommodation helps children adapt to their ever-changing environment.

The second stage in Piaget's theory, the **preoperational stage,** lasts from about 2 to 7 years of age. Preoperational children think in symbols, which permit more flexibility and planning in their problem solving. Preoperational children are egocentric in their thinking—they believe that everyone sees the world as they do. A child who hides only her or his face behind a curtain and then yells, "Come and find me," is exhibiting egocentric thinking: If I can't see you, you can't see me! Preoperational children are fooled by the appearance of an object, and their thinking is based on that appearance. For example, to a preoperational child, a half pint of milk poured into a tall, thin glass is more than the same half pint poured into a short, wide glass.

The third stage, the **concrete operational stage,** lasts from 7 to about 11 years of age. The major accomplishment of this stage is using logic to solve problems. This basic logic involves understanding that things maintain their identity even though their outward appearance may be changed. For instance, a concrete operational child recognizes that a half pint of milk poured from a tall, thin glass into a short, wide one is still a half pint of fluid because nothing has been added or taken away.

The final stage of Piaget's theory, the **formal operational stage,** begins around the age of 11. The major accomplishment of this stage is applying the logical principles first used in the concrete operational stage to more hypothetical and abstract situations. Because of this newly attained level of understanding, older children and adolescents become interested in and concerned about broad social issues and abstract concepts such as justice, equality, and fairness (Zigler & Gilman, 1998).

Literally thousands of studies have been done to test Piaget's ideas. His theory also has been expanded and refined by others, labeled *neo-Piagetians*. Neo-Piagetians (Case & Edelstein, 1993; Fischer & Bidell, 1998) have proposed theories based on the idea of stages of cognitive development, but they give more emphasis than Piaget did to the way information is processed in the brain. For instance, Case argues that children's thinking is organized into central conceptual structures—networks of concepts that allow for thinking about a variety of situations (Case & Okamoto, 1996). These structures change during development with increasing connections between different parts of the brain, which, in turn, increase memory capacity.

sensorimotor stage Piaget's first stage of cognitive development (0 to 2 years), in which the child relates to objects and people through his or her senses and motor skills

scheme a cognitive guide or blueprint for processing information about the world

assimilation directly processing information that fits a scheme

accommodation changing a scheme to fit new information from the environment

preoperational stage Piaget's second stage of cognitive development (2 to 7 years), in which children begin to think in symbols but are egocentric and perceptually bound in their thinking

concrete operational stage Piaget's third stage of cognitive development (7 to 11 years), in which children begin to use logic to solve problems

formal operational stage Piaget's fourth stage of cognitive development (begins around the age of 11), in which individuals are capable of applying logical principles to hypothetical and abstract situations

VYGOTSKY'S THEORY OF COGNITIVE DEVELOPMENT

Lev Vygotsky (1896–1934) was a Russian psychologist whose work with children with disabilities gave him an interest in issues of development (Rieber & Hall, 1998). He proposed a theory of development based on the idea that children use psychological tools such as language, numbering systems, and maps to develop higher levels of thinking. Language is particularly important to development because it allows children to develop new ideas and to regulate their behavior. Vygotsky argued that people use language to engage in internal dialogues that help them solve difficult tasks. For instance, you may say to yourself that when you finish reading this section you will take a break. Through the self-direction of your internal dialogue, you continue reading, thereby regulating your behavior and promoting the learning of the material. Vygotsky regarded this internal, or private, speech as a critical element in cognitive development and learning.

More than Piaget, Vygotsky emphasized the influence of social interaction on development. A 3-year-old boy, for example, may be unable to discuss a trip he took to the zoo, but, given a series of prompts by his mother, he can describe the animals he saw and the foods he ate during his trip. The mother acts as a skilled helper in using language to describe experiences. Similarly, a teacher may provide the information and support a student needs to carry out long division. The distance between what a child can do unaided and what a child can do through interaction with skilled helpers is called the **zone of proximal development.** It is within this zone that a person's potential for new learning is strongest.

The idea that children learn through social interactions with skilled helpers suggests that everyday experiences play a crucial role in children's development. Through their routine interactions, caregivers and teachers provide meaningful assistance to children in developing cognitive, social, and emotional skills (Stringer, 1998). For instance, caregivers often describe problem-solving strategies to children to help them guide their own behavior. As they grow older, children repeat these guidance messages to themselves, out loud at first. These messages later become the silent inner speech that is used to guide behavior (Vygotsky, 1934/1986).

INFORMATION PROCESSING THEORY

Studies of cognitive development have stimulated efforts to understand how people take in, remember, and use information from their experiences (Keil, 1998). **Information processing theory** is based on a model in which people have limited capacities for learning but can flexibly apply strategies to find ways around those limitations (Siegler, 1998).

The human information processing model, shown in Figure 2.3, has three parts. The **sensory register** allows people to very briefly retain visual, auditory, and other information taken in through the senses. **Short-term memory** holds information long enough for the person to evaluate and selectively act on inputs. The capacity of short-term memory is greater than that of the sensory register, but still only a few bits of information can be remembered (Bjorklund, 1995). **Long-term memory,** however, has an unlimited capacity for storing information over long periods of time. In long-term memory, information becomes linked to earlier memories, associations, and visual representations, creating networks that aid in recall. Individuals consciously link or classify ideas and use memory aids (such as rehearsal) to retrieve information.

Information processing theory has been particularly useful for understanding why children and adults remember information differently. For instance, 4-year-old children are less likely than adults to use memory aids and thus are less likely to process information so that it is retained in long-term memory. The theory also is helpful in understanding other changes that occur in information processing as we grow older.

---

zone of proximal development Vygotsky's term for the distance between what a child can do unaided and what a child can do through interaction with skilled helpers

information processing theory explanations for development that are based on a model in which people have limited capacities for learning but can flexibly apply strategies to find ways around those limitations

sensory register the part of the information processing system that allows people to very briefly retain information taken in through the senses

short-term memory the part of the information processing system that holds information long enough for the person to evaluate and selectively act on the input

long-term memory the part of the information processing system that has an unlimited capacity for storing information over long periods of time

FIGURE 2.3
Information Processing System

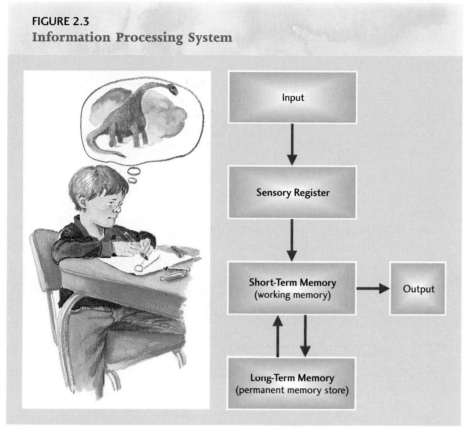

This diagram depicts the three parts of the information processing system. Can you explain what these parts are and how they work together?

WHAT ARE THE MAJOR CONTEXTUAL THEORIES OF CHILD DEVELOPMENT?

Contextual theories emphasize the interaction between the biological and environmental forces that influence behavior and development in particular contexts. Although these theories are diverse, each is based on the idea that, to truly understand child development, one must study children in their historical, social, and cultural contexts. Development occurs when a child acts within the environment to produce change.

BRONFENBRENNER'S ECOLOGICAL THEORY

Urie Bronfenbrenner (1917–present) used a concept from earth science—ecology—to outline the interplay between the child and his or her immediate social and physical environment. As shown in Figure 2.4, the child's experiences are viewed as subsystems within larger systems, or a set of nested structures (Bronfenbrenner, 1979).

The innermost circle in the **ecological model** in Figure 2.4 represents the child's **microsystem** (immediate environment) and includes influences such as physical objects (toys and technology), the structure of the environment, and the roles of and relationships among family members (Bronfenbrenner & Morris, 1998). This immediate environment has important effects on development. In a classic series of studies of the microsystem, Caldwell and colleagues (Bradley & Caldwell, 1976; Elardo, Bradley, & Caldwell, 1975) found that the quality of 6-month-old infants' physical and intellectual

ecological model Bronfenbrenner's model of the different spheres of influence

microsystem the inner sphere of the ecological model, which represents the immediate environment and includes influences such as physical objects, the structure of the environment, and the roles and relationships among family members

FIGURE 2.4
Bronfenbrenner's Ecological Model

Notice that the different spheres contain different types of influences. Bronfenbrenner believed that these different levels of influence interact to affect a person's development and behavior. This model depicts the complexity of contextual theories of development.

environments (such as the presence of appropriate play materials and opportunities for daily stimulation) related to their intellectual performance four years later. Similar results have been obtained in more recent studies (Brooks-Gunn, 1995).

The middle sphere of the ecological model is the **mesosystem,** which encompasses the connections among settings including the child and how these connections influence the child—for example, how a child's relationships at school affect her or his relationships with extended family members. In one of the first studies of mesosystem influences, it was found that children whose parents were actively involved in their hospital care were less emotionally distressed (both while in the hospital and at home up to a year later) than were children whose parents were allowed only brief visits (Prugh et al., 1953). Introducing people from one of the children's settings (the family) into another (the hospital) helped ease the transition between them.

The next circle, the **exosystem,** represents the linkages among settings, one of which does not include the child, and how these influence development. External settings include parents' social worlds, such as their employment, church attendance, and friends, and the physical environment beyond the immediate setting, such as neighborhood conditions. Researchers studying the exosystem have found, for instance, that children who live in violent neighborhoods have difficulty sleeping, have impaired cognitive performance, and often are aggressive, depressed, and fearful (Gorman-Smith & Tolan,

mesosystem the middle sphere of the ecological model, which encompasses the connections among settings including the child and how these connections influence the child

exosystem the part of the ecological model that represents the linkages among settings, one of which does not include the child, and how these influence development

1998; Horn & Trickett, 1998). The outermost circle, the **macrosystem,** represents larger societal values, historical changes, and social policies (Bronfenbrenner, 1986).

Bronfenbrenner's ecological model is based on his assumption that the environment plays a decisive role in development. But the child and his or her environment are not separate. The child interacts with the environment of which he or she is a part, and these interactions are the engine of development (Bronfenbrenner & Morris, 1998). Children meet their environment most directly in everyday situations (micro- or mesosystem interactions), but these are embedded in the larger physical, social, and cultural contexts (the exosystem), which also affect their development (Magnusson, 1995).

DYNAMIC SYSTEMS THEORY

One of the newest theories in the study of development is **dynamic systems theory** (Thelen & Smith, 1998). The basic ideas of dynamic systems come from research done outside of the social sciences, largely in physics and biology. Dynamic systems theorists assume that complex systems form from basic and simple conditions without requiring a master plan for development (Thelen & Smith, 1994, 1998). This is a new way of thinking about development. Rather than unfolding from a master plan coded by the genes, development is believed to involve self-organization, in which systems change as a result of their interactions. The individual parts of a system, called **control parameters,** interact in ways that eventually lead to advancement to a new level or a new form. Control parameters can include external as well as internal factors. In this way, dynamic systems theory emphasizes the strong interconnections between children and their environments.

Consider the development of walking as a dynamic system (see Figure 2.5). Walking is a motion of coordinated leg movements that is performed easily by most people.

FIGURE 2.5
A Dynamic Systems Model of Walking

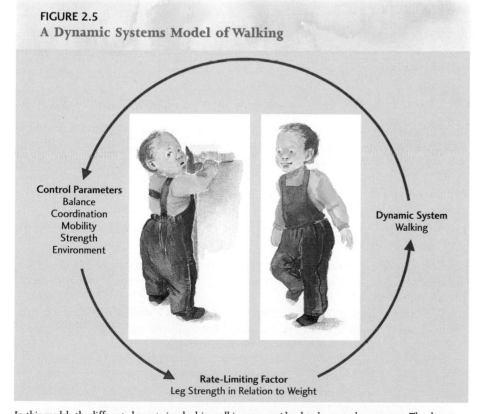

Control Parameters
Balance
Coordination
Mobility
Strength
Environment

Dynamic System
Walking

Rate-Limiting Factor
Leg Strength in Relation to Weight

In this model, the different elements involved in walking are considered to be control parameters. The slowest-developing aspect is the rate-limiting component, which limits the speed at which the behavior is acquired. Once this aspect develops, the system evolves into a new form—walking.

macrosystem the outermost sphere of the ecological model, which represents societal values and attitudes

dynamic systems theory a theory based on the idea that complex systems form from basic and simple conditions without requiring a master plan for development

control parameters the individual parts of a dynamic system

Walking also is highly variable and complex because it requires constant readjustments to allow for different surfaces and different speeds. How does a child develop these co-ordinated motions and learn to adjust them as needed? A child has acquired many components of walking before she or he actually walks—balance, coordination of the legs, stepping abilities, and leg strength. At some point, these separate pieces all come together and the child is able to propel herself or himself across the floor for a few steps, usually with great concentration and little grace.

The slowest, or last-developing, part of a system is called the **rate-limiting component;** when it develops, the system evolves into a new form (Thelen, 1989). For many children, the last part of the "walking puzzle," the rate-limiting component, is leg strength. When their legs develop adequate strength, balance improves, enabling them to shift their weight back and forth on one leg as they take a step. If assistance is provided to reduce the input of the rate-limiting (leg strength) component, such as by putting children into a walker, they can easily walk earlier than development normally would allow. Once children are walking unaided, practice at using all the parts of the system together leads to smoother and better performance. As you can see from this example, a new behavior—walking—emerges out of several different systems that eventually work together to produce this new ability. Later, with further adjustments and development of individual pieces of the motor system, brain, and body, the child will move to another new form—running.

HOW IS CHILD DEVELOPMENT STUDIED?

At 4 years of age, Bridget is a typical preschooler. Her best friend is Ivanna, and she seldom plays with boys. Bridget, like many other children, prefers to play with children who are the same sex as she. Scientists have been trying to discover why children prefer same-sex playmates (Martin, 1994), but how do they investigate a question like this? Finding an answer requires application of scientific reasoning and use of the scientific method.

SCIENTIFIC REASONING AND THE SCIENTIFIC METHOD

Scientific reasoning is similar to good everyday problem solving. When you need to solve a problem, you apply logical reasoning to minimize the number of possible explanations, with the ultimate goal of finding one probable explanation (Overton, 1998). Scientific reasoning is designed to produce results that are objective (they are measurable and observable by others), reliable (they can be replicated repeatedly), and valid (they accurately describe the phenomenon in question).

To solve the many mysteries of child development, researchers use the scientific method. The scientific method involves four steps:

1. **Formulating a hypothesis.** Through observation and study, a scientist develops an educated expectation, or hypothesis, about the phenomenon or behavior he or she is interested in.
2. **Designing a study.** The scientist strategically designs a study that tests the hypothesis. The study may involve many different methods, such as structured interviews, observations, or experiments in the laboratory.
3. **Collecting evidence.** The scientist uses the strategy that he or she has designed to collect information to test the accuracy of the hypothesis.
4. **Interpreting and reporting the evidence.** The scientist analyzes the data and interprets the patterns of the findings as they relate to the hypothesis.

Consider the hypothesis that children play with same-sex peers because they have common interests. If this hypothesis is accurate, we would expect children to play more

rate-limiting component the slowest, or last-developing, part of a dynamic system

Resonating with a Theory
Assessing Your Personal Beliefs

For some people, one theory "resonates" more than another—it makes more sense to them and just feels right. Which of the theories resonates with you? On each continuum, mark where your beliefs about the basic issues of human development fall. Then compare your answers with those that match different theoretical perspectives.

Dominant Influence: To what extent do you think biological and internal factors account for development?

Biological and Internal Influences

Minor ——————————— Major

To what extent do you think environmental factors account for development?

Environmental Influences

Minor ——————————— Major

Importance of Early Experience: Do you think that the experiences of early childhood are especially important to development?

Yes ——————————— No

Continuity/Discontinuity: Do you think development proceeds smoothly?

Yes ——————————— No

Now compare your responses to those that follow, given by theorists from different perspectives.

Issues in Development from Each Theoretical Perspective

	EMPHASIS ON BIOLOGICAL FACTORS	EMPHASIS ON ENVIRONMENTAL FACTORS	EMPHASIS ON EARLY EXPERIENCE	EMPHASIS ON CONTINUITY
Biology-Based Theories				
Evolutionary	Major	Minor	No	No
Ethology	Major	Minor	Yes	No
Attachment	Major	Major	Yes	No
Neurodevelopmental	Major	Major	Yes	No
Psychoanalytic Theories				
Freud	Major	Minor	Yes	No
Erikson	Major	Minor	No	No
Environment-Based Theories				
Classical Conditioning	Minor	Major	No	Yes
Operant Conditioning	Minor	Major	No	Yes
Social Learning	Minor	Major	No	Yes
Cognition-Based Theories				
Piaget	Major	Major	Yes	No
Vygotsky	Major	Major	Yes	No
Information Processing	Major	Some	No	Yes
Contextual Theories				
Ecological	Minor	Major	No	No
Dynamic Systems	Major	Major	No	No

This picture depicts a common scene: boys playing with other boys. Although the tendency of boys to play with other boys and girls to play with other girls is widely recognized, the reasons for it remain unclear. Can you identify the steps in the scientific method that would allow researchers to test their ideas about the reasons for these play preferences?

often with same-sex peers during gender-typed activities. For instance, a girl would be more likely to play with other girls when playing with a kitchen set than when swinging, a non-gender-typed activity. To test this hypothesis, a scientist might design a study in which a team of observers watches certain children while they play and notes the sex of the children who play with them and what they are doing at that time. After some amount of time, the scientist summarizes and analyzes the observations. The scientist then interprets the findings to determine whether the children were more likely to play with same-sex peers when they were involved in gender-typed activities than when they were involved in non-gender-typed activities. When Maccoby (1988) investigated this hypothesis, she did not find support for it. Instead, children played with same-sex playmates regardless of the type of activity. Thus, this same-sex preference appears to be due to factors other than shared interests. When a hypothesis is not confirmed, scientists often learn interesting new information, which may change theories and help them formulate different hypotheses to test.

BASIC AND APPLIED DEVELOPMENTAL RESEARCH

Basic developmental research is designed to answer broad, fundamental questions about development, such as the following:

- ✦ What are the causes of developmental disabilities?
- ✦ How is language acquired?
- ✦ What emotions are infants born with?

Applied developmental research is designed to solve practical problems, such as

- ✦ how to treat children with developmental delays
- ✦ how to improve the language skills of children who suffer head injuries
- ✦ how to help parents cope with chronically ill infants

Both types of research are necessary for understanding child development. Basic research lays the foundation for the applied research that follows. Additionally, applied research often produces questions that can be answered only through basic research (Herrmann, 1998).

TABLE 2.5

Comparing Different Research Strategies

METHOD	CONTROL AND STRUCTURE	DETERMINATION OF CAUSALITY	GENERALIZES WELL	DIRECT APPLICATION TO REAL LIFE
Case studies	No	No	No	Yes
Clinical interviews	No	No	Possibly	Possibly
Survey studies	No	No	Possibly	No
Naturalistic studies	No	No	Possibly	Yes
Correlational studies	No	No	Possibly	Possibly
Experimental studies	Yes	Yes	Possibly	No

RESEARCH STRATEGIES

For both basic and applied developmental research, scientists have developed methods, or research designs, to help them determine whether their hypotheses are correct. No single research design is perfect, and each research design has advantages and disadvantages. The following qualities vary according to the design of the study:

- ✦ Degree of control and structure
- ✦ Degree to which cause and effect can be determined
- ✦ Degree to which the findings of the study generalize to other people or settings
- ✦ Degree to which the findings directly apply to real-life events and processes

Table 2.5 outlines how these qualities apply to the six different types of research designs discussed in this chapter.

How do scientists select the methods they believe will be most useful in investigating a problem? First, the theory that guides their research may lead them to choose a particular method. Ethologists, for instance, choose methods that allow them to collect data in natural settings, because they are interested in observing the adaptive functions of behaviors as they occur in everyday situations. Learning theorists are more likely to choose controlled settings, such as laboratory experiments where they can manipulate conditions to study the effects of reinforcement on specific behaviors.

Second, the research question may dictate the best methods, leading scientists to adopt different methods at different times. For example, when first investigating a question, a scientist might examine behaviors in a natural setting. After formulating a testable hypothesis, he or she may then move into a more controlled environment where cause and effect can be tested.

Case Studies

In a **case study,** the researcher collects information about aspects of a person's life, such as medical history, family background, school grades, friendships and relationships, intelligence and achievement, personality characteristics, or dreams and desires. The advantage of this design is that it allows an in-depth view of the person. The disadvantage is that the information may not generalize to other people because of unique features of the person (Yin, 1994).

One of the earliest case studies was Charles Darwin's detailed diary study of his infant son's behavior (Darwin, 1877). Other important case studies have been based on the

case study method in which the researcher collects information about aspects of a person's life lives of famous people such as Mahatma Gandhi (Erikson, 1969). Case studies may feature people who are unusual or have a noteworthy condition, such as Victor (Chapter 1). More recently, a case study of a severely neglected and abused child named Genie provided insights into how development proceeds under extremely harsh conditions (Curtiss, 1977).

Clinical Interviews

In a **clinical interview,** the researcher asks detailed questions in interaction with the participant. The goal of the clinical interview is to identify how the individual thinks about some topic. In the following example of a clinical interview (Piaget, 1946/1969, p. 207), the researcher is exploring children's understanding of age. This interview reveals a common misunderstanding that young children have about age: that it is directly related to size.

Experimenter: *Are you the same age? (as his older sister)*

Filk (boy, age 5): *No, because we weren't born at the same time.*

Experimenter: *Who was born first?*

Filk: *She was.*

Experimenter: *Will you be the same age as her one day or will the two of you never be the same age?*

Filk: *Soon I will be bigger than her, because men are bigger than women. Then I shall be older.*

The data obtained in a clinical interview may be biased by participants telling the experimenter what they believe the experimenter wants to hear (Garbarino & Stott, 1992). Also, the method can be used only with language-proficient participants and thus is not useful with very young children or with children who have language problems. The advantage of this method is its flexibility. The clinical interview can be used to probe for new information or to gain insights into people's thoughts and feelings.

Survey Studies

A **survey study** is used to determine how a number of people respond to a set of structured questions. A survey may be conducted by phone, in person, or by mail. An advantage is that data for many people can be obtained easily, but a disadvantage is that people often respond inaccurately as they try to present themselves in the most positive way (Fowler, 1993).

If you have answered questions for a telephone poll, you have been involved in a survey study. Survey studies are popular for gathering data about demographics (age, income, marital status), beliefs and attitudes, leisure activities, political beliefs, and consumer choices. Several large-scale surveys have been done on adults. One is the General Social Survey, which covers topics such as attitudes, life satisfaction, health, religion, sex, and race. Another is the National Health Interview Survey, designed to obtain information about eating and health habits. The National Survey of Children is one of the few large-scale studies of a broad range of topics done on children (Cozby, Worden, & Kee, 1989). Every decade, the US Census Bureau conducts one of the largest surveys, encompassing almost the entire US population.

Naturalistic Studies

In a **naturalistic study,** researchers observe the behavior of people in their natural environments—homes, schools, malls, or parks. Because researchers are watching peo-

clinical interview method in which the researcher asks detailed questions while interacting with the participant

survey study method in which a number of people respond to a set of structured questions

naturalistic study method in which researchers observe the behavior of people in their natural environments ple in their familiar everyday settings, the people tend to behave normally. A disadvantage of naturalistic studies is the difficulty of generalizing from one setting to another setting. In addition, the researcher has no control over the naturalistic setting, making it virtually impossible to determine cause and effect.

Thorne (1993)conducted a year-long naturalistic study in public school classrooms in California and Michigan. She observed children's social behavior in the lunchrooms, hallways, and playgrounds. From these observations, she described how boys and girls interact. For instance, she concluded that both sexes tend to play in same-sex groups but that children cross gender lines for certain games such as "chase and kiss." Thorne's data did not enable her to draw cause-and-effect conclusions, though, because she could not systematically control for variables that might explain why children behaved as they did.

Correlational Studies

Are children who watch more television more aggressive? The important research hypothesis that they tend to be more aggressive has been difficult to test. Because so many children watch television, it is difficult to find children who do not watch television to serve as a comparison group. In such cases, researchers use correlational studies. A **correlational study** compares participants (children, in this case) on two variables to determine whether the variables relate to each other: Are children who watch more television more likely to be aggressive than children who watch less television?

To uncover patterns in variables, researchers use **correlation coefficients** calculations of the relations between variables. Correlation coefficients range from +1.0 to −1.0. A positive score represents a positive relationship between variables (a high score on one variable is related to a high score on the other). Zero represents no relationship between variables, and a negative score represents an inverse relationship between variables (a high score on one variable is related to a low score on the other). Figure 2.6 illustrates positive and negative correlations.

Although correlational studies demonstrate how variables are related, they cannot reveal whether one of the variables causes the other one. In the example of television viewing and aggression, for instance, it is impossible to know whether television viewing causes children to be more aggressive. It may be that children who are aggressive are more inclined to watch television than are less aggressive children. Or, television viewing and aggression may each be related to a third variable that has not been considered, such as parental supervision. Perhaps when parents do not supervise their children closely, the children watch more television and are also more aggressive, even though the two are not directly linked (Cozby et al., 1989).

Sometimes correlational studies provide the only ethical way to study a topic. For example, the most scientifically sound way to study the effects of spanking on children would be to have one group of parents spank their children and another group not spank theirs. But this would not be ethical. A correlational study allows researchers to ask parents about spanking practices and examine the data in relation to their children's behavior.

Experimental Studies

How do scientists investigate whether television viewing causes aggression? To answer the question of causality, scientists must use an **experimental study,** in which people are brought into a laboratory where the situation is manipulated and the effects of the manipulation are noted. The causes of behavior are easier to determine with experimental methods than with correlational methods because the scientist controls the sequence of events and any extraneous variables that may influence the findings in unexpected ways.

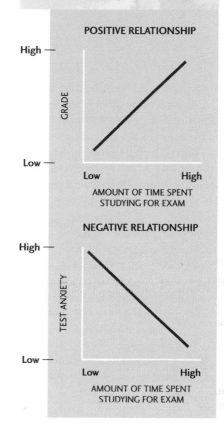

FIGURE 2.6
Examples of Correlational Relationships

Correlations provide evidence of the type of relationship between two variables. The top graph depicts a positive correlation—as students study more, their grades improve. The bottom graph depicts a negative correlation—as students study more, their anxiety about test performance decreases. Correlational research, however, cannot tell us the reasons for these relationships.

correlational study method in which researchers compare participants on two variables to determine whether the variables relate to each other

correlation coefficients calculated measures of the relations between variables

experimental study method in which scientists bring people into a laboratory where the situation is manipulated and the effects of the manipulation are noted

What Are the Ethical Concerns in Studying Child Development?

Scientists who study child development follow strict guidelines for the ethical treatment of the participants in their studies. Before running a study, scientists submit a plan for the study to the institutional review board at their college or university. This board is responsible for granting approval for and overseeing studies that involve human participants. To obtain approval, scientists must comply with the American Psychological Association guidelines for research with human participants and the guidelines for children developed by the Society for Research in Child Development. Special care is taken with children because they are assumed to be more vulnerable to stress and less able to evaluate what participation in a research program may mean. The guidelines for research with children include the following:

- **Protection from harm.** Each child must be protected from potential physical and psychological harm. No treatment or experimental condition can cause harm.

- **Protection of well-being.** In the course of research, if information that may seriously affect a child's well-being comes to the researcher's attention, the investigator has a responsibility to discuss the information with experts in the field so that the parents may arrange necessary assistance for their child.

- **Informed consent.** Each child and his or her parents have the right to know the procedures that will be used in the study and decide whether or not to be involved in the study. Informed consent also requires a description of the risks and benefits of the study.

- **Privacy.** Children involved in studies have the right to maintain their privacy. This is accomplished by allowing children to remain anonymous when they participate in studies, typically by assigning identification numbers rather than using names and by analyzing data at a group rather than an individual level.

- **Right to beneficial treatments.** Children have the right to receive any treatment that is found to be effective when used in a study. If a child is a member of a nontreated control group, she or he has the option of receiving the treatment as soon as the treatment is found to be successful.

Thinking It Through:

1. What special protections must be in place for children who participate in research, over and above those extended to adults?

2. What scientific risk is there in informing research participants about the specific nature of the study, the hypotheses, and the methods before the study begins?

---

random sampling selecting participants for a study at random

random assignment randomly assigning people to groups in a study so that the effects of uncontrolled variables will be the same for all groups in the study

independent variable condition that is assumed to be the cause of the behavior and is manipulated by the scientist

Scientists gain control over extraneous variables in several ways. One way is by trying to hold constant all other factors that may influence behavior. For instance, in a study of television violence, a scientist might hold constant the characteristics of the experimenter, the ages of the participants, the lighting, and the time of day participants are tested.

Not all variables can be easily controlled, however, especially characteristics of people. Scientists want to ensure that the effects of uncontrollable variables are randomly distributed across the groups involved in the study. For instance, a child's upbringing may influence his or her likelihood of being aggressive with other people, but it is impossible to identify and control all the variables related to a child's upbringing in any one study. To minimize the effects of these variables, scientists use randomization. They select participants at random, called **random sampling,** and they randomly assign people to groups, called **random assignment**. In this way, the effects of upbringing and other uncontrolled variables will be the same for all groups in the study.

Scientists design experimental studies by determining which variable they want to test the effects of. This is the **independent variable,** which is assumed to be the cause

How Can Results from Different Studies Be Combined?

Few single studies, no matter how well designed or analyzed, can assess the diversity of factors that influence development. Scientists therefore must review and synthesize studies that accumulate in a particular area of development (Harris, 1995). The traditional method of reviewing many studies is based on a researcher's subjective interpretation, but there is no guarantee that another researcher, reviewing the same literature, will reach a similar conclusion. Researchers now rely on the relatively new practice of using *meta-analysis* to more objectively interpret the meaning of large numbers of studies (Cooper & Hedges, 1994; Wolf, 1986).

By applying a clear set of guidelines for using statistical principles to summarize the results of previous studies, meta-analysis makes the process of reviewing child development literature (or any other literature) more a science than an art. The goal of meta-analysis is to make

the review process as replicable as any other piece of scientific work; any disagreements in the review of research studies become more a matter of method than of opinion (Wanner, 1992).

The use of meta-analysis has increased dramatically. This method has been used to address many important topics in child development, such as developmental changes (Fabes & Eisenberg, 1996), the impact of parents and peers (Lytton & Romney, 1991; Newcomb, Bukowski, & Pattee, 1993), and sex differences in behavior (Knight, Fabes, & Higgins, 1996).

One area in which meta-analysis is important is the assessment of treatment programs. For example, Lipsey (1994) examined the effectiveness of different approaches to the treatment of juvenile delinquency. The issue of concern is whether juvenile delinquents can be deterred through punishment or should be rehabilitated. Lipsey used meta-analysis

to examine the effectiveness of different treatment strategies, summarizing across 443 different studies. In general, Lipsey found that the most effective treatments are those emphasizing rehabilitation (employment, job skills, counseling). Programs emphasizing deterrence not only are less effective but actually produce greater subsequent rates of delinquency. Such applications of meta-analysis can provide guidance with important, real-life decisions.

Thinking It Through:

1. What problems does a scientist face when he or she wants to review the studies in an area of child development?
2. How can two reviewers, looking at the same literature, come to two different conclusions?
3. How can results from meta-analyses be useful to practitioners?

---

of the behavior and is manipulated by the scientist. If the independent variable is exposure to violent programming, one group of children watches a violent program and the other watches a nonviolent program. The children who watch the violent program are considered to be in the **experimental group,** whereas the children watching the nonviolent program are in the **control group.** All other variables are kept the same for both groups. The researcher then assesses whether children who received the independent variable (exposure to violent programming) differ from those who did not. The behavior thought to be affected by the independent variable is the **dependent variable**—in this case, aggressive behavior following the television viewing. Thus, in experimental studies, the "cause" is the independent variable and the "effect" is the dependent variable (Cozby et al., 1989).

Although the experimental method allows scientists to determine cause and effect, it has disadvantages. The major disadvantage is that laboratory situations often are not realistic. People may respond quite differently in a laboratory setting than in real life.

experimental group group that receives the independent variable

control group comparison group that is treated in the same way as the experimental group but does not receive the independent variable

dependent variable the behavior thought to be affected by the independent variable

Do Gifted Children Become Well-Adjusted Adults?

Many people believe that gifted children are odd and socially awkward. But is this stereotype true? One attempt to examine this issue was launched in 1920, when Lewis Terman (1877–1956) began a longitudinal study of gifted children. He was interested in discovering the origins and outcomes of being a genius. He was particularly interested in testing the popular belief that geniuses grow up to be maladjusted. This study is one of the classic longitudinal studies (Terman, 1925). Over 1000 highly intelligent (IQ scores of 140 and above, or 40 points over the average) children from California were followed from school age through the rest of their lives. Terman was involved in the study until the children were in their 40s and 50s (Terman & Oden, 1959), and then new researchers took over the study to continue following Terman's "Termites," as the participants called themselves.

Terman's participants were successful at all stages of their lives. As children, they did well in school, had satisfactory peer relationships, and showed early and intense interests in science and literature. Many more of the gifted participants finished college and obtained graduate degrees than did members of comparison groups with normal-range IQ scores. With respect to social adjustment and maturity, the gifted participants were similar to comparison groups of non-gifted people. Almost all of them married, and many had children. In their 40s, the gifted participants were at the peak of their careers.

The Termites included many distinguished scientists, doctors, lawyers, and inventors. One participant learned fifteen languages, and two others were awarded over a hundred patents. Generally, the participants seemed contented with their lives. The gifted participants did not grow up to be criminals or alcoholics; in

fact, their rates of criminal behavior and alcoholism were much lower than those for the general population. Even in their 70s, many of the participants had active and intellectually stimulating lives (Shurkin, 1992).

Thinking It Through:

1. Why is it important to test common-sense beliefs? In what ways does Terman's study dispel the myth that geniuses are eccentric?

2. If you were designing a study of the psychological adjustment of gifted children, what kinds of measures would you consider including in your study? Why is it difficult to measure adjustment?

3. Why are longitudinal studies difficult to conduct? What factors make them expensive? How do you keep participants interested in being in the study?

MEASURING CHANGE OVER TIME

Many of the most interesting questions in child development involve change over time. Is an outgoing and affectionate toddler likely to grow up to be a teenager who has many friends? Do active children become active adults? To answer these questions, scientists use methods that assess change over time.

One method for assessing change is the **cross-sectional study.** As Figure 2.7 illustrates, in cross-sectional studies, individuals of different ages are tested at the same point in time, and the results from each age group are compared. For instance, a researcher interested in developmental changes in memory capacity might test children who are 4, 6, and 8 years old. Children at each age would be shown a group of objects and later asked what they remembered about the objects. By averaging the memory scores for children at each age, researchers could get an idea how memory capacity changes.

Another method for assessing change over time is the **longitudinal study** (see Figure 2.7), in which the same group of individuals is tested at different points in time. When the results at the different points in time are compared, developmental changes become apparent. Problems of longitudinal studies include a tendency for some indi-

cross-sectional study method in which individuals of different ages are tested at the same point in time and the results from each age group are compared

longitudinal study method in which the same group of individuals is tested at different points in time viduals to drop out and for test scores to improve because of repeated testing. These studies also are expensive and time-consuming (Willett, Singer, & Martin, 1998).

Both cross-sectional and longitudinal studies have limitations in identifying age-related changes. In cross-sectional studies, the children in each age group make up a **cohort,** or unique birth group. The scientist may be unaware of important systematic ways in which cohorts differ. For instance, suppose a comparison of computer skills in 10-year-olds and 60-year-olds reveals that more of the 10-year-olds are highly skilled. The scientist might be tempted to conclude that as people grow older they lose computer skills. However, these two cohorts have experienced different historical times, which affected the amount of their exposure to computers in the first place.

To minimize problems with cross-sectional and longitudinal designs, scientists may use a combination of the two strategies, called a **cohort-sequential research design.** In this design, illustrated in Figure 2.8, a cross-sectional study is expanded so that data are collected from the same cohorts at different points in time. New participants can be added at each time point to prevent the problems of repeated testing and attrition.

MEASURING CHILDREN'S BEHAVIOR

Developmental scientists have devised many ways to measure variables of interest, such as aggression, memory, intelligence, and stress. Four broad categories of measures are used. *Physiological measures* record responses of the body, such as heart rate, hormone production, and galvanic skin response (sweating), which are used to assess arousal and anxiety. Activity in different parts of the brain can be assessed by recording electrical

To examine the influence of television on children, researchers often use experimental procedures. What are the strengths and weaknesses of the experimental method? How might a researcher examine television's influences using naturalistic procedures?

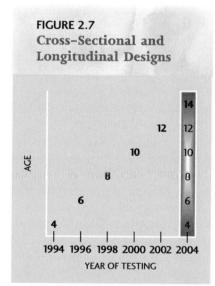

FIGURE 2.7
Cross-Sectional and Longitudinal Designs

This figure presents a graphic comparison of cross-sectional and longitudinal designs. The numbers in boldface indicate the ages at which children would be subjected to longitudinal testing: the same children would be studied every two years, from age 4 until age 14. The numbers in the boxed column represent the ages at which children would be subjected to cross-sectional testing: children between 4 and 14 years of age would all be tested at the same time. Can you identify the strengths and weaknesses of each design?

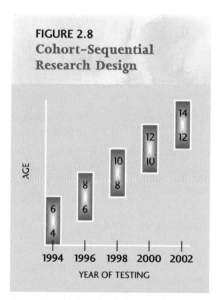

FIGURE 2.8
Cohort-Sequential Research Design

The cohort-sequential research design minimizes the problems of both cross-sectional and longitudinal designs. The figure depicts a design in which five consecutive cross-sectional studies (in the boxes) take place at two-year intervals. The same children are used, but new participants can be added at each time point to prevent the problems of repeated testing and attrition.

cohort a group of individuals who are the same age or who experience similar events at the same time

cohort-sequential research design a cross-sectional study expanded so that data are collected from the same cohorts at different points in time activity of brain. Brain cell activity is recorded through sensitive electrodes placed at various locations on the person's head and scalp.

Behavioral measures involve the direct assessment of behavior through observation. To investigate whether children have preferences for certain toys, observers watch them play to see if they choose one type of toy over another. To assess whether mothers and fathers respond to their children differently, observers watch and record how parents play with their children.

Self-reports are a third type of measure. Rather than observing children as they play with dolls or cars, a scientist might ask them which toy they prefer. Self-reports include questionnaires in which people respond to questions about their behavior, attitudes, beliefs, values, and habits. Self-report measures are the easiest type of information to gather, but people may not be accurate in reporting or may not remember the information they are asked to report on.

Projective measures indirectly assess individuals' psychological states. The typical strategy is to show a participant an ambiguous scene, such as a picture of a boy standing by a fireplace looking sad. The participant is then asked to make up a story about the boy. Or a child may be asked to draw a person or a family. From these stories and drawings, researchers infer the person's thinking and feelings. This method yields only subjective data, however, which might vary in interpretation from researcher to researcher.

As you can see, developmental scientists face many challenges as they choose a research question, theoretical basis, set of methods, and types of measures. But studying how behavior develops and changes over time can be rewarding and meaningful work.

CHAPTER SUMMARY

How do theories explain child development?

• Scientific theories are structured sets of ideas that help explain the complexities of child development, organize existing evidence, and provide guidance for future research.

• Developmental theories attempt to explain how behavior changes over time.

• Theories are judged by their usefulness, testability, ability to provide practical guidance, and ability to stimulate new research.

What are the major biology-based theories of child development?

• Evolutionary theory focuses on the idea that development of the individual is the result of the inheritance of characteristics that promote survival of the species.

• Ethological theory focuses on the evolutionary causes and adaptive value of behavior. Ethologists propose that there are critical and sensitive periods in development.

• Attachment theorists argue that early emotional ties with caregivers provide a child with an inner working model on which future relationships are based, and that attachment behaviors increase an infant's likelihood of survival.

• Neurodevelopmental theory focuses on how the brain develops and how experience influences this development.

What are the major psychoanalytic theories of child development?

• Psychoanalytic theories stress the role of unconscious internal drives as the major influences on development.

• Freud's psychosexual theory emphasized how sexual energy (the libido) develops. He argued that this energy is directed by the psyche, which consists of the id, ego, and superego, and that the libido becomes focused on different erogenous zones over five stages (oral, anal, phallic, latency, genital) of development.

• Erikson expanded on Freud's theory by emphasizing the role of social and cultural influences, recognizing developmental changes beyond adolescence, and focusing on healthy development. His psychosocial theory is based on crises that individuals undergo at different stages of development. How individuals resolve these crises influences their development.

What are the major environment-based theories of child development?

• Classical conditioning was discovered by Pavlov, who found that pairing a neutral stimulus with an unconditioned stimulus eventually elicits a conditioned response to the neutral, or conditioned, stimulus.

• Watson applied classical conditioning to the study of children's emotions and found that emotions such as fear often result from the pairing of a once-neutral stimulus with an un-conditioned stimulus that naturally elicits fear.

• Skinner focused on learning that occurs because of the consequences that follow a response (operant conditioning). Behaviors that lead to positive consequences are more likely to be repeated than those that lead to aversive consequences.

• Social learning theory emphasizes the roles of observation and imitation. Individuals develop new patterns of behavior by observing others and then modeling their behaviors. For modeling to occur, the behavior of another must be attended to, retained, reproduced, and reinforced.

What are the major cognition-based theories of child development?

• Piaget's theory of cognitive development maintains that children's thinking is qualitatively different from that of adolescents or adults.

• In Piaget's four stages, children move from an understanding of the world based on its sensory and perceptual qualities (sensorimotor and preoperational periods) to an understanding based on the application of complex and abstract logic (concrete and formal operations). Cognitive development involves adapting to one's environment, using the processes of assimilation and accommodation.

• Vygotsky's theory of cognitive development emphasizes the importance of psychological tools, such as language, in development. Vygotsky also places great emphasis on the role of the social context and how social interactions support development in a learner's zone of proximal development.

• Information processing theory focuses on both environmental input and the processing of information in the brain. The individual has limited but flexible capacities for processing information from the environment. These capacities change over time.

What are the major contextual theories of child development?

• Bronfenbrenner's ecological theory features the interplay of the individual and his or her social and physical environment. The microsystem represents the immediate environment (the family); the mesosystem encompasses the connections among settings including the child (such as school and family); the exosystem represents the linkages among settings, one of which does not include the child (the culture); and the macrosystem represents societal values and attitudes. The interactions between the child and the environment are the engine of development.

• Dynamic systems theory is a theoretical approach to understanding development that focuses on self-organization. Separate components of behavior develop at different times and then come together to produce new forms of action and behavior.

How is child development studied?

• The goals of scientific research are to produce findings that are objective, reliable, and valid. The scientific method involves four steps: formulating a hypothesis, designing a study, collecting evidence, and interpreting and reporting the evidence.

• Basic research is designed to investigate broad core developmental issues, whereas applied research is designed to solve practical problems.

• Many research strategies are available for testing hypotheses, and each has advantages and disadvantages. Case studies involve collecting information from individuals. In a clinical interview, questions are asked in a semistructured format. Survey studies are used to determine how people respond to structured questions. Naturalistic studies involve observing behavior in natural settings. Correlational studies assess the relationships between variables. Experimental studies investigate cause and effect.

• Change over time is measured through the use of developmental designs. In cross-sectional studies, individuals of different ages are tested at the same time. In longitudinal studies, the same group of individuals is followed and tested over time. In cohort-sequential studies, multiple groups of individuals are followed and tested over time.

• Different measures are used to study children's development. Physiological measures assess activity in the body, such as heart rate and electrical activity in the brain. Behavioral measures require direct observation of people's behavior. Self-reports involve asking people to answer questions about their behavior or attitudes. Projective measures use people's responses to ambiguous scenes or pictures to measure their psychological states indirectly.

KEY TERMS & CONCEPTS

accommodation *(41)*	cohort *(55)*	correlation coefficients *(51)*
assimilation *(41)*	cohort-sequential research design *(55)*	cross-sectional study *(54)*
attachment theory *(32)*	concrete operational stage *(41)*	dependent variable *(53)*
case study *(49)*	control group *(53)*	dynamic systems theory *(45)*
classical conditioning *(36)*	control parameters *(45)*	ecological model *(43)*
clinical interview *(50)*	correlational study *(51)*	ego *(34)*

ethological theory *(31)*
evolutionary theories *(31)*
exosystem *(44)*
experimental group *(53)*
experimental study *(51)*
extinction *(38)*
fact *(30)*
formal operational stage *(41)*
id *(33)*
independent variable *(52)*
information processing theory *(42)*
libido *(33)*
long-term memory *(42)*
longitudinal study *(54)*

macrosystem *(45)*
mesosystem *(44)*
microsystem *(43)*
naturalistic study *(50)*
negative reinforcement *(38)*
neurodevelopmental approaches *(32)*
operant conditioning *(38)*
positive reinforcement *(38)*
preoperational stage *(41)*
psychoanalytic theories *(33)*
psychosexual development *(34)*
psychosocial crises *(35)*
punishment *(38)*
random assignment *(52)*

random sampling *(52)*
rate-limiting component *(46)*
scheme *(41)*
sensorimotor stage *(41)*
sensory register *(42)*
shaping *(38)*
short-term memory *(42)*
social learning theory *(38)*
superego *(34)*
survey study *(50)*
theory *(30)*
vicarious reinforcement *(38)*
zone of proximal development *(42)*

ACTIVITIES & APPLICATIONS
Relating to Child Development

1. Use your knowledge of theories of development to generate explanations of the behavior of Tamika, in the chapter opening vignette. How would Bandura explain her behavior? How could Tamika's behavior be understood based on neurodevelopmental theory?

2. Where do you stand in the nature versus nurture debate? What evidence, experiences, and observations can you cite to support your position? How do your ideas on the respective roles of biology and environment in development compare with those of your classmates?

3. Think about your own behavior. Can you think of examples of behaviors that you learned through operant conditioning? Through social learning? Describe how you might have acquired these behaviors.

4. Design an individual or collaborative research project using one of the research strategies described in this chapter. Begin by posing a question that you wish to answer about child development. Try to formulate a hypothesis. Now, what methods will you use to test this hypothesis? Who will your participants be and how many will there be? What information will you need, where and how will you get it, and in what form will you record it? What ethical issues will you need to consider? What might be the outcomes of applications of your findings?

Grasping the Whole

Benchmark Characteristics of the Stages of Child Development Used in This Book

DEVELOPMENTAL STAGE	APPROXIMATE AGES	PROMINENT CHARACTERISTICS OF STAGE
Prenatal	Conception to birth	Unfolding of genetic code
		Formation of basic organs and structures
Neonatal	0–2 months	Transition to extra-uterine life
		Adaptation to external environment
		Establishment of basic emotions and social interactions
Infancy/toddlerhood	2–36 months	Transition to symbolic thought and language
		Development of locomotion
		Development of attachment relationships
Early childhood	3–6 years	Development of autonomous learning and regulated actions
		Focus on parent–child discipline
		Development of peer relationships
Late childhood	7–10 years	Transition to school
		Development of logical thinking
		Development of self-comparisons
Early adolescence	11–14 years	Achievement of puberty, growth spurt, and focus on physical appearance
		Development of risk-taking behaviors
		Interest in intimate relationships
Late adolescence	15–19 years	Development of formal logic
		Achievement of physical maturation
		Preparation for adulthood

Status Report on Child Development

This graph shows the population of the United States as a function of age, from birth to 19 years. Notice how the population increases from birth to age 5 and then begins to drop off. What factors contribute to the increased population rates in early life and the decreased population rates later in childhood and adolescence? What impact might these data have for social policy?

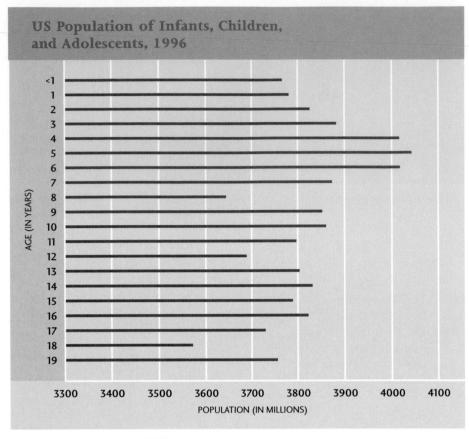

US Population of Infants, Children, and Adolescents, 1996

SOURCE: US Census Bureau, 1997.

SUGGESTED READINGS

Elder, G. H., Modell, J., & Parke, R. D. (1993). *Children in time and place.* New York: Cambridge University Press. Edited volume that focuses on how major historical events, such as war and economic depression, influence children's development. Thought-provoking analyses are presented by noted scholars who examine the link between social changes and developmental outcomes.

Jones, R. A. (1996). *Research methods in the social and behavioral sciences.* New York: Sinauer Associates. Readable volume that introduces the basic methods of conducting scientific research in the social and behavioral sciences. Jones presents a variety of research methods and issues related to them, in both general and specific terms.

Leach, P. (1994). *Children first.* New York: Alfred A. Knopf. A book that challenges our society to put families and children first. Leach offers insightful information about what our society must do, and is not doing, for today's children.

Malson, L. (1972). *Wolf children and the problem of human nature.* New York: Monthly Press Review. Fascinating accounts of wolf children—children abandoned in the wild to grow and develop on their own. Included is the complete text of *The Wild Boy of Aveyron,* Jean Itard's first-hand account of his experiences with a wolf child.

Rowe, D. C. (1994). *The limits of family influence.* New York: Guilford Press. In-depth but readable book contending that too much weight is placed on the influence of family on children's development. Rowe examines the theoretical basis of such beliefs and describes in detail what behavioral genetic studies can teach us about environmental influences.

RECOMMENDED WEBSITES

American Psychological Association (APA): The APA is the largest scientific and professional organization representing psychology in the United States. It works to advance psychology as a science, a profession, and a means of promoting human welfare. The APA Website contains valuable information on a wide variety of topics related to child development and families. <http://www.apa.org/>

Children Now: Children Now is a nonpartisan, independent voice for children, working to translate the nation's commitment to children and families into action. A large amount of up-to-date information on child development, social policy, and research makes this a valuable Website. Excellent links to other Internet sites add to its value. <http://www.dnai.com:80/~children/>

Jean Piaget Society: This Website is devoted to honoring Jean Piaget and his major theoretical and empirical contributions to the understanding of the origins and evolution of knowledge. It provides an open forum for the presentation and discussion of scholarly work on issues related to human knowledge and its development, as well as lists of relevant books and other publications. <http://www.piaget.org/>

National Council on Family Relations (NCFR): The NCFR is the leading nonprofit organization for family researchers, educators, policy makers, and practicing professionals. On the Website, its members share knowledge and information about families. <http://www.ncfr.com/>

National Human Genome Research Institute (NHGRI): The NHGRI was established to take a lead role in the Human Genome Project. Its Website contains valuable information about genetics, genetic technology, and the ethical, legal, and social implications of genetics research. <http://www.nhgri.nih.gov/>

UNICEF: UNICEF is an intergovernmental agency of the United Nations that assesses the situations of children around the world and prepares plans of action, with targets and goals, to help children. Its Website contains information, links, and publications dealing with the state of children in various parts of the world. <http://www.unicef.org/>

US Census Bureau: The Website of the Census Bureau contains a huge amount of information about the United States— its population, families, economy, and society. User-friendly methods allow individuals to have immediate, easy access to these informative materials. <http://www.census.gov/>

NATIONAL HOTLINES FOR CHILD DEVELOPMENT

American Academy of Pediatrics: 800-421-0589

Information Clearinghouse for Children: 619-260-4279

National Library of Medicine: 800-638-8480

National Resource Center for Youth Services: 918-585-2986

PART 2

Prenatal & Neonatal DEVELOPMENT

*I*t really is quite amazing, this miracle of baby-making. For one thing, I know I couldn't put a car together in nine months, much less something as complicated as a whole person. I look at the Empire State Building and find myself in awe that it was built by human beings—and yet it's nothing compared to the complexity of those human beings themselves. Add to that that each and every person is put together in a completely automated process—a little assembly-line womb—that doesn't just make my head spin, it makes it pop right off!

—C. RYWALT'S ON-LINE DIARY (1996)

I was serving spaghetti dinner when the contractions started getting much more intense, and I knew we were in business at last (I never did get to eat that dinner). . . . We arrived at the hospital and that's when I entered transition. . . . I started shaking like a leaf. My water broke and with every contraction, I got another rush of warm water—not a pleasant or pretty thing. I was in a lot of pain and told the doctor that I wanted my epidural NOW. Twenty minutes later I laid down in a bit of a fog and announced that I might be "pushing." Three minutes after that a doctor puts a baby on my tummy. I took a good look and said "how did that get here?"

—ANONYMOUS MOTHER'S ON-LINE DIARY OF GIVING BIRTH

As these new parents' comments reveal, the miracle of life and its development draws the attention, fancy, and amazement of parents, as well as poets, writers, and scientists. From a single fertilized cell, a complex individual made up of trillions of cells develops. Parents-to-be all over the world wonder whether their unborn child is a boy or girl and whether the child is healthy. Most children are born healthy, but some are born with serious disorders due to genetic or environmental factors.

Once children are born, the demands of parenting and caregiving begin. Growth and development are rapid in the early years of life, and many changes occur as the result of the birth of a child. Newborns are not as helpless and passive as we once thought them to be. Thanks to new research, our ideas of newborns have changed. Babies actively strive to meet their needs for food, comfort, and social interactions.

IN PART 2, YOU WILL LEARN ABOUT

- how genetic patterns are transmitted from parents to children
- types of genetic and chromosomal disorders
- methods of determining prenatally whether an unborn child has a genetic or chromosomal disorder
- how fertilization occurs
- the development of the embryo and fetus
- the factors that can have a negative or positive impact on prenatal development
- how pregnancy is viewed in different cultures
- how babies are born

- types of birthing methods and complications associated with childbirth
- how different members of the family experience birth
- the physical and behavioral characteristics of the newborn
- how the newborn's brain develops and the role of early experience in brain development
- how newborns perceive the world
- why some newborns are born at risk

Genetics & Prenatal DEVELOPMENT

CHAPTER OUTLINE

Sitting around the dinner table, three couples anxiously waited for the time to pass. One of the women, Anita, thought she might be pregnant, and, on a whim, two of the men at the dinner went to the store and bought a pregnancy test kit. Now, the couples were waiting to see the results. After a few minutes, the test strip appeared to change color, turning faintly pink. With a flashlight and magnifying glass, the couples agreed that the test was positive. Hugs, kisses, tears, and laughter filled the room. The couples talked about the morning sickness, weight gain, and bodily changes that were soon to come. Internally, miraculous changes were already occurring. A week later, the test was confirmed by a doctor; Anita was pregnant with her second child! Approximately nine months later, a precious baby girl was born.

Although the baby in this story is now 5 years old, vivid memories of these early events linger for each person at dinner that night. The night the three couples shared the good news about the pregnancy, Anita and her husband Bob, like many other couples, thought about the excitement and joy of having another child and about the external signs of the pregnancy. And all the while, their daughter's genetic endowment, transmitted at conception, was guiding her prenatal development as she grew from a single cell into a complex, functioning human being.

HOW DO GENES INFLUENCE DEVELOPMENT?

Since giving birth to their second child, Anita and Bob have often wondered how their two children could be so different from each other, especially since they were raised with similar expectations and goals. Their firstborn, Sarah, is muscular, introverted, and somewhat inactive. In contrast, Erin is thin, outgoing, and active. One possibility is that Anita and Bob's children inherited different genetic patterns. Like Anita and Bob, scientists are interested in these differences, and they study inheritance to learn how people develop in their appearance, thinking, and behavior.

Exciting advances in genetics are being made every day. In 1988, scientists from all over the world joined forces in the Human Genome Project to begin pinpointing the locations of over 100,000 genes on the human genome. By "mapping" genes, scientists can begin to examine how genes code for development. This knowledge can be used in many ways—for instance, in developing more effective treatments for diseases.

GENES AND CHROMOSOMES

Virtually every human cell carries a genetically programmed blueprint for development. The blueprint is coded by the **genes**, which reside on thin structures called **chromosomes**. The number of chromosomes varies dramatically across species. In normal humans, each cell contains forty-six chromosomes that work together in pairs: one chromosome of the pair is inherited from the mother and the other from the father.

The process begins as sex cells—ova and sperm—develop within the child's mother and father. Most cells multiply by creating exact duplicates of themselves through **mitosis,** which involves one duplication of chromosomes and one cell division (see Figure 3.1a).

genes the structures containing the code that provides the blueprint for development

chromosomes the structures on which genes reside

mitosis the process of cell replication involving one duplication of chromosomes and one cell division, resulting in twenty-three pairs of chromosomes (forty-six total)

FIGURE 3.1
Mitosis and Meiosis

(a) Mitosis　　　　　　　　　(b) Meiosis

Mitosis and meiosis are processes involved in the creation of new cells. Notice that meiosis, which produces sex cells, involves an extra cell division. Why is an extra cell division needed?

meiosis the process of cell replication undergone by ova and sperm, involving one duplication of chromosomes and two cell divisions, resulting in twenty-three chromosomes

karyotype a photograph of chromosomes, used by geneticists to align each chromosome with the other member of its pair

autosomes the first twenty-two pairs of chromosomes, which account for most of the body cells

sex chromosomes the twenty-third pair of chromosomes, which accounts for a person's sex

Each of the resulting cells contains the full complement of twenty-three pairs of chromosomes. Ova and sperm, however, undergo a process called **meiosis,** which involves one duplication of chromosomes and two cell divisions. Each of the resulting four cells contains half the complement of chromosomes: one member of each pair of chromosomes (see Figure 3.1b). Once conception occurs, the chromosomes of the ovum and sperm align so that the newly developing child has half his or her genes from each parent. Thus, genes provide a unique plan for development, incorporating genetic information from each parent.

Chromosomes vary in size, with some containing more genetic material than others. In a **karyotype** analysis, a geneticist photographs chromosomes and then aligns each chromosome with the other member of its pair, and the pairs are ordered by size and structure. The first twenty-two pairs of chromosomes, called **autosomes,** account for most aspects of development. The twenty-third pair, called the **sex chromosomes,** is unique in that the members may not match. For human females, the sex chromosomes normally consist of two X chromosomes. For males, the sex chromosomes normally consist of an X and a Y chromosome, which are given different labels because they look and function differently (Mange & Mange, 1994). The blueprint for development is outlined by the genes that are arranged in specific locations on the "arms" or "legs" of chromosomes. For instance, researchers have located a gene on chromosome 10 involved in hormone production whose presence increases the risk of breast cancer for women. The information detailed by human genes would fill about 116,000 textbook pages like this one. In contrast, information on the genes of a fruit fly would fill 5,600 pages (Mange & Mange, 1994).

GENETIC TRANSMISSION PATTERNS

How likely is it that a child will be tall like his father or have the same color eyes as his mother? Certain physical characteristics, such as a cleft chin, and hundreds of diseases are determined by the action of a single gene, making it possible to predict whether they will occur in offspring. Other characteristics and diseases have genetic components, but the transmission patterns are more complex and difficult to determine because they are caused by multiple genes.

A person's **genotype,** or genetic code, influences his or her **phenotype,** which is the outward expression of the genotype. But not all the information in one's genotype is expressed in one's phenotype. Because genes work in pairs, certain types of genes are more likely to be expressed than others. Both parents may contribute identical copies of a gene to their child, in which case the child is **homozygous** for the trait. Or each parent may contribute a different copy of the gene to their child, in which case the child is **heterozygous** for the trait.

As an illustration of the action of genes, consider a girl who is heterozygous for a cleft chin, having received the gene for a cleft chin from her dad and a "normal," non-cleft chin gene from her mother. This girl will have a cleft chin, because the gene for that trait is dominant. A gene whose code is expressed is called a **dominant gene.** For dominant genes to be expressed, only one copy needs to be present. A gene that is not expressed in the presence of a dominant gene is a **recessive gene,** such as the gene for a non-cleft chin. For a recessive characteristic to be expressed, both genes in the pair must be recessive. For instance, if a child inherits the homozygous pattern of a non-cleft chin gene from her mother and a non-cleft chin gene from her father, she will not have a cleft chin.

Until recently, it was assumed that characteristics such as eye color, hair color, and height were the result of the action of a single gene. Today, however, geneticists believe that each of these characteristics is determined by multiple genes. Although dark eye colors tend to be dominant over light eye colors, it is possible for two blue-eyed parents to give birth to a brown-eyed child.

Dominant Transmission

Most serious genetic diseases are not transmitted through a dominant gene, because diseased offspring would not survive long enough to transmit the characteristics to their own children. But some genetic diseases, like Huntington's chorea (a degenerative

In a karyotype analysis, geneticists align the chromosomes by pairs and identify them by number. Notice that the first pairs of autosomes tend to be larger than the higher numbered pairs. You can see that, in the sex chromosomes for this male (the twenty-third pair), the X chromosome is much larger than the Y chromosome. What factors determine whether a boy or a girl is conceived?

genotype a person's genetic code

phenotype the outward expression of the genotype

homozygous describes a child's condition with respect to a trait when both parents have contributed identical copies of the gene for that trait to their child

heterozygous describes a child's condition with respect to a trait when each parent has contributed a different copy of the gene for that trait to their child

dominant gene a gene whose code is expressed when only one copy of the gene is present

recessive gene a gene whose code is not expressed in the presence of a dominant gene

Should the Sex of a Child Be Preselected?

If you could, would you want to select or know the sex of your baby before the baby was born or even conceived? If so, you are not alone: according to one survey, 80 percent of Americans say they would do whatever was needed to ensure that the sex of their child was the one they wanted (Pooler, 1991).

Currently, there are three approaches to attempting to preselect the sex of a child. The traditional approach is based on the differences between the qualities of X and Y sperm. Y sperm are faster but live a shorter time; X sperm are slower but live longer. Timing intercourse to match these qualities may influence the likelihood of giving birth to a child of the preferred sex. Intercourse at the time of ovulation, when the Y sperm will find a waiting egg, may increase the likelihood of having a boy. Intercourse several days before ovulation may increase the likeli-

hood of having a girl because the longer-living X sperm will still be viable when ovulation occurs (Shettles & Rorvik, 1984). Another approach, however, predicts the opposite outcome, based on the mother's hormone levels at conception. According to this theory, the likelihood of giving birth to a girl should be increased if conception takes place at ovulation, when maternal levels of gonadotropins are highest. Neither method has been proven scientifically to be effective.

A third approach to sex selection is to increase the number of either X or Y sperm before intercourse. Several methods have been used to identify sperm as either X or Y and to separate one kind of sperm from the other. One method is to separate X and Y sperm in a centrifuge. Another method is to place sperm in the top of a column containing progressively more viscous layers of gel-like liquids. Sperm that

make it through all the layers are more likely to be Y sperm. With both methods, the desired sperm can then be used for artificial insemination. In one study, a 76 percent rate of births of the desired sex was reported (Ericsson & Beernink, 1987). Most scientists believe, however, that the matter of sperm selection is unresolved (Mange & Mange, 1994).

Thinking It Through:

1. What reasons might parents have for choosing the sex of their children? Are there valid reasons related to genetic risks?
2. What might be some negative consequences of allowing people to choose the sex of their children?
3. If people routinely chose the sex of their children, do you think they would choose boys or girls more often? Why?

---

neurological disease), are transmitted by a single dominant gene (on the fourth chromosome) and are maintained in the population because they often do not strike until middle-age.

Dominant transmission poses serious problems for those who carry the dominant gene for a disease. For example, suppose a woman learns that her mother had Huntington's chorea. Consideration of the possible combinations of genetic pairs contributed by her parents reveals that the woman has a 50 percent chance of having the dominant gene for Huntington's (see Figure 3.2a). In the past, this woman would have had to decide about having children before she knew whether or not she had the gene. Now she can be tested for Huntington's, but the decision to take the test can be agonizing because there is no known cure for the disease. For this reason, few members of Huntington's families choose to take the test.

Recessive Transmission

The birth into the Deford family of the first girl in over fifty years was greeted with much celebration and joy. Alex Deford was a healthy girl at birth but soon was sick all

FIGURE 3.2
Transmission Patterns

(a) Dominant Transmission: Huntington's Chorea

(b) Recessive Transmission: Cystic Fibrosis

(c) Sex-Linked Transmission

Part (a): The father is homozygous, with two healthy copies (h) of the gene, but the mother is diseased because she has one diseased copy (H) of the dominant Huntington's gene. As you can see, the offspring of these two parents have a 50 percent chance of being healthy and a 50 percent chance of being diseased. **Part (b):** The father and mother are carriers because they each have one copy of the cystic fibrosis gene (c). Their offspring have a 25 percent chance of being healthy, a 50 percent chance of being carriers, and a 25 percent chance of having the disease, because it takes two copies of the cystic fibrosis gene (cc) to have the disease. **Part (c):** The mother carries the gene for a sex-linked disease on one of her X chromosomes (**X**). The daughters have a 50 percent chance of not being carriers of the disease gene and a 50 percent chance of being carriers, with one disease copy and one normal copy of the gene. None of the daughters will have the disease, because those with a disease copy (**XX**) will have one normal copy of the gene to mask the disease copy. The sons have a 50 percent chance of being normal and a 50 percent chance of being diseased, because those with a disease copy (**XY**) will not have a normal gene on their Y chromosome to suppress the disease gene.

the time. At 4 months, Alex was tested and found to have cystic fibrosis (CF), a serious recessive genetic disease. Because no one in the family had CF, they were shocked that they had a child with CF.

As Alex grew older, her health deteriorated. She had difficulty breathing, lost weight, and developed heart and liver problems. She was continually in and out of the hospital. Alex died when she was only 10 years old (Deford, 1986).

CF is the most common autosomal recessive disease among Caucasians, affecting about 1 in 2000 newborns. It is the leading genetic cause of childhood death. About 1 in 20 people are heterozygous for CF: they have one copy of the disease gene but also

This child has cystic fibrosis, which is a very serious recessive genetic disease with no known cure. How can parents minimize their chance of giving birth to a child with a genetic birth defect?

have the normal, dominant gene that masks the effect of the recessive gene. A child with the disease has identical recessive genes—in this case, two CF genes. About 50 percent of people with CF die by the age of 24. There currently is no cure for CF, although gene therapies are being developed.

Approximately 500 characteristics and diseases are transmitted through recessive genes. Unlike dominant characteristics and diseases, which 50 percent of the offspring are likely to have, recessive characteristics and diseases like CF can remain hidden for generations because they are not expressed unless both parents contribute the gene to their child (see Figure 3.2b).

People who are heterozygous for a recessive disease or characteristic do not have the recessive disease or characteristic but are **carriers.** A child whose parents are both carriers has a 25 percent chance of having the recessive disease or characteristic and a 50 percent chance of being a carrier.

Because recessive transmission requires that both parents pass on the recessive gene, recessive diseases and characteristics tend to be more prevalent in groups that are isolated or that intermarry. For instance, people of Mediterranean origin are more at risk for *beta thalassemia*, an untreatable but prenatally detectable disease that accounts for hundreds of thousands of childhood deaths a year worldwide. Jewish people from Central and Eastern Europe and certain groups of French Canadians are more at risk for *Tay Sachs disease*, which is a serious and untreatable illness that often leads to death within the first two years of life. The risk for Jewish and French Canadian groups is about 1 in 6000 births, as compared to 1 in 550,000 births among non–Jewish American and non–French Canadian populations. Individuals with African heritage, especially those from West Africa, are more at risk for *sickle cell anemia*, a disease of the blood that causes painful joint swelling, anemia, and infections and may lead to an early death. For African Americans, the risk of having both genes for the disease is about 1 in 500 (Mange & Mange, 1994).

The genes that cause diseases such as sickle cell anemia do not die out of the population because they confer genetic advantages as well as disadvantages, thus favoring a kind of genetic diversity called **balanced polymorphism.** For example, although few individuals with sickle cell anemia survive to reproduce, those who are heterozygous for the disease are resistant to malaria. Because they increase the likelihood of survival for those who are heterozygous, genes like those for sickle cell anemia are preserved in a population (Plomin, DeFries, McClearn, & Rutter, 1997).

Sex-Linked Transmission

Hemophilia causes excessive bleeding because of failures in blood clotting. This genetic disease was frequently observed among members of European royalty. The pattern of transmission is recessive, but with a twist. In this case, as is true for virtually all cases of sex-linked transmission, the gene for the disease is found on the X chromosome. Recessive transmission is different on the sex chromosomes than on the autosomes. On the autosomes, two recessive copies of the gene must be present for the characteristic to be expressed. This is not true on the sex chromosomes. Because the Y chromosome is smaller than the X, it does not carry as much genetic material. A single recessive gene on the unmatched segment of the X chromosome may express itself, because there is no corresponding gene on the Y to suppress it. Figure 3.2c shows how sex-linked transmissions of such conditions as hemophilia, baldness, and color-blindness occur. With sex-linked transmission, females are more likely to be carriers and males are about three times more likely to have the disease. For example, **fragile X syndrome**—a common cause of mild to moderate mental retardation—occurs in 1 in 1250 males and 1 in 2500 females (Plomin, DeFries, et al., 1997). Individuals with fragile X syndrome may have protruding ears, a prominent jaw, unusual speech, and poor eye contact.

carriers people who are heterozygous for a recessive disorder

balanced polymorphism a kind of genetic diversity in which the genes that cause diseases provide certain genetic advantages as well as disadvantages

fragile X syndrome a condition passed on by sex-linked transmission and characterized by protruding ears, prominent jaw, unusual speech, poor eye contact, and mild to moderate retardation

Polygenic Transmission

Dominant, recessive, and sex-linked patterns are the most straightforward mechanisms for transferring genetic information from one generation to the next. However, many characteristics, such as a predisposition for colon cancer or diabetes, are coded by multiple genes and may require an environmental stimulus for the disease to be manifested.

WHAT ARE COMMON CHROMOSOMAL ABNORMALITIES?

The chances that a healthy mother will give birth to a healthy infant are high. Nonetheless, 3 to 5 percent of newborns have some type of genetic or chromosomal abnormality. Genetic disorders are due to flaws in one or two genes. In contrast, chromosomal abnormalities occur when a child is born with missing or extra chromosomes. Most embryos with genetic or chromosomal abnormalities do not survive until birth—they are spontaneously aborted, or miscarried, before the mother even knows she is pregnant.

DOWN SYNDROME

A common chromosomal abnormality is *Down syndrome*, which occurs in about 1 in 900 live births (March of Dimes, 1998). About 90 percent of children with Down syndrome have forty-seven chromosomes rather than the normal forty-six, with an extra number 21 chromosome (referred to as *trisomy 21*). This excess genetic material results from the failure of chromosomes to separate during meiosis. About 5,000 children are born each year with Down syndrome, and more than 250,000 people in the United States currently have Down syndrome (National Down Syndrome Society, 1997).

Most children with Down syndrome have certain physical characteristics, including wide-spaced eyes, a large protruding tongue, short stature, a round face, folds in the corners of their eyes, and unusual creases on the palms of their hands (Hassold & Patterson, 1998). Children with Down syndrome also often have heart and eye defects and may have immunological problems that make them susceptible to diseases. These physical problems account for the lower life expectancy for Down syndrome individuals, but life expectancy has increased from an average of 15 years in the 1940s to 30 or more years today (March of Dimes, 1998).

Down syndrome children have mental retardation, with intelligence scores ranging from 20 to 80 (100 is an average score), but most are in the 45 to 55 range (Plomin, DeFries, et al., 1997; Robinson, Goodman, & O'Brien, 1984). Language skills also are severely impaired (Fowler, Gelman, & Gleitman, 1994). By adolescence, language skills remain at the level of a 3-year-old (Plomin, DeFries, et al., 1997). About 50 percent of Down syndrome children develop behavioral problems as they grow older, especially boys with limited or no language skills (Tager-Flusberg, 1994).

Young mothers have little risk of giving birth to Down syndrome infants—only 1 in 2400 live births of Down syndrome infants are to mothers under 20 years of age. By age 35, the risk increases to 1 in every 365 births; and by age 40, the risk is 1 in 110 live births (National Down Syndrome Society, 1997). The most common cause of Down syndrome is a failure of sex cell division during the formation of ova (Mange & Mange, 1994; Plomin, DeFries, et al., 1997).

SEX CHROMOSOME ABNORMALITIES

Sex chromosome abnormalities include having an extra X or Y chromosome and lacking an X chromosome. Through karyotype analyses, many more cases of sex chromosome abnormalities can now be identified.

Down syndrome children tend to be identifiable by their facial features, such as a large tongue, wide-spaced eyes, and a round face. What risk factors increase a couple's chance of giving birth to a child with Down syndrome?

Turner's Syndrome

Girls born with *Turner's syndrome* are missing the second X chromosome (XO), usually as a result of cell division abnormalities in the father's sperm (Mange & Mange, 1994). Estimates vary, but there may be 1 case of Turner's syndrome in every 2500 births (Plomin, DeFries, et al., 1997). Girls with Turner's syndrome lack ovaries and have immature external genitalia. They tend to be short, with broad chests and wide (webbed) necks. This condition often can be identified at birth, but many girls are not identified until they reach puberty and fail to menstruate. Early identification is useful because hormone therapy can help. Girls with Turner's syndrome have normal verbal skills but often have poor spatial skills, difficulty sustaining attention and remembering information, and delayed social skills (McCauley, Kay, Ito, & Treder, 1987).

Klinefelter's Syndrome

Boys born with an extra X chromosome have *Klinefelter's syndrome* (XXY). The likelihood of this disorder is 1 or 2 cases per 1000 births (Plomin, DeFries, & McClearn, 1990). Boys with Klinefelter's syndrome are sterile and tend to have long limbs and immature testes (Sotos, 1997). Because they lack adequate male hormones, they do not develop masculine characteristics at puberty, such as facial and body hair, and may have femalelike breast development. Early hormone replacement therapy can produce a more typical male pattern of development. Mental retardation is common, with approximately 5 to 20 percent of cases falling below the normal range for intelligence (Jones & Cahill, 1994). Klinefelter's boys often have language deficits, attention problems, and reading difficulties (Rovet et al., 1996).

XYY Syndrome

Boys born with *XYY syndrome*, characterized by one or more extra Y chromosomes, appear normal (Jones & Cahill, 1994). XYY boys are tall, have severe acne during adolescence, are poorly coordinated, and may exhibit impulsive behaviors and lower intelligence (Kumra et al., 1998). The more Y chromosomes a boy has, the lower his intelligence is likely to be.

XYY patterns are caused by cell division problems during sperm production. About 1 in 1000 births is a boy with extra Y chromosomes (Plomin, DeFries, & McClearn, 1990).

In the 1960s, researchers identified a higher-than-expected frequency of the XYY pattern in inmates of a maximum security prison. The hypothesis was proposed that having an extra Y chromosome produces aggressive and antisocial behavior. Later studies revealed, however, that this hypothesis is wrong: male prisoners in general, regardless of the nature of their crime, are likely to have XYY patterns. These findings suggest that lower intelligence and impulsive behavior, rather than aggressiveness, may land XYY men in prison (Sutton, 1988).

HOW ARE GENETIC DISEASES DETECTED?

In the past, family planning was limited to the ability to choose whether or not to have a child. Today, with tremendous advances in the ability to detect genetic and chromosomal abnormalities, more options are available to help families plan for the future. Fortunately, in most cases the outcome of genetic testing is favorable, and families can be assured that they will have a child who is no more at risk for health problems than other children (Mange & Mange, 1994).

GENETIC TECHNOLOGY

Genetic and chromosomal disorders account for many problems that affect the health and well-being of infants. Because of the significance of these disorders for infant health, many technologies have been developed to assess the status of infants even before they are born. Some of these technologies, such as ultrasound imaging, involve visual examination of the unborn child to determine physical defects. Other technologies, such as amniocentesis, require obtaining genetic material that is used to test for genetic and chromosomal problems.

Ultrasound Imaging

A painless and virtually risk-free procedure for identifying some developmental problems is **ultrasound,** in which video images of the fetus and its internal organs are produced from the echoes of sound waves. Ultrasound can detect heart conditions and physical deformities. Ultrasound is used with other techniques when an accurate image of the fetus's location is needed. Studies show that ultrasound helps identify possible birth defects when performed by physicians with extensive training in fetal diagnosis (Crane et al., 1994).

In this ultrasound image of a fetus, features such as the head, arms, and legs are marked with arrows for easy identification. Physicians use these images to look for physical abnormalities such as neural tube defects or missing arms or legs. Can you explain how an ultrasound works?

Chorionic Villus Sampling

Since the 1980s, **chorionic villus sampling (CVS)** has been successfully used to assess genetic material in fetal cells. Either by inserting a needle through the mother's abdominal wall or by inserting a catheter through the mother's cervix, cells are removed from the projections on the chorionic membrane (a layer of protective cells surrounding the fetus); these are then analyzed for genetic defects (Wapner, 1997).

CVS can be done during the first trimester of pregnancy, usually nine to twelve weeks after conception. The risk of problems associated with CVS is very low (Salihu, Boos, & Schmidt, 1997), particularly when it is performed after the eighth week of pregnancy by experienced medical personnel (Simpson & Elias, 1994). The early detection CVS affords gives couples more time to consider their options—such as whether to continue or terminate the pregnancy.

Amniocentesis

A common method of detecting genetic problems during prenatal development is **amniocentesis,** in which a long, thin needle is inserted through the mother's abdominal wall into the fluid-filled amniotic sac surrounding the fetus. The amniotic fluid contains some skin cells of the fetus; some fluid is removed, and then these cells are examined to determine whether genetic defects are present. In addition, the analysis determines whether biochemical or metabolic imbalances are present. The sex of the child also may be identified.

Studies show that the risk of amniocentesis for the unborn child is small (Simpson & Elias, 1994). The major drawback is that the test is done relatively late in pregnancy (fifteen to nineteen weeks) and obtaining the results takes several weeks. The advantage is that it is a very accurate method of identifying a variety of prenatal developmental problems.

Detection of Alpha Fetoprotein

The mother's blood contains *alpha fetoproteins*, which can be used to screen for several developmental problems during pregnancy. If the mother has a high level of alpha fetoproteins, the fetus may have a neural tube defect (such as spina bifida), which then can

ultrasound a procedure used to identify some developmental problems, in which video images of the fetus and the fetus's internal organs are produced from the echoes of sound waves

chorionic villus sampling (CVS) a procedure used to assess genetic material in fetal cells, in which cells are removed from the projections on the chorionic membrane

amniocentesis a procedure used to determine whether genetic defects are present, in which amniotic fluid is collected

Treating a Diseased Fetus

Their first son died when he was only 7 months old. He died of an X-linked recessive disease called *severe combined immunodeficiency,* which strikes approximately 1 out of every 100,000 babies. Because it is X-linked, it strikes boys more often than girls. The disease produces a very weak immune system, increasing the child's susceptibility to infections. Most infants born with this disease die within the first year of life. When the woman became pregnant again, she was concerned that her second child would also have the disease. Using chorionic villus sampling, doctors tested the unborn child's DNA. The child, another son, was affected. In a medical first, the child was treated for the disease in utero by Dr. Alan Flake, a pediatric surgeon at Children's Hospital of Philadelphia. Using the unaffected father's bone marrow, Flake gave the fetus three transplants of cells by ultrasound-guided injections at 16, 17½, and 18½ weeks. At birth, the child seemed normal except for an easily treated rash. At 11 months, he showed no signs of the immune disease and was healthy.

Medical treatment for unborn children, or *fetology,* is a relatively new medical specialty. To date, medical treatments such as blood and bone marrow transfusions, insertion of drainage tubes, and surgical repairs have been performed in utero. Although there are risks to these prenatal treatments, early treatment can prevent symptoms of a disease and may even eliminate the disease entirely (Flake et al., 1996). Similar techniques may soon be used to treat other genetic disorders such as sickle cell anemia. With improvements in technology and medical science, it is likely that fetologists will be able to treat more and more cases in the future.

be confirmed through ultrasound. If the mother's alpha fetoprotein level is low, the fetus may have a chromosomal abnormality (such as Down syndrome), which must be confirmed through genetic testing (Simpson & Elias, 1994).

GENETIC COUNSELING

Despite the many advances that science has made in detecting genetic and chromosomal abnormalities, tens of thousands of children are born each year with birth defects. Birth defects occur in 1 of every 28 births and are the leading cause of infant death, accounting for about 22 percent of all infant deaths (March of Dimes, 1998). Table 3.1 lists the incidence of the most common types of birth defects.

Genetic counselors help couples determine the likelihood of having children with birth defects, assist them in making decisions about conception, and provide counseling for families who have given birth to infants with genetic problems. Genetic counseling is recommended of individuals in the following situations (Mange & Mange, 1994):

- ✦ Individuals who have children with a genetic disorder
- ✦ Individuals with a known genetic disorder who would like to start families
- ✦ Women who have had repeated miscarriages
- ✦ Older pregnant women
- ✦ Couples at risk for genetic diseases because of their ethnicity or ancestry
- ✦ Couples at risk for genetic diseases because they are related to each other

Genetic counseling begins with an accurate medical history and diagnosis. Karyotype analyses may be done to determine the genetic patterns of the parents, and a pedi-

TABLE 3.1
Incidence of Common Birth Defects

BIRTH DEFECT	ESTIMATED INCIDENCE
Structural/Metabolic	
Heart and circulation	1 in 115 births
Muscles and skeleton	1 in 130 births
Genital and urinary tract	1 in 135 births
Nervous system and eyes	1 in 235 births
Chromosomal disorders	1 in 600 births
Down syndrome	1 in 900 births
Respiratory tract	1 in 900 births
Cleft lip/palate	1 in 930 births
Spina bifida	1 in 2000 births
Metabolic disorders	1 in 3500 births
Congenital Infections	
Syphilis	1 in 2000 births
HIV infection	1 in 2700 births
Rubella	1 in 100,000 births
Other	
Fetal alcohol syndrome	1 in 1000 births
Rh blood incompatibility	1 in 1400 births

NOTE: All numbers are based on the best available estimates, which underestimate
the incidence of many birth defects.
SOURCE: March of Dimes, 1998.

gree analysis may be carried out to determine genetic diseases of other family members.
Genetic counselors use this information to help families make difficult decisions about
conception, pregnancy, and birth.

HOW DOES PRENATAL DEVELOPMENT PROCEED?

From the time the sperm and egg unite, miraculous changes occur that cul-
minate in the birth of an infant. How these changes are brought about, what influences
them, and how to maximize optimal outcomes are questions that confront parents and
scientists. In this section, you will learn that prenatal development is made up of many
complex and interrelated processes working together to produce a human infant.

OVULATION

For pregnancy to occur, a human egg, or **ovum,** and a sperm cell must meet and
share their genetic material. This process begins with ovulation. Each month, a woman
releases at least one ovum from her ovaries during ovulation. Ovulation occurs as a normal part of the woman's menstrual cycle. In addition to ensuring that ovulation takes
place, the menstrual cycle initiates changes in the uterus that prepare it to receive a fertilized ovum.

ovum a human egg

The average menstrual cycle is approximately equal to a lunar month but can vary greatly, from twenty-five to thirty-five days. At birth, females have approximately 400,000 to 500,000 immature ova in each ovary, and no new ova develop after birth. With an average cycle of twenty-eight days, a women ovulates about 13 ova per year, or 481 ova in the thirty-seven years of her reproductive life (Jones, 1997). How these ova are selected from the thousands contained in a woman's ovary remains a mystery.

Each menstrual cycle is divided into three main phases. The first is the *menstrual phase* (lasting four to five days), when menstruation (the "period") takes place. Menstruation occurs because the lining of the uterus degenerates and is expelled in a bloody discharge.

The second phase is the *follicular phase*, in which the lining of the uterus grows back and thickens, influenced by the female hormone estrogen. This phase continues until ovulation, which occurs on about day 14 of a 28-day cycle or day 16 of a 30-day cycle (Rathus, Nevid, & Fichner-Rathus, 1993). This is the time of the month when a woman is most likely to get pregnant.

The last phase is the *luteal phase*, lasting from ovulation until the beginning of the next menstruation (usually about fourteen days). During this phase, different hormones are secreted (such as progesterone) that prepare the uterus for the arrival of a fertilized ovum. If fertilization does not occur, the ovum disintegrates and is washed out of the body in the menstrual flow. If fertilization does occur, the fertilized ovum embeds itself in the uterine lining; menstrual cycles usually stop during pregnancy (Jones, 1997).

SPERMATOGENESIS

After puberty, men produce sperm in their testes on a daily basis throughout their lives (about 100 sperm are produced per second). Sperm develop in a process called **spermatogenesis,** which requires about seventy-two days to produce a mature sperm cell (Rathus et al., 1993). In early stages, sperm are called **spermatocytes,** and each contains forty-six chromosomes, including one X and one Y sex chromosome. These spermatocytes divide into two **spermatids,** each of which has twenty-three chromosomes, including either an X or a Y sex chromosome. Mature spermatids, called **spermatozoa,** are fully functional and capable of fertilizing a human ovum.

Approximately 200 to 500 million sperm are released at each ejaculation (Wong & Perry, 1998). A man is considered fertile if there are approximately 60 million sperm in a normal ejaculation, 60 percent are normal in shape and size, and 40 percent of these sperm are mobile (Institute of Medicine, 1990).

FERTILIZATION

The mature ovum is one of the largest cells in the human body, with a diameter of approximately 190 micrometers (about the size of a period printed on this page). As shown in Figure 3.3a, the two primary layers are an outer protective layer of cells and an inner nucleus that contains twenty-three chromosomes—the genetic material of the woman. Each month during her reproductive lifetime, a woman releases an ovum during ovulation. Once released, the ovum enters the fallopian tube and is moved toward the uterus by cilia, small hairlike structures lining the tube. The ovum cannot propel itself and so is dependent on the cilia to move it to the uterus (Glass, 1994). For fertilization to occur, an ovum must be penetrated by a sperm cell within 24 to 48 hours after ovulation.

A healthy sperm cell is about .0002 inch long and is composed of a head, body, and tail (see Figure 3.3, b and c). The head contains the genetic material, and the tail moves the sperm through the woman's reproductive system. The body contains the energy production system for moving the tail (Wong & Perry, 1998).

As noted earlier, males produce X and Y sperm. If an X sperm fertilizes the ovum, a girl is conceived; if a Y sperm fertilizes the ovum, the child will be a boy. Thus, it is

spermatogenesis the process by which sperm develop

spermatocytes sperm in the early stage of development, at which time each one contains forty-six chromosomes, including one X and one Y sex chromosome

spermatids the result of the division of spermatocytes, each one containing twenty-three chromosomes and including either an X or a Y sex chromosome

spermatozoa mature spermatids, which are fully functional and capable of fertilizing a human ovum

FIGURE 3.3
Ovum and Sperm

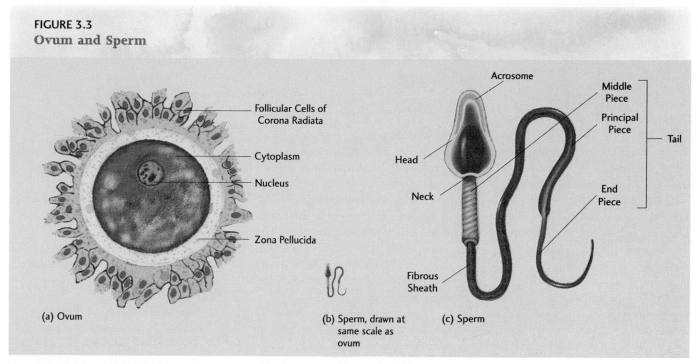

(a) Ovum

Follicular Cells of Corona Radiata

Cytoplasm

Nucleus

Zona Pellucida

(b) Sperm, drawn at same scale as ovum

(c) Sperm

Acrosome

Head

Neck

Fibrous Sheath

Middle Piece

Principal Piece

End Piece

Tail

The ovum is much larger than the sperm. The chromosomal material is in the nucleus of the ovum and in the head of the sperm. Can you explain the processes by which ova and sperm are produced?

the father's sperm that determines the child's sex (the mother contributes only X chromosomes).

Once ejaculated, the sperm begin a long journey through the female reproductive tract. Of the millions of sperm that are ejaculated, only 100 to 1000 actually reach the ovum. Thus, there is a "survival of the fittest" test that eliminates many damaged or weak sperm. For fertilization to occur, sperm must reach and penetrate the ovum within about three days of ejaculation. After this time, the fertilizing abilities of sperm decline, although in rare cases sperm can survive longer than six days (Jones, 1997).

Fertilization begins when a sperm penetrates the outer layer of an ovum. Once this happens, the ovum releases a secretion that thickens its outer layer, preventing other sperm from penetrating it. After penetration, the head of the sperm sinks into the nucleus of the ovum and the corresponding chromosomes align in pairs. Fertilization is complete once the chromosomes from the sperm and ovum combine to form twenty-three pairs that carry unique genetic instructions (Moore, 1993).

Overview of Prenatal Development

In most Western cultures, birth is considered the beginning of a person's lifetime (Rosenblith, 1992). At birth, however, infants already have been influenced by their genetic makeup and the qualities of their prenatal environment. An understanding of the changes that take place during prenatal development is needed to fully understand later development.

In this electron microscope photo, which is enlarged many times, the head of the sperm is entering the ovum; its tail is shown outside the ovum. Notice how much larger the ovum is than the sperm. What factors determine which sperm reaches and fertilizes the ovum?

Should Humans Be Cloned?

Consider the idea that in the future we will be able to produce embryos by taking a person's DNA and using it to produce an identical twin. This process is called *cloning*. In early attempts at cloning, scientists removed the genetic material from a mouse ovum, replaced it with a cell from a mouse embryo, and implanted the new cell in the uterus of an adult mouse, where it developed into an identical copy of the donor mouse embryo (Jones, 1997).

In 1996, the world was rocked by the announcement that a sheep named Dolly had been successfully conceived and born using a cloning process called *nuclear transfer* (Campbell, McWhir, Ritchie, & Wilmut, 1996). Dolly's genes came from frozen mammary tissues of a 6-year-old adult sheep (Wills, 1998). In the experiment, the chromosomes from the adult sheep were inserted into unfer-

tilized eggs. This fusion triggered the eggs' development, and the embryos were then transferred into the uterus of a host sheep. When the lambs, including Dolly, were born, they were genetically identical females—identical to the donor sheep. In the first round of experiments, only 5 of 250 embryos survived to birth and 3 of these died for unknown reasons within ten days.

Even more amazing was the news that scientists in Oregon, employing the same procedures used to clone Dolly, produced monkeys cloned from embryos. Thus, for the first time a species closely related to humans has been cloned (Baum, 1997).

The success of cloning experiments raises important moral and ethical issues about cloning human beings. It is illegal in the United States to use federal funds for human cloning projects, and other coun-

tries, such as Britain, have outlawed such efforts. Of course, being able to clone such copies is one thing; whether we should do so is entirely another matter.

Thinking It Through:

1. Under what conditions might you approve of the cloning of human beings?
2. Should all research on cloning be banned, even research that may lead to new techniques to fight cancer or other diseases? Why or why not?
3. Would you like to be cloned? What issues might you face if this opportunity existed?
4. To what extent do you think your clone would be similar to you, given what you have learned about the effects of genetics and the environment on human development?

---

germinal stage the first stage of prenatal development, which begins at conception and lasts until the fertilized egg implants itself in the uterine wall

embryonic stage the second stage of prenatal development, which begins at implantation and lasts until about eight weeks

fetal stage the third and final stage of prenatal development, which begins at about eight weeks and lasts until birth

zygote the fertilized ovum

Prenatal development, which begins at conception and ends at birth, proceeds through three stages.

- The **germinal stage** begins at conception and lasts until the fertilized egg implants itself in the uterine wall (usually about two weeks). Cell division and differentiation are the main qualities of this stage.
- The **embryonic stage** begins at implantation and lasts until about eight weeks. The developing child is referred to as an *embryo*. During this stage, the major organs and body parts develop almost daily. This stage is the most critical time in prenatal development; it is when environmental damage is most likely to occur.
- The **fetal stage** begins at about eight weeks and lasts until birth. The developing child is referred to as a *fetus*. During this stage, elaboration of the existing organs and structures occurs and the brain develops rapidly.

THE GERMINAL STAGE

The fertilized ovum, called the **zygote,** takes two to three days to reach the uterus. During this time, the zygote divides several times through mitosis, producing cells that

Finding New Ways to Make Babies

About 8.5 percent of married couples who want children are unsuccessful in their efforts. Infertility is defined as being unable to conceive after 12 months of unprotected intercourse or being unable to carry a fetus to term (Institute of Medicine, 1990). For about half of infertile couples, the problem lies with the female, and for about 30 percent, the problem lies with the father. For the remaining 20 percent of infertile couples, there are problems with both partners (Mange & Mange, 1994).

In addition to surgery and other medical procedures and adoption, several procedures for "assisted reproduction" are now available:

- **Artificial insemination.** Sperm are provided by a donor, and near the time when the woman is ovulating, a doctor uses a syringe to deposit the donor's sperm in the woman's uterus. This procedure may be repeated as many times as necessary to achieve fertilization and is often successful. About 8000 US children each year are conceived though the use of artificial insemination.
- **In vitro fertilization.** In England in 1978, baby Louise, a normal baby girl, was born after her mother's egg

was fertilized in a test tube. The basic in vitro procedure is to obtain an ovum directly from the woman's ovary, fertilize it with sperm in a culture dish, and then transfer the zygote(s) to the woman's uterus. Women are usually treated with hormones to induce ovulation of more than one egg; this increases the chances of success but also has resulted in many multiple pregnancies. The success rate for in vitro fertilization is low—only about 10 percent of such attempts end in a live birth.

- **Gamete intrafallopian transfer.** Sperm and an ovum are deposited into the woman's fallopian tube. Once they are deposited, fertilization occurs as it would normally. Rates of success are higher for this procedure than for in vitro fertilization (16 percent versus 10 percent).
- **Embryo transfer.** If both partners are infertile, embryo transfer may be suitable. In this procedure, donors provide both sperm and an ovum. Once the ovum is fertilized, the zygote is then transferred to the woman. This procedure is relatively rare, and its success rate is low.

- **Surrogate mothers.** When a couple have been unable to conceive or carry a fetus full term, a surrogate mother agrees to be artificially inseminated with sperm from the man. She carries the fertilized egg through pregnancy and gives birth, and then gives up the child to the couple.

Although they make it possible for infertile couples to have children, assisted reproductive techniques are not a solution for all couples. Procedures can be lengthy, expensive, and physically and emotionally demanding. Most physicians recommend that couples begin with the less expensive and less invasive procedures first and then attempt the more aggressive methods later (Institute of Medicine, 1990).

Furthermore, these techniques have generated important ethical and moral questions that still go unanswered. For example, what happens to their frozen embryos when couples divorce? What happens when a surrogate mother decides she cannot give up the child after carrying the child for nine months? Until these questions are resolved, interested couples need to be fully aware of the uncertainties and take steps to minimize undesired consequences (Robertson, 1996).

---

are identical to the zygote. The first cell division occurs within about twenty-four hours after fertilization. By the time the zygote reaches the uterus, it consists of twelve to sixteen cells that are beginning to separate into two layers. The inner layer of cells develops into the infant, and the outer mass of cells eventually forms the structures that support the developing infant, such as the umbilical cord and placenta (Wong & Perry, 1998). Table 3.2 outlines the major changes of early prenatal development.

After two or three days of floating freely in the uterus, the zygote implants itself in the wall of the uterus. The cells of the outer layers of the zygote develop hairlike projections

TABLE 3.2
Early Timetable of Prenatal Development

DAY	MILESTONE
0	Ovulation occurs (ovum lasts up to 24 hours; sperm last up to 6 days).
1	Fertilization occurs.
6	Zygote adheres to uterine wall.
7	Implantation begins.
10	Implantation is complete.
14	Amnion, chorion, placenta, and umbilical cord begin to develop.
15	First menstrual period is missed.

SOURCE: Adapted from Jones, 1997.

that burrow into the lining of the uterus. Eventually, these hairlike structures will transfer nutrients to the zygote. The connections established by implantation provide a source of nutrients for the zygote until the support structures are fully functional. This process is complete during the second week, and the zygote, measuring no more than 1 millimeter in diameter, now consists of a few thousand cells. Implantation also triggers hormonal changes that prevent menstruation and provide the woman with some of the first signs that she is pregnant.

Ectopic Pregnancies

Usually implantation takes place in the uterus, but sometimes it occurs outside the uterus—most commonly in a fallopian tube, but occasionally in the abdomen or ovary. This condition, known as an **ectopic pregnancy** (outside the uterus), occurs in about 1 in every 100 pregnancies (Wong & Perry, 1998). The main cause of ectopic pregnancies is damaged fallopian tubes. Ectopic pregnancies cause abdominal pain and irregular vaginal bleeding and are dangerous to the health of the mother if not terminated.

Multiple Pregnancies

Another complication of fertilization occurs when multiple pregnancies (such as twins) develop. In the United States, twins occur in about 1 in every 80 pregnancies, but in other parts of the world, the incidence varies, with a much higher rate in West Africa, for example, and a much lower rate in Japan. African American mothers are more likely to have twins, particularly fraternal twins, than are Caucasian American mothers (Wong & Perry, 1998). The incidence of twin pregnancies is up to four times greater than the rate of twin births, though, because often one of the embryos spontaneously aborts early in development (Jones, 1997).

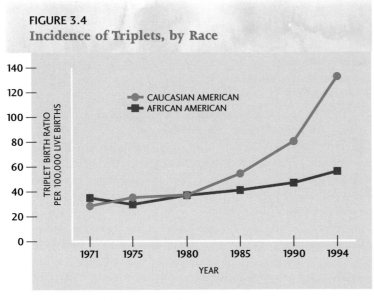

FIGURE 3.4
Incidence of Triplets, by Race

SOURCE: Centers for Disease Control, 1997c.
Notice that the rate at which mothers give birth to triplets varies by year and by the race of the mother. What factors likely contribute to these differences?

Multiple pregnancies involving more than two children are even rarer. Triplets occur once in every 8000 to 9000 pregnancies, and quadruplets occur once in every 700,000 pregnancies (Grant, 1993). Because of the increased use of fertility drugs, rates of multiple pregnancies have increased since 1970 (Centers for Disease Control, 1997c). For example, the incidence of triplets has quadrupled since 1970. The high rates of multiple pregnancies among Caucasian American women likely result from the use of fertility drugs by older women who decide to delay pregnancy and then need to overcome the greater difficulty in getting pregnant (see Figure 3.4). With increasing numbers of fetuses, the chance of survival and good outcomes decreases. But today's medical technology makes it more probable that multiple infants will survive—as in the case of Bobbi McCaughey, who, in 1997, gave birth to seven babies after she took fertility drugs to get pregnant.

ectopic pregnancy a pregnancy that occurs outside the uterus

TABLE 3.3

Milestones and Characteristics of Prenatal Development

AGE (MONTHS)	LENGTH (INCHES)	WEIGHT	MILESTONES AND CHARACTERISTICS
1	.17		Backbone and vertebrae form. Heart forms and starts to beat. Arm and leg buds form. Embryo is not yet distinguishable as human.
2	1.25	1 g	Bone cells appear. Arms and legs become distinct. Fingers and toes form. Major blood vessels form. Internal organs continue to develop.
3	3	28 g	Eyes form but eyelids are fused closed. Ears form. Arms and legs are fully formed. Heartbeat can be detected. External genitalia develop. Fingernails and toenails form.
4	6.5–7	113 g (4 oz)	Head is large relative to rest of body. Face takes on human features. Movements may be detected by mother.
5	10–12	227–454 g (.5–1 lb)	Head and body hair are visible. Head is less disproportionate to rest of body. Brain develops rapidly. Periods of sleep alternate with periods of alertness.
6	11–14	567–681 g (1.25–1.5 lb)	Layers of the cortex of the brain develop. Skin is wrinkled. Skin is pink because blood in vessels is visible.
7	13–17	1135–1362 g (2.5–3 lb)	Fetus becomes viable. Eyelids open and eyelashes form. Teeth form.
8	16.5–18	2100 g (6 lb)	Fat deposits form. Body is more rounded. Skin unwrinkles. Testes in boys descend into scrotum sac.
9	20	3178–3405 g (7–7.5 lb)	Body hair is shed. Nails reach tips of fingers and toes. Growth rate slows down. Fetus moves into position for birth.

SOURCE: Bennett and Brown, 1993; Jones, 1997; Moore, 1993.

THE EMBRYONIC STAGE

Once implantation occurs, the embryo and its support structures take shape and begin to function. Table 3.3 identifies the major accomplishments of prenatal development.

Early in embryonic development, the human embryo is indistinguishable from embryos of other species. In this photo, the 5-week-old embryo is floating within the amniotic sac. How might the resemblance of embryos of different species at this stage be used to support an evolutionary view of development?

From the inner mass of cells, two membranes form that surround and protect the embryo. The first is the **amnion,** which grows over the embryo and becomes filled with *amniotic fluid.* The amount of amniotic fluid is about 5 to 10 milliliters after eight weeks of development and increases through pregnancy to a maximum of 1000 to 1200 milliliters (Wong & Perry, 1998). This sac and its fluid provide the developing embryo with shock-absorbing protection.

The second membrane is the **chorion,** which grows to surround the embryo after about one month of development. The chorion helps form the **placenta,** a mass of tissue through which nutrients and waste products are exchanged between the mother and the developing embryo. The placenta is made up of fine blood vessels (called *capillaries*) from the mother's and embryo's circulatory systems. The mother's blood does not directly mix with that of her developing child. The developing embryo is connected to the placenta by the **umbilical cord,** the lifeline of the embryo, which consists of two arteries and one vein.

The third week of prenatal development begins with the formation of three layers of cells. The outer layer is the *ectoderm,* which later becomes the skin and nervous system. The middle layer is the *mesoderm,* which becomes the muscles, bones, and circulatory system. The inner layer is the *endoderm,* which becomes the digestive system and lungs. The formation of these layers reveals the remarkable nature of early development. Early development involves not only the change from a single cell into a creature that ultimately consists of several trillion cells but also increasing cell differentiation. Our many different types of cells—hair cells, liver cells, brain cells, and so on—all form from a single cell.

About twenty-one days after fertilization, the ectoderm begins to form a groove that develops into the *neural tube.* This tube eventually becomes the central nervous system. The front portion of the tube becomes the brain, and the back forms the spinal cord.

Within a few weeks, the embryo is about ½ inch long and looks more like a salamander than a human being. In fact, early in development it is almost impossible to distinguish embryos of different species. By the end of the embryonic period (at about eight weeks), however, human embryos look distinctively different than embryos of other species.

During the embryonic period, the brain, nervous system, circulatory system, and sensory organs develop. At four weeks, the heart, although still just a tube, begins to flutter and then beat. Arms and legs appear, first as buds and later as limbs. The liver, pancreas, and major divisions of intestines develop around this time and the embryo's face begins to form, although at this age the face is still unrecognizable. By eight weeks, the fingers and toes are visible and are noticeably webbed. At the end of eight weeks, the embryo weighs about .03 ounce and is slightly over 1 inch in length.

The 8-week-old embryo is beginning to look more human in its physical features. Why is the embryo most susceptible to damaging environmental influences during this time period?

Development during the embryonic period proceeds according to two important principles. The first is that growth occurs from the head downwards—a principle referred to as **cephalocaudal development** (see Figure 3.5). The second is that body parts closer to the central axis of the body develop first, while those that are farther away from the center of the body (such as the hands) develop later. This principle is referred to as **proximodistal development**.

By the end of the embryonic period, 95 percent of the major body structures are developed and some are even functioning, although they are incapable of sustaining the embryo independent of the mother. Because the organs and body systems are forming, the embryonic period is a time of great vulnerability to environmental influences.

FIGURE 3.5

Changes in Body Proportion During Prenatal Development

FERTILIZATION AGE IN WEEKS

9   12   16   38

SOURCE: *Moore, 1998.*

Notice that, as the embryo and fetus grow, the size of the head relative to the rest of the body changes. What other aspects of developmental change can you identify in this figure?

THE FETAL STAGE

The transition from an embryo to a fetus is gradual and signifies that the developing child is unquestionably recognizable as human. The fetal stage is marked by growth and elaboration of the structures that developed earlier. This is the final and longest phase of prenatal development—extending from about the ninth week after fertilization until birth.

Around the sixteenth week of prenatal development, many mothers first feel the movements of their unborn child. These fetal movements, known as **quickening,** are dramatic signs of pregnancy. More than a positive pregnancy test, a bulging abdomen, or even the sound of the fetal heartbeat, the movements of the fetus signal and confirm the presence of the life inside the woman. Quickening is one of the greatest sources of joy during pregnancy, and lack of fetal movements can be a source of great anxiety (Eisenberg, Murkoff, & Hathaway, 1991).

Growth during the fetal stage is very rapid, especially during the third and fourth months. The rate of growth is greater than at any other time before or after birth. By sixteen weeks, the fetus is three to four times larger and over a hundred times heavier than it was at the end of the embryonic period. It is 6 to 7 inches long and weighs about 4 ounces (Jones, 1997). As the fetus enlarges, the mother's uterus, or womb, grows; as a result, it is around the sixteenth week that her condition becomes obvious to others (see Figure 3.6).

amnion a membrane that grows over the embryo and becomes filled with amniotic fluid, which protects the embryo

chorion a membrane that grows to surround the embryo after about one month of development and helps form the placenta

placenta the structure through which nutrients and waste products are exchanged between the mother and the developing embryo

umbilical cord the lifeline of the embryo, consisting of two arteries and one vein

cephalocaudal development the principle that growth occurs from the head downwards

proximodistal development the principle that body parts closer to the central axis of the body develop first, while those farther away from the center of the body develop later

quickening fetal movements during pregnancy

FIGURE 3.6
Growth and Change of Fetus and Mother

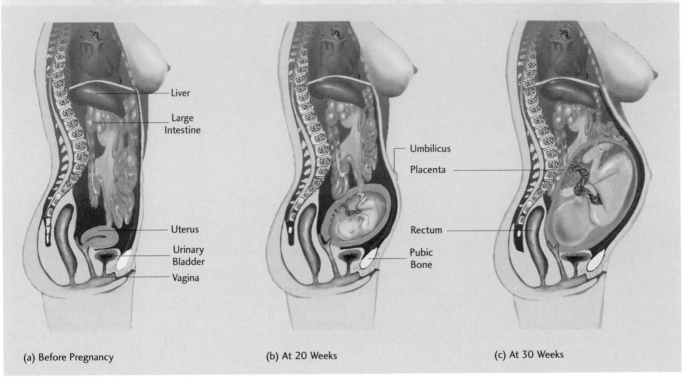

Liver

Large
Intestine

Umbilicus

Placenta

Uterus

Urinary
Bladder

Rectum

Vagina

Pubic
Bone

(a) Before Pregnancy

(b) At 20 Weeks

(c) At 30 Weeks

SOURCE: Moore, 1998.
Early in pregnancy, the embryo is small and causes few noticeable physical changes in the mother. Later in pregnancy, the physical changes in the mother increase as the baby grows larger. Can you describe how the mother's and the embryo's systems are connected?

Notice that the 8-month-old fetus is quite well developed at this point. What major changes occur during the last trimester?

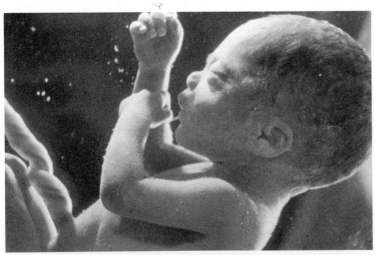

Important body changes occur during the third and fourth months. The fetus develops a penis or vagina at the beginning of the third month. In males, the process begins when the testes secrete the male hormone testosterone, which causes a group of cells to develop into the penis, scrotum, and seminal vesicles. In females, because testosterone is not secreted, these cells develop into the fallopian tubes, uterus, and vagina. Thus, boys' and girls' sex organs have the same origins but develop differently depending on the presence or absence of testosterone (Wong & Perry, 1998).

The nervous system also develops rapidly during the early part of the fetal period. By the fifth month, the cells of the brain have migrated to their proper locations and formed connections with other brain cells. These connections allow brain cells to communicate with one another and to control some bodily functions. The fetus displays simple reflexes such as sucking and swallowing and can react to disturbances of its environment, such as loud noises made outside but near the mother's uterus (Jones, 1997). Such reactions indicate that the fetus is not simply an unreactive mass of tissue but is a responsive being.

Can Fetuses Learn?

You have already learned that fetuses can hear and respond to sounds during the third trimester of pregnancy. Recordings of sounds in the uterus indicate that the fetus can clearly hear the mother's voice and heartbeat, but the father's voice is muffled. Do fetuses learn from exposure to their mother's voice during the time they spend in the womb?

In one study, thirty-three healthy pregnant women volunteered to test the hypothesis that they do (DeCasper & Spence, 1986). At about seven and a half months into their pregnancy, the women read and recorded three stories that were used later to test their children. The stories were carefully selected to be similar in length, but the common nouns in the stories were changed to ensure little overlap. Each mother was assigned one of the stories as her "target story," which she read aloud two times a day when she thought her unborn baby was awake.

After birth of these children, sixteen of the newborns participated in the rest of the study. Each infant was fitted with a headphone and a nipple to suck on. The nipple was electronically wired to monitor sucking patterns. Some of the newborns were rewarded for sucking longer by hearing a recording of a woman's voice reading the target story. When they sucked for a shorter period, they heard a woman's voice reading an unfamiliar story. Other infants were given different reward patterns. Some heard their mother's voice reading the stories, and some heard another mother's voice. The results showed that infants changed their sucking patterns more when they heard the familiar story, even when a woman other than their mother read the story.

In another study (Panneton & De-Casper, 1986), newborns who had heard "Mary Had a Little Lamb" sung to them by their mothers during the two weeks before birth showed a clear preference for this song over another after birth. The results of these studies suggest that infants develop a familiarity with auditory stimuli in utero. Fetuses learn from exposure to prefer material they hear during late pregnancy.

These findings raise an intriguing question: Does a newborn's preference for mother's rather than father's voice reflect familiarity with her voice during pregnancy? Prenatal learning may influence the development of sensory connections in the brain that then serve as a basis for later preferences (Laughlin, 1991).

Thinking It Through:

1. Can a fetus acquire preferences for music, language, or literature through experience during pregnancy? If so, would it be a good idea to "educate" fetuses? Why or why not?
2. Do the findings of these studies suggest a critical period for the development of preferences?
3. How could researchers test to determine whether a fetus develops a preference for the mother's voice over another woman's or the father's voice?

An important milestone is reached as the fetus enters the last trimester of prenatal development. Prior to this point, a fetus born prematurely has a poor chance of surviving. At about seven months, survival is possible with intensive care because the fetus's lungs and nervous system are developed enough to support breathing. Thus, the seventh month marks the **age of viability**—the point at which postnatal survival is likely (Moore, 1993).

During the last three months, the finishing touches of prenatal development are completed. At thirty weeks, the eyelids open to reveal fully formed eyes with pupils that respond to light. By thirty-five weeks, the hands have a firm grasp and the hair is growing. Increased production of fat makes the body more rounded and less wrinkled (Bennett & Brown, 1993). This increase in fat improves control of body temperature. By the end of the last trimester, the average newborn is about 20 inches long and weighs 7 to 7½ pounds.

age of viability the point at which postnatal survival is likely

WHAT CONDITIONS INFLUENCE PREGNANCY AND PRENATAL DEVELOPMENT?

Although genetic and chromosomal disorders cause some birth defects, about 80 percent of birth defects are caused by environmental problems during prenatal development. The unborn child has at least two lines of protection from environmental influences. The first is the amniotic fluid, which protects the fetus from physical injuries. The second line of protection is the **placental barrier,** created by blood vessel walls that separate the maternal and fetal circulatory systems. This barrier acts as a filter, blocking many harmful agents from entering the blood supply of the child. The placental barrier effectively blocks large agents, such as bacteria, but not smaller agents, such as viruses. The mother's hormones, any alcohol she drinks, and the nicotine from any cigarettes she smokes are among the substances that can cross the placental barrier. Thus, the protection provided by the placental barrier is incomplete.

Alcohol and cigarettes are examples of **teratogens**—agents that cross the placental barrier and cause or increase the incidence of physical malformations and behavioral and cognitive deficits in children. Many teratogens have been identified, including diseases such as smallpox and HIV, environmental agents such as X rays and pesticides, and drugs such as cocaine and alcohol. Although the effects of teratogens vary, the severity of these effects depends on at least three factors:

✦ **When the teratogenic exposure occurs.**   A particular teratogen will affect a zygote, an embryo, and a fetus differently. If the zygote is exposed to a teratogen, a spontaneous abortion may occur. During the embryonic stage, organs and body structures, which are undergoing rapid development, are likely to be damaged. Teratogenic exposure at the fetal stage, when the brain is developing quickly, may damage the nervous system and brain, affecting later behavior or intelligence (see Figure 3.7).

✦ **Amount of teratogenic exposure.**   Some teratogens, especially alcohol and drugs, are dosage dependent; that is, the more the mother takes, the greater the likelihood that the developing child will be affected. Similarly, the longer the exposure to teratogens, the greater the likelihood that development will be disrupted.

✦ **Fetal characteristics.**   Important individual differences occur in fetal reactions to a teratogen. Depending on constitution, some fetuses will perish under the influence of a particular teratogen, while others may suffer severe or mild complications.

These three factors operate together to determine the degree to which teratogens influence the developing child. Some effects are direct (for example, the fetus is exposed to alcohol when the mother drinks), and some are indirect (for example, the fetus receives less oxygen while the mother is smoking). Because many teratogenic effects occur before women even know they have conceived, a good strategy to ensure healthy offspring is for women to avoid teratogens if there is any possibility that they may be pregnant—that is, if they have had unprotected intercourse.

DISEASES

About 3 to 5 percent of birth defects are caused by infectious diseases transmitted to the developing child (Beckman & Brent, 1986). Several diseases have a dramatic impact on the developing child, even when they produce only mild symptoms in the mother. The diseases most likely to influence prenatal development are caused by viruses. Approximately 5 percent of women who are pregnant are affected by viral diseases (Gibbs & Sweet, 1994).

placental barrier a line of protection for the unborn child, created by blood vessel walls that separate the maternal and fetal circulatory systems

teratogens agents that cross the placental barrier and cause or increase the incidence of physical malformations and behavioral and cognitive deficits

FIGURE 3.7
Critical Periods for Teratogenic Effects

NOTE: *Dark portions denote highly sensitive periods; light portions denote less sensitive periods.*
SOURCE: *Moore, 1998.*
The timing of teratogen exposure is crucial. Notice that teratogens have the most impact during the embryonic stage, except on certain body parts such as the brain and ears, which continue to be at risk for teratogenic effects because they continue to grow and develop during the fetal period.

Rubella

The placental barrier does not provide complete protection for the developing child. During a mini-epidemic of rubella—a form of measles—in the 1960s, 30,000 fetuses and newborns died and over 16,000 children were born deaf or blind (Rosenblith, 1992). Rubella causes flu-like symptoms so mild that pregnant women may not even realize they are ill. Nonetheless, rubella crosses the placental barrier and interferes with normal development during early pregnancy. If the mother has rubella during the first twelve weeks of pregnancy, the child has about an 80 percent chance of showing some effects. At thirteen to fourteen weeks, the risk drops to about 50 percent; by the end of the second trimester, the risk is 25 percent (Cunningham, MacDonald, & Gant, 1993).

The dangers of rubella can be prevented through immunization prior to pregnancy. Although preventive efforts have reduced rubella-related defects in infants, an increase has occurred in recent years (National Center for Health Statistics, 1996). The incidence of rubella-related defects is especially high among Hispanic Americans and African Americans because of lower immunization rates (Kaplan et al., 1990).

Syphilis

Unlike most other bacteria, the bacteria that cause syphilis can cross the placental barrier and damage the developing child. Before effective treatments, syphilis accounted for about one-third of stillborn children. Unlike most teratogens, syphilis is more dangerous in later prenatal development, especially after the eighteenth week. Syphilis causes lesions on the eyes, leading to blindness, and on the skin and mucous membranes. Children who were exposed prenatally to syphilis also suffer retarded growth, liver damage, and problems with their nervous systems (Fletcher & Gordon, 1990).

In most states, prenatal health care includes testing for syphilis and other sexually transmitted diseases. Although antibiotics reduced the rates of new cases of syphilis in the 1960s, prenatal syphilis infection continues to be a problem, with over 2000 new cases reported in 1994 (National Center for Health Statistics, 1996). These cases tend to involve low-income women who do not receive adequate prenatal care (Gibbs & Sweet, 1994).

Pediatric AIDS

Pregnant women infected with the human immunodeficiency virus (HIV) often transmit the disease to their developing children. In the United States, most children with HIV are born to drug-addicted mothers, although the number of women infected through heterosexual transmission is rapidly increasing (Mehta & Bentrup, 1996). HIV is usually transmitted to the fetus through the placental barrier but also may be transmitted during delivery because of the infant's exposure to vaginal fluids and during breast-feeding (Committee on Pediatric AIDS, 1998). HIV-infected infants are likely to have impaired brain growth (Epstein et al., 1986), bacterial and viral infections, cognitive deficits, and weak muscles (Byers, 1989).

With over a million AIDS sufferers in the United States (Minkoff, 1994), more children will be exposed to this disease prenatally than ever before. Recent studies suggest that mothers with AIDS who take AZT during pregnancy are much less likely to transmit the virus to their newborns (Morris, 1998).

DRUGS

In the United States, 90 percent of pregnant women take some type of drug during pregnancy (Cunningham et al., 1993), including over-the-counter medications, prescriptions, and illicit drugs. Drugs influence the mother's entire body and are transmitted to the developing child during pregnancy.

Thalidomide

The negative consequences of drugs are best illustrated by the thalidomide tragedy. In Europe in the 1950s, over 10,000 children were born with arms or legs missing, hands growing from their shoulders, or feet growing from their hips. Medical researchers pinpointed the cause of these defects: the mothers had taken a mild sedative called thalidomide, prescribed to them by their doctors during early pregnancy to control nausea and insomnia. The US Food and Drug Administration had not approved the use of thalidomide because of lack of testing, so most families in the United States were spared its tragic consequences (Bower, 1995).

The timing of thalidomide ingestion was significant (Beckman & Brent, 1986). Because thalidomide interferes with development of the skeletal system, its effects are most obvious during the late embryonic period, when arms and legs are forming. Once developed, the embryo's arms and legs are not affected by thalidomide.

Alcohol

Over 5 million women in the United States drink alcohol during pregnancy. When a pregnant woman drinks, her unborn child is exposed to the teratogen ethanol—the active ingredient in alcoholic beverages. Because the fetus is less able to metabolize ethanol than the mother, the fetus's exposure may be longer and more intense. Women who drink heavily during pregnancy (five or six drinks a day) are more likely to miscarry or have low-birthweight infants (Andres & Jones, 1994). Heavy drinkers and binge drinkers also have a much higher risk of giving birth to a child with **fetal alcohol syndrome (FAS),** a constellation of problems marked by physical deformities and intellectual deficits. Characteristics of FAS include the following (Streissguth, 1997):

This 8-year-old child has fetal alcohol syndrome. He has the typical facial abnormalities associated with the syndrome, including a flat nose and small, narrow head. In some states, mothers who drink or take drugs during pregnancy are charged with child abuse. Do you agree or disagree with this policy? Why?

- ✦ Abnormally flat face and nose
- ✦ Narrow head
- ✦ Delayed and retarded physical growth
- ✦ Heart defects
- ✦ Cognitive deficits
- ✦ Hyperactivity

The most serious and consistent feature of FAS is mental retardation. In a longitudinal study of 500 FAS children followed until age 7, the children were found to have an average IQ score of 65, compared with a normal score of about 100 (Streissguth, Sampson, & Barr, 1989). Women who drink alcohol moderately (one or two drinks per day) may be at risk for giving birth to children with **fetal alcohol effects (FAE).** These children have slightly retarded physical development and may have learning disabilities (Kerns, Don, Mateer, & Streissguth, 1997).

Binge drinking may be more injurious than consistent low levels of drinking (Abel, 1996). The timing of fetal exposure to ethanol also is important. For example, facial anomalies and mental retardation are more likely to occur if the mother drinks early in pregnancy (Coles, 1994; Maier, Chen, & West, 1996). Some evidence suggests that women who quit drinking during pregnancy may prevent FAS or FAE in their newborns (Coles, 1994). No one knows how much alcohol consumed during pregnancy is *too* much, so physicians recommend total abstinence.

But even this precaution may not be enough—children may suffer effects from alcohol that was consumed before the woman became pregnant. For example, children born to abstaining mothers who previously had been drinkers had lower IQ scores than children whose mothers did not drink before or after becoming pregnant (Russell, Czarnecki, Cowan, & McPherson, 1991).

Cigarettes

Despite the warnings about the dangers of smoking, in 1992, an estimated 48 million adults in the United States smoked. The highest rates generally are found among people 25 to 44 years of age, although smoking among teen mothers has increased. Approximately 14 percent of pregnant women smoke cigarettes (National Center for Health Statistics, 1998), and with each puff they expose themselves and their unborn children to toxic substances.

Smokers ingest over 4000 chemicals in each cigarette, including known carcinogens. Some of these chemicals pass through the placenta and influence the unborn child. For example, carbon monoxide and nicotine deprive the child of oxygen, adversely influencing brain development. The danger to fetuses is especially severe when mothers smoke a pack or more a day.

fetal alcohol syndrome (FAS) a constellation of problems, including physical deformities and intellectual deficits, that may occur if a mother drinks heavily during pregnancy

fetal alcohol effects (FAE) the effects, including mildly retarded physical development and learning disabilities, that may occur if a mother drinks moderately during pregnancy

FIGURE 3.8

Smoking Among Mothers During Pregnancy and School Failure and Learning Problems for Children at Age 7

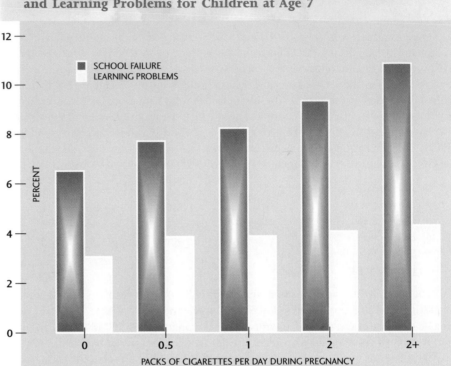

SOURCE: *Adapted from Newman and Buka, 1991.*

Notice that the rates of school failure and learning problems in children depend on whether and how much the mother smoked during pregnancy. School failure seems to be more influenced by maternal smoking than learning problems are. What can be done to decrease the rates of smoking among pregnant women?

Males who smoke may decrease their sperm production, making conception less likely. Women who smoke during pregnancy increase their risk of having a spontaneous abortion, premature birth, and complications in delivery (deHass, Harlow, & Cramer, 1991; Taylor & Sanderson, 1995). Infants born to smokers are smaller and less likely to survive.

Some studies report that children of smokers have deficits in motor coordination, physical growth, and spatial and reading abilities (Floyd, Zahniser, Gunter, & Kendrick, 1991), but these outcomes also are influenced by related lifestyle factors such as alcohol use, socioeconomic status, and nutrition (Barr, Streissguth, Darby, & Sampson, 1990). Smoking also has long-term effects (Fergusson, Horwood, & Lynskey, 1993). As indicated in Figure 3.8, children whose mothers smoked during pregnancy were more likely to fail in school and have learning deficiencies than children whose mothers did not smoke. Notice that the more a mother smoked, the more likely the child was to fail at school (Newman & Buka, 1991).

Because the effects of smoking are dosage related, they can be minimized if mothers reduce the number of cigarettes they smoke and reduce their exposure to secondhand smoke. Smokers who enroll in smoking cessation programs and reduce their smoking tend to give birth to normal-birthweight babies (MacArthur & Knox, 1988).

Cocaine

In a study of 400,000 admissions of women to drug treatment facilities in 1993, the second most common reason for admission (following alcohol use, at 44 percent) was use of cocaine, especially crack cocaine, at 26 percent (National Center for Health Statistics, 1996). Although overall use of cocaine has decreased somewhat in the last few years, rates among inner-city and minority groups have increased (National Institute on Drug Abuse, 1991). According to some estimates (Holzman & Paneth, 1994), as many as 15 to 20 percent of inner-city mothers use cocaine during pregnancy. Federal law mandates drug testing of all newborns.

Women who take cocaine during pregnancy have more miscarriages and stillbirths and lower birthweight babies than other women (Mastrogiannis, Decavalas, Verma, & Tejani, 1990), and this is especially true for mothers who use crack cocaine (Cherukuri, Minkoff, Feldman, Parekh, & Glass, 1988). Infants born to cocaine-using mothers are more at risk for physical deformities, especially of the heart and circulatory system (Chasnoff, Chisum, & Kaplan, 1988), and their brain development may be adversely affected (Hurt et al., 1995).

The effects of cocaine on prenatal development occur for two reasons (Lester, Freier, & LaGasse, 1995). First, the fetus is exposed to the cocaine because it passes through the placental barrier. This exposure interferes with information processing within the brain, increases blood pressure, and produces heart seizures. Second, cocaine affects the mother's system, in turn influencing the environment of her unborn child. For instance, cocaine decreases oxygen and blood flow in the mother, interfering with normal prenatal development (Bingol et al., 1987).

After birth, infants exposed to cocaine prenatally seldom experience withdrawal from the drug, but they may be irritable and have attention-span and motor-development problems (Chasnoff, Burns, Schnoll, & Burns, 1985; Lester, Freier, & LaGasse, 1995). They also may show less interest in learning than other infants (Alessandri, Sullivan, Imaizumi, & Lewis, 1993). Although research suggests that some children who were exposed to cocaine prenatally may have cognitive deficits, these deficits greatly depend on the family environment (Azuma & Chasnoff, 1993; Griffith, Azuma, & Chasnoff, 1994). For example, children born to mothers who use cocaine also are at greater risk of abuse and neglect than children of nonusers, and abuse and neglect, in turn, are linked to cognitive deficits (Leventhal et al., 1997). The long-term effects that can be attributed directly to a mother's cocaine use are difficult to pinpoint because cocaine use is associated with many other risk factors (Mayes, Granger, Bornstein, & Zuckerman, 1992).

Heroin

Heroin (and other narcotics such as morphine and codeine) crosses the placental barrier. Infants of mothers who use heroin are born addicted to the drug and undergo withdrawal. Addicted newborns experience sleep disturbances, hyperactivity, convulsions, fever, sweating, vomiting, diarrhea, and even death (Andres & Jones, 1994). Heroin-exposed infants are small and have behavioral problems such as irritability and excessive crying. These effects are evident at 4 months after birth, but research has not consistently found narcotic effects on behavior after about 1 year of age (Hutchings & Fifer, 1986).

Because drug-addicted parents expose their children to many risk factors, it is difficult to disentangle the effects due solely to prenatal exposure to the drug. In an interesting study, Wilson (1989) compared heroin-exposed infants with unexposed infants raised by addicted parents. Intelligence in the children related to the home environment, with the lowest IQ children being those raised by addicted parents. Thus, the effects of prenatal drug exposure may be exacerbated by caregivers who continue to use drugs and tend to have disorganized and chaotic lifestyles (Woods, Eyler, Behnke, & Conlon, 1993).

ENVIRONMENTAL HAZARDS

Lead, pesticides, radiation, and chemicals are environmental agents that may cross the placental barrier and affect the developing fetus. These environmental agents may be

FIGURE 3.9

Changes in Birth Rates, by Age and Race/Ethnicity of the Mother

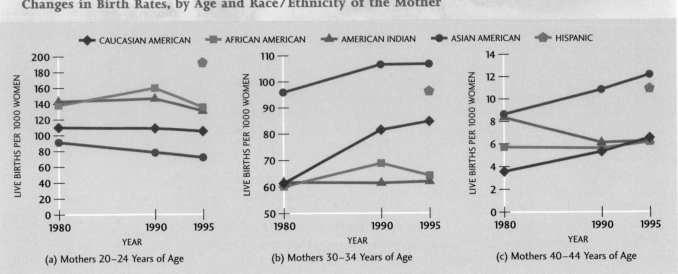

(a) Mothers 20–24 Years of Age

(b) Mothers 30–34 Years of Age

(c) Mothers 40–44 Years of Age

NOTE: Data for Hispanic mothers were not available until 1995.
SOURCE: National Center for Health Statistics, 1997.
Notice how the birth rates vary for women of different races/ethnicities. For young mothers, birth rates have been relatively steady; more African American and American Indian women have babies at a young age than do women of other ethnicities. In both groups of older mothers, there are more Asian American women than women of other ethnicities. Changes over time are seen mainly for older Caucasian American and Asian American mothers. What factors have contributed to these changes in birth rates?

hazardous to people of any age and increase the risk of cancer later in life. However, they are particularly hazardous to prenatal development.

Radiation

Radiation is a powerful teratogen. Over thirty types of birth defects, many involving the central nervous system, have been related to prenatal exposure to high levels of radiation. The most common effects are microencephaly (abnormally small brain and skull) and mental retardation. The severity and type of effect depend on the amount of radiation received and on the timing of the exposure. Following World War II, Japanese women survivors who had been closest to the sites of the atomic bomb explosions and had received high levels of radiation gave birth to physically deformed and mentally retarded children (Otake & Shull, 1984). Although diagnostic X-ray procedures involve much less radiation, a risk for birth defects remains, especially for fetuses at between 8 and 15 weeks (Cunningham et al., 1993).

Chemical Hazards

Every day we are surrounded by potentially dangerous chemicals in our air, water, and food and in the products we use. Unfortunately, pregnant women may not even be aware that they have been exposed to harmful chemicals. For example, in the 1950s, an industrial plant in Japan dumped mercury waste into the ocean, polluting the water and fish. Children born to mothers living nearby suffered severe retardation and irreversible physical and neurological impairments. Pregnant women often unknowingly expose their unborn children to high levels of lead, contained in paint, auto emissions, and coatings on blinds and shades (Vorhees & Mollnow, 1987). Research now suggests that many common products, ranging from food preservatives to insecticides and even some cosmetics, pose risks to unborn children.

MATERNAL CONDITIONS

In addition to biological and teratogenic factors that affect the developing child, characteristics of the mother can pose risks to the unborn child. A mother's physical, psychological, and social characteristics can affect the fetus by influencing her health or by altering the chemistry of her blood.

Maternal Age

More than ever before, women are delaying having their first child. As shown in Figure 3.9, birth rates have been dropping among women in their early 20s, but increasing among women in their early 30s and early 40s—particularly Caucasian American and Asian American women (National Center for Health Statistics, 1997). Today, it is not uncommon for a woman to have her first child or start a second family after 40.

Pregnancy risks increase as the mother gets older (Reichman & Pagnini, 1997). Mothers over 35 are at increased risk for having a child with Down syndrome. They also risk developing high blood pressure, gestational diabetes, and cardiovascular disease, all of which are usually controllable. Additionally, older mothers are somewhat more likely to miscarry (Johnson, Walker, & Niebyl, 1991). When an older mother eliminates as many risk factors as possible and undergoes extensive prenatal testing, however, her chances of delivering a healthy newborn are virtually as good as those for a younger mother (Yagel et al., 1998).

Maternal Stress

A pregnant woman's psychological condition influences the health of her unborn child. Like any other major life transition, pregnancy and delivery produce a moderate amount of stress, as parents-to-be must adjust to new demands and responsibilities. Stress can cause changes in the mother's blood chemistry. Research has shown that mothers who are stressed or emotionally upset produce hormones that cross the placental barrier and affect the fetus. Extreme and prolonged conditions of stress increase the risk for miscarriage, difficult labor and delivery, and prematurity (Glover, 1997).

Parity

Parity, or the number and spacing of children a woman bears, also affects prenatal development. Generally, a woman's endocrine system takes four years to return to prepregnancy condition (Cunningham et al., 1993). Infants born before the endocrine system recovers may be at a disadvantage; a pregnancy within three months of delivery is classified as a high-risk pregnancy (Eisenberg, Murkoff, & Hathaway, 1991). Infants conceived after the period of recuperation have a better prenatal environment than do firstborn children. Blood circulation is richer after a first pregnancy, and later-born children suffer fewer birth defects and complications. Furthermore, labor and delivery are quicker and less demanding for later-born children. However, the advantages of this enhanced prenatal environment are lost if later births follow too closely.

PROTECTIVE FACTORS

What can a couple do to increase their chances of giving birth to a healthy baby? Good nutrition during pregnancy is essential. Proper nutrition and weight gain increase the likelihood of giving birth to a healthy baby (Cnattingius, Bergstrom, Lipworth, & Kramer, 1998). Women need not "eat for two"; usually a woman needs only about 300

This 38-year-old woman is having her first child. What factors contribute to the increase in the number of older women starting families?

parity the number and spacing of children a woman bears

What Are the Effects of Prenatal Malnutrition?
The Dutch Famine of 1944–1945

During World War II, an inhuman experiment was carried out by the Nazis. In retaliation for a strike organized by Dutch railroad workers to impede Nazi efforts to reinforce their troops in the fall of 1944, the Nazis imposed an embargo on transports to the Netherlands. This embargo included the transport of food, producing a famine that continued until the spring of 1945. During that time, 40,000 pregnant Dutch women and their unborn children were exposed to severe malnutrition and starvation. By studying these children, scientists gained important insights into the effects of malnutrition on development.

The effects of malnourishment on the babies were dramatic. Among those exposed to malnourishment during the second or third trimester, death rates were higher than normal in their first weeks of life, and the rates continued to climb until they were 3 months old. Once the famine babies reached the age of 1 year, their risk of death returned to normal levels (Diamond, 1990).

As adults, the famine babies were physically smaller and more likely to have defects of the central nervous system. But even more sobering was the effect starvation had on the generation of children born to these famine babies. Examination of birth records revealed that women who were born to mothers starved during the Dutch famine of World War II gave birth to underweight babies. Thus, the babies were affected by the starvation of their grandmothers two generations earlier. Somehow the grandmothers' starvation had long-term effects such that, ultimately, their children's children were affected in utero. The lesson of the Dutch famine is that harm from malnourishment is not limited to the generations that experience it directly, but may be felt generations later (Diamond, 1990).

Thinking It Through:

1. What cause-and-effect relationships are implied in this case?
2. What problems exist in relying on historical situations to draw conclusions about cause-and-effect relationships?
3. What are the implications of these findings for famine victims today? For contemporary mothers-to-be?

---

additional calories (American College of Obstetricians and Gynecologists, 1990). Pregnant women have some special nutritional needs, though. To produce more blood, they need increased levels of iron, protein, and folic acid; to help fetal bones grow, they need more calcium and phosphorus. Ideally, women of average weight should gain approximately 30 pounds during pregnancy. Fit and well-nourished women may have easier childbirth, although more research is needed to definitely establish this finding (Wolfe et al., 1989).

One of the most important ways women can protect their unborn children is to have regular prenatal checkups (Johnson, Walker, & Niebyl, 1991). Regular checkups allow complications to be prevented or dealt with promptly and effectively. The number of women who receive prenatal care has steadily increased, and prenatal care has been associated with lower rates of birth complications (Moore, Origel, Key, & Resnick, 1986). Unfortunately, not every woman receives adequate prenatal care. Caucasian American women are more likely than many other women to receive prenatal care (National Center for Health Statistics, 1997).

Pregnancy is a family affair. A supportive and nurturing environment protects a pregnant woman and her unborn child by creating favorable conditions for them. Having a sympathetic partner, relatives, or friends helps minimize the negative effects of stress. Additionally, having a source of social support helps a woman deal with the physical demands or complications that arise during pregnancy.

CULTURAL INFLUENCES ON PREGNANCY

In every culture, reproduction and pregnancy are fundamental issues of human existence. Although reproduction and pregnancy are biological events that are similar all over the world, the experience and treatment of these events differ dramatically across cultures. In most Western cultures, pregnancy represents a major transition into adult life. Unlike marriage, pregnancy and birth are irreversible processes and mark a break from childhood (Fogel, 1997). But other cultures view pregnancy and birth differently. For example, West Africans view pregnancy as a divine gift, primarily signifying a couple's purity and strength (Nsamenang, 1992). Infertility among West African couples is interpreted as proof that the couple is being punished by their ancestors (Nsamenang, 1987). Most West Africans indicate that they would prefer to die in poverty and be survived by children than to die rich and childless (Nsamenang & Laosebikan, 1981).

Pregnancy and birth are biological events that occur similarly worldwide. However, the changes that occur during pregnancy and birth are viewed differently depending on cultural expectations. In this photo, Australian Aboriginal women are performing a "baby smoking" ceremony. What might be the purpose of this ceremony?

Women's Responses

Culture also affects the impact of pregnancy and the changes it brings for the parents-to-be. The fact that responses to pregnancy differ for different cultures and subcultures tells us that this biological condition is interpreted through the lens of cultural values and beliefs and institutions. In North America, many women become preoccupied with their weight gain and physical appearance during the later stages of pregnancy because of the emphasis the culture places on slenderness. North American women report feeling that they had lost control of their bodies and become embarrassingly conspicuous. Some pregnant women believe they look less attractive sexually and worry about being attractive to their partners (Fogel, 1997). In contrast, on the island of Yap in Micronesia, females are desired for their fertility, and the largeness of a pregnant woman is a symbol of her ability to produce children. In the Yap culture, the increased size associated with pregnancy is highly valued, so women do not worry about being thin (Lingenfelter, 1993).

Men's Responses

In the United States, men and women differ somewhat in their reactions to pregnancy. In one study, the majority of mothers and fathers reported that they anticipated and were curious about the upcoming birth, but fathers expressed less anxiety and less pleasure about the pregnancy than did mothers. Mothers were more likely to say they talked to or loved the unborn child (Mercer et al., 1988).

Some expectant fathers experience a sympathetic pregnancy, known by the French term *couvade*. During his partner's pregnancy, the father may suffer symptoms for which there is no recognized physiological basis, including increased or decreased appetite, weight gain, diarrhea or constipation, and headaches or toothaches. Onset is usually during the third gestational month, and the symptoms usually go away after childbirth (Holditch-David et al., 1994). In most Western cultures, *couvade* is seen as an expression of anxiety about the pregnancy, ambivalence about being a father, or envy over the attention the expectant mother receives during her pregnancy (Klein, 1991).

In some non-Western cultures, *couvade* refers to a custom whereby expectant fathers identify with their mates and make sacrifices of their own during the pregnancy. In India, for example, when the wife of a Brahman becomes pregnant, the husband traditionally stops chewing betel palm leaves until his wife gives birth. In the Philippines, an expectant father stops eating sour fruit a week before the delivery to prevent the newborn from being born with stomach problems. An expectant father in the Ifugao tribe of the Philippines is not supposed to disturb his unborn child by cutting wood during his wife's pregnancy (Meltzer, 1981).

Unfortunately, not all men share the feelings of their pregnant partners. The likelihood of extramarital sex increases during pregnancy (Thorpe, Dragonas, & Golding, 1992), and about one in six pregnant adult women is physically abused by her partner (Parker, McFarlane, & Socken, 1994). Thus, in addition to cultural differences, there are individual differences in how men (and women) react to pregnancy (Clinton, 1986).

CHAPTER SUMMARY

How do genes influence development?

- Information for development is coded by the genes, which, for humans, are found on twenty-three pairs of chromosomes. Sex is determined by the twenty-third pair, the sex chromosomes.

- Many physical characteristics and diseases result from information coded by a single gene, which can be expressed through a dominant, recessive, or sex-linked pattern.

- Most personality, behavioral, and intellectual traits are complexly determined by multiple genes.

What are common chromosomal abnormalities?

- About 3 to 5 percent of newborns have some type of genetic or chromosomal abnormality. One of the most common is Down syndrome, which results from an extra chromosome on the twenty-first pair.

- Sex-linked chromosomal abnormalities are those characterized by extra or missing sex chromosomes. Children with these disorders usually have abnormal development of sexual organs and often have behavioral problems.

- Genetic disorders can be detected using methods that allow visual inspection of the unborn child, such as ultrasound imaging, and methods that directly assess the unborn child's genetic material, such as chorionic villus sampling and amniocentesis. Genetic counselors help couples determine their risks for genetic disorders.

How does prenatal development proceed?

- Fertilization occurs when an egg and sperm cell meet and share their genetic material. The window of time for fertilization is only a few days around ovulation.

- Each menstrual cycle is divided into three phases—the menstrual, follicular, and luteal phases. Ovulation occurs in the middle of the woman's menstrual cycle.

- Sperm cells undergo a process of development, called spermatogenesis, in which cells initially containing forty-six chromosomes divide until they contain only twenty-three.

- The first stage of prenatal development is the germinal stage, which begins at fertilization and lasts until the egg implants in the mother's uterus. Cell division and differentiation are the hallmarks of this stage.

- The second stage is the embryonic stage, which begins at implantation and lasts until eight weeks. Because 95 percent of the organs and body parts develop during this stage, the embryo is most vulnerable to environmental damage.

- The third stage, the fetal stage, lasts from eight weeks until the end of pregnancy. During this stage, elaboration of the existing organs and structures occurs and the brain develops rapidly.

- Development is directional. Parts of the body close to the head develop first, and those farther away from the head develop later (cephalocaudal development). Additionally, growth occurs from the center of the body outward (proximodistal development).

- The seventh month of prenatal development marks a critical juncture—the age of viability. A child born during this stage is likely to survive.

What conditions influence pregnancy and prenatal development?

- Teratogens are agents that cross the placental barrier and harm the developing child. Teratogens include certain kinds of diseases, drugs, and environmental toxins. The effects of teratogens depend on their timing and amount and on the characteristics of the fetus.

- About 5 percent of birth defects are due to infectious diseases transmitted by the mother to the developing child. Diseases such as rubella, syphilis, and AIDS can seriously affect the health and well-being of the developing child.

- Many women take drugs during pregnancy. Alcohol, cigarettes, cocaine, prescription drugs, and illicit drugs cross the placental barrier and can harm the developing child.

- Environmental hazards such as radiation and chemicals and maternal characteristics such as age and stress can affect the conditions of both the mother and the developing child.

- Eating well, getting exercise, undergoing regular prenatal checkups, and having support from family and friends increase a woman's chances of having a healthy child.

- Although reproduction and pregnancy are biological events that are similar all over the world, the *experience* of pregnancy varies according to the culture one lives in.

KEY TERMS & CONCEPTS

age of viability *(85)*
amniocentesis *(73)*
amnion *(82)*
autosomes *(66)*
balanced polymorphism *(70)*
carriers *(70)*
cephalocaudal development *(82)*
chorion *(82)*
chorionic villus sampling *(73)*
chromosomes *(65)*
dominant gene *(67)*
ectopic pregnancy *(80)*
embryonic stage *(78)*
fetal alcohol effects (FAE) *(89)*

fetal alcohol syndrome (FAS) *(89)*
fetal stage *(78)*
fragile X syndrome *(70)*
genes *(65)*
genotype *(67)*
germinal stage *(78)*
heterozygous *(67)*
homozygous *(67)*
karyotype *(66)*
meiosis *(66)*
mitosis *(65)*
ovum *(75)*
parity *(93)*
phenotype *(67)*

placenta *(82)*
placental barrier *(86)*
proximodistal development *(82)*
quickening *(83)*
recessive gene *(67)*
sex chromosomes *(66)*
spermatogenesis *(76)*
spermatids *(76)*
spermatocytes *(76)*
spermatozoa *(76)*
teratogens *(86)*
ultrasound *(73)*
umbilical cord *(82)*
zygote *(78)*

ACTIVITIES & APPLICATIONS
Relating to Pregnancy and Prenatal Development

1. Interview a woman who is pregnant with her first baby. Ask her how she feels about the pregnancy. How does she feel about her own physical and emotional condition? Are any of her concerns based on cultural beliefs and attitudes? To what extent does she engage in behaviors that promote healthy development of the unborn child? What concerns does she express about the health of the baby? After your interview, consider what conditions in the baby's total environment might influence prenatal development.

2. Review how you are similar to and different from your grandparents, parents, and siblings. To what extent do you think genes versus family environment contributed to those differences? Discuss with your family members the genetic factors in your family history that might be relevant to your medical history. What might you do to offset genetically related health risks?

3. What factors contribute to a couple's ability to conceive? How do these factors differ for women and men? Collect information on techniques that help couples who have trouble conceiving. Which of these procedures would you consider if you had trouble conceiving?

4. Collaborate with classmates on a research project to identify (a) factors that can prevent conception, (b) ethical dilemmas in genetic counseling, or (c) optimal nutrition during pregnancy.

Birth & Neonatal DEVELOPMENT

CHAPTER OUTLINE

"*Good night,*" I said. Two hours later . . . "*wake-up, wake-up, your mom is going to have a baby. You could have a brother tonight!*" my Nana said as I got dressed. I was so tired, it was after midnight. I was hungry too, but all I could think about was my mom and dad. At the hospital, I asked Nana if she remembered when I was born. She said it was one of the best days of her life. All of a sudden, my dad came rushing into the waiting room and yelled "*Baby girl!*" I was stunned, I never thought I'd have a sister. I imagined having a brother to play with and show him how *to do things. To my surprise when I saw my sister she was so cute. When they brought her home, I had to be very quiet and couldn't run around the house like I used to. That was OK though, I liked watching her grow and do things.*

—Anonymous 8-year-old boy's on-line account of the birth of his sister

For most individuals, the birth of a child into the family is an unforgettable and mysterious event, and family members continue to tell stories about the birth of their babies long after the children have grown up. This 8-year-old's story about the birth of his sister reminds us that even children marvel at the birth of a baby and the early changes that occur. It also reminds us that family and personal lifestyles are altered dramatically by the arrival of a newborn.

How Is a Baby Born?

The birth of a child is a complex and exciting event. For approximately nine months, the expecting parents anticipate the event. During that time, the unborn child has been developing in preparation for life outside the mother's womb. Even with nine months' notice, many expecting parents are caught off guard by the events associated with birth. How do newborns make the transition from the prenatal to the postnatal world? How do parents react to the birth of a child?

THE BIRTH PROCESS

When a woman finds out she is pregnant, her doctor will count 280 days from the first day of her last period and pronounce this to be her due date. Only about 3 percent of all women give birth on their due date, but over 45 percent give birth within one week before or after that date. Although most children are delivered at between thirty-seven and forty-one weeks' gestation, a sizable number are delayed or are preterm (see Figure 4.1). Girls tend to be born a few days earlier than boys, and women who have shorter menstrual cycles tend to have shorter pregnancies, although the reasons for these differences are not clear (Jones, 1997).

One of the many mysteries surrounding childbirth is what causes it to begin. Much of our present understanding of how labor begins comes from observations of sheep. For some time, sheepherders in Idaho had noticed that pregnant ewes grazing in certain pastures failed to give birth on time. Looking for the causes of this delay, researchers

FIGURE 4.1
Distribution of Gestation Among US Women

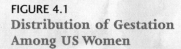

Postterm (42 weeks or more) 9%

Preterm (28 to 36 weeks) 10%

Extremely Preterm (less than 28 weeks) 1%

Term (37 to 41 weeks) 80%

SOURCE: Adapted from National Center for Health Statistics, 1997.
What conclusions can you draw about the likelihood that a mother will give birth on or close to her due date?

Here a woman in labor is attended by a midwife. What are the symptoms of true labor? What factors influence when labor starts and how long it lasts?

discovered that the newborn lambs had underdeveloped adrenal and pituitary glands. These abnormalities occurred because the pregnant ewes were eating plants containing high levels of a chemical that crossed the placenta and harmed the glandular development of the fetus. As a result, the fetus secreted lower-than-normal levels of adrenal steroid hormones. Subsequent research confirmed that fetal steroids initiate labor. Injections of fetal hormones into pregnant ewes any time during the second half of their pregnancy resulted in early delivery (Nathanieisz, 1995).

Like the sheep, human newborns who are delivered early tend to have larger adrenal glands and those delivered late tend to have underdeveloped glands. However, the mother's body also may trigger labor by releasing prostaglandins, a group of fatty acids widely distributed throughout body tissues (Nathanieisz, 1995). Other evidence suggests that oxytocin, a hormone secreted by the mother's pituitary glands, stimulates uterine contractions and hastens labor. In fact, as you learned in Chapter 3, many women are given synthetic oxytocin (pitocin) to hasten labor contractions. Other evidence indicates that, along with hormones, maturation of the placenta controls the onset of labor (Jones, 1997). The variety of possible causes of birth suggests that we still have much to learn about the factors that determine when birth occurs.

Women all over the world experience the same general biological changes associated with birth. About two to three weeks before birth, many women report that they suddenly can breathe more easily and feel more comfortable. This relief is referred to as **lightening** and occurs when the fetus drops into the pelvic cavity, decreasing pressure on the mother's diaphragm. In a few hours to a week before the onset of labor, the baby's head moves further down into the mother's pelvis in preparation for birth.

The birth process is divided into three stages: (1) dilation of the cervix, (2) birth of the baby, and (3) expulsion of the placenta, or "afterbirth." The first stage lasts the longest, but the length of each stage varies considerably from birth to birth. For mothers who are having their first child—**primiparous women**—the entire birth process usually lasts from 10 to 16 hours. The average length of time is shorter (6 to 11 hours) for women who have previously given birth—**multiparous women**. Any duration up to 24 hours is considered normal (Wong & Perry, 1998).

Stage 1: Dilation of the Cervix

Throughout pregnancy, and especially during the last month or two, women experience mild, irregular contractions of the uterus, called **Braxton-Hicks contractions.** During late pregnancy, women sometimes experience **false labor** in the form of contractions that may be moderately intense and rhythmic. The contractions associated with

lightening when the fetus drops into the pelvic cavity, decreasing pressure on the mother's diaphragm

primiparous women women who are having their first child

multiparous women women who have previously given birth

Braxton-Hicks contractions mild, irregular contractions of the uterus experienced throughout pregnancy, especially during the last month or two

false labor moderately intense, rhythmic contractions late in the pregnancy false labor decrease over time, especially when women exercise. The true contractions of labor mark the beginning of the first stage of the birth process. Early contractions last about 30 to 60 seconds and occur at 5- to 20-minute intervals. By the end of labor, the interval is only about 1 to 3 minutes and the duration and intensity of contractions are greater (Cassidy, 1993).

Early in labor, the muscle contractions of the uterus pull the sides of the uterus upwards, increasing the size of the opening of the uterus, called the *cervix*. Dilation of the cervix is necessary for the fetus to move through the birth canal. The cervix dilates from a diameter of .3 centimeter at the beginning of labor to about 10 centimeters at the end. The entire dilation takes about 8 to 14 hours in a primiparous woman, but takes only 4 to 6 hours in a multiparous woman because her cervix is more pliable.

Early in the first stage, the mucous plug that ordinarily blocks the cervix is dislodged and some blood from the vagina is produced (often referred to as the "bloody show"). Also during this first stage, a small tear usually appears in the amniotic sac and the fluid trickles or gushes from the sac through the vagina. This tearing of the sac is often called "breaking water," and it is one of the sure signs that labor is beginning. Sometimes, however, the sac remains intact after labor has advanced, and the doctor will puncture the amnion to release the fluid (this does not hurt the mother or fetus). Ideally, to avoid infection, birth should occur within 12 hours of breaking the sac. Parents are often instructed to start timing the contractions when the water breaks. Once contractions are about 5 minutes apart, the woman needs to move to the birthing area.

The last part of dilation, called *transition*, is the most difficult part—the severity of the contractions is greatest and the pain is the worst. Women often have an urge to push the baby out, but at this point it is too early to push because the cervix is still dilating. Transition is the time when most women receive some kind of medication to cope with the pain. Until recently, sedatives and general anesthesia were widely given to women in labor to help them sleep, rest, and manage the pain. Unfortunately, these medications cross the placenta and affect the baby. If large dosages of sedatives or anesthetics are used, the baby may be restless and withdrawn for days after birth (Brazelton, Nugent, & Lester, 1987). Heavy use of drugs during birth is related to learning disorders among school children (Brackbill, McManus, & Woodward, 1985); however, most evidence indicates that low levels of medication used during birth do not significantly affect healthy babies (Rosenblith, 1992).

Instead of anesthesia and sedatives, which affect the mother's whole body, regional pain control is used for most births in the United States today. A common method for controlling the pain of labor is the **epidural block,** in which a local anesthetic is delivered to block pain in the region from the waist to the feet (Thorp & Breedlove, 1996). Recent innovations in the form of smaller needles, new medications, and a new delivery method, which includes a drip epidural on a wheeled cart, provide pregnant women with fewer side effects, more mobility, and more soothing effects while in labor (Shutte, 1997).

In deciding whether they want to receive medications during labor, mothers must weigh the benefits of pain relief against their concerns about drug effects. Although over 80 percent of women in childbirth in the United States receive some form of pain medication, many mothers feel ambivalent about taking medication:

> . . . the nurse checked my cervix and informed me that I was 4 cm and asked me if I wanted an anesthetic. I said that I didn't want any yet and might not ever want it. Then the next contraction hit, and I said the magic word—"epidural." Honestly, I was not crazy about the idea of taking drugs for this, but I wasn't sure how I would get through the next few hours without it.
>
> —ANONYMOUS MOTHER'S ON-LINE
> BIRTH STORY

Transition is the period of time that is most difficult for the fetus as well. In order to assess how the fetus is managing, its heart rate is monitored by placing small box-shaped sensors on the mother's abdomen. If the heart rate goes too high or too low, emergency procedures may be needed to quickly remove the baby (Cassidy, 1993).

epidural block a common method for controlling the pain of labor, in which a local anesthetic is delivered to block pain in the region from the waist to the feet

In this picture, the second stage of birth has just occurred; a healthy newborn was just delivered. Can you describe the other two stages and the events that take place in all three stages?

Stage 2: Expulsion of the Fetus

In the second stage of the birth process, the tempo of activity changes. During the first stage, the mother was relatively passive; she experienced uncomfortable contractions for many hours while waiting for the cervix to open completely. In the second stage, the mother begins the intense physical effort of pushing the baby through the birth passage (Sleep, 1993).

The second stage begins when the cervix is fully dilated and ends with the baby's birth. Contractions now help push the baby through the birth canal. The contractions decrease in intensity a bit and last about 60 seconds, with 1- to 3-minute rest periods in between. The second stage can be quite quick (as short as 5 minutes) for some mothers, particularly multiparous women, but it usually lasts about 1 to 2 hours for primiparous women.

As the fetus moves through the cervix and vagina, the mother may feel some urge to push and will be encouraged to do so by the doctor or midwife. To push, the mother applies pressure using her diaphragm. **Crowning** occurs when the top of the baby's head becomes visible. The baby's head is large and difficult to deliver. To help the fetus pass through the birth canal, the baby's head undergoes **molding,** in which the bones of the baby's skull, which are not yet fused, press together and may even overlap. Molding gives the newborn's head an elongated shape, which usually disappears soon after delivery. To create a larger opening for the head, the doctor may perform an **episiotomy**—that is, make a small incision in the skin below the vagina. This procedure prevents tearing of the vaginal tissues as the baby emerges.

Once the baby's head emerges, with the face toward the mother's back, the doctor or nurse suctions out the fluids in the air passages and checks to see if the umbilical cord is around the baby's neck—a common occurrence that poses no special danger if detected at this time (Jones, 1997). The baby then turns so that the shoulders can fit through the vaginal opening. After the shoulders are delivered, the rest of the baby slides out, and he or she takes a first breath and usually emits a rousing cry. The old tradition of slapping the back side of the newborn to stimulate breathing usually is not necessary. The umbilical cord is then clamped about 3 inches from the baby's abdomen and cut. Because there are no nerve endings in the umbilical cord, neither the mother nor the infant feels this happen.

Stage 3: Expulsion of the Placenta

Contractions continue after the baby is born, helping the placenta move through the birth canal. About 15 to 30 minutes after the baby has been delivered, the placenta is expelled. The doctor checks the placenta to ensure that it is intact, because any remaining pieces may lead to uterine infections.

BIRTHING METHODS

Birth is a significant event in every culture, but social customs and birthing methods vary widely across cultures and at different times in history. Women in Nepal, for example, are rubbed with oil to make them more comfortable, and they wear a waist cloth tied above their stomachs to "prevent the child from going up to the mother's mouth" (Escarce, 1989). In some cultures, women give birth alone, but the more common pattern is for a group of people to assist. Nepalese women are assisted by other women who have had children but not by men or children. In contrast, in Laos, women's primary helpers are the husband and mother-in-law (Muret-Wagstaff & Moore, 1989).

Practices in the United States have varied over time. In the nineteenth century, most women gave birth at home with midwives. By the 1950s, the trend had reversed, with most women giving birth at a hospital and almost all newborns being delivered by physi-

crowning when the top of the baby's head becomes visible

molding when the bones of the baby's skull, which are not yet fused, press together and even overlap to accommodate passage through the birth canal

episiotomy a small incision made in the skin below the vagina to prevent tearing of the vaginal tissues as the baby emerges cians. Modern practices have reduced the risks that women and infants face during birth. Many fewer women and children die in childbirth than did in the past (see Figure 4.2).

In the United States, a wide range of settings and options are available for childbirth. Many families choose to give birth in a hospital room that looks like a bedroom. Some families select a specially designed bathtub filled with warm water as the site for delivery. Before labor begins, families need to consider the delivery options available to them.

The range of options depends on the mother's risk factors—her age, weight, and general health. Certain women are at risk for complications during delivery:

+ Adolescent girls
+ Older women, particularly those over 35 or 40 who are having their first child
+ Women who have certain conditions or diseases
+ Women carrying twins, triplets, or other multiple fetuses

Women who are at risk have limited options because they must have the full range of support systems available in case of an emergency.

Lamaze Childbirth

During World War II, Russian doctors were faced with a problem; they did not have any pain medication they could administer to women who were giving birth. To help these women through labor and delivery, they applied the principles of classical conditioning (see Chapter 2). Through breathing and muscular relaxation, they conditioned the women to respond positively to their contractions (Wong & Perry, 1998). These techniques were adopted by Dr. Fernand Lamaze and introduced around the world.

Lamaze classes usually involve six weekly sessions in which the participants prepare for birth by learning

+ how the childbirth process works
+ how to breathe during labor and delivery to control pain and discomfort
+ how to focus on relaxing thoughts and feelings
+ how fathers can help in labor and delivery

The goal of the classes is to help women manage the pain of labor and delivery and to maximize the enjoyment of the parents of the birth of their children.

Leboyer: Birth Without Violence

A complementary birth approach was developed by Dr. Frederick Leboyer, a French physician. The focus of this technique is on the infant's, rather than the parents', birth experience. Leboyer developed techniques that minimize the infant's trauma of being born by mimicking the conditions of the mother's womb. The bright lights of the operating room are replaced with dim, indirect lighting; the temperature of the usually cool delivery room is raised so that it is closer to the mother's body temperature. After delivery

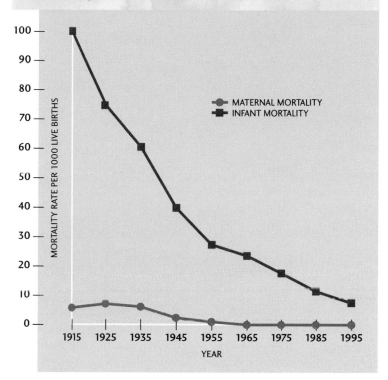

FIGURE 4.2
Historical Trends in US Infant and Maternal Mortality Rates

SOURCE: National Center for Health Statistics, 1996.
What factors have contributed to the decreasing rates of infant and maternal mortality in the United States?

and before the umbilical cord is cut, the naked infant is placed on the mother's bare belly, providing direct physical contact. The infant is then given a warm bath, in an effort to re-create the experience of the prenatal environment.

How well do the Lamaze and Leboyer methods meet their goals? The existing evidence is conflicting. Some research reports that, when parents are Lamaze trained, mothers experience less pain and parents have more positive feelings about the birth experience (Leventhal, Leventhal, Shacham, & Easterling, 1989; Mackey, 1990). Other research fails to find such differences (Copstick, Taylor, Hayes, & Morris, 1986; Hodnett & Osborn, 1989). Part of the reason for these different findings is that parents are individuals with different needs and no program will consistently meet the needs of all parents.

Some couples who try the Lamaze or the Leboyer childbirth technique do not succeed in having unmedicated births (Shute, 1997). When this happens, they often feel guilty for not being tough enough or angry because they were not told how much it would hurt.

To provide couples with more choices in birthing methods, birthing centers have been developed. These centers provide an out-of-hospital, family-centered setting where labor and delivery are treated as normal life events to be shared with whomever the mother likes. Many centers encourage mothers to walk, eat, drink, and get into positions that are comfortable for them during labor and delivery. Certified nurse-midwives provide most of the care, but many centers have close connections with hospitals in case of an emergency. Only women with low-risk pregnancies are accepted at birthing centers. Birthing centers usually cost less than a hospital birth: nationally, the cost of a birth at a birthing center averages $3300, whereas the average cost of a vaginal birth in a hospital is $6430 (Krajeski, 1996).

Despite the conflicting evidence, it appears that alternative birthing techniques, if properly supervised, can be safe and enjoyable (Mackey, 1990). The best advice for parents-to-be is to choose a birth method carefully—obtaining all available information on the method, just as you would when choosing a physician or hospital.

BIRTH COMPLICATIONS AND RELATED PROCEDURES

> Amanda Sue was in trouble. I had yet to meet her: my wife was in her tenth hour of labor, and the fetal monitor attached to her stomach indicated that our baby's heart rate was dipping alarmingly low. . . . The first few hours in the labor room were so easy, they could have been a Lamaze teacher's dream. . . . But in the last hours leading up to this moment, the pain had become agonizing. . . . I did not have to talk to the doctors to know they were concerned. . . . Just before two-thirty Dr. Charles said he wanted to try to deliver the baby. . . . In an instant Amanda Sue was there . . . and in good health. . . . Dr. Charles said . . . "I almost decided to do a caesarean 3 times. Ten years ago I would have had to, but these new fetal monitors are so sophisticated—the monitor told me that the baby was bouncing back okay every time, so I knew it would be all right to go ahead."
> —BOB GREENE (1984, PP. 3–6)

The experience of childbirth is usually positive for family members, as they celebrate the entry of a healthy newborn into the world. But, as Bob Greene's diary depicts, childbirth can be stressful and frightening for some families. Many complications can occur during delivery.

Caesarean Sections

Although most births involve the fetus descending through the mother's vagina, many do not. In a nonvaginal birth, known as a **caesarean section,** the fetus is delivered through an incision in the mother's abdomen. In general, a caesarean section is used

caesarean section procedure by which the fetus is delivered through an incision in the mother's abdomen

If there were potential complications with the birth of your child, would you lean toward choosing a c-section to be safe or waiting and trying alternative approaches?

TABLE 4.1

Conditions Under Which Caesarean Delivery May Be Recommended

1. Breech presentation
2. Unfavorable shape of pelvis
3. Large fetus (over 8 pounds)
4. Premature rupture of amniotic sac
5. Active genital herpes
6. Fetal distress (significant increase or decrease in fetal heart rate)
7. Prolonged pregnancy (more than 42 weeks)

SOURCE: Cunningham et al., 1993; Korte and Scaer, 1992.

whenever it is believed that further delay in delivery would seriously compromise the health of the fetus. Table 4.1 lists some of the conditions under which caesarean sections are recommended.

Although the conditions for performing caesarean sections have not changed much in recent years, the number of caesarean sections performed in the United States has increased dramatically since the 1970s. Figure 4.3 shows that caesarean deliveries accounted for about 5 percent of all deliveries in 1970 but about 21 percent in 1995 (National Center for Health Statistics, 1997). About 1 million caesarean deliveries are performed each year in the United States, making it the most common type of major surgery performed. European rates are about one-fourth to one-half the US rates (Korte & Scaer, 1992).

Many factors account for the rise in caesarean births. By the 1960s, increasing emphasis was being placed on the health of the fetus. At the same time, advances in medical care had made caesarean deliveries safer to perform. As a safe alternative to normal deliveries, caesarean sections became a practical way to improve the outcome of difficult pregnancies. Another contributing factor was the rising number of repeat caesareans. More than 98 percent of women in the United States who have had a caesarean delivery undergo caesareans for subsequent pregnancies (National Center for Health Statistics, 1996). Furthermore, doctors' concerns about being sued for malpractice, should something go wrong with the delivery, increased the likelihood that a caesarean section would be used at the slightest indication of fetal distress (Korte & Scaer, 1992).

Today, most parents and doctors are urged to exercise caution in the use of caesarean sections. A caesarean section represents major surgery. Compared to a normal delivery, it is costly, involves a longer recovery period, has a higher risk of infection, and may be more likely to make infants or their mothers ill (Haynes de Reght, Minkoff, Feldman, & Schwartz, 1986). Alternative methods are available for dealing with fetal distress and prolonged labor, and these can be tried before moving

FIGURE 4.3

Caesarean Deliveries as a Percentage of All Births

SOURCE: Adapted from National Center for Health Statistics, 1996; 1997; Taffel, Placek, and Moien, 1989.

What factors have contributed to the increased rates of caesarean deliveries since 1970? What factors should a mother and her doctor consider before deciding on a caesarean delivery?

In the past, family members were less involved in childbirth than they are today. What factors do families have to consider when deciding about the setting for childbirth?

forward with surgery. However, when the mother or her unborn child is at risk, complications can be avoided with early and aggressive surgical intervention.

Induced Labor

During some pregnancies, situations arise in which the prolongation of the pregnancy is not in the best interests of either the mother or the fetus. In these situations, labor may be induced. Pitocin or other medications may be given to start labor and delivery. These drugs have been found to be effective (Prysak & Castronova, 1998), and long-term studies show no higher chances that infants delivered after labor is induced will develop physical problems (Bramadat, 1994). However, because labor may signal the maturity of the fetus, its absence may indicate that the fetus is not quite ready for life outside the mother's womb. Although there clearly are times when allowing a pregnancy to continue is dangerous for mother or child, decisions to induce labor must be made carefully.

Breech and Transverse Presentations

In 95 percent of all births, the fetus is delivered in the head-down position. In 3 to 4 percent of births, however, the fetus is positioned with buttocks or feet leading the way (National Center for Health Statistics, 1997). This position is referred to as the **breech presentation.** Breech deliveries usually involve longer periods of labor but often occur with no difficulties. Sometimes, however, breech presentation requires caesarean delivery. In 1 out of 200 births, the fetus is positioned with shoulders and arms leading the way—known as the **transverse presentation.** In these cases, a caesarean delivery almost always is necessary (Cunningham et al., 1993).

(H OW IS CHILDBIRTH EXPERIENCED?

Mothers, fathers, and newborns experience childbirth differently. As with all the major life events, the birth of a child has a lasting impact on the family, and mothers, fathers, and newborns each face a different set of challenges as they adjust to the changes brought about by birth.

THE MOTHER'S PERSPECTIVE

As a first-time mother I still find myself, more than half a year later, remembering my birth experience. I think I am finally coming to an understanding of the many feelings I had then and accepting the miserable ones as well as the elation.

—KORTE AND SCAER (1992, P. 182)

In the words of this new mother, the experience of birth is intense and mixed. Although having a baby is a joyous time for most women, many new mothers feel anxious, fragile, and overwhelmed after giving birth. The "baby blues" are not an inevitable part of having a baby, but they are very common, affecting about 70 to 80 percent of women giving birth. New mothers often cry unexpectedly and feel sad or angry without knowing why. A number of factors contribute to these blues, including the following (Eisenberg, Murkoff, & Hathaway, 1991):

✦ **Biological changes.**   The postpartum period is a time of great changes in a woman's body. Levels of female hormones drop sharply after childbirth.
✦ **Fatigue.**   The strains of labor, delivery, and care of the newborn, combined with a loss of sleep, contribute to mothers' feeling overwhelmed and exhausted.

breech presentation fetal position in which the buttocks or feet lead the way

transverse presentation fetal position in which the shoulders and arms lead the way

✦ **Loss of attention.** The baby takes center stage, and mothers no longer receive the attention they had while pregnant.

✦ **Increased demands at home.** New mothers may feel overwhelmed by the responsibilities at home, particularly if there are other children in the family.

✦ **Sense of anticlimax.** After the long pregnancy and all the excitement generated, the "big event" may not live up to the mother's expectations.

✦ **Feelings of inadequacy.** Concern about her ability to care for the newborn may raise the mother's levels of confusion, guilt, and anxiety. In addition, changes in her physical appearance and body may raise the mother's doubts about her attractiveness.

For most mothers, these feelings usually begin a day or so after birth but rarely last more than a week or two and go away without the need for treatment.

For about 10 percent of new mothers, unfortunately, these feelings do not subside quickly or easily. In contrast to the baby blues, **postpartum depression** is marked by intense feelings of sadness, anxiety, or despair that disrupt the new mother's ability to function and interact with her child (Carro, Grant, Gotlib, & Compas, 1993). Postpartum depression can affect the newborn child. In one study, newborns of mothers who experienced postpartum depression showed poor motor activity and were more irritable (Abrams, Field, Scafidi, & Prodromidis, 1995).

It is not known why some women become depressed after childbirth and others do not. One important factor is biology. Because some women are more sensitive to the biological changes that accompany birth, they may be more prone to postpartum depression. Stressful life events (unwanted pregnancy, single parenthood, lack of social support) and delivery complications also increase the chances of postpartum depression (Cohn, Campbell, Matias, & Hopkins, 1990). If depression and anxiety do not go away and begin to interfere with the mother's functioning, treatment may be needed.

Research findings tell us that, all in all, it is common for mothers to experience a brief period of fear and anxiety after childbirth. Such feelings are quite common and do not mean that the new mother is a failure or that she is mentally ill. For the most part, these feelings are the result of the changes, both physical and psychological, brought about by the birth of a child.

THE FATHER'S PERSPECTIVE

Probably one of the most memorable moments with Jeremy . . . was being able to be there for his birth and to hold him for the first time right after he was born. To cradle a newborn life in your arms that you know is yours and that you created—you really can't describe it. You don't want to put him down. You don't want to let him go. . . . A lot of other experiences have come since then, but that has got to be one of the most enjoyable.

—ANONYMOUS FATHER'S ON-LINE STORY OF
THE BIRTH OF HIS SON

As this birth story reveals, for most contemporary fathers, experiencing the birth of their children does not mean pacing the hospital hallway with a pocketful of cigars to hand out as soon as word comes down. Today, many fathers take an active role in the birth process. In childbirth classes, fathers frequently serve as coaches for their partners, providing both physical and emotional support.

How a father experiences the birth of his child is strongly influenced by his emotional reactions and the degree to which he believes he is able to support his partner. Many men report that assisting in the birth of their child was a wonderful experience but at the same time made them feel helpless, particularly in dealing with their partner's labor. The more involved fathers become in the birth process, the more often they report feelings of closeness to their spouse and to their newborn child (Doherty, 1997).

postpartum depression intense feelings of sadness, anxiety, or despair experienced by a mother after the birth of a child

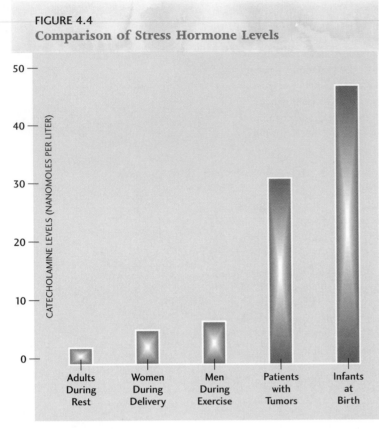

FIGURE 4.4
Comparison of Stress Hormone Levels

CATECHOLAMINE LEVELS (NANOMOLES PER LITER)

Adults During Rest | Women During Delivery | Men During Exercise | Patients with Tumors | Infants at Birth

SOURCE: *Adapted from Lagercrantz and Slotkin, 1986.*
Why are stress hormone levels so high at birth? Notice that women giving birth have rel-atively low stress hormone levels.

The involvement of the father in the birth also in-fluences how mothers feel about the birth experience. Fathers who are supportive during birth and labor have partners who are less anxious and distressed and are not as likely to need medication (Biller, 1993). Although the determinants of a father's level of involvement in the birth process and with his very young child are com-plex, fathers with greater psychological, social, and eco-nomic resources tend to be more involved and more satisfied with their involvement (Daly, 1993; Wood-worth, Belsky, & Crnic, 1996).

THE NEWBORN'S PERSPECTIVE

How does the newborn experience birth? Most of us would imagine that birth is a grueling and frighten-ing experience. The baby is squeezed through the birth canal for several hours, during which time his or her head is compressed and put under considerable pres-sure. Then, the baby is delivered from the warm, moist, and protected environment of the womb into a bright, loud, and chaotic world. As Figure 4.4 shows, newborns produce "stress" hormones, called *catecholamines*, at levels 20 times higher than those found in adults—levels higher even than those found in adults who have seri-ous medical conditions (Lagercrantz & Slotkin, 1986).

Despite these conditions, the stress of a normal de-livery usually is not harmful (Gunnar, 1989). Evidence suggests that the fetus is well equipped to withstand this stress and that the chemicals produced by the stress may prepare the newborn to survive outside the mother's womb. For example, the surge in stress hormones helps clear the newborn's lungs and promotes normal breathing. Additionally, the surge in hormones increases the newborn's metabolism and energy supply (Slotkin, Kudlacz, Hou, & Seidler, 1990). One result of the increased metabolism and energy supply is that the newborn is born alert and aroused. By causing the newborn to be alert, the hormonal surge may promote the development of emotional ties between parents and their new-born during the first hours of life (Slotkin & Seidler, 1989).

PARENT-NEWBORN BONDING

This was bizarre. We were standing there laughing at the doctor's story and two feet away Amanda Sue lay moving against my wife's chest. Susan looked up at me and let out a long breath. And then, for the first time, I reached down and touched my daughter.

—BOB GREENE (1984, P. 6)

As this diary entry indicates, touching or holding their newborn for the first time is a moving event for most parents. But human parents are not the only ones who do this. These tender scenes between parents and newborns occur in many species—chimps and gorillas are just two examples (Bard, 1994). Parents' early contact behaviors may be part of intuitive parenting, some aspects of which may be determined by genetically driven responsiveness to infants.

When mothers and newborns spend time together right after birth, do they create a special bond that then helps the baby to develop? Conversely, are children who are deprived of early bonding, because they were adopted or sick, at risk for later developmental problems or even child abuse? These questions arose in the 1960s, after two decades during which mothers generally gave birth in cold and sterile hospital rooms, usually after taking pain medications that decreased their awareness of the birth process. Once the baby was born, she or he was whisked away to a nursery. Every 4 hours or so during the four or five days that mother and child stayed in the hospital, a nurse would bring in the baby for mom to feed. Thus, early contact between mother and child was limited.

Because of their concerns about these childbirth procedures, Klaus and colleagues (Klaus, Kennell, Plumb, & Zeuhlke, 1970) compared mothers and newborns who went through this typical procedure to a group of mothers and newborns who had extended contact immediately after birth. After one month, the mothers with extended contact were more likely to be responsive to their newborns. Based on these results, Klaus and Kennell (and others) proposed that there is a sensitive period immediately following birth during which mothers and infants bond through close physical contact. When bonding is interrupted, parenting failures are more likely and the child is at greater risk for abuse, neglect, and poor parenting.

As a result of these findings, there have been many positive changes in birthing practices, such as allowing babies to room in with their mothers. The scientific basis for bonding has not held up over time, however. Studies conducted since the 1970s have not supported the original findings (Goldberg, 1983; Lamb, 1982a; 1982b; Myers, 1984). For mothers who may be at risk for developing poor relationships with their newborns, however, having extra time with their infants may promote healthy interactions (Perusse, Neale, Heath, & Eaves, 1994).

No one denies the importance of parents' and infants' spending time together. Establishing a healthy parent-child relationship has many phases; spending the first hours together may be one of these phases. If parents miss this first step, they still have many other opportunities to develop healthy parent-child relationships. There is no evidence of a critical period for human bonding—success or failure in the parent-child relationship does not hinge on a few brief moments in time (Goldberg, 1983). The emotional tie between infants and their significant caregivers develops over a long period of time and is not dependent only on the early interactions.

Notice how comfortable the father in this photo appears to be in holding his newborn and how alert the baby is. How do fathers experience birth? How has fathers' experience of birth changed in the past fifty years?

CULTURAL DIFFERENCES IN THE EXPERIENCE OF CHILDBIRTH

Societies have unique responses to the event of birth, based on their beliefs, values, and customs. In the United States, birth generally is considered a very private affair, with only a few people involved. Until recently, this meant that mothers went through almost the entire birth process in the presence of only medical personnel. Only in the last twenty years or so have fathers and other close family members or friends attended births. At the other extreme, the Jahara of South America believe that the birth of a child is an event of interest to the entire community. They celebrate birth as a public event—mothers give birth under a shelter and in full view of the entire village, even small children (Fogel, 1997).

In many cultures, specific ceremonies surrounding birth reflect the traditions and values of the culture. Morris Opler (1981) describes one interesting example of such a ceremony for children born into the Jicarilla Apache Indian tribe. This event usually is conducted within four days of birth, to bond the child both to the family and to protective supernatural powers. Called "water has been put on the top of his head," the ceremony marks the first time water touches the baby. Only water mixed from sacred "male" and "female" rivers is used. The newborn is bathed in the sacred water and songs are sung. The parents' and siblings' faces are painted with red ochre. This face painting is like a prayer and is considered a blessing in Jicarilla culture. When all have been painted, the singer presents the newborn to the father, saying "This is your baby." This announcement publicly establishes the sacred obligation of the father to his newborn child and his mate. The father then gives the baby to the mother.

This birth rite illustrates how one's culture attributes meaning to birth. Because birth is such a powerful and profound event in most people's lives, many customs have developed that link it to the fabric of culture. These customs signify that birth is a social as well as a physical event and highlight the significance a culture places on bringing forth new life. Perhaps the remarkable thing is the ability of parents and newborns to adapt despite the diversity of rituals their cultures prescribe.

WHAT ARE THE CHARACTERISTICS OF A NEWBORN?

The adjustments a newborn must make to a new world are complex and demanding. After nine months as a protected and dependent being inside the mother's womb, the newborn must adapt to life outside the womb. The term **neonate** refers to infants who are making this adjustment—usually within their first one to two months. To survive, newborns must accomplish four major tasks:

+ **Breathing on their own.**   The newborn's first challenge is to obtain the oxygen necessary for survival. To do this, the infant must switch from relying on oxygen provided by the blood in the umbilical cord to breathing on his or her own. A newborn's mouth and nose are filled with fluid before birth, and this shift requires that the fluid be drained and the airways opened for breathing. Childbirth itself forces some of the fluid out during the tight squeeze through the birth canal. The doctor or nurse clears out the remaining fluid to help the baby breathe.
+ **Changing blood circulation.**   The infant's circulation pattern must also change to allow for breathing. Before birth, the placenta supports the infant. When the link to the mother is severed, circulation changes so that blood flows, for the first time, to the lungs. This change shifts the pressure of blood in the heart, which then changes the direction of blood flow. This is why newborns have irregular heartbeats and unstable blood pressure.
+ **Controlling body temperature.**   Unlike the uterine environment, which has a steady, warm temperature, the environment outside the womb is susceptible to extreme changes in temperature. To survive, infants must control their body temperature and adjust to shifting temperatures.
+ **Ingesting food.**   During prenatal development, the fetus obtains nutrients through the placenta. After birth, the newborn must obtain nourishment a different way—through his or her mouth. Normally, infants quickly adapt to oral feeding because they are capable of sucking when they are born and their digestive systems are developed enough to process the nutrients they need.

PHYSICAL APPEARANCE

Many parents are surprised by the appearance of their newborn child—he or she does not look like the babies they've seen on television! Newborns on average range in length from 19 to 21 inches, and their length at birth depends more on the size of the mother's uterus than on genetic inheritance. This is why a small mother can carry the child of a very large father. The average weight for newborns is 7 to 7½ pounds. After a vaginal delivery, the baby's head often is misshapen, the face swollen, and the nose flattened from the pressures of moving through the birth canal. The newborn also may be covered in a white, waxy covering, called the **vernix caseosa**, which provides protection from bacteria. Many infants have uneven coloring, often having bluish or grayish fin-

neonate an infant who is in the first one to two months of life

vernix caseosa a white, waxy covering that provides the infant with protection from bacteria

TABLE 4.2

Apgar Scoring System

SIGN	0 RATING	1 RATING	2 RATING
Heart rate	Absent	Slow (below 100)	Over 100
Respiration	Absent	Slow and irregular	Good, crying
Skin color	Blue or pale	Extremities blue, trunk pink	Completely pink
Muscle tone	Limp	Some flexion of extremities	Active movements
Reflex response	No response	Grimace	Vigorous crying

SOURCE: Adapted from Apgar, 1953.

gers, nose, and feet as a result of poor blood circulation. Because of the presence of maternal hormones, the newborn may have enlarged genitalia.

She had microscopic fingernails, a scrawny, funny ducktail hairdo, and tiny replicas of a wizened old man's hands. . . . She had weighed six pounds, fifteen ounces at birth, and had been twenty-one-and-one-half inches long. . . . I leaned over and started whispering to her and stroking her head. She looked up at me and I kept whispering. . . . Amazing. Forty-eight hours ago she hadn't even been born.

—Bob Greene (1984, pp. 11–12)

Like most new parents, Bob Greene began his assessment of his newborn with a quick examination of her size, fingers, and head. Medical personnel also do a quick examination of the general well-being of the infant, to determine whether any type of emergency intervention is needed. The most commonly used procedure was developed by an anesthesiologist, Dr. Virginia Apgar. The **Apgar Scale** is a simple and effective method of diagnosing potential problems in full-term and preterm newborns (Hegyi et al., 1998). At 1 minute and 5 minutes after birth, the baby is examined for five vital signs: respiration, reflex responsiveness, muscle tone, color, and heart rate (see Table 4.2).

To test her new system, Dr. Apgar attended hundreds of births and meticulously recorded her findings. Newborns who scored from 8 to 10 usually emerged from the birth canal with a lusty cry and adjusted on their own. Babies who scored from 4 to 7 needed help or close observation until their scores improved. Those who scored from 0 to 3 were limp and unresponsive. To survive, they needed CPR. For example, a child who has been oxygen deprived during labor and delivery is likely to have blue- or gray-colored skin, may have arms and legs that droop because of lack of muscle tone, and may not be breathing immediately after birth. Fortunately, only 1.4 percent of newborns have Apgar scores of less than 7 (National Center for Health Statistics, 1997).

NEONATAL REFLEXES

Infants are born with simple, coordinated, unlearned responses, called **reflexes,** that provide limited ways for them to interact with their environment. Some reflexes aid survival because they orient the infant toward food or protection. Protective reflexes include coughing, sneezing, blinking, and muscle withdrawal (see Table 4.3).

Apgar Scale a method of diagnosing potential problems in full-term and preterm newborns, in which five vital signs are examined: respiration, reflex responsiveness, muscle tone, color, and heart rate

reflexes simple, coordinated, unlearned responses

TABLE 4.3
Some Neonatal Reflexes

NAME	STIMULUS	RESPONSE	DEVELOPMENTAL COURSE
Blink	Puff air at baby	Closes eyes	Permanent
Sucking	Place object in infant's mouth	Sucks rhythmically	Changes to voluntary sucking by 2 months
Stepping	Hold baby under the arms in upright position, with feet on the ground; move baby forward	Steps by alternating legs	Disappears at 2 to 3 months
Babkin	Gently squeeze baby's palms with baby lying on back	Closes eyes, opens mouth, and turns head to middle of body	Disappears around 3 to 4 months
Rooting	Tickle baby's cheek with finger or nipple	Turns head toward finger or nipple and tries to suck	Disappears around 3 to 4 months
Tonic neck	Lay baby down flat	Turns head to one side, with arm and leg extended on that side and other arm and leg bent inward	Disappears around 3 to 4 months
Palmar grasp	Press finger against baby's palm	Grasps the finger	Declines after 3 to 4 months

(Continued)

TABLE 4.3 *(Continued)*

NAME	STIMULUS	RESPONSE	DEVELOPMENTAL COURSE
Moro	Make sudden loud noise or let infant's head drop slightly	Arches back, throws arms out, and then draws them in, legs extended	Disappears around 5 to 6 months
Swimming	Place infant face down in water	Moves arms and legs rhythmically, exhales through mouth	Disappears around 6 months
Babinski	Gently stroke sole of baby's foot from heel to toe	Spreads out and curls toes, turns foot inward	Changes at 12 months

SOURCE: *Adapted from Prechl and Beintema, 1965.*

Feeding reflexes include the rooting and sucking reflexes. The *rooting reflex* is seen when you rub your finger against a newborn's cheek: the baby turns toward the stimulation in search of a nipple to suck. The *sucking reflex* is seen whenever something touches an infant's lips: the baby tries to suck on it. Sucking is a surprisingly complex behavior that involves coordinating breathing and swallowing as well as coordinating the movements of the tongue, lips, and jaw to create a vacuum.

Other reflexes include the *Moro reflex*, a startle reaction to loud noises in which infants fling their arms out and then draw them in, arch their backs, and extend their legs. The *palmar grasping reflex* is elicited by touching the inside of the baby's hand, which causes the fingers to curl around the object. Parents of newborns are often surprised at how powerful this grasp reflex is—newborns can be lifted by using their grasping reflex.

Because reflexes help a newborn survive, an assessment of reflexes provides important insights into problems that some babies may face. An infant's reflexes can be used as indicators of the development of the nervous system. Reflexes that are too strong or too weak or that do not show expected developmental changes may indicate that the child has a problem. Babies who have been exposed to medications during delivery may fail to show some of the reflexes, such as sucking, but catch up soon after birth. As the infant's brain develops, the infant begins to take over voluntary control of actions and some reflexes disappear, usually between 4 and 8 months. The normal development of reflexes has been charted, and deviations from this pattern may signal that an infant has neurological problems. For instance, infants who have brain damage caused by cerebral palsy may continue to show a reflex after it should have disappeared (Allen, 1996).

Neonatal States

If you have ever spent time with a young infant, you have probably observed rapid changes in her or his **state of arousal**—the degree to which the infant is alert, attentive, and awake. Infants rapidly drift in and out of wakefulness, excitement, drowsiness, and sleep. As shown in Table 4.4, these different states can be described in terms of six major categories, from high to low arousal: fussing/crying, nonalert waking,

The newborn's ability to nurse involves many complex skills. What reflexes of a newborn are involved in nursing? Can you identify some of the protective reflexes?

state of arousal the degree to which an infant is alert, attentive, and awake

TABLE 4.4
Infant States of Arousal

STATE	DESCRIPTION	TIME IN STATE (WHILE ALONE)
Fussing/crying	Low-intensity fussing or higher intensity crying	3%
Nonalert awake	Eyes open but unfocused, body movements, isolated fussing	3%
Alert awake	Attentive, looking around, eyes open	7%
Drowsiness/ sleep-wake transition	Little motor activity, eyes closing and opening	7%
Active sleep	Eyes closed, uneven breathing, rapid eye movements, smiling, grimacing	50%
Quiet sleep	Eyes closed, regular and slow respiration, limited activity	30%

SOURCE: Adapted from Thoman and Whitney, 1990.

alert waking, drowsiness/sleep-wake transition, active sleep, and quiet sleep (Thoman & Whitney, 1990).

Understanding states of arousal is important for several reasons:

✦ States of arousal influence infants' interactions with others and with their environment. In a quiet alert state, infants learn better and seem particularly tuned in to the environment.

✦ Infant states of arousal provide information about individual differences. Some infants sleep more than others whereas some are more alert, and these differences are seen even during prenatal development (Groome et al., 1997). These differences in states of arousal also provide insight into the behavioral traits of young infants. As you will learn, some infants are passive and react little to their environment, whereas others are more responsive and easily irritated.

✦ The regularity of states of arousal provides a window on the maturity of the nervous system. Neonates who are very irregular in their states of arousal are at risk for later developmental problems (Thoman, 1990).

Infant states vary depending on the qualities of the caregiving they receive. In a classic study, Sander and colleagues (1972) found that newborns cried more and showed altered arousal patterns when they were introduced to new caregivers who responded differently than their previous caregivers had. These findings suggest that infant states of arousal develop through an interaction between their biological tendencies, such as the maturation level of the nervous system, and their environment, such as the quality of caregiving they receive.

NEONATAL SLEEP PATTERNS

You get so tired. In the middle of the night something interrupts your sleep; it is that cry again, and you don't know how you're going to make it out of bed to hold the baby.

—BOB GREENE (1984, P. 21)

Should Babies Sleep with Their Parents?

In the United States, most newborns sleep alone. In many countries, infants and mothers sleep together during the first few years of the infant's life. For instance, in a study of twelve communities, researchers found that only in the United States did young infants regularly sleep away from their parents (Whiting & Edwards, 1988). Co-sleeping occurs in both technologically advanced and less advanced societies. For instance, Japanese children sleep next to their mothers in early childhood and often continue to sleep with a member of the family until they are 15 years old. Co-sleeping is not due to limited space but instead is due to cultural beliefs about the importance of having a sleeping partner.

One study compared the sleeping patterns and beliefs of US parents and Highland Mayan parents (Morelli, Rogoff, Oppenheim, & Goldsmith, 1992). The typical pattern among Caucasian American families was separate sleeping. After three months of sleeping near the parents in a crib or bassinet, about 60 percent of Caucasian American infants moved to their own room, and after six months, 80 percent of the infants had their own room for sleeping. In contrast, 100 percent of the Mayan infants slept in bed with their mother and more than half with their father as well. Infants tended to sleep with their mother until the next child was born.

Mayan parents differ from US parents in their beliefs about sleeping arrangements. Mayan families believe that co-sleeping is the only reasonable way for babies and parents to sleep. When they heard about the US style of separate sleeping, some Mayan parents were shocked and strongly disapproved, suggesting that this may be tantamount to child neglect. Caucasian American parents reported that they believe separate sleeping arrangements are necessary both because they need to go back to work and because the practice fosters independence in their children. Furthermore, many US parents worried that sleeping together would be a difficult habit to break and might be unsafe (the baby might be crushed).

The cultural differences between Mayan and Caucasian American families may relate to problems in sleeping. In the United States, parents commonly report that infants have difficulty sleeping, and a number of programs have been designed to train infants to soothe themselves and regulate their own sleep (Ferber, 1986). In Mayan families, infants go to sleep easily and parents do not complain of sleep difficulties.

Perhaps the bedtime difficulties experienced by US parents relate to the infants being separated from the social interactions of family life in the evening to sleep alone in their own room. Additionally, such infants feed less often, as mothers nurse their infant three times more frequently when the two sleep together than when the infant sleeps in an adjacent room (McKenna et al., 1994). The co-sleeping that occurs in so many other cultures allows infants to be involved in social interactions, since they sleep when others do, and it may alleviate infants' fears and ease their transition to sleep (Morelli et al., 1992).

Thinking It Through:

1. What advantages and disadvantages can you think of for sleeping with an infant? For sleeping apart from an infant?

2. What explanations can you hypothesize for cultural differences in family sleeping arrangements?

3. What rituals for going to bed were part of your sleeping routine when you were young? Which of these rituals could be due to cultural beliefs and practices?

A newborn child averages about 16 hours of sleep a day. Nonetheless, as Bob Greene's diary entry reveals, parents of newborns often are bleary-eyed and tired because they do not get enough sleep. This is because newborns do not sleep 16 hours all at one time. In Figure 4.5, you can see that the typical adult sleeps for one long period of about 7 to 8 hours and is awake for the rest of the day. In contrast, the typical newborn sleeps six or seven times a day for about 2 to 3 hours at a time (Thoman & Whitney, 1989). Even this picture is somewhat misleading, because newborns may fall asleep for a few

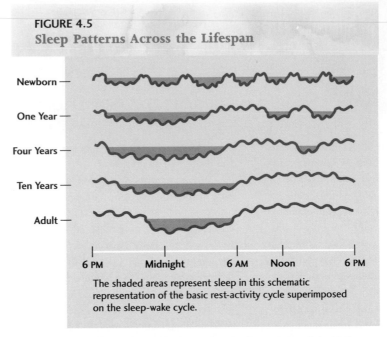

FIGURE 4.5
Sleep Patterns Across the Lifespan

Newborn —

One Year —

Four Years —

Ten Years —

Adult —

6 PM   Midnight   6 AM   Noon   6 PM

The shaded areas represent sleep in this schematic representation of the basic rest-activity cycle superimposed on the sleep-wake cycle.

SOURCE: Bornstein and Lamb, 1992. Reproduced with permission of the McGraw-Hill Companies.
Notice how the sleep patterns of newborns are different from those of older children and adults. What factors contribute to these differences?

minutes or a few hours at almost any time of the day. By the end of two weeks, neonates begin to sleep somewhat longer during the night than during the day.

Young infants awaken because they are hungry or uncomfortable and often fall asleep soon after being fed or changed. As they grow older, the time they spend sleeping decreases. The timing of sleep also changes as they get older. Older infants sleep more hours at night and fewer hours during the day, matching adult patterns more closely.

The length of time an infant sleeps at night may be an indicator of brain development (Zaiwalla & Stein, 1993). Indices of brain activity show that changes in sleeping and waking occur in the first months of life (Hoppenbrouwers et al., 1988). For instance, the brain activity patterns associated with drowsiness are not found in very young infants but are found in infants 5 to 8 months of age (Berg & Berg, 1987). The changes in sleep-wake cycles may signal important changes in the brain's ability to process information, which increase the infant's responsiveness to his or her environment (Sigman, Beckwith, Cohen, & Parmelee, 1989).

NEONATAL IMITATION

One of the most surprising capabilities of newborns is that they can imitate facial expressions. Stick out your tongue at a newborn and the child probably will stick her or his tongue out too. Although this sounds easy, it is quite an amazing and difficult accomplishment. Think about trying to imitate a scary facial expression. You can try to match the face you have seen, but you cannot know for sure that you have copied that scary face. Unless you have a mirror, there is no way to monitor the imitation process visually.

Despite this difficulty, neonates are capable of imitating facial expressions such as pursed lips. Even 1- and 3-day-old infants can imitate simple expressions and head movements, and will continue to imitate them for a short time after the display stops (Meltzoff

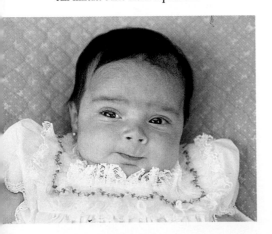

In this photo, the young infant is imitating an adult (off camera) who is pursing his lips. The infant tries several times before she is successful. What kind of information about newborns' capabilities is gained from the fact that newborns can imitate basic facial expressions?

TABLE 4.5
Brazelton's Neonatal Behavioral Assessment Scale (Revised)

REFLEX ACTIONS ASSESSED	BEHAVIORS ASSESSED
palmar grasp	orientation to a visual stimulus
Babinski	orientation to an auditory stimulus
standing	alertness
automatic walking	pull-to-sit
tonic neck reflex	cuddliness
Moro	irritability
rooting	activity
sucking	smiling
	self-quieting activity

Babinski

Tonic Neck Reflex

Irritability

Smiling

SOURCE: Adapted from Brazelton, Nugent, and Lester, 1987.

& Moore, 1994). Cross-cultural studies provide additional evidence: in rural Nepal, 1-hour-old newborns imitate lip-widening and lip-pursing (Reissland, 1988). It appears that neonates have an internal code that they use to match what they see with what they do. This code is not programmed at birth; instead, neonates use others' behaviors as a guide to help them construct their responses (Meltzoff & Moore, 1994).

By 6 weeks of age, infants not only imitate those in their immediate presence but also show evidence of **deferred imitation**—imitation of behaviors that occurred in the past (Meltzoff & Moore, 1994). Infants' ability to imitate someone after a delay indicates that they remember something about that individual, which sets the stage for additional interactions.

BEHAVIORAL ASSESSMENT OF NEONATES

A neonate's behavior provides insight into his or her development and health. For this reason, many instruments have been developed to assess their behavior. The most widely used instrument is the **Neonatal Behavioral Assessment Scale,** developed by a pediatrician, Dr. T. Berry Brazelton, to measure a newborn's responses to the environment, especially reactions to others. The assessment is conducted with simple equipment by a trained examiner, who reviews the newborn's reflexes, motor capabilities, abilities to control attention and behavior, and responses to interaction with others (see Table 4.5). For instance, to assess cuddliness, the examiner holds the baby close and assesses to what extent the baby relaxes or curls up to cuddle. To assess self-quieting abilities, the

deferred imitation imitation of behaviors that occurred in the past

Neonatal Behavioral Assessment Scale a measure commonly used to assess a newborn's responses to the environment examiner observes the actions a baby takes after he or she has become fussy: Does the baby suck his or her thumb to settle down?

The scale is used to identify newborns who have difficulties adjusting to their new environment outside the womb. After difficulties are identified, appropriate interventions can be developed. For instance, a neonate with impaired brain development may be hypersensitive to stimulation and react in a disorganized manner. Better control over the kinds of stimulation the infant receives may help the baby develop the ability to organize responses to the environment. The scale provides useful information even for infants who are not at risk, because it helps identify each baby's capacity for receiving and using stimulation from the environment (Brazelton, Nugent, & Lester, 1987).

HOW DOES EARLY BRAIN DEVELOPMENT PROCEED?

Danelle leans over her 2-month-old infant, catches Tracy's attention, and moves a stuffed bear in front of Tracy's face. The baby watches intently, moving her eyes from side to side as the bear travels back and forth. Inside Tracy's brain, thousands of brain cells send information from her eyes to the visual centers in the brain and from her brain to the muscles that control her eyes. Danelle thinks she is only playing with her daughter, but she is giving Tracy the kind of experience that stimulates brain development.

About half of all human genes are involved in building the brain by providing the codes for its basic structures and functions (Robinson, 1996). Once brain development has been set in motion, the genetic code goes only so far before the child's environment makes a tremendous impact on the brain's development. An infant who has an enriched environment, in which she or he is exposed to many people, to music, to language, and to play opportunities, develops under optimum conditions.

PROGRESSIVE EVENTS IN BRAIN DEVELOPMENT

By the time a baby is born, the parts of the brain that control many important survival-related functions, such as breathing, swallowing, sucking, and maintaining a heartbeat, are functioning. The sensory areas of the brain also develop early, allowing newborns to smell, taste, feel, see, and hear things going on around them. Only later do areas of the brain develop that are thought to be involved in regulating emotions, acquiring language, and reasoning. During early infancy, the size of the brain increases dramatically and it becomes capable of controlling more and more complex behaviors.

A newborn's nervous system is formed from the neural tube (see Chapter 3). Very early in prenatal development, the neural tube generates **neurons,** which are the nerve cells that make up the communication system of the brain (Begley, 1996). These brain cells migrate outwards to specific areas of the brain, to form its structure. At birth, a newborn's brain has over 100 billion neurons (Nash, 1997).

As you can see in Figure 4.6, a neuron is composed of a cell body, many **dendrites** for receiving messages, and a long **axon** for sending messages. After migrating to their appropriate locations in the nervous system, neurons spin out axons and dendrites that allow for the transmission of information between them. At this point, each neuron produces many different connections with other neurons. Information is transmitted through electrical impulses that travel down the length of a neuron, causing it to produce a chemical response to the impulse. This chemical messenger then transmits the information from one neuron to the next through small gaps, or spaces, between the cells, called **synapses.** With the wealth of new sensory information that is available to the newborn, neurons form synaptic connections at a very fast rate (see Figure 4.7).

neurons the nerve cells that make up the communication system of the brain

dendrites parts of a neuron that are located on the cell body and receive messages from other neurons

axon long part of a neuron that is located at the cell base and sends messages to other neurons

synapses small gaps, or spaces, between the cells through which information is transmitted from one neuron to the next

FIGURE 4.6
Brain Cell and Synaptic Connections

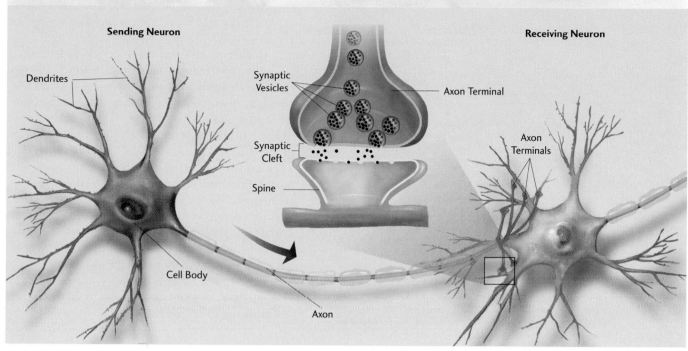

The dendrites of the neuron receive messages, and the axons send messages. How are these messages sent?

FIGURE 4.7
Development of Neural Connections, from Birth Through 15 Months of Age

(a) Newborn   (b) 3-Month-Old   (c) 15-Month-Old

What differences are apparent in the depictions of the neural connections of young children at different ages? What factors contribute to these differences?

FIGURE 4.8
Development of the Brain

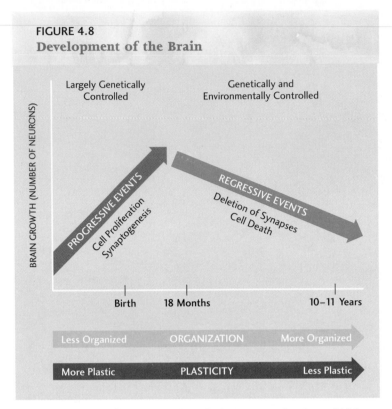

This model illustrates different events in brain development. How does this model help you understand the impact that children's environment can have on their development?

Progressive events involved in early brain development, such as the proliferation and migration of neurons, add structure to the developing brain. Unfavorable environments (such as prenatal exposure to drugs or alcohol) can disrupt these early progressive events (see Figure 4.8).

Another process that occurs in the early years of brain development is **myelination,** in which the neurons are sheathed in smooth layers of fatty proteins (myelin). Electrical impulses travel about three times faster along myelinated pathways. Myelination occurs first in parts of the brain that control reflexes and later in parts that control voluntary movements (Cratty, 1999). After birth, those parts that are used to process sensory information (such as the visual system) myelinate first, and the parts that control attention, memory, self-control, and learning myelinate later. Research has linked myelination to behavioral and cognitive development. For instance, particular brain locations in the cortex (the outer layer of the brain) are myelinated at 15 to 24 months of age, which corresponds to the time when children make tremendous advances in their cognitive and language skills (Konner, 1991).

BRAIN PLASTICITY

Infant brains are more flexible than adult brains. The flexibility, or plasticity, of the brain allows it to fine-tune through interaction with its environment. Because of this plasticity, infant brains adjust to many different situations and are able to recover from serious assaults. We know about the benefits of brain plasticity from clinical cases. Recall from Chapter 1 the case of Brandi Binder, who, because of severe epileptic seizures, had the entire right side of her cortex removed when she was 6 years old but still managed to become talented in art, math, and music. With age, some of the brain's plasticity is lost. Adults who have the operation Brandi had lose much more functioning (Goodman & Whitaker, 1985).

REGRESSIVE EVENTS IN BRAIN DEVELOPMENT

During early development, the brain generates about two to three times more neurons and connections between neurons than are needed to survive and function. Pruning then takes place to decrease the number of cells and connections. Although cells and connections are lost, those that are maintained are strengthened and the brain becomes increasingly organized.

Pruning is influenced by both genetic and environmental factors, but the connections lost during pruning are those that are not reinforced by the child's environment. That is, connections that a child does not use disappear. Early experiences play a crucial role, therefore, in the formation of neural pathways (Greenough, Black, & Wallace, 1987).

ENVIRONMENTAL EFFECTS ON BRAIN DEVELOPMENT

The story of brain development suggests how our genetic inheritance sets up critical or sensitive periods that act as windows of opportunity for learning from early experiences. These early experiences actually change the structure and functioning of the brain. In fact, experience may be the chief architect of the brain (Nash, 1997).

myelination the process in which a neuron is sheathed in a smooth layer of fatty proteins (myelin)

Because of the rapid growth of the brain during the early years of life, children are most vulnerable to the effects of the environment during this time (Nelson & Bloom, 1997). Unfavorable conditions, such as poor nutrition or exposure to drugs or diseases, increase the risk of problems in brain development. Disruptions of growth and development during the brain's growth spurt can have a variety of serious outcomes:

- Permanent reduction in brain size
- Reduction in the number of neurons
- Reduced myelination of cells
- Decreased numbers of synaptic connections

Damage or disruption in the development of the brain during the early years may increase the likelihood that a child will have difficulties in school, lack the ability to handle stress well, and have poor motor and sensory functioning (Cratty, 1986). One source of this type of disruption is inadequate stimulation during sensitive periods. For example, infants who have depressed mothers and who receive less social interaction have brains that are less active (Nash, 1997). Animal studies support the idea that environmental stimulation has a strong effect on brain development. Animals that live in enriched environments—with playmates and toys to interact with—have 25 percent more connections between neurons than do animals in impoverished environments (Greenough, Black, & Wallace, 1987).

The implications of the newest research on brain development are profound. The idea that the environment is central in fine-tuning the brain suggests that early development may be even more important than previously thought in influencing both healthy and unhealthy developmental outcomes.

HOW DO NEONATES PERCEIVE THEIR WORLDS?

Neonates perceive sights, sounds, textures, smells, and tastes, but their abilities to experience these sensations are not as fully developed as adults'. Newborns' senses of taste and smell are more developed after birth than their senses of vision and hearing are. Because their sensory systems are not yet fully developed, low-intensity stimuli, such as pale colors and soft sounds, may not be noticed at all. High-intensity stimuli, such as bright light or loud noise, may cause newborns to withdraw. Stimuli that are moderately intense are the "gentle magnets" that draw the attention of neonates (Stern, 1992).

THE VISUAL WORLD OF THE NEWBORN

Because the womb is a dark place, fetuses have little exposure to visual information before birth. Until the 1960s, people did not really know what or how newborns could see. Many parents have noticed that their newborns stare at them right after birth and sometimes follow movements with their eyes. But just what does the world look like to a newborn?

Newborns have poor visual acuity; what they see at 20 feet is what an adult with good vision sees at 300 to 800 feet (Aslin, 1987). The optic nerve and parts of the brain that process visual information are not fully developed at birth. Within six months, visual acuity improves to adult levels. Soon after birth, although their vision is blurry, neonates can see and track slow-moving objects within their visual range—about 7 inches in front of the face. While tracking an object, newborns move their eyes with jerky motions, which are gradually replaced with smoother movements as they gain control of their eye muscles.

Look at the picture of the flag. What aspects of the photo draw your attention? How would a newborn visually scan this picture?

Notice how intensely this neonate is looking at the mobile. What features of the mobile make it effective in catching the visual attention of the newborn?

When adults visually scan objects, their eyes make very small and rapid movements to shift from one point of fixation to another. These movements allow them to take in visual information about the whole object, collecting enough small images that they recognize an object for what it is.

Just as adults do, newborns systematically scan objects, especially faces. A few simple rules sum up how neonates visually scan the world around them (Kellman & Banks, 1998):

+ They look for edges, using broad, jerky sweeps across their visual field.
+ If they find an edge, they keep looking at it.
+ They sweep their eyes across the edge again and again.
+ If they cannot continue scanning one edge, they look for another.

As infants grow older, their scanning moves from the external edges to the more internal parts. Generally, younger infants attend to the most striking aspect of an object—the part that is moving, the brightest part, or the largest part. This is why mobiles that are bright and feature high-contrast colors are the ones young infants find most attractive. Parents holding a newborn often notice that she or he seems to look above their eyes. This is due to the newborn's fascination with areas of highest contrast—the hairline or eyebrows. Newborns often look right into a caregiver's eyes because the eyes are very striking and appealing.

As newborns develop greater control over the movements of their eyes, they are able to seek out and fix their attention on objects that appeal to them. The increased control occurs as the result of the maturation of the neonate's nervous system. Importantly, caregivers respond to these changes with increased attention and affection toward the infant. Caregivers often report that their infant is looking at them "for the first time" and that this is an expression of affection on the part of the infant. Caregivers find this immensely appealing. They cannot tell you what has changed, but are aware that something is different. This interplay shows how changes in the maturation of the infant's nervous system bring about changes in the infant's social and emotional relationships (Bertenthal, 1996).

Infants are born with capacities that direct them to learn about and orient to people and events that are crucial for their survival. Infants are especially attentive to faces, particularly when held close. They prefer curved lines and moderate complexity, as found in faces, and areas of high contrast, as found in eyes and mouths. Caregivers elicit the infant's attention by holding their face close to the infant's face in the same orientation and by interacting with the infant. The infant's visual capabilities combine with the caregivers' tendencies to interact with the baby in ways that provide mutually rewarding visual interactions.

THE NEWBORN'S WORLD OF SOUND

The structures needed for hearing are more developed at birth than the structures needed for vision are. By 1 year of age, an infant's auditory system generally is similar to an adult's (Kellman & Banks, 1998). But what do newborns hear? From birth, babies can hear sounds that are whispered, but not sounds softer than that; adults can hear much softer sounds (Nozza, 1995). Newborns cannot hear sounds of short duration as well as adults can, and they prefer relatively high-pitched sounds, such as the sound of a woman's voice (Fernald, 1985). Even newborns can localize sounds; for instance, they can identify the location of a rattle by hearing that the sound is coming from the left side rather than the right side (Aslin, Jusczyk, & Pisoni, 1998). Infants seem particularly attuned to human voices, especially the sound of their own mother's voice (DeCasper & Spence, 1986).

As discussed in Chapter 3, newborns prefer the sounds they were exposed to during prenatal development. Within two days of birth, infants show a preference for hearing their own language rather than another language. They also prefer the sounds of intrauterine heartbeats to many other sounds, and they prefer melodies their mother

Do Newborns Prefer to Hear Their Own Language?

As you have learned, newborns have preferences for certain sounds; they like to listen to their mother's voice, heartbeats, and stories that they listened to while they were still in the womb. Do unborn children also pay attention to the language that they hear spoken? Can they distinguish it from another language? If a mother and father speak only English during pregnancy, will their newborn prefer to listen to English rather than another language?

Eight 2-day-old infants who were born into monolingual English homes and eight 2-day-old infants who were born into monolingual Spanish homes were tested to determine whether they could discriminate between their own and another language. A contingent reinforcement procedure was used, in which infants learned to control the presentation of audio recordings of women speaking in either Spanish or English by sucking on a pacifier that was connected to a computer. The harder and longer the infants sucked, the longer they could control the length of time they heard the voices. After spending about 12 minutes learning how to control the voices through sucking, twelve of the sixteen infants showed the expected pattern: they activated the recordings in their native language for longer periods than they did the recordings in the foreign language (Moon, Cooper, & Fifer, 1993). The two days over which the infants were exposed to their native language after birth may have influenced their preferences, but the researchers believe that it is more likely that their prenatal experiences determined their preferences for their native language.

Thinking It Through:

1. Why would newborns have a preference for their own language?
2. What differences would you expect in the pattern of findings if 2-*month*-old infants were studied instead of 2-*day*-old infants? Would it be more difficult to determine when the infants' preferences developed?
3. Why did the researchers use infant sucking behavior to answer their research questions? What other behaviors could they have measured as indicators of preferences?

---

sang during pregnancy to other melodies. Prenatal exposure to sounds appears to "set" infants' preferences for sounds after they are born (Aslin, 1987).

THE NEWBORN'S WORLD OF TASTE, SMELL, AND TOUCH

Neonates have well-developed senses of taste, touch, and smell. Newborns can distinguish among tastes that are sweet, salty, bitter, and sour. They prefer sweet solutions over all other tastes, and they show disgust or distress when tasting something bitter or sour (Rosenstein & Oster, 1988). Although their numbers increase after birth, taste buds form early in prenatal development, suggesting that this sensory system functions even before birth. Further confirmation of the early functioning of the sense of taste comes from the findings that premature newborns pucker their lips when they taste something sour (Tatzer, Schubert, Timischl, & Simbruner, 1985) and premature and full-term neonates are calmed by sweet-tasting substances (Smith & Blass, 1996; Zeifman, Delany, & Blass, 1996). Early in life, babies have a wider distribution of taste buds than adults do—taste buds are found even on the tonsils and in the back of the throat.

Newborns can distinguish between smells such as vinegar and alcohol. They turn away and make faces when presented with strong or unpleasant smells (vinegar) and turn toward more pleasant smells (Lipsitt, Engen, & Kaye, 1963).

Smells may be one of the first and most basic connections between neonates and their caregivers (Fabes & Filsinger, 1988). Within six days after birth, infants will turn their heads toward the smell of their mother's breast milk rather than that of other mothers (MacFarlane, 1975). Breast-fed infants show particular sensitivity to their mother's smells, such as her perfume and underarm odor (Cernoch & Porter, 1985; Porter, Makin, Davis, & Christensen, 1992). Mothers have a similar sensitivity for their infant's smells and can identify the smell of their infant soon after birth. When presented with clothing worn by their own baby and identical clothing worn by other babies, mothers are most likely to pick the clothing of their own baby by the smell (Porter, Cernoch, & McLaughlin, 1983).

Early in prenatal development, the fetus responds to a light touch—moving, for instance, when touched by an instrument. The parts of the nervous system that process information about touch develop very early. At birth, the presence of reflex responses to touch suggests that the newborn is particularly sensitive on the face, hands, soles of the feet, and abdomen (Reisman, 1987). Newborns are sensitive to changes in temperature and respond to cooling temperatures by waking up and moving around, which increases their heat production. A full-term newborn may sweat when the temperature is hot, but a preterm infant does not, suggesting that the cooling mechanism of sweating matures more slowly than other responses to temperature (Harpin, Chellappah, & Rutter, 1983). When infants are hungry, they will root toward warmth. For example, when warm glass tubes are held close to their cheeks, they move their heads and open their mouths toward the tubes (Reisman, 1987). This finding suggests that temperature cues are used by infants to locate nourishment.

The extent to which newborns experience pain has important consequences for their treatment. For many years, medical personnel assumed that infants were buffered from pain, at least for a short time after birth. Because of this assumption, they avoided giving newborns anesthesia or pain medication for surgical procedures to reduce the risk of complications. Today, however, we know that newborns do experience pain. When they are circumcised or receive injections, newborns become distressed. They hold their breath and cry, their arms and legs and bodies become rigid, their faces show "pain" expressions, and they have difficulty sleeping (Anand & Hickey, 1987). Neonates' bodies respond to surgical procedures by producing more stress hormones (Gunnar, Fisch, Korsvik, & Donhowe, 1981). If a newborn needs to undergo surgical procedures, the American Academy of Pediatrics (1989) recommends that physicians use anesthesia and analgesics, following the same guidelines as for other high-risk groups. These procedures effectively and safely reduce the pain and distress experienced during surgery (Stang et al., 1997).

THE "DANCE OF PERCEPTION"

Newborns respond to meaningful stimuli, and their responses facilitate the development of close relationships. Babies curl up in their caregivers' arms, look at their caregivers and appear interested in what they see, and respond to their caregivers' touch. When an infant cries, the mother's breasts respond with increased blood flow, facilitating milk production. In turn, caregivers' responses reinforce and shape the infant's subsequent responses. Thus, as in a dance, each partner mutually leads and follows the other's responses.

Additionally, caregivers respond to babies in ways that facilitate interactions. By holding a baby in the crook of their arm, they place the baby at just the right distance for the baby's eyes to focus. By speaking in a high-pitched, melodious voice, they draw the baby's attention and soothe his or her distress. As this "dance of perception" between the young infant and the caregivers continues, each partner in the dance fine-tunes his or her responses to adapt to the other's nuances.

WHY ARE SOME NEWBORNS AT RISK?

Donald was born seven weeks early and weighed only 3½ pounds. Similar to other low-birthweight babies, he had respiratory distress, apnea (stoppage of breathing), and jaundice (yellowing from poor liver function) and was unable to suck. Donald was placed in an incubator in the intensive care unit. He also was placed on a ventilator, treated with fluorescent lights for jaundice, and fed through a tube inserted into his nose. Donald's parents, Jackie and Fred, traveled 4 hours from their rural ranch to the hospital every week to see Donald. Jackie brought her refrigerated breast milk so that Donald could be fed her milk when she was not there. Jackie and Fred took Donald home when he was 8 weeks old and weighed 5 pounds. He was active and alert, and his respiratory problems were under control. Jackie says that she hardly slept at first: "I kept getting up to make sure he was breathing." She and Fred eventually relaxed, after realizing they were capable of taking care of Donald and his problems. "We know he's going to be slower developing than other babies," said Fred, "but we aren't in any hurry. He can take his time."

—ADAPTED FROM WIDERSTROM, MOWDER,
AND SANDALL (1991)

Donald was lucky. He survived being born early and weighing less than is optimal for a newborn. As with other infants who are born early, his systems were not all fully developed, especially his respiratory system (lungs and ability to breathe). Not all children are as lucky as Donald.

An important distinction is made between infants who are **preterm** (or **premature**)—those born prior to 37 weeks' gestation—and infants who are **low birthweight**—those born after 37 weeks' gestation but weighing less than 5½ pounds. Low birthweight usually is a more significant risk factor than prematurity, accounting for 75 percent of the poor postnatal outcomes (Fanaroff, Martin, & Miller, 1994). Prematurity is a risk factor largely because of the many disabilities often associated with it (Allen, 1993). A baby like Donald, born at thirty weeks, takes eight weeks to reach the same developmental level as a baby born at thirty-eight weeks. The combination of being both preterm and low-birthweight places a newborn at the greatest risk for negative outcomes (Bardin, Zelkowitz, & Papageorgious, 1997).

Rates of low-birthweight and premature babies vary by racial/ethnic group (National Center for Health Statistics, 1997). As depicted in Figure 4.9, African American mothers have a higher incidence of low-birthweight, very-low-birthweight (less than 3.3 pounds), and premature deliveries than any other ethnic group. The reason for this difference is unclear, but some factors that increase the likelihood of African American mothers' delivering low-birthweight and premature infants seem not to affect other ethnic groups, even other minority groups. A list of the factors that place a newborn at risk for prematurity and low birthweight appears in Table 4.6.

In 1995, about 20,000 infants in the United States were born two to three months premature and weighed less than 1000 grams (2.3 pounds). These infants are referred to as "kilogram kids," and they spend their first few months fighting for their lives. In the past, virtually all of these newborns died, but over 40 percent of them now survive (National Center for Health Statistics, 1995b). However, almost 9 out of every 10 infants who weigh less than 500 grams at birth do not live, whereas about 75 percent of those who weigh 1000 grams survive.

Prematurity and low birthweight interact with cultural and social variations in caregiving environments to influence children's developmental outcomes. For instance, Bradley and colleagues (1994) found that the percentage of low-birthweight children living in poverty who were adaptive and resilient was very low (about 10 percent). This percentage is considerably lower than the 40 percent of preterm children from more affluent, nonpoverty households who were adaptive and resilient. These findings are particularly

preterm or **premature** term describing infants born prior to 37 weeks' gestation

low birthweight term describing infants born after 37 weeks' gestation but weighing less than 5½ pounds

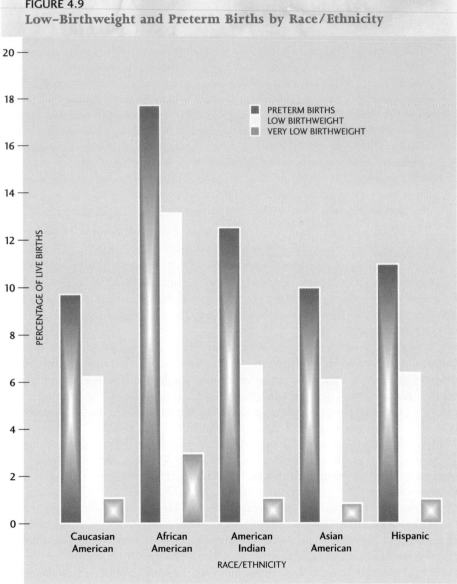

FIGURE 4.9
Low–Birthweight and Preterm Births by Race/Ethnicity

SOURCE: Adapted from National Center for Health Statistics, 1997.
What factors contribute to differences among the groups in the percentages of low-birthweight and preterm births?

noteworthy given that the researchers did not include children with serious chronic medical problems (such as cerebral palsy). The odds that a premature, low-birthweight child living in poverty will show early evidence of the ability to tolerate adverse conditions are "for all practical purposes, nil" (Bradley et al., 1994, p. 357). These findings provide evidence that certain environmental conditions, such as poverty, can increase the vulnerability of an already vulnerable child (Fang, Madhavan, & Alderman, 1999).

CONSEQUENCES OF LOW BIRTHWEIGHT AND PREMATURITY

Most infants who are born too early or weigh too little at birth develop normally and become healthy and thriving children. The positive outcomes for many of these chil-

TABLE 4.6

Factors That Place Newborns at Risk

BIOLOGICAL RISK FACTORS	ENVIRONMENTAL RISK FACTORS
Prematurity	Poverty/unemployment
Intracranial hemorrhage	No medical insurance
Growth retardation	Teenage mother
Brain abnormalities	Mental retardation or emotional
Biochemical abnormalities	disturbance in parent or caregiver
Infections	Substance abuse by caregiver
Lung disease	History of child abuse or neglect in
Neonatal seizures	family
Maternal substance abuse during	Family dysfunction
pregnancy	Lack of parenting skills
	Parent-child separation (divorce,
	maternal incarceration)

SOURCE: Adapted from Allen, 1993.

dren relate to the plasticity of an infant's nervous system, which recovers from early trauma more quickly and easily than an adult's nervous system. Nonetheless, as a group, these infants are more likely to show a variety of physical problems, including the following (Hack, Klein, & Taylor, 1995):

+ Subnormal growth
+ Mental retardation
+ Blindness
+ Deafness
+ Cerebral palsy
+ Health problems

The smallest infants are at a higher risk for having low intelligence scores and deficits in cognitive abilities when they grow up, even when neurological and social risk factors are taken into account (Doussard-Roosevelt et al., 1997). Very-low-birthweight babies (weighing less than 3½ pounds) are particularly at risk for problems in specific areas, such as memory and fine motor skills, with verbal abilities being less impaired (Hack, Taylor, Klein, & Eiben, 1994; Schothorst & van Engeland, 1996).

Low-birthweight babies also have more difficulties in school, and the number of difficulties seems to increase as the weight of the child at birth decreases. Very-low-birthweight children are particularly vulnerable to problems in mathematics and specific learning disabilities (Koller et al., 1997; Taylor, Klein, & Hack, 1994); in addition, they have an increased risk of needing special education classes (Hack, Klein, & Taylor, 1995). Very-low-birthweight children who are premature show the greatest impairments in intelligence, motor performance, and attention (Korkman, Liikanen, & Fellman, 1996).

Very-low-birthweight children also may have more behavior problems than other children, and the lower the birthweight, the more problems reported (McCormick, Gortmaker, & Sobol, 1990). The problems include hyperactivity, poor social skills, and conduct disorders (Young, 1996).

Can a Breathing Bear Help Preterm Infants?

Premature infants have difficulty with many tasks that full-term babies do not; they have difficulty breathing, sucking, and maintaining normal body temperature. Some interventions with premature babies have been designed to mimic life in the womb, which is assumed to be ideal for healthy development. One clever strategy is to use breathing bears—teddy bears that make audible breathing sounds. If premature infants have a breathing partner, as they would have if they had stayed longer in the womb, do they develop more quickly? Thoman and colleagues (1995) tested this idea with infants who were 33 gestational weeks old. Half these premature infants were given breathing bears, and the other half were not. After two weeks, the premature infants with the breathing bears were awake less often, slept quietly more often, and cried less than the infants in the control group. These findings suggest that a simple intervention—the introduction of an audible breathing partner—can help premature infants develop (Thoman, Hammond, Affleck, & Desilva, 1995).

Thinking It Through:

1. Do you think a breathing bear would benefit full-term babies as well? Why or why not?
2. In what other ways could a preterm baby's environment be made more like the prenatal environment?

NEONATAL INTENSIVE CARE

Like Donald, whose case was highlighted at the beginning of this section, most preterm newborns with developmental problems are put in a neonatal intensive care unit. The first step is to stabilize the newborn's body temperature and place her or him in an isolette to prevent loss of warmth. If respiratory problems are evident, the new-

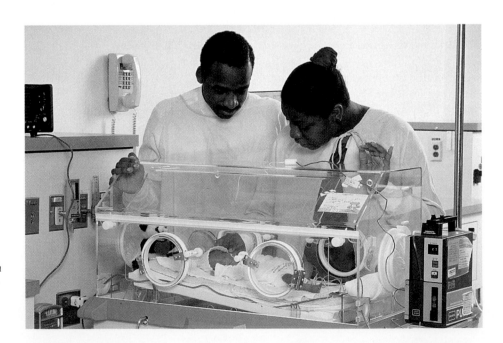

Notice that this infant is in an incubator, which helps keep him warm. How has technology improved the survival chances of newborns needing intensive care? What ethical issues does this technology raise?

Reading Premature Babies' Signals

Premature babies in intensive care need to have a carefully controlled environment, but the level of stimulation they need for optimal development has been difficult to determine. A current perspective is that premature newborns differ in the amount of stimulation they need, depending on their stage of development and their medical condition. Dr. Heidi Als (1984) proposed that caregivers learn to attend to premature infants' signals so that they can tell whether their newborns need to have time away from stimulation or are content with the level of stimulation they are receiving. Parents who learn to read these cues will feel more competent and will promote their baby's behavioral orga-

nization. Parents who are inaccurate in reading cues may feel frustrated and unrewarded in their parenting efforts.

Following are some common signals (Hussey, 1988). When premature infants are ready for stimulation, they tend to be

- happy and attentive
- alert and vocalizing
- relaxed
- looking at people

When premature infants are trying to regulate their level of stimulation, they tend to

- suck on their fingers or hands to soothe themselves

- go to sleep to shut out sounds and sights
- curl up to feel more secure

When premature infants are uncomfortable and need a change, they

- spread their fingers apart
- frown
- grunt or make faces
- salute with their hands over their eyes
- yawn, cry, or look away

---

born is given oxygen. Heart, respiration, and other vital signs are closely monitored. Treatment for apnea or infection is given. After the infant is stabilized, she or he can be moved to an intermediate-level care facility. Upon reaching 5½ pounds, babies graduate from their special care facilities and can go home.

Approximately 2 to 9 percent of newborns require intensive care, and most of these are very-low-birthweight infants (Hack et al., 1995; Widerstrom, Mowder, & Sandall, 1991). Most of these newborns spend between fifteen and fifty days receiving special care in the neonatal intensive care unit, with the longest stays for the lightest babies (Gottfried, 1985). Changes in medical care, especially neonatal intensive care, have dramatically improved the survival rates for very-low-birthweight infants.

Not long ago, newborns in intensive care units experienced the frantic pace of hospital life and continuous monitoring, without concern for their special developmental needs or their families' needs (Young, 1996). Today, medical personnel are more sensitive to these newborns' special requirements and attempt to provide an environment that mimics the conditions of the prenatal environment. Lights are turned down, infants are swaddled in hammocks, and medical personnel know when to encourage or limit interactions with the infants. Importantly, parents are encouraged to be involved in their infant's care (Gottwald & Thurman, 1990). Breast-feeding and supplemental touching and caressing appear to be particularly valuable for premature and low-birthweight babies (Bier et al., 1997; de Roiste & Bushnell, 1996). These interventions are effective in shortening the length of the premature infant's stay in intensive care.

Preterm infants often have difficulty breathing and may experience short periods when they stop breathing. How does a breathing bear help preterm infants? Can you describe the ways in which this preterm baby looks different from a full-term baby?

Should There Be Limits to Neonatal Treatment?

Rapid improvements in medical care for newborns have led to an increase in survival rates for very small and very-low-birthweight infants. The advent of neonatal intensive care procedures has also increased the number of high-risk newborns who survive but have disabilities (Hack et al., 1995). In addition to the ethical issues, there also is a medical question concerning the provision of extensive medical treatment to extremely immature newborns. Is there a limit to the effectiveness of treatment?

Several studies have investigated infant survival rates to determine whether a cutoff point exists in treatment effectiveness. In a study of infants born between 1988 and 1991 at twenty-two to twenty-five weeks' gestation, it was found that outcome depended on gestational age. As the table shows, the likelihood of survival varied dramatically with age, as did the chance of having severe brain damage (Allen, Donohue, & Dusman, 1993). The researchers concluded that aggressive medical care (such as resuscitation) is in-

dicated for infants born in the twenty-fifth gestational week, but not for those born in the twenty-second gestational week. To determine the indicated treatment level for those in between, the researchers recommended opening discussions with parents, health care providers, and society at large. Concerns about which infants receive intensive medical care are likely to become more pressing as scarce health care resources are evaluated and reallocated (Hobar & Lucey, 1995).

Thinking It Through:

1. How does society determine which—and whether—very small and very early newborns will receive expensive and demanding medical interventions?
2. Should parents be asked to consider the costs to society of caring for a high-risk infant whose chances of surviving are very low?
3. Because medical interventions for very small or early infants are expensive, should society make certain these interventions are available to all who need them?

Rates of Survival and Brain Damage in Premature Newborns

GESTATIONAL AGE	SURVIVAL RATE	RATE OF BRAIN DAMAGE
22 weeks	0%	—
23 weeks	15%	98%
24 weeks	56%	79%
25 weeks	79%	31%

SOURCE: Allen et al., 1993.

CAREGIVING AND HIGH-RISK INFANTS

I cried constantly. After the doctors came and didn't give us much hope, I just felt so helpless. Justin was born almost three months early and was about the size of my hand. You dream about holding your new baby and here we were, separated and unable to hold him for weeks. Justin couldn't respond because he was so medicated and on a ventilator. We would visit as often as we could, talk and touch him through the portals. The hardest thing was feeling that there was nothing I could do. And, worst of all, it made me wonder if this baby was really a person and was really ours.

—ANONYMOUS ON-LINE STORY OF A MOTHER
WITH A SON IN NEONATAL INTENSIVE CARE

Preventing SIDS

After the first few days of life, the most common cause of unexpected death in infants is sudden infant death syndrome (SIDS). When an infant dies in his or her sleep and there is no other ready explanation, SIDS is often the diagnosis. Other possible causes of death, such as child abuse and overheating, must be ruled out. SIDS is not well understood; apparently, many different factors can cause an infant to die in the first months after birth. Some of the suspected causes of SIDS include drug use by the mother during pregnancy, an undetected fast-acting viral or bacterial infection, oxygen deprivation during pregnancy, hormonal imbalance, and cigarette smoking in the home. More infants die of SIDS within the first few months of birth than later, suggesting that infants may be less susceptible to SIDS once certain developmental changes have occurred. Certain infants seem to be at risk for SIDS: boys, infants with brothers or sisters who died of SIDS, preterm infants, low-birthweight infants, infants with low Apgar scores, and infants with respiratory problems (Barness & Gilbert-Barness, 1992). Recommendations made to parents to reduce the likelihood of an infant's dying of SIDS include placing the infant in a face-up position rather than a face-down position to sleep and sleeping with the infant. Sleeping with an infant has been shown to help the infant regulate his or her breathing (McKenna et al., 1994).

Even in the best of circumstances, adjusting to the birth of a child is difficult and stressful for parents and other family members. As the mother's story on page 130 reveals, adjusting to the birth of a high-risk infant means additional emotional, psychological, and physical challenges. Seeing your infant in an intensive care unit can be frightening and overwhelming, and parents often are not prepared for this. Preterm and very-low-birthweight babies look different than healthy, full-term babies; the tubes, machines, and isolettes are foreign and unsettling to most parents (Fleming et al., 1994). Even in well-functioning families, parents who give birth to fragile children experience chronic or recurrent stress (Clubb, 1991).

Once a high-risk infant is taken home, the family faces many new challenges. The baby may have short-term health care needs, such as a need for someone to monitor apnea episodes, or long-term needs, such as a need for a ventilator. High-risk newborns require a great deal of parents' time and energy, and many parents report that family life deteriorates: spouses have less time for each other and parents have less time to attend to the needs of their other children (Diehl, Moffitt, & Wade, 1991). Family functioning also can be affected by financial concerns, which mount as the care for the fragile child continues. For families with high-risk infants, problems with finances are a common source of stress (Wegener & Aday, 1989).

In interactions with their parents, preterm infants are less responsive, alert, and active than their full-term peers. Yet parents of preterm infants take a more active role in interactions than parents of full-term infants do (Goldberg & DiVitto, 1995). For example, parents of preterm infants stay closer, hold and touch more, and provide more stimulation. These findings suggest that parents of a preterm infant sometimes compensate for the low responsiveness of their infant by taking more direct action to engage the infant. This compensation provides a basis for secure parent-infant relationships as the preterm infant gets older and healthier. Nonetheless, parents of very-low-birthweight infants or of preterm infants who have a lasting illness (such as a heart defect) are more likely to have difficulties establishing secure relationships with their newborn (Plunkett, Meisels, Stiefel, Pasick, & Roloff, 1986).

INFANT MORTALITY

Many infants worldwide do not live long enough to celebrate their first birthday. In 1996, Niger and Sierra Leone had two of the highest rates of infant mortality. In the United States, the infant mortality rate was relatively low, with only 8 children out of 1000 not surviving until their first birthday. However, despite the excellent medical facilities in the United States, the US infant mortality rate is still higher than that of many other developed countries—twenty countries have lower rates (UNICEF, 1998).

Within the United States, some groups have much higher rates of infant mortality than others. Compared with the mortality rate for Caucasian American infants—6.3 deaths per 1000 live births—mortality rates are 132 percent higher for African American infants and 43 percent higher for American Indian infants. The mortality rate for Hispanic infants is comparable to that for Caucasian American infants, whereas Asian American infants have a mortality rate that is 16 percent lower (National Center for Health Statistics, 1998). Why the infant mortality rates for these groups differ is as yet unknown, but one likely reason is differences in access to and use of prenatal and postnatal care. Cultural values and family support are important, too, as evidenced by the lower rates of infant mortality among Hispanic infants, despite lower socioeconomic status and less prenatal care (Balcazar, Peterson, & Krull, 1997).

CHAPTER SUMMARY

How is a baby born?

• There are three stages of labor. In the first stage, contractions of the uterus cause the cervix to dilate.

• In the second stage, the baby is born. The baby moves through the birth canal and is expelled through the vaginal opening. The baby's head molds as it passes through the birth canal.

• In the third stage, the placenta is expelled.

• There are many birthing methods to choose among, including the Lamaze method, which focuses on educating the parents and teaching relaxation techniques, and the Leboyer method, which focuses on lessening the trauma of childbirth for the infant by using quiet and dimly lit rooms.

• Infrequently, birth complications occur, for a variety of reasons. A woman may require a surgical method of birth (caesarean section) to safeguard her baby's health, an infant may be born in an unusual position, or birth may have to be induced.

How is childbirth experienced?

• A mother's experience of childbirth encompasses both positive and negative feelings. The mother feels excitement and the pain of labor and also may experience baby blues or postpartum depression due to biological changes, fatigue, loss of attention, and the increased stresses on family life.

• A father's experience of childbirth depends on whether or not he feels confident of his ability to support his partner. Today, many more fathers are present when their children are born; they feel closer to their partners and children for having shared the experience.

• Newborns produce high levels of stress hormones during birth, but they are well equipped to manage the birth process. These hormones cause infants to be alert and attentive immediately following birth.

• Parents may feel a special closeness to their child after birth, but the scientific evidence does not support the idea that there is a critical period for initial bonding.

What are the characteristics of a newborn?

• Newborns face four challenges after birth: breathing on their own, controlling their body temperature, changing their blood circulation, and ingesting food.

• Newborns' physical characteristics differ from those of older infants: they have misshapen heads and faces, uneven coloring, and enlarged genitalia.

• The Apgar scale is used to assess whether newborns need emergency medical care.

• Newborns have automatic behaviors, called reflexes, some of which help them to survive. Assessment of reflexes provides information about the condition of the baby's nervous system.

• Newborns shift among states of arousal. These states influence the quality of interactions between caregivers and newborns.

• Newborns sleep 16 hours a day, spread out over the day and night. Sleep and wake cycles may indicate brain development.

- The ability of newborns to imitate facial expressions indicates that they have some internal code that allows them to match what they see with what they do.
- Brazelton's Neonatal Behavioral Assessment Scale allows medical personnel to evaluate the development and health of newborns.

How does early brain development proceed?

- Progressive events in brain development—cell generation and the formation of billions of synaptic connections—are genetically controlled.
- Neurons allow communication among the various areas of the brain. Myelination of neurons helps them send and receive information more quickly and efficiently.
- Regressive events include cell death and the loss of connections between neurons. Which connections are lost and which develop more fully depend on early experiences. Thus, the infant brain is more plastic than the adult brain.

How do neonates perceive their worlds?

- Newborns' vision is blurry compared to that of adults. Newborns like to look at areas of high contrast, especially edges of things, and they like to look at faces.
- Newborns can hear fairly well at birth. They like to listen to familiar and high-pitched voices and sounds.

- The senses of smell, taste, and touch are well developed by the time the child is born. Newborns can distinguish many tastes and smells, and they prefer sweet tastes and pleasant smells.
- Newborns feel pain and show signs of distress when they are in pain.

Why are some newborns at risk?

- Preterm, or premature, babies are born too early—before 37 weeks. Low-birthweight babies weigh too little—less than 5.5 pounds—when they are born. The combination of these two risk factors is more serious than either alone.
- Some newborns require intensive medical care, which is usually provided in neonatal intensive care units. The nature of the care has changed greatly over the last twenty years.
- High-risk infants usually develop into healthy children, but some have physical and cognitive problems. These problems are more likely to occur if the infant is of very low birthweight.
- Taking care of high-risk infants is challenging and, depending on the nature of the infant's problems, can be very stressful for families.
- In the United States, infants have a good chance of surviving their first year of life, but in many countries and for some groups within the United States, the infant mortality rate is high.

KEY TERMS & CONCEPTS

Apgar Scale *(111)*
axon *(118)*
Braxton-Hicks contractions *(100)*
breech presentation *(106)*
caesarean section *(104)*
crowning *(102)*
deferred imitation *(117)*
dendrites *(118)*
epidural block *(101)*
episiotomy *(102)*

false labor *(100)*
lightening *(100)*
low birthweight *(125)*
molding *(102)*
multiparous women *(100)*
myelination *(120)*
Neonatal Behavioral Assessment
    Scale *(117)*
neonate *(110)*
neurons *(118)*

postpartum depression *(107)*
preterm *(125)*
premature *(125)*
primiparous women *(100)*
reflexes *(111)*
state of arousal *(113)*
synapses *(118)*
transverse presentation *(106)*
vernix caseosa *(110)*

ACTIVITIES & APPLICATIONS
Relating to Birth and Neonates

1. How have birthing practices changed over time? Talk to your parents and their friends about their childbirth experiences, and compare them to those of parents who have given birth within the last ten years. What changes have occurred in attitudes, practices, and technology? How have these changes altered the experience of childbirth? What type of birth method would you choose? Why?

2. Reread Bob Greene's diary entry about the birth of his daughter Amanda Sue (page 104). What are the sources of fetal stress at birth? What criteria would have determined whether or not Dr. Charles performed a caesarean? What changes have occurred in the United States that have increased the number of c-sections?

3. Arrange to observe a newborn, and watch for the characteristics of a neonate identified in this chapter. Design a rating chart on which to record the characteristics you observe. You might also attempt to assess the newborn's behavior, using information in this chapter. On the basis of your observations, develop a research question on a topic in neonatal development that interests you.

4. Use your imagination and the information in this chapter to try to experience a physical and social environment the way a newborn would. What is your visual world like? What do you hear, taste, smell, and feel? How do others' interactions with you influence your "dance of perception"? How do you interact with the world?

Grasping the Whole

Benchmarks in Prenatal and Neonatal Development

	PHYSICAL/MOTOR DEVELOPMENT	COGNITIVE DEVELOPMENT	SOCIAL/EMOTIONAL DEVELOPMENT
Conception	Genetic transmission Sex determination	Genetic basis of intelligence	Genetic basis of personality and behavioral traits
Prenatal			
Germinal	Development of zygote Cell division and differentiation Development of placenta and umbilicus Implantation		
Embryonic	Critical time for teratogenic effects Cephalocaudal and proximodistal growth Development of sensory and internal organs	Beginning of brain and central nervous system development	Pregnancy confirmed Parental excitement about pregnancy Feelings of concern for health of child
Fetal	Rapid growth of body and brain Development of external genitalia Age of viability Preparation for birth Reflexes functioning	All senses functioning to some degree Well defined stages of arousal REM sleep	Mother's condition becoming obvious Family preparing for arrival of new child
Birth	Labor and dilation of cervix Crowning and molding Afterbirth Beginning of breathing and body temperature control	Exposure to sensations from world outside the uterus	Parental, societal, and cultural expectations for birth Addition of new family member
Neonate	Reflexes Rapid brain development Continuation of perceptual development Cycling through states of arousal Initial weight loss followed by weight gain	Innate preferences Perceptual memory Ability to learn simple contingencies Ability to imitate facial expressions	Parent-newborn bonding Caregiving Individual differences in behavioral traits becoming evident

Worldwide Rates of Infant Mortality

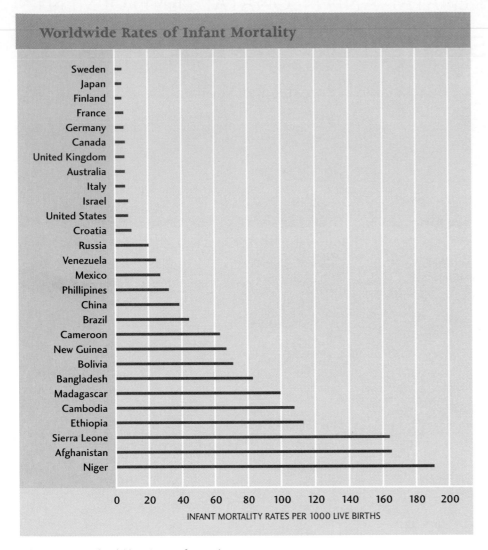

INFANT MORTALITY RATES PER 1000 LIVE BIRTHS

NOTE: Rates are for children 1 year of age or less.
SOURCE: UNICEF, 1998.

Status Report on Prenatal and Neonatal Development

Countries vary tremendously in their infant mortality rates. What are some factors that may account for these differences?

SUGGESTED READINGS

Brown, J. E. (1997). *Nutrition and pregnancy.* New York: Lowell House. Step-by-step guide to the dietary requirements of pregnancy, birth, and lactation.

Eisenberg, A., Murkoff, H. E., & Hathaway, S. E. (1994). *What to expect when you're expecting.* New York: Workman. Readable guide for expecting parents. Readers are reassuringly led, month by month, through a wealth of information incorporating recent developments in medicine and medical science.

Payne, R., & Cobb, S. (1996). *The American Medical Women's Association guide to fertility and reproductive health.* New York: Dell.

State-of-the-science medical guide written by doctors who are on the front lines of women's health. The volume provides comprehensive information on solutions to fertility problems.

Vaughan, C., & Fylling, M. (1997). *How life begins: The science of life in the womb.* New York: DTP. Informative text and vivid full-color pictures of the miracle of human reproduction. Interviews with leading scientists chronicle the latest in prenatal research.

RECOMMENDED WEBSITES

The Baby Center: This comprehensive site for parents and family care workers is reviewed by a medical advisory board. <http://www.babycenter.com/>

Childbirth: Designed to help readers become good consumers with respect to pregnancy and childbirth, this Website has many links to educational, informational, and personal resources. <http://www.childbirth.org/>

NOAH on Pregnancy: This comprehensive New York Online Access to Health (NOAH) Website gives consumers high-quality health information that is accurate, timely, relevant, and unbiased. NOAH currently supports English and Spanish. <http://www.noah.cuny.edu/>

OBGYN Net: A comprehensive site run by the Association of Labor Assistants and Childbirth Educators, OBGYN offers up-to-the-minute reference information, an events calendar, clinical reference collections, powerful search tools, discussion forums, electronic journals, and recent articles. <http://www.obgyn.net/>

On-Line Birth Center: Abstracts, articles, and resources appear on midwifery, pregnancy, birth, and breast-feeding. <http://www.efn.org/~djz/>

Pregnancy Place: Information is provided on fertility, infertility, and all aspects of pregnancy and childbirth. <http://www.preg.com/>

SIDS Network: A growing collaborative effort, this site offers up-to-date information as well as support for those who have been touched by SIDS. <http://www.sids-network.org/>

NATIONAL HOTLINES FOR PREGNANCY, PRENATAL, AND NEONATAL DEVELOPMENT

SIDS Network: 800-860-1454

March of Dimes Birth Defects Foundation: 888-663-4637

Planned Parenthood Federation of America: 800-230-7526

PART 3

Infant & Toddler DEVELOPMENT

"Watch this," Susan said tonight as Amanda was sitting on the floor in her diapers. "Where's your toe?" Susan said. Amanda took her first finger and touched her big toe. "Does she really know?" I said. "You try it," she said. "Amanda," I said, "show me your toe." Without hesitation, she touched her finger to her big toe again. "Where'd she learn that?" I said. "What do you think we do all day?" Susan said . . .

When I leave for work now, she follows me to the door. She stands and waves and says "Bye-bye, Da-da." She doesn't say it like an adult would say it. . . . Each syllable is pronounced in exactly the same slightly exaggerated tone,

something like

"BYE!—BYE!—DA!—DA!" It's not so much a farewell; it's a request that I not leave yet. . . . I find myself very slow to leave the house these days.

—BOB GREENE'S JOURNAL ENTRY ABOUT AMANDA AT 1 YEAR OF AGE (1984, pp. 299, 304)

From the moment they are born, infants are bombarded by sights, sounds, smells, and tactile sensations. A major task of the first two years of life is to develop ways of making sense of and organizing these sensations. As the brain develops and infants gain experience, they increasingly acquire abilities to integrate and understand the world around them. Eventually they learn to understand words, such as *toe*, and to coordinate their eyes and hands so that they can reach out to grab something they want, as Amanda did when she touched her toe.

Infants also face the task of developing ways of interacting with their social world. Parents, caregivers, siblings, other family members, and friends interact with infants, and the quality of these interactions has important implications for infants' development. In turn, infants' actions and responses affect how others interact with them. Bob Greene's reluctance to leave when Amanda says her good-bye is a good example of the influence infants and toddlers have on those they interact with. This reciprocal interaction forms the basis for much of the development that occurs during this stage of life.

IN PART 3, YOU WILL LEARN ABOUT

- how infants develop in size and weight and the factors influencing their development
- how infants' motor capabilities develop and the dynamic system of factors that interact to produce these capabilities
- how infants' health and safety can be improved
- infants' nutritional needs and the advantages of feeding infants human breast milk
- the perceptual competencies of infants
- how infants learn through contingencies and how they remember over a long period of time
- the stages through which infants pass as their cognitive abilities develop
- how infants' cognitive development is enhanced through interactions with skilled caregivers

- how infants develop language skills and the important role that caregivers play in helping children learn language
- how emotions develop during infancy and toddlerhood and how they come to be expressed
- the enduring characteristics of infants and toddlers that make up temperament and how these characteristics help us understand individual differences in very young children
- how attachments to significant others develop, how these attachments are measured and assessed, the factors that influence them, and the consequences for later development
- the effects of day care on infants and toddlers and the factors that contribute to these effects
- factors related to child maltreatment and how maltreatment might be prevented

CHAPTER 5

Physical & Cognitive Development in INFANCY AND TODDLERHOOD

*A*s a newborn, Gabrielle weighed 8 pounds and 4 ounces, was 20 inches long, and had a full head of black hair and big cheeks. She cried, ate, and slept, but mainly cried. When she was 2 months old, she would stare intently at new toys. By 5 months, when she was given a duck that squirted water out of a hole in its belly, she was so fascinated with that duck she remembered how to make it squirt even weeks later. By the time she walked, Gabrielle understood what to do when I asked her to "bring me your cup," and she could say, "milk," "kitty," and "bye-bye."

She grew so quickly. When she was 2 years old, she was 35 inches tall, weighed 28 pounds, had long brunette hair, and could speak simple sentences. One of her favorite games was chasing her cat and picking oranges off trees in the yard. Not only had she become a real little person with likes and dislikes, she could now plan and remember activities, like when we have a picnic.

—*Anonymous mother's on-line notes (1998)*

Twenty years ago, little was known about the capabilities of infants. Most people assumed that their worlds were filled with confusion—they could not see or hear very well, nor could they learn very easily. That picture has changed dramatically. Today, we recognize that infants are actively learning about the people and objects they encounter, and much of this learning occurs in the context of routine interactions with those people. For example, Gabrielle's intense staring at new toys at 2 months of age shows us that she selectively attended to things that interested her.

HOW DO INFANTS AND TODDLERS DEVELOP PHYSICALLY?

Growth in height and weight and dramatic changes in motor skills occur rapidly during the first two years of life, more rapidly than for older children. Infants' proportions are different from those of older children and adults. Their heads are much larger relative to the size of their bodies. A newborn's head is about one-quarter of his or her body size, whereas an adult's head makes up about 12 percent of his or her body size. Relative to head size, infants have a large forehead, small flat nose, and large eyes. They have a distinctive body shape as well, with a protruding stomach; short, bowed legs; and relatively high amounts of fat (Cratty, 1999).

Like Gabrielle's mother in the opening story, parents are very aware of changes in their children's physical growth. This is true in part because growth is so noticeable but also because growth is an indication of children's health. Pediatricians use growth charts to follow changes in children's height and weight over time and to compare one child's growth to that of other children. Each line of the chart in Figure 5.1 represents a different growth pattern. The bottom line represents a child who is growing more slowly than other children. This child is ranked in the 5th percentile, meaning that only 5 percent of children of the same age are shorter (or weigh less). The blue line in the middle represents an average growth pattern. If a child is in the 50th percentile, half of the other children are taller and half shorter. The top line represents the growth of a child in the 95th percentile, who is taller (or heavier) than almost all other children. For most children,

FIGURE 5.1

Growth Charts for Height and Weight (birth to 36 months)

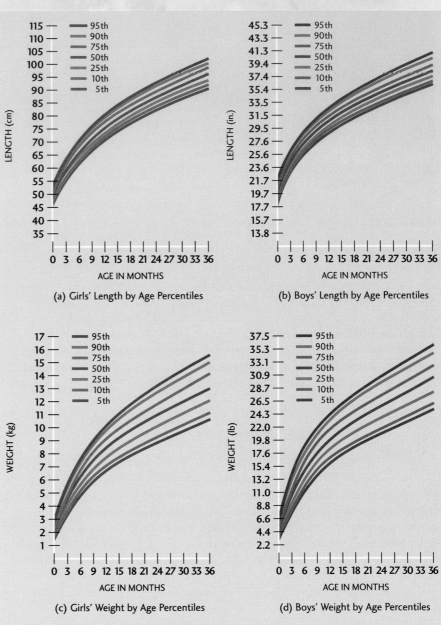

SOURCE: National Center for Health Statistics, 1976.
Notice that infants tend to grow very rapidly in both weight and height. Girls and boys show similar growth patterns in the first two years of life.

growth patterns remain similar over time, so a child who is average in height at age 3 is likely to be average at age 5.

GROWTH PATTERNS IN INFANTS AND TODDLERS

By their first birthday, most children gain 15 pounds and grow 9 inches. After prenatal growth, there is no other period of life in which children grow as quickly as they do during the first year. As you can see in Figure 5.1, infant boys and girls continue to grow rapidly during the first three years, and their growth patterns are similar. By age 2, boys reach about 50 percent and girls 53 percent of their adult height. Birth weight usually doubles by 5 months, triples by the end of the first year, and quadruples by about 30 months of age. It takes ten years for children to reach half their adult weight.

Genetic factors play a major role in determining a child's growth pattern, especially for height and body type and to a lesser extent for weight. Generally, tall parents have children who are tall and short parents have children who are short.

The conditions in which a child is raised also influence growth patterns. Children who do not receive adequate nutrition during their early years do not achieve optimal height. Changes in diet can alter trends, however. For example, because of improved diets, Japanese children born after World War II grew too large to fit into the school desks that their parents had used as children. Americans, too, are taller than their ancestors because of improved diets; children born after World War II tend to be about 1 inch taller than their parents (Roche, 1979).

MOTOR DEVELOPMENT IN INFANTS AND TODDLERS

Tickle a newborn's foot and the baby will move his or her whole body in response, but tickle a preschooler's foot and the child will move only his or her leg. This difference illustrates how infants' movements become more localized and specialized during the first few years of life. Major developments in motor activity occur during the first year or two as infants acquire the abilities to sit, crawl, stand, and walk. But before they can acquire these abilities, infants must gain control over their muscles and learn to cope with the forces of gravity.

During the first year, infants' reflexes become inhibited as the brain develops and they gain voluntary control over many of their movements. The process is complex, and the rate at which they develop motor skills depends on many factors. After the first year, motor development mainly involves practicing and mastering previously learned skills. Infants gain greater control and precision in movement as their ability to integrate information from the senses and the muscles increases. But there are dramatic individual differences in motor development. Some infants are advanced and others are delayed in demonstrating skills, and the "normal" range is broad.

Lifting the Head and Sitting

Infants raise their head before they learn to stand up. The cephalocaudal trend—by which development proceeds from head to tail—is apparent in the development of motor control and stability (see Table 5.1). Infants first gain control over their head, later their trunk, and even later their balance, enabling them to stand and walk.

Caregivers often are cautioned to support the head when they hold a newborn. There are good reasons for this. At birth, infants have little control over their head and neck muscles and cannot hold up their head. Within a month, most infants can hold up their head if someone supports the base of the neck. Three-month-old Kirra can raise her chest off the floor when placed on her stomach. In another two to three months, she gains enough control over her upper trunk to be able to sit with support. By the time she is 7 or 8 months old, Kirra's control extends to her lower trunk, and she can sit erect (Gallahue & Ozmun, 1995).

Crawling, Creeping, and Standing

Five-month-old Manuel is lying on his stomach. When he reaches for a toy in front of him, this motion causes his head and chest to rise, and then his outstretched arm pulls him forward. In a month or so, these motions will turn into crawling, in which he will

This baby can stand, but only while being held up. How has her ability to control her muscles changed thus far? What other motor skills does she need to begin to stand on her own?

cruise in infant development, to move around while holding onto things for support

TABLE 5.1

Major Milestones of Motor Development in Infancy

ABILITY	APPROXIMATE AGE OF ONSET
Turns head to one side	One week
Holds head with support	First month
Lifts head and chest	Second month
Supports head well when lying on stomach	Third month
Sits with support	
Crawls	Sixth month
Stands with support	
Rolls over from front to back	Eighth month
Sits alone	
Creeps	Ninth month
Stands alone	Twelfth month
Walks alone	Twelfth to fifteenth month

SOURCE: Adapted from Gallahue and Ozmun, 1995.

move with his stomach on the floor. Several months later, when he is stronger and more coordinated, Manuel's crawling will change into creeping, in which he will move on his hands and knees without his stomach touching the floor. Like most infants, Manuel will be able to stand at about 6 months, but only while someone holds him up under the arms. He will then begin to stand by holding onto furniture and pulling himself up. By 11 to 13 months, Manuel will stand well on his own.

Walking

Eleven-month-old Sheri was playing in a wading pool with her older sister. Much to the surprise of her parents, Sheri stood up, holding on to the side of the pool, and then let go of the edge and took her first steps. The excitement and story surrounding her first steps now are a part of Sheri's family history.

Like Sheri's, most families respond to an infant's first steps with excitement, recognizing that walking is the most spectacular feat of early motor development. The increased mobility infants gain when they learn to walk leads to many new opportunities for learning, as well as danger. The relationship between infants and their caregivers changes once this important developmental milestone is reached.

Learning to walk progresses in stages. Not long after infants start to creep and pull themselves to a standing position, they begin to **cruise**—moving around while holding onto things for support. At 10 to 15 months, children make tentative and unsteady efforts to walk unassisted, usually with their arms held shoulder high and their feet spread apart and pointed outward. This first walking motion involves wobbly movements as children shift their weight from one foot to the other to move forward, giving them an unsteady toddling motion. Gradually, they lower their arms, turn their feet forward, and narrow their stance (Cratty, 1999). During their second year, children try many variations in their movements, including walking sideways, backwards, and on their toes.

Children's motor development, especially with respect to walking, is well described by a dynamic systems perspective (see Chapter 2). Recall that this perspective focuses on

Assessing Development in Infants and Toddlers

The Denver Developmental Screening Test II is used to assess children's development in four areas: gross motor skills, fine motor skills, language skills, and social/emotional skills. The test can be given to children from birth to 6 years of age and is simple to administer (Frankenberg, Dodds, Archer, Shapiro, & Bresnick, 1992). Items on the test are scored according to the age at which 75 percent of children are able to pass the item. Some sample items are given below.

Gross motor skills:
- by 12–14 months—stands alone well; stoops and recovers
- by 24–30 months—jumps up; throws ball overhand
- by 36–40 months—balances on each foot for 1 second; broad jumps
- by 48–52 months—balances on each foot for 3 seconds; hops

Fine motor skills:
- by 12–14 months—scribbles; puts block in cup
- by 24–30 months—builds tower from six cubes
- by 36–42 months—wiggles thumb; copies circle
- by 48–54 months—draws a person with three parts

Language skills:
- by 12–14 months—says words other than *mama* and *dada*
- by 24–30 months—combines words; names six body parts
- by 36–42 months—knows two adjectives; names one color

Personal-social skills:
- by 12–14 months—indicates wants; plays ball with examiner
- by 24–30 months—washes and dries hands
- by 36–42 months—puts on T-shirt

---

how each action is made up of bits and pieces of experience and how an action is dynamic because it changes every time it is performed (Adolph, 1997; Fogel, 1996). For instance, infants can walk on smooth floors as well as carpets because the complex actions required for each step are subtly adjusted to accommodate the different types of floor (Thelen & Smith, 1994). Rather than assuming that advances in motor development are accounted for solely by maturation of the brain, dynamic systems theory assumes that the components leading to motor actions act in concert to produce changes, with each component important and necessary for producing change.

Research shows that infants have many of the motor capabilities involved in walking long before they put them all together and begin to walk. But why don't infants walk earlier? One reason is that they are unable to support their weight on one leg. Watch as adults walk and you will see that they shift all their weight from one leg to the other. Thus, each leg must be able to support the weight of the body, which requires muscle strength and balance. As infants' fat-to-muscle ratio changes over the first year, they achieve a critical combination of strength and balance that enables them to put the necessary components together to walk (Fogel & Thelen, 1987). Because infants' fat-to-muscle ratios vary, the timing of walking varies from one child to the next. Dynamic systems theory is useful for explaining how a minor change in balance and strength results in the reorganization of capabilities to develop a much more complex behavior—walking.

Implications of Walking for Infants and Families

When infants begin to walk, new worlds open up to them. At the same time, a new emotional climate develops in the home. For example, once they can move about by themselves, infants react with increased frustration and anger when they cannot quite

When do you think this infant will begin walking? What factors contribute to an infant's developing the motor skill of walking? Why do some infants walk before others?

145

When infants begin walking, their movements are unsteady. Many toddlers direct their movements by leaning in the direction they want to go. What are the other differences between toddlers who have just started walking and those who have been walking for months?

reach an attractive goal or an object they set out to get (Campos, Kermoian, & Zumbahlen, 1992). Their increased ability to locomote also heightens infants' sensitivity to the presence of caregivers. Infants who can walk show greater levels of distress when separated from caregivers and greater affection when in their presence.

Parents, too, change their emotional reactions once infants begin to walk. The expression of anger increases; some parents report that the onset of walking coincides with the first time they express anger toward their infants. As they see their infants develop independence, parents increasingly hold them responsible for their actions, expecting the infants to comply when told "No, stop that!" Parents also express more affection toward their walking infants, as a result of the pride they feel in their infants' new accomplishments (Campos et al., 1992).

Walking provides a good example of the interrelated nature of the domains of development. To be able to walk, children must accomplish a series of complex motor and physical tasks involving coordination, balance, and strength. Moving about freely changes children's expectations about what they can do, thereby changing their emotional responses. The new level of independence children achieve as walkers changes their parents' expectations about them. Thus, changes in childrens' physical development can bring about changes in their social and emotional relationships with others.

BOWEL AND BLADDER CONTROL

During the first year of life, infants have no control over the muscles involved in elimination and have little, if any, awareness of the physical signs that signal elimination. In the middle of the second year, many children make the connection between the feelings of impending elimination and their outcome (Leach, 1997). The potential to be toilet trained increases at the end of the second year or the beginning of the third year, once toddlers can anticipate elimination. Control over bowel movements usually is accomplished earlier than bladder control.

When to start toilet training is a serious concern for many parents. Junko was very anxious because her son, who had just turned 3, was not yet toilet trained. She wondered what she should do about this. Research shows that there are large individual differences in when children become toilet trained (Taubman, 1997). Most children learn to control their bladders and bowels when they are ready, just as they learn to sit and walk. For example, shortly after Junko voiced her concerns, her son seemed to spontaneously become toilet trained.

When Junko's son was ready for toilet training, he responded positively and quickly to it. Starting to train him earlier would have lengthened the process and probably not produced earlier bowel or bladder control. Four percent of children are toilet trained by age 2, 60 percent are trained by age 3, and only 2 percent are not trained by age 4. Boys generally take longer to be trained than girls. If a child is not trained by 42 months, caregivers may want to seek the advice of a pediatrician (Blum, Taubman, & Osborne, 1997).

WHAT FACTORS INFLUENCE INFANT HEALTH AND SAFETY?

Infants' health issues vary depending on their age, genetic inheritance, condition at birth, and living conditions. The leading causes of death for children under 1 year of age are congenital anomalies, sudden infant death syndrome (SIDS), and disorders related to low birthweight or premature birth (see Chapter 4). After children learn to walk, the leading cause of death is physical injuries, which account for about one-third of all deaths for children 1 to 4 years of age (National Center for Health Statistics,

1997). Many health problems that children experience can be prevented through the use of vaccines to ward off diseases and safety devices to protect them from injuries. Between 1994 and 1995, increased vaccination rates contributed to a 6.4 percent drop in cases of childhood tuberculosis (Centers for Disease Control, 1997). Another health issue for young children is exposure to environmental hazards, such as exposure to lead and radon gas. Children who live in impoverished environments are most at risk for health and safety problems because of a lack of health care and the unsafe conditions in which they live (Huston, 1994).

PROMOTING HEALTHY DEVELOPMENT AND GROWTH

In order to promote their healthy development and growth, children should receive six "well-child" visits during the first year of life, six visits over the next four years, and then a visit every other year until the age of 20. These visits should include the following (American Academy of Pediatrics, 1991):

◆ An assessment of the child's growth
◆ A review and update of the child's medical history
◆ A physical examination and health screening
◆ Guidance on feeding, sleeping, accident prevention and safety, and behavioral problems

In the United States, all states require that children receive basic immunizations before entering school. However, approximately one-third of children under 3 do not receive immunizations (Centers for Disease Control, 1997), and inner city, low-income children are least likely to be immunized (Perrin, Guyer, & Lawrence, 1992). Unfortunately, many US children lack access to health care, and the number of children without any form of health insurance has increased over the last twenty years (Monheit & Cunningham, 1992). Hispanic children are less likely to have health insurance than Caucasian American or African American children (US Census Bureau, 1998). The lack of health insurance among Hispanic children may be due to cultural factors—because of social and cultural barriers (such as limited English proficiency or fear of deportation), immigrant families may not seek health coverage.

AVOIDING ACCIDENTS

Infants are at risk for many kinds of accidents. Before they crawl, infants may fall off changing tables or beds or get caught in crib rails. Baby appliances such as walkers, rockers, and jumpers can cause injuries if used improperly (Smith, Bowman, Luria, & Shields, 1998). Unsupervised crawling and walking infants may hurt themselves by falling down stairs, falling into swimming pools, or walking out into the street. Infants also may be hurt or killed in car accidents. Caregivers need to be particularly cautious about car safety; babies should be restrained in car seats attached to the back seat. Infants also may be poisoned by dangerous chemicals in the house. Because infants are prone to explore, caregivers should babyproof and toddlerproof their homes.

INFANT NUTRITION

Because infants grow most rapidly in the first year, adequate nutrition during that period is essential. Most infants obtain adequate nutrition from breast milk or formula. Human milk has evolved to provide the best nutrition for an infant, and it changes in composition to match the infant's needs. Even a mother who is malnourished produces milk that is sufficient to meet her infant's nutritional needs for the first few months of life (Brown, Robertson, & Akhtar, 1986).

Should Babies Be Taught to Swim?

Drowning is one of the most common accidents of childhood. In addition to falling into swimming pools, rivers, and lakes, children have drowned by toppling into toilets or buckets with just a few inches of water in them. In an effort to "drownproof" them, some parents enroll their children in infant swimming programs. Other parents enroll their infants in these programs because they believe that there is a critical period for learning to swim.

These programs should be viewed with caution for several reasons. First, parents must realize that their children will never be "drownproofed" because no one, regardless of age or skill, is com-pletely safe around water (Langendorfer, 1987). Second, scientific evidence does not support the idea of a critical period for acquiring swimming skills. Third, although few experience this rare condition, some babies will suffer hyponatremia (water intoxication) if they ingest large quantities of water during swimming. Symptoms of hyponatremia are lethargy, weakness, vomiting, and seizures, and victims may die (Burd, 1986). A more common problem is that children may catch giardia, an intestinal parasite that causes severe diarrhea. Because of these concerns, the YMCA Division of Aquatics (1984) and the American Academy of Pediatrics (1999) recommend that parents wait until children are 3 years old before enrolling them in organized aquatic programs (Gallahue & Ozmun, 1995).

Thinking It Through:

1. Why might people think that infancy is an ideal time to teach swimming skills?
2. What were your experiences in and around water as a baby or young child? If you can swim, when and under what circumstances did you learn to swim?
3. What guidelines might you follow to prevent the accidental drowning of an infant or toddler in your care?

Benefits of Breast-Feeding to Infants

Human milk provides all the protein needed by a baby for the first six months of life. It also contains a balance of amino acids and minerals that differs from that in other nutritional sources. Human milk contains more cholesterol than cow's milk or formu-las, and cholesterol is essential for promoting myelination within the brain. Also important for brain development is human milk's higher concentration of lactose, which provides the fuel needed by the infant's rapidly growing brain. Although human and cow's milk are both low in iron, the iron in human milk is absorbed better, reducing the likelihood of iron deficiencies. Human milk also is more digestible than cow's milk.

Breast milk also provides an array of protective benefits to infants. Breast-fed infants are more resistant to infections than bottle-fed infants. One reason is cleanliness. Contaminants are more likely to be a problem with bottle-feeding, especially in countries that have very hot climates (which promote bacteria growth) or that have contaminated water (Lifshitz, Finch, & Lifshitz, 1991). Another reason is that breast milk contains substances that fight off infections. Breast-feeding is especially useful in transferring the mother's immunities to the infant in the first weeks of life and stimulating the infant's own immune system. During the first few days of the baby's life, the mother's breasts produce **colostrum,** a pre-milk substance containing antibodies from the mother that protect the baby from infections. The advantages of breast-feeding may last a long time; breast-fed infants have less risk of some diseases later in life, including coronary artery disease, allergies, and diabetes (Lifshitz et al., 1991).

Breast-fed newborns tend to be more irritable, reactive, and physiologically adap-tive than bottle-fed babies. Research shows that this is an optimal pattern of responsive-

colostrum a pre-milk substance containing antibodies from the mother that protect the baby from infections

148

ness (DiPietro, Larson, & Porges, 1987). Longer term effects of breast-feeding include scoring slightly higher on intelligence tests, even when family economic backgrounds are taken into account (Fergusson, Beautrais, & Silva, 1982). Babies breast-fed longer than eight months show increases in IQ and reading comprehension scores at 8 and 18 years of age as well (Horwood & Fergusson, 1998). It is unclear, however, whether it is the composition of breast milk or the interpersonal interactions involved in breast-feeding that affects later cognitive development (Doyle, Rickards, Kelly, Ford, & Callanan, 1992; Lucas, Morely, Cole, Lister, & Leeson-Payne, 1992). This does not mean, though, that caregivers should be concerned if they cannot or do not breast-feed. As you will learn, many other factors, such as providing an enriching intellectual environment, play important roles in influencing children's intellectual growth.

Notice that the mother is holding the infant and gazing at him. Beyond providing infants with optimal nutrition, what aspects of breast-feeding may be pleasant for mothers and encourage attachment for infants?

Benefits of Breast-Feeding to Mothers

In addition to conveying nutritional and protective benefits to infants, breast-feeding also has benefits for mothers. Many women enjoy breast-feeding their infants because of the pleasure and closeness they experience during feeding sessions. Women who breast-feed lose more weight and experience nonpainful uterine contractions, which help them to recover from childbirth more quickly than women who do not breast-feed. Breast-feeding also delays ovulation, which is beneficial for mothers who do not use or have limited access to birth control. Convenience also is a factor: breast milk does not need to be heated up or cooled down, and it is portable and usually plentiful. In developing countries, families attempting to bottle-feed may spend 50 percent of their income on infant formula (Lifshitz et al., 1991), so breast-feeding is economically advantageous as well. Also, parents do not have to worry about the potentially fatal consequences if formula is limited or water is contaminated.

Breast-feeding is not an option for all women, however. For example, it is difficult to maintain while working outside the home, although breast pumps allow women to express their milk for later use. Some women are advised not to breast-feed because of the medication they are taking or diseases they might transfer to their infants through breast milk. Mothers with AIDS, for instance, may pass the disease on to their infants through their milk (Sizer & Whitney, 1997). Additionally, breast-feeding can be demanding on mothers—using a bottle allows other family members to help and participate in the care of the infant.

Prevalence of Breast-Feeding

In the 1970s, only about 25 percent of new mothers in the United States breast-fed their babies; today, about 60 percent of mothers breast-feed (Ryan, 1997). Breast-feeding has become especially popular among college-educated, higher income women (Life Science Research Office, 1995). Mothers also are breast-feeding for longer periods of time than they did in the 1970s. Today, 20 percent more mothers breast-feed for 5 or 6 months (Ryan, 1997). Experts on nutrition would like to increase to 75 percent the number of mothers who breast-feed for the first few weeks and increase to 50 percent the number who continue until the babies are 4 to 6 months old (Sizer & Whitney, 1997).

In the 1940s and early 1950s, pediatricians recommended that parents feed their infants on a rigid 4-hour schedule, with the idea that this routine would increase infants' self-regulation of hunger. Today, most pediatricians recommend feeding "on demand"—that is, feeding infants whenever they are hungry. Feeding on demand allows infants to control their own nutritional intake and satisfaction (Drewett, 1993).

WEANING AND FEEDING INFANTS AND TODDLERS

The recommended timing for introducing solid foods into an infant's diet has changed since the 1970s, when mothers were encouraged to offer cereal to infants as young as 6

Notice that this baby has smeared his face with food. Why should infants be allowed to feed themselves? When should caregivers begin to let infants feed themselves?

weeks of age. Pediatricians now recommend delaying solid foods until the child has reached at least 13 to 14 pounds (double the average birth weight) or is between 4 and 6 months old. Before that time, infants' digestive systems are not sufficiently developed to digest starchy foods. Undigested solid foods may sensitize the child to proteins that cause food allergies. Infants signal their readiness for solid foods by demanding to be fed more frequently than every 2 hours and by drinking large quantities of milk (Lifshitz et al., 1991). Although "baby teeth" begin to erupt between 5 and 9 months of age and most infants have six teeth by their first birthday, their first foods need to be soft because infants are unable to chew well until their second year.

Children need high-calorie foods because they have high energy needs for rapid growth. Most parents start by introducing cereals, which are digested easily and rarely cause food allergies. Later, fruits and vegetables are added to an infant's diet. Protein foods such as cheese, yogurt, egg yolks, and pureed meats can be introduced at 6 to 8 months. Whole eggs, milk, and more table foods can be introduced when babies are 1 year old (Sizer & Whitney, 1997).

Throughout the toddler years, children make a gradual transition to their family's regular diet and develop more mature eating habits and skills. Toddlers need to eat frequently, and their diet must include nutrient-dense foods to ensure that their nutritional needs are met while they are growing rapidly. For example, low-fat milk is not appropriate for an infant. Reducing fat and cholesterol in the diet, restricting high-calorie foods, and limiting between-meal snacks may be recommended for many older children and adults, but for infants such restrictions can contribute to inadequate nutrition and failure to thrive (Lifshitz et al., 1991).

FAILURE-TO-THRIVE INFANTS

Failure to thrive (FTT) is a term used to describe infants and children who do not appear to be ill or abnormal but who do not grow at the expected rates (Casey, 1992). Children whose growth is below normal or whose growth rate slows down drastically may be FTT infants (Lifshitz et al., 1991).

The most common causes of FTT are undernutrition, in which children do not have enough food to eat, and malnutrition, in which children do not receive the appropriate nutrients. The quality of the interactions children have with their caregivers also may be a factor (Powell, Low, & Speers, 1987). Once treated with adequate nutrition and calories, FTT children return to normal growth patterns (Bithoney & Newberger, 1987), although children with FTT generally are shorter and lighter than those without FTT, even fourteen years after the initiation of treatment (Oates, Peacock, & Forrest, 1985).

Failure to thrive is more than a growth problem. Children with FTT also are likely to (Powell et al., 1987):

+ show abnormal behaviors
+ lack nurturing caregivers
+ be passive and inactive
+ be shy and withdrawn
+ show little expression of emotion
+ avoid close physical contact and cuddling
+ show unusual eating behaviors

Mothers of FTT children may be depressed or may have serious psychological problems that interfere with caregiving activities, including feeding. Families of children with FTT often have disorganized homes and experience social isolation or multiple stressors (Casey, 1992).

Several studies show that FTT children lag behind their peers in language development, reading, verbal intelligence, and social maturity, even years after treatment. The outcomes for the individual child depend on how long the child had FTT, the ongoing quality of caregiving, and the child's home environment (Casey, 1992).

failure to thrive (FTT) a term used to describe infants and children who do not grow at the expected rates

HOW DO INFANTS' PERCEPTUAL ABILITIES DEVELOP?

Infants are bombarded by sights, sounds, smells, tastes, and tactile sensations. From this array of stimuli, they perceive and make sense of their world by selecting some types of information and ignoring others. Selective perception requires interpreting sensory information by actively sorting and organizing the information into meaningful units. Making meaning is an innate capability in humans, and many of the changes that occur in perception are due to the maturation of the nervous system and brain (Kellman & Banks, 1998).

PERCEPTION OF COLORS, PATTERNS, AND FACES

In Chapter 4, you read how newborns are attracted to high-contrast stimuli that are moderately intense, complex, and sharply defined. With increased visual acuity, development of their visual system, and better control of eye movements, infants between 2 and 4 months expand the range of their attention to include stimuli that are colorful, meaningful, and patterned.

By 2 months of age, infants discriminate red, blue, and green (Adams, 1989). They perceive patterns in place of the simple lines and shapes seen by newborns; that is, they observe the relationships among the lines and shapes. Several studies indicate that by 3 months of age infants take notice of patterns that are "different" or misaligned, but 1-month-old infants do not (Van Griffin & Haith, 1984). These findings suggest that between 1 and 3 months infants begin to see the organization of visual displays rather than only their details.

As you learned in Chapter 4, newborns like looking at contrasting areas of faces. Infants' preferences for faces increase as they grow older and learn to recognize how a whole face should look. By 12 weeks of age, infants prefer faces over nonface stimuli, even when the complexity of the two pictures is equal (Dannemiller & Stephens, 1988; see Figure 5.2). By 5 months, infants treat their own faces as familiar, social stimuli (Legerstee, Anderson, & Schaffer, 1998), suggesting that they recognize themselves through facial cues.

When shown schematic drawings of faces, infants exhibit a preference for looking at typical faces rather than faces with distorted features (Maurer & Barrerra, 1981). Surprisingly, even infants as young as 3 months prefer attractive adult faces over less attractive faces (Langlois et al., 1987; Samuels & Ewy, 1985), and by 6 months they prefer attractive faces of infants and adults of diverse races (Langlois, Ritter, Roggman, & Vaughn, 1991).

Although young infants recognize and prefer to look at faces, they are not very good at reading emotions displayed on faces. Until they are about 6 months old, they recognize only simple and clearly displayed emotional expressions. For instance, they recognize a smile only if it is broad and open-mouthed (Kuchuk, Vibbert, & Bornstein, 1986). Not until they are 18 to 24 months old do infants understand that facial expressions reflect others' emotional states (Repacholi & Gropnik, 1997; Saarni, Mumme, & Campos, 1998).

PERCEPTION OF MOVING OBJECTS

Infants prefer to watch moving objects rather than stationary ones. When shown moving and stationary objects or patterns, infants prefer to look at patterns or objects that move at a moderate rate. Infants' abilities to detect motion improve in the first three months; by about 6 months of age, infants are good at coordinating their movements with the movements of objects (Aslin, 1987). For instance, they will grasp at a moving object within a twentieth of a second of the moment it touches their hand (von Hofsten, 1983).

Infants also recognize and prefer complex patterns of motion made by people (such as walking or running). To test infants' abilities in this area, researchers devised an unusual experiment in which a person was outfitted with small lights to mark the locations

FIGURE 5.2
Face and Nonface Stimuli Used to Study Infants' Face Preferences

SOURCE: Dannemiller and Stephens, 1988. Early studies of face preferences compared infants' responses to faces and to other patterns, but it was unclear whether the complexity of the stimuli influenced their responses. To ensure that the amount and complexity of visual information did not bias their results, Dannemiller and Stephens (1988) controlled for the amount of dark and light areas in each figure that infants were shown. Infants show face preferences even when the information is controlled.

Why will this infant avoid crawling over the "cliff"? What changes must take place in the visual system for an infant to be able to detect depth?

of the major joints (such as shoulders and hips). The outfitted person was then filmed running and walking in a very dark room so that only the points of lights were visible on the film. When shown these moving light displays along with computer-generated lights moving in nonhumanlike patterns, infants from 3 to 5 months of age preferred to watch the human patterns of motion (Bertenthal, Proffitt, Kramer, & Spetner, 1987).

DEPTH PERCEPTION

Does an infant recognize that stairs drop off? Will he or she try to crawl down the stairs or be afraid of falling? The classic study of depth perception involved placing infants on a **visual cliff apparatus,** which uses a checkerboard pattern covered with Plexiglas to create an illusion of depth. On the "cliff" end, the checkerboard pattern drops off several feet but the Plexiglas continues level. If an infant can detect height, will she or he crawl over the "edge" of the cliff?

By 7 months, most infants avoid the cliff area of the apparatus, even when their mother calls them from across the "abyss." This suggests that infants of this age respond to changes in depth (Walk & Gibson, 1961). Prior to this age, infants often show interest in the cliff but may or may not avoid it. Seven-month-old crawling babies begin to show fear of heights, and infants who push themselves around in walkers also develop a fear of the cliff (Bertenthal & Campos, 1984).

Infants detect depth and distance before they can crawl, probably because of changes that occur in the visual system between 3 and 7 months of age. Depth and distance cannot be perceived unless the viewer is able to compare images from both eyes. At birth, the visual system receives input from both eyes in the same part of the brain, but by 6 or 7 months, separate locations develop for input from each eye (Kellman & Banks, 1998).

Researchers use looming and zooming objects to assess infants' responses to distance. Around 3 months of age, infants respond to looming objects—those that seem to be coming toward them—by blinking. When an object is zooming away from them, they do not blink (Banks, 1988). Seven-month-old infants begin to use visual cues to determine depth (Kellman & Banks, 1998). The relative size of an object, for example, provides information about whether the object is close or far away.

HOW DO INFANTS AND TODDLERS LEARN AND REMEMBER?

The motor and perceptual changes that infants undergo in their first two years expand their foundations for learning. Infants have many more opportunities to learn about their world as they gain increased access to it by walking. Changes in their nervous system and increased tendencies to organize information into patterns also give them ways to represent and store information in more useful and memorable units. Infants are able to learn associations even at birth, and their memories improve as they grow older.

Not all associations are learned. When newborn Patrick searched for the nipple after being tickled on the cheek, he was exhibiting a reflex, not a learned behavior. By 7 months of age, he shows evidence of learning when he becomes excited and attentive when placed in his high chair. Patrick has learned and remembers the contingency

visual cliff apparatus a checker-board pattern covered with Plexiglas, used to create an illusion of depth

"When I am put in this chair, I get food," and he acts accordingly. Many behaviors that older infants and toddlers exhibit, such as playing pat a cake or peek-a-boo, result from learning to associate one event with another.

LEARNING THROUGH CONTINGENCY AND ASSOCIATION

In Chapter 2, you learned about Albert, the young boy who was conditioned to be afraid of a white rat. Albert initially was unafraid of the rat, but when researchers paired a loud, unpleasant noise with the rat, Albert learned to associate the two. After making that association, he responded to the sight of the rat with fear, even when no noise occurred.

Human newborns as young as 2 hours old can be trained through classical conditioning methods to expect a contingency. In one study, newborns were gently stroked on the head for ten seconds before they were fed sweetened water. Initially, the stroking had no effect on sucking behavior, but once infants learned the association, stroking caused them to orient their head, pucker their lips, and suck more than infants who had not been provided with the same contingency (Blass, Ganchrow, & Steiner, 1984). When the infants in the contingency group were given a different contingency—they were stroked, but the feeding was stopped—they often cried, became angry, or whimpered, indicating that their expectancies had been violated.

Infants also learn through operant conditioning, in which they associate their actions with particular consequences (see Chapter 2). When a baby experiences a pleasant or rewarding consequence for a behavior, he or she is likely to act in the same way again. In studies of infants, the actions most commonly measured are sucking, kicking, gazing, and head turning. Infants are particularly quick to learn about consequences that have to do with feeding or that allow them to hear their mother. For instance, infants have been taught that if they suck longer or harder, they can listen to a sound they like, such as their mother's voice (DeCasper & Fifer, 1987). They have learned to associate their behavior (sucking) with a positive consequence (hearing mother's voice).

LEARNING WHAT'S FAMILIAR: HABITUATION AND NOVELTY RESPONSES

When infants find something fascinating, they turn their attention to this stimulus and gaze intently at it. Beyond sensing objects and perceiving their forms, what do infants gain from such focused attention? Scientists who study infants' information-processing abilities are interested in whether there are differences in the ways they pay attention to stimuli and what kinds of information they acquire while they focus so attentively.

To gain her infant's attention, Marta repeatedly dangles a stuffed bear in front of her daughter and then removes it. At first, her daughter Celina stares at the bear for a long time, but with continued presentations, Celina looks at the bear for shorter periods of time, as if she is getting bored. This behavior provides evidence of **habituation**—a decrease in attention to a stimulus that has been presented repeatedly (Bornstein & Ludemann, 1989). Now Marta replaces the bear with a clown, and Celina shows renewed interest. Celina's increase in attention to this new stimulus after habituation to a previous stimulus, a response called **dishabituation,** shows that she distinguishes between the two stimuli, the bear and the clown.

When babies habituate and then dishabituate, they demonstrate that they remember, at least for a short time, an object they have been shown and can compare that memory with a new stimulus (Schneider & Bjorklund, 1998). To assess infants' short-term memories, researchers use habituation-dishabituation tasks and measure visual behavior, sucking rates, and heart and respiration rates. Because infants cannot use words to tell us about their perceptions, thoughts, and memories, the habituation task is important in assessing these abilities.

habituation a decrease in attention to a stimulus that has been presented repeatedly

dishabituation an increase in attention to a new stimulus after an infant has habituated to a previous stimulus

Notice that this infant has a ribbon tied to her foot and to the mobile. She has learned that when she kicks she turns the mobile. Why is this method useful for assessing infants' memories? What factors influence whether infants will remember the contingency?

Evidence of habituation is found very early in life: newborns habituate to repeated visual presentations (Slater, Mattock, Brown, & Bremner, 1991). The fact that habituation occurs so early allows researchers to test what kinds of things infants discriminate, including social categories. For example, in one study, infants habituated to faces of men and dishabituated when presented with faces of women. This finding suggests that by 9 months of age infants distinguish between the appearances of men and women (Leinbach & Fagot, 1993).

As infants grow older, they habituate to new stimuli more quickly. A newborn might take 5 to 10 minutes to habituate, but a 6-month-old habituates in 30 seconds (Bornstein, 1985). Among infants of the same age, the rate of habituation varies, and these differences are stable over the first three years. Faster habituation may reflect an ability to process information more effectively, which may be critical to memory later in life (Schneider & Bjorklund, 1998).

LONG-TERM MEMORY

Fetuses can learn associations in the last months of prenatal development and remember them after birth. Newborns are capable of learning basic survival-related information, such as the sources of nourishment and the smells and sounds of their mother. However, young infants have fragile memories—they are unlikely to remember information for very long, and their memories are constrained by the context of learning. Marked improvements occur at 2 to 3 months and at 6 to 10 months of age. These improvements are linked to increased myelination of the neurons, the increased number of synapses formed in the brain, development of the frontal cortex, and increased attention span. Another improvement occurs at around 18 to 20 months of age, when babies use language to aid memory.

Try to remember experiences that occurred during the first three years of your life. Few people, if any, can do this. The inability to recall events that occurred very early in life is called **infantile amnesia**. Why do we remember so little from our earliest years? Initial research on this question suggested that young infants need repeated exposure to ensure memory that lasts for even a few days. In one study, mothers repeated phrases to their 2-week-old infants sixty times a day for two weeks. After over 800 exposures, infants remembered the information for almost two days (Ungerer, Brody, & Zelazo, 1978). If it takes this many exposures to learn something for two days, it is no wonder that we remember so few childhood experiences! Encouraging them to reenact events or parts of events, though, can remind very young children of past experiences and inoculate them against forgetting these experiences over long periods of time (Hudson & Sheffield, 1998).

Research has shown that memory is improved when the procedures are more familiar to children. Consider 6-month-old Yi Ling, who participates in an experiment in which one end of a ribbon is tied to her leg and the other end to an interesting mobile above the crib. After five minutes, Yi Ling recognizes the contingency: when she kicks, the mobile turns (Rovee-Collier & Fagen, 1981). Two weeks later, Yi Ling returns to the laboratory, and the mobile-and-string set-up is tried again. Will Yi Ling remember that kicking her foot makes the mobile move? Unlike many of the testing situations used in early research to assess infants' long-term memory, this situation closely resembles her everyday experiences, and she remembers the contingency.

When infants are placed in familiar situations and are motivated to remember, they learn with less repetition (or fewer exposures) and remember for longer periods of time. For instance, in a series of studies, 2- and 3-month-old infants were trained in two nine-minute sessions to learn the contingency that leg-kicking will make a mobile turn. When their memories were tested within one or two weeks of learning the contingency, most babies remembered it, but the longer the time between learning and testing, the less likely they were to remember. Generally, 2-month-old infants remembered the contingency when tested one week after learning it. The 3 month old infants remembered it

infantile amnesia inability to recall events that occurred very early in life

Do Infants Display Memories for Gender-Typed Behavior?

Nicholas, a 25-month-old toddler, watched intently as an adult showed him how to "diaper a bear" by putting a teddy bear on a diaper, wiping the bear, shaking on powder, and then folding the diaper on the bear. Then the adult showed Nicholas how to shave a teddy bear by squirting shaving cream onto the hand, rubbing the cream on the bear's face, shaving the bear (using a toy razor), and wiping the bear's face. Two weeks later, Nicholas and other toddlers of both sexes who had been shown these sequences (and several others) were brought back to the laboratory. The experimenter brought out the diapering props and later the shaving props and gave them to Nicholas. Would Nicholas be able to remember both sequences of events and imitate them after the two-week delay?

The research question in this study was whether children would remember as much about "gender-inconsistent" sequences as about "gender-consistent" ones. Gender-consistent sequences are those that fit the stereotypic expectations for the child's sex; gender inconsistent sequences are those that fit the stereotypic expectations for the other sex. In the United States, most people believe that face shaving is a masculine activity and diapering a feminine one. Of course, both men and women shave and can diaper babies, but children may still develop stereotypic beliefs about these activities. If they do, will it influence the activities they choose to engage in? Will Nicholas be as likely to remember how to diaper the bear as how to shave the bear?

Cognitive theories about gender development propose that once children realize they are boys or girls, they begin to pay attention to and remember information that fits the expectations for their own sex (Martin & Halverson, 1981). Because memory is difficult to test in infants and toddlers, until recently no studies had assessed memories for gender-consistent and -inconsistent information. In 1993, Patricia Bauer used the method described above to investigate toddlers' memories for gender-consistent and gender-inconsistent sequences. Bauer used an elicited imitation task in which toddlers watched an adult perform a series of sequentially ordered events using props. Immediately after watching the events, the toddlers were asked to repeat the sequence using the props. Some time later, the toddlers were given the props again and watched to ascertain whether they would spontaneously use the props to act out the sequence of events.

The children in Bauer's study were equally likely to imitate the masculine and feminine actions immediately after they were presented. After a two-week delay, however, a different pattern was found: boys selectively remembered masculine events better than feminine events, whereas girls showed similar memories for both events. In other words, the boys remembered how to shave a teddy bear better than how to diaper the bear.

Why would boys remember these events differently? The diapering and shaving events involved similar props—teddy bears and washcloths—so it was not the props that made a difference in memory. The boys must have decided that shaving was a masculine activity and therefore an activity that they could engage in, but that diapering was a feminine activity that they should not engage in. Additional support for this conclusion came from the boys' behavior during testing: two of the ten boys refused to interact with the props for the feminine sequences, and a third boy acted out shaving when he was given the props for diapering!

Thinking It Through:

1. How do very young children learn their sex? Do you think parents label children's sex for them?

2. How do very young children learn stereotypic expectations? Do you think all of the boys had watched their fathers shave? What about boys who do not have a man living in the house?

3. Do you think the boys chose shaving because it was a more fun activity? What did Bauer do to minimize this possibility when she designed the study?

two weeks later, but after that time they acted as though they had never seen the mobile (Rovee-Collier, Enright, Lucas, Fagen, & Gekoski, 1981). Other studies show that older infants, like Yi Ling (6 months), can remember the contingency up to seven weeks later when reminders are given (Rovee-Collier & Shyi, 1992).

Infants, like all learners, remember best when the testing conditions are similar to the original learning situation. Thus, infants' memories are context-bound—that is, strongly tied to situational cues. The importance of situational cues in infant memory has been confirmed by another series of leg-kicking studies. In these studies, some infants were shown a reminder (a moving mobile) on day 13 after they first learned the kicking contingency—one day before they were likely to completely forget it. The "reminded" infants remembered the contingency better the next day than infants who had not been reminded about their earlier learning or those who had been shown only a still mobile or a ribbon (Hayne & Rovee-Collier, 1995). Similarly, when infants were tested in an environment that differed from the one in which learning took place, such as a crib with a different colored bumper, they were less likely to remember the contingency than when tested in the same environment (Butler & Rovee-Collier, 1989; Hayne, Rovee-Collier, & Perris, 1987).

Deferred imitation, in which there is a delay between seeing an action and imitating it (see Chapter 4), provides evidence of infants' long-term memory, because it requires that the infant have a way of representing an observed action in memory and recalling it. A child who watches her father make cookies and the next day pretends to make cookies is showing that she remembered the previous day's cookie-making actions. Research indicates that infant's abilities to engage in deferred imitation improve during their first two years. Infants from 11 to 20 months old show deferred imitation of novel actions for up to twelve months (Meltzoff, 1995).

Longitudinal studies support the finding that infants are capable of long-term memory. In one study, 6-month-old infants were trained to reach for a toy whenever it made a noise. The training took place in a laboratory room under two situations—with the lights on and with the lights off. Two years later, the same children and other children serving as a control group were asked if they remembered being in the earlier study. None of them did. Some of the children were reminded of the earlier study by being shown the toys that had been used. Then, while sitting with their mothers, the children were tested in the dark and in the light to see whether they would reach for the toy that made the sound, as they had done two years before. The children who had participated in the earlier study were much more likely than the other children to reach for the toy (Perris, Myers, & Clifton, 1990).

This study shows that unusual situations may be memorable to young children for a long period of time, especially when the events are novel and involve smells, sounds, and movements. Infantile amnesia may occur because adults are seldom in the same situations as they were when infants, because adults and infants represent information differently, and because brain development and cognitive abilities are different for adults and infants (Hayne & Rovee-Collier, 1995; Schneider & Bjorklund, 1998).

HOW DO COGNITIVE ABILITIES DEVELOP DURING THE SENSORIMOTOR PERIOD?

Important changes occur in purposeful behavior during infancy. At 2 months, infants do not reach out to grab a rattle, but by 18 months, they experiment with problem solving. During the first two years of life, infants move from narrow and repetitive reflex actions to the flexible use of symbols to represent objects and people. During this time, infants and toddlers also come to recognize that other people and objects are separate from themselves. At 8 to 12 months, infants begin to show the first signs of truly intelligent behavior; for example, they plan and try out different actions to obtain a goal. According to Piaget, these changes characterize the first period of cognitive development: the *sensorimotor period* (see Chapter 2). Piaget described the rapid changes that infants and toddlers undergo in terms of six stages (Piaget, 1936/1963). Each stage builds on the skills acquired in the previous ones (see Table 5.2).

TABLE 5.2
Stages in the Sensorimotor Period

STAGE	AGE	CHARACTERISTICS
Stage I	Birth to one month	Practices reflex actions
Stage II	1 to 4 months	Engages in primary circular reactions—repetitive actions centered on the infant's body
Stage III	4 to 8 months	Uses visually guided reaching for greater exploration Engages in secondary circular reactions—repetitive actions centered on objects
Stage IV	8 to 12 months	Shows first signs of intelligence by using intentional behavior to solve problems
Stage V	12 to 18 months	Engages in tertiary circular reactions—modified repetitive actions designed to explore qualities of objects
Stage VI	18 to 24 months	Achieves greater flexibility in problem solving by using symbols to represent objects

STAGE I: USING REFLEXIVE SCHEMES (BIRTH TO 1 MONTH)

In stage I, neonates spend their time using the reflexive behaviors that they were able to perform at birth. As you learned in Chapter 4, many neonatal reflexes, such as grasping, looking, and sucking, help them survive. Piaget viewed these reflexes as the basic schemes, called *sensorimotor schemes*, that provide children with ways to interact with and know about the world around them. Infants' first knowledge of the world is derived from these schemes. For example, through their experiences in applying their "sucking" scheme, infants come to know the shape of a nipple. By grasping a toy, infants come to know its shape. In Piagetian terms, infants assimilate information by using schemes.

Although sensorimotor schemes are repetitive and automatic behaviors, they are not applied rigidly: infants make them fit the situation, such as by changing the shape of their lips to fit around a differently shaped nipple. According to Piaget, infants accommodate their schemes to meet the demands of different situations. At this point, however, infants' behavior is not purposeful—they do not have goals in mind while exercising reflex actions.

STAGE II: EXPLORING MOVEMENTS OF THE BODY (1 TO 4 MONTHS)

In stage II, infants act somewhat more purposefully. By 2 to 3 months, many infants recognize that their actions have specific effects, as seen in the foot-kicking studies described earlier. They discover these effects through repetitive actions, which Piaget described as primary circular reactions. **Primary circular reactions** are repetitive actions that are centered on an infant's own body and motions. These actions, such as thumb-sucking, first occur accidentally, but infants find them pleasurable and so continue the actions. For example, Piaget described how his son Laurent began sucking his thumb. Laurent's hand accidentally landed near his mouth while he was being held. Seeing this interesting object, Laurent tried to suck on it, but his arm slipped away. After many tries, Laurent moved his arm so that his thumb was near his mouth, and he began sucking his thumb (Piaget, 1936/1963).

STAGE III: EXPLORING OBJECTS (4 TO 8 MONTHS)

At around 4 months, stage III infants begin to combine primary circular reactions into more coordinated patterns. For instance, they coordinate schemes so that they can

primary circular reactions
repetitive actions that are centered on an infant's own body and motions

grasp objects they see. To do this, infants must make the connection among what they see, the movements of their arms, and the movements of their hands. The coordination of vision and movement schemes allows infants much more flexibility to explore.

During a meal, 7-month-old Noah drops a spoon off the edge of his tray onto the floor. He finds the sound interesting, so he repeats this action each time his mother puts the spoon back on his tray. Noah's behavior indicates that he is exploring the qualities of objects—in this case, the spoon. Noah, like other stage III infants, demonstrates that he can use a new type of circular reaction, called a secondary circular reaction. **Secondary circular reactions** are repetitive actions focused on the qualities of objects, such as the noises they make or their shapes and colors. Like primary circular reactions, these reactions begin accidentally, but through them infants explore the characteristics of objects rather than those of their own body. The sound a spoon makes when it hits the floor or the sound a plastic duck makes when squeezed becomes the focus of attention, and infants will repeat the action time and time again to reproduce this interesting property.

Infants in this stage want to make appealing sights and sounds continue. Piaget (1936/1963) describes how, at 7 months, his son Laurent used all his skills to make an interesting event happen again. After watching his father drum on a tin box, Laurent turned toward the box, shook his arm in front of the box, and shook his head, trying out all of his movements to make the phenomenon reoccur.

These actions illustrate how infants become goal-oriented and more tuned in to their environments as they mature cognitively. Because of these changes, everyday activities become increasingly challenging and interesting. The highly repetitive, structured, and predictable games that caregivers and infants often engage in during feeding, bathing, and diapering provide infants with opportunities to learn contingencies and elicit smiles of obvious pleasure. In turn, caregivers respond positively to the increased pleasure displayed by infants, creating a mutually rewarding context for interactions.

STAGE IV: ACTIVE PROBLEM SOLVING (8 TO 12 MONTHS)

According to Piaget, infants in stage IV show the first signs of intelligence, marked by the intentional application of schemes to reach a goal. Like stage III infants, stage IV infants use familiar schemes, but they are now purposeful in applying those schemes. Older infants set out to accomplish a task and often have a goal in mind before starting an action. One indication of purposeful behavior in infants is the desire to complete activities they begin. Unlike a younger infant, who might be easily distracted by other interesting objects, an infant in stage IV who fails to accomplish his or her task is likely to be upset. For instance, 10-month-old Stacie becomes upset after her father picks her up and moves her away from the cat she is trying to catch. A few months earlier, Stacie would have been easily distracted by this movement and would have happily lost interest in the cat. Unfortunately for the cat, Stacie now has a pre-set goal, and her actions are based on achieving this goal.

STAGE V: CREATIVE PROBLEM SOLVING (12 TO 18 MONTHS)

Infants in stage V are creative problem solvers. For the first time, they are capable of applying entirely new strategies to solve problems rather than simply using combinations of previously learned schemes. Infants' creativity during this stage stems from their use of **tertiary circular reactions,** in which infants systematically modify their behaviors in subtle ways to explore the effects of those modifications. Noah, who earlier dropped a spoon off his high chair to explore the qualities of the spoon, begins to explore these qualities in a new way as he grows older. He now experiments with different trajectories of the spoon: dropping it, throwing it gently, and flinging it across the room. Noah acts as a budding scientist, interested in finding out how variations in his behavior influence the qualities of the spoon. Now he might squeeze a toy duck to make it quack, then sit on it, and finally bite it to find out what happens.

secondary circular reactions repetitive actions focused on the qualities of objects, such as the noises they make or their shapes and colors

tertiary circular reactions subtle modifications infants make in their behavior so as to explore the effects of those modifications

The ability to conduct tertiary circular actions provides children with the means to learn from their actions. Because stage V infants are capable of trying many ways to solve a problem, they are more likely to hit upon a successful solution than are younger infants who use more rigidly applied schemes.

STAGE VI: USING SYMBOLS TO REPRESENT REALITY (18 TO 24 MONTHS)

After 18 months of age, toddlers develop a new and important ability that changes the way they approach and solve problems. Stage VI toddlers begin to use mental symbols to represent objects, called **symbolic representation**. They no longer need to act out a sequence of events to discover the outcome—they can imagine the actions beforehand. Thus, problem solving now can take place inside the child's mind before he or she takes any action.

Piaget described how his daughter Lucienne solved a problem using mental symbols. Piaget inserted a metal chain into a matchbox and then handed the matchbox to Lucienne. The matchbox was left partially open, and Lucienne began exploring the box by turning it over. She then tried to grasp the chain through the opening. When those actions were unsuccessful, she tried a new way to solve the problem: she inserted her index finger into the opening, grabbed a small part of the chain, and then pulled the whole chain out. Piaget then repeated this experiment, this time leaving a smaller opening in the matchbox. Lucienne tried to solve the problem the same way she did before, but this time her solution did not work because the opening was too small. She then paused and seemed to think about how to solve the problem. During this pause, Piaget noticed that Lucienne was opening her mouth, at first a little and then wider and wider. This indicated to him that Lucienne recognized that she needed to increase the size of the opening in the matchbox so that her finger would fit in it. Lucienne then used her finger to widen the opening and successfully applied her previous scheme of grasping the chain. She did not have to try many different actions before finding a solution; Lucienne "thought" through the problem, using symbols for the object and actions, and decided which actions were most likely to be successful.

Stage VI toddlers thus rely less on motor actions and more on symbols for solving many everyday problems. With their increased use of symbols, toddlers are more capable than infants of thinking about the past and future, thinking about problems quickly and flexibly, and remembering actions to use in new situations.

INFANTS' UNDERSTANDING OF THE PERMANENCE OF OBJECTS

There was that first long stage when she didn't pick anything up at all, and everything had to be handed to her. . . . Now it's different. If she is playing with a toy, and it slips out of her hand, she will follow it with her eyes; we can see her wondering what has become of it. A month ago it would have stayed on the floor, no longer a part of her consciousness; now, most of the time, she will return to it and pick it up again. She understands that even though it's out of her hand for the moment, it's still a part of her world.

—BOB GREENE'S JOURNAL ENTRY ABOUT
AMANDA AT 8 MONTHS (1984, P. 229)

Knowing that people and objects have an independent existence beyond one's own perception of them is called understanding **object permanence**. Infants are not born with an understanding of object permanence; they have no idea that objects or people continue to exist outside of their own perception of them. When Bob Greene's daughter was younger, she did not bother to look for objects she dropped because they were no longer part of her consciousness. This lack of understanding of object permanence extends to infants' bodies: they are unaware that the objects flying in front of their face are their own arms and hands.

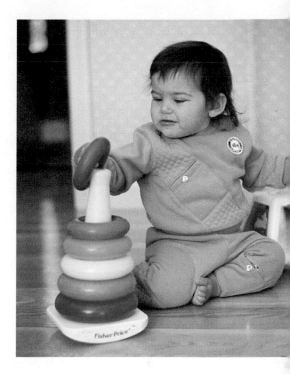

How do infants explore the qualities of objects during play? Why is play so important for cognitive development?

symbolic representation the use of mental symbols to represent objects

object permanence the concept that people and objects have an independent existence beyond one's own perception of them

Over the first two years of life, infants gradually develop an understanding of object permanence by coming to realize that objects have form and depth and that they are solid. Toward the end of the sensorimotor period, infants become capable of acting on that knowledge by actively searching for objects that have disappeared.

Searching for Hidden Objects

Piaget assumed that an important indicator of infants' understanding of object permanence was whether they tried to find a hidden object. Based on the studies he conducted on infants' searching strategies, Piaget outlined how infants develop an understanding of object permanence and how this understanding relates to the stages of sensorimotor cognitive development.

In stages I and II (0 to 4 months), infants show no evidence of realizing the independent existence of objects. An infant who drops a rattle outside her or his field of vision will not cry in frustration or even look for the toy. If someone covers a toy with a cloth while a stage I or II infant watches, the infant does not try to uncover it; as far as the infant is concerned, the toy has disappeared.

In stage III (4 to 8 months), infants search for an object that is partially in view but not one that is completely hidden. Because infants at this age do not search for hidden objects, Piaget suggested that they still do not realize the permanence of objects.

Infants' behavior during stage IV (8 to 12 months) is puzzling and intriguing. They show some understanding of object permanence, but their understanding is far from complete. Vonnie's mother hides a doll under a washcloth several times, and Vonnie finds it. Then, Vonnie watches her mother hide the doll under a washcloth and, from there, under a blanket. Where will Vonnie look for the doll? You might guess that she would look under the blanket, assuming that the last hiding place is the best bet for finding the toy. Stage IV infants, however, show a surprising pattern: they look in the first place the object was hidden. Thus, Vonnie looks under the washcloth. The tendency to search in the first hiding place (A) while ignoring the second (B) is called the **A-not-B error.**

Why would an infant like Vonnie search in the first hiding spot? This question has intrigued researchers for years. According to Piaget, infants remember the object as an "object + action"—that is, the object takes on the characteristics of the action performed on it. In this case, the doll becomes doll-under-a-washcloth, and an infant with this concept is unlikely to search for doll-under-a-washcloth by looking under a blanket. Research shows that this error may be due to infants' inability to inhibit actions they have performed before (such as searching in the A hiding place) until a certain level of brain development has occurred (Diamond, 1991).

By the time they reach stage V, infants are capable of searching for hidden objects that have been moved several times. The only limit to their understanding is that they must see each movement of the object to be able to find it. By 18 months, stage VI toddlers have overcome this limitation and have a fully developed concept of object permanence. They now can follow multiple movements of objects, even when the movements cannot be seen. For instance, when Sean watches his mother place a toy cow in a plastic cup and then place the plastic cup under a blanket, he still knows where the cow is. Although Sean does not see that the cow is hidden under the blanket, he infers that the cow continues to exist even though it is hidden in the cup and then infers that the cow must still be wherever the cup is, which in this case is under the blanket.

Remembering the Location of Hidden Objects

The search task requires that infants coordinate several schemes, including their vision and reaching schemes, to find a hidden object. Maybe infants younger than 18 months understand object permanence but cannot master the coordination of schemes well enough to demonstrate what they understand. The issue of children's *performance versus competence* is a recurring one in developmental research. Researchers often have to infer what infants or children know from what they do; if their actions are limited,

A-not-B error infants' tendency to search in the first hiding spot (A) while ignoring the second (B)

inferences about their knowledge may be inaccurate. A solution to this problem is to simplify the tasks that infants and children are asked to perform. Rather than having infants search for hidden objects, an alternative approach is to examine their visual attention to different objects. Remember that infants pay more attention to surprising and novel experiences than to familiar ones. Based on this preference, researchers have devised clever visual attention studies that allow them to assess infants' understanding of objects without the performance demands involved in Piaget's search studies.

In one of these studies (Baillargeon & Graber, 1988), 7- to 8-month-old infants were shown objects that appeared and disappeared. During one of these presentations, however, the sequence of events was "impossible." As depicted in Figure 5.3, infants first saw an object located on one of two placemats. Next, a screen was pushed in front of each placemat, hiding the object from the infants' view. Fifteen seconds later, a hand reached behind one of the two screens and pulled out the object. For one event, the object was pulled from behind the screen that covered the placemat on which the infant had seen the object—the "possible sequence." For the other event, the object was pulled out from behind the screen that had *not* hidden the object—the "impossible sequence." Infants stared longer at, and were more surprised by, the impossible sequence than the possible one. This result indicates that the infants remembered the location of the hidden object and were surprised when it was not where it was supposed to be.

FIGURE 5.3
Baillargeon and Graber's Possible and Impossible Events

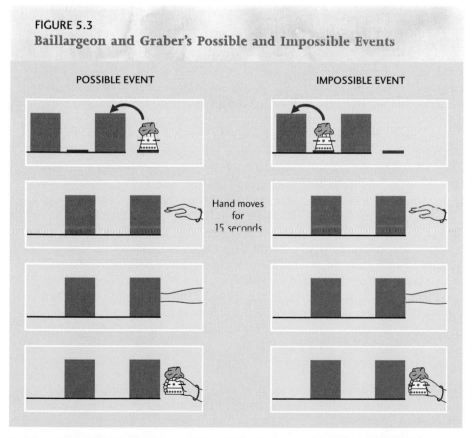

SOURCE: Baillargeon and Graber, 1988. Copyright © 1988 by the American Psychological Association. Adapted with permission.

Infants in this study were shown possible and impossible events to determine whether they had an understanding of object permanence. In the possible event, the screen on the right covers the object, and a hand reaches behind the screen and removes the object. In the impossible event, the screen on the left covers the object, but the hand reaches behind the screen on the right and removes the object. Infants were surprised by and paid more attention to the impossible event. How can we use this reaction to determine what infants know?

TABLE 5.3
Stages in Understanding of Object Permanence

STAGE	AGE	KNOWLEDGE	ACTION OR LIMITATION
Stages I & II	0 to 4 months	Loses awareness of objects when they disappear By 3 to 4 months, understands inertia and gravity	Loses interest and does not search
Stage III	4 to 8 months	Recognizes continued existence of hidden objects Understands solidity of objects	Cannot find completely hidden objects
Stage IV	8 to 12 months	Remembers last location of a hidden object	Shows A-not-B error—will search for object in the first hiding place but not the second
Stages V & VI	12 to 24 months	Coordinates knowledge and performance Recognizes complex hiding patterns	Can search for and find hidden objects, even if they are hidden in two places

By using simplified methods, researchers have found evidence of object permanence in even younger infants (Haith & Benson, 1998; Munakata, McClelland, Johnson, & Siegler, 1997). Additionally, 5-month-old infants were more surprised and paid more attention when a wall appeared to move *through* a solid object than when the wall stopped upon coming into contact with the object (Baillargeon, Spelke, & Wasserman, 1985). Other studies have shown that 3- and 4-month-old infants understand basic principles of objects and motions, such as gravity and inertia (Spelke, Breinlinger, Macomber, & Jacobson, 1992). These studies suggest that, very early in life, children develop basic concepts about the world that are then expanded and elaborated later in development (see Table 5.3). Piaget, however, was accurate in describing how infants act on objects around them. By 6 to 12 months, infants begin to demonstrate in their actions what they know about objects (Goubet & Clifton, 1998). This change is likely due to development of the frontal cortex of the brain (Diamond, 1991). It is not until the end of their second year, however, that infants can completely integrate their knowledge of objects with their actions (Small, 1990).

Thousands of studies have tested Piaget's ideas about cognitive development. Although much of his work has been substantiated, some findings have led to conclusions different from those Piaget originally suggested. For example, infants' abilities are more variable and context-dependent than Piaget initially proposed. Also, as you have seen, infants' understanding of object permanence is more complex and cumulative than Piaget thought.

INFANTS' UNDERSTANDING OF NUMBER CONCEPTS

Infants' cognitive accomplishments include more than problem solving and understanding objects. Research has demonstrated something few people thought possible: infants have a basic understanding of the concept of number. Wynn (1992) used a version of the possible-impossible event procedure to explore infants' understanding of numbers. After being habituated to displays of one or two items, one group of 5-month-old infants watched an "addition situation," in which one object was added to another, and another group watched a "subtraction situation," in which one of two objects was removed (see Figure 5.4). In both situations, one outcome was a possible event and one was impossible. In the addition situation, for instance, a screen was lifted to hide one Mickey Mouse doll. Infants then saw a hand place another identical mouse doll behind

FIGURE 5.4
Wynn's Possible and Impossible Events

SEQUENCE OF EVENTS: 1 + 1 = 1 OR 2

1. Object placed in case
2. Screen comes up
3. Second object added
4. Hand leaves empty

THEN EITHER:

(a) Possible Outcome   OR   (b) Impossible Outcome

5. Screen drops . . .
6. revealing 2 objects
7. Screen drops . . .
8. revealing 1 object

SEQUENCE OF EVENTS: 2 − 1 = 1 OR 2

1. Objects placed in case
2. Screen comes up
3. Empty hand enters
4. One object is removed

THEN EITHER:

(a) Possible Outcome   OR   (b) Impossible Outcome

5. Screen drops . . .
6. revealing 1 object
7. Screen drops . . .
8. revealing 2 objects

SOURCE: Wynn, 1992.
To test their understanding of addition and subtraction, Wynn showed infants possible events (1 + 1 = 2; 2 − 1 = 1) and impossible events (1 + 1 = 1; 2 − 1 = 2). In both cases, the infant paid more attention to the impossible event. Do you think that infants can subtract and add? If so, how else might these accomplishments be tested? If not, how do you explain Wynn's results?

the screen. In the possible event, the screen dropped to reveal two dolls (1 + 1 = 2). In the impossible version, the screen dropped to reveal only one doll (1 + 1 = 1). Infants spent more time looking at the impossible event; that is, they stared longer at 1 + 1 = 1 than at 1 + 1 = 2. These findings suggest that even 5-month-old infants have a basic understanding of addition and subtraction. However, infants may simply have basic visual concepts of what a small number of objects looks like and exhibit surprise when objects do not match these expectations (Haith & Benson, 1998).

PERCEPTION AND EARLY COGNITIVE DEVELOPMENT

Piaget theorized that infants form concepts from their direct experience with objects. Other researchers, however, believe that infants may develop basic concepts about the world around them from perceptual knowledge alone (Mandler, 1992). According to this view, infants' early concepts come from their perceptions of objects rather than their direct physical actions on them.

Infants as young as 6 months spend a great deal of time looking back and forth between two new objects, as if they are contemplating similarities and differences between them (Ruff, 1986). This visual scrutiny increases as they grow older (Mandler, 1990). What are infants doing during these intense visual inspections of objects? Mandler believes that infants may be comparing similarities and differences between objects and forming **image schemas**—primitive notions, based on the visual appearance of objects, that lay a foundation for thinking about them. For instance, infants may have an up-down schema, a container schema, and a part-whole schema. A container schema has an interior, an exterior, and a boundary; infants with a container schema understand that containers hold things and are surprised if they do not. Infants may use image schemas to develop perception-based concepts that help them quickly learn about the world without requiring actions on their part.

THE SOCIAL CONTEXTS OF EARLY LEARNING AND COGNITIVE DEVELOPMENT

Much of infants' knowledge of the world is gained through their many daily interactions with others, particularly caregivers. The Russian scientist Lev Vygotsky believed that social interactions are essential for learning and that infants develop cognitive skills through interactions with others more skilled than themselves (Vygotsky, 1978). Older children and adults serve as role models for thinking, provide stimulating environments for children, and encourage children's learning by guiding them to solutions.

In Vygotsky's view, children develop their cognitive abilities though socially mediated learning. As you learned in Chapter 2, Vygotsky used the concept of the *zone of proximal development* to represent the range in learning that a child is capable of with help from more skilled and experienced partners (Rogoff, 1990). Through interactions with skilled partners, children expand their cognitive competencies.

Children's cognitive development is influenced by daily interactions within a cultural community (Rogoff, 1990). Parents and other adults in the community involve children in guided participation in everyday activities, which become the context for an "apprenticeship in thinking." Through these apprenticeships, children learn about their own culture and develop enhanced cognitive skills. Adults from all over the world use many of the same methods to guide their children's participation in daily events.

Caregivers provide structure and support for children's thinking through informal teaching methods, called **scaffolding**. Just as steel and wooden scaffolding provides the support needed to construct a building, caregivers' cognitive scaffolding provides the support children need to extend their current skills to a higher level of competence. The type of scaffolding used by caregivers changes as infants' understanding increases, and it varies according to the caregiver's preferences (Bruner, 1983). For instance, caregivers often help infants interpret situations through their actions, emotions, and tone of voice. With older children, some mothers prefer a social style of scaffolding in which they draw attention to themselves ("watch me do it"), whereas other mothers use an activity-oriented method in which they draw attention to objects or events ("find the piece of the puzzle that matches the color of the one next to it") (Bornstein & Tamis-LeMonda, 1990).

Mothers and fathers are equally effective in their ability to supply scaffolding for their children's emerging skills (Connor, Knight, & Cross, 1997), and they begin these interactions soon after the child's birth. By 2 months of age, infants already have developed a

image schemas primitive notions, based on the visual appearance of objects, that lay a foundation for thinking about them

scaffolding informal teaching methods that guide children's participation in daily events basic understanding of what patterns to expect in these interactions. In one study (Murray & Trevarthen, 1986), mothers and their 2-month-old infants were videotaped, and the babies were given the chance to watch the live interactions with their mothers on a video monitor. The babies responded positively by making eye contact and moving their mouths. When the live video was replaced with a taped replay of their mothers' reactions in a former exchange, the babies were distressed and looked away. Although the mothers were responding as they had before, their responses were not contingent on their infants' actions—they were not in synchrony—and this was distressing to the babies.

Like synchrony, joint attention between "teacher" and "learner" facilitates cognitive development. Because they share a focus of attention, caregivers and infants have a common ground for interpreting and understanding interactions (Rogoff, 1998). By about 6 months, infants and their caregivers begin to share and negotiate learning tasks during play. Ten- to 12-month-old infants and their caregivers work out the details of interactions quite well and are well practiced in their routine interactions (Corkum & Moore, 1998; Rogoff, 1990). The ability of parents to successfully engage their children in joint attention on a task influences their children's later cognitive development. Toddlers whose mothers engage them in effective joint attention at 6 and 12 months have comparatively higher IQs (Hunter, McCarthy, MacTurk, & Vietze, 1987). In general, caregivers who are responsive and sensitive to their children's interactions encourage cognitive development (Bornstein & Tamis-LeMonda, 1997).

THE CULTURAL CONTEXTS OF EARLY LEARNING AND COGNITIVE DEVELOPMENT

Do caregivers all over the world use scaffolding to encourage their children's cognitive development? To answer this question, Rogoff and colleagues (Rogoff, Mistry, Goncu, & Mosier, 1993) examined the use of scaffolding by middle-class parents in cities in Utah and Turkey and by parents in small communities in India and Guatemala. In all four communities, the two parents and their children jointly took part in structuring learning situations.

Striking cultural variations in the use of scaffolding were found. In Utah and Turkey, parents were more likely to provide verbal instructions and activity lessons that were removed from the ordinary context of adult life. For instance, parents in these communities interacted with their children around toys and games but did not take their toddlers into their workplaces. In India and Guatemala, however, children were less likely to receive direct instruction during play but were more likely to be observant of, and take primary responsibility for, learning and participating in adult activities. These differences relate to the expectations and demands of the children's communities. In communities in which children spend most time with their parents, children are expected to learn the specific economic skills of their parents, such as weaving, and their training involves watching and participating in these activities. In other communities in which children spend less time with their parents, children are expected to learn varied skills and to spend years in school. The focus is on motivating children to learn through praise and verbal instruction. Both methods of scaffolding produce the desired result of socializing children to become effective members of the community in which they are raised (Rogoff et al., 1993).

HOW DO INFANTS AND TODDLERS DEVELOP LANGUAGE SKILLS?

We talk to her all the time. I will come home at the end of the day, and I will say, "Well! Amanda Sue Greene! What have you been doing all day?" . . . In a way, this all seems useless. . . . On the other hand . . . I keep thinking that all of these words are going to her brain, and that something must be happening there. It's not happening yet; but of all the words we speak to her, some of them must be sticking. . . . When she does learn to talk, though, it will be because of these nonstop, one-way conversations we have with her.

—BOB GREENE'S JOURNAL ENTRY ABOUT
AMANDA AT AGE 5½ MONTHS
(1984, P. 180)

Language is a social tool consisting of a complex set of rules for using symbols (Owens, 1996). With a limited number of words, we can generate an infinite number of different messages. Thus, language is creative and flexible, and children show evidence of this when they generate words to say things they probably have never heard. For example, when 24-month-old Brandon experienced his first snowfall, he referred to it as "milk rain"—generating his own unique description of the event. Language also can be used to refer to events that happened in the past or to describe future events.

Infants are exposed to language during social interactions, even before they understand what individual words mean. When adults carry on a conversation in front of a young infant, the infant is likely to hear them speaking around 150 words a minute, making 12 to 30 sounds per second (Lieberman, 1984). From these exchanges, infants learn to recognize speech sounds, words, and what words mean. Before they even utter a word, children practice many skills that relate to mastering language. During the first year, infants' language production consists of cooing, babbling, and gesturing—using sounds and motions to communicate their desires. In the second year, the range and flexibility of infants' language abilities expand rapidly as they begin to use their first words and phrases to express themselves. By the time they are 5 years old, most children are competent speakers of their native language.

To become speakers of a language, children must be able to master four language-related domains (Gleason, 1993):

+ **Distinguish sounds and sound patterns.**   A child who is a competent speaker of a language recognizes and distinguishes the basic sounds of that language, or **phonemes.** In English, phonemes include the /sh/ sound, which is distinct from the /s/ sound. Competence in language also involves being able to produce these sounds so that others can understand them.

+ **Learn the meanings of words.**   **Semantics** refers to the meanings associated with words. Children accomplish an amazing feat when they learn how to use cues from others and from the environment to make sense of a sound and associate it with a particular word.

+ **Learn to put words together.**   **Syntax** is the grammar, or rules, of a language. Competent speakers of English realize that "I store am going" is not a grammatical sentence. As part of mastering their language, children must learn to arrange words in meaningful order and use the parts of speech as prescribed by the rules of the language.

+ **Learn to use language in a social context.**   **Pragmatics** refers to the practical rules guiding the use of verbal and nonverbal communication in differing situations. A child who commands his grandmother to take him to the playground has not yet learned that in this situation the polite use of language is more likely to bring success than a command is. To become competent speakers, children must learn the rules of using language with others, such as waiting for pauses in conversations to speak and taking turns in a discussion.

phonemes the sounds of a language that are the basis for word construction

semantics the meanings associated with words

syntax the grammar, or rules, of a language

pragmatics the practical rules guiding the use of verbal and nonverbal communication in differing situations

BEFORE THE FIRST WORDS

Infants are actively engaged in learning language. Before they utter words, infants must become proficient in distinguishing and producing the sounds of their native language, and they need to identify individual words and their meanings from the streams of sounds they hear spoken around them.

Distinguishing the Sounds of Speech

Children must be able to discriminate the sounds of language before they can put sounds together in a meaningful way. Each language uses a subset of the 100 to 150 possible phonemes; for instance, English uses about forty-five phonemes (Owens, 1996). Languages differ in terms of the number and types of phonemes they contain (Menyuk, 1988).

Because each language involves only some of the sounds that are possible, scientists have asked whether infants learn to hear only the sounds from their native language or have the ability to hear all sounds. Research has demonstrated a surprising pattern—newborns are able to discriminate and attend to the sounds from all languages, but by 10 months of age, infants no longer attend to phonemes unless the phonemes occur in the speech they hear every day (Werker & Tees, 1984). Infants therefore appear to have a sensitive period in which their capabilities are fine-tuned to the particular language (or languages) they are exposed to in early life (Best, 1995). The processes underlying this fine-tuning and the extent to which it occurs have yet to be determined (Aslin, Jusczyk, & Pisoni, 1998; Jusczyk, 1997).

Children also acquire **phonemic awareness**—knowledge of permissible and nonpermissible strings of sounds in their native language. For instance, English combines s + p in words such as *speak* and *spring* but not s + r. As they listen to the language around them, infants and toddlers are exposed to the many sound combinations of their native language (Menyuk, 1988). From this exposure, children learn the statistical regularities in speech—the sounds that occur together—and this helps them extract information about words and their boundaries (Saffran, Aslin, & Newport, 1996). Infants also achieve phonemic and semantic competence through their attention to the rhymes and rhythms of language. For example, *intonation*—rising and falling speech patterns—gives clues about meaning. Universally, adults tend to use exaggerated intonation and a higher pitch when speaking to infants. Caregivers use rising intonations when they want infants to pay attention to something (Fernald, 1989).

Producing the Sounds of Speech

By 2 months of age, many infants make their first noncrying sounds. They begin **cooing**, making soft, repetitive vowel sounds such as "aah" and "ooh." Around 6 months of age, infants begin to produce sounds combining consonants and vowels, such as "ba" and "da." Between 6 and 10 months of age, they begin **babbling,** repeating consonant-vowel combinations such as "mama" and "dada." Many caregivers interpret these babbles as words, but at this age infants do not associate these sounds with particular meanings.

Intentional Communication

Ten-month-old Ray looks at his father, points to a teddy bear, and grunts. The message is clear: he wants his father to hand him the teddy bear. Even before they utter a word, infants communicate their needs through gestures and vocalizations. As they grow older, children add verbal interactions as another way to communicate (Owens, 1996).

Infants' abilities to communicate develop in concert with their cognitive abilities and based on the responses they receive to their communication attempts. For instance, the cognitive ability to understand cause-and-effect relationships goes hand in hand with realizing that behavior can be used to achieve an effect or a goal. A 10-month-old infant understands cause and effect and uses gestures to communicate needs and desires. In response, caregivers demand more precise communication from their older infants: they expect them to communicate more directly, such as by pointing to objects.

phonemic awareness knowledge of permissible and nonpermissible strings of sounds in one's native language

cooing making soft, repetitive vowel sounds such as "aah" and "ooh"

babbling repeating consonant-vowel combinations, such as "mama" or "dada," two or more times

Can Babies Communicate Through Hand Signals?

Most 1-year-olds are limited in their ability to express their desires because they know only a few words. Does this mean that infants are unable to let their caregivers know when they are cold or what they want to eat? For most infants, these would be difficult messages to convey. Some babies, however, have learned how to communicate complex messages through the use of simple gestures, called *baby signs.*

Baby signing as an area of study arose from Linda Acredolo's experience with her 1-year-old daughter Kate, who began to sign for flowers by wrinkling her nose and sniffing. With encouragement, Kate learned twenty-nine signs in the next six months and became able to communicate many complex ideas. As she grew older and her verbal skills developed, she stopped using signs.

Because of her experience with Kate, Acredolo and her colleague, Susan Goodwyn, began a study of baby signs in 140 families. They found that children who used signs were helped in their language development rather than hindered, and that their parents responded more positively toward them because of their increased ability to communicate their needs to sleep or eat or have a book read to them. They also found that girls were more likely to develop signs than boys and that parent-child interactions were important in helping children to learn signs. By 16 to 18 months of age, children averaged about four signs that they used frequently (Acredolo & Goodwyn, 1988). Infants who use signs may be less frustrated because their needs can be addressed more quickly. For example, one child in the study who was afraid of dogs could easily signal this fear to parents and be comforted promptly.

Infants can be encouraged to use signs they invent themselves, or caregivers can teach signs to children. For instance, *noisy* can be represented by pointing a finger to the child's ear, *go out* by pretending to turn a doorknob, and *cold* by hugging the arms to the body (see the figure). Acredolo and Goodwyn recommend that caregivers start with a few simple physical signs, say the words as they make the signs, and repeat the signs often to increase likelihood of the child's using them (Acredolo & Goodwyn, 1996).

Thinking It Through:

1. Why might effective nonverbal communication benefit infants and toddlers and their relationships with parents?

2. How might effective nonverbal communication promote the development of language and thinking?

3. What signs and signals did you learn and use as a young child? What five signs would you regard as the most important to teach a baby?

Baby Signs

Drink/Bottle
Description:
Thumb to mouth, tilting up
Mimics a drinking motion
Possible Situations:
To request a bottle;
to request juice or water

Food/Eat
Description:
Fingertips to lips
Depicts putting food in mouth
Possible Situations:
To request something to eat;
to label food or someone eating

Sleep
Description:
Head tilted,
hands against cheek
Mimics head on pillow
Possible Situations:
Request to take a nap;
request to go to bed

SOURCE: Acredolo and Goodwyn, 1996.
Baby signs are often related to the activities and immediate needs of the infant. Many of the signs are made by performing the action to be communicated or by indicating a part of the body (for example, noisy might be indicated by pointing to the ear). Which signs do you think infants are most likely to use?

First Words

Children's understanding of language, called **receptive language,** precedes their ability to produce language, **expressive language**. For example, long before they can utter the word *cat*, infants respond to "Where's the cat?" by looking at the cat. Many children understand single words at around 8 to 9 months of age (Owens, 1996). This is most reliably demonstrated by their response to being called by their name or to being told "No!"

Although infants communicate through gestures and produce and respond to word-like sounds during the first year, they usually do not begin to say real words until they are about 12 months old (Bloom, 1998). Children's first attempts to speak real words are important because they signal that the child understands the symbolic significance of words. Speaking words is not an easy task. To produce a word, children must be able to recognize the sounds that make up the word and the order in which these sounds need to be produced. They must remember the sounds and integrate them into a smooth-flowing word.

First words usually are the names of common objects or people. The importance of children's social environment as a setting for language development is apparent: their first words often describe the important people and objects with which they are most familiar, such as *mama, dada,* names of pets, or names of categories (*hat, doggie*). For some children, first words include action words (*bye-bye, all gone*) and, of course, the word *no* (Bloom, 1994; Nelson, 1981).

The ability to say words indicates a remarkable increase in children's level of abstract thinking—they now understand the correspondence between a mental concept and the set of sounds (the word) that has been assigned to that mental concept (Woodward & Markman, 1998). In addition, their first words are packed with meaning. A child's first words are **holophrases,** individual words that convey as much meaning as sentences. For instance, a child is likely to say "doggie" to announce that the dog is entering the room or to convey her desire that the dog come play with her. *Doggie* means much more than simply "the dog."

Development of Vocabulary

Once children understand the sound-word connection (between 12 and 18 months), they add around three words per month to their vocabulary. After 18 to 24 months, a vocabulary explosion often occurs, in which children quickly acquire a large number of words at a rapid rate (Bates, O'Connell, & Shore, 1987; see Figure 5.5). They also begin to use words for social rituals, such as saying "bye-bye" (Gopnick, 1988) Around age 2, children include words that indicate an understanding of success ("hooray") and failure ("uh-oh") (Gopnick & Meltzoff, 1986). Because children's vocabularies are limited, they invent new words by, for instance, changing a noun to a verb. A child who sits in a rocker chair might say "Rocker me, mommy" (Clark, 1997).

First Sentences

At about 18 months, many children begin to produce sequences of words, usually separated by long pauses. By the end of the second year, these sequences give way to true sentences (Bloom, 1998). The shift from using holophrases to actually producing sentences marks another tremendous accomplishment of the toddler years. In true sentences, children do not randomly string words together. Instead, the order of the words represents their first application of grammar—the use of rules to convey meaning. Constructing sentences is taxing and requires much effort for young children; this probably explains why early sentences are produced haltingly and why children often repeat the same sentence over and over with only minor changes (Cartwright & Brent, 1997).

Two-word sentences contain the information that is available in each word as well as the information implied in the order of the words (Braine, 1963). Children's early sentences emphasize meaning and usually refer to actions or objects (Bloom, 1998). When

receptive language children's understanding of language

expressive language children's ability to produce language

holophrases individual words that convey as much meaning as whole sentences

FIGURE 5.5
Growth of Young Children's Vocabulary

NOTE: Data for 8 to 16 months and for 18 to 30 months came from different samples of children.
SOURCE: Fenson et al., 1994.
Notice that after children learn about fifty words, they tend to show a spurt in vocabulary learning. How do you think children learn so many words so quickly? What role do caregivers play in children's word learning?

discussing actions, children talk about who performs the action, where it is done, and the object used to perform the action. When discussing objects, children talk about the names and characteristics of the objects, their locations, and their ownership. A construction that children commonly use is an agent and its action, such as "daddy go" or "doggie bark." Examples of 2-year-olds' two-word sentences are shown in Table 5.4.

Children's earliest sentences are called **telegraphic speech** because they contain only the most essential and informative words and seldom include less informative words, such as *a*, *an*, or *the*. Telegraphic speech gradually becomes elaborated as children develop more sophisticated language skills.

How is children's language acquisition explained?

How do children so quickly and easily develop the skills needed to hear the sounds of a language and learn its rules? Many different explanations have been proposed. Some emphasize the special role of the human brain in interpreting language,

telegraphic speech early language in which only highly informative words are used and less informative words are neglected

TABLE 5.4

Examples of Children's Two-Word Sentences

SEMANTIC RELATION	ENGLISH	GERMAN	SAMOAN
agent–action	teddy fall	puppe kommt (doll comes)	pa'u pepe (fall doll)
action–object	hit ball	tur aufmachen (door open)	tapale 'oe (hit you)
possessor–possession	mama dress	mein ball (my ball)	lol a'u (candy my)
rejection–action	no wash	nicht blasen (not blow)	le 'ai (not eat)

SOURCE: *Adapted from de Villiers and de Villiers, 1992.*

whereas others emphasize the role of rewards for grammatical speech. To better understand the issues of language development, consider the case of Genie, a girl who was denied exposure to language, along with satisfaction of her other basic needs, during eleven years of her life.

One day in 1970, a slumped and disheveled child weighing approximately 60 pounds entered a welfare office in Los Angeles with her almost blind mother. What social workers thought might be an autistic child of 5 or 6 years turned out to be a 13-year-old who had been hidden away in a back room since the age of 2. Genie's father believed she was brain damaged and forced her to live virtually alone for her whole life. Genie's only contacts with humans were brief and unpleasant: her father would sometimes bark at her, but little was ever said to her directly. She was strapped into a crib at night and onto a potty chair for most of her days.

Genie was immediately removed from this horrible environment and admitted to a children's hospital. She was weak, unable to walk very well, and not toilet trained. Psychologists, social workers, linguists, and therapists all worked with Genie, trying to assess her capabilities and help her develop the social, emotional, and intellectual skills that should have been a natural part of her upbringing. In addition to her physical problems, Genie could not utter more than a few sounds. Would she be able to learn language and adapt to her new environment? The following sections explore the theoretical stances on language acquisition and how these theories might predict outcomes for Genie.

INNATE THEORIES: BIOLOGICAL INFLUENCES ON LANGUAGE ACQUISITION

Biological theories suggest that a special capacity for understanding language resides within the human brain. The dominant biological theory was proposed by Noam Chomsky (1965, 1986), who argued that children are born with a **language acquisition device (LAD)** in their brain that allows them to understand the properties—the universal grammar—of all human languages. The LAD acts as a guide, or blueprint, for recognizing language input and detects the regularities in language. Children develop a sense of universal grammar merely by being exposed to language.

Some indirect evidence in support of Chomsky's ideas comes from the similarities in the ways children all over the world acquire language. Scientific evidence supports Chomsky's assumptions about the importance of the brain in language acquisition. Although the LAD part of the brain has not been identified, people with various kinds of

language acquisition device (LAD) in biological theory, a part of the brain that allows children to understand the properties of all human languages brain damage show very specific language disorders, which suggests that different aspects of language are processed in specific locations in the left hemisphere of the brain. For instance, people with damage to Broca's area of the brain (see Figure 5.6) can express meaning but are unable to produce sentences with grammatical rules. Damage to Wernicke's area does not prevent people from forming grammatically correct sentences, but they convey nothing meaningful in their sentences. Recent studies suggest that the brain is involved in very complex ways in processing language (Maratsos, 1998; Seidenberg, 1997). For instance, studies using brain imaging techniques show that different sites within the brain are activated for processing nouns and for processing verbs (Damasio & Damasio, 1992). None of these studies, however, has addressed the question of whether humans are born with a special capacity for understanding language.

Biological factors, specifically brain development, may play a powerful role in language acquisition. According to Lenneberg (1967), there is a critical period for language development, from about the age of 2 to puberty, during which the brain is primed for processing language. Without exposure to language during this critical period, a person will never develop language, because thereafter the brain loses its ability to acquire language through simple exposure.

Evidence in support of Lenneberg's critical period hypothesis has been obtained in studies of immigrants' language abilities. When people move to the United States from other countries, they are placed in a new environment and need to learn a new language to function effectively. How easily do non-English-speaking immigrants learn to speak English? Research on second language learning suggests that age at arrival in a foreign country relates to mastery of the language, even after decades of practice with the lan-

FIGURE 5.6
Language–Related Areas of the Brain

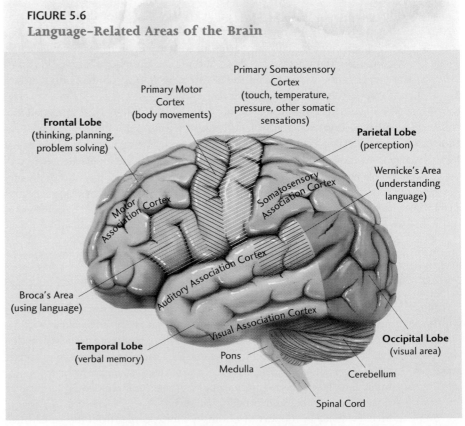

The figure shows the areas of the brain that are thought to be heavily involved in processing language-related information. What does recent research tell us about the complexity of language processing?

guage. In one study, Korean children who arrived in the United States before age 7 mastered English as well as native English-speaking children; those who arrived here between 8 and 15 years of age were less capable; and adolescents and adults who arrived between 17 and 39 years of age did not master English very well at all (Johnson & Newport, 1989). These findings suggest that learning a new language is easier for children than it is for adults.

Biologically based theories have dominated much of the scientific thinking about language development. Although these theories explain many of the interesting features of language development, they may not provide the whole explanation. Language development occurs more gradually than is implied by innate theories, and the universal features that Chomsky believes underlie all languages have been difficult to identify (Moerk, 1989).

The case of Genie was a natural test of innate biological theory, because Genie was not exposed to language during the critical period. According to biologically based theories, the prognosis for Genie would be pessimistic. Genie might be unable to acquire language, even with rigorous training.

LEARNING-BASED THEORIES OF LANGUAGE ACQUISITION

In contrast to theories of biological influences on language development, learning-based theories emphasize a child's environment as the key to developing language skills. The leading proponent of this theory was Skinner (1957), who suggested that children learn language through reinforcement of correct and grammatical forms of speech. Other behaviorists suggest that language is learned through observation—by watching and listening to others (see Chapter 2).

Rewards and punishment are involved in important ways in language development: caregivers encourage infants to talk and reinforce their talking with praise, affection, and attention. Thus, reinforcement motivates children's communication efforts (Owens, 1996). Imitation also is important to language acquisition in that children grow up speaking the language they hear around them; they imitate idioms and dialects. For instance, children in parts of the South might say "I'm fixin' to go to school," meaning that they are getting ready to go to school.

Although they are useful in explaining some aspects of language acquisition, learning-based theories do not adequately explain the development of grammar. Parents seldom reward or punish grammaticality in children's speech; they are more likely to reinforce children for what they say than how they say it (deVilliers & deVilliers, 1992). Also, children produce so many new and unusual sentences that it is unlikely that they have heard and borrowed them from others or have been reinforced for these sentences (Clark, 1997). For instance, after taking a bath, 30-month-old Jake told his mother that he was "barefoot all over," referring to the fact that he was naked. It is unlikely that Jake had ever heard anyone refer to being naked in this way.

To the extent that observational learning, rewards, and punishments account for language development, the prognosis for Genie would be somewhat hopeful. If she was presented with many instances of speech from all the concerned people trying to help her and was rewarded for producing grammatically correct sentences, she might slowly acquire language, although it could take years of training for her to become a competent speaker of English.

SOCIAL INTERACTION THEORIES OF LANGUAGE ACQUISITION

Caregivers support language acquisition in many important ways beyond rewarding children and providing models for language use. Social interaction theories of language development suggest that the social context of language is a fundamental part of language development (Bohannon & Warren-Leubecker, 1989). Thus, children acquire language in interaction with parents and other skilled speakers of the language. Many studies confirm the importance of social interaction in language acquisition. For instance, a child may watch foreign-language television for hours a day but will not learn the language unless he or she interacts with others using that language. Simple exposure to language is not enough to allow one to learn it (Bloom, 1998).

Children's active participation in social interactions is also vital to their developing complex forms of language. Deaf children raised by hearing parents who do not use a form of sign language may create their own language (home signing), and they will learn at about the same rate as other children. But they will not develop complex language abilities (such as the ability to ask wh- questions), even though they have had opportunities to interact with others. Language acquisition seems to require children's participation in the activities that the language is helping to create (Cole, 1992). For children to acquire anything more than the basics of language, they must actively participate in everyday social interactions using language.

Another way in which caregivers foster children's language acquisition is through exposure. By talking to them, caregivers expose infants to the rules, contexts, and patterns of language. Early in language development, mere exposure makes a critical difference (Owens, 1996). In a two-year longitudinal study of US families with toddlers, Hart and Risley (1995) found that the average family spent 28 minutes an hour interacting with their child when he or she was very young and even more time when the child began to speak words. Parents addressed their children an average of 325 times per hour, although the rate varied from 56 to 793 times per hour (Hart & Risley, 1995). Thus, in a 14-hour day, one child may hear about 700 utterances while another hears over 11,000 utterances! Over several years, the language environments of these two children will grow even more discrepant. It is no wonder that the researchers found that, by age 3, children exposed to more utterances a day knew more words than children exposed to fewer utterances a day (Hart & Risley, 1995). The powerful message of this research is that the sheer quantity of language interactions to which a child is exposed in her or his social environment makes a difference in early language development.

Another role of caregivers is in providing many examples of language near the child's own level of understanding. They talk to and interact with their children in specific ways that seem to facilitate language development (Vygotsky, 1962). The version of language that caregivers use with their children has been termed **child-directed speech** or *motherese*; it consists of simple, repetitive sentences spoken in attention-getting ways. Child-directed speech is spoken in a higher-pitched voice and uses exaggerated intonations to direct and maintain the child's attention (see In Research Focus). Child-directed speech has a simple vocabulary and focuses on present events (see Table 5.5). Many stud-

child-directed speech a special version of language that caregivers use with their children; also called motherese

TABLE 5.5
Qualities of Child–Directed Speech

LINGUISTIC QUALITIES	PRODUCTION QUALITIES
Fewer words per utterance	Higher pitch
More repetitions	Slower tempo
Less complexity	Longer pauses
Greater use of idiomatic speech ("Let's go potty")	Louder volume
Simpler vocabulary	More emphatic stress

Is There a Signing Version of Child-Directed Language with Deaf Children?

All over the world, caregivers use similar patterns to simplify their speech when addressing infants and young children. Because child-directed language is repetitive and simpler than speech addressed to adults, children pay attention to and learn from these examples better than from more adultlike forms of speech.

When communicating with young deaf children, do mothers use a different form of sign language than they use with older deaf children? Is there a signing version of child-directed language? In one study, eight deaf women proficient in Japanese sign language were observed

and videotaped in two sessions. In one session, they interacted with their profoundly deaf infants, and in the other session, with a deaf woman. The researchers wanted to see whether mothers interacted differently with adults than with their own infants. Striking differences were found. In interactions with their infants, these mothers used a slower tempo of signing, tended to repeat signs more readily, and exaggerated the movements in the signs. Both deaf and hearing infants showed greater attentional and emotional responsiveness to infant-directed signing than to adult-directed signing (Masataka, 1996, 1998).

Like spoken child-directed language, sign child-directed language helps children identify the important features of language (Masataka, 1992).

Thinking It Through:

1. What events in communication help children identify the important features of a language?
2. How might deaf children learn semantics, syntax, and pragmatics?
3. Do you think children learn signs and words the same way? What study might you design to find out?

---

ies indicate that not only caregivers but also older children use child-directed speech (Hoff-Ginsberg, 1986).

In child-directed speech, words that may be difficult for the child to understand are modified; for instance, a parent might say "tummy" for "stomach" and "grandpa" for "grandfather." Caregivers also simplify the grammar in sentences and use active constructions, such as "baby eats carrots" rather than "the carrots are going to be eaten by the baby." In these ways, child-directed speech exposes children to simplified language that is still more complex than what they may already understand and use (Bruner, 1983).

Studies suggest that use of child-directed speech is related to enhanced language skills in children (Gleitman, Newport, & Gleitman, 1984). Further, studies show that infants whose mothers try to elicit language from them ("Tell me what this is called" and "Is that a horse or a cow?") develop larger vocabularies than many of their peers do (Jones & Adamson, 1987). A longitudinal study of language development in the first three years of life indicated that children whose mothers allow them to take turns in conversations learn language more rapidly (Menyuk, Liebergott, & Schultz, 1995).

Caregivers differ in their use of child-directed speech. Compared to older mothers, adolescent mothers speak fewer words to their infants, and their infants vocalize less than those of older mothers (Culp, Osofsky, & O'Brien, 1996). Additionally, children of depressed mothers, who do not use exaggerated intonation patterns when talking to their infants and who are less responsive, verbalize less than children of non-depressed mothers (Bettes, 1988). Although caregivers all over the world use child-directed speech, cultural differences are apparent in its specific forms (Ingram, 1989). For instance,

Korean mothers emphasize action-oriented speech rather than object-oriented speech with their infants. Korean infants understand more verbs than do English-speaking infants (Choi & Gopnick, 1995).

Caregivers use subtle methods to illustrate complex forms of grammar—for instance, **expansion** of the child's own utterances. When an infant says "cup," a caregiver is likely to respond by saying "Yes, that is your cup." By expanding the child's one or two words to a complete sentence, the caregiver is presenting the child with an opportunity to understand and acquire the complexities of the language.

Caregivers' use of expansions and child-directed speech acts as scaffolding for learning language. The scaffolding changes as parents offer ever more advanced versions of the language, thereby providing an optimal language-learning environment for children. The social context, especially active interactions with caregivers, provides children with a learning environment that supports their language development. However, it is unlikely that the social context provides a full explanation for all aspects of language development. Not all children have optimal social interactions, and yet most children learn language.

According to social interaction theories, Genie's prognosis would be somewhat hopeful. Genie had little exposure to people during her early years and so had few opportunities to engage in language within a social context. Over time, Genie might gradually gain language skills through intensive social interactions with concerned caregivers if they provide motivation and appropriate levels of child-directed language and expansions of her speech.

GENIE'S OUTCOMES

Soon after Genie appeared in the welfare office, she began working with Susan Curtiss, a graduate student in linguistics. Curtiss kept records of Genie's vocalizations and conducted testing of her language skills (Curtiss, 1977). At first, Genie's vocalizations were high-pitched, monotone whimpers or squeaks. After many outings with Curtiss, Genie acquired new words that represented some of her favorite things, such as *pail* for the plastic containers she liked to play with and *store* for the places she liked to visit.

Genie quickly developed a variety of social skills, and she learned a number of new vocabulary words in a relatively short time. One year after Genie was admitted to the hospital, her grammar resembled that of an 18-month-old child; six months later, she was using plurals and could produce some two- and three-word sentences. The linguists working with Genie were excited about the possibility that she would learn grammar despite being beyond the critical period, but in three more years Genie's speech did not improve very much. Unlike most 3-year-olds, Genie could not correctly form sentences using *why, where,* or *what*. For example, she produced word strings such as "Where is may I have a penny?" or "I where is graham cracker on top shelf" (Rymer, 1993).

In tests conducted to assess Genie's brain functioning, researchers discovered an abnormality: her left hemisphere, which in most people is involved in processing language, did not function at all. Her right hemisphere processed language. Genie's brain could not handle language input normally.

After living with a string of researchers and foster parents, Genie today lives in a home for adults with mental impairments. Now in her forties and without the special attention researchers provided, Genie seems to have lost her hard-won social skills along with her battle to acquire language (Rymer, 1993).

How can we explain Genie's developmental successes and failures? It is difficult to draw firm conclusions because of the severe physical and emotional abuse and neglect she suffered at the hands of her parents. The abuse, including malnourishment, may have interfered with her ability to learn language. Or, she may have been brain damaged in

expansion taking young children's simplified language and adding complexity and completeness to it some way before the abuse started, the brain damage hampering her ability to learn language and causing her father to think she was mentally retarded. Despite developing cognitive and social skills, Genie may have found it hard to learn grammar and syntax because of her brain dysfunction. In addition, Genie missed the early years of language learning, possibly limiting her ability to ever acquire language skills. Genie's story suggests that exposure to language may be important for normal brain development, as well as for language acquisition. For many years Genie lacked the stimulus of social interaction and appropriate language models to observe and follow. She was never reinforced for using language, and she never heard child-directed speech. Thus, in the triumph and ultimate tragedy of Genie's story, you can see how each theory of language acquisition provides insights about how children acquire and learn to use language.

CHAPTER SUMMARY

How do infants and toddlers develop physically?

- Growth in height and weight is more rapid during infancy than at any other time in the lifespan, except for prenatal development. Infants' growth is influenced by genetics and their living conditions.

- Infants gain control over muscles in a cephalocaudal pattern, beginning with the neck and head and moving down toward the feet.

- By 6 months, most infants crawl. At 8 or 9 months, infants creep and cruise, holding onto furniture for balance. By 10 to 15 months, most infants begin unassisted walking. Walking is the major motor milestone of infancy and is one of the last major motor skills that infants master.

- Children do not have control or awareness of the physical symptoms associated with elimination until the middle of their second year. Most children are toilet trained by the age of 3.

What factors influence infant health and safety?

- Many accidents and health problems of infants can be prevented with proper safety precautions and immunizations.

- Because of their rapid growth, infants require a healthy and nutritious diet. Breast milk is the ideal food for young infants and protects them from diseases. In the United States, breast-feeding is more common today than it was in the 1970s, and mothers are breast-feeding their infants for longer periods of time.

- Failure-to-thrive infants have slower than normal growth because of undernutrition or malnutrition. Given adequate diets, these children grow normally. Failure-to-thrive children experience many difficulties with family interactions and with their behavior and cognitive functioning.

How do infants' perceptual abilities develop?

- At around 3 months of age, infants begin to discriminate colors; recognize patterns; prefer faces, especially attractive ones; and recognize human-generated motion.

- By 5 to 7 months of age, infants begin to recognize depth and distance by using visual cues.

How do infants and toddlers learn and remember?

- Infants learn about the world through associations with existing behaviors, as in classical conditioning, or through associations of their actions with particular consequences, as in operant conditioning.

- Habituation is characterized by decreasing responsiveness to a stimulus that has been presented repeatedly. Scientists use infants' increased interest in new events and decreased interest in familiar events in habituation studies to assess infants' concepts and categories.

- Infants have fragile memories. Their memories are more dependent on situational cues than adult memories are. Infants generally remember better when given reminders and visual cues that mimic the original learning situation.

- Deferred imitation tasks have been used to document long-term memories in toddlers. Infantile amnesia is likely due to the facts that adults are seldom in the same situations as they were when infants and adults have different cognitive abilities than infants.

How do the cognitive abilities of infants and toddlers develop during the sensorimotor period?

- From birth to 2 years of age, infants are in Piaget's sensorimotor period of cognitive development, which is further divided into six stages.

- In stage I (0 to 1 month), infants practice their reflex actions.

- In stage II (1 to 4 months), infants demonstrate that they can repeat interesting actions centering on their body, called primary circular reactions.

- In stage III (4 to 8 months), infants coordinate schemes so that they can reach for interesting objects that they see. They also demonstrate secondary circular reactions, in which their repetitive actions focus on the noises or shapes of objects rather than on their own body.

- Stage IV (8 to 12 months) infants show the first signs of true intelligence by intentionally applying a scheme to reach a goal.

- In stage V (12 to 18 months), infants are creative in their problem solving—they vary their strategies and assess the outcomes of the variations. These systematic variations are tertiary circular reactions.

- In stage VI (18 to 24 months), infants begin to use symbols for the first time. Symbols allow them much greater flexibility in problem solving—they can mentally consider outcomes without having to act them out.

- Children's understanding of objects undergoes dramatic changes during infancy and toddlerhood. Infants move from having no concept of the permanence of objects to having a partial understanding. Only later in infancy do they acquire a full understanding of object permanence. Measurements of children's understanding of objects vary depending on the testing procedures used and whether the children must act on their knowledge.

- Mandler proposed that infants develop concepts from their perceptions of objects rather than from their direct experiences with them, as Piaget suggested.

- Social interactions, especially with knowledgeable adults, expand the range of children's cognitive abilities, as indicated by Vygotsky's zone of proximal development. Parents use scaffolding and bridging to maintain children's attention on a task and to structure tasks so that children can successfully complete them.

How do infants develop language skills?

- To become speakers of a language, children must master four domains: (1) phonology—the sounds of the language;

(2) semantics—the understanding of word meaning; (3) syntax—the rules for forming sentences; and (4) pragmatics—the practical applications of language in different situations.

- Even before they utter their first words, infants engage in many language-related activities, including cooing, babbling, and intentional communication through gesturing.

- During the first year, experience with language helps fine-tune children's abilities to distinguish phonemes.

- Infants' first words, spoken around 12 months, are usually words that label important and familiar people or objects. These words are called holophrases because they convey a sentence's worth of meaning.

- Infants begin to form two-word sentences when they are around 2 years old. First sentences are grammatical and telegraphic (only the most important and informative words are included).

- Chomsky's innate theory of language acquisition emphasizes that humans are specially equipped with a language acquisition device that allows them to understand and process the regularities of language. Lenneberg's innate theory assumes that there is a critical period in language development during which children must be exposed to language. Innate theories best account for the creativity and universal features of language.

- Learning theories emphasize the roles of modeling and reinforcement in language development. Learning theories best account for idioms, first words, and dialects.

- Social interactions in everyday life play an important role in children's language development by providing a rich language-learning environment. Caregivers support children's language development mainly through the use of simplified and exaggerated speech, called child-directed speech.

KEY TERMS & CONCEPTS

A-not-B error *(160)*
babbling *(167)*
child-directed speech *(174)*
colostrum *(148)*
cooing *(167)*
cruise *(144)*
dishabituation *(153)*
expansion *(176)*
expressive language *(169)*
failure-to-thrive (FTT) *(150)*

habituation *(153)*
holophrases *(169)*
image schemas *(164)*
infantile amnesia *(154)*
language acquisition device (LAD) *(171)*
object permanence *(159)*
phonemes *(166)*
phonemic awareness *(167)*
pragmatics *(166)*

primary circular reactions *(157)*
receptive language *(169)*
scaffolding *(164)*
semantics *(166)*
secondary circular reactions *(158)*
symbolic representation *(159)*
syntax *(166)*
telegraphic speech *(170)*
tertiary circular reactions *(158)*
visual cliff apparatus *(152)*

ACTIVITIES & APPLICATIONS
Relating to Infants and Toddlers

1. Recall Gabrielle's achievements in the vignette at the beginning of this chapter. Where and how did she learn to make the duck squeak? How did she learn to recognize the words *kitty* and *bye-bye* when she heard them?

2. At what age did you first walk unassisted? In what physical environment and social context did you accomplish this feat? At what age did you first use words to communicate? What were your first words and sentences, and in what social and cultural contexts did you say them? Did your family members use child-directed language with you? Do you use child-directed language with children or pets today? What does it sound like?

3. Observe an infant or toddler to identify his or her perceptual abilities. You might interact with or test the baby informally to try to determine perception of colors, patterns, faces, movement, or depth. Try to identity the baby's stage of sensorimotor development. What perceptual, motor, and cognitive abilities characterize this stage? For example, does the baby understand object permanence? number concepts? How could you tell when the baby entered the next stage of sensorimotor development? How could you or others best stimulate this development?

4. Investigate and report on a nutrition, health, or safety issue concerning infants or toddlers. For example, you might research a topic such as immunizations, baby foods, SIDS, lead exposure, baby toys, furniture and appliances for babies, infant car seats, or FTT babies.

CHAPTER 6

Social & Emotional Development in INFANCY AND TODDLERHOOD

CHAPTER OUTLINE

Two 11-month-old boys, Jamal and Kyle, are at a birthday party for another child who is turning 1. Although both boys find themselves in a similar situation, their reactions are dramatically different. Jamal is curious and interested in the goings on at the party. He easily separates from his mother and explores the interesting and new environment. When a balloon bursts suddenly and makes a loud noise, he becomes upset and goes to his mother for comfort. Once in her arms, he is quickly soothed and soon smiles and returns to exploration and play.

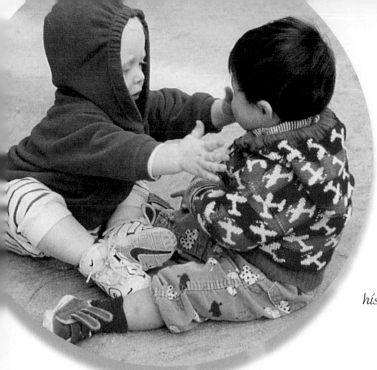

In contrast, Kyle is timid and fearful in this new situation and does not explore his new environment. Kyle clings to his mother and becomes upset when separated from her, even for a short time. But when his mother picks him up to comfort him, Kyle pushes and fusses in her arms and becomes angry. When the balloon pops, he becomes intensely distressed and is not easily comforted by his mother.

The period of infancy and toddlerhood is a time when children make major strides in the development of social and emotional competencies (Saarni, Mumme, & Campos, 1998). Infants and toddlers must develop the social and emotional skills that allow them to get and hold the attention of adults and other important figures in their lives, express affection and annoyance when appropriate, establish relationships, and adapt to the demands of increasingly complex environments. Establishing trust and some measure of independence are important outcomes (Erikson, 1968). The characteristics infants and toddlers bring to these environments—and the ways significant people treat them—have important consequences for their development. For children like Jamal, the period of infancy and toddlerhood is an exciting time of growth, change, and challenge. For children like Kyle, however, this period often is fraught with insecurity and uncertainty—and sometimes even victimization.

HOW DO EMOTIONS DEVELOP DURING INFANCY AND TODDLERHOOD?

For many years, people believed that newborns and young infants expressed only one emotional state—general excitement (Bridges, 1932)—and that other emotions appeared gradually with age and experience. New research suggests, however, that many of the basic emotions are present at birth. As you can see from Table 6.1, the basic emotions of interest, sadness, and disgust are present at birth, and joy, anger, surprise, and fear develop during the first eight months. Although researchers sometimes disagree as to the precise timetable for the development of emotions (Malatesta, 1990), it is clear that by the end of the first year of life infants have a wide range of emotional capacities and express emotions in increasingly complex ways (Kochanska, Coy, Tjebkes, & Husarek, 1998).

Children also become more social and independent over the first two years of life—the clingy behavior of infants eventually is replaced by more mature forms of social behavior, such as making a verbal request or moving about to get something one wants. Children's behavior also changes in response to the demands of their environments. Very young infants often get the attention of their parents by crying, but older infants use other means, such as showing a toy to a parent or expressing affection, as they face increased expectations for age-appropriate behavior.

TABLE 6.1

The Appearance of Emotions in the First Year of Life

EMOTION	AGE
Interest	Birth
Sadness	Birth
Disgust	Birth
Joy	Months 1–2
Anger	Months 2–3
Surprise	Months 3–4
Shyness	Months 4–5
Fear	Months 6–8

SOURCE: Adapted from Izard and Malatesta, 1987.

This 1-month-old infant's reflex smile involves just the muscles of her lower face. Notice that only her mouth is smiling—her eyes are not. To get a sense of this, cover half the picture with your finger. What does the mouth convey to you? What do the eyes convey?

The social smile of this 3-month-old child involves the entire face—the grin is from cheek to cheek, and the eyes are bright and wide open. What changes occur in the parents' responses when their infant begins to smile like this?

endogenous smile smile that is triggered by changes in nervous system activity and involves only the lower face muscles

exogenous smile smile that is triggered by external stimuli

social smile smile that is triggered by social stimuli (such as the mother's face)

SMILING AND LAUGHTER

When you're drawing up your list of life's miracles, you might place near the top the first moment your baby smiles at you. . . . Today, she looked right at me. And she smiled. . . . Her toothless mouth opened, and she scrunched her face up and it really was a grin. . . . The sleepless nights, the worries, the crying—all of a sudden it was all worth it. . . . She is no longer just something we are nursing and carrying along—somewhere inside, part of her knows what's going on, and that part of her is telling us that she's with us.

—BOB GREENE'S JOURNAL ENTRY ABOUT
AMANDA AT 7 WEEKS OF AGE (1984,
PP. 33–34)

As Bob Greene's journal entry suggests, an infant's smile not only conveys a sense of well-being and pleasure but also reminds us that young infants have meaningful internal states (Greenspan & Greenspan, 1985). In fact, smiling may be one of the most significant aspects of social and emotional development during the first six months of life. Similar to many other aspects of early development, smiling develops through a series of maturational changes (Super & Harkness, 1991). Table 6.2 outlines these changes. As you can see, newborn children sometimes smile, but their smiles are not enduring or strong and occur most often while they are asleep. Such a smile is called an **endogenous smile** because it is triggered by changes in nervous system activity. Endogenous smiles are reflexive and involve only the lower face muscles.

By 2 to 3 weeks, infants smile when gently stimulated by high-pitched sounds or by soft stroking of their abdomens. This gentle stimulation increases the level of nervous system excitement and elicits a tiny reflex smile (Sroufe, 1977). This reflex smile is labeled an **exogenous smile** because it is triggered by external stimuli (Wolff, 1963).

Over the next few weeks, infants smile when they are fully awake and attentive. These alert smiles are fuller and more expressive than the earlier smiles and may be a response to a combination of visual, tactile, and auditory stimulation (Stack & LePage, 1996). Playing pat-a-cake, for example, might elicit twenty to thirty smiles, whereas auditory or visual stimuli alone might elicit only eight to ten smiles (Rosenblith, 1992).

By 6 to 8 weeks, an important change takes place—the **social smile** first appears. Now, the infant smiles upon seeing mother's or father's face or hearing her or his voice. Social smiles are longer lasting and involve the entire face; the grin goes from cheek to cheek, and the eyes widen and brighten (Izard & Malatesta, 1987).

At about 10 weeks of age, infants' smiling becomes *instrumental*—they use their smiles to achieve a goal, such as getting mom, dad, or other caregivers to smile back (Bower, 1982). Smiles are powerful social reinforcers for both infants and caregivers. When an infant smiles, the caregiver tends to smile back and repeat the behavior that elicited the smile. Infants learn about the power of their smiles, and they begin to use their smiles to gain control over their environment (Brazelton, 1991). For example, 10-month-old infants are more likely to smile at their mother when the mother is attentive to them than when she is not, suggesting that infant smiling is responsive to the social context (Jones, Collins, & Hong, 1991). Additionally, the mutually reinforcing smiles between an infant and his or her caregiver foster the development of attachment.

Infants' laughter appears at about 4 months of age. At first, laughing occurs in response to physical stimulation, such as tickling or being swooped up high in mom's or dad's arms (Sroufe & Waters, 1976). After 6 months of age, infants increasingly laugh at visual and social stimuli, such as playing peek-a-boo or seeing sister make a funny face. As toddlers, children laugh at events that earlier made them cry, such as seeing dad wear a mask. These milestones reflect the child's developmental progression from laughter based on physical stimulation to laughter based on cognitive interpretations (Snow, 1989). Laughing also is mutually reinforcing and fosters positive feelings and interactions between the infant and others in the social environment.

TABLE 6.2
The Development of Smiling and Laughing

AGE	RESPONSE	STIMULATION	TIME TO ONSET	CONDITIONS
Smiling				
Neonate	Corners of mouth	No external stimulation		Due to nervous system fluctuations
Week 1	Corners of mouth	Low-level, modulated sound	6–8 sec	During sleep, boosting of tension
Week 2	Mouth pulled back	Low-level, modulated voices		When drowsy, satiated
Week 3	Grin, includes eyes	Moderate-level voices	4–5 sec	When alert, attentive (nodding head with voices)
Week 4	Grin, active smile	Moderate or moderately intense sounds	Reduced	Vigorous tactile stimulation effective
Weeks 5–8	Grin, active smile, cooing	Active stimulation, first visual stimulation	Less than 3 sec	Nodding head, flicking lights, stimulation that must be followed
Weeks 9–12	Grin, active smile, cooing	Inactive visual stimulation, moderately intense	Short	Trial-by-trial effects, recognition
Laughter				
Month 4	Laughter	Multisensory, vigorous stimulation	1–2 sec	Touch, tickling, auditory
Months 5–6	Laughter	Intense auditory stimulation and touch	Immediate	Items that may previously have caused crying
Months 7–9	Laughter	Social, visual stimulation	Immediate	Tactile, auditory decline
Months 10–12	Laughter	Visual, social	Immediate or anticipatory	Visual incongruities, active participation

SOURCE: Sroufe and Waters, 1976. Copyright © 1976 by the American Psychological Association. Adapted with permission.

Although the development of smiling and laughter is similar across cultures, the behaviors used by parents in different cultures to elicit smiling vary. For example, American mothers rely largely on toys and objects to elicit smiling in their infants, whereas Japanese mothers are likely to engage infants in social stimulation. Mothers in both cultures are equally effective in eliciting smiles in their infants, but they do it in different ways because of different culture-based parenting goals. In the United States, mothers place high value on promoting autonomy and independent exploration of the object world. Japanese mothers, in contrast, place high value on strengthening mutual dependency and making the infant an extension of themselves. Thus, they engage their infants differently (Bornstein, Tal, & Tamis-LeMonda, 1991).

Soothing a Crying Infant

A variety of techniques are used to soothe crying infants (Amato, 1997; Rosenblith, 1992; Wolke, 1993):

- **Holding a crying infant.** Picking up and holding a crying infant is one of the most effective methods of getting the infant to stop crying. Holding the infant up high, in a front-to-front position so that the infant looks over the caregiver's shoulder, is one of the most effective positions.
- **Providing auditory stimulation.** Talking, singing, and providing background noise are effective methods of soothing a crying infant. The kind of auditory stimulation depends in part on the age of the infant. For newborns, nonsocial auditory stimulation (the humming noise of a clothes dryer or vacuum cleaner) is most effective. For older infants (after 3 months of age), social auditory stimuli, such as the caregiver's voice, are more effective than nonsocial stimuli.

- **Providing visual stimulation.** After 3 to 4 months of age, a crying infant is effectively soothed by visual stimulation. At this age, seeing the face of a caregiver or a toy will soothe a crying child. After an infant reaches 4 months, the combination of both visual and auditory stimulation is more effective than either one alone. At this age, presenting him or her with an attractive toy that makes noise often soothes a crying infant.
- **Rhythmic physical stimulation.** Providing the infant with rhythmic physical stimulation, such as rocking or patting, is often effective. Generally, rocking an infant from side to side is more effective than rocking the infant up and down. Increasing the pace of rocking is more effective than decreasing the pace. Many parents have found that taking their crying infant for a ride in the car is soothing, partially because of the

rhythmic stimulation provided by the movement of the car.
- **Use of a pacifier.** A pacifier is effective in soothing a crying infant because it stimulates the sucking response, which is incompatible with crying. The rhythmic nature of sucking helps the infant reorganize his or her behavior and calm down.
- **Removing distressing stimuli.** Changing an infant's wet diaper, feeding a hungry infant, or removing a scratchy blanket or other irritant from around an infant will reduce crying.

None of these techniques works all of the time with every infant, and techniques that were effective with newborns become less effective with older infants. Thus, it is no wonder caregivers complain that as soon as they figure out how to soothe an infant, the infant changes, forcing them to figure him or her out all over again.

CRYING

Crying is an infant's most effective way of communicating. This is true from the moment the child is born—the cries of the newborn tell the mother, doctor, and nurse that the newborn's lungs have filled with air. The cries also tell something about the status of the newborn's nervous system. Differences in pitch, duration, or pattern of crying may reveal abnormalities in a newborn's functioning. For example, newborns with high-pitched, shrill cries may have *cri du chat* (cry of a cat) syndrome, indicating brain damage or other nervous system disorders. Crying is the mechanism by which infants communicate their needs. Infants who are placid and rarely cry may be at risk of poor growth because their parents are not always made aware of the need to feed them (Skuse, Wolke, & Reilly, 1992).

Crying begins as a reflex response that has survival value and progressively becomes more controllable. Moreover, the significance of crying changes over the course of infancy and toddlerhood.

Characteristics of Cries

Mothers frequently report that they can distinguish different types of cries their infants make. Researchers also have identified different characteristics of infants' crying (Wasz-Hockert, Michelsson, & Lind, 1985; Wolff, 1969). The basic cry is a rhythmic pattern of crying followed by a brief silence, a short inhalation whistle, and then another brief silence. Anger cries differ from the basic cry in that excess air forced through the vocal cords gives the cry a more breathy sound. The pain cry is distinguishable through its sudden and loud onset and duration, followed by a period of breath holding. A fourth cry—the hunger cry—is similar to the basic cry, but it tends to be rhythmic, have a braying sound, and be accompanied by kicking in the same rhythm as the crying (Wolff, 1969).

The amount of crying varies dramatically from infant to infant and from day to day (St. James-Roberts & Plewis, 1996). Crying increases over the first six weeks of life and then decreases. Figure 6.1 shows that crying peaks in the first three months and then decreases by about half by the end of the first year. On the average, infants cry more in the first three months of life than at any other time, averaging about 2 hours of crying each day. Although some babies cry more than others, what most infants have in common is a period of fussiness late in the day, beginning at 3 to 12 weeks (Zeskind, 1985). Figure 6.1 also reveals that infant crying initially is greatest in the evening, when the infant's nervous system overloads (Amato, 1997) and then shifts toward feeding times as the infant

From birth, crying is an infant's most effective way of communicating. How should caregivers respond to infants' crying? What consequences might be associated with such responses?

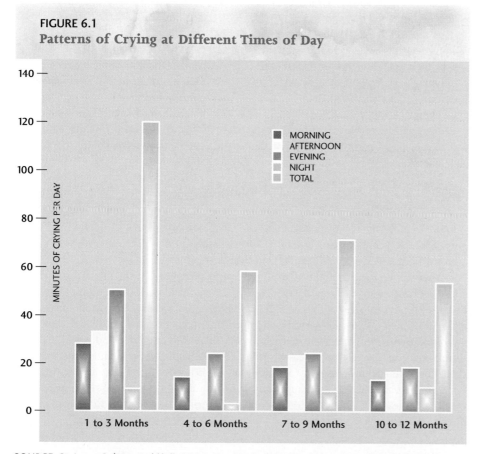

FIGURE 6.1
Patterns of Crying at Different Times of Day

MINUTES OF CRYING PER DAY

MORNING
AFTERNOON
EVENING
NIGHT
TOTAL

1 to 3 Months   4 to 6 Months   7 to 9 Months   10 to 12 Months

SOURCE: St. James-Roberts and Hall, 1991. Reprinted with the permission of Cambridge University Press.
Both the total amount of crying and the times of day during which crying occurs change over the course of the first year of life. What developmental changes take place that might account for these differences?

Should a Crying Baby Be Soothed?

Caregivers are very motivated to soothe crying infants and often try a variety of techniques (Wikander & Helleday, 1996). How to soothe a crying infant is one question; whether to soothe a crying infant is another, and it is one that has been hotly debated. Caregivers often ask, "If I always pick up my crying baby, won't she cry more often just to be cuddled?" According to learning theory (Gerwitz & Boyd, 1977; Landau, 1982), the answer is yes. Caregivers reinforce crying by attending to it and thereby increase its frequency. In contrast, other theories of caregiving, such as attachment theory, emphasize the need for prompt, efficient responses to infants' crying (Bell & Ainsworth, 1972; Brazelton, 1991). Some research shows that infants whose mothers respond promptly to their cries in the first three months of life cry *less* later in their first year than do infants whose mothers do not respond promptly.

These infants also are more likely to use noncrying modes of communication during the first year (Bell & Ainsworth, 1972; Hubbard & van IJzendoorn, 1991).

One possibility is that, although prompt responses may reinforce infant crying, they may reinforce only mild crying or precry behaviors such as pouts, frowns, or moans. When a caregiver is slow to respond, an infant's crying is likely to become stronger and more disagreeable. When the caregiver responds only after the crying has become too unpleasant to bear, she or he reinforces noxious, enduring demand crying (Gustafson & Harris, 1990). Furthermore, crying is not good for babies: it saps their energy, increases their blood pressure, and depletes their supply of oxygen (Anderson, 1984; Green, Gustafson, & McGhie, 1998).

A weighing of the evidence suggests that spoiling an infant by responding to

his or her cries is not a serious risk. The most important consequence of quick attention to an infant's cries is that the baby develops a sense of trust in caregivers and a sense of efficacy in determining what happens to him or her (Erikson, 1968). Infants who do not acquire this sense may develop feelings of helplessness and lose their desire to act (Fincham & Cain, 1986).

Thinking It Through:

1. What criteria would you use to decide how long to wait before responding to a baby's cries?
2. Cries represent infants' wants and needs. How can caregivers' responses to cries influence the development of efficacy and trust?
3. If caregivers always respond to infants' cries, how do infants learn to soothe themselves?

gets older (St. James-Roberts & Halil, 1991). These patterns of infant crying are similar across different Western cultures (St. James-Roberts, 1993).

As with the development of smiling, crying progresses from internal to external sources of stimulation (Snow, 1989). During the neonatal period, infants cry primarily because of physical needs—because they are hungry, in pain, or physically uncomfortable. Additionally, there are periods when infants cry for no apparent reason. As infants get older, their crying gradually becomes more related to cognitive and emotional conditions than to physical ones (Lester, 1985). For example, older infants might cry because they are scared or angry or because they do not want to be left alone. Caregivers' perceptions of infant crying change with age—as infants get older, caregivers perceive more complex and individualized needs and motives in the cries they hear (Leger, Thompson, Merritt, & Benz, 1996).

Culture and Infant Crying

People in different cultures, and in the same culture at different times, have contrary ideas about appropriate responses to a crying infant. In some cultures, crying is thought

To keep children calm and to minimize their crying, Navajo caregivers confine them on a cradleboard. Notice how the infant is tightly swaddled to reduce movement and decrease the chance of becoming upset and aroused.

to be good for the infant. Some Mexican mothers believe that crying cleanses the child of illness or disease and that letting the child cry strengthens the child's lungs and nervous system (Atkin, Olvera, Givaudan, & Landeros, 1989). In other cultures, caregivers believe that infants should not cry and that their needs should be constantly and consistently attended to. For example, traditional Navajo caregivers believe that infants should be kept calm and quiet. To prevent crying, they often wrap Navajo infants onto a cradleboard for the first 10 months of life. These swaddled infants, who are in a lower state of arousal, sleep longer and cry less (Chisholm, 1989).

ANGER AND TEMPER TANTRUMS

Although there is some debate as to when infants first express anger, it is clear that by the end of the first year children can and do become angry (Buss & Goldsmith, 1998). At about 9 months of age, infants begin to develop a sense of control, and angry crying and temper tantrums are signals of their frustration when things are not to their liking (Wolf, 1996). As infants move beyond the first year of life, they become aware of, and are frustrated by, the limits they experience. For example, 14-month-old Ethan used to play happily in his high chair and car seat, but he now cries and flails his arms and legs when put in either one. Ethan is a physically active infant who is mobile and agile. The restrictiveness of the car seat and high chair is frustrating, and he reacts angrily to it. Similarly, 16-month-old Josephina enjoys playing with her mother's car keys. But her smiles turn to screams of protest when her mother needs the keys and takes them from her. Josephina becomes rigid, throws herself to the ground, and kicks and yells. These behaviors give an infamous reputation to the toddler years, commonly referred to as the "terrible twos and threes."

Three important changes take place during the toddler years that contribute to the defiant reputation toddlers have (Hoyt, 1996; Schaefer & DiGeronimo, 1995):

+ **Increased ability to express anger.**   As toddlers' communication skills increase, so does their ability to express anger and frustration. Their vocabulary increases dramatically, although they have not yet learned to censor themselves. They now are more capable of telling caregivers when things are not to their liking. The amount of angry crying decreases, but defiant language increases (Kopp, 1992).

Dealing with Temper Tantrums

Temper tantrums peak during the second year, often are short-lived, and occur most often because children are tired, hungry, or frustrated. Until about 3 years of age, these tantrums have minimal aftereffects. With increasing age, children tend to sulk and be resentful (Brooks, 1998). Dealing with tantrums can be difficult and sometimes embarrassing when they take place in public. Here are some practical tips for dealing with young children's angry and manipulative tantrums (Schaefer & DiGeronimo, 1995; Schulman, 1997; Wolf, 1996):

- *Keep your cool.* Staying calm in the face of screaming and kicking is difficult but essential. Count to 10, or take deep breaths to settle yourself down.
- *Don't give in.* Try to ignore the tantrum, even in public. Distract or soothe the child if possible, but refuse to give in to the child's angry demands. Giving in reinforces the angry behavior.
- *Help the child find words for her or his feelings.* Talking about feelings teaches a child to use words rather than behavior to express anger. Using words helps a child gain a sense of mastery over the situation.
- *Give yourself and the child some breathing room.* If possible, separate yourself from the child by crossing or leaving the room or by having the child sit down until he or she calms down. This separation gives both parties a chance to collect themselves.
- *Remind yourself that tantrums reflect the child's growing developmental competencies.* Although tantrums may be irritating and difficult to deal with, they are normal reactions to the increasingly demanding environments in which children find themselves. Tantrums also show that limits are placed on the child's behavior and that the child feels secure enough to express himself or herself.

◆ **Limitations in social understanding.** Although toddlers have many increased capacities, they do not yet understand concepts such as waiting, sharing, or patience. Thus, hunger, boredom, or fatigue can cause angry outbursts.

◆ **Strivings toward autonomy.** Toddlers increasingly strive to express their newfound abilities and their desire to be individuals (Erikson, 1968). This independence often conflicts with what is required of them or what is best for them. For example, 30-month-old Dori constantly struggles with her mother over getting dressed. Dori only wants to wear her red skirt and cries angrily when she has to wear anything else.

Two types of temper tantrums have been identified (Turecki & Tonner, 1985): **manipulative tantrums,** in which children use the tantrum to manipulate others into giving them what they want, and **temperamental tantrums,** in which children respond with anger because some aspect of their style of interacting has been violated. For example, Reese, who has a low tolerance for change, threw several temper tantrums when household routines were disrupted during his grandparents' visit. The best ways to respond to the two types of tantrums differ. It is important not to give in to manipulative tantrums, but it is important to help the child cope with situations giving rise to temperamental tantrums (Brooks, 1998).

SELF-AWARENESS AND EMOTIONS

By 18 to 24 months of age, children understand that emotions are connected with what one wants or does not want (Wellman & Woolley, 1990). Toddlers' temper tantrums

manipulative tantrums tantrums children throw to manipulate others into giving them what they want

temperamental tantrums anger response when some aspect of a child's style of interacting has been violated illustrate that young children can and do use an emotional reaction to try to get what they want. Thus, children's first understanding of emotions is based on associations with their desired goals and outcomes (Stein & Trabasso, 1989).

Toddlers also begin to express **self-conscious emotions,** such as pride, shame, embarrassment, and guilt. Self-conscious emotions are those that involve injury to or enhancement of one's sense of self (Lewis, 1993). For example, at about 24 months, children show signs of embarrassment when they are caught violating a rule—they may lower their eyes, hang their head, and hide their face with their hands.

Self-conscious emotions require several important advances in self-awareness and cognitive development. For these emotions to develop, children must have the following characteristics (Lewis, 1993):

Notice the look of shame and guilt on this 2-year-old's face. Once children understand that there are standards for their behavior, self-conscious emotions appear. What other changes bring about the development of self-conscious emotions?

◆ They must have a conscious awareness of themselves as distinct from others.
◆ They must recognize that there are certain rules to be followed and standards or expectations to be met.
◆ They must be able to evaluate their behavior in relation to these standards.
◆ They must have a sense of responsibility for meeting or not meeting these standards.

When children see themselves as responsible for success in meeting a standard, they experience pride. When they view themselves as responsible for failing to meet a standard or follow a rule, they may feel guilt, embarrassment, or shame. Thus, at about age 2, children have a rudimentary understanding that their behaviors lead to others' approval or disapproval, and they feel emotions that reflect this anticipation (Frolund, 1997). After age 3, children begin to react independently to these standards; they feel pride or shame as they develop the ability to reflect on and compare their behaviors to standards they set for themselves. Three-year-olds still depend on others' reactions for these feelings; they beam with pride because mom is proud of them. It is not until about 8 years of age that children say they feel proud or ashamed of themselves independently of others' approval or disapproval (Stipek, Recchia, & McClintic, 1992).

From toddlerhood on, girls are more likely than boys to show shame when they fail at a task (Lewis, Alessandri, & Sullivan, 1992). What is particularly interesting about this finding is that girls often show more shame than boys do even though they perform as well as the boys; that is, girls show more shame than boys do despite a lack of difference in their abilities. Research indicates that the same is true in adulthood: women express more shame than men do (Tangney, 1990).

These findings suggest that gender differences in the expression of shame appear early and persist throughout life. One reason is that girls and women are more likely than boys and men to be taught to assume personal responsibility for failure (Dweck & Leggett, 1988). Additionally, girls are more likely than boys to receive negative feedback from caregivers and teachers (Lewis, 1987). Thus, there is good reason to believe that early socialization experiences account for the gender differences in the expression of shame and other self-conscious emotions.

PLAY AND EMOTIONAL DEVELOPMENT

Fifteen-month-old Ben tries to get his 4-year-old sister's attention by taking one of her dolls and offering it to her. When his sister fails to respond, he drops the doll and laughs. When his sister again fails to respond, he does this a second and third time. Soon his sister tells him to stop bothering her, and Ben becomes upset and takes the doll to the kitchen, where his mother is. He shows the doll to his mother, and she asks, "Is the doll hungry?" Ben first looks sad, then smiles and says "yes." His mother gives him a piece of carrot, which Ben tries to feed to the doll. When he cannot get the carrot in the doll's mouth, he gets upset until his mother suggests that he put the baby to sleep. Ben then puts the baby on the chair and puts a napkin over it.

self-conscious emotions those emotions that involve injury to or enhancement of one's sense of self (such as pride and shame)

Ben's story provides vivid evidence that many of children's early emotional responses occur in the context of play. Even before the toddler years, infants smile and laugh when mother plays with them while they are being bathed or diapered. Play provides young children with the opportunity to experiment with emotions in a relatively stress-free environment (Sutton-Smith, 1998).

Play also provides young children with an opportunity to learn about their world. Ben, for example, learned that he can use play to attract others' interest and attention. It may not always work and sometimes produces feelings of frustration and sadness, but Ben's understanding of the world is enhanced by these playful interactions (Sutton-Smith, 1994).

Infants' and toddlers' play often is repetitive and ritualistic. Initially, it revolves around the child's body and physical actions, such as when 6-month-old Teriqua repeatedly splashes water in the bath and laughs each time. By 12 months, children begin to use objects and involve others in their play (Goncu, 1993). These playful interactions can be emotionally intense, and they can quickly lead to anger and aggression because of the egocentric and impulsive nature of toddlers. But even these negative interactions help children learn about their emotional worlds—they provide children with opportunities to gain self-control and cope with negative social interactions and feelings (Eisenberg, Fabes, & Guthrie, 1997).

HOW DOES TEMPERAMENT INFLUENCE DEVELOPMENT DURING INFANCY AND TODDLERHOOD?

From the moment of birth, infants differ in their responses to their environment. Some infants cry frequently and intensely; others cry rarely and relatively quietly. Some infants get on a schedule very quickly and adapt easily to changes in their environment; other infants are unpredictable and do not easily adjust to change. These differences in infants' responses to their environment often are considered to be linked to biological and genetic processes that predispose them to respond in certain ways. The predisposition to respond in certain enduring and characteristic ways to one's environment is known as **temperament** (Wachs & King, 1994).

An important aspect of temperament is its consistency; temperament sometimes shows stability from infancy through adolescence and even adulthood (Caspi, Henry, McGee, Moffitt, & Silva, 1995; Caspi & Silva, 1995). Research suggests that temperamental differences are present prenatally—more active fetuses are more unpredictable and unadaptable as infants (DiPietro, Hodgson, Costigan, & Johnson, 1996). The heritability of temperament distinguishes it from the closely related concept of personality, which refers to a person's unique behavioral, motivational, and temperamental ways of responding. Thus, *personality* is a broader term, and a person's personality is more likely to be a product of diverse influences (Strelau, 1994).

TEMPERAMENTAL TRAITS

A variety of components of temperament have been identified (Buss & Plomin, 1984; Rothbart, 1989), but the most famous and widely used are the nine components identified by Thomas and Chess (1970, 1977):

+ **Rhythmicity:**   the regularity of basic functions, such as sleep, wakefulness, excretion, and hunger. Some children function on regular cycles; they eat, sleep, and defecate on schedule almost from birth. Other children are less predictable.
+ **Activity level:**   the intensity and frequency of motor movements. Some children are very active. They kick and move a lot, even before they are born; they

temperament   the predisposition to respond in certain enduring and characteristic ways to one's environment move around a great deal in their cribs; and as toddlers, they are nearly always running. Other children are much less active.

✦ **Approach-withdrawal:**   the degree to which a child accepts or rejects new people, objects, or situations. Some children are excited when they experience something new; others withdraw from new situations. A first airplane trip makes some children laugh with excitement but makes others cry; a new food is quickly accepted by one child but spit out by another.

✦ **Persistence:**   the amount of time a child devotes to an activity. Some children play happily with a toy for a long time; other children move quickly from one activity to another.

✦ **Adaptability:**   how quickly and easily a child adjusts to change. Some babies adjust quickly; others are upset at even the slightest disruption of their routine.

✦ **Quality of mood:**   the extent to which a child expresses positive or negative emotions. Some children are consistently upbeat and happy, even in the face of trying circumstances. Others are consistently unhappy; they whine or become sad at a moment's notice.

✦ **Distractibility:**   the degree to which stimuli in the environment alter a child's behavior. Some children stop crying if they are given a toy; other children fuss regardless of what one does to draw their attention.

✦ **Threshold of responsiveness:**   the intensity of stimulation needed to elicit a response. Some infants are sensitive to almost any noise, light, or touch; others seem unaware even of bright lights or loud noises.

✦ **Intensity of reaction:**   the energy level of a child's response. Some infants whimper softly when they cry, others scream and cry loudly.

Temperamental traits are thought to be stable and enduring throughout the life span, particularly after 24 months (Lemery, Goldsmith, Klinnert, & Mrazek, 1999). To the extent that this is true, children who are intense and negative in mood as infants will continue to be intense and negative in mood as older children, adolescents, and adults. Table 6.3 presents examples of how different temperamental qualities may be expressed over time. For example, an infant who is high in adaptability will enjoy his or her first bath. As a preschooler, this child will play happily with new peers. As a school-aged child, she or he will look forward to beginning a new school year.

Although there is considerable evidence that temperament is consistent across development (Braungart-Rieker & Stifter, 1996; Caspi & Silva, 1995), temperament does not always follow a predictable course. Thomas and Chess (1985) found that some children in their study showed consistency in temperamental traits, other children were consistent in certain aspects of temperament but inconsistent in others, and still other children changed completely in a number of temperamental qualities. These findings suggest that the expression of one's temperament may be modifiable and that socialization and other environmental influences affect the temperament we observe in others (Wachs & King, 1994).

PATTERNS OF TEMPERAMENTAL RESPONDING

Based on their longitudinal observations, Thomas and Chess (1985) identified three general patterns of temperamental responding. Using different combinations of temperamental traits, Thomas and Chess classified 65 percent of the infants in the study into one of three temperamental groups (see Table 6.4):

✦ **The easy child.**   Infants in this group behave predictably and respond positively to new situations. These infants easily get on a schedule and quickly adapt to changes in their routine. They smile a lot, accept frustration with little protest, are easily comforted, and generally are a joy and a pleasure to caregivers. About 40 percent of infants display this type of temperament.

TABLE 6.3
Examples of Temperamental Qualities Expressed over Time

TEMPERAMENTAL QUALITY	RATING	2 MONTHS	1 YEAR	10 YEARS
Rhythmicity	Regular	Has been on 4-hour feeding schedule since birth; has regular bowel movements	Naps after lunch each day; always drinks bottle before bed	Eats only at mealtimes; sleeps the same amount of time each night
	Irregular	Awakes at a different time each morning; size of feedings varies	Will not fall asleep for an hour or more; moves bowels at a different time each day	Falls asleep at a different time each night; food intake varies
Approach-withdrawal	Positive	Smiles and licks washcloth; has always liked bottle	Approaches strangers readily; sleeps well in new surroundings	Went to camp happily; loved to ski the first time
	Negative	Rejected cereal the first time; cries when strangers appear	Cries when placed on sled; will not sleep in strange beds	Was severely homesick at camp during first days; does not like new activities
Adaptability	Adaptive	Was passive during first bath, now enjoys bathing; smiles at nurse	Was afraid of toy animals at first, now plays with them happily	Likes camp, although homesick during first days; learns enthusiastically
	Not adaptive	Is still startled by sudden, sharp noises; resists diapering	Continues to reject new foods each time they are offered	Does not adjust well to new school or new teacher; comes home late for dinner even when punished
Intensity of reaction	Mild	Does not cry when diapers are wet; whimpers instead of crying when hungry	Does not fuss much when clothing is pulled on over head	When a mistake is made in a model airplane, corrects it quietly; does not comment when reprimanded
	Intense	Cries when diapers are wet; rejects food vigorously when satisfied	Laughs hard when father plays rough; screams and kicks when temperature is taken	Tears up an entire page of homework if one mistake is made; slams door of room when teased by younger brother
Quality of mood	Positive	Smacks lips when first tasting new food; smiles at parents	Likes bottle; reaches for it and smiles; laughs loudly when playing peek-a-boo	Enjoys new accomplishments; laughs when reading a funny passage aloud
	Negative	Fusses after nursing; cries when carriage is rocked	Cries when given injections; cries when left alone	Cries when unable to solve homework problem; is very "weepy" if not getting enough sleep

SOURCE: Thomas, Chess, and Birch, 1968.

TABLE 6.4

Categorization of Children's Temperament

TEMPERAMENTAL QUALITY	EASY CHILD	SLOW-TO-WARM-UP CHILD	DIFFICULT CHILD
Rhythmicity	Very regular	Varies	Irregular
Approach-withdrawal	Positive approach	Initial withdrawal	Withdrawal
Adaptability	Very adaptable	Slowly adaptable	Slowly adaptable
Intensity of reaction	Low or mild	Mild	Intense
Quality of mood	Positive	Slightly negative	Negative

SOURCE: Adapted from Thomas, Chess, and Birch, 1968.

✦ **The difficult child.**   These infants are almost the opposite of the easy child: they are irregular in their schedules and bodily functions, are slow to adapt to change, cry longer and louder than other infants, and generally are wary of new people or situations. Difficult infants require a lot of patience and energy from caregivers. About 10 percent of infants display this type of temperament.

✦ **The slow-to-warm-up child.**   Infants in this group are characterized by mild intensity of positive and negative reactions. They tend to be active but initially do not respond well to new situations or people. Over time, however, these infants make the appropriate adjustment and display increased interest and enjoyment. About 15 percent of infants display this type of temperament.

Not all children can be classified into one of the three temperamental groups (35 percent are unclassified). In addition, most children display a wide range of responses to their environment and do not fit neatly into a particular category. Easy children are not always easy, and difficult children are not difficult in all situations (Thomas & Chess, 1985). For these reasons, the concept of a difficult temperament has been questioned (Bates, 1987). Is a difficult temperament a pattern of traits in the child or a social perception on the part of the caregiver? What is considered difficult by one caregiver may not be by another, although a difficult temperament at 18 months is predictive of behavior problems ten years later (Guerin, Gottfried, & Thomas, 1997).

The perception of temperamental qualities in an infant also is influenced by cultural factors. For example, in areas of Brazil where infant mortality is very high because of impoverished conditions, caregivers show a preference for difficult infants (Schepher-Hughes, 1987). This preference is based on the perception that difficult infants are stronger than placid, easy infants and are therefore more likely to survive the harsh conditions. Similarly, difficult infants born into the Masai tribe in Kenya are preferred over easy infants because they are viewed as potential warriors for the tribe, a role that is highly valued (DeVries, 1984). Thus, caregivers' perceptions of and responses to infant temperaments are influenced by the context in which they live (Wachs & King, 1994).

HOW DO PARENT-INFANT ATTACHMENTS INFLUENCE DEVELOPMENT?

During infancy and toddlerhood more than at any other time in their development, children are dependent on their parents to meet their basic needs for healthy growth and development. Although the influence exerted by parents is just one of many,

What Are the Early Roots of Shyness?

"My daughter and I have never been close.... I gave up my career to do special things with her and we often times clash. She prefers doing things alone instead of playing with me.... She now is very passive at school, does not want group attention, prefers to play alone but likes to watch others play.... I feel that Julie was born this way" (Rubin & Asendorpf, 1993, pp. 3–4).

In this excerpt from a letter, a mother comes to the conclusion that her daughter's shyness and social withdrawal have a genetic basis, were present from birth, and are part of her temperament. This mother's conclusion is consistent with research findings on the early roots of shyness. For example, Kagan and colleagues (Kagan, 1989; Kagan, Snidman, & Arcus, 1993) found that about 15 to 20 percent of healthy 1- to 2-year-old Caucasian children are extremely and consistently shy, timid, and fearful when they encounter unfamiliar situations. These children hesitate in their approach to objects, remain quiet with new people, and stay close to their mother. Longitudinal studies indicate that over 75 percent of these children retain this shyness through the eighth year of life (Kagan et al., 1993). By contrast, approximately 30 percent of Caucasian children are fear-

less, uninhibited, and outgoing. They approach objects without hesitation, talk spontaneously to unfamiliar persons, and spend little time close to their mothers.

In comparing shy children with those who are not, Kagan found that a combination of temperamental traits, including high motor activity and frequent crying upon novel stimulation, predicts early shyness. These qualities are thought to reflect differences in inherited physiological processes. Using these predictors, Kagan and colleagues identified two groups of infants, who were seen at 4 and 14 months of age. At 4 months, one group of infants showed frequent and vigorous motor activity, such as flexing and extending their limbs, arching the back, and crying frequently. The second group of infants showed low levels of motor activity and rarely cried (Kagan et al., 1993). At 14 months, the two groups of infants were observed in situations likely to produce fearful reactions, such as being presented with a noisy metal robot. Over 60 percent of the infants who were active and cried a lot at 4 months were fearful at 14 months. In contrast, only 12 percent of the infants who were low in temperamental reactivity at 4 months were fearful at 14 months.

These findings suggest that some children have a biological predisposition

to respond with fear and withdrawal to new or strange environments. The relationship between the 4-month profile of motor activity and crying and later signs of shyness was not due to differences in gestational age at birth, health, or stressful conditions. Instead, it appears that the children's nervous systems made them vulnerable to anxiety and distress. This does not mean, however, that children cannot learn to control these feelings and the urge to withdraw. The environment appears to play a more substantial role in helping children overcome their tendencies toward shyness than in making them shy in the first place (Kagan et al., 1993).

Thinking It Through:

1. Were you or one of your siblings shy as a young child? (Offer evidence for your answer.) If so, what were some consequences of shyness for your (or your sibling's) development?
2. What learning principles might explain how shyness develops in children? How might shyness be overcome?
3. Why was it important for Kagan to control for gestational age, health, and stress? What roles might these factors play in the development of shyness?

---

most people believe that different child-rearing experiences early in development relate to differences in the way children turn out. These early parental influences relate primarily to **attachment**—an enduring emotional tie characterized by a tendency to seek and maintain closeness to a specific figure (the attachment figure), particularly under conditions of stress (Ainsworth, 1973). Children's patterns of attachment to their caregivers help explain their individual differences.

In the opening to this chapter, you met two 11-month-old boys, Jamal and Kyle, who were attending a birthday party. Although both boys found themselves in a similar situa-

attachment an enduring emotional tie characterized by a tendency to seek and maintain closeness to a specific figure (the attachment figure), particularly under conditions of stress tion, their reactions were noticeably different. Jamal was curious and readily explored the new environment, whereas Kyle was timid and did not explore his surroundings.

Jamal's and Kyle's reactions reflect important differences in how they perceive and respond to their environments. Jamal appears to have a strong sense of security that enables him to explore and be curious about his world, even in situations that are new and potentially stressful. Kyle, however, appears anxious and uncertain about his world, and this anxiety and uncertainty inhibit his ability to cope successfully with new and demanding environments.

Jamal and Kyle provide evidence that infants react differently to their environments. Temperament theorists explain these differences primarily as a product of differences in biological dispositions. Another explanation focuses on the quality of the relationships infants have with their caregivers. Based on the work of John Bowlby (1969) and Mary Ainsworth (1973), attachment theory was developed to account for individual differences in personality, social development, and interpersonal relationships. Unlike temperament theory, attachment theory places great emphasis on the caregiver child relationship as the foundation for individual differences. In contemporary Western societies, attachment theory is widely regarded as one of the most promising theories of personality and social development (Colin, 1996).

ATTACHMENT THEORY

Attachment is a long-lasting relationship, not a product of transient enjoyment or comfort. For most people, the best example of this relationship is the tie that usually develops between an infant and his or her primary caregiver (most often the mother). Evidence of this attachment is seen in a child's attempts to seek out and maintain contact with the primary caregiver and in the child's distress when separated from that person.

Attachment is distinct from bonding (see Chapter 4), which generally refers to the caregiver's tie to the infant. Some scientists believe that bonding occurs in the first hours or days after birth (Klaus & Kennell, 1982), although evidence in humans is scarce. Human parents have the ability to bond with their child even when they do not have contact with the child early in life. Adoptive parents, for example, form deep and meaningful emotional ties to their adopted children (Juffer & Rosenboom, 1997), even when the adoption occurs years after the child is born (Brodzinsky, Lang, & Smith, 1995) or when children are adopted after living in extreme institutional conditions, such as Romanian orphanages (Chisholm, 1998).

When not stressed, infants naturally seek interaction with their environments; they are intrigued and curious about their world. They explore their worlds contentedly if attachment figures are present, but become distressed and stop exploring when separated from attachment figures (Posada et al., 1995). Infants do not have to be in physical contact with the attachment figure for exploration and curiosity to occur—just knowing that the attachment figure is near seems sufficient to support play and exploration. Thus, infants use attachment figures as a base from which they attend to, learn about, and explore their worlds. When a threat arises, the attachment figure serves as a source of security and safety.

As the example of Jamal and Kyle shows, not all infants form the same kind of attachment to their caregivers. Infants differ in their ability to use attachment figures as a secure base and in the intensity and quality of emotions they feel toward attachment figures. Caregivers also differ considerably in how they respond to their infants and in the feelings they hold toward their infants.

THE DEVELOPMENT OF ATTACHMENT

Based on her observations of infants in the African country of Uganda and in Baltimore, Maryland, Mary Ainsworth (1973) identified phases in the development of early

TABLE 6.5

Ainsworth's Phases of Attachment

PHASE	AGE (IN MONTHS)	CHARACTERISTICS OF PHASE
1. Preattachment	0–2	Nondiscriminate responses to caregivers; reflexive rather than voluntary behaviors; positive response to both social and nonsocial stimuli
2. Attachment-in-the-making	2–6	Clear preference for social stimuli; positive response to familiar caregivers but not to unfamiliar ones; no single attachment preference observable
3. Clear-cut attachment	7–12	Clear preference for a single attachment figure; evidence of stranger and separation anxiety
4. Goal-corrected partnership	48	Recognition that caregivers have feelings or goals that may be different from the child's; attempts to change caregivers' plans and goals and become a partner in planning how the relationship proceeds (discussed in Chapter 8)

attachment relationships (see Table 6.5). Most of these phases take place during infancy and toddlerhood. Despite the large cultural differences between the two groups of infants, Ainsworth found that the sequences of development of attachment were very similar; subsequent research on infants raised in other cultures confirms her basic findings (Colin, 1996).

The Preattachment Phase

During the first eight weeks of life, infants are sometimes referred to as "asocial" because both social and nonsocial stimuli produce positive responses. Infants at this age rarely protest when caregivers leave and do not distinguish among the various caregivers who attend to them (Thompson, 1998).

Ainsworth called this first phase the *preattachment phase*, referring to the fact that young infants do not discriminate in their responses to caregivers. There is little evidence that infants consistently prefer the primary caregiver to any other person. Recall from Chapters 4 and 5 that infants are drawn to human faces and to the human voice but at first do not associate these with any particular person. Although infants' responses to caregivers generally are reflexive rather than voluntary, their reflexive behaviors strengthen the emotional tie with caregivers and draw caregivers to them.

The Attachment-in-the-Making Phase

After a period of indiscriminate responding, infants around 2 to 6 months of age gradually begin to direct their responses to familiar rather than unfamiliar people. This shift characterizes Ainsworth's second phase. In this *attachment-in-the-making phase*, infants more often smile at, look at, reach for, and are soothed by familiar rather than unfamiliar people.

Despite their increased preference for familiar caregivers, Ainsworth did not consider infants in this phase to have full-fledged attachments. By definition, attachments cannot occur until the child understands that people and objects have an independent existence—that is, until the infant develops the concept of object permanence. As you learned in Chapter 5, for a young infant, a parent who is "out of sight" is "out of mind." Thus, in the second phase of attachment, infants may recognize caregivers and respond to them with a delight and pleasure they do not show to strangers, but attachment has not yet fully developed.

The Clear-Cut Attachment Phase

Important changes that take place around 7 months of age enable infants to develop clear-cut attachments to their primary caregivers. Evidence of these changes comes from studies of infants placed in foster care. If infants are placed in foster care prior to 7 months of age, they usually adapt to a new caregiver quite easily. In contrast, infants placed in foster care after 7 months of age do not adjust quickly or easily (Colin, 1996). These findings provide us with evidence of a developing attachment—disruption of this attachment elicits specific and adverse responses.

What changes at 7 months of age? In addition to developing a sense of object permanence at around this age, infants become able to set goals (see Chapter 5)—they make planned efforts to achieve contact with the attachment figure, protesting when separated or lifting their arms to be picked up. These early efforts at making contact and influencing caregivers are primitive, however. An infant may pull a book out of mother's hand if she is reading or may pull the telephone cord while father is talking. As children mature, they find more sophisticated and acceptable ways to achieve contact. But in all cases, children are finding ways of satisfying their needs for help and comfort (Maccoby, 1980).

Stranger Anxiety

Stranger anxiety, a characteristic of the clear-cut attachment phase, is a wary and fearful reaction to strangers, which appears at about 7 months. Until that time, infants often respond positively to strangers, but after forming attachments, they become fearful of strangers. The intensity of their responses peaks between 8 and 10 months of age and then gradually declines during the second year (Thompson, 1998). Stranger anxiety may not completely subside; even some 4-year-old children show signs of wariness when encountering a stranger, particularly in an unfamiliar setting.

Although most children show some stranger anxiety, this wariness of strangers is not universal or consistent. For example, an infant is less likely to respond negatively to a stranger if the caregiver is holding the child, if the caregiver greets the stranger in a warm and pleasant tone of voice, or if the caregiver talks to the child about the stranger in a soothing voice (Gunnar, 1980). Additionally, infants who are exposed regularly to large numbers of adults show less stranger anxiety than other infants (Colin, 1996). Infants who have few encounters with strangers may associate strangers with negative experiences, such as going to the doctor for a vaccination.

Separation Anxiety

Another response that appears during the clear-cut attachment phase is **separation anxiety,** in which negative protests accompany separation from the attachment figure. Protests over the attachment figure's leaving usually peak in frequency and strength between 12 and 18 months of age, but such protests commonly remain strong through the second year of life (Colin, 1996). Studies of infants in diverse cultures reveal similar patterns: before 7 or 8 months of age, infants rarely protest when separated from their caregivers. Separation anxiety then increases during the second year of life and declines thereafter (Kagan, 1976). Infants protest and show distress when attachment figures depart and express joy and relief when reunited with them. These responses are not shown when strangers depart or reappear. Thus, separation from attachment figures

stranger anxiety a wary and fearful reaction to strangers

separation anxiety a response in which negative protests accompany separation from attachment figures

Handling Early Separation

Saying good-bye to an infant can be trying, not only for the infant but also for the caregiver. In one study, fathers and mothers reported equally high levels of separation anxiety (Deater-Deckard et al., 1994). Here are some suggestions for handling inevitable early separations (adapted from Hall & Schmidt, 1996):

- Understand that children react differently depending on their temperament, their age, and the situation. For instance, what works when you leave a child home may not work when you leave a child at day care.
- Make separations as stress-free as possible. Try to plan so that the child is rested and content when you have to leave.
- Gradually build up the amount of time you spend away from the child. Start slowly, and increase the length of the separation over time.
- Try to set a schedule for the separation, and stick to it if you can. Establishing a routine helps the child develop a sense of predictability.
- Understand that separation is difficult for the caregiver as well as for the child. In fact, early separations may be more difficult for caregivers than they are for infants.
- If possible, try to use the same substitute caregiver. Establishing trust with the substitute caregiver is important for both the primary caregiver and the child.
- Try not to leave without saying good-bye. Communication is important, even with a preverbal child.
- Make leaving a game. Saying good-bye gets easier with practice. Games like peek-a-boo and hide-and-seek provide playful ways of experiencing separation.
- Use transitional objects. Special toys or comforting objects (such as blankets) can help smooth difficult separations and other transitions.

---

represents a significant source of stress for infants—and their caregivers (Deater-Deckard, Scarr, McCartney, & Eisenberg, 1994).

The final phase of attachment shown in Table 6.5 is not reached until 4 years of age, when children begin to negotiate relationships more directly. This phase is discussed in Chapter 8.

ASSESSING PATTERNS OF ATTACHMENT IN THE STRANGE SITUATION

The most common method of assessing attachment was developed by Ainsworth; it is based on characteristic responses of infants to the presence or absence of caregivers and strangers. Ainsworth's purpose was to create a situation that would activate infant attachment behavior not routinely observed in the home. The **Strange Situation** is a procedure used with infants between 11 and 18 months of age (Ainsworth, Blehar, Waters, & Wall, 1978). Carried out in an environment that is unfamiliar to the infant, this procedure consists of eight 3-minute episodes involving exploration, separation, and reunion sequences with a caregiver (usually the mother) and an adult stranger. Table 6.6 describes the eight episodes of the Strange Situation.

In Episode 1, rapport is established. During Episode 2, observers assess the extent to which the infant uses his or her mother as a secure base for exploring the new room and toys. Reactions to a stranger are assessed in Episode 3. Separation anxiety is assessed in Episode 4, when the mother leaves the infant with the stranger. In Episode 6, separation responses are observed in a more stressful context, when the infant is left alone. If the in-

Strange Situation a procedure used to assess infants' attachment behavior under conditions of increasing stress due to separations from caregivers and strangers

TABLE 6.6
Ainsworth's Strange Situation Procedure

EPISODE	PEOPLE PRESENT*	PROCEDURE
Setup	E	Appropriate for infants 11–18 months old, the procedure requires an unfamiliar room with two chairs, an attractive collection of toys, and space for the infant to move about. Two chairs and the toys are on the three points of a triangle, far enough apart so that the observer can determine whether the infant is nearer the caregiver, the toys, or the other adult.
Episode 1	I, C, E	E shows C where to put I and where to sit, then leaves. If necessary, C gets I to start playing with the toys.
Episode 2	I, C	C does not initiate interaction with I but may respond if necessary.
Episode 3	I, C, S	S enters, sits quietly for 1 minute, talks with C for 1 minute, and engages I in interaction or play for 1 minute.
Episode 4	I, S	C exits. S lets I play. If I needs comfort, S tries to provide it. If I cries hard, the episode is terminated early.
Episode 5	I, C	C calls to I from outside the door; C enters, greets I, and pauses. If I needs comfort, C may provide it. When I is ready to play with the toys, C sits in a chair. If I is very upset and needs extra time, the episode can be extended.
Episode 6	I	C exits. I is left alone. If I cries hard, the episode is terminated early.
Episode 7	I, S	S enters, greets I, and pauses. If I is OK, S sits. If I needs comfort, S tries to provide it. If I cries hard, the episode is terminated early.
Episode 8	I, C	C calls to I from outside the door; C enters, greets I, and pauses. If I needs comfort, C may provide it. C lets I return to play when ready.

*I = Infant, C = Caregiver, E – Experimenter, S = Stranger
SOURCE: Adapted from Colin, 1996.

fant becomes highly upset, these episodes are terminated early. The infant's responses to being reunited with the mother are observed in Episodes 5 and 8, and the infant's ability to be soothed by the stranger is assessed in Episode 7. Thus, Ainsworth devised a series of episodes that allow researchers to compare and contrast infants' responses to the presence and absence of their mother (or other caregiver) and the presence and absence of a stranger. Based on the responses observed over the eight episodes of the Strange Situation, four patterns of attachment were identified. These four patterns are outlined in Table 6.7.

Secure Attachment

Jamal's behaviors described at the beginning of this chapter illustrate the first pattern, **secure attachment.** When he and his mother went through the Strange Situation, he explored the new room and the new toys right away (Episode 2). He often vocalized and showed the toys to his mother. When the stranger came in during Episode 3, Jamal looked intensely at her, moved closer to his mother, and resumed his play. When his mother left, Jamal stopped playing and became upset. When the stranger tried to comfort him, he accepted the contact and stopped crying but showed little interest in playing. Upon his

secure attachment pattern in which infants use their attachment figures as a secure base, obtaining comfort from their presence and becoming distressed by their absence

TABLE 6.7
Ainsworth's Patterns of Attachment

PATTERN	CHARACTERISTICS
Secure	Uses caregiver as secure base for exploration Seeks and maintains contact with caregiver at reunion Shows little or no resistance to contact with caregiver Shows clear distress during separation If distressed, seeks caregiver and is soothed by contact
Avoidant	Does not seek or maintain contact with caregiver Responds positively to stranger Shows little distress at separation from caregiver Often shows some avoidance of caregiver at reunion
Ambivalent	Appears nervous and timid in exploration episodes Seeks contact with and resists release from caregiver but also is openly resistant to interaction with caregiver Is distressed during separations but has difficulty settling down during reunion episodes Often shows angry behavior—hits, kicks, or squirms while being held by caregiver Sometimes appears passive, unhappy, or helpless
Disorganized/ Disoriented	Often shows avoidance and resistance Sometimes freezes in place in odd postures Shows bizarre repetitions of behavior Lacks a coherent strategy for handling separations and reunions Responds inconsistently in Strange Situation May exhibit behaviors reflecting child abuse and neglect

SOURCE: Colin, 1996; Thompson, 1998.

mother's return, Jamal smiled, rushed to meet her, and eagerly accepted her comfort. Afterward, Jamal returned to playing with the toys.

When left alone during Episode 6, Jamal immediately stopped playing, began to cry, and crawled to the door. When the stranger entered during Episode 7, Jamal resisted attempts to be comforted, and his mother's final return was met with clear signals that he wanted to be picked up and his cries were soothed right away. Jamal resumed playing with the toys until the end of the final episode.

These responses show that Jamal uses his mother as a secure base from which he can separate to some degree to explore his environment. Securely attached infants seek out their attachment figures, obtain much pleasure and comfort from their presence, and are distressed and bothered by their absence. Approximately 68 percent of middle-class American infants are classified as securely attached infants.

Avoidant Attachment

The second pattern of attachment is referred to as **avoidant attachment.** Infants who fall into this pattern show conspicuous avoidance of contact or interaction with the caregiver, as is seen in the case of Trisha. Like Jamal, Trisha readily separated from her

avoidant attachment pattern characterized by conspicuous avoidance of contact or interaction with the caregiver mother and explored the toys during Episode 2. But the entrance of the stranger during Episode 3 was met with a smile. After her mother left, Trisha continued to play contentedly. During Episode 5, Trisha reacted neutrally to her mother's return and quickly turned back to the toys. In contrast to Jamal, Trisha did not seek physical contact with her mother when she returned. When left alone during Episode 6, Trisha became unhappy and fussy. This negative response disappeared when the stranger entered. When her mother returned in the final episode, Trisha barely took notice of her.

On first glance, Trisha appears to be very independent. She did not respond to the presence or absence of her mother. Trisha clearly disliked being left alone, but she was as easily calmed by the stranger as she was by her mother. Does this mean that avoidant infants like Trisha are truly indifferent to their attachment figures? After much consideration, Ainsworth and colleagues concluded that avoidant infants may be masking the insecure distress they feel and suppressing their impulses to seek comfort from their mother. Studies examining the physiological responses of these infants show that they are aroused—their heart rates rise—during the stressful segments of the Strange Situation (Sroufe & Waters, 1979). Their behaviors may suggest that these infants are unresponsive, but their internal responses reveal the discomfort they feel (Colin, 1996). Approximately 20 percent of infants are classified as exhibiting avoidant attachment.

Ambivalent Attachment

The third pattern, **ambivalent attachment,** is reflected in Kyle's responses to the Strange Situation. During Episode 2, Kyle was reluctant to leave his mother's side and explored the new room and toys very little compared to either Trisha or Jamal. He was noticeably anxious when the stranger entered. When his mother first left, Kyle cried angrily and rejected the stranger's attempts to comfort him. When his mother returned, she was greeted with a cry and clear signals that he wanted to be picked up. When Kyle's mother picked him up, he wrapped his arms around her but also pushed, kicked, and cried. The second departure of his mother during Episode 6 elicited immediate and strong protests from Kyle. He cried angrily and threw himself to the floor. When the stranger came in, Kyle screamed and struggled against being held by her. His mother was sent back in early, and Kyle went crying to her with his arms held up, indicating that he wanted to be picked up. But again, when his mother picked him up, Kyle began to squirm in her arms and push away from her as if he wanted to get down. When set down, Kyle screamed even louder, clung to his mother's skirt, and thrashed out at her. When picked up again, Kyle continued to be upset and was stiff and uncomfortable in her arms. After a period of time of being held even more tightly by his mother, Kyle began to relax in her arms. Eventually, Kyle did resume playing with the toys.

Kyle's behavior toward his mother is inconsistent. He appears to want to be comforted by his mother but also seems to receive little comfort once in her arms. His responses are ambivalent—both desiring and resisting her contact and comfort. Kyle and other infants who fall into the ambivalent attachment category are often unmistakably angry. About 12 percent of infants are classified as ambivalently attached.

Disorganized/Disoriented Attachment

An attachment pattern that was not part of Ainsworth's original classification system has been added (Main & Solomon, 1990). The **disorganized/disoriented attachment** classification was devised in response to the concern that a high percentage of infants who had been abused and/or neglected were classified as securely attached (Crittenden, 1988). Many researchers doubted that maltreated infants could have secure attachments, and closer examination of their behaviors in the Strange Situation revealed some abnormalities.

Infants classified as disorganized/disoriented in their attachments have no coherent strategy for handling separations from and reunions with their mother. Consequently,

ambivalent attachment pattern characterized by inconsistent behavior toward a caregiver

disorganized/disoriented attachment pattern characterized by lack of a coherent strategy for handling separations from and reunions with the caregiver their behavior is inconsistent, disorganized, and disoriented (Carlson, 1998). For example, when Brooks was assessed in the Strange Situation, she first approached her mother upon reunion and then froze and became dazed, avoiding her completely. When her mother returned, she began to cry. During the exploration phase (Episode 2), Brooks approached her mother with a toy but then became apprehensive toward her.

Why an abused or neglected infant like Brooks might react to the Strange Situation with this type of behavior is clear: she has the same need for contact and warmth from the caregiver that other children have, but her prior experiences of maltreatment have taught her that the caregiver may ignore or punish her bids for contact (Crittenden & Ainsworth, 1989). Thus, Brooks' inconsistent and disorganized responses reflect both her need for closeness and her expectations that her mother's behavior will be aversive.

CAREGIVER AND CHILD FACTORS AFFECTING ATTACHMENT

What influences account for the differences in the attachments Jamal, Trisha, Kyle, and Brooks formed with their caregivers? Many factors influence the quality of attachment, but two important influences are the sensitivity of the caregiver and the characteristics of the child.

Caregiver Sensitivity

Based on her research, Ainsworth concluded that what matters the most is the caregiver's sensitive responsiveness to the infant (De Wolff & van IJzendoorn, 1997). Sensitive responsiveness includes the ability to notice signals from the infant, interpret these signals accurately, and then respond appropriately. Securely attached infants like Jamal come to believe that their signals will elicit the attention they want and that their needs will be met (Isabella, 1993). Insensitive caregiving does not necessarily imply coldness or hostility; it refers to caregivers who fail to respond accurately and supportively to their infants' needs. For example, infants whose mothers are depressed will probably not have their needs met and will therefore be more likely to develop insecure attachments (Cicchetti, Rogosch, & Toth, 1998). Insensitive caregivers teach infants that their signals are ineffective (Susman-Stillman, Kalkose, Egeland, & Waldmen, 1996).

Infant Characteristics

Ainsworth and her colleagues believe that the quality of attachment depends solely on the caregiver's behavior. Other researchers, however, believe that characteristics of the infant play a role in influencing caregivers' behavior. Do some infants invite and others resist the caregiver behaviors that lead to secure attachments? Theories of temperament suggest that infants react very differently; for example, some children are more responsive to their environments than others, and some are more resistant to being held and cuddled than others (Seifer et al., 1996). Such characteristics shape the behaviors of their caregivers. Infants who like to be held, cuddled, and looked at foster caregiver sensitivity, whereas those who are difficult to soothe or are easily overstimulated may discourage it (Bridges, Connell, & Belsky, 1988; Seifer & Schiller, 1995).

Additional evidence of the role that infant characteristics may play in the formation of attachment comes from studies of children who have disabilities or are at risk. For example, deaf or blind infants often are slow to develop secure attachments to their mother (Meadow-Orlans, 1995). Compared to nondisabled children, these infants may respond in ways that are less likely to promote sensitive caregiving: blind infants, for instance, cannot use their gaze to attract their caregivers the way sighted infants can. Similarly, very-low-birthweight preterm infants are likely to be insecurely attached because they are less socially responsive and more difficult to soothe than are full-term infants (Mangelsdorf et al., 1996). Although disabled and at-risk infants can form healthy attachments, their behaviors do not encourage caregiver responsiveness to the same extent that other infants' behaviors do.

THE ROLE OF CULTURE IN ATTACHMENT

Attachment theory was proposed as a universal theory of development. However, because child-rearing goals, values, and behaviors vary from culture to culture, attachments may not have the same meaning in different cultures. For example, infants who rarely experience separation from their mother may react differently to the Strange Situation than do infants who experience separation more frequently. Japanese infants, who are encouraged to be dependent on their mothers, are more likely than US infants to cry and become passive when left alone. Correspondingly, Japanese mothers are more likely than US mothers to hold and maintain contact with their infants (Takahashi, 1990). Because of the increased stress experienced by Japanese infants in the Strange Situation, a higher percentage of Japanese infants than US infants are classified as ambivalently attached.

Research has confirmed different patterns of attachments in infants from different cultures (Miyake, Chen, & Campos, 1985). Figure 6.2 shows how the percentage of infants classified as secure, avoidant, or ambivalent varies from one culture to the next. In Germany, for example, where parents press infants to behave independently and rebuff their bids for contact, a sizable percentage of children are classified as avoidant. In contrast, in Japan, where mothers value contact and dependence, almost no children are classified as avoidant. In Israel, where children have only infrequent contact with unfamiliar people, almost half of the infants are classified as ambivalent. Compare this to the pattern of attachments found in Sweden, where children are exposed to large numbers of unfamiliar people.

American cultural diversity also leads to differences in attachment behaviors and patterns. European American mothers place a great deal of emphasis on self-confidence and self-reliance. These values reflect the individualism of the traditional European American culture. In contrast, Puerto Rican mothers place more emphasis on respect, obedience, and remaining connected with others (Harwood, Miller, & Irizarry, 1995). As a result, Puerto Rican infants are more likely to be classified as ambivalently attached than are European American infants.

CONSEQUENCES OF ATTACHMENT

How much does the nature of early attachment matter for children's development? The answer to this question is a subject of debate. Kohlberg and Kramer (1969) questioned the impact of early relationships on later development unless these relationships were extreme and traumatic. They maintained that the quality of early relationships is greatly transformed by the cognitive changes that take place later in life. It is therefore difficult to imagine how an infant's attachment early in life can have a strong effect on her or his development later in life.

Other researchers, however, believe that early attachments play an important role in influencing later development (Thompson, 1998). Children like Jamal, who have secure attachments, see themselves as lovable and feel their needs will be met. These children act in ways that are consistent with this benevolent view of the world (Belsky, Spritz, & Crnic, 1996). In contrast, Trisha, Kyle, and Brooks, who have insecure attachments, tend to develop a dramatically different view of themselves and their environments. They believe that the world is unsupportive, inconsistent, and rejecting. These beliefs, feelings, and behaviors link their past experiences and attachments with the present (Cassidy, Kirsh, Scolton, & Parke, 1996).

Studies support a link between early attachment and later development. For example, securely attached children get along better with their peers, tolerate frustration more successfully, and more fully express a wide range of emotions than do children who are not securely attached (Belsky & Cassidy, 1994; Sroufe, 1996). Older children who had secure attachments as infants approach their environments with interest and pleasure, are comfortable in seeking help from others, follow directions easily, and seldom cry, fuss,

FIGURE 6.2
Cultural Differences in Patterns of Attachment in Children

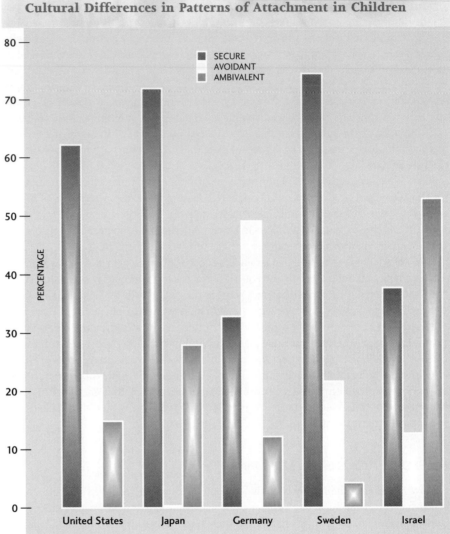

SOURCE: Miyake, Chen, and Campos, 1985.

Notice how the patterns of attachment vary from one culture to the next. What child-rearing and cultural factors contribute to these differences?

or become angry when encountering frustrating circumstances (Elicker, Englund, & Sroufe, 1992). In addition, attachment is related to later adjustment. For example, children with disorganized attachment are likely to experience later behavior problems and psychiatric problems (Carlson, 1998). Infant attachment also relates to later intellectual functioning; securely attached children remember positive events better than negative ones, whereas the reverse is true for insecurely attached children (Belsky et al., 1996). Thus, attachment histories can affect the kind of information that is attended to and remembered, and this can have long-term effects on later relationships.

ATTACHMENT TO FATHERS

In the United States, fathers spend considerably less time interacting with their infants than do mothers (Bailey, 1994). This difference has been found across a wide range of culturally diverse populations (Fracasso, Lamb, Scholmerich, & Leyendecker, 1997). There are, however, large individual differences among fathers, with some very involved in caregiving and others almost completely disengaged (Jain, Belsky, & Crnic, 1996). As children get older, father involvement increases (Coltrane, 1995; Cooksey & Fondell, 1996).

Not only do fathers and mothers spend different amounts of time with their infants, but they interact differently with their infants, too. Fathers typically interact as playmates, rather than as protectors, comforters, or care providers (Bornstein & Lamb, 1992). When infants need caring for, many fathers let the mother take over (Parke, 1995). But despite these differences in the nature of interactions, infants develop secure attachments with fathers (Belsky, 1996).

Research comparing infants' responses in the Strange Situation suggests that infants cry when both mothers and fathers leave the room, but do not cry when strangers leave the room. When reunited with either parent, infants show relief and comfort. Exploration of the room is greater when either mothers or fathers are present than when they are gone (Colin, 1996). Although infants' reactions generally are less intense with their fathers, they treat fathers as attachment figures who serve as secure bases (Doherty, 1997; Parke, 1995). Thus, when given the opportunity, fathers have as much capacity as mothers to form intimate ties with their infants, to be sensitive to their needs, and to be competent in nurturing them (Beitel & Parke, 1998).

Do infants who are securely attached to their mother also develop a secure attachment to their father? According to a meta-analysis of studies that examined the relationship between infant-mother and infant-father attachment, there is some consistency (Fox, Kimmerly, & Schafer, 1991). Infants who are securely attached to one parent tend to be securely attached to the other parent, and infants who are anxiously attached to one parent are anxiously attached to the other. Thus, mothers and fathers generally provide caregiving behaviors that mutually support the development of attachment. This consistency also suggests that one sensitive parent may buffer the infant from deficiencies in the other parent's behavior, thereby promoting secure attachments to both parents (Colin, 1996).

HOW DOES DAY CARE INFLUENCE INFANTS' AND TODDLERS' DEVELOPMENT?

In the United States, there are over 20 million children under the age of 6, and the parents of about 12 million of these children work outside the home (Center for the Future of Children, 1996). This situation is radically different from that in the 1950s, when only 12 percent of married women with preschool children worked outside the home. Until 1975, the Census Bureau did not even collect labor force data on mothers with infants or toddlers because it was assumed that few mothers worked (National Issues Forum, 1989). Now, about 60 percent do so, largely for economic reasons. The increase in the number of working mothers with children less than 3 years of age is especially dramatic. More than half of all mothers with children under age 1 are in the work force, either full or part time (Center for the Future of Children, 1996). The rapid entry of women into the labor force over the past few decades has altered the way very young children are raised, and the demands for—and concerns about—day care have soared.

PATTERNS OF DAY CARE USE

Although it is popularly believed that most infants and toddlers with working mothers are cared for in group day care centers, the fact is that the majority are cared for in homes by relatives, such as fathers, mothers, siblings, grandparents, uncles, aunts, or cousins (US Department of Commerce, 1996). As Figure 6.3 indicates, children under 3 are more likely to be cared for by relatives than are older children. As shown in Figure

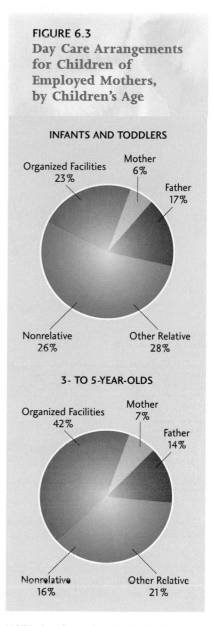

FIGURE 6.3
Day Care Arrangements for Children of Employed Mothers, by Children's Age

INFANTS AND TODDLERS

Organized Facilities 23%
Mother 6%
Father 17%
Other Relative 28%
Nonrelative 26%

3- TO 5-YEAR-OLDS

Organized Facilities 42%
Mother 7%
Father 14%
Other Relative 21%
Nonrelative 16%

NOTE: Care by mothers includes that of mothers working at home and away from home. Other relatives include siblings, grandparents, uncles, aunts, and cousins.
SOURCE: US Department of Commerce, 1996.

Compare the figures for infants and toddlers to those for preschool children. Notice especially the increase in the percentage of older children who receive care from someone other than a relative. What factors contribute to these differences?

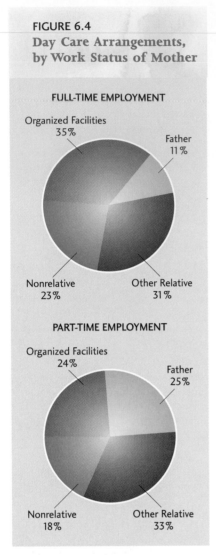

FIGURE 6.4
Day Care Arrangements, by Work Status of Mother

FULL-TIME EMPLOYMENT

Organized Facilities
35%

Father
11%

Nonrelative
23%

Other Relative
31%

PART-TIME EMPLOYMENT

Organized Facilities
24%

Father
25%

Nonrelative
18%

Other Relative
33%

NOTE: Other relatives include siblings, grandparents, uncles, aunts, and cousins.
SOURCE: US Department of Commerce, 1996.
What differences do you see when you compare the figure for mothers who are employed full time to those who work part time? What aspects of working full time account for these differences?

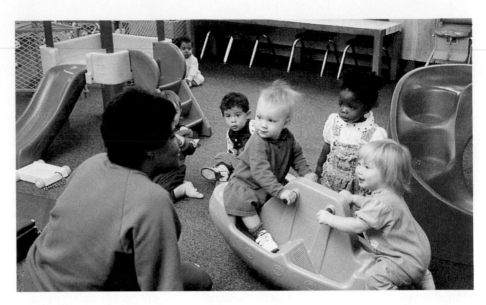

More young children than ever before are being cared for by someone other than their parents. What social changes contribute to this increase in nonparental care? How do you feel about this? What factors should parents consider when looking for high-quality care for their young children?

6.4, preschoolers are more likely to be cared for by relatives, particularly the father, if the mother works part time rather than full time. Mothers who work full time are more likely to rely on organized day care centers or nonrelatives to care for their children (US Department of Commerce, 1996).

With the exception of government-sponsored programs for children from poor families, child care (particularly infant care) in the United States is privately owned and operated (Lamb, Sternberg, & Ketterlinus, 1992). Nationwide regulations have never been mandated by the federal government, and existing state and local regulations generally only establish minimal levels to ensure that children are protected from harm (Phillips, Lande, & Goldberg, 1990; Scarr, 1998). According to some estimates (Whitebook, Howes, & Phillips, 1989), 67 percent of child care centers are "barely adequate" in quality. Infants from high-income families, as well as those from low-income families that receive subsidies, are more likely to receive high-quality day care than are infants from middle-income families (NICHD, 1997).

EFFECTS OF DAY CARE

With so many infants and toddlers spending so much time away from their parents, particularly their mothers, how might children's development in general and their attachments in particular be affected? As you might expect, this question is not easily answered.

Attempts to examine the effects of early child care have led to contradictory conclusions. The results from several studies show that day care may benefit low-income children and have benign, sometimes even beneficial, effects on middle-class children (Clarke-Stewart, Allhusen, & Clements, 1995; Hausfather, Toharia, LaRoche, & Engelsmann, 1997). Day care generally enhances the intellectual performance of low-income children, increases their curiosity and concentration, and fosters independence, social competence, and cooperativeness (Lamb et al., 1992; NICHD, 1996; Phillips, McCartney, & Scarr, 1987). But the results from other studies have not been as positive. For example, some studies report that day care increases children's aggression and decreases their compliance (Vandell & Corasaniti, 1990).

How Does Day Care Affect Infants' Emotional Development?

Questions about the effects of infant day care on children's development have fueled much research and debate. Research has produced inconsistent results—sometimes finding positive outcomes and sometimes finding negative ones. Egeland and Hiester (1995) proposed that these inconsistencies may be due to differences in the quality of infant-mother attachments. Because securely attached infants may feel anger or ambivalence in response to repeated separations from their mother, these children may be adversely affected by early day care. In contrast, children who are insecurely attached may be less affected by the separation from their mother and show positive responses to day care.

To test their predictions, Egeland and Hiester chose 12-month-old infants who did and did not have early day care experience. The mothers and infants came from a sample of high-risk poverty families. To assess attachment, the infants and their mothers were observed in the Strange Situation. Based on a longitudinal design, measures of emotional health, anger, aggression, anxiety, and self-control were obtained from observations and teacher reports collected yearly through third grade and again when the children were in sixth grade.

When they were 3 ½ years of age, home-reared children who had been securely attached as infants displayed fewer negative emotions and less avoidance of mothers than did day care infants who had been securely attached. These findings continued to hold for securely attached children when they were in kindergarten. However, the reverse pattern was found for those insecurely attached as infants: home-reared children were more withdrawn and less confident than day care children. These effects of day care and attachment decreased over time, disappearing by third grade.

Egeland and Hiester concluded that the separation of mother and child necessitated by day care has different effects on securely and insecurely attached infants, at least during the early years of life. Repeated separations appear to make securely attached infants vulnerable to experiencing anger and aggression. Early day care may, however, be a protective factor for insecurely attached infants, enhancing their social and psychological development. One possible reason for this difference may be that the care children receive in day care is different from that received from their mothers. Securely attached children are likely to find day care providers less sensitive and responsive than their mothers. But for in-securely attached children, day care may compensate for poor relationships with their mothers and provide more stability and consistency than they get at home.

Security of attachment and day care experience did not predict outcomes beyond first grade. Egeland and Hiester suggest that the lack of findings for older children may be best explained by the influence of elementary school. By the second grade, children have experienced a similar daily environment for an extended time, regardless of their experiences with their mothers or with day care. Thus, school may have a leveling effect, making children more similar.

Thinking It Through:

1. The children and mothers in this study came from a sample of high-risk families in poverty. Would you expect the same results with children and mothers from high-income families? Why or why not?
2. What kinds of experiences do children have in school that would weaken the effects of early day care?
3. What significance do the findings of this study have for making social or political policy decisions about day care?

Beginning in the late 1980s, the accumulation of evidence regarding the impact of infant day care on mother-infant attachment led some researchers to conclude that day care has adverse effects on attachment. Specifically, Belsky (1988, 1990) concluded that infants may be at risk for insecure attachments if they spend more than 20 hours per week in nonmaternal care during their first year of life. When observed in the Strange Situation, infants with early extended day care experiences were more likely to avoid and ignore their mothers.

Belsky's conclusions have drawn intense criticism (Clarke-Stewart, 1992). One criticism is that Belsky's conclusions are too strong: the majority of infants with early extended day care experiences are securely attached to their mothers (Thompson, 1991). Other researchers note that it is not day care itself that leads to insecure attachments but rather the comparatively greater stress that parents who rely on early extended infant care may be experiencing. Families under stress report that they spend less time researching day care options, need longer hours of day care for their infants, and accept poorer quality day care (Lamb, 1998; Phillips & Howes, 1987).

Howes (1990) found that the quality of care was a better predictor of later functioning than was the age at which children entered day care. Secure relationships with day care teachers have been found to enhance children's play, competence, and social relationships (Howes, Hamilton, & Matheson, 1994). A more recent large-scale study, involving 1300 families in ten different states over five years, found that early child care itself did not harm mother-infant attachment (NICHD, 1996). Additionally, sensitive and responsive mothering is more strongly predictive of positive outcomes for young children in day care than are child care factors (NICHD, 1998). Thus, what transpires in a young child's family appears to be more important than the day care itself in determining how children are affected by day care.

This debate highlights the need for affordable, high-quality day care (Scarr, 1998). Even Belsky (1990) notes that affordable, high-quality day care is not as available as it needs to be and that it is inappropriate to conclude that only mothers can care for their infants or that day care is bad for infants. Evidence from countries like Sweden, where high-quality infant day care is readily available, shows that infants with day care experience have more positive developmental outcomes (such as greater social skills and intellectual competence) than infants without such experience (Broberg, Hwang, Lamb, & Ketterlinus, 1989; Field, 1991). In the United States, where most child care is a for-profit enterprise, parental decisions regarding day care are more often determined by cost and availability than by quality (Griffin & Fein, 1996).

CULTURE AND DAY CARE

Variations in caregiving and day care for infants and children in different countries reflect different political, cultural, and social values. In the People's Republic of China, many day care policies reflect the collectivist values mandated by the central government as well as traditional values emphasizing obedience and respect. Because of China's overpopulation problems and one-child policy, most contemporary families are made up of six adults (four grandparents and two parents) and one child. The child therefore becomes the center of adult attention and care. To cultivate the correct socialistic spirit, day care is designed to train children in developing self-control, good habits, and obedience (Lee, 1992). By 2 or 3 years of age, children are learning how to satisfy others and behave according to formal and rigid standards, which mandate behaviors rarely expected of toddlers from Western cultures (such as sharing).

Very different child care conditions exist for children and families in Brazil, where three-quarters of the people live in impoverished urban areas. Intense urbanization has not been matched by corresponding increases in job, educational, health, or housing opportunities. Often, small children are confined in cramped spaces with little food, while adults and older siblings work long hours. Thus, there is great need for *creches* (day care), but only about 23 percent of preschool-aged children attend such programs. For the very young, such care is even less available; only about 10 percent of infants and toddlers attend *creches* (Campos, 1992). As you might imagine, in most of the *creches*, particularly those serving low-income families, children are placed in large groups supervised by relatively untrained staff. Although some improvements have been made, the unfavorable economic conditions and overcrowding lead to rigid routines in the *creches*, with little tolerance for child initiative and autonomy (Goncalves, 1990).

Judging the Quality of a Day Care Program

With so many children now attending some type of day care, it is critical to be able to judge the quality of these programs. Adults need to know how to identify good child care in order to make certain that a program is right for their child. Below are some guidelines to use in judging the quality of day care programs for young children (Child Care Action Campaign, 1996; Gonzalez-Mena & Eyer, 1993; NAEYC, 1995):

- *Give yourself time.* Finding high-quality child care takes time. Look at many different programs, and properly investigate a program before placing a child in it. Talk to relatives, friends, neighbors, and colleagues about their own child care arrangements. Get information from child care resources and referral agencies in the community. Visit a program at various times and watch the children: are they happy and content? If the program director discourages you from visiting or restricts your visit, look elsewhere.
- *Examine the physical environment.* Child care settings should be safe. Look for fences around the outdoor playground and well-constructed play equipment. Dangerous and toxic substances should be locked up, out of the children's reach. Electrical outlets and radiators should be covered. The child care workers should wash their hands before feeding, before handling food, before and after diapering, and after washing surfaces. A system for identifying the parent or guardian responsible for picking up the child should be well established and adhered to.
- *Take notice of the adult/child ratios and group size.* The more adults present, the more individual attention children receive. Younger children need more adults present than do older children. The total size of the group also is important. There should be no more than eight in a group of infants, and no more than twenty in a group of 5-year-olds. For each adult, there should be no more than the following number of children:

    3–4 infants or toddlers
    4–6 2-year-olds
    7–8 3-year-olds
    8–9 4-year-olds
    8–10 5-year-olds

- *Ask about the training of the staff and the licensing of the program.* Licensing and training requirements vary from state to state. Although compliance does not guarantee quality, the program should be in compliance with your state's requirements. Some professional organizations (such as the National Association for the Education of Young Children) accredit programs that meet high standards of quality. Ask for evidence of such accreditation. Qualified staff should have some direct education in early childhood education or child development.
- *Make certain the curriculum is developmentally appropriate.* The materials provided to children should be appropriate for their age and level of development. For infants and toddlers, there should be soft, washable, colorful toys that can be looked at or sucked. There should be no small parts that could come off and be swallowed. Preschoolers should have access to books, as well as toys, blocks, and equipment that emphasizes gross motor development.

In the Kenyan community of Morongo, where infant mortality is very high, infants and toddlers are never left alone. An infant is carried by his or her mother until about 6 months of age, at which time the child is taken care of by others in the family or community. This "dense caretaking environment" in early childhood reflects the Morongon child care strategy, which seeks to maximize survival in a high-mortality context during the most vulnerable period of the child's life (LeVine et al., 1994). The differences among child care in China, Brazil, and Kenya demonstrate how child care and its impact on children are influenced by the broader cultural, social, political, economic, and physical environments in which children and families find themselves.

How Does Day Care in an Israeli Kibbutz Affect Infant Development?

In Israel, many children are reared in a kibbutz, where they are cared for by trained child care specialists and are brought up in special quarters separate from their parents. A kibbutz is a village with a population ranging from 20 to 1500. Property is communally owned except for a few personal belongings, and work is centrally organized. Children stay with their mother during early infancy, but afterwards they move into houses with other children of their own age, occasionally sleeping with their parents. Thus, children of the same age from different families grow up together, and siblings of different ages live, eat, sleep, and play separately. This system allows mothers to participate fully in the extrafamilial work and citizenship duties of the kibbutz. Nevertheless, there are strong family ties; children and parents spend a great deal of leisure time together (Ben-David, 1983).

When Israel became an independent state in 1948, the founders believed that Israeli children would be the foundation on which the new culture and society would be built. Child care in the kibbutz is based on the belief that child rearing is best done by specially chosen and trained educators called *metapelets* (Rosenthal, 1991). The kibbutz style of education and child rearing focuses on cooperation, responsibility, and devotion to work. These qualities are considered important to the goals and functioning of the kibbutz and Israeli society in general (Sagi et al., 1997).

Research generally does not find consistent differences between children reared in a kibbutz and other Israeli children (Auerbach et al., 1989). There is, however, some evidence that kibbutz children who slept with their parents are more securely attached than those who slept in the infant houses (Sagi et al., 1994). In that study, however, there was not a single case of an avoidant attachment observed in any of the children. It appears that the kibbutz style of infant care eliminates active avoidance of, and anger toward, mothers, whether or not the infants sleep with their parents.

Many Americans have difficulty believing these results. Because they expect care providers and mothers to become rivals for the child's affection, they assume that attachment relationships would be severely disturbed by this child care arrangement. In Israel, however, a relationship with both the care providers and the mother is fostered and desired by the kibbutz collective, and these values minimize the risk (Devereux et al., 1983).

Thinking It Through:

1. How would you feel about being raised on a kibbutz? How might you be different if you had been raised on one? Why?
2. Would you consider raising your children in a communal environment such as a kibbutz? Why or why not?
3. Why would Americans be reluctant to accept a kibbutz-style child-rearing arrangement?

WHY ARE CHILDREN ABUSED AND NEGLECTED?

Katy was shaken so hard as a baby that her brain was smashed inside her skull. The damaged areas eventually had to be cut out, leaving her with half a brain. . . . A stroke at age 4 left her partially paralyzed. Tests revealed problems with Katy's pituitary gland and thyroid. . . . She goes to the hospital twice a week for 2 hours of occupational and speech therapy. Her sister, Micki, escaped the wrath of their angry father . . . while Micki was getting taller and slimmer, Katy was squat. Micki stands as testimony to what Katy's life might have been.

—ADAPTED FROM K. BLAND (1997)

Katy's story illustrates the horror and tragedy of the abuse and neglect of a child. The media have flooded us with stories of infants and children who have been abandoned, beaten, or killed by their caregivers; deprived of essential emotional and physical comfort; or sexually molested and abused. Such reports have increased the public's awareness of the incidence and severity of child abuse. In 1976, only 10 percent of Americans surveyed considered child abuse to be a problem; less than 20 years later, that figure had risen to over 90 percent (Finkelman, 1995). Although the stories attract tremendous attention and outrage, they fail to reveal the complex interplay of factors that make up the causes and consequences of child abuse and neglect.

DEFINITIONS OF CHILD ABUSE AND NEGLECT

Four categories of child maltreatment generally are distinguished: (1) **physical abuse,** in which caregivers cause death, serious physical harm, or imminent risk of serious harm to children; (2) **sexual abuse,** in which caregivers engage in sexual activity with children; (3) **neglect,** in which children's physical or emotional well-being is jeopardized by the failure to provide shelter, clothing, or protection; and (4) **psychological maltreatment,** in which caregivers emotionally abuse children by threatening them or conveying that they are worthless, unloved, or unwanted (Berliner & Elliot, 1996; Kolko, 1996; National Research Council, 1993). According to the scientific evidence, psychological maltreatment often is the strongest predictor of harmful developmental outcomes for the child (Hart, Brassard, & Karlson, 1996).

Caregivers who maltreat children often abuse or neglect them in more than one way (Belsky, 1993). In one study (Kaufman & Cicchetti, 1995), not one of the seventy physically abused children had experienced physical abuse alone. Each type of maltreatment has its own rates of occurrence, factors that influence it, and potential consequences. Because researchers and therapists tend to focus on one type of abuse or another, we know little about the extent to which different types of child abuse and neglect share common factors or respond to different types of treatment (National Research Council, 1993).

INCIDENCE OF CHILD ABUSE AND NEGLECT

The findings of the Third National Incidence Study of Child Abuse and Neglect (Sedlak & Broadhurst, 1996) indicate a sharp increase in the scope of the child maltreatment problem. Using a broad definition of maltreatment, this study estimated that the total number of US children who were reported as abused or neglected in 1994 was 2,815,600. Today, more than 3 million children are abused or neglected (NCCAN, 1999). This total reflects a 98 percent increase since 1986. The incidences for the various categories of abuse increased as follows:

+ The number of sexually abused children rose from 133,600 in 1986 to 300,200 (a 125 percent increase).
+ The number of neglected children increased from 917,200 in 1986 to 1,961,300 (a 114 percent increase).
+ The number of physically abused children increased from 311,500 in 1986 to 614,100 (a 92 percent increase).

Sadly, not all cases of alleged child abuse and neglect are investigated: in only 28 percent of the cases where children were harmed by abuse and neglect did an investigation take place.

CHARACTERISTICS OF VICTIMS OF CHILD ABUSE AND NEGLECT

Certain children face greater risk of experiencing abuse than others. Of course these children are not responsible for their abusive conditions; however, they possess characteristics known to increase the chance that abuse will occur. Following are some findings

physical abuse abuse that causes death, serious physical harm, or imminent risk of serious harm

sexual abuse abuse that involves engaging in sexual activity

neglect failure to provide shelter, clothing, or protection for a child

psychological maltreatment emotional abuse caused by threatening harm or conveying to an individual that she or he is worthless, unloved, or unwanted about how child and family characteristics are related to child abuse and neglect (Goodman, Emery, & Haugaard, 1998; Wiese & Daro, 1996):

✦ **Gender.**   Girls are sexually abused more often than boys. This gender difference in the incidence of sexual abuse leads to higher rates of abuse in general for girls.

✦ **Age.**   Young children are more at risk for maltreatment than older children. The lower rates as children get older reflect the reality that older children have more opportunities to escape, defend themselves, or retaliate.

✦ **Ethnicity.**   Generally, rates of child maltreatment do not differ as a function of children's race or ethnicity. However, ethnic minority children are likely to experience more severe types of maltreatment than Caucasian children.

✦ **Temperament.**   Children with difficult temperamental qualities (such as negative moods or intense crying) may tax parental tolerance, increasing the risk of abuse.

✦ **Income.**   Children living in families that earn less than $15,000 annually are 25 times more likely to experience some form of maltreatment than children in families earning $30,000 or more. (This statistic may be due to reporting bias.)

✦ **Family size.**   Children from large families are more likely to be abused and neglected than children from small families.

✦ **Disabilities.**   Children with disabilities are 4 to 10 times more likely to experience abuse or neglect than their nondisabled peers. Similarly, children with medical or health problems (such as birth complications, prematurity, or asthma) are more likely to experience abuse or neglect.

These findings tell us that some children are more at risk than others for maltreatment, often because they place more stress or demands on parents. Although they may not do so evenly, child abuse and neglect cross all social class, racial, religious, and educational boundaries (Wolfner & Gelles, 1993).

CHARACTERISTICS OF CHILD ABUSERS

The image most people have of a child abuser is a person with a serious psychological disturbance, but the research evidence does not support this conclusion. In fact, less than 10 percent of child abusers evidence extremely disturbed symptoms (Murphy & Smith, 1996). What, then, are the characteristics of those who commit child abuse and neglect? From the existing research (Kolko, 1996; Lutzker, 1998; Sedlak & Broadhurst, 1996), the following conclusions can be drawn:

✦ Parents are more likely than any other group to abuse children (see Figure 6.5). Although the popular press highlights cases where nonparental caregivers and foster parents perpetrate abuse, they are the adults least likely to do so.

✦ Probably because children most often live with their biological parents, biological parents are responsible for the majority of the cases of child abuse and neglect. Sixty-two percent of abuse cases and 91 percent of neglect cases are perpetrated by biological parents.

✦ Because mothers carry the major responsibility for child care, they tend to abuse more often than fathers (although fathers are more often involved in sexual abuse). However, the severity of the injury or impairment that a child experiences as a result of maltreatment is not related to the sex of the perpetrator.

✦ Single parents have a particularly high rate of committing abuse and neglect.

✦ Children are more likely to be abused by younger than by older caretakers.

✦ Adults who commit child abuse tend to be isolated, lack family and peer support networks, and not be involved in community activities.

FIGURE 6.5
Perpetrators of Child Abuse

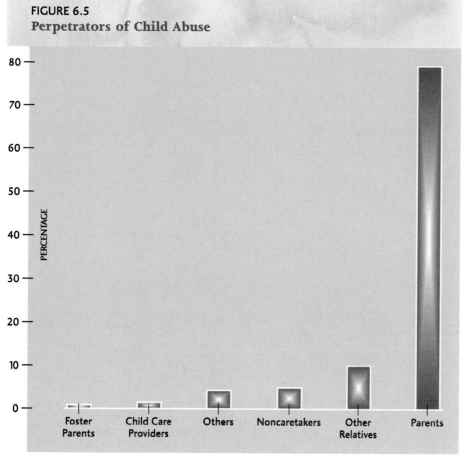

SOURCE: *US Department of Health and Human Services, 1998.*
There is a dramatic difference between the rates at which child abuse is perpetrated by parents and all others.
What impact might such findings have for intervention and prevention programs?

✦ Abusive adults have limited knowledge of caregiving, have unrealistic expectations for children's behavior, find child rearing difficult, have a low tolerance for infant behaviors (such as crying), and tend to use harsh disciplinary practices.

✦ Although committing child abuse is not consistently associated with alcohol use, it is associated with drug use. The rate of child maltreatment is about 46 percent higher for drug users than for those who do not use drugs.

One of the most consistently reported findings regarding characteristics of child abusers is that they are likely to have experienced abuse themselves when they were children. Approximately 30 percent of abused children grow up to be abusive, compared to 4 percent of the general population (Gelles, 1987; Maxfield & Widom, 1996). Additionally, child abuse often occurs in a general context of family violence. When a child is abused, it is likely that a spouse is also abused (Appel & Holden, 1998; McCloskey, Figueredo, & Koss, 1995). Child abuse thus frequently reflects an atmosphere of violent and abusive family relationships.

Together, these findings present a complex picture of the person who commits child abuse and neglect. Although they suggest that some individuals are more at risk for committing child abuse than others, the potential for acting abusively is present in varying degrees in many individuals (Wolfner & Gelles, 1993). No single profile fits all child abusers.

FIGURE 6.6
Ecological Model of Child Abuse and Neglect

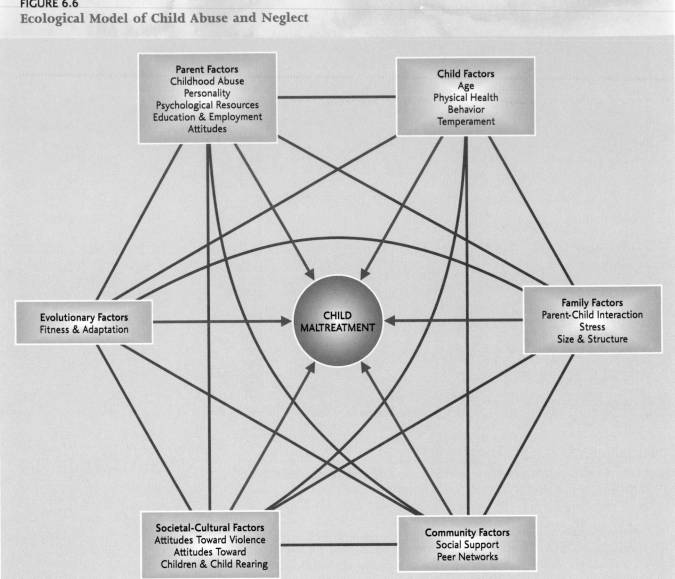

SOURCE: Belsky, 1993.
This model illustrates how different contextual factors might interact to increase children's risk for abuse and neglect.
How does this model help us understand the dynamics of child maltreatment? How might this model be used to design effective intervention and prevention programs?

To address the complex causes of child abuse, Belsky (1980, 1993) developed an ecological model showing different pathways leading to child maltreatment (see Figure 6.6). According to Belsky, child maltreatment is most likely to occur when the stressors outweigh the supportive conditions in a person's environment. These stressors and supports take many forms and include a variety of parent factors (personality, attitudes), child factors (temperament, age, health condition), family and community factors (stress, family structure, social support), cultural norms (attitudes toward parenting and toward violence), historical developments (children's rights), and evolutionary factors (fitness).

As an illustration of the broad array of factors that influence child abuse and neglect, consider the case of Amos. Amos was born to parents who were fundamentalist in their religious beliefs and who approached parenting with a traditional and physical style of parenting (Melzak, 1992). At the time of Amos's birth, his mother was preoccupied with her new relationship with Amos's father and with a custody battle she was having over her eldest son from a prior marriage. Amos's mother was an insecure, intelligent, anxious woman, and his father was a gentle, quiet man who often was humiliated by his wife. Amos was described as an active, difficult-to-manage child who did not sleep regularly and did not live up to his elder brother's model of maturity, obedience, and self-control. Beginning sometime after his first birthday, Amos was beaten at home by both parents and sometimes by his grandparents. When Amos began preschool, he often got in trouble and was severely beaten with a belt by his parents for doing so. The parents reported that this was how they were punished when they were children.

The case of Amos reveals the complex factors that contribute to abuse. Amos's parents came from a background where physical punishment and physical control of children were acceptable. The facts that Amos also was beaten by his grandparents and that intense physical punishment was used by the grandparents on Amos's parents when they were children reflect an intergenerational history of abuse. Additionally, because of the stress associated with the new marriage and the custody battle, Amos's parents had limited abilities to cope with the stress of child rearing. Faced with a sensitive, impulsive, and out-of-control little boy, Amos's parents were overwhelmed.

Amos's case supports Belsky's (1993) proposal that child abuse and neglect are multiply determined by the interaction of processes associated with various individual, familial, cultural, and historical factors. There is no one cause of child maltreatment, and no single determining factor or profile of a child abuser or a victim has emerged from the literature. The most consistent conclusion seems to be that child abuse, its causes, and its consequences result from the transaction of risk and protective factors that exist at multiple levels (Korbin, Coulton, Chard, Platt-Houston, & Su, 1998). The exact conditions that contribute to child abuse, however, vary from family to family and from situation to situation.

EFFECTS OF CHILD ABUSE AND NEGLECT

In the United States in 1994, 1271 children died from maltreatment, more than 3 children every day, and the rate is up 48 percent since 1985 (Wiese & Daro, 1996). Younger children are more at risk of loss of life from maltreatment than are older children—88 percent of the fatalities from maltreatment occurred in children under 5 years of age, and 46 percent occurred in children under 1 year of age. As Katy's story at the beginning of this section reveals, even if young children survive maltreatment, it can have irreparable effects on their development (Emery & Laumann-Billings, 1998).

Even when there is no evidence of neurological or physical impairment, the consequences of child abuse can be devastating. Abused and neglected children sometimes show delayed intellectual development, particularly in the area of verbal intelligence (Augoustinos, 1987); poor school performance (Kendall-Tackett & Eckenrode, 1997; Leiter & Johnsen, 1997); and deficits in attention and information processing (Dodge, Bates, & Pettit, 1990).

Child abuse and neglect also have strong effects on children's psychological and social development, and these consequences are extremely powerful in the early stages of development (National Research Council, 1993). Early child abuse and neglect may harm the development of children's attachments, sense of security, self-esteem, and emotional stability (Trickett & McBride-Chang, 1995). Children who have been abused or neglected also may have negative mental health outcomes, such as depression, anxiety disorders, and aggressiveness (McCloskey et al., 1995). A consistent finding is that sexually abused young children exhibit inappropriate sexual behavior (Trickett & McBride-Chang, 1995).

PREVENTING CHILD ABUSE AND NEGLECT

As the number of victims increases, there is a growing awareness of the need to prevent child abuse and neglect. Unfortunately, most efforts are devoted to helping children only after a major incident of maltreatment has been identified (Wolfe, 1993). Yet, because of the high financial and human costs associated with child maltreatment, preventing it is critical.

Prevention is commonly categorized as primary, secondary, or tertiary. **Primary prevention** is directed at the population as a whole. Educational programs that sensitize society to basic issues of maltreatment or that provide essential parenting skills to all individuals before they become parents are examples of primary prevention programs (Daro, 1996). **Secondary prevention** targets a specific segment of the population thought to be at high risk for child maltreatment. Generally, these programs are designed to provide support for poor single mothers and fathers, helping them cope with the demands of child rearing. **Tertiary prevention** is directed at situations in which child maltreatment already has occurred. The goal is to prevent or decrease its reoccurrence. Providing parenting skills training programs to individuals who have committed child abuse is an example of tertiary prevention (Dubowitz, 1989).

Most prevention efforts focus on parent training (National Research Council, 1993). Training parents in child management (such as discipline techniques), child care, and self-control skills (such as managing frustration and anger) has been effective in promoting positive parent-child interactions (Britner & Reppucci, 1997). There also is some evidence that parent training reduces parental distress, thereby reducing the chances of abuse and neglect (Shifflett & Cummings, 1999). When parenting programs are combined with efforts to provide families with services that address critical family needs—such as for child care, mental health counseling, social support, and home improvements—the effectiveness of the intervention is improved (Reuter, Longer, & Ramisetty-Mikler, 1999; Striefel, Robinson, & Truhn, 1998).

Unfortunately, given that reports of child abuse and neglect are increasing, it seems that prevention efforts have been relatively ineffective (Emery & Laumann-Billings, 1998). In fact, there is some evidence that one-third or more of the abusive parents served by prevention programs maltreated their children while in these programs (Cohn & Daro, 1987). To date, most interventions have been designed to address child abuse and neglect using secondary or tertiary prevention rather than primary prevention. In Scandinavian countries such as Sweden and Denmark, nationwide primary prevention programs provide support and services to all families. In these countries, rates of child abuse and neglect are about eight times lower than those in the United States (Pransky, 1991). Thus, it appears we can do something about the rates of child abuse and neglect in the United States, but it will take broader interventions and policies to make a difference.

primary prevention efforts targeted at the population as a whole, to sensitize people to basic issues or to provide particular skills

secondary prevention efforts targeted at a specific segment of the population thought to be at high risk

tertiary prevention efforts directed at preventing or decreasing the reoccurrence of an event that has already occurred

CHAPTER SUMMARY

How do emotions develop during infancy and toddlerhood?

• Many of the basic emotions are present at birth or shortly thereafter.

• Smiling is an important emotional behavior because it is a powerful social reinforcer. By about 6 to 8 weeks, infants move from reflexive smiling to social smiling. Laughter appears about a month later.

• Crying is an infant's most effective way of communicating. Several different types of cries have been identified, based on their characteristics—basic, anger, pain, and hunger cries. Crying increases over the first six weeks of life and then decreases.

• Caregivers who respond quickly to their infants' crying have infants who do not cry as often or as intensely. Caregivers' responses to crying often are influenced by their culture.

• Infants increasingly respond to the limits of their abilities and their environments with anger and temper tantrums. Tantrums are brought about in part by important developmental changes, such as increased ability to express anger and strivings toward independence, couple with limited social understanding.

• The self-conscious emotions of shame, embarrassment, and pride, which appear at about age 2, reflect young children's increased self-awareness and cognitive development.

• Play provides infants and toddlers with opportunities to explore emotional development, and many early emotions occur in the context of play.

How does temperament influence development during infancy and toddlerhood?

• Temperament refers to individual differences in how people respond to their environments. A variety of components of temperament are thought to be present at birth and are constant over time and situations.

• Three patterns of temperamental qualities—easy, difficult, and slow to warm up—reflect differences in styles of responding to the demands of the environment.

• The expression of temperament can be modified by social and cultural environments.

How do parent-infant attachments influence development?

• Attachments are enduring emotional ties characterized by the tendency to seek closeness to a specific attachment figure. The mother usually is the first attachment figure.

• Attachment theory suggests that attachment is a long-lasting relationship. Evidence of attachment is seen in children's attempts to seek out and maintain contact with attachment figures and in children's distress when separated from attachement figures.

• Ainsworth proposed that attachments develop in phases. The preattachment phase is the first eight weeks of life, when infants do not discriminate in their responses to caregivers. The attachment-in-the-making phase lasts until about 7 months and is a period in which infants discriminate familiar from unfamiliar caregivers. The clear-cut attachment phase is next and reflects a clear preference for a particular caregiver.

• Two characteristics of the clear-cut attachment phase are stranger anxiety and separation anxiety.

• Attachment is assessed using the Strange Situation—a series of separations from and reunions with a caregiver and a stranger. Securely attached infants use the attachment figure as a secure base, respond with distress when separated from that person, and are relieved and joyful at reunion.

• Avoidant attachments are characterized by a lack of contact or interaction with the caregiver.

• Ambivalent attachments are characterized by both a desire for comfort and a resistance to contact.

• Disorganized/disoriented attachments are characterized by avoidance, resistance, and bizarre repetitions of behavior.

• Caregiver sensitivity, infant characteristics, and cultural factors influence the quality of parent-child attachment.

• Attachment affects later development. Infants with secure attachments generally are more socially and emotionally competent.

• Infants become attached to their fathers, despite having less contact with them than with their mothers. Given the opportunity, fathers can be as sensitive and nurturing as mothers.

How does day care influence infants' and toddlers' development?

• There has been a dramatic increase in the number of infants and toddlers cared for by individuals other than their parents. The rapid entry of women into the work force is primarily responsible for this change.

• The majority of infants and toddlers with working mothers are cared for by relatives. As children get older and as women work longer hours, children are more likely to be placed in organized group day care.

• Concerns have been raised about the possibility that day care could have an adverse effect on infants' attachments, especially for infants who have caregivers other than parents for more than 20 hours per week. These concerns have been challenged; the challenges point out the need for high-quality, affordable day care.

• Caregiving arrangements for very young children vary considerably across cultures. The types of care provided to infants and toddlers are influenced by the values of a culture and by economic, political, and health conditions.

Why are children abused and neglected?

- Four categories of child maltreatment are physical abuse, sexual abuse, neglect, and psychological maltreatment. Recent statistics reveal increases in the rates of reported child maltreatment.

- Certain children face greater chances of experiencing maltreatment than others. Girls generally are maltreated more often than boys; in particular, they are more likely to be sexually abused. Younger children are more at risk for maltreatment than are older children.

- Child abuse and neglect cross all social class, racial, religious, and educational boundaries. Most child abusers are not psychologically disturbed. Because they carry out the majority of child rearing, biological parents, particularly mothers, are the adults most likely to abuse and neglect children. Most abuse does not occur in day care or foster care.

- Adults who commit abuse are low in child-rearing knowledge, have unrealistic expectations and low tolerance for children's behavior, and rely on physical punishment for discipline. They also tend to be socially isolated and to have been abused themselves as children.

- The effects of child maltreatment can be devastating, and sometimes fatal. Even when there is no evidence of physical impairment, social, psychological, and intellectual damage may occur. These consequences are particularly powerful early in development.

- Three types of prevention models have been identified: primary, secondary, and tertiary. Most prevention efforts focus on parent training, but these have been relatively ineffective.

KEY TERMS & CONCEPTS

ambivalent attachment *(201)*
attachment *(194)*
avoidant attachment *(200)*
disorganized/disoriented
    attachment *(201)*
endogenous smile *(182)*
exogenous smile *(182)*
manipulative tantrums *(188)*

neglect *(211)*
physical abuse *(211)*
primary prevention *(216)*
psychological maltreatment *(211)*
secondary prevention *(216)*
secure attachment *(199)*
self-conscious emotions *(189)*
separation anxiety *(197)*

sexual abuse *(211)*
social smile *(182)*
Strange Situation *(198)*
stranger anxiety *(197)*
temperament *(190)*
temperamental tantrums *(188)*
tertiary prevention *(216)*

ACTIVITIES & APPLICATIONS
Relating to Infants and Toddlers

1. Consider the story at the beginning of this chapter about Jamal and Kyle at the birthday party. What information in this chapter helps you to describe and discuss the differences between the two boys' emotional and social behaviors? How might you use information in this chapter to explain those differences? What effects might the differences have on Jamal's and Kyle's development?

2. How would you describe your temperament? What were some socioemotional and behavioral expressions of your temperament when you were a baby or young child? How would you characterize your pattern of attachment with your primary caregiver? How do you think your attachment

pattern might have influenced your social and emotional development?

3. Arrange to observe infants and toddlers in a day care program, especially at the beginning and the end of the day, when they are being dropped off and picked up. Observe and record the behavior and social and emotional responses of parents, children, and day care workers. Before you observe, however, you should develop a research design. What will be your research question? What, exactly, will you observe, when, and for how long? How will you systematize and interpret your observations to answer your research question?

Grasping the Whole

Benchmarks in Infant and Toddler Development

PHYSICAL/MOTOR DEVELOPMENT	COGNITIVE DEVELOPMENT	SOCIAL/EMOTIONAL DEVELOPMENT
Rapid growth, particularly in lower portions of body	Coordination and integration of reflex actions into more complex schemas	Evidence of early individual differences in temperamental and emotional characteristics
Increased voluntary control of muscles and movements	Evidence of color, pattern, face, motion, and depth perception and preferences	Increasing evidence of attachments to significant caregivers
Improved control of trunk; ability to roll over	First evidence of problem solving	Socialization through experience, primarily with family members
Reaching of motor milestones— creeping, crawling, sitting, standing, cruising, walking, and running	Development of the concept of object permanence	Enhanced experience with peers and nonfamilial caregivers
	Development of prelanguage skills—cooing, babbling	Greater probability of being a victim of abuse and neglect
	Acquisition of true language— one-word stage (holophrase)	

Status Report on Infants and Toddlers

Child maltreatment is greatest at the youngest ages and decreases as children get older. Can you suggest some reasons why?

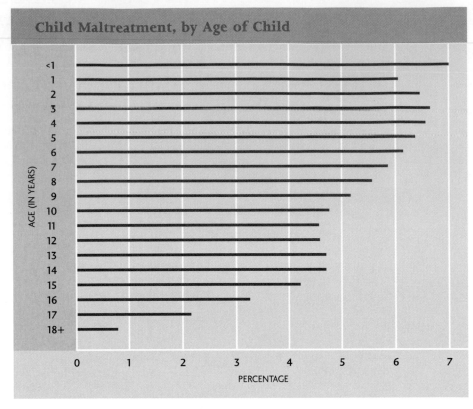

Child Maltreatment, by Age of Child

AGE (IN YEARS): <1, 1, 2, 3, 4, 5, 6, 7, 8, 9, 10, 11, 12, 13, 14, 15, 16, 17, 18+

PERCENTAGE: 0 1 2 3 4 5 6 7

SOURCE: US Department of Health and Human Services, 1998.

SUGGESTED READINGS

Acredolo, L., & Goodwyn, S. (1996). *Baby signs: How to talk with your baby before your baby can talk.* New York: Contemporary Books. Thoughtful and digestible account of how one can use the natural communication abilities of a baby to foster language development.

Brazelton, T. B. (1994). *Touchpoints: Your child's emotional and behavioral development.* Reading, MA: Addison-Wesley. A famous physician's readable account of early development and the important roles of father, mother, and caregiver in a young child's life.

Lamott, A. (1994). *Operating instructions: A journal of my son's first year.* New York: Fawcett Books. An honest and enjoyable book reflecting the changes, challenges, and demands of single parenthood.

Stern, D. (1992). *Diary of a baby.* New York: Basic Books. The story of what goes on inside a baby's mind, by a noted authority on infant development.

RECOMMENDED WEBSITES

Attachment Theory and Research Center: Maintained by the State University of New York at Stony Brook, this site contains information about infant-mother attachment. It includes comments, bibliographies, measures, and artifacts from John Bowlby and Mary Ainsworth. <http://www.psy.sunysb.edu/attachment/>

Child Abuse Prevention Network: Maintained by Cornell University, this network is dedicated to providing comprehensive Internet resources for the prevention of child abuse and neglect and to reducing the negative conditions in the family and community that lead to child maltreatment. <http://child.cornell.edu/>

International Society on Infant Studies: This Website, devoted to the scientific study of infant development, provides information about infant journals, conferences, and newsletters. <http://www.isisweb.org/>

KidsHealth: Created by medical experts at the Nemours Foundation, this rich Website is devoted to the health of children. It has accurate, up-to-date information about growth, food, and fitness; childhood infections; immunizations; lab tests; medical and surgical conditions; and the latest treatments. <http://KidsHealth.org/>

La Leche League: This Website, sponsored by La Leche League International, is dedicated to providing education, information, support, and encouragement to women who want to breast-feed. <http://www.lalecheleague.org/>

National Association for the Education of Young Children: This Website is devoted to providing information on issues surrounding early childhood care and promoting excellence in early childhood education. <http://www.naeyc.org/>

Temperament.com: A clearinghouse for research and practical information about temperamental characteristics, this site is for parents, students, professionals, and others who have an interest in temperament. <http://www.b-di.com/>

Zero to Three: Dedicated to the healthy development of infants and toddlers, this interactive Website contains helpful information for parents and professionals on a wide variety of topics related to very young children. <http://www.zerotothree.org/>

NATIONAL HOTLINES FOR INFANTS AND TODDLERS

Child Abuse Hotline: 800-422-4454

La Leche League: 847-519-7730

Women, Infants, and Children (WIC): 800-445-5818

PART 4

Early Childhood DEVELOPMENT

Eight 4-year-olds attending preschool sit around a table at snack time. The teacher brings over a tray with peanut butter, jelly, and crackers on it. Of the eight children, five ask for peanut butter and jelly on their crackers and three want plain peanut butter.

After they make their crackers, the teacher asks, "What did we make more of? Did we make more peanut butter and jelly crackers or more crackers with just plain peanut butter?"

One of the children who wanted only peanut butter says, "I know! More peanut butter. I like only peanut butter, so it's more."

The teacher tries again. "I'll count the children who are eating peanut butter and jelly: 1 . . . 2 . . . 3 . . . 4 . . . 5. Now I'll count the children eating plain peanut butter: 1 . . . 2 . . . 3.

Now, are there more eating peanut butter and jelly or plain peanut butter?"

The same boy answers: "Everybody has peanut butter, so there's more with only peanut butter." The child licks his peanut butter cracker and shows his peanut butter–covered tongue to his peers. They all start to laugh, and the teacher tries to figure out how her question "misfired."

D uring early childhood, children experience an increase in the complexity with which they think about and participate in their worlds. Although family members, particularly parents, remain important, children begin to experience life outside the family. They are increasingly exposed to non–family members and influences such as school and television. Most of these experiences involve peers, and most peer interactions take place in the context of play.

Children make significant advances in their cognitive development in early childhood. Their reasoning becomes more abstract and less bound by motor actions. Their language and communication skills increase, and they can ask and answer many rich and complex questions. Their reasoning, however, remains limited compared to that of older children and adults. As the peanut butter story reveals, young children's thinking is dominated by their own perceptions, feelings, and perspectives. They have difficulty understanding that others have views different from their own, as evidenced by the child who said that more children had only peanut butter on their crackers because that is what he had. These new ways of thinking set the stage for even more advanced forms of reasoning and understanding.

IN PART 1, YOU WILL LEARN ABOUT

- how preschoolers' bodies change in size and appearance
- how young children develop gross and fine motor skills
- what the nutritional and health needs of preschool children are and how childhood accidents and diseases can be prevented
- how preschool children's ways of thinking and solving problems are different from those of older children and adults
- how caregivers can expand the range of children's cognitive development by providing challenging environments and experiences for children
- the challenges that preschoolers face in learning language

- how young children develop a sense of self and come to associate positive and negative feelings with their developing sense of self
- how young children come to see themselves as a boy or a girl and the theories that explain gender development
- how young children deal with anger and aggression and develop prosocial emotions and actions
- how parenting behaviors influence young children
- how young children understand and are affected by family transitions such as divorce and remarriage
- how young children relate to and play with other children, including brothers and sisters
- the role of television in young children's development

CHAPTER 7

Physical, Cognitive, & Language Development in EARLY CHILDHOOD

CHAPTER OUTLINE

▶ How Do Children's Bodies and Motor Skills Develop During Early Childhood?

▶ What Are the Nutritional and Health Issues for Young Children?

▶ How Do Young Children Think and Solve Problems?

▶ What Changes Occur in Young Children's Language Development During Early Childhood?

First my dad buys the spaghetti macaroni and then he cooks it. He puts it in the oven at 25 or 10 degrees. He cooks it about one minute. Then he blows on it and I eat it.

—Macaroni recipe by Brandon, age 4

To make bread, you put all the dough in the breadmaker. Then you turn it on and go to sleep. While you sleep, the maker comes alive and mixes up the bread and cooks it. Then it goes back to sleep until we need to make more bread.

—Jasmine, age 3

when you make cookies, you have to be careful not to break them after they are cooked. If they break, they don't taste as good.

—Kari, age 4

Ovens cook at 25 or 10 degrees, inanimate objects come alive, and broken cookies don't taste as good as whole ones. These examples of young children's beliefs about cooking show the remarkably different ways in which they think about the world. Children's physical development is not as dramatic as it is during infancy, but the changes are still very apparent—they no longer have their "babyish" appearance. Unlike infants, preschoolers can dress themselves, draw pictures, throw a ball, and run forward and backward. Language development occurs rapidly during this time, as children master many complexities of grammar and the use of language. As you will see in this chapter, cognitive, language, and motor skills develop best in the context of social interactions with caregivers and other adults in the community.

HOW DO CHILDREN'S BODIES AND MOTOR SKILLS DEVELOP DURING EARLY CHILDHOOD?

Consider the following scene. Tracy, age 4, throws a large red ball to her 15-month-old sister, Kim. Kim reaches for it, but is unable to catch it. Kim leans forward to retrieve the ball and toddles unsteadily. Tracy runs toward her, picks up the ball, hands it to Kim, and says, "Now you throw it to me." Kim tries to throw the ball, but it falls out of her hand and rolls away.

Leaner and taller preschoolers like Tracy move more quickly and steadily than infants like Kim and can run, jump, and throw a ball with good accuracy. What changes take place over the span of a few years that allow children to look so different physically and move so much more competently?

CHANGING BODY SIZE AND APPEARANCE

Remember the general physical characteristics of infants, which we discussed in Chapter 5—protruding stomach, short bowed legs, and a large head relative to body size. Compared to infants, the most notable physical feature of preschool children is that they lose their babyish appearance. Body fat decreases to approximately 12 percent of body weight, the stomach flattens as muscles strengthen, arms and legs grow longer and slimmer, and the body grows in size relative to the head.

During the preschool years, growth is not as rapid as it is during the infant years, but most children grow approximately 3 inches a year and gain 4 pounds a year. Girls and boys are very similar in their patterns of physical growth and development during the preschool years. The average 3-year-old boy is 38 inches tall and weighs 33 pounds, and the average 3-year-old girl is slightly smaller and lighter (Tanner, 1978).

Some children grow taller and develop more quickly than other children. What factors account for these differences? As you learned in Chapter 5, children's genetic endowment influences growth and development, with taller children being born to taller parents. In the United States, African American children tend to be taller than Caucasian American children, and both groups tend to be taller than Asian American children. However, children born in the United States, regardless of ethnic and racial background, tend to be taller than almost all other children around the world (Cratty, 1986). In addition to genetic endowment, good nutritional habits and better health care tend to foster taller children.

BRAIN DEVELOPMENT

During the preschool years, a child's brain develops quickly, reaching 75 to 90 percent of adult size by age 5. The brain grows larger during this time because the neurons grow more interconnections, increasing the number and size of nerve endings (Nosphitz & King, 1991). Another change is an increase in myelination, which allows information to move more quickly between the cells in the brain (see Chapter 4). The rate of development of many children's skills and abilities may depend on myelination. For instance, the areas of the brain involved in hand-eye coordination are not completely myelinated until around the age of 4 or 5 (Konner, 1991; Tanner, 1978).

The largest part of the brain is the cerebral cortex, which has many folds, or convolutions, throughout its surface. The cerebral cortex controls higher thought processes such as problem solving, consciousness, and language abilities. The cortex is the last part of the brain to finish growing. Because of its slower rate of growth, the cortex may be more susceptible to environmental influences than other parts of the brain. The cerebral cortex is divided into two halves, called hemispheres, each of which has areas specialized for certain functions. For most people, the left hemisphere is specialized for language processing, whereas the right hemisphere is specialized for recognizing spatial relationships (reading maps, for instance). Hemispheric development occurs unevenly. The left hemisphere develops rapidly around the age of 2; the right hemisphere, with its visual recognition systems, does not develop at the same rate. The growth spurt for the right hemisphere occurs around the age of 4 or 5 (Borsting, 1994; Fischer & Rose, 1994). Also around age 5, the connections between the two hemispheres increase in number and become more efficient, allowing children to better coordinate functions involving both sides of the brain and body (Huttenlocher, 1990; 1994).

GROSS MOTOR SKILLS

After a year of coordinating all the systems required for standing and walking, toddlers take another year to perfect walking. Soon after, children begin trying many variations in their movements, including walking sideways, walking backward, and walking on their toes. New skills are emerging rapidly in the third year. With little training, children learn to run, throw balls, and jump. How do they acquire these skills?

One key factor in the development of motor skills is the development of children's visual systems. Areas of the brain associated with the ability to focus the eyes and with eye movements continue to develop through early childhood. The development of visual pathways, combined with improving communication between the hemispheres, results in advances in eye-hand coordination and allows preschoolers to become better at left-right directions.

The Development of Handedness

Parents often wonder whether their children will be right or left handed. Most children and adults (92 percent) are right handed (Coren & Porac, 1977). Some research suggests that preferential right-handedness has its evolutionary origin in the tendency of mothers to hold infants on the left side, where the child is soothed by the sound of the mother's heart. Mothers who were right handed would be more skillful at manipulating objects with their free hand and would be selectively favored (Huheey, 1977). More recent research suggests that handedness is influenced more by genetics than environment (McManus & Bryden, 1992).

Infants do not show strong hand preferences; instead, they vary their use of hands. Stable preferences emerge for most children around 3 to 4 years of age. Some evidence suggests that an early (4 to 6 months of age) and strong hand preference may indicate that the infant has a neurological problem (Harris, 1992). To test a preschooler's hand preference, it is best to use a task that is somewhat challenging, because either hand may be used for a simple task such as reaching for an object. For children, the tasks commonly used to assess handedness include writing, drawing, eating, pointing, and throwing.

Tests of 3- to 4-year-olds show that the proportion of right-handed children is close to the level of right-handedness seen in adults. Also, studies indicate that there is stability in preferences, at least after age 3 (Harris, 1992).

In adults, questionnaires and performance tests are used to assess handedness. For instance, adults are asked the preferred hand for various activities such as eating, writing, drawing and erasing, hammering, and throwing a ball. In some cases, adults are asked to do unusual tasks (such as moving pegs and tapping their fingers), with the idea that these tasks are not subject to the effects of prior practice.

An indeterminate number of children and adults are ambidextrous—they switch preferred hands depending on the task they need to do. Even for the same task, they will sometimes prefer the right hand and other times the left hand (Porac, Coren, & Searleman, 1986).

For many generations, left-handedness was actively discouraged in schools. Even today, our environment is structured to favor right-handers, but parents are encouraged to let children's natural handedness prevail (Coren, 1993).

Another important factor for motor development is balance, which contributes greatly to the proliferation of skills children exhibit during the preschool years. Children with visual or inner-ear problems may have difficulty integrating the sensory information necessary for good balance (Hatton, Bailey, Burchinal, & Ferrell, 1997). A lack of balance interferes with the stability they need to perform more complex skills like kicking and throwing. Practice, imitating others, and others' expectations and encouragement also play important roles in motor development. For example, children with older siblings develop motor skills more rapidly than other children (Samuels, 1980).

Although some children take longer to develop motor skills than others, a small group of children are clumsy—they are unable to coordinate parts of their bodies for activities such as throwing a ball, hopping, or drawing. Because clumsy children may be improperly labeled as learning disabled or may suffer from teasing, early identification of motor development problems and referral to treatment programs can benefit children (Bertenthal & Clifton, 1998).

Running and Jumping

Although young children sometimes appear to be running, it is not until they are 2 to 3 years of age that they show true running, during which both feet leave the ground. Even then, they are not well-controlled runners, because they are unable to stop or start quickly. By the time children are 4 to 5 years old, their running ability has greatly improved, and most can run twice as fast as they did when they were 2 (Cratty, 1986).

FIGURE 7.1
Developmental Changes in Throwing

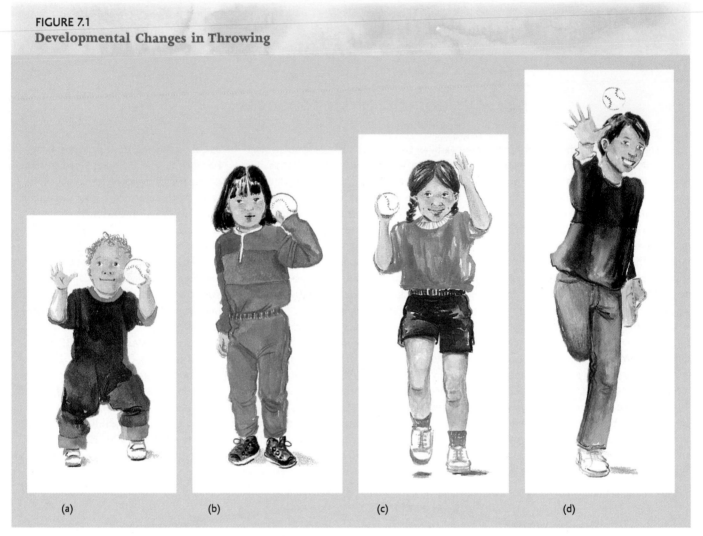

(a)   (b)   (c)   (d)

SOURCE: Cratty, 1979. © 1979 by Allyn & Bacon. Adapted by permission.
Throwing proceeds from (a) a toddler's accidental letting go of an object to (b and c) 2- to 4-year-olds' variable throws to
(d) a mature throw accompanied by a step with the foot opposite the throwing arm. Throughout late childhood, girls are
less likely than boys to involve their whole body in throwing.

Children's first attempts at jumping are one-footed steps off an object, usually occurring at around 18 months of age. By 2, most children can use a two-footed take-off to propel themselves off an object, but they are not very efficient in using their arms to help their motion. By 4, most children can jump on level ground, using their arms appropriately to help propel them. And by 5, most children can jump a distance of 3 feet (Cratty, 1986).

Throwing and Catching

Throwing and catching a ball are complex motor skills that develop in stages over the early childhood period (Marques-Bruna & Grinshaw, 1997). Throwing gradually comes to involve more of the body and greater body rotation. Mature throwers rotate around the central axis of their body and shift their weight forward. In contrast, 2- to 3-year-olds often use a rigid underhand toss with no body movement. By 3½ years, children can throw overhand with some body rotation, but they keep their feet firmly on the ground. By 5 or 6, most children step with the opposite foot and shift their weight when throwing, and their speed and accuracy improve with age (see Figure 7.1).

Children's ability to catch a ball also develops during childhood, with better visual tracking of the ball, more flexible positioning of their arms during the "catch," and faster reaction times. Very young children tend to hold their arms stiffly in front of them to catch a ball and sometimes close their eyes or turn their head away to avoid the ball. By 4, most children watch the ball coming and hold their hands open to receive it. By 5 to 5½ years of age, most children hold their arms and elbows flexibly to absorb the force of the ball.

FINE MOTOR SKILLS

To be able to cut with a pair of scissors or fold pieces of paper, children must be able to organize the coordination of their hands and eyes, using the small muscles in their hands precisely. These fine motor skills develop markedly during the early childhood period.

Although infants can grasp small objects between their forefinger and thumb, precise movements of individual fingers take several more years to achieve (Geraldson & Hopkins, 1997). Biological factors play a role in finger differentiation: children with brain damage often cannot use each finger individually and instead use their hands as though they were encased in a fingerless mitt (Cratty, 1986).

The developmental progression in fine motor skills from less to more differentiation, coordination, and control is apparent during the preschool years. For instance, 2-year-olds can scribble, put on some articles of clothing, turn pages in a book, and construct towers consisting of six to eight blocks. Three-year-olds have better developed fine motor skills: they can eat with a spoon, copy a circle, and pour from a pitcher. By 4, children can dress themselves, draw tadpolelike human figures (see Figure 7.2), and cut on a line with scissors. Most 5-year-olds can fasten buttons, draw letters, unzip a zipper, and string beads.

CULTURAL AND RACIAL INFLUENCES ON MOTOR DEVELOPMENT

Children with African origins typically are more advanced in motor development than children with European origins: they throw farther, balance better, and are better able to run (Cratty, 1986). The reasons for these differences are varied and complex. Genetic factors may play a role, specifically in influencing the length and proportions of arms, legs, and the overall body size. Cultural factors—including parenting practices, nutrition, and the perceived importance of motor skill development—also play a role, however. Mothers in Nigeria, Uganda, Sierra Leone, India, and Pakistan encourage their children to walk and stand up more quickly and train them in motor development. For instance, Nigerian and West Indian mothers use passive stretching movements, massage, and active encouragement in the first year of a child's life to promote motor development (Hopkins, 1991). Interestingly, in two African groups that do not encourage early motor development (the Baganda and the Somia), the infants and children show slower development of motor skills than Caucasian children in the United States (Kilbride, 1980).

Cultural and biological factors likely interact to influence children's motor development. For instance, African American infants show early motor precocity and are especially reactive, which may, in turn, contribute in a transactional way to caregivers' encouragement of their motor skills (Rosser & Randolph, 1989).

WHAT ARE THE NUTRITIONAL AND HEALTH ISSUES FOR YOUNG CHILDREN?

Children's growth and motor development depend on good health and nutrition. Because preschoolers are not growing as fast as they did as infants, their appetites are not as strong. Caregivers often worry that children are not eating enough to obtain adequate nutrition. However, the nutritional requirements of young children can be met with small, healthy meals. An average preschooler requires about 1700 calories per day, with less than 35 percent of the calories coming from fat.

FIGURE 7.2
Tadpole People

SOURCE: Gardner, 1980. Copyright © 1980 by Howard Gardner. Reprinted by permission of BasicBooks, a subsidiary of Perseus Books Group, LLC.

About how old were the children who drew these "tadpole" people? What physical characteristics do these children represent in their drawings? What aspects of the physical development of young children do the drawings represent?

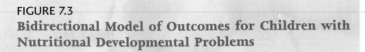

FIGURE 7.3
Bidirectional Model of Outcomes for Children with Nutritional Developmental Problems

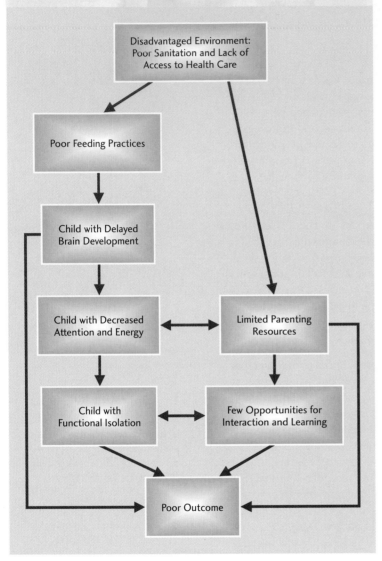

SOURCE: Lozoff et al., 1998.

Notice that a disadvantaged environment has multiple effects, both direct and indirect, on children's development. The bidirectional effects can be seen in the interplay between children's having less energy and paying less attention and caregivers' having limited resources and lowered expectations. Each factor is an action as well as a reaction to the other factors.

iron-deficiency anemia a nutrient deficiency common in infants and toddlers

functional isolation the increased disengagement from one's social and physical environments that may result from a poor environment and inadequate nutrition

UNDERNOURISHMENT AND MALNOURISHMENT

Inadequate nutrition is implicated in more than half the child deaths worldwide (UNICEF, 1998). Almost 200 million of the world's children below 5 years of age are underweight and likely to be suffering from undernourishment. Undernourishment is more common in parts of Africa and Asia than elsewhere in the world (UNICEF, 1998; Pollitt et al., 1996). Undernourishment is closely associated with economic impoverishment, limited health care and educational opportunities, and poor living conditions. When food is scarce, children's diets consist largely of cereals and legumes, and they eat few fruits, vegetables, and animal products. Thus, undernourished children often are malnourished as well—they do not receive adequate proteins, vitamins, and minerals.

Approximately 13 million children in the United States are malnourished—about 1 in 4—and most of these children are from low-income families (UNICEF, 1998). A common problem for young children who do not eat enough meats and green vegetables is lack of iron, which results in chronic fatigue. Serious iron deficiencies lead to **iron-deficiency anemia,** a common nutrient deficiency. Some children may be malnourished even though they consume enough calories. These children fill up on "empty" nonnutritional calories (such as those found in cookies and potato chips) and fail to eat enough healthy foods.

Undernutrition among preschoolers and school-aged children is a serious health concern because of the many adverse consequences associated with it. Undernourished children tend to have stunted growth and delayed motor development (Simeon & Grantham-McGregor, 1990). They also are at risk for cognitive disabilities such as low levels of attention, learning impairments, and poor academic and school-related performance (Wachs, 1995).

Why do undernourishment and malnourishment have such pervasive and negative effects on children? One idea that may explain these effects is **functional isolation**—malnourished children become increasingly disengaged from their social and physical environments (Brown & Pollitt, 1996). Functional isolation results from direct and indirect effects of poor environments and inadequate nutrition. If children's diets lack iron, for example, their brain development is impaired and delayed. Diminished brain development—accompanied by attempts to reduce energy expenditures by withdrawing from stimulation—influences children's behavior. The children may become more wary, easily tired, less attentive, and less playful, and they rarely show delight and pleasure (Lozoff et al., 1998). Because these children are not very responsive, caregivers do not interact with them much. Caregivers expect less from these children, so the children receive even less stimulation. Over time, they withdraw from their physical and social environments, increasing the likelihood that outcomes will be poor (see Figure 7.3).

TABLE 7.1

Calories and Fat in Popular Fast Foods

FAST FOOD	CALORIES	FAT (GRAMS)	% CALORIES FROM FAT
Cheeseburger	318	15	42
Chicken fingers	236	13	50
Fries (medium)	341	20	53
Chocolate shake	326	10	28
Fish sandwich	440	20	41
Nachos (with cheese and beef)	568	31	49
Pancakes (with butter and syrup)	519	14	24
Pizza (cheese) (1 piece)	260	10	27
Taco	370	21	50
Tuna fish sandwich	584	28	43

SOURCE: Bowes, Church, and Pennington, 1994; Sizer and Whitney, 1997.

Some children with inadequate nutrition live in families that cannot afford the food they need. However, many children lack nutritious diets even when food is abundant. Because of increased demands on family time, families often stop for fast food meals or prepare high-fat convenience foods at home, thereby including high levels of fat and sodium in the diet (see Table 7.1). Caregivers can limit children's fat and sodium intake by screening convenience foods based on their labels, curtailing fast food consumption, and carefully selecting the fast foods that are offered.

ACCIDENTS AND DISEASES

Children today are generally healthier than children of twenty years ago. Death rates from diseases such as influenza and pneumonia have decreased. Many dangerous and contagious childhood diseases (measles and polio, for instance) were virtually eliminated in the United States by the 1980s because of routine vaccinations given during childhood. However, some caregivers, especially those from low-income families, have not ensured that their children receive these vaccinations, with the result that 1 in 4 children is not protected against rubella, polio, mumps, and measles (Centers for Disease Control, 1997b). Diseases reemerge in the population if children do not receive their sequence of vaccinations (Kassianos, 1998).

The leading cause of death in the preschool years is accidents, often automobile accidents. In the United States, children are required to wear seat belts. Until they are 5, children should travel in special car safety seats that protect them from injuries (American Academy of Pediatrics, 1999a). Automobile manufacturers offer airbags and side-impact protection. Because the force of an opening airbag can harm children, young children should always be in the back seat of the car. Disarming airbags is not recommended. Restraint laws have been quite effective in protecting children: children who are not restrained are much more likely to die in automobile accidents than are children who are properly restrained (American Academy of Pediatrics, 1999a; Decker, Dewey, Hutcheson, & Schaffner, 1984).

Helping Young Children Become Healthy Eaters

To help caregivers make better food selections for their children, several consumer groups have assessed popular children's foods. In one assessment of children's convenience foods, ten non-diet foods were identified by nutritionists as having relatively low fat, low sodium, and low cholesterol. These healthy foods were tested and found to be foods young children enjoyed. The nutritionists discovered, however, that many foods that are tasty to children, especially convenience soups, are high in sodium. Parents can increase the nutritional value of these foods, usually by adding a vegetable side dish (Sizer & Whitney, 1997). The following table presents information on some of these relatively healthy convenience foods.

Calories, Fat, and Sodium in Convenience Foods That Children Enjoy

CONVENIENCE FOOD	CALORIES	% FAT	SODIUM (MG)
Light vegetable pizza	240	26	500
Fat-free deli sliced turkey breast pack (1 oz)	360	33	225
Fish fillets (3 oz)	130	21	220
BBQ chicken meal	370	7	670
Chicken nuggets, corn, pudding	360	33	500
Prepared rice or noodle dishes	420	10	760

Many accidents occur in homes. Children fall into swimming pools, drink poisonous substances, are burned in fires, are cut by broken glass, fall into bathtubs, injure themselves on sharp corners of furniture, and fall down stairs. Accidental poisonings have decreased markedly in the last twenty years; nevertheless, 500,000 children ingest some type of poison every year, and 2000 die from the poison.

Lead poisoning is a common health problem for young children in the United States. Although the incidence of lead poisoning has decreased, it continues to be a significant health issue. About 5 percent of young children (approximately 900,000) have a toxic level of lead in their blood (American Academy of Pediatrics, 1999b). Lead can be found everywhere—in paints, gasoline, foods, water, dust, and soil. The most common route of exposure for children is through lead-based paint in older homes. Children with high levels of lead are at risk for many behavioral problems. They may be hyperactive, impulsive, easily frustrated, or withdrawn. Even low levels of exposure increase the risk for social withdrawal and disinterest (Mendelsohn et al., 1998). Children who live in older neighborhoods and homes or who play on old playground equipment may be exposed to lead. Not surprisingly, children who live in the inner city are more likely to suffer elevated lead levels and anemia than other children (Adams, Geva, Coffman, Palfrey, & Bauchner, 1998).

What health and safety risks do these children face? What is the most common kind of playground injury? How can it be prevented?

Playgrounds also pose health risks for children. Between 1983 and 1987, over 300,000 children were treated in emergency rooms for playground-related injuries. The most common accidents involve falling off playground equipment and result in skull and brain damage (Sacks et al., 1989). Protection can be provided by ensuring that the ground is covered with 8 inches or more of an impact-absorbing material (for example, mats or wood chips).

HOW DO YOUNG CHILDREN THINK AND SOLVE PROBLEMS?

Four-year-old Ginny, like other children her age, can identify many kinds of dinosaurs. She knows that some dinosaurs eat only plants and others only meat. She is more knowledgeable about dinosaurs than many adults. She also can easily be fooled by appearances: she thinks that a tall, thin glass holds more grape juice than a small, wide glass of the same volume. Ginny thinks differently than infants, older children, and adults. When it comes to dinosaurs, she is an expert; but when it comes to understanding physical laws of nature, she is a novice with little understanding of the world. To fully understand young children's thinking, we must consider the physical, social, and cultural contexts they experience, as well as how they interpret problem-solving situations.

PREOPERATIONAL THINKING

According to Jean Piaget, young children have made tremendous strides in their understanding of the world, and their thinking is qualitatively different from that of infants. As you learned in Chapter 5, infants do not fully understand that objects continue to exist when they are not directly experiencing them, but young children have no difficulty comprehending object permanence. Infants experience the world in the here and now, with little comprehension of the past or future, but preschoolers can think about the future and discuss the past.

Young children have moved into the *preoperational stage* of cognitive development (2 to 7 years of age). At this stage, they use **symbolic representations**—they can mentally

symbolic representations mental representations of objects and people that can be manipulated in the mind

Why will this 4-year-old say that the snake has more clay in it than the ball? What property of physical objects is not being conserved? According to Piaget, what is this child's stage of cognitive development?

represent objects and people and manipulate these representations. Children first show this ability at the end of the sensorimotor period (Chapter 5). Because of their ability to use symbolic representations, young children are not confined, as infants are, to thinking in the present. Young children's symbolic capacities are illustrated in how they play, what they remember, and their increasingly sophisticated use of language. For instance, children in the preoperational stage often imitate behaviors they have seen in the past. Four-year-old Lynna provides an example of deferred imitation. Days after she saw her friend Maria trying a ballet pose, Lynna tried the same pose for the first time. Lynna remembered Maria's actions from days earlier and reproduced these actions.

Children at this stage show remarkable ability to communicate with language, which requires the use of symbols. Young children's thinking is no longer dominated by motor actions; they can use symbols to manipulate information mentally, allowing for faster and more flexible thinking. Before an action occurs, children can anticipate the outcome. Unlike infants, preschoolers have better memories for past events such as a family trip, and they can plan for the future, thinking about whom they will invite to a birthday party that is still weeks away.

According to Piaget, young children, unlike older children, adolescents, and adults, are preoperational thinkers because they are unable to apply **operations**—actions internalized as symbols that can be reversed and coordinated. The ability to use operations is based on the ability to apply basic logic to problem solving. Preoperational children are able to internalize actions in symbols, but cannot yet reverse and coordinate these symbols.

Conservation Tasks

To illustrate the difference between operational and preoperational thinking, Piaget used **conservation tasks.** These are tasks in which children are shown an object, watch a transformation of that object, and then decide whether the transformed object is the same as or different from what it was before it was transformed. For instance, 4-year-old Jason is shown two balls of clay, both of which are exactly the same size and shape. One ball is then rolled out into a long thin snake shape, and Jason is asked to decide if one piece has more clay in it than the other or if they have the same amount. His answer may come as a surprise to many adults: he is likely to say that the long skinny shape has more clay in it than the ball.

In recognizing that the snake and the ball have the same amount of clay, adults apply basic logical principles regarding the conservation of matter. In contrast to Jason, older children understand that an object transformed into a new form contains the same amount of matter so long as nothing is added or taken away. Older children and adults understand the **identity concept,** which involves recognizing the essential "sameness" of an object despite physical changes to it.

Jason, like other preschool children, does not consistently apply the idea of identity to problem-solving experiences. Because young children do not use logical operations, their reasoning often seems flawed to us. Young children's thinking exhibits **centration**—the tendency to focus attention on the most obvious and striking characteristic of an object while ignoring others. They see the snake as having more clay than the ball, for example, because it is longer. Young children centrate on the length of the snake while ignoring its comparative thinness. Their thinking is guided by appearances—what things look like—rather than by logic. Eight-year-old Carol used to take advantage of her 4-year-old sister's tendency to centrate on size (and lack of knowledge of money) by trading big nickels for her sister's small dimes. To her younger sister, bigger meant more.

Static Thinking

The focus on one dimension also is obvious in children's **static thinking**—their tendency to attend to the outcome rather than to the changes that produced the outcome.

operations actions internalized as symbols that can be reversed and coordinated

conservation tasks tasks used to assess children's use of operations, in which children must decide whether a transformed object is the same as or different from what it was before

identity concept the essential "sameness" of an object despite physical changes to it

centration the tendency to focus attention on the most obvious and striking characteristic of an object while ignoring others

static thinking the tendency to attend more to the outcome than to the changes that produced the outcome

For example, a preschool child may watch her friend dress in a monster costume at Halloween and then focus only on the final state; that is, she may become scared of the monster who has magically replaced her friend. Children may even make up unbelievable stories about what happened during a transition. When asked what had happened to her friend, the child might say that her friend had gone home. Young children often exhibit static thinking when they tell stories: they focus only on the beginning of the story and its end. Three-year-old Erin's favorite story is "Once upon a time there was a princess. The end."

Precausal Reasoning

Young children's reasoning about the causes of events does not match adults'. Adults reason *inductively*, from particular examples to the general principle, or *deductively*, from the general principle to the specific example. For instance, inductive reasoning would suggest that if every swan you've ever seen is white, then all swans are white. Deductive reasoning would be used to determine that if all swans are white, and this bird is a swan, then this bird must be white. Piaget argued that young children are more likely than adults to use a different form of reasoning, called **transductive reasoning.** Transductive reasoning suggests that if two particular examples or events occur together, they must be causally related. For example, when Joshua sees his mother pick up her bagged lunch and leave for work, he may believe that the bagged lunch caused her to leave the house. Because the events occurred at the same time, he believes that one caused the other. Also, young children seem to infer that all things happen for a reason, so they search to find a cause, even when events are unrelated or arise by chance.

Understanding Concepts and Categories

Preschoolers' simple classifications of objects and people are based on partial concepts (sometimes called preconcepts) that allow them to make distinctions among global categories, such as animals, food, and people (Mandler, Bauer, & McDonough, 1991). In simple situations, young children can categorize on the basis of a single attribute, but their ability to vary strategies when necessary is limited (Freund, Baker, & Sonnenschein, 1990). Young children's ability to understand differences within a category also is limited. They may distinguish between dogs and elephants, for example, but have difficulty distinguishing different kinds of dogs.

Young children have difficulty understanding some of the more complex aspects of categorization. They have trouble with multiple classification; that is, they fail to understand that one person or object may belong to multiple categories simultaneously. For instance, they may not understand how their mother can also be a daughter. Young children also have difficulty with categorization problems involving **class inclusion,** or part-whole relations of categories. For instance, when 4-year-old Elsie is shown ten brown dogs and five white dogs and is asked whether there are more brown dogs or more white dogs, she is likely to answer the question correctly. However, when asked whether there are more brown dogs (a subclass) or more dogs (the whole class), she is likely to say there are more brown dogs. Elsie's answers show that she can make comparisons within a classification level (brown versus white dogs), but she cannot make comparisons across different levels of classification (brown dogs versus all dogs combined).

Egocentrism

One of the most interesting aspects of preschoolers' thought is their tendency toward **egocentrism;** they assume that their own perspective is shared by other people. Preschoolers rely on their own perception of events rather than recognizing that other people may have a different perception. The result is that they fail to take another person's

transductive reasoning the inference that if two particular examples or events occur together, they must be causally related

class inclusion part-whole relations of categories

egocentrism the assumption, characteristic of most preschoolers, that their own perspective is shared by other people point of view into account (Piaget & Inhelder, 1958). Egocentrism is evident in many aspects of preschoolers' thinking. When 3-year-old Kirra pulled a blanket over her head and announced that we should try to find her, she exhibited egocentric thinking. She reasoned that if she could not see us, we could not see her.

Piaget and Inhelder (1956) designed a special task, called the three-mountain task, to assess whether children can adopt another's point of view. In this task, a child and a doll sit at opposite sides of a table with a view of a scene of three mountains varying in size and appearance. From the child's perspective, the tallest mountain has a different location in the scene than it does from the doll's perspective. The child examines the scene from each position around the table, including the doll's, and then is shown pictures representing all views. When asked which view the doll sees, preschoolers are likely to select the scene that best matches the view from their seat, not the doll's seat. Their egocentric thinking leads them to believe that others see things the way they do.

Children's lack of ability to recognize another's point of view influences their social interactions. Young children often have difficulty communicating effectively, especially on the telephone, because they do not understand that the other person does not see what they see or know what they know. Also, they may have difficulties dealing with others' emotions because they do not understand that others feel differently than they do.

Another feature of egocentric thought is **animism**—attributing lifelike qualities to objects that are not alive. By the preoperational stage, children recognize that most inanimate objects are not alive but have difficulty with inanimate objects that move freely. A 4-year-old girl, asked whether a river is alive, may assert that the river is alive because the water moves. When children talk about the moon being happy or the sun going to

FIGURE 7.4
Three–Mountain Egocentrism Task

Why will this 3-year-old assume that the stuffed animal sees exactly what he sees? What term did Piaget give to this kind of thinking? Does this experimental result mean that a young child is not capable of taking the perspective of another person? Why or why not?

animism attributing lifelike qualities to objects that are not alive sleep, their comments suggest that they believe that the moon or sun is alive. According to Piaget, preoperational children's egocentric thinking inhibits their ability to distinguish between things that are alive and those that are not.

EVALUATING PIAGET'S THEORY OF PREOPERATIONAL DEVELOPMENT

Piaget's ideas about development were unlike those of his predecessors; they were so unusual and surprising that many studies were designed to replicate his findings. Even with children from other countries, Piaget's ideas have been confirmed when the same procedures have been used. Children go through the stages described by Piaget, in the order he outlined. Nonetheless, Piaget may have underestimated children's abilities in some ways. Many of Piaget's tasks may have been too demanding or confusing for preschool children. Developmental researchers have simplified Piaget's tasks to explore whether children will perform the simpler tasks the same way they do the more difficult versions (Gelman & Baillargeon, 1983). The implication is that if children show higher levels of problem solving on simplified tasks, we must reconsider the meaning of Piaget's earlier research.

Children's egocentric thinking has been examined using tasks simpler than the three-mountain task. In one set of studies conducted by Hughes (cited in Donaldson, 1978), children were shown a four-room house without a roof. Two police officer dolls were placed in different locations in the house, and the children were asked to hide a boy doll from the officers' sight. Piaget's theory would predict that preschool children could not succeed at this task, just as they do not succeed at the three-mountain task. Surprisingly, most of the 3-year-olds and almost all of the 4-year-olds were successful in placing the boy doll in a position that neither adult doll could see. Making the task more understandable and providing some practice may improve children's ability to adopt another's perspective. Even 3-year-old children are able to imagine others' perspectives on tasks that involve familiar scenes (such as a pond or farmhouse with animals) and familiar characters (such as Grover from *Sesame Street*) (Borke, 1975).

Young children also are more likely to demonstrate an understanding of conservation when tasks are simplified. When children do not witness the transformation (making the snake from clay), they sometimes respond as though they have conserved (Rose & Blank, 1974). Some children can be trained to conserve, especially when simpler tasks are used, but younger children respond less to training than older children (Case, 1998).

Animistic thinking is less evident when children are asked about familiar concrete objects (such as dolls and rocks) rather than the less familiar objects Piaget used (such as the sun or moon). In tasks with familiar objects, young children recognize the qualities associated with being alive earlier than Piaget expected. For instance, young children realize that movement, growth, and emotions are associated with people but not with rocks or dolls (Massey & Gelman, 1988).

When familiar and comfortable situations are used for testing, children's understanding of causality also is more sophisticated than Piaget believed (Bullock, 1984). For instance, most preschool children know that causes precede outcomes, or effects. When shown an apparatus in which a Snoopy doll pops up if a marble is dropped into the left side but not the right side, 3-year-old children understand that the cause (dropping the marble) must occur prior to the effect (Snoopy's appearance) and select the correct side in which to drop the marble (Bullock & Gelman, 1979; Bullock, Gelman, & Baillargeon, 1982).

Children exhibit higher levels of categorization skills under simplified conditions. They can solve some kinds of class inclusion problems when the wording is changed or when simpler versions of the task are used. For instance, young children recognize that a person would have more to color in a picture if he or she colored the whole bird rather than just its wings (Siegler, 1998).

These studies show that Piaget underestimated young children's capabilities to solve problems using logical principles. Nevertheless, his theory still provides us with a good description of many of the ways in which young children's thinking differs from that of older children and adults. Piaget's ideas about preoperational development are a good starting point for understanding children's problem solving, and they guide us in the right direction for conducting new studies on how young children think about the problems they face every day.

YOUNG CHILDREN'S MEMORY

Four-year-old Abe and 8-year-old Mabel just visited the zoo with their parents. On the car ride home, Abe says he saw a bear and some snakes. Mabel recites a much longer list; she reports that they also saw elephants, birds, monkeys, zebras, kangaroos, and lions. The children's parents remember even more of the animals than either of the children. This example illustrates a typical pattern: young children remember less than older children. Do young children fail to pay attention, or do older children have special capabilities for remembering?

Have you ever noticed that as soon as you read a phone number out of the telephone book and dial it, you forget it? Conversely, are you surprised at how vividly you remember some things? For instance, many people say they can remember exactly what they were doing when they heard that Princess Diana of Great Britain was killed in an automobile crash in Paris. However, these same people may not remember what they ate for lunch the day before. Why are some memories so vivid, whereas others are so fleeting?

People have different ways to store memories, which determine the likelihood that the memories will be remembered later. In Chapter 2, you learned that the memory system has three components: sensory storage, short-term memory, and long-term memory. A phone number you want to dial immediately after looking it up would be held briefly in short-term memory; it would never be transferred to long-term memory, because you have no need to remember it for a longer time period. In contrast, an event such as your wedding or an automobile accident you witnessed is likely to be moved into long-term memory, because it is reviewed, involves visual imagery, evokes emotions, and may be important to remember. Like older children and adults, young children have a three-component memory system that allows them to store information in their memories. Why, then, do they remember less than older children and adults?

All humans have limits on their capacities to process information. When people are distracted or tired or are presented with too much information, they will not remember it as well as when they are attentive and alert and are presented with less information. However, young children's capacities are more limited than older children's and adults' for three basic reasons:

◆ **Tendency to be easily distracted.**   Young children are more easily distracted than older children. Children who are distracted by loud noises or colorful scenes will not pay as much attention as children who can focus their attention more systematically. Attention to relevant information increases between 3 and 8 years of age (DeMarie-Dreblow & Miller, 1988).

◆ **Failure to use memory strategies.**   Memory strategies are techniques used to improve memory, such as **rehearsal** (reviewing information), **organization** (clustering information into groups of similar objects or into meaningful categories), and **elaboration** (thinking of associations among objects). These strategies help move information into long-term memory. Consider how you study for an exam. To increase the likelihood of doing well on an exam, you might rehearse new terms and try to think of ways to relate them to meaningful concepts. For instance, you might study terms concerning prenatal development in the order in which developments occur month to month. The use of

rehearsal memory strategy involving the reviewing of information

organization memory strategy involving the clustering of information into groups of similar objects or into meaningful categories

elaboration memory strategy involving the forming of associations among objects strategies develops during childhood. Toddlers show evidence of using very simple precursors to memory strategies (DeLoache, Cassidy & Brown, 1985). Preschoolers begin to develop memory strategies, but use rehearsal, organization, or elaboration only rarely to help them remember information.

✦ **Lack of awareness of memory.** Young children are unlikely to use **metacognition;** that is, they are less likely than older children to be aware of memory and to monitor their memory performance. Around age 5, children begin to be aware of their learning processes, probably because of their school experiences, and this awareness grows throughout childhood. The better children monitor their memory and learning processes, the more likely they are to store and retrieve information effectively (Siegler, 1998).

Young Children's Understanding of Everyday Events

By the time a child is 5, she or he may have taken hundreds of baths, eaten at fast food restaurants many times, and helped bake cookies a dozen times. What do children remember from these kinds of events? Do they understand that the actions involved in everyday interactions take place in some order? Do they understand which pieces of information are essential and which are not? For instance, in a fast food restaurant, a child can order a hamburger one day and chicken pieces the next, but in both cases, she or he must place the order and pay before picking up the food. The causal sequence of events is crucial, while the type of food is not (Schlottmann, 1999).

The concepts that people form about routines involved in everyday interactions and events may be thought of as **scripts.** As children experience these activities, they have opportunities to learn the sequencing of events (Nelson, 1986). By the age of 3, children begin to develop rudimentary scripts. For example, 3-year-old Jenny may describe the script for grocery shopping as "First, we go to the store, and then we pick out food we like." This basic script has little detail, but reveals Jenny's understanding that going to the store happens before picking out food. As children mature, they develop more elaborate scripts with more details and more sequencing of events (Farrar & Goodman, 1992; Mandler, 1993). For instance, a 5-year-old may remember the script for going to the store as driving to the store, parking the car, getting a cart for the food, picking out food, paying, going to the car, going home, and putting the groceries away (Hudson, Shapiro, & Sosa, 1995). Children's first successes at planning future events are based on their script based knowledge of events (Hudson & Fivush, 1991).

Children's memory for everyday routines and activities influences how they remember specific information. Young children may inaccurately remember an uncommon event by distorting their memories in the direction of a familiar script. For instance, children who have eaten at a nice restaurant may inaccurately report that the food was paid for before they ate, because this is what they experienced in fast food restaurants. Familiarity with the fast food restaurant script colors their memory (Siegler, 1998). As children grow older, they become better able to distinguish between actual and script memories.

Parents help children develop and remember scripts by asking them to recall past events and by asking questions about the activities that occurred (Hudson, 1990). In this way, parents provide children with hints about what kinds of information are important to remember and give them cues about the ordering of events (Nelson, 1993; Price & Goodman, 1990).

Young Children as Experts

Despite their limitations in remembering information, young children are able to learn a large amount of information on topics that interest them. Some children learn enough information in an area to become experts, developing a vast store of knowledge about dinosaurs or becoming a chess whiz. One study focused on a 4½-year-old dinosaur

metacognition awareness of memory and monitoring of memory performance

scripts concepts that people form about routines involved in everyday interactions and events

Can Young Children's Eyewitness Testimony Be Believed?

In 1988, Margaret Michaels was convicted of sexually abusing preschool children at the school where she worked in New Jersey (*State v. Michaels*, 1988). She was accused of molesting children during regular school hours over a period of seven months. None of the alleged acts had been noticed by staff or parents, and none of the children had reported any instances to their parents. The first suspicion occurred when a 4-year-old former student told a nurse who was taking his temperature rectally, "That's what my teacher does to me." This started a series of investigations, and many other children began to disclose similar stories, but only after they had been repeatedly interviewed by case workers. On the basis of testimony provided by nineteen child witnesses, Michaels was convicted of 115 counts of sexual abuse and sentenced to serve forty-seven years in prison. An Appeals Court reversed her conviction, and the New Jersey State Supreme Court upheld this reversal (*State v. Michaels*, 1994), ruling that in order to retry the case, the prosecution would first have to convince the court that the child witnesses could provide reliable testimony. The prosecution then dropped all charges against Michaels (Ceci & Bruck, 1995).

The Michaels case is not an isolated case. There have been many similar cases, some of which you may remember because of the extensive media coverage they received. Often the sole witnesses are preschool-aged children who disclosed the abuse only after a long delay and after intensive interviewing. Usually, no corroborative evidence is found and the defendants maintain their innocence (Ceci & Bruck, 1995). Can the testimony of young children be believed?

Children can be reliable witnesses, but many conditions influence the accuracy of their testimony:

- *Suggestibility and vulnerability to leading questions.* Existing research indicates that preschoolers are more vulnerable than older children to leading questions and are more suggestible. This is not to say that young children cannot provide accurate and reliable testimony, but they are more susceptible to a variety of factors that contribute to unreliable testimony (Ceci & Bruck, 1998). A child who is repeatedly asked about how her teacher touched her in a "bad" place may be led into believing that this happened, even if it did not.

- *Desire for approval from adults.* Young children are very reliant on adults for approval and are eager to please them. It is common for a preschooler to provide a desired answer to an adult's question just to win the adult's approval (Garbarino & Stott, 1992). For example, when an adult asks young children to select a suspect from a series of photographs that does not contain a picture of the actual suspect, children rarely acknowledge that they do not recognize any of the photographs. They are likely to make a false identification because they want to please the adult. This is true even when children are warned that the lineup may not contain a picture of the suspect (King & Yuille, 1987).

- *Repeated questioning.* Young children's testimony is less likely to be distorted after one interview than after several interviews (Ceci & Bruck,

1995). The constant questioning, and sometimes leading questions, may cause children to think that they are supposed to answer questions in certain ways. Repeating questions to young children may make them feel that their previous answers were wrong. A child who initially answered that the teacher didn't do anything "bad" may eventually say that the teacher *did* do something bad, simply because an adult asked repeatedly. The child may think that if his or her initial answer had been OK, then the adult would not have asked the question again and again. Children's desire to please adults may lead them to change their answers to what they believe the adult wants rather than what is accurate.

Of course, older children and adults also are suggestible and vulnerable to leading questions. However, because of their limited memory skills, dependence on adults, and limited experiences, young children are more easily influenced by the suggestions and leading questions. The impact of persistent and suggestive questioning is likely to be especially powerful on children (Ceci & Bruck, 1998).

Thinking It Through:

1. Why did prosecutors drop their appeal in the Margaret Michaels case?
2. What are the three main factors that can lead to inaccuracy in children's testimony, and why do they decrease accuracy?
3. How can young children's reports of sexual abuse be obtained with the fewest inaccuracies?

expert who had been exposed to information about dinosaurs for a little over a year. This child could name and recognize over forty types of dinosaurs and describe where they lived, their diets, and their forms of locomotion (Chi & Koeske, 1983).

Children and adults who are experts on a specific topic retain more details about that topic and think about that topic both more extensively and differently than other people (Chase & Simon, 1973). Most importantly, an expert organizes information differently. For instance, chess experts are better than nonexperts at remembering the positions of chess pieces in real games, but they do not have an advantage when the pieces are randomly arranged on the board (Chi, 1978). This suggests that a chess expert's better memory for chess is due not to better memory abilities overall but to a better understanding of chess.

Just as experts remember information relevant to their area of expertise better than novices, children remember familiar information better than unfamiliar information (Harris, Durso, Mergler, & Jones, 1990). When information is familiar, children can apply new strategies more efficiently. With practice, these strategies become more automatic and require fewer processing demands. Because processing demands are minimal, children develop the capacity to apply memory strategies to unfamiliar content (Siegler, 1998).

Why do some children become experts on dinosaurs? How does their knowledge of dinosaurs differ from that of someone who is not an expert?

THEORY OF MIND: YOUNG CHILDREN'S UNDERSTANDING OF MENTAL EVENTS

Tammy, age 3, played a trick one day with the help of her father. She called for her uncle to come into the room, knowing that as soon as he opened the door wide enough to enter, he would be hit by the pillow that she and her father had balanced on the top of the door. For Tammy to enjoy this trick, she had to recognize that her uncle did not know what was about to happen and would be surprised when the pillow dropped on him. Which he was.

Tammy's behavior indicates that she has some understanding of mental states—what people know, think, and feel. Preschoolers often use the words *think, pretend,* and *imagine,* providing clues that they have ideas about the inner mental events that people experience (Bartsch & Wellman, 1995). An understanding of inner mental events means that children have developed a **theory of mind;** that is, they understand that people think, imagine, pretend, and wonder about the world around them.

Developing a theory of mind represents a tremendous accomplishment in which children learn to separate the external world from the inner workings of the mind (Wellman & Gelman, 1998). This achievement influences many aspects of children's lives, including how they distinguish pretend and real events, understand deception and lies, interpret other people's behavior, and distinguish between beliefs and desires. For instance, children who have a theory of mind are likely to understand how to anger or entertain a younger sibling (Dunn, 1988) and how to ensure that their communications have been understood (Shwe & Markman, 1997). The extent to which children all over the world develop a theory of mind is unclear. Cultural factors such as schooling, emphasis on science, and group cohesiveness may influence how and whether members of a culture develop and use beliefs about others' minds and behaviors (Gauvain, 1998; Lillard, 1998).

For North American children, whose understanding of theory of mind has been studied the most extensively, understanding of inner mental states increases in sophistication

theory of mind the understanding of inner mental events—that people think, imagine, pretend, and wonder about the world around them during early childhood. Three- and 4-year-old children realize that people, but not objects, can "think" and that thinking is an internal process. By 5 years of age, children tend to believe that people think using their brains and realize that one can think about things that are not present (Flavell, Green, & Flavell, 1987). In addition, young children's theory of mind gives rise to fantasy play, as they now can pretend and imagine what others feel or think (Taylor & Carlson, 1997).

One of the ways scientists have studied children's theories of mind has been to investigate their understanding of others' beliefs (Cassidy, 1998). Suppose two 4-year-olds, Maria and Jeremy, are shown a bag of cookies. Then when Jeremy is out of the room, the cookies are taken out of the bag and replaced with erasers. When Jeremy returns, Maria is asked what Jeremy thinks is in the bag. Will she recognize Jeremy's false belief that there are cookies in the bag (since he did not observe the change to erasers)? Or will she say that Jeremy knows what she knows—that there are erasers in the bag?

By the age of 4, Maria is likely to recognize Jeremy's false beliefs. Maria also is capable of misleading someone intentionally using her theory of mind. To mislead someone, children must understand that the other person does not know what they know. When simple and concrete situations are used, even 3-year-olds can intentionally mislead someone (Chandler, Fritz, & Hala, 1989). However, young children's understanding of mental states is not sophisticated nor is it applied consistently. They may be poor at inferring from a situation what others are thinking (Flavell, Green, & Flavell, 1995). For example, Tammy continued to try to fool her uncle, not recognizing that he now knew the pillow trick. Preschool children also fail to realize that people tend to focus their thinking on one topic at a time rather than on many.

Young Children's Understanding of Pretend and Real

Given that children spend much of their time playing "make believe" and watch many hours of fantasy situations on television, it is important to determine how well they can distinguish between pretend and real situations. The answer depends on the type of fantasy-reality comparison that is made. Children often are quite capable of making these distinctions. When 2½-year-old children are involved in fantasy play using make-believe substances such as "tea" in a cup, they recognize the fantasy nature of the play and respond appropriately—maybe even wiping up imaginary spilled tea after they watch another "spill" it (Harris & Kavanaugh, 1993; Leslie, 1987). Similarly, by age 3, young children understand the difference between a real object and a "play" toy (Woolley & Wellman, 1990).

Children do, however, have difficulty identifying an object when its appearance conflicts with its true identity. When children are shown a deceptive object, such as a sponge that looks like a rock, they are confused by the object's appearance and do not pay attention to its true nature (Flavell, 1988). At age 3, most children do not distinguish the appearance of deceptive objects from their reality, even after training (Taylor & Hort, 1990). However, in simplified situations, even 3-year-olds may recognize these distinctions (Rice, Koinis, Sullivan, Tager-Flusberg, & Winner, 1997). Children's ability to make more difficult discriminations increases with age (Flavell, Green, & Flavell, 1987). By age 5, children generally make these distinctions, even in cognitively demanding situations (Martin & Halverson, 1983). The boundaries children draw between fantasy play and reality also become more differentiated between 2 and 6 years of age: whereas younger children might scare themselves playing monster, older children will not (DiLalla & Watson, 1988).

The Social Context of Cognitive Development

As you learned in Chapter 5, infants gain knowledge through interactions with other people. The social context continues to play an important role in young children's cognitive development. In Piaget's view, children are explorers who discover many interesting and valuable ideas through their interactions with people and objects. According to the Russian psychologist Lev Vygotsky, children and caregivers discover ideas together.

Just as parents of infants and toddlers can scaffold their learning of language, parents of preschoolers can promote their cognitive development through the use of a scaffolding system. This cognitive scaffolding provides a continually evolving, moderately challenging learning environment, which changes in response to the child's developing cognitive competencies.

Scaffolding involves many different strategies, including engaging the child's attention, reducing the number of steps in a task, motivating the child, and demonstrating the skill to be performed (Karpov & Haywood, 1998). To see how caregivers' scaffolding strategies work, consider the way Anita helps her 4-year-old daughter Rachel with a challenging animal puzzle. To make the task easier, Anita breaks it into more manageable units. After turning all the pieces right side up, Anita suggests that Rachel select the pieces that have straight edges, because these pieces make up the border of the puzzle. Then Anita gives Rachel strategies for putting the pieces together. As Rachel selects each piece, Anita describes the color and the animal on the piece, giving Rachel clues to help her decide where the piece might fit. At each step, Anita provides subgoals for finishing the puzzle, which help Rachel avoid frustration. She also suggests ways to think about the puzzle pieces, providing Rachel with keys to the thinking process.

Anita is extending Rachel's problem-solving abilities and understanding about puzzles by working within Rachel's zone of proximal development (Chapter 5). The next time they get a puzzle out, Anita waits to see whether Rachel turns the pieces right side up before suggesting this strategy. Anita also is less likely to discuss the colors of each piece, and Rachel is more likely to mention these qualities herself as she tries to fit pieces together. Anita and Rachel continually renegotiate strategies, with Anita tuning in to Rachel's skills each time they play.

If Anita tried the same strategies with a much more challenging game, Rachel probably would not complete the game. Both probably would feel frustrated in their efforts because they would be working outside of Rachel's zone of proximal development. If Anita tried the same strategies with a simple game that Rachel had already mastered, Rachel's cognitive skills would not be facilitated. By working within the frame of Rachel's abilities and providing a nurturing context, Anita gives Rachel a challenging experience, and Rachel's problem-solving abilities improve (Tappan, 1998).

When Rachel works on the puzzles, an interesting thing takes place: Rachel talks out loud to herself. Her tendency to talk about the puzzle aloud when she is alone demonstrates Vygotsky's idea of **private speech,** which individuals speak to themselves when solving problems. Piaget assumed that children's tendency to talk to themselves simply indicated egocentrism, and so he labeled this **egocentric speech.** Vygotsky, however, believed that private speech is an internalized voice that helps guide thinking. In solving the puzzle, Anita suggested strategies ("Let's put the straight-edged pieces together first"), which Rachel used to put the puzzle together. Later, when Rachel worked on the puzzle alone, she repeated out loud the strategies that her mom had proposed. Over time, these conversations become internalized and children can, on their own, use them to help direct their behavior (Winsler, Diaz, & Montero, 1997).

Recent research has confirmed and expanded upon the idea of private speech (Duncan & Pratt, 1997). Children use private speech more often to direct their actions than to make egocentric remarks. As children grow older, their private speech becomes quieter (Berk, 1994).

CULTURAL INFLUENCES ON YOUNG CHILDREN'S THINKING

Just as caregivers provide learning environments for children's cognitive development, so too do the communities or cultures in which children are raised (DiMaggio, 1997). Children's learning takes place through active participation with others. One can

private speech Vygotsky's term for speech directed toward the self, used when solving problems

egocentric speech Piaget's term for speech directed toward the self think of children as apprentices who are actively involved in organizing and supporting their own learning experiences by working with other people in everyday cultural activities (Rogoff, Mistry, Goencue, & Masier, 1993). Through apprenticeships with adults, children essentially become experts on their own culture; they learn the skills, the background knowledge, and the values and norms of their community.

Given the great diversity of cultures and communities, it is not surprising that children's exposure to their own culture results in specific experiences and scripts that differ from those of children raised in different cultures. How do children learn the specific cognitive skills and values associated with their own culture?

+ **Through exposure.**   To learn cultural scripts, children need exposure to the situations associated with the scripts. In their day-to-day experiences and interactions with others, children are exposed to their culture's values regarding particular skills (Jacobs, 1997). For instance, the Inuits, who live near the Arctic Circle, often demonstrate the value of knowing one's whereabouts as a survival skill, and so their children learn to use spatial skills to navigate their environment.

+ **Through practice.**   Children also learn cultural scripts through practice (DiMaggio, 1997). A young child raised in a rural environment, for example, is more likely than a city child to learn about the care of farm animals. Similarly, children who are raised with the cultural expectation that they will learn certain skills, such as weaving, receive many opportunities to practice such skills.

+ **Through regulation.**   Cultural differences in child-rearing practices include variations in the extent to which adults control and regulate children's roles in everyday activities. Children may be allowed or required to observe a valued activity before practicing it. As children become more accomplished and skilled, adults may increase children's involvement in the activity. Providing graded levels of exposure to valued activities helps children learn the details needed to perform them (Rogoff et al., 1993).

+ **Through encouragement.**   Adults provide different learning experiences for children by encouraging them to become involved in certain activities (Cole, 1997). Encouragement may be indirect and social or direct and material. In Zimbabwe, many parents encourage their children to learn about marketing, because trading is an important part of daily life. In contrast, young children in the United States receive little parental encouragement to become involved in trading. Thus, children from Zimbabwe develop sophisticated cognitive scripts for and knowledge of trading more readily than children from the United States do.

+ **Through assignment of responsibility.**   Cultures vary in the extent to which parents and adults structure the learning environment. In some cultures, adults provide structure by guiding children's attention, motivation, and involvement and by providing lessons in important activities. This greater level of parental involvement is typical in societies in which children's participation in adult life is delayed until they are much older. Children learn skills that are assumed to help them later, when they take on adult roles (Rogoff et al., 1993).

In other cultures, children direct their own attention and motivation and determine for themselves their level of involvement in adult activities. The role of adults is to provide feedback in response to children's requests but not to try to direct the children. For instance, in a Mayan Indian town in Guatemala, children routinely observe their mothers' involvement in adult economic activities—for example, weaving and sewing. Children are responsible for watching the activities and deciding whether and when to enter into them. While the mothers respond to children's questions and requests, typically they do not give direct instruction (Rogoff et al., 1993). Children raised in traditional Native American cultures learn through quiet observation. A Navajo girl may decide she

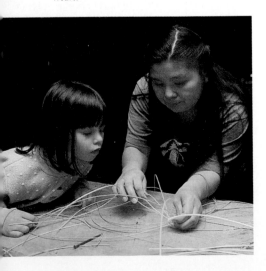

In what way is this child taking primary responsibility for learning to weave? By what means do children learn the scripts associated with their culture? How would cultural differences change this scene if you were learning to weave?

is ready to weave after spending time watching her mother, but without receiving direct instruction in weaving (Collier, 1988).

EDUCATING YOUNG CHILDREN

Young children's cognitive development is influenced by the stimulation and interactions that caregivers provide for them. Some of these interactions are very direct, such as those discussed earlier in which caregivers provide scaffolding for their children. Caregivers also act as teachers and facilitators of learning by providing stimulating environments for their children. Outside the home, children experience opportunities to learn in preschool and kindergarten settings.

Parents as Teachers

How do children grow up to become gifted or talented in a particular cognitive area? Do their parents treat them in any special ways to help encourage their talents? Not surprisingly, parents play a very important role in encouraging the cognitive abilities of their children. In a fascinating study of twenty five famous mathematicians, it was discovered that twenty one of these talented individuals had experienced early intellectual stimulation (Fowler, 1986). For example, the father of René Descartes (1596–1650; credited with unifying algebra and geometry) began René's intensive intellectual stimulation when he was only 14 months of age. Blaise Pascal (1632–1662; credited with developing the first calculating machine and famous for his work on probability theory) and Karl Gauss (1777–1855; considered to be the father of modern mathematics) had parents who intensively schooled them to calculate, read, and write early and engaged them in many intellectual discussions. Almost all of these great mathematicians were, as children, exposed to highly intellectual adults who stimulated their cognitive development.

Parents promote cognitive development by constructing an optimal learning environment in the home—they provide materials, experiences, and encouragement that help children to become curious explorers of their worlds. An instrument designed to measure these aspects of a stimulating environment is called the Home Observation for Measurement of the Environment (HOME) Scale. Studies using the HOME Scale have investigated the roles in children's cognitive development of parental encouragement of learning and the physical environment to which the child is exposed (see Table 7.2).

TABLE 7.2
Assessing the Home Environment

SUBSCALE	SAMPLE ITEMS
Stimulation of academic behavior	Child is encouraged to learn colors
Variety in daily stimulation	Child is frequently taken on outings with other family members
Access to toys and games for stimulation	Home has toys and games
Encouragement of maturity	Child is encouraged to be responsible and sociable
Language stimulation	Parent teaches child about language through the use of games, books, puzzles
Punishment methods	Parent does not spank or slap child during visit
Physical environment	Rooms are clean and uncluttered
Pride and acceptance	Parent is proud of child

SOURCE: Elardo and Bradley, 1981.

TABLE 7.3

Stimulating Young Children's Intellectual Development

- Read to children and let them see you read.
- Visit the library and allow children to select their own books.
- Set limits on television viewing to encourage more conversational skills and reading.
- Provide pencils, crayons, and markers for children to practice drawing and writing.
- Ask children questions and listen to their answers.
- Take children to museums, art galleries, and historical sites.
- Encourage children to think critically and solve problems.
- Explore and play with children.

SOURCE: National Association for the Education of Young Children, 1995.

Higher scores on the HOME Scale relate to better outcomes for children. When children are exposed to many varieties of learning materials in a safe environment and when they receive encouragement for learning, they score higher on tests of language development and cognitive development than do children with less stimulating environments (Bradley & Caldwell, 1981). African American, Caucasian American, and Hispanic children show similar relationships between HOME features and cognitive development (Bradley et al., 1989).

During the early years, parents can encourage children's cognitive development in many ways. Probably the most important is spending time with children (see Table 7.3). Although most parents are aware of the importance of reading to their children, not all parents routinely provide this type of experience. As illustrated in Figure 7.5, many children are read to very little or not at all during the early years.

Young Children's Educational Experiences

Since the first public nursery schools for children were opened in the United States in the early 1900s, the idea of an education-oriented setting for young children has become increasingly popular. Even with fewer children being born today in the United States than in past decades, enrollment in preschools has risen dramatically, from about 20 percent in the 1970s to about 50 percent today.

A good preschool uses developmentally appropriate practices. This means that the activities are based on knowledge about the developmental level of children within a particular age range. At the same time, a good preschool encourages and recognizes the unique qualities that each child brings to the educational experience. Activities in the preschool curriculum foster children's physical, social, cognitive, and emotional development.

A good preschool does not mimic older children's elementary education classes. Instead, a good preschool is geared specifically for the active young child. Rather than sitting at desks and being guided by a teacher, children should be encouraged to actively explore their environments. Some children might play with water containers, others listen to a story, and still others build a block fortress. Teachers can facilitate children's involvement by asking questions or offering suggestions. A good preschool focuses on the individual needs of each child and on enhancing children's self-esteem and self-control.

The effectiveness of preschool programs has been studied extensively. High-quality preschool programs have low student-teacher ratios, a well-educated staff, and developmentally appropriate activities. Children in such programs show advances in cognitive

FIGURE 7.5
Percentage of Young Children Who Were Read to in the Previous Week

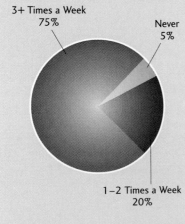

SOURCE: National Center for Education Statistics, 1996.

What generalization can you draw from this figure? Does research support a connection between being read to and achieving literacy?

Notice that the children in this class are not sitting at desks studying. How do children learn in preschool? What are some developmentally appropriate methods for encouraging cognitive development in preschool children?

and social skills compared with children from the same kind of backgrounds who do not attend preschools (Clarke-Stewart, 1984). This is especially true for disadvantaged children (Burchinal, Lee, & Ramey, 1989). In one study, the cognitive and social advantages of preschool were still apparent after three years of elementary school (Howes, 1988). Children who attended high-quality preschools had fewer behavior problems and better academic skills in first grade than did children who did not attend high-quality preschools.

Clearly, a major issue for parents must be the quality of care that their children receive. Given the importance of a good preschool, it is essential that parents learn how to assess the quality of preschools so that children have the optimal early childhood education experience. Table 7.4 outlines some of the features that parents should look for in preschools.

Children's first experience with formal schooling usually occurs in kindergarten. The first kindergartens, opened in the mid-nineteenth century, were designed to nurture young children. Today in the United States, kindergarten has become another tier of the public education system. Many people believe that children's cognitive development needs to be accelerated, and one means of doing so is to increase the academic emphasis in kindergarten. These people see preschools and kindergartens as obvious places to

TABLE 7.4

Indicators of a High-Quality Preschool

Licensing/Accreditation	The program is licensed by the state. If the program is accredited by the National Association for the Education of Young Children, it is a top-notch program.
Setting	There is a safe, fenced, outdoor play area, well equipped for many activities. The indoor area has space for many different activities and a wide variety of toys, books, puzzles, and games.
Teacher-Child Ratio	The number of children supervised by a team of two teachers is not greater than 18 to 20. Each teacher is responsible for no more than 8 to 10 children.
Teacher Qualifications	Teachers have college-level training in child development or early childhood education.
Parent Involvement	Parents are encouraged to drop in to observe the children and to participate in activities with them. Teachers frequently review and discuss children's development with parents.

SOURCE: National Association for the Education of Young Children, 1997.

When Are Young Children Prepared to Start School?

"By the year 2000, all children in America will start school ready to learn." These words were uttered in 1989 by then President Bush and the state governors, who established this as the top goal for American education. Few would argue with this goal, but how *readiness* is defined and how this goal is reached are hotly debated (Gredler, 1997; Shepard, 1997).

Readiness to learn has been conceptualized as the level of development at which a child is prepared to undertake the learning of specific material and content. For most preschoolers, learning is an active and enjoyable process. Most enter kindergarten ready to learn, but this readiness does not always guarantee success in school (Lewit & Baker, 1995).

Historically, chronological age has served as the major criterion for school entry. In the United States, although some children enter kindergarten at age 4, the majority enter at between 5 and 6 years of age, with about 8 percent held back each year to begin school after they are 6 (National Center for Education Statistics, 1993). The tendency to hold children back has been increasing; in recent years, almost 16 percent of first-grade children were held back for one year (Brent, May, & Kundert, 1996). Because some aspects of development, such as language skills, are strongly correlated with age, older children, particularly boys, do better in school during the early grades than do younger classmates. However, these differences tend to disappear by third grade (Shepard & Smith, 1988). Age generally is not a good predictor of academic success (Morrison, Alberts, & Griffith, 1997).

Although there is no agreement as to what constitutes readiness for school, being physically healthy, having adequate communication skills, having an interest in learning, being able to sit still, and controlling one's impulses have been identified as key components (Lewit & Baker, 1995). According to a large-scale study of kindergartners and their parents (National Center for Education Statistics, 1993), only 63 percent of kindergartners had all of these school readiness qualities. These findings are in line with an earlier study in which kindergarten teachers said that 65 percent of their students were not ready to participate successfully in school (US Department of Education, 1993). In addition, when teachers were asked to compare the readiness of their current students with that of their students five years ago, only 25 percent said that today's kindergartners were more ready; 42 percent said fewer students were ready now than before.

School readiness does not reside solely with children. Families, schools, and communities have the responsibility to ensure children's school readiness. Supportive environments that promote healthy, concerned, developmentally appropriate interactions with young children are likely to produce the most active and eager learners in kindergarten and beyond (May & Kundert, 1997)

Thinking It Through:

1. What kinds of things can parents and teachers do to promote young children's school readiness?
2. What individual characteristics of young children enhance their readiness to enter school?
3. In your opinion, what are the most important qualities that determine a young child's readiness to enter kindergarten? What factors put children at risk for not being ready to enter school?

begin academic training and promote readiness for school. Many experts in child development, however, oppose an emphasis on early academic training in reading, writing, and arithmetic (Charlesworth, 1989; Elkind, 1987, 1988), primarily for two reasons. One reason relates to the belief that children learn best when they are actively involved in learning. Good kindergarten and preschool programs lay the foundation for later cognitive skills by encouraging developmentally appropriate play and supplying hands-on experiences. Another reason is that children who are pushed academically at a young age may lose interest in learning, which has serious long-term consequences for children's education.

EARLY INTERVENTION AND YOUNG CHILDREN'S COGNITIVE DEVELOPMENT

Young children's cognitive development is stimulated and nurtured when they are exposed to intellectually challenging environments and have positive role models to emulate. For instance, children are more likely to be interested in reading if they observe their parents routinely reading for pleasure in the home. Unfortunately, not all children have such ideal conditions for cognitive development. Many young children are in stressful, distracting environments that lack intellectual stimulation. These children do not have the kinds of early experiences that foster the development of competent intellectual performance and achievement. For instance, they may not be taken to libraries or read to often because the parents are overworked or in poor health. Can these unstimulating environments be overcome or supplemented?

Head Start

Project Head Start originated in 1965, during America's "War on Poverty," and was designed to serve preschool-age children from economically disadvantaged backgrounds. In 1998, there were over 40,000 Head Start classrooms serving 793,809 children. The program has serviced almost 17 million children since 1965. In 1994, approximately 61 percent of Head Start families had an annual income of less than $9,000. Of the children enrolled in Head Start, 36 percent were African American, 31 percent were Caucasian American, 26 percent were Hispanic, 4 percent were Native American, and 3 percent were Asian American. Head Start serves about 30 percent of all eligible children (ACYF, 1998).

Children living in low-income families are at risk for failure in school because these families may not give priority to academic values or encourage children to think critically. The families simply may not have the resources to promote cognitive development. To overcome these problems, Head Start programs were developed. Children begin Head Start classes at age 3 and can continue for two years. Although Head Start is more than an educational program, one of its stated goals is to provide environmental interventions that stimulate children's cognitive growth. For this reason, much of the research on the effectiveness of Head Start has focused on the intellectual performance of the young children enrolled in the program (Raver & Zigler, 1997).

Studies of the immediate effects of Head Start showed that young children's IQ scores rose by at least 10 points and that their achievement levels sometimes rose after just a few weeks of attending Head Start (Datta, 1985). Unfortunately, findings on later effects were not as optimistic. Research found that young children attending Head Start did not continue to do better on cognitive tests or in school (Nieman & Gaithright, 1981). These reports dashed the hopes of those who believed that early intervention in the form of intellectually stimulating preschools could improve children's success in school permanently. In fact, plans were drawn up to discontinue Head Start (Lubeck, De-Vries, Nicholson, & Post, 1997).

Fortunately, parents of the preschoolers enrolled in Head Start protested, and their actions saved the program. Soon afterward, new research was undertaken using more sophisticated designs and techniques. These studies found that young children who attend Head Start show an initial boost in intellectual performance that sometimes lasts for years, but that this initial boost often fades over time (Barnett, 1998).

Why might children's intellectual performance fade over time? One answer may be the formal education these children receive after the preschool years. Low-income families often live in communities where schools do not receive adequate funding. These children thus may find themselves in inferior educational settings and less than stimulating environments. The drop in performance may therefore be a by-product of the relatively poor school environments disadvantaged children encounter (Zigler & Styfco, 1998).

The research also showed, however, that important lasting effects of Head Start exist in other areas. Specifically, participants of Head Start were found to compare favorably in the following ways with low-income children who did not attend Head Start (Consortium for Longitudinal Studies, 1983; Gamble & Zigler, 1989):

+ They were less likely to be assigned to special education classes.
+ They were less likely to be held back a grade in school.
+ They had fewer school absences.

The focus on the intellectual benefits of Head Start for disadvantaged young children obscures the benefits of Head Start in other areas. Preschoolers who attend Head Start show improved physical health, nutritional status, family interactions, and social-emotional behaviors (Raver & Zigler, 1997). Thus, there are considerable benefits to the early interventions provided by Head Start.

Head Start is expanding its services to include children younger than 3 years of age. The rationale for this extension is clear: waiting until a child is 3 or 4 years old is too late (Kagan & Neuman, 1998). With children beginning Head Start earlier, it may be possible to provide preventive services that are more effective than the remedial services provided after problems arise. Children who are healthy, who have positive relationships with caregivers, and who receive adequate stimulation have the foundations for learning in preschool and beyond.

Sesame Street

Television reaches many eligible children that Head Start does not reach. Because of its wide acceptance and use, television is viewed by educators as a "teacher" in every home. Between 1960 and 1970, Congress passed legislation funding the construction of public educational television stations and the development of educational programming. Today, public television provides a wide range of educational programming, and almost every US family has access to these programs.

Most children know and recognize the characters Grover and Big Bird, attesting to the popularity of the highly successful educational program *Sesame Street*. *Sesame Street* is watched by almost half of all preschoolers on a weekly basis. Over 10 million children between the ages of 2 and 5 view an average of three episodes each week (A. C. Nielsen, 1990). *Sesame Street* was the first educational program that combined the attention-holding qualities of commercial television with developmentally appropriate educational material designed to help prepare children for school. The goal of *Sesame Street* is to promote the intellectual growth of preschoolers, particularly disadvantaged preschoolers.

Sesame Street is successful in teaching children many skills; regular viewing increases young children's understanding of numbers, letters, and vocabulary and boosts their reasoning skills. Children from varied racial, social, geographic, and educational backgrounds all seem to learn from watching *Sesame Street* (Children's TV Workshop, 1991; Rice, Huston, Truglio, & Wright, 1990). In addition, mothers of preschoolers are pleased with the educational benefits provided by it (Yankelovich & White, 1989).

The influence of *Sesame Street* is stronger on 3-year-old children than on 5-year-olds, suggesting that the effects of *Sesame Street* may be greatest when children first begin to watch it. Early on, some critics of *Sesame Street* argued that its apparent effectiveness was due to children's watching the show with parents who used the television show as a means to teach their children (Cook et al., 1975). However, in more recent research (Rice et al., 1990), parents reported that they watched *Sesame Street* with their preschoolers only 25 percent of the time that the preschoolers watched the program. Thus, 75 percent of the time preschoolers spent watching *Sesame Street* was without their parents. *Sesame Street* provides young children with valuable educational experiences that they can profit from on their own, as well as when they watch with their caregivers (Comstock & Paik, 1991).

Sesame Street is not just an American phenomenon. The show has been adapted for use all over the world and is recognized as beneficial in many countries. In its various adaptations, *Sesame Street* plays in over eighty countries around the world. In each country, *Sesame Street* has been tailored to meet educational goals specific to children in that cultural setting:

+ The Arabic version of *Sesame Street*, *Iftah Ya Simsim*, focuses on bridging the gap between the informal language that Arabic-speaking children are exposed to in their homes and the classic Arabic language used in the schools. *Iftah Ya Simsim* makes learning formal Arabic fun as well as interesting (Ezzaki, 1990).
+ In Portugal, *Sesame Street* is called *Rua Sesamo*. Because only 30 percent of children in Portugal go to preschool, *Rua Sesamo* plays a greater role in early education than *Sesame Street* does in the United States (Brederode, 1990).
+ The Turkish version of *Sesame Street* is called *Susam Sokagi*. In Turkey, concern about illiteracy—particularly among women and people who live in rural areas—is great. One goal of *Susam Sokagi* is to get mothers to watch with their children, so that both the mothers and the children will learn to read and write (Sahin, 1990).

The variations in *Sesame Street* reflect cultural differences in values, education, and economic conditions. Regardless of the culture, research evidence shows that *Sesame Street*, in its different versions, successfully meets the wide variety of educational needs of children in various countries (Children's Television Workshop, 1991).

WHAT CHANGES OCCUR IN YOUNG CHILDREN'S LANGUAGE DEVELOPMENT DURING EARLY CHILDHOOD?

Most children are competent speakers of their native language by the age of 5. They have learned many of the subtleties of language; for example, they can distinguish between two similarly worded sentences that have quite different meanings, such as "The bird is in the tree" and "The bird is in the dark." They learn the meanings of thousands of words during the early preschool years. Language development is a primary focus of socialization in a culture. **Social communicative competence** is the ability to effectively convey an intended message to others (Wilcox & Terrell, 1985). Children whose social communicative competence is low are at risk for problem behaviors and poor social relationships (Rice, Hadley, & Alexander, 1993).

VOCABULARY

Children's vocabularies expand rapidly during the preschool years and even faster during the school years. Researchers estimate that before first grade, children learn about five words a day, but in first grade to third grade, they learn about twelve words a day. Children average about 10,000 words in their vocabulary by first grade and about 20,000 words by third grade (Anglin, 1993).

Although young children have a much larger vocabulary than toddlers, they still experience the frustration of not being able to get adults to understand their meaning. There are some words that children want to say but cannot. Some sounds are difficult for them to produce, and children around the world will avoid words that they find difficult to say (Ingram, 1989). Often children create words to better express themselves. For instance, a 4-year-old said, "Try to be more rememberful, mom" when disappointed by his mother's forgetfulness (Clark, 1993).

social communicative competence
the ability to effectively convey an intended message to others

SOLVING THE MYSTERY OF WORD MEANING

Every time children hear a new word, they must act like detectives, trying to solve the mystery of the meaning that is intended by the word. Young children are smart word learners and understand the meanings of novel nouns quickly (Akhtar, Carpenter, & Tomasello, 1996). One way children learn word meanings is through **fast mapping,** in which they learn to associate the sound of the word with the concept the word stands for, sometimes in a single exposure (Markson & Bloom, 1997). Mappings are more likely to occur, and are more accurate, for concrete objects than for abstract information (Rice, 1990). Children's abilities to attend and remember enhance their ability to learn new words (Samuelson & Smith, 1998). Children also use cues from social interactions to attach meaning to new words (Tomasello, Strosberg, & Akhtar, 1996).

The speed of the mapping process increases with age, such that preschoolers are more likely than toddlers to learn words in a single exposure. In one study, children were asked to play a hiding game with a puppet. They were shown three objects—two familiar objects and one new object called a *koob*—and three hiding places. The children were asked to hide each object in a designated spot. After hiding the two familiar toys, the children were directed to "hide the koob under the bowl." They were then asked questions about the objects and the objects' names. The results revealed that almost all of the children fast mapped the name *koob* to the new object (Dollaghan, 1985).

Although fast mapping helps children learn new words, it does not provide solutions to more subtle aspects of the word meaning mystery (Woodward & Markman, 1998). Listen to young children's speech and you will note that their use of words is often quite different from adults'—especially the way they relate a word to a class of objects. Sometimes children use words to refer to objects or things that are outside the bounds of the category named by the word, in a process called **overextension** (Anglin, 1985). A child who uses the word *doggie* to refer to all furry animals with four legs—a cat, a dog, a lamb—is overextending the bounds of the meaning of the word. The child is nonetheless demonstrating the ability to map a set of sounds (doggie) to a meaningful grouping (small furry animals). The tendency to overextend words is very common among young children (Woodward & Markman, 1998). When children use words to refer to a smaller group than the word actually names, they are exhibiting **underextension** (MacWhinney, 1989). For instance, a child who uses *shoe* to refer only to the shoes in the closet but not to the shoes he or she wears is underextending the range of the meaning of *shoe* (Clark, 1981) (see Figure 7.6). Children pay particular attention to the forms of objects and their functions when trying to solve the mystery of word meaning.

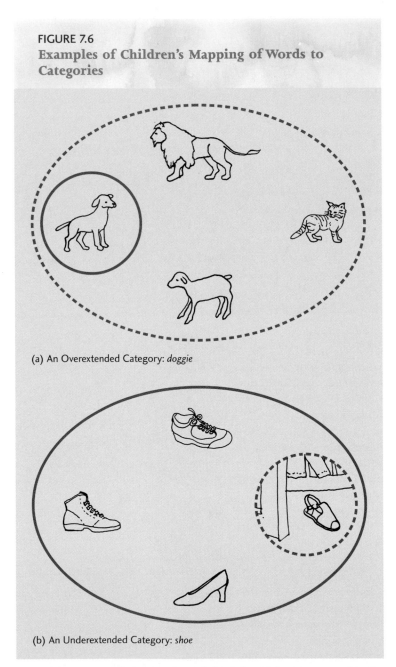

FIGURE 7.6

Examples of Children's Mapping of Words to Categories

(a) An Overextended Category: *doggie*

(b) An Underextended Category: *shoe*

When children overextend, their use of a word extends beyond the category named by the word. In (a), the child has extended "doggie" to mean any animal with hair. When children underextend, their use of a word is narrower than the category named by the word. In (b), the child has narrowed the meaning of "shoe" to only shoes in closets—not shoes on people's feet.

Children also must determine the level of meaning intended by a word (Woodward & Markman, 1998). When Kurt was 2 and first met his friend's cat, Simon, he heard the labels "Simon," "cat," and "animal." Each label is correct, but each has a different level of meaning. How does Kurt know which word stands for the individual animal and which stands for the whole category of small and furry creatures?

One way children learn the meanings associated with alternative words for the same object is through cues that others provide in their speech. When children hear the cue word *the*, they know that the following word refers to a category of objects rather than a single unique object (Callanan, 1989). When Kurt heard "See the cat," he had a way to recognize that *cat* must refer to the category rather than a name. In contrast, when he heard "This is Simon," the preceding words acted as a cue that *Simon* was the proper name of the object (Gelman & Taylor, 1984).

Another way children resolve the category-level problem is through certain assumptions they make about words and objects. Around age 2, children make the assumption that only one name applies to each object. When they hear a new word associated with an object, they assume that word is the name of the object (Merriman & Bowman, 1989). Given another word, they are unlikely to think it is also the name of the object. Instead, they assume that it refers to another aspect of the object. Children show an order of preference for mapping new words to objects and attributes. They first assume the new word is an object name. If it is not an object name, they then assume the new word refers to a part of the object. If that is not correct either, they assume the word refers to an unusual aspect of the object, such as its texture or shape (Marcus et al., 1992). Using these assumptions and the cues others give, children eventually learn that multiple labels can be used to represent people and objects (Deak & Maratsos, 1998; Hall & Graham, 1998).

As you might suspect, it is difficult for children to understand the meanings of words that refer to abstract concepts—such as *tall* and *short*, *high* and *low*—because these words are not associated with any particular object (Woodward & Markman, 1998). Think about a child who hears the word *tall* associated with a building and with a person. What will this child likely infer about the meaning of the word *tall*? A person may be tall relative to a chair but is short in comparison to a building. *Tall* is not associated with a person in the same way that *adult* might be. So it is not surprising that children have difficulty mastering these descriptive terms.

At about what age did Kurt realize that "Simon" is the name of this particular cat? What cues would Kurt have used to understand that the word "Simon" is this cat's name rather than a label for the category?

YOUNG CHILDREN'S LANGUAGE STYLES

Two types of language styles have been identified in middle-class US families. Children with a **referential language style** develop a vocabulary that includes many object names and use these labels to name the things in their environments. Children with an **expressive language style**, however, use words to regulate social interactions with adults and have fewer object names in their vocabulary (Nelson, 1973). The vocabulary explosion is likely to occur at the end of the second year for children with a referential style, who quickly add many names of things to their vocabulary at this time (Goldfield & Reznick, 1990).

All children use both referential and expressive styles of language on occasion, but some children emphasize one style over the other. Mothers of expressive children direct and control their children's actions through the use of language. For instance, a mother might say, "Say 'good-bye' to your grandmother." In contrast, mothers of referential children comment on aspects of the environment and name activities and objects their children interact with—for example, naming the different toys a child picks up during play (Goldfield, 1987). A child's interests may contribute to the mother's use of language. The mother of a child who shows special interest in a certain toy may encourage that interest by providing names more freely than does the mother of a child who shows less interest (Bridges, 1986).

fast mapping associating the sound of a word with the concept the word stands for, sometimes in a single exposure

overextension the use of words to refer to objects or things that are outside the bounds of the category named by the word

underextension the use of words to refer to a smaller group than the word actually names

referential language style language style focused on developing a vocabulary that includes many object names

expressive language style language style focused on using words to regulate social interactions with adults

BEYOND TWO-WORD SENTENCES

As children grow older, their understanding and use of language become increasingly sophisticated. Sentences grow longer than two words, allowing children much more flexibility in communicating their ideas and desires. Between 2 and 3 years of age, many children form sentences of three words or more, using an agent-action-recipient word order to convey meaning. For instance, they might say, "I hugged the cat." Three-year-olds can use negatives such as *no, not, can't,* and *don't.* They may ask questions using *what* and *where,* but they are unlikely to form questions using *why* or *how.*

During the preschool years, children show evidence of trying to discover and apply grammatical regularities to their speech (Owens, 1996). They gain mastery over many rules of grammar, indicating past tense by adding *-ed* to the end of a verb and forming the plural by adding *-s* to the end of a noun. Their application of these rules becomes obvious when they use them in situations in which the rules do *not* apply, in a process called **overregularization.** At around 3 to 4 years of age, English-speaking children may begin to apply the rules for regular forms to irregular cases. Children overregularize infrequently, and when they do, it tends to be with words that parents do not use often (Fenson et al., 1994; Marcus et al., 1992). A child might say, "My teeths hurt" or "I breaked my toy." Caregivers' attempts to correct overregularizations are often ineffective. For example, when 3-year-old Brenda said, "I goed to school today," her mother tried to correct her by saying "You mean you went to school today." Without missing a beat, Brenda replied, "Yeah, I goed to school today."

Even in completely unfamiliar situations, children assume that rules for regular plural forms apply. In one study, children were first shown a picture of a birdlike creature called a *wug* and then shown a picture depicting two of the creatures. The children were asked to finish the sentence "There are two ____." Most children said, "There are two *wugs*" (Berko, 1958). They assumed that the plural of *wug* would follow the regular form and be *wugs.*

An interesting twist on children's application of grammatical rules is that younger children correctly use the appropriate plurals and past tenses for even the irregular forms. It appears that very young children memorize the irregular forms and reproduce them accurately. Later, when they learn the rules for the regular forms, they assume that these apply to the irregular forms. Even later, they learn to distinguish between the regular forms and the irregular forms and produce both correctly.

Around 4 years of age, children begin to use connectives to conjoin two events in a complex sentence, such as "You watch television and I'll play with my doll." Use of the connective word *and* is one of the first ways children combine simple sentences. As they mature, children learn to form complex sentences in which two events occur sequentially in time, such as "Let's go to the store and buy some cookies." Even later, children form complex sentences expressing causality. Children use *and* as an all-purpose connective word, but they begin to add others, such as *then* and *when* to represent temporal orderings of events and *because* and *so* to represent causal events (Bloom, 1998).

Five-year-old children have an amazing mastery of language and can use language to entertain and tell stories. Nonetheless, subtle aspects of syntax elude them, and they struggle with some forms of grammar such as the past tense of *to be* (*was* and *were*), possessive pronouns (*his, her, your*), and infinitives ("I want *to go* now") (Owens, 1996). Children gain mastery over the more complex and subtle aspects of grammar and vocabulary during the school years.

UNDERSTANDING CONVERSATIONAL RULES

Six-year-old Robbie sat at the dinner table with a group of adults, patiently trying to find a time when he could break into the conversation to make a point. By the time he found an opening in the conversation, he had forgotten what he wanted to say. For

overregularization application of language rules when they do not apply

Does Abuse or Neglect Influence Children's Language Acquisition?

Given that parents provide a social context for language development (Huttenlocher, 1998), what happens to children who have disruptions in their parent-child relationships? Several studies have been done to investigate language development in children who have been physically abused or neglected.

In one study, the language abilities of seventy-four preschoolers were assessed (Culp et al., 1991). About half the children were girls and half boys; approximately half were Caucasian American and half African American. Most of the families were of low socioeconomic status. Twenty of these children had been physically abused, forty-one had been neglected (inadequate supervision, their well-being not provided for) but not physically abused, and thirteen had been both abused and neglected.

Compared to the norms developed for language acquisition, the abused children were approximately 0 to 2 months delayed, the abused and neglected children were approximately 4 to 8 months delayed, and the neglected children were 6 to 9 months delayed. Children who

were neglected showed delays in both understanding and producing language. Surprisingly, children who were maltreated did not suffer other cognitive developmental delays; instead, the effects seemed to be mainly in their language abilities. Language development may be more sensitive than cognitive development to disruptions in parent-child interaction.

You may be surprised that abused children showed minimal delays in language development compared to neglected children. The researchers suggest that the qualities of abuse and neglect have different outcomes for parent-child interactions. Although abusive parents may have a few violent outbursts and withdrawals, neglected children tend to experience persistent parental withdrawal and lack of support (Culp et al., 1991). Other studies have shown similar language-delay problems, but they have also shown that children who were severely abused were more delayed than children who suffered less severe abuse or neglect (Fox, Long, & Langois, 1988).

To understand how parents influence their children's language develop-

ment under such adverse conditions, future research needs to look at development in families over an extended period of time, using longitudinal research designs (see Chapter 2). Only then will it be possible to determine the extent to which children's delays are due to lack of contact with the parent rather than emotional problems arising from the abuse and neglect.

Thinking It Through:

1. Were you surprised by the findings of this study? How do the findings seem to contradict common sense?
2. Why did the researchers have to be concerned about the effects of abuse and neglect on cognitive development as well as on language development?
3. Why might neglect have a more severe impact on language development than abuse does?
4. Using the information in this feature, create a chart or graph to show the findings in this study.

---

adults, most of the rules of conversation are so ingrained that they do not think about them. They know when they can take a turn in the conversation. But young children face the challenge of learning to follow conversational rules while at the same time applying the rules for forming sentences.

Young children are surprisingly good at following basic conversational rules. Even at the age of 2, most children realize that they should begin speaking once someone has spoken to them, and they recognize that certain statements require specific answers (yes or no) (Bloom, Rocissano, & Hood, 1976). By the age of 4, many children are aware that they must adjust their speech to fit the speaker; in other words, they must be mindful of whether the person they are speaking to can understand them. For instance, young children shorten their sentences, simplify their vocabulary, and speak more slowly when talking to even younger children (Tomasello & Mannie, 1985). The ability to adjust to

Strategies for Helping Children Learn Language

Caregivers find many ways to provide an optimal learning environment for preschool children's language acquisition (Owens, 1996). Following are some important strategies for helping children learn language.

- *Recast and expand children's own sentences into longer and more correct forms.* If a child says, "The dinosaur walked in the woods," a caregiver might expand and recast the sentence by saying "That dinosaur walked a long time in the woods, didn't it?" Or a parent might expand a child's statement "I breaked my new doll" into "I'm sorry that you broke your new doll." These variant forms of sentences maintain the basic meaning but display it in a new sentence structure, as well as in correct grammatical form. Children learn

more rapidly about language when parents use these methods (Farrar, 1990). Caregivers use more complex expansions with preschoolers than with toddlers (Hoff-Ginsberg, 1985).

- *Maintain the child's attention to verbal tasks.* Children learn about conversations when caregivers provide topic continuity and reintroduce topics.
- *Build language activities into everyday routines.* For example, while baking cookies, a caregiver might describe every step in the process. By using language skills for everyday activities, children develop scripts for these events that include the use of language.
- *Provide a moderately challenging language environment for the child.* Caregivers should not adjust their language level down to the child's at

all times, but instead should regularly expose the child to a combination of moderately challenging and highly challenging language environments.

- *Encourage the child to experience many language partners.* Children who are encouraged to speak to a wide range of social partners are more likely to hear varied types of input at different levels than are children who speak with fewer partners.
- *Encourage the child's own style of language learning.* Some children are likely to imitate others, and some children tend to avoid imitation. Some children like to make a game out of naming objects. Try to determine the methods the child uses and then incorporate them into everyday language experiences.

---

the level of the listener continues to develop during childhood. It is important to remember, though, that these skills are not used all the time by all speakers: even adults are not always mindful of the capabilities of their listeners.

THE SOCIAL CONTEXT OF LANGUAGE DEVELOPMENT

Social experiences continue to play an important role in children's language acquisition after infancy (Huttenlocher, 1998; Wilcox, Hadley, & Ashland, 1996). Parents direct children's language exposure when they read to children and engage in a scripted activity like tea party. They provide opportunities for children to be involved in conversations by asking them to comment on activities and experiences. For instance, to prompt Sarah to begin a conversation with her father, Sarah's mother asks her at the dinner table, "Can you tell Daddy about the toy we bought for Erin?" Both parents are likely to continue to focus her attention on this topic by asking questions about the shopping trip. Caregivers use more sophisticated and complex forms of expansion as a way of encouraging children to pay attention to the grammatically challenging aspects of their speech (Bloom, 1998). Caregivers also socialize politeness in children's language. A father might say to his child,

"Say, 'Please may I have a cookie' " to encourage appropriate manners (Gleason, Ely, Perlmann, & Narasimhan, 1996).

Beyond parent-directed language activities is the larger social context of language use, which involves both the child and the caregiver as active agents who negotiate the activities of daily living (Ninio & Snow, 1996; Tomasello, 1992; Tomasello & Akhtar, 1995). Children play a more active role in directing speech than early research suggested. In fact, children may be the primary force in directing language interactions and often take the lead in their everyday conversations with adults and caregivers (Bloom, Margulis, Tinker, & Fujita, 1996). Caregivers are more likely to respond to children than to initiate conversations with them.

As children grow older, they spend more time with their siblings, and this new, expanded social context influences language development. Siblings' speech among themselves is different from caregivers' speech to children—it is more playful and includes more reciprocal verbal interchanges (Brown & Dunn, 1992). Having a variety of language partners, each with a particular language style and vocabulary, encourages and supports children's language development.

Thus, language learning occurs in a social context, driven by children's need to communicate and share meaning with others. Caregivers, siblings, peers, and teachers all contribute to learning by responding to the meanings children communicate, providing scripted language experiences, and being responsive partners in communication. Children's desire to communicate, opportunities to connect with others through language, and changes in cognitive development converge to facilitate language development (Bloom, 1998).

CHAPTER SUMMARY

How do children's bodies and motor skills develop during early childhood?

- Physical growth is fairly rapid during early childhood and is affected by many factors, including genetic inheritance, nutrition, family income, and ethnic group.

- A child's brain develops in structure and function during the preschool years. New neural connections form, and the increase in myelination of the axons allows for more efficient communication across different areas of the brain.

- The left hemisphere of the brain, which is specialized for language processing, develops rapidly in the first two years. The right hemisphere, which is specialized for spatial information, develops rapidly around the age of 5.

- Preschool children make tremendous advances in their gross and fine motor skills. The improvement in skills is due to brain development, a better sense of balance, and increased eye-hand coordination.

- Motor development is influenced by practice, parental expectations, imitation, genetic inheritance, brain development, and ethnicity.

What are the nutritional and health issues for young children?

- Many children are undernourished and/or malnourished because they do not receive adequate nutrition. Undernourishment is associated with economic impoverishment, limited health care and educational opportunities, and poor living conditions.

- Many low-income children in the United States suffer from malnourishment. Serious lack of iron can lead to iron deficiency anemia, a nutritional deficiency common in children.

- Undernourished and malnourished children have stunted growth and motor development, learning impairments, and poor school performance. These effects may be due to functional isolation, whereby children become disengaged from their social environments because of impaired brain development and lack of responsiveness.

- Preschoolers generally are healthy. Accidents are the leading cause of death for preschoolers, and many can be avoided.

- Lead poisoning is a common health problem for young children. It occurs most often in children living in older neighborhoods where lead-based paints have been used.

How do young children think and solve problems?

- In the preoperational stage of cognitive development, children think using symbols. This greatly increases their abilities to consider the past and the future, anticipate actions, and think flexibly.

- Preoperational thinking is best illustrated using conservation tasks. These tasks show that young children tend to be fooled by the appearance of an object, rather than recognizing that transformations may not change the identity of the object.

- Preschoolers tend to think egocentrically, assuming that other people's perspective is the same as theirs.

- Although Piaget's ideas have been confirmed in many studies that used the same tasks, later studies with simpler tasks indicate that young children may be more advanced in their problem solving than Piaget believed.

- Young children tend to have shorter memories than older children because they are easily distracted, do not consistently use memory strategies, and are less likely to monitor their memory performance.

- Children tend to have good memories for scripted events, especially those they experience frequently. Children's ability to remember scripts increases with age, especially as reflected in better memory for details and sequencing.

- Children show variable levels of understanding, with high levels of expertise in some domains and less understanding in others.

- During the early years, North American children improve in their ability to understand the inner workings of the mind such that they recognize that people think, pretend, deceive, and imagine.

- Young children have some understanding of pretend versus real situations. They are more likely to confuse pretense and reality when an object's appearance conflicts with its true identity.

- Children's cognitive development is influenced by their caregivers, who transmit cultural information and direct their learning experiences. Children eventually direct their own actions through the use of private speech, which is similar to the speech that caregivers used with them earlier.

- Children can be encouraged to develop their cognitive skills through exposure to preschool and kindergarten programs as well as educational television. Good preschool and kindergarten programs provide experiences and activities that are based on the children's developmental levels.

- Head Start programs have played a very important role in the education of young children from economically disadvantaged backgrounds. Lasting effects have been found for children who participated in Head Start programs.

- *Sesame Street* is a successful educational television series that improves children's learning of numbers, letters, and vocabulary.

What changes occur in young children's language development during early childhood?

- By the age of 5, most children are competent speakers of a language and have mastered the basics of semantics, syntax, and pragmatics of the language.

- A child's vocabulary expands rapidly during the preschool years. Children use fast mapping to relate new words to objects.

- To learn words, children must solve the mystery of word meaning, determining how words relate to concepts and understanding the level of meaning intended by a word.

- Preschool children master more complexities of grammar, such as the ability to negate a sentence, use plurals, and use past tense markers. They occasionally apply grammatical rules even when they are not appropriate.

- Having responsive communication partners is crucial for children's language development. Children guide and direct many interactions with their caregivers. They learn best from experiences that are relevant to them.

KEY TERMS & CONCEPTS

animism *(236)*
centration *(234)*
class inclusion *(235)*
conservation tasks *(234)*
egocentric speech *(243)*
egocentrism *(235)*
elaboration *(238)*
expressive language style *(253)*
fast mapping *(252)*
functional isolation *(230)*

identity concept *(234)*
iron-deficiency anemia *(230)*
metacognition *(239)*
operations *(234)*
organization *(238)*
overextension *(252)*
overregularization *(254)*
private speech *(243)*
referential language style *(253)*
rehearsal *(238)*

scripts *(239)*
social communicative
 competence *(251)*
static thinking *(234)*
symbolic representations *(233)*
theory of mind *(241)*
transductive reasoning *(235)*
underextension *(252)*

ACTIVITIES & APPLICATIONS
Relating to Young Children

1. Go to a playground and observe children of different ages playing. Are the preschool children able to throw, jump, and catch with greater maturity than the younger children? How can you tell that their behavior is more highly developed? Do you notice some children who seem less skilled for their age than others?

2. Watch Saturday morning television for children and notice the kinds of food advertisements that are shown. Then go to the grocery store and read the nutritional information on these foods. Are children being encouraged to eat and drink nutritious foods? How might you remedy this situation if you were a parent?

3. Try some Piagetian tasks with a 4- or 5-year-old child. Ask the child about why the stars shine at night. Does the child give an egocentric response? Try a conservation task with the child. Does the child think a piece of clay that is long like a snake has more clay in it than one shaped like a ball? Give the child a choice between a broken and an unbroken cookie and see if he or she thinks the unbroken one would taste better.

4. Listen to a parent and young child in a problem-solving situation. Does the parent or the child seem to be directing the conversation topics? Does the parent encourage politeness, expand the child's sentences to make them more complex, or repeat the child's ideas back to her or him? In what ways does the parent help in the child's problem solving and in the child's use of language?

CHAPTER 8

Social & Emotional Development IN EARLY CHILDHOOD

CHAPTER OUTLINE

*B*arry and Hector, both age 5, watch as their teacher introduces a new computer game that allows them to create their own insects and learn about them in the process. Hector eagerly waits while the teacher sets up the game, but Barry is noticeably reluctant and nervous. Both children are able to put the first two or three parts of the insect together, but after that the game becomes more difficult. Barry tries to add the next piece. After some unsuccessful attempts, he pounds on the

*table, begins to sob, and cries out, "I hate this; I can't do it!"
In contrast, Hector persists at the game until he discovers the correct movements to make the pieces fit. He
smiles proudly, shouts "I did it!" and starts another
game. Barry, however, clearly feels bad and is quiet and
withdrawn for some time afterward.*

During early childhood, children's social and emotional lives become increasingly complex as they encounter a broader array of people, situations, and environments. This rich array of interactive partners and contexts provides many opportunities to learn about social interactions, about their own and others' emotions, and about their capabilities and characteristics. As Hector and Barry's story reflects, preschoolers' social and emotional lives are often playful and positive, but they can also be tumultuous and uncertain.

HOW DOES SELF-AWARENESS CHANGE DURING EARLY CHILDHOOD?

During early childhood, dramatic changes occur in children's awareness and image of themselves and in their feelings of self-worth. For some children, these changes lead to a positive view of self: they see themselves as active, independent, and persistent. For other children, these changes lead to a negative view of self, filled with uncertainty, helplessness, and failure.

The actions and feelings of Barry and Hector in the opening story are not rare or unique. Barry has difficulty coping with challenging and possibly frustrating events. His negative view of himself contributes to his feelings of inadequacy and defeat. In contrast, Hector's positive self-image helps him face the challenge of the game without becoming upset and frustrated. He has an image of himself as being able to solve problems, so he does not fear failure.

DEVELOPING SELF-CONCEPT

Self-concept refers to an individual's beliefs about the attributes and capacities she or he possesses (Coopersmith, 1967; Lynch, 1981). The fundamental requirement for a concept of self is the recognition that you are distinguishable from others. By age 2, most toddlers recognize themselves as individuals—they can state their own name, identify themselves in a mirror, and distinguish and label themselves in pictures that include other children of the same age and same sex (Snow, 1990; Wolf, 1990).

self-concept an individual's beliefs about the attributes and capacities she or he possesses

Important advances in rudimentary self-concept are made during early childhood as children develop an awareness of their own characteristics. Three-year-old children first describe themselves in global terms, based on external qualities ("I'm fast") rather than psychological qualities ("I'm kind"). This global tendency leads young children to think that if they are good at drawing they also are good at puzzles, running, or singing; that is, self-definitions are generalized to other contexts. By 4 years of age, children's judgments are more specific and differentiated (Measelle, Ablow, Cowan, & Cowan, 1998). They acknowledge that they are good at one skill, but not so good at others. Or they may acknowledge that they are good at doing something in one situation but not in other situations (Harter, 1998). For instance, older preschoolers may believe that they are good at puzzles but not at drawing or that they are good at playing basketball with other preschoolers but not with older children.

Young children often describe themselves in an all-or-none fashion, failing to recognize that traits can co-occur. Thus, children ages 3 to 5 view themselves as either good or bad, but not both good and bad. Likewise, young children believe that they cannot feel both happy and sad at the same time (Ruble & Dweck, 1995). Between 6 and 8 years of age, children begin to acknowledge that two traits or feelings can co-occur, but only sequentially; that is, one quality is initially experienced, followed by the other.

By about age 8, children acknowledge that two opposing qualities of the self can exist simultaneously. However, at this age, children typically attach one quality to one situation and another quality to a different situation (such as "I'm smart in reading but dumb in math"). It is not until age 10 or later that children recognize simultaneous positive and negative qualities in the same situation—for instance, one can be both nice and mean to the same person or in the same situation (Harter, 1998).

Older children and adults recognize that their characteristics and traits are fairly stable over time and situations. Preschoolers, however, rarely describe themselves in terms of stable traits, and when they do, they use very global terms. Instead, their descriptions are likely to be based on characteristics and behaviors that change from time to time ("I'm clean" or "I'm happy").

Based on our discussion of cognitive development in Chapter 7, we could say that preschoolers lack "conservation of self." Just as young children do not recognize that a ball of clay retains its identity (contains the same amount of clay) when it is transformed from a ball to a snake, they do not recognize that their identity can be consistent in different situations and at different times (Bales & Sera, 1995). One consequence of this lack of recognition is that young children often overestimate their abilities, remaining confident even in the face of negative feedback (Stipek, Recchia, & McClintic, 1992). Given young children's tendencies to inaccurately estimate their abilities, caregivers should be skeptical when young children claim that they can do something that seems too advanced for them. By late childhood, a child's self-concept reflects an understanding of enduring qualities and traits and is more accurate and realistic in its representations of the child and the child's characteristics (Schuster, Ruble, & Weinert, 1998).

DEVELOPING SELF-ESTEEM

Self-concept and self-esteem are closely related. Self-concept refers to the mental picture we develop about ourselves. **Self-esteem** refers to the value we attach to the mental pictures of ourselves (Coopersmith, 1967). Children with high self-esteem have positive feelings about themselves—they see themselves as confident, worthy, and effective. Children with low self-esteem have negative feelings about themselves—they feel uncertain, timid, and sad.

As children enter early childhood, they are increasingly capable of making judgments about themselves, but these judgments are global and vary depending on the situation. Young children's self-esteem revolves around feelings of good and bad—feeling "good" when they succeed in a task and feeling "bad" when they fail (Ruble & Dweck,

self-esteem the value an individual attaches to the mental picture of himself or herself

1995). Hector and Barry show clear signs of making evaluative judgments. Hector persists at the challenging computer game, is elated when he succeeds, and is motivated to play the game again. Barry feels bad when he begins to fail, becoming frustrated and helpless. Their evaluations of themselves are based on meeting a single standard, such as completing or failing at a task. As children get older (around age 7 or 8), they move away from this global good-bad evaluation of themselves and begin to make more complex assessments, evaluating themselves in comparison to others or in relation to the difficulty of the task (Pomerantz, Ruble, Frey, & Greulich, 1995). With age, children become more focused on distinguishing unique aspects of themselves (Daniels, 1998; Mintz, 1995).

Recent research suggests that self-esteem can be understood as a combination of two qualities: worthiness (feelings of being valued) and competence (feelings of being effective). Mruk (1995) put these two qualities on a matrix and used the various combinations of high and low worthiness and competence to identify four types of self-esteem. The matrix is presented in Figure 8.1.

For the first two types of self-esteem, high self-esteem and low self-esteem, there is a match between feelings of competence and worthiness. A combination of high competence and high worthiness results in high self-esteem. Children with high self-esteem are better prepared to face challenges because they have acquired feelings about themselves that are associated with success and positive worth. In contrast, children with low self-esteem feel unworthy and have ineffective interactions, producing feelings of unhappiness and anxiety.

In Mruk's two other types of self-esteem, there is a discrepancy between feelings of worthiness and competence. These types of self-esteem demand that children "defend" their sense of self against others' view of them. Defensive self-esteem I combines high worthiness and low competence. Children with this pattern feel valued despite the fact that they lack the accomplishments or abilities to be successful. Thus, worthiness is not deserved. Children who possess this pattern of self-esteem often behave in ways that might be labeled spoiled, stuck-up, or self-centered.

The other discrepant type of self-esteem, defensive self-esteem II, combines high competence and low worthiness. In this case, children may be quite skilled, but their feelings of unworthiness distort their view of themselves. They tend to worry about performance and failure (performance anxiety), and they have difficulty experiencing satisfaction in their achievements. These children feel they must constantly prove their worth (Mruk, 1995).

Young children derive their feelings of competence and worthiness primarily from significant others, especially parents and other caregivers. Statements and expressions that affirm (or disaffirm) a child's accomplishments and value are rooted in how significant others regard the child and his or her particular behaviors and achievements. In a sense, competence is a measure of how effectively the child responds to the world, and worthiness is a measure of how the world responds to the child. In both cases, the values and judgments of children's social environments influence their self-esteem.

INFLUENCES ON YOUNG CHILDREN'S AWARENESS OF SELF

How do children develop positive concepts and feelings about themselves? What factors contribute to

Notice how this young child's smile reveals the pride she feels in her accomplishment. How does this pride contribute to her self-concept and self-esteem?

FIGURE 8.1
Matrix of Self Esteem

HIGH WORTHINESS

Defensive Self-Esteem I (self-centered)

High Self-Esteem

LOW COMPETENCE

HIGH COMPETENCE

Low Self-Esteem

Defensive Self-Esteem II (performance anxiety)

LOW WORTHINESS

SOURCE : Mruk, 1995. Springer Publishing Company, Inc., New York 10012. Used with permission.
According to this model, patterns of self-esteem are made up of combinations of competence and worthiness. Can you explain the different combinations? Can you assign combinations to yourself and people you know?

the differences observed between Barry's and Hector's reactions? According to research, young children's self-concept and self-esteem are influenced by their own characteristics, their family and peer relationships, and the environments in which they live (Frome & Eccles, 1998).

Physical Appearance

Even at a young age, a person's physical appearance predicts self-esteem (Feingold, 1992). Individuals who are more physically attractive have higher levels of self-esteem than those who are less physically attractive, and this relationship is consistent throughout the life span (Harter, 1998). This correlation is just as high in special populations such as the intellectually gifted and the learning disabled (Harter, 1993; Serketich & Dumas, 1997). Thus, from an early age, those who are judged to be attractive by societal standards receive more positive attention than those judged to be less physically attractive. Young children are well aware of societal standards and incorporate them into their sense of self early in life.

The importance of physical appearance is first evident in infancy. Parents react to the physical appearance of their infants and toddlers, responding more positively to children who are more physically attractive (Langlois, 1981). During early childhood, girls and boys are equally satisfied with their appearance. Boys continue to evaluate their appearance positively as they move through the school years, but girls' evaluations begin to decline during elementary school (Harter, 1993). Girls' self-esteem also declines with age, and it becomes particularly low for those girls whose self-esteem hinges on their looks.

Society and the media place great importance on physical appearance at every age and for both sexes (Kilbourne, 1994; Wheeler & Kim, 1997). The standards are particularly narrow and rigid for women—emphasizing unrealistic ideals of thinness and desirable body characteristics (Henderson-King & Henderson-King, 1997). These standards are difficult for women and girls, even young girls, to live up to, and they create a situation in which females are likely to become dissatisfied with their physical appearance. In turn, their self-esteem may suffer.

Relationships with Caregivers and Peers

Children who have warm and secure relationships with their parents and other caregivers generally have positive concepts and feelings about themselves. In contrast, children who are rejected, overprotected, dominated, or neglected develop a negative self-concept and low self-esteem (Sroufe, 1990; Mruk, 1995).

In addition, children with good peer relationships develop a positive self-concept and positive self-esteem. Being accepted by peers affirms a sense of being liked. Having positive peer relations also provides children with support and affection. In contrast, children who are rejected by peers may develop doubts about being able to relate to others, which can lead to low self-esteem, withdrawal, victimization, and aggression (Asendorpf & van Aken, 1994; Egan & Perry, 1998; Hartup, 1996).

Social and Cultural Conditions

How individuals view and feel about themselves is tied to the social and cultural conditions in which they are raised. Young children who are raised in stressful or threatening environments are at greater risk for developing a poor self-concept and low self-esteem. For example, children who live in poverty face a variety of stressors, such as violence, overcrowding, and inadequate nutrition, that more affluent children do not. These stressful conditions undermine individuals' sense of dignity, value, and self-worth. As discussed in Chapter 6, conditions of abuse or neglect also damage children's self-esteem (Stern, Lynch, Oates, O'Toole, & Cooney, 1995).

Is Self-Esteem Lower in African American and Hispanic Children?

Because self-esteem is influenced by what other people think, it is sometimes assumed that minority children have lower levels of self-esteem than Caucasian American children. What is not considered, however, is that many minorities do not compare themselves to the larger society. Their self-esteem may be based less on what the general society thinks of them than on the perceptions of their family and friends and other important people in the minority community. Some of the current research has identified the factors that account for the healthy development of self-esteem in African American and Hispanic children.

African American Children. African American children are likely to live in close proximity to their relatives. These relatives often are an important source of affection, care, and support for African American children. The additional caregiving also serves as a source of comfort and help in times of stress (Scherman, Goodrich, & Kelly, 1988). The increased support and nurturance provided by this extended family network promotes positive self-esteem.

The presence of a father plays an especially important role in the development of self-esteem among African American children—particularly African American boys. An African American child who lives in a home where the father is absent is likely to exhibit low self-esteem (Espinoza & Ehrlich, 1989).

African American children with a poor sense of ethnic identity—recognition and acceptance of membership in an ethnic group—suffer from low self-esteem (Ogbu, 1991). Some people believe that young children are "color blind," but as early as 4 years of age, children are capable of distinguishing different ethnic groups (Aries & Moorehead, 1989). Children whose parents teach them about being African American and instill in them a sense of pride show healthy and positive self-esteem (Bowman & Howard, 1985). These parents help their children cope with the negative stereotypes and harassment they encounter (Walker, Taylor, McElroy, & Phillip, 1995).

Hispanic Children. Like African American families, Hispanic families provide supportive and nurturing environments that often buffer children against the assaults that occur in the broader society (Solis, 1995; Valdez, 1996). Hispanics place a high value on family support (Sabogal, Marín, & Otero-Sabogal, 1987), and this support is provided not only by parents but also by grandparents, uncles, aunts, and cousins. Often, no sharp distinction is made between relatives and friends, with friends being considered family if a close relationship has been formed (Chilman, 1993). The term *compadrazo* is often used to describe this relationship. Children living in these relatively large families have extensive networks of support and nurturance that protect and enhance their self-esteem.

Another important characteristic of Hispanic families that helps their children develop positive relationships and self-esteem is their traditional preference for smooth and pleasant social relationships. The term *simpatía* refers to the high regard the Hispanic culture has for feelings and actions geared to safeguarding the dignity of individuals by showing respect and striving for harmony. This does not mean that Hispanic families and children do not express anger, aggression, or frustration. However, when situations have the potential for conflict, particularly among family members or friends, solutions are sought that avoid confrontation, hurt feelings, and loss of self-respect. *Simpatía* and supportive extended families foster the development of positive self-esteem among Hispanic children (Marín, 1994).

Although minority children generally have positive and healthy self-esteem, they face greater threats to their self-esteem than do Caucasian American children. These threats appear to be due to economic and social conditions rather than minority status *per se.*

Thinking It Through:

1. How does being a member of a minority group influence self-esteem differently than being a member of a majority group?
2. Why is it important to understand the development of self-esteem among minority children? What implications does this understanding have for social policy?
3. How do parents and other family members influence minority children's self-esteem?

People in different cultures are strikingly different in how they see themselves (Raeff, 1997). For example, the North American representation of self is based on an appreciation of how one is different from others and on the importance of asserting oneself.

In contrast, the Japanese representation of self is based on fitting in with others and the importance of being connected with them (Markus & Kitayama, 1991). The factors that contribute to a positive self-concept and high self-esteem for North American children and Japanese children differ in accord with the cultural values and practices to which they are exposed. Japanese culture, for instance, values *suano*—a term used to describe the development of cooperation and the yielding of personal autonomy (White & LeVine, 1986). Unlike North Americans, the Japanese do not view *suano* as a sign of weakness; it is thought to reflect maturity, self-control, and healthy adaptation. For Japanese children, therefore, *suano* forms an important basis for self-concept and self-esteem. In Western cultures, however, independence and autonomy are highly valued. Consequently, the self-concepts and self-esteem of children in North America are determined in part by the degree to which the children reflect these characteristics (Markus & Kitayama, 1991).

Within North American cultures, there are important differences among the values and practices of different subcultures (Frable, 1997). Various religious groups (such as the Quakers) and ethnic groups (such as Native Americans) explicitly value and promote interdependence to a greater extent than does the larger culture. In addition, children who live in small, rural communities are more likely to be exposed to values and practices that emphasize connectedness than are children growing up in larger metropolitan communities (Sampson, 1989).

HOW DO YOUNG CHILDREN DEVELOP A CONCEPT OF GENDER?

During the preschool years, children come to understand which gender group they belong to and that this is a stable part of one's self-concept (Frable, 1997). Learning this fundamental aspect of the self is only the beginning. Children also learn about the roles and expectations associated with their own and the other sex. These beliefs, roles, and expectations are shared cultural constructs, but each child develops her or his own set of individual beliefs about the sexes.

An important part of young children's self-concept is **gender identity**—the understanding and acceptance that one is a boy or a girl. Gender identity is based on the understanding that there are different sexes and that a person's gender group is stable over time and situations (Kohlberg, 1966). For most children, understanding of gender progresses through three stages:

1. By about 30 months of age, children engage in **gender labeling**—they label themselves and others according to their gender group. At this time, children call themselves *boys* and *girls* and use pronouns that correctly match the gender group.
2. By 3 to 4 years of age, children understand **gender stability**—they know that gender is stable over time. A boy who has achieved gender stability knows that he will always be a boy and will grow up to be a man, not a woman.
3. By 4 to 5 years of age, children understand **gender consistency**—they know that gender does not change despite changes in appearance or activities. For instance, a child who has achieved gender consistency understands that a boy who dresses as a girl remains a boy despite his appearance.

Not all children develop gender identity easily. Because of certain genetic disorders, a small number of children are born with ambiguous-looking genitals. Early research found that children with ambiguous-looking genitals have problems developing gender identity if their gender group is assigned late in childhood (Money & Ehrhardt, 1972). However, some of these children have fewer problems if they are assigned to a gender group early in life (by 18–36 months), are raised consistently with their gender group

gender identity understanding and acceptance that one is a boy or a girl

gender labeling labeling oneself and others on the basis of gender group

gender stability understanding that gender is stable over time

gender consistency understanding that gender does not change despite changes in appearance or activities assignment by their parents, and are given surgical or hormonal support for their assigned gender group. Surprisingly, even children who are raised to be one sex but are genetically the other sex can develop a stable gender identity. This is not always the case, however, and research has been undertaken to decide how best to determine gender group assignments (Diamond & Sigmundson, 1997).

Questions regarding the relative contributions of biological and social influences to gender identity development are being raised because of a rare genetic disorder first found in children in the Dominican Republic. In this disorder, boys are born with female-looking genitals and are usually raised as girls. At puberty, the male hormone testosterone is released and these children develop masculine features and attributes. Thus, these children, who were raised as girls, suddenly look like boys. Surprisingly, many of these children adjust to a male gender identity with little difficulty, probably because in their culture being a male is more highly valued than being a female. These cases suggest that a stable gender identity may not be fully developed until adolescence and that raising a child to be one sex does not always offset the biological influence of genes (Imperato-McGinley, Peterson, Gautier, & Sturla, 1979).

Young Children's Gender Stereotypes

Gender stereotypes are the beliefs people share about the typical characteristics of males and females. As early as age 2½, children have learned basic stereotypes about the sexes, including information about appearance and activities. For instance, young children think that girls have long and curly hair and that they cry a lot (Intons-Peterson, 1988). They think that boys are taller and stronger than girls and hit people more (Kuhn, Nash, & Brucken, 1978). Young children even believe that softness is associated with being female and hardness with being male (Leinbach, Hort, & Fagot, 1997). Young children do not, however, think that males and females differ in personality, except in very concrete terms such as being strong or being nice.

Gender stereotypes influence children in many ways. First, children (and adults) use them to make judgments about other people, especially when their information about the other people is limited (Martin, 1989; Martin, Woods, & Little, 1990). These judgments often have to do with familiar activities and roles. For instance, 4-year-old Claudia decides that her new neighbor, Polly, might be fun to play with because she is a girl and therefore will probably like the kinds of things that Claudia likes.

Second, young children's stereotypes influence what they remember. Generally, children remember information that fits their stereotypic beliefs (Stangor & McMillan, 1992). After being shown pictures of girls and boys engaged in many activities, children better remember the pictures of children engaged in stereotypic activities (such as a boy playing with a car) than those of children engaged in counter-stereotypic activities (such as a boy playing with a doll). Young children also remember more about people of the same sex than about people of the other sex (Signorella, Bigler, & Liben, 1998).

Several studies have shown that children experience memory distortions; that is, they misremember information with a bias toward their stereotypes (Martin & Halverson, 1983; Signorella & Liben, 1984). For example, when 5- to 9-year-old children of both sexes saw television commercials of a boy playing with a doll and a girl playing with a truck, over half the children distorted the sex of the actor in one of the commercials and 25 percent distorted the sex of the actor in both commercials (Stangor & Ruble, 1989).

Many caregivers hope that their children will not learn gender stereotypes if they see many examples of people who break from gender stereotypic expectations. The fact that children distort information to fit their gender stereotypes, however, makes it difficult to change stereotypes. Rather than breaking stereotypes, their memories respond in ways that confirm gender stereotypes. It seems unlikely that caregivers can change young children's stereotypes merely by exposing them to examples of people engaging in counter-stereotypic behaviors and activities. Instead, parents and caregivers may need to

gender stereotypes beliefs people share about the typical characteristics of males and females take more active measures, such as teaching children that not all people believe gender stereotypes or act on the basis of them (Bem, 1983).

YOUNG CHILDREN'S GENDER-TYPED PLAY PREFERENCES

By 2 years of age, girls and boys show preferences for different toys (Ruble & Martin, 1998). By the age of 3 or 4, girls play more often than boys with dolls, tea sets, art materials, and domestic toys (ironing boards, kitchen sets). Evidence for these preferences is found in a classic study of letters children write to Santa Claus requesting the toys they want for Christmas. Table 8.1 summarizes the toy requests in 750 such letters to Santa Claus from children primarily under 8 years of age (Richardson & Simpson, 1982). As can be seen in Table 8.1, both boys and girls request sex-typed toys. Notice that girls request boys' toys more often than boys request girls' toys, perhaps reflecting the greater acceptance of cross-gender activities in girls than in boys.

One reason children prefer stereotypic toys and activities is because they have a history of playing with them and are familiar with them. Parents give children toys that are gender-stereotyped and encourage them to play with these toys (Ruble & Martin, 1998). Children also prefer toys and activities that reinforce their own gender identity. For example, when a toy that children have never seen before is described as a toy that is liked by others of their own sex, both girls and boys prefer that toy. If the new toy is described as being liked by members of the other sex, the toy often is avoided (Bradbard, Martin, Endsley, & Halverson, 1986).

TABLE 8.1

Percentages of Boys and Girls Requesting Stereotypic Boys' and Girls' Toys from Santa Claus

TOY	PERCENT OF BOYS REQUESTING	PERCENT OF GIRLS REQUESTING
Boys' Toys		
Cars, trucks	45.5	8.2
Sports equipment	25.1	15.1
Soldiers or other military toys	23.4	0.8
Race cars	23.4	5.1
Action figures (humanoids)	22.8	5.1
Tricycles, bicycles	15.3	9.7
Outer space toys	7.5	0.3
Girls' Toys		
Adult dolls	0.6	27.4
Baby dolls	0.6	23.0
Clothes	11.1	18.9
Doll houses	1.9	16.1
Doll accessories	1.1	12.5
Clothing accessories	2.2	15.3
Stuffed animals	5.0	9.7

SOURCE: Richardson and Simpson, 1982.

Children are particularly likely to avoid toys gender-stereotyped for the other sex if they are discouraged from or punished for playing with them (Langlois & Downs, 1980). This avoidance reaction is so strong that children will stay away from even very attractive toys if they think the toys are intended for the other sex (Martin, Eisenbud, & Rose, 1995). For instance, Joe chose to play with a deflated football rather than a new kitchen set. Ian happily played with a race car until the helmet of the driver fell off, revealing a woman with long blonde hair. Ian immediately dropped the car like a "hot potato." Such findings suggest that children use stereotypic expectations to decide whether or not they like specific toys. These expectations prevent children from learning about the toys and activities used by the other sex (Boston & Levy, 1991).

SIMILARITIES AND DIFFERENCES BETWEEN YOUNG GIRLS AND BOYS

Gender stereotypes are based on beliefs about differences between the sexes in behavior, appearance, and personality. But to what extent do boys and girls really differ? Observable differences between the behaviors of boys and girls generally have not been found before age 2 (Huston, 1983). Thus, if you were brought into a room full of young infants and could not tell by their appearance which were boys and girls, you would not consistently be able to distinguish girls from boys based on their behavior. Interestingly, although there are no noticeable differences between very young boys and girls, parents often say that their young sons and daughters *are* different. Based on these perceptions, parents may interact with their sons and daughters differently, thereby setting the stage for sex differences to emerge.

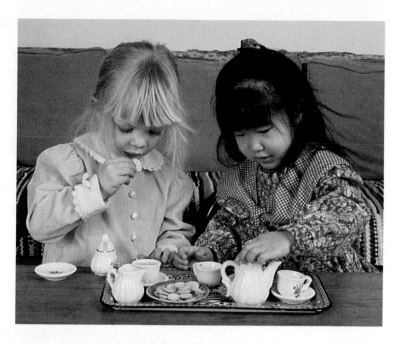

Children often prefer toys and activities that reinforce their own gender identity. What factors contribute to this preference? How might children be encouraged to play with more cross-sex toys?

In a classic review, Maccoby and Jacklin (1974) concluded that there are four sex differences found consistently in children and adolescents. On average, males have better visual-spatial skills (such as map-reading skills), have better mathematical reasoning abilities, and are more physically aggressive, whereas females have better verbal skills. Maccoby and Jacklin (1974) also noted that these differences tend to be small and highly variable within each sex—girls, for example, are as different from one another as they are from boys.

The results of recent research suggest that sex differences occur in more areas than Maccoby and Jacklin originally identified (Ruble & Martin, 1998). For instance, boys tend to be more active than girls (Eaton & Enns, 1986), although the level of activity varies considerably depending on the situation and age. Boys also are more likely to take risks (Ginsburg & Miller, 1982) and engage in rough play, such as wrestling (Braza, Braza, Carreras, & Munoz, 1997; Pellegrini & Smith, 1998). Gender differences in forms of play increase with age, are observed in cultures all around the world (Whiting & Edwards, 1988), and are even found in monkeys, apes, and rats (Meaney, 1988).

Boys throw a ball with considerably more accuracy and velocity than girls, whereas girls have better fine eye-motor skills and flexibility (Thomas & French, 1985). Girls and boys also exhibit different types of nonverbal communication (Hall, 1984). Girls are more likely than boys to smile, and boys are more likely than girls to stare at others.

Gender differences also are found in social behavior and personality. Girls generally are more socially oriented, are more easily influenced, and are seen by teachers as more dependent than boys (Ruble & Martin, 1998). Boys tend to show more aggression and anger, and girls show more fear (Eisenberg, Martin, & Fabes, 1996).

The reasons for these differences are complex. As you will soon learn, many different theories have been proposed to explain why males and females differ. Some of these theories focus on the effects of biological and physiological differences (Kimura, 1993; Levy & Heller, 1992), whereas others focus on environmental and social factors (Bussey & Bandura, 1992) or cognitive processes (Martin, 1991).

WHAT ARE THE CONTEMPORARY THEORIES OF GENDER DEVELOPMENT?

During early childhood, critical changes take place affecting children's gender development. Several contemporary theoretical approaches have been developed in an attempt to explain these changes. Each theory provides insight into why boys and girls behave differently and the ways they use their knowledge of gender. Although the theories differ in the aspects of gender they emphasize, all the theories consider gender to be an important part of development.

BIOLOGICAL THEORIES

Biological theories focus on specific physiological or biochemical processes that affect gender development. The biological influences that have been studied most extensively concern the actions of hormones, and the most commonly studied hormones are androgens, especially testosterone. These hormones often are referred to as "male hormones" because they occur at higher levels in males than in females. When animals are exposed to androgens during prenatal development, they show more male-typical behaviors, such as aggression, and fewer female-typical behaviors, such as nurturance (Collaer & Hines, 1995). Prenatal androgens are thought to masculinize the brain as it develops, making it more sensitive to some types of environmental stimulation and less sensitive to others. As a result, males and females may be predisposed to develop different skills, abilities, and personalities.

Levels of hormones vary in humans, and some children are exposed to higher than normal prenatal levels of androgens, usually because of genetic disorders. An example is girls who have congenital adrenal hyperplasia (CAH). These girls may be born with somewhat masculinized genitals, but they usually are raised as girls and receive treatment and sometimes surgery to offset the masculine hormones. Parents report that their CAH daughters behave as tomboys and the girls prefer to play with boys' toys (Berenbaum & Snyder, 1995). Many researchers believe that the behavior of CAH girls is the result of their exposure to high prenatal levels of androgens.

Biological theories suggest that children's abilities, behaviors, and personality may all be influenced by levels of hormones, especially those that are present during prenatal development. Some people worry that if biological factors influence gender development, then there is no way to change girls' or boys' behavior. However, this is not the case—some biological influences can easily be changed. Furthermore, most researchers believe that even if gender development is influenced by biological factors, environmental factors such as socialization and reinforcement can influence the course of a child's development (Hoyenga & Hoyenga, 1993).

SOCIAL LEARNING THEORIES

The basis of social learning theories is that children learn gender roles through two processes: direct learning and observation. In direct learning, children learn gender roles from the rewards and punishments they receive (Mischel, 1966). Children may be rewarded for exhibiting stereotypic traits and engaging in stereotypic activities and punished for behaving in ways deemed gender inappropriate. Thus, their gender-related behavior is conditioned. For instance, when Jason is teased for playing with a baby doll, he discovers that this behavior is regarded as inappropriate for him and quickly learns to avoid baby dolls in favor of trucks or blocks.

Many research studies have shown that boys and girls receive different rewards and punishments for gender-related behaviors. Parents and peers reward girls and boys for different activities, but in both cases, stereotypic activities are encouraged more than counter-stereotypic ones (Trice & Rush, 1995). Interestingly, boys are more likely than girls to be punished for engaging in cross-sex behaviors and activities, suggesting that boys are held to more rigid standards than are girls (Burnett, Anderson, & Heppner, 1995). Parents treat their sons and daughters differently by presenting gender-stereotypic toys and assigning gender-stereotypic chores (Lytton & Romney, 1991; Ruble & Martin, 1998). Girls are more likely to be assigned kitchen and cleaning chores, and boys are more likely to be assigned yard work. Surprisingly, there is little evidence that parents treat boys and girls differently in other ways, such as encouraging daughters to be dependent or encouraging sons to be aggressive and dominant.

Children also learn gender roles by observing others (Bandura, 1976). When Lucas observes children tease Jason for playing with a doll, he too learns that boys should avoid dolls. By observing the consequences that befell Jason, Lucas learns without directly experiencing the same consequences.

Children do not pay equal attention to, and learn equally from, everyone. A reasonable supposition would be that children observe and imitate the behavior of others of the same sex, which would explain why girls act differently than boys. It is not so simple, though. Children imitate same-sex models if the models are familiar but not if they are unfamiliar. However, they also imitate behaviors if they view many same-sex models, even if they do not know the people (Bussey & Bandura, 1984; Bussey & Perry, 1982). Because children pay attention to people who are prestigious and nurturant—such as sports and movie stars, teachers, and family members—they are likely to imitate these individuals (Lockwood & Kunda, 1997). Sometimes children imitate the behaviors of other-sex people; girls are more likely to do this than boys. Boys will imitate girls only if they are shown to be powerful (Bussey & Bandura, 1984).

COGNITIVE THEORIES

Cognitive theories contribute to our understanding of gender development by considering children to be actively involved in learning gender roles and motivated to adhere to them (Ruble & Martin, 1998). The earliest cognitive theory was proposed by Kohlberg (1966) and is based on the idea that children's understanding of gender emerges as part of their general cognitive development. Kohlberg argued that children's understanding of gender provides the key to the development of gender-stereotypic behavior. As children learn about their gender, they are motivated to behave in ways that are consistent with their gender group. Kohlberg believed that once children develop the idea that gender is a stable attribute, they will show stronger stereotypic behavior, pay more attention to same-sex models, and have better memory for stereotypic information than do children who lack basic gender knowledge (Stangor & Ruble, 1987).

A recent extension of cognitive-developmental theory is gender schema theory. People use **gender schemas,** which are mental representations about the sexes, to guide their behavior and thinking (Bem, 1981; Martin, 1991; Martin & Halverson, 1981). As children interact with their world, their experiences are filtered through gender schemas. Over time, everything comes to be interpreted through these male-female schemas. Children then behave according to their interpretation of what it means to be male or female.

gender schemas mental representations about the sexes

FIGURE 8.2
Model of Schematic Processing

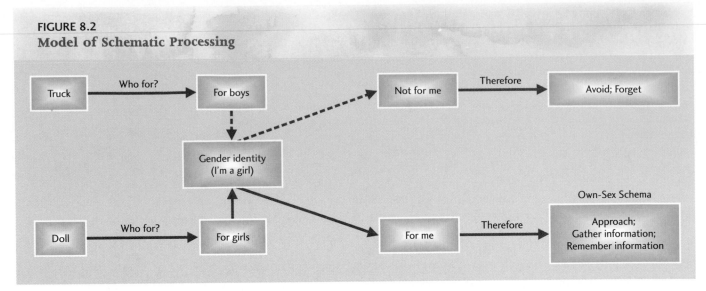

SOURCE: Martin and Halverson, 1981. Reprinted by permission.
This model illustrates how children's schemas influence their memory, attention, and behavior. In this example, a girl decides to play with a doll because she believes it is a toy appropriate for girls. How does this model help in understanding the influence of gender schemas and stereotypes?

Most children have extensive gender schemas, which become more elaborate as they grow older. For instance, as part of her gender schema, 4-year-old Shawntel has information that girls like to make cookies and paint their toenails and boys like to play with trucks and spaceships. With this information, she can form ideas about what is appropriate for her to do.

Gender schemas influence what children pay attention to, what they remember, and how they behave (Martin, 1991). The influence of gender schemas is best summarized by the principle of **schematic consistency,** referring to the tendency of children's behavior and thinking to match their schemas (see Figure 8.2). For instance, children pay more attention to and better remember information if it is relevant to their own gender group (Signorella, Bigler, & Liben, 1998).

HOW DO EMOTIONS DEVELOP DURING EARLY CHILDHOOD?

As you saw in Chapter 6, even newborns express a variety of emotions. During early childhood, children's emotional lives become increasingly differentiated and rich. Young children become better at communicating their emotions, more emotionally responsive to others, and more aware of emotions in themselves and others.

DEALING WITH CONFLICT, ANGER, AND AGGRESSION

As young children become actively involved in social relationships, it is not surprising that they encounter more situations that elicit conflict, anger, frustration, and aggression. During the second year of life, young children begin to confront their parents and siblings with increasing frequency. For example, conflicts between children and their mothers double in frequency between 18 and 24 months of age (Dunn & Munn, 1987).

schematic consistency the tendency of children's behavior and thinking to match their schemas

Children's aggressive acts also increase during the first three years of life, although the patterns vary depending on the type of aggression studied.

Young Children's Angry Conflicts

Most expressions of anger and aggression occur in the context of interactions with others. For young children, conflicts involve struggles over objects and possessions (Fabes & Eisenberg, 1992). As children mature, their conflicts increasingly have social causes, such as being rejected, ignored, or challenged (Ross & Conant, 1992). Angry tantrums and outbursts peak at about 2 years of age and are relatively uncommon after age 4. For 2-year-olds, the most common cause of anger is parents' attempts to establish household routines (such as for eating or sleeping). Among older preschoolers, anger is likely to be caused by difficulties with playmates (Laursen, Hartup, & Koplas, 1996).

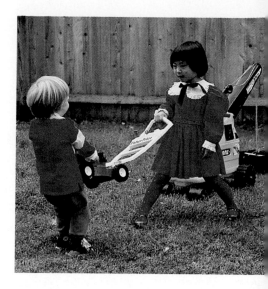

Children's conflicts at this age revolve primarily around possession of objects and space. The frequency of conflicts increases during the preschool years. What factors account for this increase?

Changes in the frequency of conflicts reflect changes in children's cognitive and social competencies. As children grasp social rules and order, they respond to violations of these with anger and frustration. Children's developing sense of autonomy during the second and third years also intensifies their negative reactions to others' attempts to control them. During this time, children begin to understand that rules can be questioned (Dunn & Slomkowski, 1992). In addition, their enhanced understanding of intentions makes it more likely that children will hold others responsible for their actions when there is no indication that the behavior was accidental. Holding others responsible increases the chance that a child will become angry when someone acts in a way that she or he does not like. These factors combine to increase the significance of others' behaviors in relation to young children's goals and desires.

Children respond to conflict in a variety of ways that change over the course of early childhood. When a conflict occurs, young children might become physically aggressive, try to reason out a solution, stand around, cry or throw a tantrum, go for help, or try to assert themselves (such as by taking back a toy that was taken from them). Interestingly, physical aggression in response to conflict is rare among young children; less than 20 percent of conflicts include acts of aggression such as hitting or kicking. As language develops, children increasingly rely on verbal strategies, such as negotiating, to resolve conflicts (Ross & Conant, 1992). In addition, as children gain a better understanding of social relationships, they begin to look for ways to resolve conflicts that do not damage their ongoing interactions—that is, they try to find a cooperative solution (Ashley & Tomasello, 1998).

Young Children's Aggression

Aggression is commonly defined as a behavior intended to harm or injure another (Grusec & Lytton, 1988). Although infants get angry and sometimes strike people and objects, it is difficult to say they are aggressive. Consider the following excerpt from Piaget (1952), describing what happened when he offered a matchbox to his 7-month-old son Laurent, but held his other hand in front of the matchbox so that Laurent could not reach it:

> I present a box of matches above my hand, but behind it, so that he cannot reach it without setting the obstacle aside. But Laurent, after trying to remove or lower it, . . . suddenly tries to hit my hand as though to remove or lower it. . . . Laurent tries to reach the box, and bothered by the obstacle, he at once strikes it, definitely lowering it until the way is clear.
>
> —JEAN PIAGET, 1952 (P. 217)

Laurent's behavior looks very much like aggression, but is it? It is unlikely that Laurent intended to harm his father; rather, it is more likely that he treated his father's hand as an obstruction that needed to be removed. Laurent's goal seems to have been focused more on possessing the interesting object than on inflicting harm or pain.

Near the end of the second year, things begin to change. Maccoby (1980) identified at least five kinds of information a child must master before the child's behavior can be judged as aggressive:

+ that other people experience distress and feel pain
+ that the child's own actions can cause distress
+ which actions cause distress in other people
+ how to carry out distress-producing actions
+ that distress can cause other people to act the way the child wants them to

These types of information are learned during early childhood, some earlier than others. As children master these types of information, their ability to act aggressively increases.

Different kinds of aggression have been identified. Physical aggression, such as hitting, kicking, and pushing, decreases between 2 and 4 years of age, while verbal aggression, such as threatening and name calling, increases (Coie & Dodge, 1998). The aggressive behavior of children 4 to 6 years of age often is aimed at the retrieval of objects or territory (Fabes & Eisenberg, 1992). This type of aggression is referred to as **instrumental aggression**—aggression used for a specific purpose. Kindergarten children (6 to 7 years of age) show less overall aggression, but they are more likely to aggress in ways that are designed to harm another person. This type of aggression is sometimes called **hostile aggression,** referring to the fact that it is directed against another person and is often used in retaliation for another's actions. Because hostile aggression requires that a child understand others' intentions, this type of aggression occurs less often in younger children.

Gender Differences in Aggression

The issue of gender differences in aggression has been of interest for decades (for an early example, see Green, 1933). In several reviews (Hyde, 1984; Knight, Fabes, & Higgins, 1996; Maccoby & Jacklin, 1980), boys were found to be both more physically and more verbally aggressive than girls. These findings are not restricted to studies conducted in the United States. Boys have been found to be more aggressive than girls in Switzerland, Ethiopia, Kenya, India, the Philippines, Mexico, and Japan (Smith & Green, 1974; Whiting & Whiting, 1975). Thus, there is considerable evidence that boys are more aggressive than girls. The cross-cultural consistency of these findings suggests that there may be biological contributions to aggressive behavior.

Is it possible that girls express aggression differently than boys do? Crick and her colleagues (Crick & Grotpeter, 1995) suggest that girls may exhibit unique forms of aggression that have been overlooked in past research. Crick agrees that boys may be more physically and verbally aggressive than girls. She argues, however, that because girls are more likely than boys to focus on establishing close relationships with others, they are more likely than boys to harm others through relational aggression. **Relational aggression** is defined as aggression that is designed to damage someone's relationships with others by withdrawing friendship, excluding someone from a group, and so on. Several studies have found that girls use relational aggression more than boys do (Crick & Grotpeter, 1995; Fabes, Eisenberg, Smith, & Murphy, 1996). These findings suggest that both young boys and young girls are aggressive, but they display distinct forms of aggression.

DEVELOPING CARING FEELINGS AND ACTIONS

A recently divorced father drops off his 3- and 4-year-old daughters, Aimee and Erin, at his former wife's house. Aimee and Erin burst out of the car and run into the waiting arms of their mother. The father clearly is sad, and Erin, the older daughter, notices her father's sad expression, becomes sad herself, and goes to tell her dad that she will miss him. She hugs him and says, "Things will be OK."

instrumental aggression aggression used for a specific purpose

hostile aggression aggression directed against another person, generally in retaliation for his or her actions

relational aggression aggression designed to damage someone's relationships with others, by withdrawing friendship, excluding someone from a group, and so on

Erin feels sorry for her father and attempts to comfort him, an example of prosocial emotions and actions. **Prosocial behavior** refers to voluntary actions intended to benefit another person. Prosocial emotions motivate prosocial behavior (Eisenberg & Fabes, 1998). As you will see, it is during early childhood that prosocial emotions and actions increasingly become a part of the ways children relate to others.

Prosocial Emotions: Empathy and Sympathy

Empathy refers to an emotional state that matches another person's emotional state—for instance, feeling bad because someone else feels bad (Eisenberg & Strayer, 1987). In contrast, **sympathy** involves feeling sorry or concerned for other people because of their emotional states or conditions (Eisenberg & Fabes, 1991). When Erin felt sad at the sight of her father's sadness, she was displaying empathy. When she felt sorry for him, she was displaying sympathy. Sympathy frequently, but not always, results from empathy.

Empathy and sympathy are important to study because they often motivate prosocial behaviors and actions (Roberts & Strayer, 1996). Because of Erin's feelings of empathy and sympathy for her father, she felt compelled to help her father feel better. The link between sympathy or empathy and prosocial behavior has been confirmed by research in the United States (Eisenberg & Miller, 1987; Eisenberg & Fabes, 1998) and in countries as diverse as Germany (Trommsdorff, 1995), Brazil (Carlo, Koller, Eisenberg, Pacheco, & Longuercio, in press), and Japan (Ando, 1987).

Empathy appears fairly early and increases across childhood. Although infants cannot distinguish their own feelings and needs from those of others, they occasionally respond to others' emotions. For example, they often cry when they hear the cry of another infant (Sagi & Hoffman, 1976), although this tendency is not consistent or universal (Zahn-Waxler, Radke-Yarrow, Wagner, & Chapman, 1992).

Early in childhood, children tend to act and think in an egocentric manner. Thus, they are likely to respond to another's distress in ways that they themselves might find comforting. When 3-year-old Thomas saw his mother crying, he became sad and brought her his favorite stuffed animal to cheer her up. In this situation, Thomas projected his own needs onto his mother. Thomas's response is not purely egocentric, however, because his attempt to cheer up his mother is based on empathy for his mother's emotional state.

As children develop the capacity to take the perspective of others, they become increasingly aware that other people's feelings are independent of, and sometimes different from, their own. Four-year-old Erin's response to her father's sadness reflected her understanding of her father's needs, and she responded appropriately. Until later childhood, however, children's empathic and sympathetic responses are limited to the feelings of familiar persons in familiar or directly observed situations. Preschoolers, for example, are most likely to be emotionally responsive to everyday events (such as getting scratched or being made fun of) that cause distress to familiar people or animals (Szagun, 1992). During later childhood, the scope of children's concerns widens to include the conditions of unknown others who are less fortunate than they are (Damon, 1988; Hoffman, 1982).

Helping, Sharing, and Acting Responsibly

Prosocial actions appear early in development. Two-year-olds share toys and food with others, often without prompting. They also begin to help take care of their younger siblings and spontaneously help with some household chores (Garner, Jones, & Palmer, 1994; Rheingold, 1982). For example, 3-year-old Maggie responds to the cries of her younger sister by saying "Sister is crying; let's go to her. Let me hold her. You'd better nurse her, Mommy. Does she have to burp?" Maggie is trying to comfort and care for her younger sister. Maggie's ability to meet the needs of her baby sister is limited, but her responses show genuine concern for her sister's well-being and a desire to help. Across

prosocial behavior voluntary actions intended to benefit another person

empathy an emotional state that matches another person's emotional state—for instance, feeling bad because someone else is feeling bad

sympathy feeling sorry or concerned for other people because of their emotional states or conditions

During the preschool years, children's prosocial emotions and behaviors become more advanced and appropriate. Children become genuinely concerned about the well-being of others. What can be done to foster and promote such feelings and behaviors?

the preschool years, these acts of caring become more common. Preschoolers also act in more responsible ways; they are more likely to comply with parents' requests and are less likely to ignore or defy parental demands (Power, McGrath, Hughes, & Manire, 1994).

Reasons and motives for helpful and responsible behaviors also change during early childhood. When asked why they share or help, young preschoolers often explain their behavior by referring to the other person's needs ("I gave him some crackers because he's hungry") or practical reasons ("I helped clean up because the table was dirty"). Thus, they appear to be motivated by an understanding of another's situation or needs. At other times, children focus on the task at hand or other practical aspects of the situation (Eisenberg, 1992). Older preschoolers occasionally justify prosocial behaviors by referring to their relationship with the person who needs help ("I helped her carry the toys because she's my friend") or their desire for others' approval ("I gave him some of my blocks so he'll like me"). Four- and 5-year-olds also justify prosocial behavior on the basis of selfish reasons ("If I share with him, the teacher will let me play outside"). With maturity, children recognize the social nature of helping relationships. It is not until later childhood that children's reasons for helping become altruistic, reflecting the desire to help others without any apparent personal gain or benefit (Damon, 1988).

Socialization of Prosocial Emotions and Behavior

Caregivers have considerable influence on young children's prosocial responses. Children who have warm and secure relationships with their caregivers are more likely to show prosocial feelings and behaviors (Kestenbaum, Farber, & Sroufe, 1989). In contrast, if the parents express anger and hostility and use physical punishment, the children are less empathic and less prosocial (Denham, Renwick-DeBardi, & Hughes, 1994; Denham, Zoller, & Couchoud, 1994).

When caregivers frequently talk to and reason with children about prosocial activities and the importance of feeling concern for and helping others, the children are more empathic and prosocial. Children also learn about acting prosocially by watching the actions of their caregivers. But parents' talk must be backed by action; parents or caregivers who preach prosocial behavior but do not model it have little effect on children's prosocial development (Bryan & Walbek, 1970). It is important to note that children also can learn to be uncaring by imitating the selfish or uncaring behaviors modeled by adults (Eisenberg, 1992).

HOW DO PARENTING BEHAVIORS INFLUENCE YOUNG CHILDREN'S DEVELOPMENT?

During early childhood, children's attachments change significantly. Preschoolers come to understand that caregivers have feelings and plans that often differ from their own. This understanding enables preschoolers to attempt to change caregivers' plans

Fostering Children's Concern and Caring for Others

Based on the existing research, Schulman and Mekler (1985) have identified a number of ways to help young children develop prosocial emotions and behaviors. Some of their important suggestions follow:

- Draw the child's attention to other people's feelings. Encourage the child to imagine how he or she would feel in someone else's situation.

- Talk about the impact of the child's actions on other people's feelings, including yours.
- Explain why other people feel the way they do.
- Let the child know that you expect her or him to be considerate and responsible and that these qualities are important to you.

- Give approval when the child is considerate and helpful; show disapproval when he or she is not.
- Share your own empathic feelings with the child. Stress the good feelings that come from caring about other people.

and goals. Ainsworth (1972) referred to this new type of attachment relationship as a **goal-corrected partnership.** In this new, emerging relationship, the child becomes a partner in planning how the relationship develops. This change in attachment places greater emphasis on how caregivers respond to children's more active behaviors. Caregivers' behaviors influence children's development in many other ways (Parke & Buriel, 1998). For example, through parents or their substitutes, young children learn the ways and values of their society (Bugental & Goodnow, 1998).

DISCIPLINING YOUNG CHILDREN

When you think of the term *discipline*, punishment may be the first thing that comes to mind. However, punishment is only one type of discipline. In the context of child rearing, **discipline** refers to any attempt by parents to alter children's behaviors or attitudes. The goal of discipline is to help children develop self-control and act in ways that society deems acceptable and appropriate. Before the age of 2, children are rarely disciplined. After children reach the age of 2, however, disciplinary encounters dominate parent-child interactions, and parents increasingly expect children to be able to obey their rules. According to one estimate (Minton, Kagan, & Levine, 1971), almost half of all parent-child interactions after the age of 2 center around discipline, and disciplinary encounters between parent and child occur an average of 9 times per hour.

Children may behave appropriately for different reasons. **Compliance** occurs when children obey and act appropriately because they know that they are being watched or that they will be rewarded or punished for their actions. **Internalization** occurs when children's obedience is based on internal controls and standards that they have incorporated into their own expectations of themselves. That is, they act appropriately because they want to (internalization), not because they have to (compliance).

How discipline is used influences whether or not children internalize standards. Discipline is more effective if it is *consistent* (Deal, Halverson, & Wampler, 1989), is not

goal-corrected partnership an attachment relationship in which the child becomes a partner in planning how the relationship develops

discipline attempts by parents to alter children's behaviors or attitudes

compliance obedience brought about by external pressures (such as the knowledge that one will be rewarded or punished for actions)

internalization obedience based on internal controls and standards that children have incorporated into their own expectations of themselves threatening to the child's well-being (Weiss & Dodge, 1992), and occurs as soon as possible after the child's misbehavior (Grusec, 1988). Supportive discipline does not create anxiety, helps children see the consequences of their actions, and aids internalization and adaptation (Pettit, Bates, & Dodge, 1997).

Although there are many ways to discipline children, the most common methods fall into three general categories:

✦ **Power assertion** encompasses attempts by parents to use physical force or threats of physical force to control children's behavior. It includes physical punishment, taking away of privileges or possessions, and threatening such acts. About 90 percent of parents report using some type of power assertion technique at some time over the course of their children's lives (Simons, Johnson, & Conger, 1994). Boys are spanked more often than girls, mothers do more spanking than fathers, children under the age of 7 are spanked more often than older children, and African American mothers (but not fathers) spank more often than Caucasian American mothers (Day & Peterson, in press). Excessive use of power assertive discipline—particularly harsh or frequent use—puts children at risk for a variety of psychological and behavioral problems, including aggression, delinquency, and peer rejection (Peterson & Haan, 1999; Straus & Donnelly, 1994).

Reinforcing good behavior also is a type of power assertive discipline because it is based on a difference in power between parents and their children. Just like the overuse of punishment, the overuse of rewards can have detrimental effects on children. In one study, children whose parents relied on rewards to get them to act appropriately were less helpful and generous when rewards were no longer offered (Fabes, Fultz, Eisenberg, Plumlee, & Christopher, 1989). Children may see rewards as "bribes" and comply only to get the rewards rather than because of their internal motivation (Kohn, 1993).

✦ **Love withdrawal** refers to attempts by a parent to gain obedience by ignoring or isolating the child, withholding affection, or expressing lack of love for the child. Love withdrawal can be effective in the short term because of the threat of losing the caregiver's love. In the long term, however, the constant anxiety about being rejected or abandoned has negative consequences for children's internalization (Grusec & Goodnow, 1994).

✦ **Inductive reasoning** is a disciplinary technique in which parents use reasoning and verbal communication for the purpose of changing children's behavior (McGrath, Wilson, & Franssetto, 1995). Parents' use of inductive reasoning may include the following: explanations of rules and standards expected of children ("You need to stay close to me because you might get lost"), moral persuasion ("It's nice to help others"), personal appeals ("It will make Mommy happy if you help your brother"), explanations of the hurtful consequences of children's actions for others ("It hurt your sister's feelings when you wouldn't let her play with you"), and character attributions ("A kind boy like you helps his friend"). During early childhood, as children develop the cognitive ability to understand their parents' reasoning, parents begin to favor the use of inductive reasoning (Kuczynski, Kochanska, Radke-Yarrow, & Girnius-Brown, 1987). Children whose parents use inductive reasoning tend to be more prosocial and popular and have more internalized values and acceptable behavior (Hart, DeWolf, Wozniak, & Burts, 1992).

INFLUENCES ON PARENTS' USE OF DISCIPLINE

The reasons a parent chooses one disciplinary technique over another are not entirely clear. Parents have different beliefs and values about how to discipline children and

power assertion disciplinary techniques in which parents use physical force or threats of physical force to control children's behavior

love withdrawal disciplinary techniques in which parents ignore, withhold affection from, or express lack of love for the child

inductive reasoning disciplinary techniques in which parents use reasoning and verbal communication for the purpose of changing children's behavior what is or is not effective. Consider the following comments on an anonymous online message board where parents talk to one another about parenting issues:

"I spanked my daughter once in her whole life and you know what? She hit me right back, proving that violence creates more violence."

—MOTHER OF A 5-YEAR-OLD DAUGHTER

"I can't say that I've never spanked my sons, but I think spanking just gets them to mind you because you are bigger and more powerful or, worse yet, you have a weapon. That's the only lesson they learn."

—MOTHER OF 3-AND 7-YEAR-OLD SONS

"Kids need to know that if they hurt someone else or put themselves in extreme danger, the consequence is immediate and powerful. And if you've ever seen your child reaching for an electrical outlet, you know that you want to make sure it never happens again. A spanking is just the thing."

—MOTHER OF A 3-YEAR-OLD SON

The first mother reports that spanking her daughter produced a similar response in the daughter, leading her to believe that children whose parents spank them become aggressive themselves. The second mother points out that although children may comply with you because of the punishment, it does not promote internalization of good behavior. The third mother believes that spanking is a way for children to learn that their misbehaviors have powerful consequences. Clearly, these parents differ in their attitudes about disciplinary practices. What factors determine parents' preferences for certain types of discipline?

Caregivers vary considerably in their attitudes toward and choices about discipline. Even within a family, mothers and fathers may have very different approaches to discipline. Can you identify some of the factors that contribute to such differences?

Nature of the Misbehavior

The discipline parents use varies depending on the nature of the child's misbehavior. For example, parents might use a combination of power assertion and inductive reasoning in response to lying and stealing, whereas they might use inductive reasoning alone when children fail to show concern for others (Grusec, Dix, & Mills, 1982; Trickett & Kuczynski, 1986).

Characteristics of the Child

Parents use different disciplinary techniques with different children. They are more likely to use power assertion with their sons than with their daughters because they often expect their sons to be harder to control (Leve & Fagot, 1997). Similarly, parents are more likely to use power assertion with children who are difficult to manage than with children who are easy to manage (Greenwald, Bank, Reid, & Knutson, 1997). Parents are more likely to reason with older children, who can recognize and respond to parents' intentions. Moreover, as children mature, they are less tolerant of parental demands in areas they regard as outside the legitimate control of parents, such as the types of clothes they wear and the appearance of their rooms. Thus, parental discipline changes in response to children's increasing autonomy and cognitive development (Smetana, 1988).

A similar trend is found in other cultures. For example, in mainland China, early childhood is divided into two periods: *budongshi*, the age of innocence (the first 6 years), when children lack cognitive understanding, and *dongshi*, the age of understanding (after age 6). Chinese parents rely on power assertive techniques during *budongshi* but use them less often once children reach *dongshi* (Stevenson, Chen, & Lee, 1992).

Cultural, Ethnic, and Social Values

Disciplinary methods vary across cultures and among ethnic groups, in part because of different parenting goals and values. For example, many Hispanics and Asian Americans believe that children should be obedient, so they use power assertive discipline more than other groups of parents (Carter & Middlemiss, 1992). In contrast, Japanese moth-

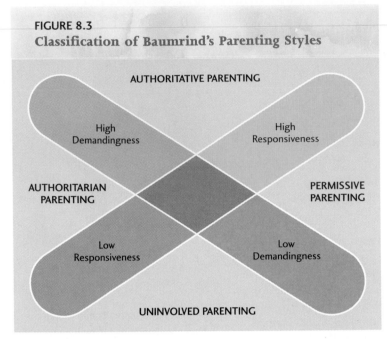

FIGURE 8.3
Classification of Baumrind's Parenting Styles

Baumrind's parenting styles were based on differences in demandingness and responsiveness. Can you describe the qualities of parents within each classification and the impact the different styles have on children?

ers tend to indulge their children, with the intention of promoting a strong sense of dependency on the family—an outcome that is valued more in Japanese than in American culture (Azuma, 1986).

Among Aka pygmies, a hunter-gatherer tribe in the tropical rain forests of central Africa, parents seldom use power assertion. They are accepting of and responsive to their children but do not firmly or consistently enforce standards for behavior. Because of the demands of their environment, Aka children must be able to care for themselves at an early age. Aka parents value the development of autonomy more than obedience and respect for elders, and their disciplinary practices reflect these values (Hewlett, 1992).

Contextual and social factors also influence parents' choice of discipline. One factor that is associated with power assertive parenting is socioeconomic status. In general, poor parents, regardless of their ethnic background, are likely to stress obedience and to use power assertion (Fox & Solis-Camera, 1997; Kelley, Sanchez-Hucles, & Walker, 1993). Parents' ability to rear competent children may be undermined by the stress and strain of the undesirable conditions associated with poverty (McLoyd, 1998).

PARENTING STYLES

Although parents' disciplinary methods vary, there are consistencies in their use of discipline. One of the most prominent studies of parents' styles of discipline was carried out by Diana Baumrind. In a long-term study of how parents influence children's development, Baumrind identified two important parenting characteristics (Baumrind, 1967, 1971, 1989). One is **demandingness**—the tendency to exert firm control over children, requiring them to act in mature and appropriate ways. The other is **responsiveness**—the tendency to be warm, accepting, and willing to take into account the wishes and feelings of the child. On the basis of these two characteristics, Baumrind identified four main parenting styles (see Figure 8.3).

Authoritarian Parenting

Authoritarian parenting is characterized by efforts by parents to shape, control, and judge the behaviors and attitudes of their children according to rigid standards of conduct. These parents usually value obedience and favor harsh, forceful measures, including physical punishment, to ensure that children comply with their rules. These parents discourage verbal give-and-take, believing that children should accept their word for what is right. Thus, authoritarian parents are high in demandingness and low in responsiveness. They set the rules, and children are to obey these rules because the parents say so. Preschoolers from authoritarian homes have low levels of self-control and independence, and they tend to be aggressive, anxious, and resistant to correction (Baumrind, 1971; Kochanska & Askan, 1995).

Permissive Parenting

Parents who practice **permissive parenting** make few demands on their children—they are accepting and tolerant of their children's impulses and desires. These parents

demandingness the tendency of parents to exert firm control over children, requiring them to act in mature and appropriate ways

responsiveness the tendency of parents to be warm, accepting, and willing to take into account the wishes and feelings of the child

authoritarian parenting a style of parenting in which parents try to shape, control, and judge the behaviors and attitudes of their children according to rigid standards of conduct

permissive parenting a style of parenting in which parents make few demands on their children—they are accepting and tolerant of their children's impulses and desires

How Does Poverty Affect Parenting?

In his moving and unforgettable book *Rachel and Her Children*, Jonathan Kozol (1988) describes family life among the very poor. In one instance, he discusses the case of Wanda and her family. Wanda is the mother of four young children. The five of them live in a 9-foot by 12-foot room. There is no cooking area or refrigerator, and Wanda has no food stamps or restaurant allowance because of a mix-up at the welfare agency. She and her children are dressed in tattered and worn sweaters and have only one mattress with no sheet for the four of them. Wanda's children are described as "wilted leaves" who sit on the floor and do not talk, play, or even move. When asked whether they are sick, Wanda tells Kozol that they have not had anything to eat. Wanda herself suffers from hypoglycemia (low blood sugar) and without treatment is often tired and depressed.

Wanda's situation is not unusual for families that face severe economic hardships. Poverty diminishes parents' psychological well-being and their capacity for supportive parenting (McLoyd, 1998). You can see this in the case of Wanda. Adults like Wanda who are poor are more likely to experience physical and mental health problems than are their economically advantaged counterparts. In addition, parents who are poor face a variety of negative life conditions—the threat of eviction, criminal assault, poor nutrition, inadequate housing, and so on—that increase their frustration and stress (Hashima & Amato, 1994). Poverty also is associated with single-parenting, and those who have to care for children alone face additional stress (Huston, 1991). What are the implications of these conditions for parenting behaviors and the children subject to them?

As a family's economic situation worsens, the parent or parents exhibit less nurturance and more negative discipline toward the children (Elder, Conger, Foster, & Ardelt, 1992; Flanagan, 1990). Poor parents are more likely to issue commands without explanation, less likely to consult children about their wishes, and less likely to reward children for behaving in desirable ways (Conger et al., 1994; McLoyd & Wilson, 1991). This is especially true if poor parents do not have a network of social support—friends or relatives they can rely on (Hashima & Amato, 1994). Not surprisingly, these parenting practices can have negative consequences for the well-being of their children.

Importantly, however, not all parents who are poor are depressed or disengaged parents. Many poor parents effectively buffer their children from the potentially detrimental effects of poverty (McLoyd, 1998). When poor parents have the psychological strength to manage the demands of being a parent, they can and do provide their children with supportive and responsive parenting behaviors. It is important to remember that stress in any family, regardless of how much money the family might have, can undermine the quality of parenting. Unfortunately, it is the nature of poverty to cause increased stress in parents and thus potentially influence their parenting negatively.

Thinking It Through:

1. How could Wanda be helped to be a better parent?
2. How does poverty undermine a parent's ability to parent? What social policy changes could minimize these effects?
3. What effects might harsh economic conditions have on parents and parenting behaviors? How could you test these effects?

view themselves as resources to be used as their children wish rather than as agents responsible for shaping or altering their children's behavior. Permissive parents avoid the use of force to accomplish their goals and thus are low in demandingness and high in responsiveness. Because permissive parents fail to set limits on their children's behavior, preschoolers raised by permissive parents resemble those from authoritarian homes. They tend to be relatively immature, demanding, rebellious, impulsive, aggressive, and less socially competent (Baumrind, 1971).

Uninvolved Parenting.

Uninvolved parenting describes the style of parents who make few demands on their children but are unresponsive or rejecting as well. Uninvolved parents do whatever they can to minimize the costs of being a parent and put little time and effort into interactions with their children (Maccoby & Martin, 1983). Parents' efforts relate more to their own immediate comfort and convenience than to the long-term development of the child. For example, these parents are unlikely to establish and enforce rules about bedtime or children's diets. At the extreme, uninvolved parents may be neglectful. Parental depression is sometimes related to uninvolved parenting; depressed parents tend to be withdrawn, disengaged, and unresponsive to their children (Lee & Gotlib, 1995). As you might expect, children from homes where the parents are uninvolved, neglectful, or depressed do not fare very well. These children tend to be noncompliant, aggressive, withdrawn, and insecure in their attachments to others (Egeland & Sroufe, 1983; Miller, Cowan, Cowan, Hetherington, & Clingempeel, 1993).

Authoritative Parenting

Authoritative parenting is exhibited by parents who encourage verbal give-and-take and share with their children the reasons behind discipline and household rules. These parents value conformity to their rules and exert consistent and firm—but not excessive—control to bring it about. Authoritative parents are loving and supportive, and they recognize the importance of children's individual interests and needs. Authoritative parents can be classified as high in demandingness and high in responsiveness. Preschool children raised in authoritative homes tend to be friendly, cooperative, socially competent, confident, and self-reliant (Dekovic & Janssens, 1992; Hinshaw et al., 1997).

Thus, authoritative parenting produces the best outcomes for children. But why is that the case? Baumrind (1989) argues that the optimal parent-child relationship at any stage of development is characterized by reciprocity—the tendency to engage in mutual give-and-take. Authoritative parenting is associated with a pattern of family functioning in which children are required to be responsive to parental demands and parents accept a reciprocal responsibility to be as responsive as possible to the reasonable demands of their children. Authoritative parents maintain a balance between structure and control on the one hand and warmth and respect on the other, and they encourage the same balance in their children. In Western cultures, this balance represents competent parenting, and parents who cannot provide the necessary control and guidance have children who are difficult to manage (Belsky, Woodworth, & Crnic, 1996).

Because different cultures hold different values, it is not surprising that the degree to which parents are authoritative or authoritarian differs across cultures and subcultures. Authoritative parenting is more prevalent in two-parent nondivorced families than in single-parent families or stepfamilies (Hetherington & Clingempeel, 1992). Authoritarian parenting is more common among families experiencing financial difficulties and among ethnic minorities (Steinberg, Mounts, Lamborn, & Dornbusch, 1991). Moreover, parents who adhere to conservative religious beliefs tend to adhere to an authoritarian parenting style more often than do parents who are less conservative in their religious beliefs (Day & Peterson, in press). These findings indicate that parenting styles and their impact on children are influenced by family circumstances and cultural beliefs and attitudes.

uninvolved parenting a style of parenting in which parents make few demands on their children and are unresponsive or rejecting

authoritative parenting a style of parenting in which parents encourage verbal give-and-take and share with their children the reasons behind discipline and household rules

HOW DOES DIVORCE AFFECT YOUNG CHILDREN'S DEVELOPMENT?

Divorce is more commonplace today than at any time in the past. Although marriage is still viewed as a lifelong commitment, many people believe that couples who are unhappy should not be forced to stay together, not even for the sake of the children.

When a sample of young mothers was interviewed in 1962, half of them said that couples with children should stay together, even if they did not get along. By 1989, fewer than 1 in 5 women gave that answer when asked the same question (Arland, 1989).

Divorce rates in the United States generally have increased since the 1960s. Approximately 1,191,000 divorces were granted in 1994 (Centers for Disease Control, 1995b). This trend is not unique to the United States. Table 8.2 presents divorce rates in selected countries for 1960, 1970, and 1988. As you can see, the divorce rates increased over time in all countries listed, in some cases more than tripling.

In the United States in 1991, just over half of divorcing couples had children who were under 18 years of age at the time of their divorce; one quarter of divorcing couples had two children (Centers for Disease Control, 1995a). By some estimates (Hutchinson & Spangler-Hirsch, 1989), nearly half of all children will experience the divorce of their parents and will live some of their life in a single-parent household, in most cases with their mother. Divorce has both short- and long-term consequences for an individual's development and adjustment. For example, a 70-year longitudinal study showed that children from divorced families grew up to have a higher risk of premature mortality (Tucker et al., 1997).

TABLE 8.2

Divorce Rates in Selected Countries (divorces per 1000 married women)

COUNTRY	YEAR		
	1960	1970	1988
United States	9.2	14.9	20.7
Belgium	2.0	2.6	8.4
Canada	1.8	6.3	12.9
Denmark	5.9	7.6	13.1
Japan	3.6	2.9	5.4
Netherlands	2.2	3.3	8.1
Sweden	5.0	6.8	11.7
United Kingdom	2.0	4.7	12.3

SOURCE: National Center for Health Statistics, 1990.

YOUNG CHILDREN'S UNDERSTANDING OF DIVORCE

As the following examples show, young children have strong reactions to divorce and parental separation that reflect their difficulty in understanding the situation.

"I think my Dad will come home soon and that my Mom and him will never, ever divorce again."

—FOUR-YEAR-OLD GIRL

"I live with only my Mommy and sister now. Daddy isn't in my family anymore."

—FOUR-YEAR-OLD BOY

"I wake up scared a lot. If my Dad would come back I'd feel better. I promised him never to leave my room a mess again if he comes home."

—THREE-YEAR-OLD GIRL

From these examples, you can see that divorce and separation are difficult concepts for children to grasp. Divorce is an abstract concept, and children's understanding of divorce is influenced by their ability to understand abstract ideas (Hetherington & Clingempeel, 1992).

The first example illustrates preschoolers' difficulty in distinguishing between inner motives and outward appearances. They see divorce as one parent moving away—they do not understand the complex motivations underlying the behaviors of both parents (Johnston, Breunig, Garrity, & Baris, 1997). Preschoolers view parents as possessions that belong to them and have only vague notions as to how parents relate to each other. They do not understand why their parents have to live apart, and they do not comprehend that divorce is usually permanent. School-age children, however, are more likely to understand the motives of their parents and that divorce is a permanent state in which parents grow apart from each other (Kurdek, 1988).

The second example illustrates the fact that young children's conception of family is concrete and is limited to those people who live together (Wedemeyer, Bickhard, & Cooper, 1989). The idea of blood relations is often too abstract for them to understand.

When Dad leaves home because of a divorce or separation, it is not uncommon for young children to consider him no longer a family member. This reasoning reflects their tendency to focus on the observable qualities of a situation rather than the underlying and unseen qualities. Older children come to define families and family transitions such as divorce in psychological rather than physical terms (Mazur, 1993).

The third example shows that divorce can be emotionally upsetting and frightening to young children. Because young children are more dependent on the people they live with than are older children, the possibility of abandonment poses a more serious threat to them. As the comments of the third child reveal, the egocentric nature of young children's thinking leads them to see themselves as at least partly to blame for their parents' separation. Children who feel this way may try to undo the situation by making amends. Similarly, when a parent stops visiting, the young child may think that it is because of something he or she did and feel unloved or rejected. Older children are more likely to recognize that the reasons for the divorce have little to do with them and that the divorce reflects the incompatibility of their parents (Kurdek, 1988).

EFFECTS OF DIVORCE ON YOUNG CHILDREN'S BEHAVIOR AND ADJUSTMENT

Divorce can generate painful emotions, uncertainty, and confusion (Guidubaldi, 1988; Maccoby & Mnookin, 1992). Divorce forces mothers, fathers, and children to adapt to changes that can affect nearly every aspect of their lives. Two households must be established where there was only one before. Family finances and schedules are radically altered. Family loyalties are divided. Parental roles and responsibilities change dramatically. How do these changes affect young children's behavior and development? What factors influence young children's adjustment to these changes?

Nearly all children react with shock and are extremely upset when they learn of their parents' breakup. Even when parents are openly fighting, young children often do not grasp the significance of these behaviors and cannot envision a separation. Most parents do not inform their young children of an impending separation until shortly before it occurs (Furstenberg & Cherlin, 1991).

In a series of longitudinal studies, Wallerstein and Kelly (1975, 1976, 1980) found that children respond to divorce differently, according to age. Young preschoolers (2½ to 3½ years) are likely to show increased aggression; middle preschoolers (3½ to 4½ years) are likely to show increased irritability, aggression, self-blame, and confusion; and older preschoolers (5 to 6 years) are likely to show increased anxiety and aggressive behavior. Many of these negative behaviors ended within a year or two for children who experienced stable caregiving environments. However, 44 percent of the preschoolers continued to show emotional distress and poor psychological adjustment a year or two following the divorce.

Because of findings such as these, some researchers have labeled the first two years following a divorce as a "crisis period" for children and adults (Chase-Linsdale & Hetherington, 1990). Young children have special needs during this crisis period. First, they need additional emotional support as they try to adapt to the new and frightening challenges brought about by their parents' divorce. Second, they need the predictable daily structure they had previously in their pre-divorce home life. Many single parents, however hard they may try, cannot meet these needs. Parents often lack the emotional energy to comfort children as they try to sort out their own anger, depression, and anxiety. The increased demands of single-parenthood often cause schedules to change from day to day. As a result, young children lose some of the support and structure they need, which may increase their aggression, fear, and uncertainty. In young children, the increased stress and confusion can result in regressed behavior, such as bed-wetting or sleep problems, that did not exist before the divorce (Benedek & Brown, 1995).

The adverse consequences of divorce appear to be greater for young boys than for young girls (Chase-Linsdale & Hetherington, 1990). It is possible that boys fare worse because they typically live with their mother, and there is some evidence that children adjust better after a divorce if they reside with the same-sex parent (Emery, 1988). Girls may be no less affected by divorce, though. Their responses (depression and withdrawal) may simply be less noticeable than boys' responses (aggression and hostility), and problems stemming from divorce may not appear until years after the breakup (Furstenberg & Cherlin, 1991).

FACTORS THAT AFFECT YOUNG CHILDREN'S ADJUSTMENT TO DIVORCE

Several factors influence how well children adapt to a divorce. Some of the important research findings can be summarized in terms of several main factors (Hetherington, Bridges, & Insabella, 1998):

✦ **Amount of conflict between the parents.** Children who are exposed to overt parental conflict (both before and after a divorce) have more adjustment problems (Cummings & Davies, 1996; Davis, Hops, Alpert, & Sheeber, 1998). When parents have hostile battles in front of young children, children's stress and anxiety increase. In fact, there is some indication that moving from a household with two parents who always are fighting in front of the children to a stable one-parent household can lead to better adjustment for children (Peterson & Zill, 1986). When divorced parents maintain civil and cordial relationships, children's adaptation to divorce is enhanced (Walsh & Stolberg, 1989).

✦ **Effectiveness of the parents.** A critical factor in children's short- and long-term adjustment to divorce is how effectively the ex-spouses (particularly the custodial parent) function as parents. Divorced parents experience more stress because of the increased demands and more limited resources they face, and as a result, the relationships between parents and their children can deteriorate. In divorced families, parent-child relationships generally are more negative (especially between mothers and their sons) and parenting is less authoritative than in nondivorced families (Parke & Buriel, 1998). Mothers tend to become more authoritarian after a divorce, whereas fathers become more permissive. The better able parents are to cope with the disruptions brought about by a divorce, the less likely they are to dramatically alter their parenting styles and the more capable they are of providing their children with the structure, consistent discipline, and love they need (Katz & Gottman, 1997).

✦ **Characteristics of the child.** Some children react more negatively to divorce than others. As discussed earlier, age and sex are important determinants of children's responses. Recall from our discussions in Chapter 6 that children's reactivity to and resiliency in stressful environments vary. Children who are sensitive to changes in their environment and do not readily adapt may be more affected by divorce than are children whose temperaments are more adaptive to change. Similarly, children who are moody and irritable may react to divorce more negatively than children who are less emotionally sensitive and less easily upset (Monahan, Buchanan, Maccoby, & Dornbusch, 1993). Children's perception of the quality of the relationship between their parents also influences their response to marital conflict and divorce (Fincham, 1998).

✦ **Relationship of the child with the noncustodial parent.** Young children's adjustment to divorce is enhanced when both parents are able to maintain relationships with them. In many cases, the father, who often is the noncustodial parent, may break off the relationship with his children, or the mother may actively try to undermine this relationship. Loss of the father's relationship generally has a greater impact on boys than on girls. Also, the younger the child is when separated from a parent, the more affected the child is by the loss (Stanley, Weikel, & Wilson, 1986). When a noncustodial parent is able to maintain an active and supportive parenting relationship, children are better off. Part of the reason for this is that noncustodial parents who maintain regular contact with their children also are likely to keep paying child support (Peters, Argys, Maccoby, & Mnookin, 1993). Additionally, the more often a father sees his children, the better he feels about the visits and the less likely problems are to occur (Arditti & Keith, 1993). Despite visitation and custody arrangements, contact with noncustodial parents drops off sharply over time. According to some estimates, by the end of the second year after a divorce, only one child in six sees his or her father as often as once a week, and close to half have not seen their father at all over the course of the preceding year (Furstenberg & Cherlin, 1991).

CHILD CUSTODY ARRANGEMENTS

Until recently, the dominant legal standard for awarding custody of children, particularly young children, favored mothers. This practice was based on the "tender years" doctrine, which assumed that child rearing during the early years should be undertaken by women (Maccoby & Mnookin, 1992). Today, however, the "best interests of the child" standard has replaced the tender years doctrine in most states (Clingempeel, Shuwall, & Heiss, 1988). This doctrine is based on the notion that the custody arrangement should be the one that best suits the child. The increased recognition that fathers' involvement with their children is beneficial to them is a reason many states have adopted joint-custody statutes.

Several different types of custody arrangements are available (see Table 8.3). These arrangements vary in the degree to which both parents are involved in physical care of and decision making for the children. As you can see from the charts in Figure 8.4, the majority of children are placed in sole custody of the mother (National Center for Health Statistics, 1995). Joint custody is awarded in a small number of cases; the percentage of arrangements in which sole custody is given to the father is even smaller. These charts also show that African American children are more likely than Caucasian American children to be placed in sole custody of their mother.

TABLE 8.3
Types of Custody Arrangements

TYPES OF CUSTODY	DESCRIPTION
Sole legal custody	Custodial parent is assigned all legal rights, duties, and powers and is responsible for all decisions regarding child's welfare. Noncustodial parent has limited rights and powers.
Sole physical custody	Custodial parent has primary physical custody of child. Noncustodial parent is usually awarded visitation rights.
Joint legal custody	Both parents retain rights to make decisions regarding child's health and welfare.
Joint physical custody	Both parents retain rights to share in day-to-day physical care of child. Child spends substantial amount of time with each parent.
Divided custody	Each parent has child for a portion of the year or in alternating years. Each parent has legal rights and makes decisions when child is with that parent.
Split custody	Each parent has sole legal and physical custody of one or more children. Noncustodial parent has visitation rights.

SOURCE: Kelly, 1994.

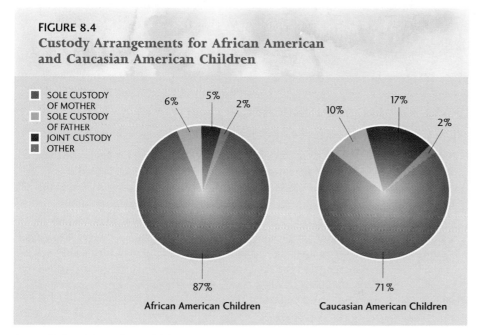

FIGURE 8.4

Custody Arrangements for African American and Caucasian American Children

- SOLE CUSTODY OF MOTHER
- SOLE CUSTODY OF FATHER
- JOINT CUSTODY
- OTHER

6% 5% 2%

87%

African American Children

10% 17% 2%

71%

Caucasian American Children

Source: National Center for Health Statistics, 1995.

Compare the figures for African American and Caucasian American children. Notice that joint custody and father custody are more common among Caucasian American children than among African American children. What factors contribute to these differences?

YOUNG CHILDREN'S ADJUSTMENT TO REMARRIAGE

When parents remarry, children must share them with a widening circle of other people—stepparents and stepsiblings. After a divorce, between 70 and 80 percent of parents do remarry. As many as 35 percent of children, 54 percent of women, and 60 percent of men live in stepfamilies (US Census Bureau, 1993).

The changes brought about by remarriage are dramatic. Newly remarried parents report experiencing twice the stress of nondivorced parents. The changing dynamics of family life after remarriage lead to changes in parenting behaviors. For example, mothers report that they are less emotionally responsive to their children and more punitive in their discipline than they were before remarrying (Hetherington, Hagan, & Anderson, 1989).

In contrast to the findings on divorce, girls have more problems than boys in making the transition to the new family. Young girls, who are likely to have enjoyed a good relationship with their single mother, may become angry and resentful of the new husband. Competition for the mother's time and attention increases the daughter's rivalry with the stepfather, regardless of how supportive the new father is (Hetherington et al., 1989).

Young children seem to adapt more readily to their parents' remarriages than do older children and adolescents (Hetherington, Arnett, & Hollier, 1988). Because young children define a family as the people who live together under the same roof, they are more accepting of new parents, brothers, and sisters than older children are. Also, because young children are more dependent on adults than older children and adolescents are, issues related to independence and resistance to authority are less likely to erupt.

At the same time, young children lack the abilities and resources of older children to adapt to the many transitions and stressors brought about by divorce and remarriage. If the parent's response to remarriage is to invest heavily in the new marriage at the expense of the child, a young child's ability to cope may be overtaxed. Thus, the quality of young children's relationships with their parents and stepparents may be crucial to their adjustment to remarriage and stepfamily life.

Does Custody Make a Difference?

Proponents of joint custody argue that it gives both parents legal rights with regard to their children and reduces the chances that one parent will abduct the children. Each year, over 280,000 children are abducted by the noncustodial parent (Vanished Children's Alliance, 1995). Joint custody also eliminates the "winner takes all" mentality of sole custody. In contrast, opponents of joint custody argue that it disrupts the continuity of care that children receive, increases children's sense of loss of control, and increases interparent conflict.

The few studies that have been conducted show modest benefits at best for children who are in joint custody arrangements. For example, joint legal custody does not necessarily increase the father's decision-making authority or involvement in child rearing (Furstenberg & Cherlin, 1991), although fathers with joint custody generally are more satisfied with their arrangement than noncustodial fathers (Arditti, 1992). Similarly, joint physical custody has not necessarily been found to be better for children's overall adjustment (Maccoby, Depner, & Mnookin, 1990). Former spouses often have difficulty co-parenting and end up avoiding each other. In addition, conflict among joint custody couples is as high as it is among sole custody couples (Maccoby & Mnookin, 1992). What seems to matter for children's well-being is not the custody arrangement, but how much conflict there is between parents and how well the parents function as parents.

Based on this information, Furstenberg and Cherlin (1991) conclude that joint custody, particularly joint physical custody, should be encouraged only in cases where both parents voluntarily agree to it. Joint physical custody may be especially difficult for young children who, because of their limited cognitive and perspective-taking skills, find the different living arrangements and changing schedules confusing. Joint custody usually does little harm, however, and a legal preference for it may send a message to fathers that our society respects and encourages their roles and responsibilities in the care of their children.

Thinking It Through:

1. What factors would you use to decide which type of custody was best for a child?
2. What are the advantages and disadvantages of each type of custody arrangement?
3. How are young children likely to respond to each type of custody?

HOW DO PEER AND SIBLING RELATIONSHIPS DEVELOP DURING EARLY CHILDHOOD?

As children develop, their social relationships widen to include people other than family members. There is a gradual shift in the importance of peers and friends after infancy. By the end of childhood, nearly 50 percent of children's social activities involve peers (Grusec & Lytton, 1988).

A child's peer group consists of other children who are about the same age and who have similar interests and activities. Relationships with peers differ in important ways from family relationships (Hartup, 1996):

- ✦ Peer relationships are voluntary relationships chosen by the child.
- ✦ Peer relationships are based on equality and mutual give-and-take, whereas family relationships, particularly parent-child relationships, are based more on the authority of parents or older siblings.

✦ Children learn things from peers that they are less likely to learn from adults, such as cooperation and reciprocity, as well as competition, lying, cheating, and fighting.

✦ Families tend to love and care for children no matter what they do; peers are not so accepting.

The quality of peer relationships affects children's development. Children who have poor peer relationships are more likely than others to drop out of school, become delinquent, and suffer many kinds of psychological and behavioral problems (Parker & Asher, 1987). Young children enjoy the companionship provided by peers, and those who lack friends and companions report being lonely (Cohn, Lohrmann, & Patterson, 1985).

YOUNG CHILDREN'S FRIENDSHIPS

The following excerpt is taken from the conversation of two 4-year-old children at play (Parker & Gottman, 1989):

Eric: [shouting] I'm a skeleton! I'm a skeleton!

Naomi: I'm your friend, the dinosaur.

Eric: Oh, hi, Dinosaur. [subdued] You know, no one likes me.

Naomi: [reassuringly] But I like you, I'm your friend.

Eric: But none of my other friends like me. They don't like my new suit. It's really just me. They think I'm a dumb-dumb.

Naomi: I know what. He's a good skeleton.

Eric: [yelling] I am not a dumb-dumb.

Naomi: I'm not calling you a dumb-dumb. I'm calling you a friendly skeleton.

This exchange reveals important elements of young children's conceptions of friendships. At first, Eric plays a skeleton and tells Naomi, who plays a dinosaur, that nobody likes the skeleton. He then confesses that it is he, not the skeleton, whom children think is dumb. In doing so, Eric shows that young children understand that disclosing personal information to friends is appropriate. Naomi's response shows that they understand that friends care about and support one another.

Friendships consist of mutual emotional bonds expressed through interactions that have qualities different from those of interactions with nonfriends. For example, friends express more positive and negative emotions to one another than they do to nonfriends, and they are likely to continue to interact even after a disagreement (Newcomb & Bagwell, 1995).

Friendships provide children with opportunities to learn effective interpersonal skills such as sharing, cooperating, and resolving conflicts, which then serve as the basis for other relationships (Hartup, 1996). Friendships also provide opportunities to gain experience in displaying and controlling emotions and in responding to others' emotions (Parker & Gottman, 1989). In addition, friends share information and ideas and engage in social problem solving (Azmitia & Montgomery, 1993).

During toddlerhood, children begin to seek out specific children and develop with them special relationships that are mutually satisfying. They may have one to two friendships, however, that are fragile and dependent on the context. For example, toddlers who are friends may engage in a give-and-take encounter where one toddler plays with a toy while the other watches, and then they change places. If this pattern of play breaks down, so does the interaction and the friendship. After age 2, children have expanded capabilities to communicate and interact. As a result, their friendships are more flexible, and the number and stability increase. By age 3, children differentiate friends from playmates, and friendships become a basis for many of their decisions about their social interactions (Howes, 1989).

The major developmental advances during early childhood that lead to these changes in friendship patterns include the abilities to manipulate symbols, use language, and engage in pretend play. These cognitive advances allow older preschoolers to share understandings about relationships with a wider range of children (Roffey, Majors, & Tarrant, 1997). Children's ability to control their emotions also increases during early childhood, and they become better able to respond appropriately and effectively to both positive and negative social interactions (Fabes et al., 1996).

During early childhood, friendship is based on the exchange of common interests and activities. Friends are children who are readily accessible, pleasurable, and entertaining and who have nice toys (Furman, 1996; Gottman, 1983). Young children usually make friends with children of similar age, sex, race, interests, and values (Poulin et al., 1997). When they make friends with a child who is dissimilar (such as someone of the other sex), the friendship tends to be short-lived (Maccoby, 1990).

Young children's friendships are fluid and changeable. Friends are those you are sharing a game with at the moment. Consider the following exchange among three 5-year-old girls:

Bethany: [*talking to Maria, who is playing in the block area with Claudia*] *What are you playing, Maria?*

Maria: *Claudia and I are playing Pocahontas. You can't play with us.*

Bethany: *Why can't I play?*

Maria: *Cause we're friends and we're playing.*

Bethany: *Well, Maria, . . . do you remember when we were playing together yesterday? You said I was your friend.*

Maria: [*initially looks confused and then brightens*] *I know; we can all be friends and you can play!*

In this example, Maria and Bethany negotiate the status of their relationship. Maria at first resists Bethany's attempt to play with her and Claudia, because she and Claudia are friends. When Bethany reminds Maria that they played together the day before, Maria resolves the dilemma by acknowledging that one can have more than one friend at a time and invites Bethany to join them. A younger child might not have been as flexible in her view of friendships.

Although young children are more likely than older children to define friendships according to the situation, their friendships can be quite intense and involving. Young children express distress at being separated from or losing a friend (Howes, 1988). It is not until mid–elementary school, however, that children recognize that friendships are based on mutual sympathy and loyalty and that the relationship between friends is stable and enduring even if they do not see each other for some time (Newcomb & Bagwell, 1998; Youniss, 1980).

YOUNG CHILDREN AT PLAY

Play among young children is observed in virtually every human culture. Even in societies where there is little time for play, children somehow manage to integrate it into their work routines. For example, in the Kipsigis community in Kenya, children have many chores that take up considerable amounts of their time. Yet, Kipsigis children incorporate play into their chores by playing tag while they watch cows or climb trees (Harkness & Super, 1983).

Although play is universal among children, there are differences in the amounts and kinds of play observed across and within cultures (Roopnarine, Lasker, Sacks, & Stores, 1998). Families in various cultures encourage different types of play and attach different meanings to play activities. For instance, differences were apparent in a study that compared how Japanese and American mothers interacted with their young children in a free-play situation (Tamis-LeMonda, Bornstein, Cyphers, Toda, & Ogino, 1992). Japan-

Why Do Boys and Girls Prefer Same-Sex Playmates?

Even a casual glance at young children's playgrounds reveals an interesting pattern: boys play with boys, and girls play with girls. Children as young as 2 show a preference for playing with children of the same sex (Maccoby & Jacklin, 1987). The preference for same-sex playmates becomes stronger during early childhood. Four-year-old children play with same-sex peers about three times as often as with other-sex peers, but by age 6, they play with same-sex peers eleven times as often (Maccoby, 1987). So what do children learn from the many hours they spend playing with others of their own sex?

Observations of young children's peer interactions show that boys and girls play differently and have different preferences for activities and toys. Boys engage in very active and boisterous play, fighting and chasing one another (such as rough-and-tumble play). Boys use direct commands to influence others, and they work hard to determine who is dominant in the group (Maccoby, 1988, 1990). For example, boys often discuss the issue of "who is the boss" of the others. A group of boys in one kindergarten class spent many hours trying to decide whether Darth Vader or Luke Skywalker was "the boss" in *Star Wars* (Paley, 1987).

In contrast, girls play quietly, use cooperative strategies with each other rather than dominance, use polite suggestions to influence others, and encourage each other to be involved in the group (Leaper, 1994; Maccoby, 1988, 1990). For instance, girls playing house spend time enacting roles that each has chosen, such as mother feeding the baby.

Boys and girls spend so much time with others of their own sex that they learn much more about the "culture" of their own gender group than about that of the other. They learn especially how to communicate and interact using styles practiced repeatedly with others of the same sex (Maccoby, 1990). Because boys' culture focuses on dominance and girls' culture focuses on cooperation, girls and boys develop different skills within their peer groups (Maccoby, 1990). Girls' cooperative strategies and polite suggestions are more effective with other girls and with adults than with boys, and their ability to influence boys decreases during early childhood (Serbin, Sprafkin, Elman, & Doyle, 1984). Boys' style of interaction is often too rough for girls, whom they begin to avoid. These early gender differences in interactive strategies and styles can cause confusion and difficulty in cross-sex communication, even as children grow older.

Thinking It Through:

1. Why do boys and girls like to play with peers of their own sex?
2. How do each of the contemporary theories (biological, social learning, cognitive) explain same-sex play preferences?
3. What are some outcomes of socialization in same-sex play groups? Do you think the early play styles may influence behavior and interactions between men and women?

---

ese mothers encouraged their young children to engage in pretend play—suggesting, for example, that the child kiss a doll or offer the doll some food. American mothers emphasized the functional uses of the toys—"Push the bus"—and spoke more about the toys as objects than did Japanese mothers. Japanese mothers viewed the play situation as an opportunity to teach their children how to interact with others, whereas American mothers used play to teach their children about the world and how to explore it on their own (Tamis-LeMonda et al., 1992).

The amount of time children spend in various play activities also is influenced by their cultural environments. For example, American children and young children growing up in the Marquesas Islands in the South Pacific allocate different amounts of time to various play activities. Figure 8.5 presents a breakdown of these differences. As you can see in this figure, Marquesan children spend considerably less time in pretend play and more time in physical and object play than do American children. This difference is

FIGURE 8.5

Percentages of Time Marquesan and American Children Spend in Different Types of Play

SOURCE: Martini, 1994.

What differences do you see when you compare the figures for Marquesan and American children? What accounts for the high rate of pretend play among American children?

solitary play play in which a child is alone, even if surrounded by other children

onlooker play play in which one child watches another child or children but does not directly participate

parallel play play in which two or more children engage in the same activity at the same time and place, but each child still plays separately

associative play play in which various children engage, but with different goals

cooperative play play in which two or more children engage, with a common goal that requires social interaction

due in part to cultural differences in their views of social status. Because Marquesan children are taught to be cautious about forming status hierarchies, they avoid play that requires distinct leaders, preferring activities that do not require much individual competition (Martini, 1994). Pretend play requires cooperation and structure; Marquesan children are more likely to engage in types of play that do not include these elements. They prefer play that is object oriented (pounding rocks to make noise) or physical (searching for insects or eels, chasing waves). Their preferences reflect the cultural values of the society in which they are reared.

Development of Social Play

The amount of time spent in play depends on the age of the individual—it begins to increase in early infancy, peaks during childhood, declines during adolescence, and all but disappears by adulthood (Pellegrini & Smith, 1998). The form of play also changes with age. In a classic study, Parten (1932) identified five forms of play relating to the level of involvement with other children. Her observations were so keen that her categories of play are still used as measures of children's social maturity.

✦ In **solitary play,** the lowest level of social play, the child plays alone, even if surrounded by other children. This type of play is typical of 2-year-olds; Parten found that approximately half of 2-year-olds' play was solitary.

✦ In **onlooker play,** the child watches another child or children playing but does not directly participate. Two-year-olds engage in a considerable amount of onlooker play, sometimes even asking questions or offering suggestions to the children playing.

✦ In **parallel play,** the child engages in an activity that another is engaged in at the same time and place, but each child is still playing separately. The children play side by side but not with each other. Parallel play is commonly observed in preschoolers.

✦ In **associative play,** the child engages in play that involves other children, but each child has a different goal. Associative play involves a considerable amount of social interaction, turn-taking, and expressive communication. Associative play is occurring when two children draw pictures at the same table, sharing crayons and commenting on each other's picture. Each child has his or her own design and goal in mind, but they share and socialize with each other as they draw. Associative play is common among 3- and 4-year-olds.

✦ In **cooperative play,** two or more children engage in a play activity with a common goal that requires social interaction. For instance, two children might dig through sand with their bare hands, opposite each other, with the goal of meeting in the middle to form a tunnel. Cooperative play represents the highest level of social play.

It is best not to think of these categories as discrete developmental stages of play. Although their play becomes increasingly social and interactive as children develop, even toddlers engage in cooperative play, and most children display a blend of all varieties of play (Howes & Matheson, 1992). Also, the kind of play children engage in is not always a measure of social maturity. For example, the meaning of solitary play depends on what the child is doing (Coplan & Rubin, 1998; Coplan, Rubin, Fox, Calkins, & Stewart, 1994) and on the physical environment (Frost, Shin, & Jacobs, 1998). Solitary play may be appropriate for a 4-year-old child when cutting and pasting paper but not when engaging in pretend play. Thus, if a child is engaged alone in an activity that is best done as a group, then solitary play may be detrimental to the child's development.

The culture children grow up in influences the amount of time they spend immersed in the different forms of play. Marquesan children almost never play alone, whereas American children spend about 35 percent of their time engaged in solitary play (Martini, 1994). Because the play of American preschoolers is almost always supervised by adults who set limits, they are not exposed to the dangers Marquesan children face. Large play groups are necessary for the protection and safety of Marquesan children.

In this example of parallel play, notice how these children are playing the same thing but are not taking notice of each other. What factors contribute to the development of more advanced forms of social play?

Young Children's Pretend Play

Much of children's play is **pretend play**—play based on make-believe situations and fantasies. In pretend play, children let objects or persons symbolize things or people they are not. Pretend play appears by age 3 and peaks around age 6 or 7. Because of its infinite themes and variety, pretend play may be the most important type of play for children's development (Slade & Wolf, 1994).

Pretend play undergoes several changes during the early childhood years (Lyytinen, Poikkeus, & Laasko, 1997). Initially, the pretend play of 2- to 3-year-olds centers on their solitary actions (such as pretending to go to sleep). As children become less egocentric, they are increasingly able to pretend that other people or objects (such as Mom or stuffed animals) are sleeping or eating. After age 3, children's pretend play becomes less self-focused and more social (Hughes, 1995). Because of their concrete and literal way of thinking, young children have trouble letting an object serve as a symbolic representation of something else. For example, 2- or 3-year-old children have difficulty pretending that a paper cup is a hat—to them, a cup is for drinking.

The roles children take in pretend play also change during the preschool years. At first, 2- and 3-year-olds play roles that are very familiar to them, such as mother or baby. Older preschoolers, because of their increased experience and ability to think abstractly, are able to incorporate roles that are less familiar or that they have never directly experienced, such as doctor or police officer.

YOUNG CHILDREN'S SIBLING RELATIONSHIPS

Almost 80 percent of children in the United States have siblings (Dunn, 1992). But the arrival of a new brother or sister is not an easy adjustment for children, and it sometimes leads to increased withdrawal, aggression, or dependency (Teti, 1992). There is evidence that mother-child attachment security decreases following the birth of a sibling (Teti, Sakin, Kucera, Corns, & Eiden, 1996). These negative reactions are especially likely among preschool-age children who have a limited understanding of their relationship to the new baby. Young children may react strongly to the stress brought about by the new demands. Furthermore, because parents often pay a lot of attention to the newborn, at the expense of the preschooler, the preschooler may feel neglected.

pretend play play in which children let objects or persons symbolize things or people they are not

When siblings are similar in age, marked changes in the nature of their relationship begin to appear during early childhood. Between 3 and 4 years of age, children become more interested in their siblings (Brown & Dunn, 1992)—they collaborate, cooperate, and play together with increasing frequency. They also fight and struggle more than they did before, and they get along better with friends than with each other (Volling, Young-blade, & Belsky, 1997).

Dynamics of Sibling Relationships

Siblings spend considerable time interacting with one another and therefore influence one another in a variety of ways. Siblings are a source of comfort and support, as well as conflict and antagonism, and they serve as role models, helping children learn new behaviors. Positive sibling relationships foster healthy adaptation in a variety of settings (Richman, Stevenson, & Graham, 1982). Negative sibling relationships also have pervasive effects. For example, children who are aggressive with their siblings are likely to have poor peer relationships (Dishion, 1990).

Sibling relationships change as children move through different developmental periods. When siblings are more than a few years apart in age, the older sibling assumes roles that are more parentlike than peerlike, often acting as teacher and caregiver for the younger brothers and sisters (Brody, Stoneman, MacKinnon, & MacKinnon, 1985; Dunn, 1988). During early childhood, children begin to share intimate feelings and thoughts with their siblings and are quite dependent on each other for companionship and support. Older siblings often become particularly important to young children in families that have recently immigrated to the United States, especially when the parents have less understanding of the new culture than the older siblings do (Perez-Granados & Callanan, 1997). During later childhood and adolescence, friends and peers take on more of these roles, and siblings are less important sources of intimacy and support. This is not to say that siblings are not important after early childhood, but their relative importance compared to peers decreases somewhat (Buhrmester, 1992).

Differences in the Quality of Sibling Relationships

As early as young childhood, striking differences in sibling relationships appear. Some siblings are very close, others extremely antagonistic. There are at least three factors influencing the quality of sibling relationships (Dunn, 1992):

1. **Temperaments of the siblings.**   The temperamental qualities of the siblings influence the level of conflict between them. Children who are active, intense, or unadaptable in temperament are likely to have antagonistic sibling relationships. The temperament match between siblings also is important: siblings who are temperamentally similar are more likely to have positive relationships (Boer, 1990; Munn & Dunn, 1988).

2. **Parental treatment.**   Negative relationships between siblings often are attributed to the parents' favoritism toward one of the siblings (Brody, Stoneman, & McCoy, 1992; McHale, Crouter, McGuire, & Updegraff, 1995). Often it is difficult to avoid treating children differently, especially if siblings are of different ages. If 4-year-old Erin is sent to bed earlier than her 9-year-old sister Sarah, for example, she may accuse her parents of favoring her sister. But if they are both sent to bed at the same time, Sarah may find this unfair because she was not allowed to stay up so late when she was 4. However, the effects of differential treatment become more profound if one sibling is treated with less warmth and affection or with more punishment. That child is more likely to behave in an aggressive, rivalrous, and unaffectionate manner toward his or her sibling (Boer, Goedhart, & Treffers, 1992; Volling & Elins, 1998). Children are less likely to respond negatively if they perceive that the differential treatment was justified (Kowal & Kramer, 1997).

3. **Family life events.** Sibling relationships can be influenced by stressful events affecting the family, such as divorce, job loss, or death (Erel, Margolin, & John, 1998). For example, sibling relationships often deteriorate in families that experience a divorce. Because of changes in caregiving following a divorce, older siblings are likely to engage in more caretaking behavior with their younger siblings; younger siblings may reject this caregiving, thereby setting the stage for conflict (MacKinnon, 1989). Sibling relationships also may become more hostile as siblings compete for the limited time and attention of their parents (Hetherington et al., 1988). The stress and new demands of making the transition to school also are likely to negatively affect siblings' relationships (Dunn, 1992).

HOW DOES TELEVISION INFLUENCE YOUNG CHILDREN'S EMOTIONAL AND SOCIAL DEVELOPMENT?

You learned in Chapter 7 that television viewing affects young children's cognitive development. As you might expect, children's social development also is influenced by television. Television plays a central role in the life of most contemporary families and often provides people with common points of reference for relating to others. Many of the themes in young children's play revolve around what they see on television.

During early childhood, many children begin to spend a large amount of time watching television. The amount of time children spend watching television and the content of many television programs have generated concerns and questions about the impact of television on family life and children's emotional and social development.

EFFECTS OF TELEVISION ON FAMILY LIFE

The acceptance and popularity of television began slowly and then exploded. In 1950, only 5 percent of US households owned a television set, but within ten years, almost 90 percent of households owned one (Van-Evra, 1998). Today, only 2 percent of households do not own a television set, and about two-thirds of households own two or more sets.

Time spent watching television has steadily increased. The television set is now on for an average of almost 7 hours per day (A. C. Nielsen Media Research, 1995). Although almost everyone watches some television, low-income families watch more television than middle- or upper-income families; television is relatively cheap entertainment, and low-income families may not have the money to spend on other sources of entertainment (Huston et al., 1992).

Most children are exposed to television from the time they are born. As you can see in Figure 8.6, children's television viewing time increases during the preschool years to an average of 2.5 hours each day and continues to increase through the elementary-school years. Viewing time peaks at about 4 hours per day just before the start of adolescence, when competing activities reduce the number of hours adolescents spend in front of

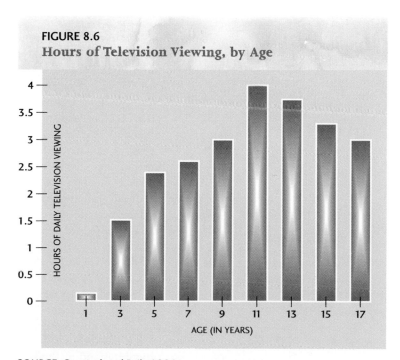

FIGURE 8.6
Hours of Television Viewing, by Age

HOURS OF DAILY TELEVISION VIEWING

AGE (IN YEARS)

SOURCE: Comstock and Paik, 1991.
Notice the increase in rates of viewing early in development. What factors contribute to this increase? Why does television play such a large role in everyday family life?

Television viewing, which increases during the preschool years, has important effects on children's development and family life. Can you identify these effects? How are they produced?

the television set (Condry, 1989). Similar patterns have been found in other countries (Liebert & Sprafkin, 1988).

The dramatic rise in the popularity of television and the time devoted to watching it has had a significant effect on family life. Compared to families that do not own television sets, families that watch television spend less time sleeping, visiting others outside the home, having conversations, cleaning the house, participating in community or school activities, and pursuing hobbies or sports (Robinson, 1981; Williams, 1986). More than half of all elementary school children watch television while eating meals, and an even larger percentage watch while doing their homework (Sheehan, 1983). Children's television viewing is inversely related to parental instruction, the number of books in the home, and school readiness; children who watch more television spend less time reading and do not value reading as much as those who watch less (Clarke & Kutz-Costes, 1997; Koolstra, van-der-Voort, & van-der-Kamp, 1997). By the time children graduate from high school, they have spent more time watching television than in any other waking activity (Josephson, 1995).

Although parents express concern about the time their children spend watching television and the effects it may have on them, they do little to control their children's viewing (Sprafkin, Gadow, & Abelman, 1992). Over half the parents in one survey indicated that they "only occasionally" or "never" restrict the amount of viewing or what their children watch (Bower, 1985). Moreover, 54 percent of US children have a television set in their bedroom, making it difficult for parents to monitor what their children watch (A. C. Nielsen, 1995).

EFFECTS OF TELEVISION VIOLENCE ON CHILDREN'S AGGRESSION

Despite efforts at regulation, children's television still contains a good deal of violent content. Violent acts typically are defined as any deliberate acts of physical or verbal force to achieve a goal (Center for Media and Public Affairs, 1994). During an 18-hour period on ten network and cable channels in 1994, an average of almost 15 scenes of violence per hour was recorded. Rates of violence were almost twice as high on cable programs as on network programs—34 versus 19 acts per hour (Center for Media and Public Affairs, 1994). For children's programs, the rates of violence are even higher. By some estimates, children's shows contain 20 to 25 violent acts per hour (Murray, 1995). By the time they reach adolescence, children have witnessed over 100,000 acts of televised violence, including over 20,000 murders (American Psychological Association, 1993).

Young children hold mixed views about the violence in television programs. Some find the violence attractive. Some do not view a program as being violent unless there is bloodshed. Others disapprove of the violent behaviors portrayed and realize that the violent themes and messages conflict with what is good. Thus, young children interpret and define television violence in different ways, and these differences affect their responses to it (Wilson & Smith, 1998).

Scientific evidence supports a relationship between children's exposure to violent television content and their own aggressive and risky behaviors and attitudes (Huston et al., 1992; Potts, Doppler, & Hernandez, 1994). This relationship has been demonstrated in studies of thousands of children of different ages and backgrounds, using a variety of procedures and methods (Hearold, 1986; Paik & Comstock, 1994). The link between television violence and children's aggression has been found worldwide (Huesmann & Eron, 1986).

Practical Guidelines for Supervising Children's Television Viewing

Given the attractiveness of television and its dominant role in American family life, what guidelines can caregivers follow to establish positive viewing habits in children? Here are some practical ideas (Davis, 1990/1991; Fabes, Wilson, and Christopher, 1989; and Murray, 1995):

- *Start early.* The younger children are, the easier it is to establish positive television viewing habits.
- *Set daily limits.* Most professionals suggest that children be limited to a maximum of 2 hours of television per day.

- *Encourage planned viewing.* Have children select programs you approve of from television schedules.
- *Don't locate a television set in a child's room.* It encourages isolated television viewing.
- *Remember that children learn from their caregivers and other role models.* If caregivers watch a lot of television, children are likely to watch a lot of television.
- *Watch television with children.* Encourage children to discuss what they see on television and how they feel about it. Let them know what you think about it.

- *Talk to children about television advertising.* Tell children that the purpose of advertising is to sell as many products as possible to as many viewers as possible.
- *Read to children rather than watching television.* Reading to children fosters more intimate interactions and enhances children's appreciation of books and reading.
- *Use V-chip technology.* This technology allows caregivers to block out shows that are offensive or inappropriate for children.

With literally thousands of studies showing a relation between television violence and children's aggressive behaviors and attitudes, what conclusions can be drawn? Several important themes are highlighted in the research (Huston & Wright, 1998):

✦ Children's aggressive tendencies are likely to be increased by violence on television when it is portrayed realistically (Atkin, 1983), when it is portrayed by human rather than cartoon characters (Hayes & Casey, 1992), when it is not subject to critical commentary (Peracchio, 1993), and when the aggressive behavior is seen as justified or rewarded (Perry, Perry, & Rasmussen, 1986).

✦ Increased arousal after viewing violent television disposes children to behave more impulsively (Zillmann, 1982), and implied violence elicits as much arousal as does actual violence (Kalamas & Gruber, 1998).

✦ Children who are abused, emotionally disturbed, or predisposed to act aggressively are more influenced by television violence than others (Sprafkin et al., 1992).

✦ Television violence can have long-term consequences. Children with high levels of exposure to television violence were likely to be aggressive ten years later and were more likely to be arrested or convicted for violent crime or abuse twenty two years later than children with less exposure to television (Eron, 1982; Eron, Huesmann, Lefkowitz, & Walder, 1996).

Although exposure to television violence relates to children's aggressive behaviors and attitudes, many factors influence this relationship. Debate continues about the extent to which we can conclusively say that television violence *causes* increased aggression in children (Josephson, 1995).

EFFECTS OF TELEVISION ON CHILDREN'S PROSOCIAL BEHAVIOR

Not all behavior on television is violent or aggressive; acts of kindness and cooperation are common. Rates of prosocial behaviors generally are comparable to rates of aggressive and violent behaviors (Greenberg, Edison, Korzenny, Fernandez-Collado, & Atkin, 1980).

Some of the programs designed for young children (such as *Sesame Street*, *Barney*, and *Mr. Rogers' Neighborhood*) specifically focus on teaching prosocial behavior. Soon after these shows were introduced, scientists became interested in determining their effectiveness in increasing children's prosocial behavior. They found that preschoolers who watched characters on *Sesame Street* or *Mr. Rogers' Neighborhood* cooperated with and helped each other more than those who did not (Friedrich-Cofer, Huston, Kipnis, Susman, & Clewett, 1979; Singer & Singer, 1998). However, simply exposing young children to prosocial television characters is not enough to strongly influence their prosocial behavior. The extent to which young children learn prosocial lessons and behaviors from television depends on two factors related to presentation:

✦ **Environmental cues and supports.**   A parent or teacher may need to supplement prosocial television programming with related materials (puppets, costumes) that promote role playing. Verbal discussions and labeling of prosocial behavior also are effective, but role playing is most effective in helping young children apply television content to their own behavior (Friedrich & Stein, 1975).

✦ **Competing messages in the program.**   In many television programs, characters display both prosocial and aggressive behaviors. Story lines often continue over several programs, with characters displaying conflicts and maladaptive behaviors as well as helpful and sympathetic responses. Young children learn best when the prosocial message clearly replaces aggressive behavior. Combined prosocial and aggressive messages sometimes lead to increased aggressive behavior in children, perhaps because children find the aggressive action more interesting and memorable than the prosocial lessons contained in the program (Lovelace & Huston, 1983).

Without environmental cues and clearly contrasting depictions of prosocial behavior, young children may not be able to apply the prosocial lessons they watch on television to their own lives.

CHAPTER SUMMARY

How does self-awareness change during early childhood?

• Although their self-concepts become increasingly complex and differentiated, young children rarely see themselves in terms of stable traits and qualities.

• As children enter early childhood, they become better able to make evaluative judgments about themselves. These judgments, however, are global, vary considerably from situation to situation, and may overestimate their abilities.

• Self-esteem can be understood as a combination of worthiness and competence. Different combinations produce four types of self-esteem: high self-esteem (high in both), low self-esteem (low in both), defensive self-esteem I (high in worthiness, low in competence), and defensive self-esteem II (high in competence, low in worthiness).

• Important influences on young children's self-concept and self-esteem include their physical appearance, their relationships with parents and peers, and the social and cultural conditions, values, and practices they experience.

How do young children develop a concept of gender?

• Children label themselves as boys or girls by 2½ years of age. By the end of the preschool years, children understand that gender is stable and constant. A mature gender identity does not develop until children are at least 4 to 5 years of age.

• Young children learn gender stereotypes as early as age 2½, and these stereotypes become increasingly complex with age.

- Boys and girls have different abilities, skills, and interests, but the magnitude of these differences often is small and the variation within each sex is large.

What are the contemporary theories about gender development?

- Biological theories focus on how biological, physiological, and biochemical processes (such as hormones) affect characteristics and abilities.
- Social learning theories attempt to explain how direct learning and observation mold and shape gender development.
- Cognitive theories view gender development as an outcome of normal cognitive development. Gender schema theory suggests that children actively construct their concept of gender by building schemas—networks of associated information—and then use these schemas to guide their behavior and thinking.

How do emotions develop during early childhood?

- As young children become socially active, they are likely to get into more conflicts with others and become angry as a result.
- Young children respond to conflicts in a variety of ways depending on the type of conflict. As they get older, they are likely to resolve conflicts in ways that are less harmful to others.
- Aggression changes in frequency and form across early childhood, with physical and instrumental aggression decreasing and verbal and hostile aggression increasing.
- Increased social interactions foster prosocial emotions and actions. Initially, children have difficulty distinguishing their own emotional needs from those of others, but as they develop perspective-taking abilities, they increasingly respond to others' emotional states in caring and appropriate ways.
- Children's motivations for helping others change from pragmatic and approval-based reasons during the preschool years to altruistic reasons in later childhood.
- Children develop prosocial emotions and actions in the context of secure relationships with caregivers.

How do parenting behaviors influence young children's development?

- As preschoolers become more independent and active, parental disciplinary efforts increase. Disciplinary methods used include power assertion, love withdrawal, and inductive reasoning.
- Three factors influence caregivers' choice of disciplinary practices: the nature of the misbehavior, characteristics of the child, and cultural and ethnic values.
- Baumrind identified four parenting styles that differ in the degree of parental responsiveness and demandingness. Authoritarian parents are high in demandingness but low in responsiveness; permissive parents are the reverse; uninvolved parents

are low in both; and authoritative parents are high in both. In contemporary western cultures, authoritative parenting is associated with optimal outcomes for children.

How does divorce affect young children's development?

- Young children's understanding of divorce is limited; they respond emotionally and fail to understand the permanence of the situation. Because of their egocentric thinking, young children are likely to believe that they somehow caused the divorce.
- Young children initially show some adjustment problems, but most adjust after a period of time.
- The quality of a young child's adjustment to divorce depends on the amount of conflict between parents, characteristics of the child, and the ability of the child to maintain a relationship with the noncustodial parent.
- When parents remarry, children often experience a difficult adjustment period. The quality of the relationships children have with their caregivers influences their adjustment to stepfamily life.

How do peer and sibling relationships develop during early childhood?

- As young children widen their social relationships, peers become increasingly important influences in their lives.
- Children's conceptions of friendship change over early childhood. The basis of friendships changes from mutual interests to mutual sympathy and loyalty, with an understanding of the stability and intimacy between friends.
- Most peer interactions take place in the context of play. Play takes many forms, including solitary, onlooker, parallel, associative, cooperative, and pretend play.
- Young children become more responsive to their siblings during early childhood. This responsiveness can lead to enhanced caring and prosocial interactions, as well as more conflict and fighting.
- Sibling relationships are influenced by the temperaments of the siblings, parental treatment, and family life events.
- Positive relationships with peers and siblings are beneficial for children, whereas poor peer and sibling relationships are associated with negative outcomes.

How does television influence young children's emotional and social development?

- Television attracts children's attention at a young age. By high school graduation, children have spent more time in front of the television than in any other waking activity.
- Television changes the ways families interact and schedule their activities. Parents do little to control children's television viewing.

- Children who watch more television have lower reading comprehension and interest in reading and decreased readiness for school.

- Television contains a lot of violent content that can increase children's aggressive behavior and attitudes. Television also con-

tains considerable prosocial content that can positively affect young children's behavior.

KEY TERMS & CONCEPTS

associative play (292)
authoritarian parenting (280)
authoritative parenting (282)
compliance (277)
cooperative play (292)
demandingness (280)
discipline (277)
empathy (275)
gender consistency (266)
gender identity (266)
gender labeling (266)
gender schemas (271)

gender stability (266)
gender stereotypes (267)
goal-corrected partnership (277)
hostile aggression (274)
inductive reasoning (278)
instrumental aggression (274)
internalization (277)
love withdrawal (278)
onlooker play (292)
parallel play (292)
permissive parenting (280)
power assertion (278)

pretend play (293)
prosocial behavior (275)
relational aggression (274)
responsiveness (280)
schematic consistency (272)
self-concept (261)
self-esteem (262)
solitary play (292)
sympathy (275)
uninvolved parenting (282)

ACTIVITIES & APPLICATIONS

Relating to Young Children

1. In light of what you have learned, reinterpret the story about Barry and Hector at the beginning of this chapter. How might the different aspects of social development (parenting behavior, peer relationships, divorce, television, and siblings) influence children's self-concept and self-esteem?

2. Using Baumrind's definitions, describe the parenting styles of your parents. Identify the specific parenting behaviors that you used to classify your parents in one of the four categories. Discuss the difficulties you had in classifying them. What effects do you think your parents had on your development? What style of parenting will you use with your own children?

3. Arrange to observe preschool children playing on a playground. What kinds of play can you identify? Who do the children play with? What kinds of activities do they engage in with their peers? Why are some children more likely than others to play with peers?

4. Watch some children's television shows and record the numbers of aggressive and prosocial acts. How did you define these behaviors? What kinds of characters displayed these behaviors? What impact might these televised acts have on young children's development?

Grasping the Whole

Benchmarks in Early Childhood Development

PHYSICAL/MOTOR DEVELOPMENT	COGNITIVE DEVELOPMENT	SOCIAL/EMOTIONAL DEVELOPMENT
More adultlike physical appearance and body proportions	Increased symbolic representation; development of preoperational thinking and problem solving; egocentrism; perception-based reasoning; lack of conservation	Concept of self based on external qualities, situational changes, and others' feedback
Growth rapid but not as rapid as in earlier years		Maturing concept of gender
Increased myelination in brain and development of neural pathways	Improved memory but easily distracted and misled in recall; limited ability to use memory strategies for better recall	Increased social interactions and resulting angry conflicts; prosocial emotions and caring actions
Improved coordination and development of advanced gross and fine motor skills	Enhanced understanding of mental events; development of theory of mind	Changing attachments and parental disciplinary efforts; increased responsiveness to changing family relationships (such as divorce or remarriage)
Increased risk for accidents, injuries, and poor nutrition	Increased responsiveness to social context of learning; preparedness for school	Development of friendships and peer and sibling relationships, particularly during play
		Greater experience with mass media, particularly television

Status Report on Early Childhood

Many factors contribute to whether or not preschool children are ready for school. Compare and contrast the views of parents and teachers regarding school readiness. What trends do you see? What factors may contribute to any differences found?

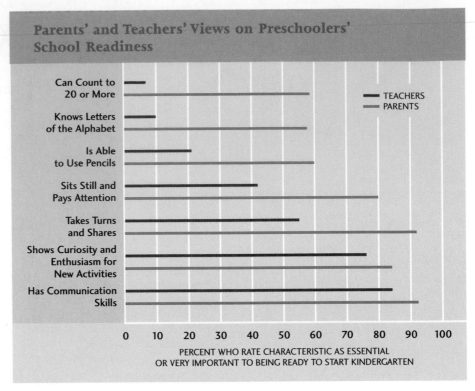

Parents' and Teachers' Views on Preschoolers' School Readiness

- Can Count to 20 or More
- Knows Letters of the Alphabet
- Is Able to Use Pencils
- Sits Still and Pays Attention
- Takes Turns and Shares
- Shows Curiosity and Enthusiasm for New Activities
- Has Communication Skills

— TEACHERS
— PARENTS

0　10　20　30　40　50　60　70　80　90　100

PERCENT WHO RATE CHARACTERISTIC AS ESSENTIAL OR VERY IMPORTANT TO BEING READY TO START KINDERGARTEN

SOURCE: Lewit and Baker, 1995; National Center for Education Statistics, 1993; US Department of Education, 1993.

SUGGESTED READINGS

Eisenberg, N. (1992). *The caring child.* Cambridge, MA: Harvard University Press. Informative account of how children develop prosocial intentions and actions, the factors that influence young children's moral development, and what parents and educators can do to instill prosocial motives and teach caring behaviors.

Garbarino, J., Stott, F. M., and the faculty of the Erikson Institute. (1992). *What children can tell us: Eliciting, interpreting, and evaluating critical information from children.* San Francisco: Jossey-Bass. Comprehensive, readable, and thoughtful guide to understanding children's communication and the factors that influence it. The authors show how professionals in diverse fields can better understand, interview, and access information from children.

Gottman, J. (1997). *The heart of parenting: Raising an emotionally intelligent child.* New York: Simon & Schuster. Clear and usable guidance on teaching children how to understand and regulate their emotions, drawn from information gleaned from two 10-year studies.

Paley, V. (1991). *Bad guys don't have birthdays: Fantasy play at four.* Chicago: University of Chicago Press. Exploration of the fantasy play of preschoolers, by a MacArthur Prize–winning educator. Real-life conversations with children provide valuable insights into the world of fantasy play and children's needs and values.

Siegler, R. S. (1996). *Emerging minds.* New York: Oxford University Press. Up-to-date account of the current understanding of the development of young children's thinking. Anyone who is curious about children's thinking, language, and memory will find something of value in this interesting and detailed elaboration of the process of change in children's thinking.

RECOMMENDED WEBSITES

Action Alliance for Children: This site provides information about current trends and policy issues affecting children and their families. The agency publishes the news magazine *Children's Advocate* and coordinates conferences and training courses. <http://www.4children.org/>

Center for Media Education: This national nonprofit organization is dedicated to improving the quality of electronic media on behalf of children and families. The site presents summaries of the research on the use of interactive technologies by children. <http://tap.epn.org/cme/>

Children's Defense Fund: The Children's Defense Fund serves as an advocate for the children of America, paying particular attention to the needs of poor and minority children and those with disabilities. The site contains key facts about the welfare of children in the United States and information about how to improve their lives. <http://www.childrensdefense.org/>

Children's Health Environmental Coalition Network: This Website is dedicated to protecting children and preventing childhood cancers and other illnesses. It provides information on the risk children face from environmental toxins and how to prevent them from being exposed, research facts, and practical suggestions for learning more about the environmental threats to children and doing something about them. <http://www.checnet.org/chec/>

Culturally and Linguistically Appropriate Services (CLAS): The Early Childhood Research Institute, at the University of Illinois at Urbana-Champaign, identifies, evaluates, and promotes early intervention and preschool practices that are sensitive to culturally and linguistically diverse young children and their families. <http://clas.uiuc.edu/>

National Institute of Child Health and Human Development (NICHD): This federal institute is part of the National Institutes of Health, US Department of Health and Human Services. The site provides useful information on the biological, developmental, and behavioral processes that determine and maintain the health of children, adults, families, and populations. <http://www.nih.gov/nichd/>

National Parenting Center: One of America's foremost parenting information services, this center is dedicated to giving parents guidance from some of the world's most renowned child-rearing authorities. Information, chat rooms, and materials are provided to expand parenting skills and strengths. <http://www.tnpc.com/>

NATIONAL HOTLINES FOR PRESCHOOL CHILDREN

Better Hearing Institute: 800-424-8576

Federal Office of Child Support Enforcement: 201-401-9373

National Association for the Education of Young Children: 800-424-2460

Late Childhood DEVELOPMENT

To go to school, Aléjan-dro wakes up at 4 a.m. so his father can drop him off at his co-madre's (godmother's) apart-ment . . . where he waits from 5:00 until 8:00 when school begins. His evenings are spent cleaning their new apartment and struggling through incompre-hensible homework and written punishments for low test scores in a class with a teacher unprepared to teach a limited-English-proficiency student. . . . He was a student embodying many characteristics seen as chal-lenging to educators: urban Mexican-American background, of low and threatened economic income, having very little parental schooling or literacy at home, bilingual yet not possessing a strongly de-veloped first or second language. . . . A simple daily event like receiving mail . . . is a struggle in Aléjandro's family. He is relied on to deci-pher what arrives at home, but he still lacks the decoding skills to comprehend accurately.

—C. L. CARGER (1996, pp. 6–8)

During the school-age years, children undergo pervasive changes, affecting their physical and psychological well-being. New contexts provide additional impetus for change. When children enter school, they are exposed to a wide variety of new intellectual and social demands. Teachers, other students, principals, classes, homework, and extracurricular activities take on added significance. Family members remain important, but the amount of time children spend with family members drops and the amount of time they spend in school and with peers increases. Thus, children experience important changes in the nature of the environmental influences and social transactions that they face.

School-age children often find their performance compared to that of others. They are evaluated by teachers, and their parents receive reports about their performance and behavior in school. Tests, homework, and assignments take up more of children's time and provide additional sources of comparisons with others. New acquaintances, friends, and enemies develop. Many of these challenges and stressors were not present before children entered school. Thus, during late childhood, children have to develop new coping strategies to deal with the stress and demands placed on them by their changing environment. Many children cope easily and adjust well. But some children, like Alejandro, are overwhelmed by their environment and lack the skills and support to cope effectively. Alejandro's story reminds us that children's cultural backgrounds affect how they cope with the demands of their environments, as well as influencing the types of challenges they face.

IN PART 5, YOU WILL LEARN ABOUT

- how children develop physically during late childhood
- how lifestyle choices, nutrition, and family relationships influence children's health and fitness
- how older children solve problems and understand concepts such as conservation and seriation
- how culture, everyday experiences, and families influence children's cognitive development
- how children's language develops during the school years
- how children master reading and writing
- how children's intelligence is defined and assessed and how creativity can be encouraged in children
- how children develop a more complex understanding of people and social situations

- how the school experience influences children's intellectual development
- how older children develop a sense of morality and moral behaviors
- the developmental changes that cause stress in children's lives and how they cope with this stress
- the emotional and psychological disturbances of late childhood
- the qualities of family life that affect older children's development
- how the school environment and teachers influence older children's social and emotional development
- the factors that influence older children's peer relationships

CHAPTER 9

Physical, Cognitive, & Language Development in LATE CHILDHOOD

CHAPTER OUTLINE

"*Wow, that math test was tough. I'm not sure how good I did. I'm going to have to spend more time doing my homework,*" *says fifth-grader Jaya to her classmates Peter and Trish as they wait for their ride home after school. Jaya then laughs and says, "But that can wait until tonight. Can you two come over and play after we get home?"*

Peter shakes his head and says, "No, I have to go home and get my mom to take me to the library so I can finish my report on the rain forests."

"Me either," says Trish. "I have a piano lesson and then I have to work on my science project."

"How about tomorrow?" inquires Jaya.

Peter considers it and then says, "Can't. I have soccer."

Trish also declines, saying that she has to stay at school for drama practice.

Jaya shrugs and says, "We used to play all the time. School sure makes life complicated."

The hallmarks of cognitive development in late childhood include learning to read, write, think, create, and solve problems. As the discussion among the carpool partners reveals, the formal process of acquiring such skills in school is hard work. Peter's and Trisha's busy schedules suggest that when children enter school, their lives are changed by the many new demands placed on them. Exams, reports, homework, and grades become important and take up a good bit of their time. Additionally, extracurricular activities such as playing sports and practicing creative arts become a part of their daily routines. Children's lives are significantly influenced by the physical and cognitive changes that take place when they enter late childhood.

HOW DO CHILDREN DEVELOP PHYSICALLY DURING LATE CHILDHOOD?

During late childhood, physical changes are not as obvious as they were during early childhood. Although growth is slower during this period, motor and physical abilities improve significantly. This period of the life span is one of the healthiest; older children are less likely than younger children, adolescents, or adults to get sick or injured.

BRAIN DEVELOPMENT

In children from 6 to 8 years of age, the brain continues to develop. By the time a child reaches age 8, the brain is approximately 90 percent the size of an adult's brain. During the school years, the functioning of a child's brain improves (Black, 1998). Information is processed more efficiently because of increased myelination of the nerve fibers of the brain and increased lateralization of the two hemispheres of the brain (see Chapter 5). Redundant synaptic connections between neurons continue to be pruned, increasing the organization of the brain (Case, 1992).

BODY SIZE AND APPEARANCE

Children grow more slowly during the school years than they did as younger children—usually about 2 to 3 inches and 3 to 6 pounds a year—and this slower rate of growth continues until preadolescence. During the elementary school years, boys and girls develop very similarly: the arms and legs grow longer relative to the trunk of the body, and the body lengthens and fills out. One effect of this slower growth rate is that children have time to become accustomed to their bodies. This brings about gains in motor control and coordination (Gallahue & Ozmun, 1995).

At this age, individual differences among children's bodies are striking, and these differences tend to remain relatively constant over time. Research shows that, generally, children's body builds remain about the same through childhood and into adolescence. Height is usually more constant than weight and musculature, which are more influenced by exercise and diet.

Few studies have examined the relation of body build to athletic ability. Observations of Olympic athletes suggest that certain sports require particular body builds. For instance, most gymnasts are short and small-boned, whereas most volleyball players are tall. Although in many countries trainers try to select the "perfect" body build for each type of athletic performance (especially for early identification of possible Olympic athletes), predicting the performance of an average-looking child based only on his or her body shape and size is very difficult (DiGirolamo, Geis, & Walker, 1998). How muscular a child is, however, does relate to physical performance: children who are more muscular usually perform physical tasks somewhat better than children who are less muscular.

MOTOR DEVELOPMENT

During the early school years, children show remarkable improvements in their motor skills. Basic motor skills become fine-tuned and coordinated (Cowden, Sayers, & Torrey, 1998). Whereas young children have difficulty jumping, older children can jump without losing their balance. A 6-year-old might throw a ball 10 feet, but an 11-year-old can throw 30 feet (Cratty, 1986). Older children have more strength, agility, and balance than younger ones. In each of these areas, improvements can be seen every year until preadolescence, when improvement slows down. Despite children's improved coordination and agility, though, not all activities are easily learned. Children need considerable practice to master tasks that require high levels of hand-eye coordination, such as striking a ball with a bat. During the school years, children also gain better control of their fine motor movements. Their writing becomes neater, and their ability to master difficult and intricate tasks, such as knitting or playing a musical instrument, increases.

School-aged girls and boys perform similarly in almost all motor activities, although there are some differences. Boys generally have somewhat more upper body strength than girls and throw faster and more accurately than girls (Thomas & French, 1985). Girls are more flexible in their hip joints and so may be more agile than boys (Plimpton & Regimbal, 1992). Biological factors and different experiences of boys and girls may account for some performance differences. Boys' leisure activities involve more sports than do girls', giving them more time to practice motor skills (Cratty, 1986).

PHYSICAL FITNESS AND SPORTS

Since the 1950s, when fitness comparisons showed that 55 percent of American children were unfit versus only 15 percent of European youth, much attention has been paid to assessing children's fitness in the United States. Concerns about children's fitness are still warranted today—more than one-half of children and adolescents are not vigorously active on a regular basis (Surgeon General, 1996).

Why are so many children physically unfit? One reason is that many children prefer sedentary activities, such as watching television or playing video games. Another is that a significant number of children live in urban settings that limit opportunities for exercise. Although many children are sedentary, the rise in popularity of sports partici-

How does involvement in organized sports such as baseball have both positive and negative influences on children's development? How can baseball-related injuries be prevented?

pation over the last twenty years has been phenomenal. Approximately 46 million children and adolescents in the United States participate in some type of sport (Griffin, 1998). Besides simply enjoying themselves, children who participate in sports benefit from regular activity and establish habits and skills that help them enjoy physical activities throughout their lives (Telama, Yang, Laakso, & Viikari, 1997). In team sports, children also learn how to cooperate with other children.

Children's involvement in sports can also have a downside: they can sustain acute injuries, from sprained ankles to spinal cord injuries. There is no clear evidence, however, that these injuries occur more often in organized sports than in free play (Bijur et al., 1995). For example, children playing on trampolines or in-line skating are particularly at risk of injury (American Academy of Pediatrics, 1998; Smith & Shields, 1998). Some organized sports are riskier than others. Children who are involved in gymnastics, baseball, or basketball, for instance, are more likely to be injured than children who play other sports (O'Neill & Micheli, 1988). In 1995, about 162,000 children in the United States were treated in hospital emergency rooms for baseball-related injuries, with about 33 percent of these classified as severe (Consumer Product Safety Commission, 1996).

Another downside is that sports injuries may damage the growth of children's long bones, which can result in permanent joint deformities or delay in growth. However, these injuries are relatively infrequent and rarely are associated with involvement in organized sports. Children's sports injuries are more likely to be due to overuse, in which repetitive action causes stress and strain to the joints and muscles. Most of these injuries can be successfully treated, and few result in permanent damage (Watkins & Peabody, 1996).

Because of fear of injuries, pediatricians used to urge parents not to let their children participate in organized sports too early. Today, the focus is on improving sports safety. For example, the Consumer Product Safety Commission (1996) recommends that softer balls and new kinds of batting helmets be used to reduce the number of baseball-related injuries.

NUTRITION

Because children continue to grow in size and weight throughout the elementary-school years, a healthy diet continues to be important for optimal growth. During the school years, children need approximately double the calories and protein (per pound) that adults need. Children also need to obtain adequate zinc, calcium, and iron because these minerals are crucial for facilitating growth (Lifshitz, Finch, & Lifshitz, 1991).

What causes childhood obesity? How is it treated? What are some consequences of obesity for children's physical development? for children's social and emotional development?

Adult standards of healthy eating may not be appropriate for children. For instance, nutritional guidelines for adults recommend avoiding fats and cholesterol, but these are essential for the healthy development of children, especially for optimal brain development. Children on reduced-fat diets may develop nutritional deficiencies. Red meat and eggs, often avoided by health-conscious adults, are excellent sources of minerals such as iron and zinc, essential for children's growth. These minerals are not easily obtained from alternative food sources such as grains and pasta. For example, to obtain minerals equivalent to those a 3-ounce steak provides, a child would have to eat 3 to 7 cups of pasta (Lifshitz et al., 1991). Avoidance of red meats may contribute to the prevalence of iron deficiencies in children, who need more iron for their weight than adults do.

OBESITY

After a move from Maine to New York, 8-year-old Paul, who had always been slightly chubby, gained 20 pounds. He lost interest in playing with friends and spent most of his time indoors watching television and eating high fat snack foods. After consulting a pediatrician, Paul was put on a supervised health plan, which included tennis twice a week, riding a stationary bike, and fewer high fat foods. Paul could eat some favorite snacks, but not while watching television. After a lot of effort on everyone's parts, Paul lost 15 pounds and his relationships with his peers improved.

—LIFSHITZ ET AL. (1991)

Paul's story is not unusual. According to a national report on nutrition in the United States, children from 6 to 9 years of age are heavier and fatter today than they were twenty years ago (Life Sciences Research Office, 1995). Those children (and adults) who weigh more than 20 percent over their ideal weight (based on height, sex, and body composition) are defined as **obese** (Wisniewski & Marcus, 1998). National surveys show that about 9 percent of boys and 13 percent of girls are overweight, and that the number of overweight children and adults is markedly higher today than it was in the 1970s and 1980s (Life Sciences Research Office, 1995). Obese children are at risk for serious health problems that result in shorter life spans, including heart disease, diabetes mellitus, cancer, and respiratory diseases (Gunnell, Frankel, Nanchahal, Peters, & Davey, 1998; Rossner, 1998).

Why do children become obese? Genetics plays a role—children inherit a predisposition for obesity from their parents. Sedentary lifestyles are another major contributor. Studies show that active children have less body fat than sedentary children and that obese children are less active than those who are lean (Rowland, 1991). Family distress also contributes to obesity. Children in families experiencing chronic stress are more at risk for obesity because of the tendency to eat and low activity levels that accompany stress (Dietz & Gortmaker, 1985; Lifshitz et al., 1991). Programs that are successful in dealing with children's obesity are multicomponent ones. They often involve parents, teachers, and health workers, and they include education about nutrition, counseling, and opportunities for physical activity (Golan, Weizman, Apter, & Fainaru, 1998).

HOW DO OLDER CHILDREN THINK AND SOLVE PROBLEMS?

At roughly age 6 or 7, most children move to the next stage of thinking identified by Piaget—called *concrete operations*—and continue to function at this level until they are around 11 or 12 years of age. In the concrete operational stage of cognitive development, children show remarkable advances in their thinking and problem-solving strategies. For the first time, they can apply logic to solve problems in an adultlike manner. Older children's thinking is more flexible and reversible and less egocentric than

obese weighing more than 20 percent over one's ideal weight (based on height, sex, and body composition) preschoolers'. The older child considers multiple dimensions of a problem rather than focusing on only one dimension, as preoperational children do. These advances allow for more sophisticated and systematic methods of solving problems. Older children's problem solving is somewhat more constrained than the problem solving of adolescents and adults, though, because older children can apply logic only to concrete or familiar situations.

CHILDREN'S LOGICAL PROBLEM SOLVING

For Piaget, the best indicator of concrete operational thinking is a child's use of logical principles. These principles are most vividly demonstrated when children solve conservation problems. As you learned in Chapter 7, understanding of conservation of mass is assessed by showing children two identical balls of clay and then rolling one ball into a snake. To demonstrate an understanding of conservation of mass, children must infer that the two shapes still contain the same amount of clay even though they look different. Preschool children do not draw this conclusion. Centrating on one dimension (such as length), they assume that the snake must have more clay in it than the ball because it is longer. Between 6 and 7 years of age, children begin to solve conservation problems. To do so, they must be able to do the following (Siegler, 1998):

+ **Mentally represent the action.** Concrete operational children can mentally visualize the changes that occur in conservation tasks. In the clay example, they recall how the clay was transformed from a ball into a snake.
+ **Focus on more than one dimension.** The concrete operational child has the ability to think about both the length and the height of the clay, rather than focusing on only one dimension.
+ **Recognize that appearances can be deceiving.** Unlike preschoolers, who are easily deceived by the appearances of objects, concrete operational children recognize that what they see can sometimes be misleading. They can use logic to override misleading appearances.

According to Piaget, an older child draws the same conclusion as an adult about the clay by applying operations. Most children who correctly answer conservation questions use the concept of identity; that is, they reason that because no clay was added or removed, there has to be the same amount, regardless of any apparent changes in appearance (see Chapter 7).

Children also use other concepts, such as reversibility and compensation, to solve conservation problems. **Reversible thinking** reflects an understanding that actions can be undone or reversed. For instance, in a conservation task, the child can mentally return the changed object to its original form (the snake can be made back into the ball). Through **compensation,** the child decides whether one change offsets another—that is, is a change in the height of a piece of clay compensated for by a change in its width?

Children master many kinds of conservation during the school years (Goswami, 1998), including conservation of number. In one conservation of number task, a child is shown two rows of five dimes, placed 1 inch apart, and watches as an adult spreads the dimes in the second row 2 inches apart. Which row contains more dimes, or do they contain the same number? Children who conserve number respond that the two rows contain the same number of dimes. Children who do not conserve number respond that the longer row has more dimes.

Other types of conservation tasks are shown in Figure 9.1. Most children understand conservation of solid and liquid quantity, number, and length by the age of 6 or 7 years. Children can solve area and weight conservation problems at around 8 or 9, and volume conservation problems at around 10 or 11. The exposure children have to different types of conservation may explain why they learn them at different rates.

reversible thinking the understanding that actions can be undone or reversed

compensation the understanding that one change can offset another

FIGURE 9.1
Examples of Different Types of Conservation Tasks

What cognitive advances must children make to solve conservation problems? At what stage of cognitive development are most children when they start first grade?

CHILDREN'S UNDERSTANDING OF CATEGORIES AND CONCEPTS

During the concrete operational stage, children's understanding of categories and concepts becomes more sophisticated. Unlike preschool children, who are inflexible in classifying objects, concrete operational children can vary their strategies when necessary (Freund et al., 1990). In addition, concrete operational children no longer have difficulty with class inclusion problems—making comparisons between a whole class of objects and subsets within the class. Recall the class inclusion problem discussed in Chapter 7, in which children were asked to compare the whole class "dogs" with the subclass "brown dogs." Unlike his preoperational 4-year-old sister Tammy, 8-year-old Jonathan understands that the category "dogs" is more inclusive than the subset based on the dogs' color.

Older children's ability to consider several dimensions at once is illustrated by their solutions to multiple classification problems. Children are shown an array of objects that differ in two or more ways and are asked to select the missing object that best fits the array. To accurately answer the question, children must consider the two dimensions of the objects simultaneously. In Figure 9.2, for example, the objects in a matrix differ in shape and color. After examining the objects and their layout, children are asked to place an object in the blank space. A child who has mastered multiple classification will choose a blue triangle as the solution.

In a classic study comparing classification strategies of preschoolers and older children, Inhelder and Piaget (1964) found that most preschoolers used only one dimension in selecting the missing object; that is, they might select any blue shape or a triangle of any color. In contrast, older children tended to select the object that satisfied both criteria.

CHILDREN'S UNDERSTANDING OF SERIATION

Older children understand the logic of serial position. When 4-year-old Tammy is shown a group of sticks that vary in length and asked to arrange them in order from the longest to the shortest, she is likely to arrange them slowly in a discontinuous way, usually by comparing pairs of sticks (see Figure 9.3).

Preoperational children like Tammy do not understand the comparative length of a number of objects and are likely to be distracted by other dimensions, such as visual alignment. As a result, they cannot accurately place all the sticks in sequence by height. But concrete operational children like 8-year-old Jonathan can control for apparent height by aligning the bases of the sticks and focusing on their actual length.

CULTURE AS A CONTEXT FOR CHILDREN'S LEARNING

Culture and community influence children's cognitive development in a number of ways (see Chapter 7). Children are exposed to scripts of daily activities and events valued in their culture, and they have opportunities to practice and learn how to carry out activities valued by their community. To what extent do cultural variations influence children's performance on cognitive tasks?

Children from nonindustrial cultures often fall behind children from industrialized cultures in their abilities to conserve, to take others' perspectives, and to understand causal relationships (Segall, Dansen, Berry, & Poortinga, 1990). Based on these findings, some researchers wondered whether concrete operational thinking may be characteristic only of children in industrialized countries.

To understand why children from nonindustrialized cultures perform differently on these cognitive tasks, two issues need to be considered. The first has to do with communication. Not surprisingly, children who are interviewed in their native language show better performance than children interviewed in a language they use but do not know as well (Nyiti, 1982).

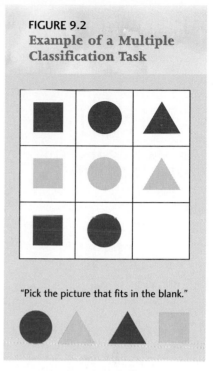

FIGURE 9.2
Example of a Multiple Classification Task

"Pick the picture that fits in the blank."

SOURCE: Inhelder and Piaget, 1964.
In this task, children are asked to classify objects on two dimensions. Why might young children classify objects in this task differently than older children? What stage of cognitive development does mastery of the task indicate? Consider how mastery of the multiple classification task may relate to concept development and the understanding of categories.

FIGURE 9.3

Example of a Seriation Task

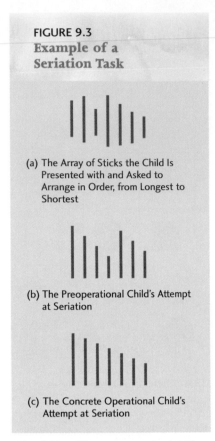

(a) The Array of Sticks the Child Is Presented with and Asked to Arrange in Order, from Longest to Shortest

(b) The Preoperational Child's Attempt at Seriation

(c) The Concrete Operational Child's Attempt at Seriation

What skills enable concrete operational children to seriate correctly? How do those skills transfer to academic tasks in the school years?

Peruvian child vendors are business whizzes compared to most European children of the same age. What accounts for their better understanding of commerce and business practices?

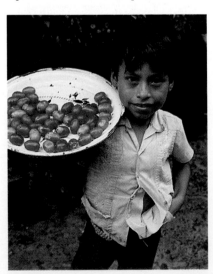

The second issue has to do with experience. Children's cognitive abilities relate to their culture and the types of experiences they have in their culture. If the ability does not match experience well, its development may be slower. If the cognitive ability matches well with experience, its development may be advanced. Children in nonindustrialized societies may display more advanced development than children in industrialized societies if the cognitive tasks selected tap into specialized experiences of their own culture. For instance, when 9- to 12-year-old children from Zimbabwe were evaluated on their understanding of profit, over three-quarters of the children understood the need to sell a product for more than one paid for it. In comparison, only about half of the same-age Scottish children understood the concept. This difference is likely due to the Zimbabwe children's greater experience in helping their families buy and sell things in the public market (Jahoda, 1983).

When children are tested in appropriate situations and when their own cultural "specialties" are assessed, the results support the notion that people in every culture reach concrete operational levels of understanding. The differing patterns that have been found are related to communication difficulties and to the types of tasks that are used to assess cognitive development.

HOW DO LANGUAGE AND LITERACY DEVELOP DURING THE SCHOOL YEARS?

By the time children enter school, they have mastered many of the basic building blocks of language. They have a large vocabulary, use many grammatical rules in their speech, adjust their speech to fit their listeners, and understand how to communicate many of their needs to others. During the school years, children's language skills continue to develop, but the changes are more subtle than those that occurred during the preschool years. Compared to the preschool child, the school-aged child is able to communicate more effectively over a broader range of contexts, use and understand more complex grammatical forms, and think about better ways to communicate using language. Additionally, a dramatic advance occurs during these years—children learn to read.

DEVELOPMENT OF SYNTAX

During the school years, children's understanding and use of grammar expand to include more complex forms of sentences, such as passive sentences. If preschool children overhear, "Big Bird was followed by the children," they are likely to picture in their mind Big Bird following behind children, rather than the accurate scenario. Preschool children often are confused by a passive sentence, probably because young children rely heavily on word order and interpret the sentence as being in the active voice. That is, they expect the object of the action to follow the verb in a sentence. By the age of 5, children understand passive sentences with action verbs ("was bitten"), but only during the school years do they come to understand passive sentences with non-action-oriented verbs ("was followed by"). Children's understanding of passive sentences continues to develop through the school years, but the full range of understanding is not usually acquired until adolescence (Bloom, 1998).

Some children learn to understand passive sentences earlier. Children who speak Sesotho (an African dialect) understand passive sentences by age 3. Compared to English-speakers, Sesotho-speakers use passive constructions for sentences much more frequently. For instance, there is no way to ask a question except in a passive form. Instead of asking, "Who asked you?" a Sesotho child must say, "Whom were you asked by?" (de Villiers & de Villiers, 1992). This cultural difference suggests that children learn more quickly those forms of language to which they are exposed (Demuth, 1990).

Are There Cultural Differences in Children's Reasoning?

Do children all around the world reason in the same way? Attempts to answer this question have sent researchers to many different countries to ask children about how they think and solve problems. One of Piaget's students, Pierre Dasen (1994), conducted a study of Australian Aboriginal children. The Aborigines were the first inhabitants of Australia. Today, many Aborigines still live in harsh environments, covering a very large territory as they move from place to place in search of water and food. Because they are continually on the move, they own few objects. They have an active and complex spiritual life, which includes elaborate rituals, myths, and symbolic art forms. For instance, they draw and paint map-like scenes that they call "dreamtime stories," containing symbols for important physical features in the environment and for movements between locations. These scenes bear no obvious resemblance to landscape scenes drawn by European artists.

Given the many differences between Aboriginal life and the lives of most European children, Dasen set out to determine whether there were differences in the ways they reason about the world. For the study, Dasen tested Aboriginal children from 8 to 14 years of age who had been in school. Several of Piaget's tasks were used. The tasks assessed conservation skills, spatial understanding, and the ability to view a scene from another person's perspective. In one spatial task, the child was shown a landscape scene with an animal in it. The child then had to find where the animal would be in a second scene, which was the original scene is shifted 180 degrees. The second spatial task involved a bottle half filled with water, which was tilted (with the water level hidden behind a screen). The child had to match the water level to a series of pictures.

For European children, the ability to understand the liquid conservation task appeared around the age of 6 or 7. Aboriginal children showed the same changes as the European children in moving from preoperational thinking to concrete operational thinking, but the shift to understanding liquid conservation did not occur until they were between 10 and 13 years of age. Even some Aboriginal adolescents and adults failed the liquid conservation task. Similar results were found for the other conservation tasks.

Although the Aboriginal children were "behind" European children in their level of understanding of conservation, their understanding of the spatial task was quite advanced. Aboriginal children moved through the stages of understanding of this task more quickly than European children did.

To try to understand these results, Dasen considered the different cultures of the two groups of children. In European countries, quantification of amounts is important. Children may learn these skills more quickly because they are of value in the culture. Children in European countries count many things, and they begin doing so when they are young. In contrast, Aboriginal culture places less value on quantification. Counting things beyond five is unusual. Because of this difference in the cultural emphasis on quantification, it is not surprising that European children can solve conservation problems earlier than Aboriginal children can.

The differences in spatial tasks also may be due to cultural variations in lifestyles. European children tend to be more sedentary and certainly are not nomadic like the Aboriginal children. Aboriginal children travel through difficult landscapes, often separately, and meet up again at the end of the day. Finding water is crucial for survival. Without good spatial skills, they would be unable to roam as freely in search of food or to find water as easily. Their spatial abilities are also fostered and reinforced by their "dreamtime stories," in which they attach meaning to physical features of the landscape.

Thinking It Through:

1. How did Dasen's study reveal the impact of culture on children's development of cognitive skills?

2. Why do European children learn conservation of quantities at an earlier age than Australian Aboriginal children do? Why is the reverse true for spatial skills?

3. How do you think Aboriginal and European children would compare on other tests of reasoning?

Young children use a variety of strategies for understanding spoken language. One example is the **minimal distance principle (MDP),** in which children assume that the noun most closely preceding the verb is the subject of the sentence. For instance, using the MDP, children would correctly interpret the sentence "Aladdin told Jasmine to eat the

minimal distance principle (MDP)
the assumption that the noun most closely preceding the verb is the subject of the sentence

Is this how a 6-year-old would understand the sentence "Big Bird was followed by the children"? Why would a young child make this mistake while an older child would not?

bread" to mean that Jasmine will be the person eating the bread. However, some verbs are exceptions to the rule, and when children use the MDP to help them understand a sentence with such a verb, they incorrectly interpret it. For example, if the MDP is applied to the sentence "Jasmine promised Aladdin to feed the dog," it will be misinterpreted to mean that Aladdin will feed the dog—when, in fact, the intended meaning is that Jasmine will feed the dog. It isn't until around 8 or 9 years of age that most children learn that *promise* sentences are exceptions to the MDP.

DEVELOPMENT OF SEMANTICS

Children's understanding of word meanings continues to develop during the school years (Hoff-Ginsberg, 1997). They add new words to their vocabulary, and their understanding of these new words often is acquired by listening to the context in which the words are used. By the time they enter first grade, children know about 10,000 words, and by fifth grade, they know about 40,000 words. Between first and third grade, children learn approximately eight to ten new words a day (Anglin, 1993).

Not all children learn that many words a day or have 40,000 words in their vocabulary by fifth grade. The variation among children is great, and the differences become larger with age. The variation is likely due in part to the relationship between reading and vocabulary size. Children who like to read when they are young develop larger vocabularies than other children (Nagy, Anderson, & Herman, 1987), and then, because these children continue to read more than other children, they continue to learn more words (Robbins & Ehri, 1994).

School-age children become increasingly sophisticated in their ability to understand subtle aspects of meaning, such as the double meanings some words carry. Terms such as *cold*, *bright*, and *sweet* have a physical meaning ("The pie is *sweet*") and also a psychological meaning ("She is a *sweet* person"). Not until children are 7 or 8 years old do they use these terms to refer to people, and complete mastery of these terms may not be achieved until a child reaches 12 years of age (Bloom, 1998).

Children also learn to understand the meanings expressed by idioms, which cannot be interpreted literally. If 4-year-old Tara heard her mother say "It's raining cats and dogs," she might run to the door and look to the sky to witness this amazing sight of dogs and cats falling from the sky. Or, overhearing her father say, in a conversation about someone at work, "She hit the ceiling," Tara might imagine a woman pounding her fist on the ceiling. These and other English idioms are difficult for young children—and people learning English as a second language—to understand. Children misinterpret these sentences because they interpret them literally. For instance, when a third-grade child participating in a study of word meanings was asked the meaning of *moneybags*, the child said, "It means that money goes into bags, and they have like dollar signs on them, and usually people bring moneybags to rob banks and stuff . . . " (Anglin, 1993, p. 110). To understand idioms, children must ignore the literal meaning of the words and instead rely solely on the context to infer the meaning of the phrase. They gradually develop an understanding of idioms, but full understanding does not occur until adolescence.

DEVELOPMENT OF PRAGMATICS

The basic knowledge that children acquired as preschoolers about the pragmatics of language is refined and expanded during the school years. Children become more skilled in these aspects of communication because they come to recognize more of the unwritten "rules" of conversations (Holzman, 1996).

During the school years, two changes in children's understanding of the pragmatics of language are particularly noteworthy. The first change is the school-aged child's increased ability to maintain a conversation (Bloom, 1998). Older children will continue to converse on one topic longer than young children will. Also, unlike preschoolers, who maintain the flow of a topic by repeating information, older children introduce new and relevant information into a conversation to maintain the topic.

The second change is school-aged children's growing ability to be sensitive and "repair" conversations when listeners do not understand what they are saying. Although preschool children have some ability to clarify messages to help listeners understand, they do not deal well with repeated requests to clarify messages. Older children, on the other hand, continue to add information to make their message clear to the listener. By 9 years of age, children also provide definitions or background information as cues to help listeners understand their statements (Ninio & Snow, 1996).

CHILDREN'S LITERACY

One of the most dramatic changes that occurs in many cultures during the school years is that children learn to read and write. Unlike speech, which is universal and is quickly and easily acquired by most children all over the world, reading and writing are not common to all cultures and usually require extensive training before they are learned (Liberman, 1996). Both reading and writing require that children develop many complex skills involving attention, perception, memory, and background knowledge.

Cracking the Code: Learning to Read

Reading depends on a complex set of skills that children learn gradually as they grow older (Adams, Treiman, & Pressley, 1998). These skills help children to crack the code of written words and their meanings.

Children move through phases in learning to read (Chall, Jacobs, & Baldwin, 1990). The first phase occurs during the preschool years. During this time, children master many of the skills required for reading, such as learning the letters of the alphabet, recognizing some words, and writing their names. The second phase starts when children are 7 to 8 years old, when they begin to read fluently. At this point, reading does not require as much effort as it did earlier. In the third phase, which arises between ages 9 and 13, children are able to use reading to obtain information. Reading becomes automatic enough so that they have the cognitive capacity to give more attention to the content of their reading. Instead of learning to read, children are now reading to learn (Heiberg & Raphael, 1996).

What skills do children need to learn to become successful readers? One important skill that children need to understand is that the written words they *see* are related to the language they *hear*. Just because a caregiver holds a book while conveying a story to a child does not mean the child understands that the book has in it the words to tell the story. Caregivers can help children understand this connection by showing children that they are reading words from the book and that the words provide the story to be told (Foorman, Francis, Fletcher, Schatschneider, & Mehta, 1998).

Some of the skills involved in reading come easily to children. English-speaking children readily acquire the following specific prerequisite knowledge about reading:

+ Words are read from left to right across the page.
+ Words continue from the extreme right of one line to the extreme left of the next line down.
+ Spaces between chunks of letters indicate words.

Other skills do not come so easily. Many children, for instance, have difficulty discriminating letters. To discriminate letters, children must be able to recognize the unique form of each letter and its orientation on the page. Mastering the orientation of letters

How will this activity help the child develop an awareness of phonemes? Why is phonemic awareness a prerequisite for learning to read? What other activities contribute to children's reading readiness?

can be quite taxing for young children because few things in their world depend on orientation to define them. A child looks around and sees a cat; a cat is a cat, regardless of its position—lying down, sitting, or standing facing to the right or the left. The same cannot be said about letters. A *b* is not a *b* when it faces in the other direction; it becomes a *d*. Children's lack of attention to orientation can be seen in their earliest attempts at "writing" where the letters they draw are scattered on the page, slanted, and even placed on their sides. It is not surprising, then, that over 50 percent of 5- and 6-year-old children reverse letters and numbers. Only about 10 percent of 7-year-olds do so (Kaufman, 1980). Even after they learn letters, many children confuse those that differ only in orientation, such as *b* and *d* (Adams et al., 1998).

Another challenge for children is mastering phonemic awareness (see Chapter 5). To read a word, children must recognize the sounds associated with the letters and be able to blend these sounds together to form a word (James, 1990). The ability to recognize the correspondence between sounds and letters relates to reading achievement in the early grades (Bruck, 1992). Preschool children are not very aware of these correspondences but school-age children become more skilled at recognizing them.

How can children's awareness of phonemes be improved? Exposure to nursery rhymes or other rhyming activities promotes phonemic awareness, as children hear the subtle variations in the sounds of similar words. Rhyming games also increase children's general awareness that words consist of various sounds (McBride-Chang, 1995). Phoneme deletion exercises, such as asking a child to say *cat* without the *c* sound, can also improve children's understanding of phonemes. Training preschool and kindergarten children in phonemic awareness leads to improved reading skills up to four years later (Byrne & Fielding-Barnsely, 1995).

Children's Reading Readiness

Pushing children to read before they are ready may cause them to become discouraged. Instead, caregivers should be on the lookout for general cues that their children are ready to read. Following are some of the cues that indicate readiness to read (National Association for the Education of Young Children [NAEYC], 1998):

◆ Attempting to tell stories while scanning and turning pages in a ▢k
◆ Understanding that stories start at the front of the book and move to the back in order, page by page
◆ Recognizing written labels or signs
◆ Pointing out individual letters
◆ Showing interest in seeing his or her name in print

Once children have shown that they are ready to read, caregivers can arrange many activities to encourage reading (see In Everyday Life). The complex skills involved in reading are best practiced and learned in the social context of interactions with caregivers, peers, and siblings. Competence in reading is fostered by practice and experience in all language domains. Reading to children certainly encourages reading skills, but so do other language-related activities such as carrying on conversations with them.

Controversies About Teaching Children to Read

Reading has been taught in many different ways, but controversy today surrounds the relative merits of two methods (Freppon & Dahl, 1998). In the **phonics approach,** children are trained to translate letters and groups of letters into sounds. For instance, children practice sounding out words that they cannot initially pronounce. Only simple and basic materials are used to study individual words. In the **whole language approach,** learning to read is assumed to be a natural process that occurs most

phonics approach technique used to teach children to read, in which children are trained to translate letters and groups of letters into sounds

whole language approach technique used to teach children to read, in which learning to read is assumed to be a natural process that occurs most effectively in a print-rich environment

Helping Children Learn to Read and Write

Caregivers can provide children with many opportunities to learn to use written and spoken language. Below are some recommendations for activities that caregivers can use to help their children become successful readers and writers (Itzkoff, 1996; NAEYC, 1998):

- Read to children regularly. Ideally, caregivers should read to their children every day. Bedtime stories are only one means of providing a recurring opportunity to share the reading experience with them.
- Provide reading and writing materials in the home. In addition to making books, paper, and pencils readily accessible, caregivers need to establish reading and writing traditions, such as writing thank-you notes for presents, giving books for special occasions, and making routine visits to the library.
- Provide display areas for writing and drawings. Caregivers encourage their children's attempts to write and draw when they proudly display the children's work, even on the refrigerator door.
- Provide good role models for reading and writing. Children need to observe caregivers involved in reading and writing activities so that they realize the importance of these skills.
- Work with children during reading times. For instance, a caregiver and child might read out loud together. If the child makes a mistake, the caregiver can repeat the difficult word and encourage the child to repeat it as well. This kind of paired reading has been shown to be very successful in improving children's reading skills.
- Provide regular times for reading and writing. Caregivers can provide children with routine opportunities to experience books and writing. The television should be turned off and other distractions minimized.
- Work in partnership with children's teachers. Caregivers can facilitate children's learning about reading and writing by becoming a part of the schooling process. Caregivers can check over their child's homework, make sure that assignments are carried out, and maintain communication with the child's teacher.

effectively in a print-rich environment. Children become readers by guessing the meanings of words based on each word's context within the passage and their prior knowledge (Smith, 1992). Associated with this approach is the idea of **emergent literacy,** which assumes that children naturally develop the skills involved in written and oral language over the years and gradually improve these skills as they grow older (Teale & Sulzby, 1985). Although many educators have adopted the whole language approach, research provides little support that this method facilitates children's reading (Vellutino, 1992).

Rather than focusing on one approach to the exclusion of the other, some researchers argue that the best method is to incorporate aspects of both approaches (Pressley, 1998). For instance, the developmental approach to reading proposed by Spear-Swerling and Sternberg (1994) allows for changes in the method as children grow older and as their reading competencies change. In the earliest phase, children use visual cues to learn words. In the next phase, they make limited use of phonetic features of words. In the final phase, which begins around 6 or 7 years of age and continues through adulthood, children achieve automatic word recognition. At this point, the most important skills to stress are those involving comprehension of the material (Adams et al., 1998).

The whole language and phonics approaches appear to help different kinds of children. The whole language approach particularly benefits children with low initial reading scores, whereas those with high initial reading scores benefit more from a phonics approach (Sacks & Mergendoller, 1997).

emergent literacy educational approach in which it is assumed that children will naturally develop the skills involved in written and oral language and gradually improve these skills as they grow older

WHAT CHARACTERISTICS DEFINE CHILDREN'S INTELLIGENCE AND CREATIVITY?

A pair of twins is given a date in the future—say, August 17, 3040. Almost instantly, they announce the day of the week on which the date falls. Or, give them a thirty-digit number to remember and they can report it back as accurately as if it had only three digits (Sacks, 1970). In another case, a young boy sets up a laboratory in his basement in which he invents burglar alarms and fixes radios. As an adult, he deciphers a Mayan Indian code and solves physics problems (Feynman, 1985). These people seem to be extraordinarily gifted, and we might assume they have high levels of intelligence. But, to what extent do these capabilities actually relate to intelligence? In the cases just discussed, not very well: although the young inventor, Richard Feynman, grew up to win the Nobel prize in physics, the twins had low IQ scores (around 60) and were institutionalized.

If you ask people on the street what makes someone intelligent, they are likely to suggest that there are three facets to intelligence: practical problem-solving abilities (reasoning logically), verbal abilities (reading comprehension, being a good conversationalist), and social abilities (being sensitive to social cues). Many scientists, but not all, agree that there are several different types of intelligence.

MEASURING INTELLIGENCE

Few children graduate from high school without having taken at least one intelligence test. Intelligence tests were first developed at the beginning of the twentieth century by Alfred Binet and Theodore Simon. These tests were designed for pragmatic reasons, especially to differentiate between those children who would benefit from standard schooling and those who might need special types of instruction.

Today, many types of intelligence tests exist, but the most popular individual test for school children is the Wechsler Intelligence Scale for Children—III, or WISC-III (Sattler, 1992). The WISC has two major components (see Table 9.1). The first component is verbal intelligence, which is measured by assessing general world knowledge ("How many pennies make a dime?"), vocabulary, comprehension of written passages, digit span memory (how many numbers the child can remember), and arithmetic. The second component is performance intelligence. To assess performance intelligence, many different tasks are used, including finding what is missing in a picture, arranging pictures in order so that they tell a sensible story, arranging blocks to reproduce a particular design, and unscrambling pieces of objects. The child receives scores on the two major components. The WISC also provides a profile of skills that the child possesses.

Intelligence quotient (IQ) was originally used to express the relationship between the number of items passed and the child's age. The method used today compares a child to other children of the same age. This method assumes that intelligence is normally distributed across the population (see Figure 9.4), with most people falling in average ranges and fewer people falling in the upper and lower ends of the scale. Children who score 100 have an IQ equal to or greater than that of 50 percent of children of the same age. Children with a score of 70 have an IQ equal to or greater than that of about 2 percent of children of the same age (Bjorklund, 1995).

UNDERSTANDING THE LIMITS OF IQ SCORES

For many children, especially highly verbal children, IQ scores predict school achievement and success (Sattler, 1992). IQ tests also accurately identify children who need special help in school and those who are especially bright. Despite these encouraging results, the usefulness of IQ tests has been questioned. For example, IQ scores do

TABLE 9.1

Sample of Subtests from the Wechsler Intelligence Scale for Children—III

SUBTEST	TYPE OF TASK
Verbal Subtests	
Information	Children are asked general information questions, such as "What is steam made of?"
Vocabulary	Children are asked to define words.
Comprehension	Children are asked questions to assess their general understanding and common sense. For example, a child might be asked, "What is the advantage of keeping money in a bank?
Similarities	Children are asked to think abstractly to describe how two objects are similar. For example, a child might be asked, "In what way are an hour and a week alike?"
Performance Subtests	
Picture Arrangement	Children are asked to order pictures in a logical manner to tell a meaningful story.
Picture Completion	Children are asked to find what is missing in pictures, which requires that they organize and analyze information visually.
Block Design	Children are asked to arrange blocks to match pictures, which requires spatial skills and visual-motor coordination.

SOURCE: Wechsler, 1991.

not predict life outcomes for many individuals. People who score high on IQ tests tend to complete more years of school and have more prestigious occupations (Morris & Levinson, 1995), but within normal ranges, IQ does not relate to success in a career (Mc-Clelland, 1993). Career success is due to many factors such as motivation and social skills (Sternberg & Wagner, 1993).

Because IQ scores do not always predict life success, IQ testing has come under scrutiny in federal courts and several state legislatures. Furthermore, IQ tests may not be used similarly for all children. In California, for example, because disproportionate numbers of African American children were placed in special education classes on the basis of IQ scores, the court has banned the use of these scores for student placement. The irony here is that tests designed to help decide a child's placement are now banned from the use for which they were designed (Weinberg, 1989).

The reasons IQ tests are questioned are many, but one of the most common reasons is that they are culturally biased—that is, they test material that is more important or familiar to people from one culture than people from another (Ogbu, 1994). For many years, researchers have attempted to develop culture-free tests in which general abilities are assessed rather than the knowledge that has been acquired through one's specific culture. One example is the Raven Progressive Matrices Test, which presents material in pictorial form. Although this test eliminates many of the problems of culture-bound tests, such as heavy reliance on language skills, it still relies on some culturally relevant material. For instance, it requires children to recognize that three-dimensional objects can be represented in two dimensions, which is not a typical skill for children in nonliterate societies (Deregowski, 1980). Another alternative has been to try to devise tests that are culture-fair—that

FIGURE 9.4
Distribution of IQ Scores

Intelligence is assumed to be normally distributed in the population. Explain what this means. What percentage of children have an IQ greater than 130?

is, they assess aspects of functioning that are common to all cultures. These tests, however, still favor the skills of some cultures over the skills of other cultures (Anastasi, 1988).

Today, many educators and researchers believe that the assumptions underlying IQ tests are flawed and that the best approach is to use an IQ test as only one part of a comprehensive assessment of an individual's functioning (Howe, 1997). Instead of using an IQ test as the sole indicator of a child's abilities, an educator should carry out a full assessment of each child, taking into consideration her or his everyday behavior outside of school, opportunities for schooling, and classroom performance (Weinberg, 1989). In fact, some scientists suggest that a better indicator of children's developmental status is social or emotional IQ (Salovey & Sluyter, 1997).

IDENTIFYING THE COMPONENTS OF INTELLIGENCE

When Steven was growing up, I didn't know he was a genius. Frankly, I didn't know what the hell he was. I'm really ashamed, but I didn't recognize the symptoms of talent. For one thing—and he'll probably take away my charge accounts for saying this—Steven was never a good student. Once, his teacher told me he was "special"—and I wondered how she meant it.

—LEAH ADLER (MOTHER OF STEVEN SPIELBERG, WHO
HAS MADE SOME OF THE MOST FAMOUS MOVIES OF
ALL TIME—ET, JAWS, RAIDERS OF THE LOST ARK, AMIS-
TAD, SCHINDLER'S LIST, AND SAVING PRIVATE RYAN)

Whether an individual succeeds in life may depend on aspects of functioning that are not captured in the typical IQ test. For that reason, several theorists have proposed that people differ in various components of intelligence. For instance, in his *triarchic theory of intelligence*, Robert Sternberg (1985) proposes that people differ in three components that relate to how they process information:

♦ **Performance.**   This component involves encoding and interpreting information and retrieving information from memory. Consider the following problem: Cake is to ice cream as eggs are to (a) bacon or (b) pie. Solving this analogy first requires encoding the words and their meanings. Next, the relation between cake and ice cream has to be inferred (often eaten together). Then, the relation between cake and eggs has to be determined (both foods) and then related to the choices. For this analogy, the reasoning might be that eggs and bacon are often eaten together just as cake and ice cream are.

♦ **Knowledge-acquisition.**   This component involves strategies for gaining and acting on information. Successful problem solving requires that relevant information be distinguished from irrelevant information. Consider the following problem: A person spends $20 buying 5 grocery items. The oranges cost $.50 each, and each box of cereal costs $4.00. How much did the person pay for 3 oranges? To solve this problem most effectively, children should attend only to the price of the oranges and ignore the irrelevant information about the numbers of items on the shopping list and the cost of cereal. Gifted children tend to be more selective in attending to information than nongifted children (Davidson & Sternberg, 1984).

♦ **Metacomponents.**   Metacomponents are abilities that allow for monitoring of task performance and constructing of strategies to solve problems. Metacomponents permit the transfer of information from one context to another. Older children, children with higher IQs, and children with greater expertise are better able to apply information from one situation to another (Siegler, 1998).

Intelligence involves all of these components working together to help solve problems. Research has demonstrated that individuals differ in these three components and that the triarchic theory provides a useful way to think about changes in intelligence as children grow older.

TABLE 9.2

Gardner's Seven Frames of Mind: Examples of Abilities and People Who Exemplify Them

FRAME OF MIND	ABILITIES	PEOPLE
Linguistic	Good conversationalist; has learned several languages; writes well	T. S. Eliot
Logical-Mathematical	Able to solve logical and mathematical problems; analytical	Marie Curie, Albert Einstein
Musical	Plays several instruments; understands music theory; composes music	Wolfgang Mozart, John Lennon
Spatial	Good at visualizing, solving visual problems, and negotiating directions; artistic	Pierre Renoir
Bodily-Kinesthetic	Good athlete or dancer; has good motor skills	Jackie Joyner-Kersey, Alvin Ailey
Interpersonal	Socially competent; understands others' feelings	Sigmund Freud
Intrapersonal	Knows himself or herself	Mahatma Gandhi

SOURCE: Adapted from H. Gardner, 1983.

In contrast to Sternberg's focus on processing strategies, Gardner (1983) emphasizes *multiple intelligences*—that is, intellectual domains in which individuals may have different strengths. As you can see in Table 9.2, Gardner proposed seven "frames of mind," or distinct areas of skill that are relatively independent of one another. In any of these, a person can display talent or genius. Only three of these frames of mind are assessed in standard IQ tests (Simonton, 1994). The frames-of-mind approach is useful for thinking about intelligence across cultures and throughout time. In some cultures, it may be adaptive to have good spatial skills so that one can be a successful hunter. In most western cultures, linguistic and logical-mathematical skills are especially valued.

The seven frames of mind were identified from research on brain-damaged individuals and from studies of exceptional children. Individuals who have particular forms of brain damage due to strokes or injury will exhibit normal skills in some areas but have extremely limited skills in other areas. For instance, a person with damage to the frontal lobes of the neocortex may have very limited interpersonal skills but intact logical-mathematical functioning. Similarly, some children—like the twins who could associate days with dates—are known as **savants** because they show exceptional abilities in one domain of intelligence but are incompetent in some other domains. One popular example of a savant is the autistic man played by Dustin Hoffman in the movie *Rainman*. He could memorize the cards perfectly during a game of blackjack but could not carry on a conversation with his brother. Children called **prodigies** show exceptional abilities at a very young age in one domain but not necessarily in others. Wolfgang Amadeus Mozart was a musical prodigy who composed keyboard pieces at age 5, published a composition by age 7, and wrote symphonies and operas by age 15. Otherwise, he was a typical, playful child and teenager (Simonton, 1994).

CREATIVITY IN CHILDREN

Four-year-old Christene and her mother were waiting for their dinner at a restaurant. Using the pad and pen they brought along, Christene drew a puzzle for her mother to solve. After her mother tried but could not solve the puzzle, Christene explained, "The answer to the puzzle is me! These lines stand for my wavy hair, the numbers show that I'm four going on five, and the rest doesn't stand for anything at all!"

—T. M. AMABILE (1993, p. 18)

Creativity is novel and appropriate behavior, different from what the person has done before or seen before (Amabile, 1992). According to this definition, Christene's actions

savants people who show exceptional abilities in one domain of intelligence but have retarded mental development in some other domains

prodigies children who show exceptional abilities at a very young age in one domain of intelligence but not necessarily in others

creativity novel and appropriate behavior that is different from what the person has done or seen before

FIGURE 9.5
Christene's Puzzle: Is It Creative?

SOURCE: T. M. Amabile, 1993.
"The answer to the puzzle is me! These lines stand for my wavy hair, the numbers show that I'm four going on five, and the rest doesn't stand for anything at all!" Do you think this puzzle depicts creativity? How might this puzzle fit the definition of creativity?

What skills does this child need to be creative? Are all children creative? How should creativity be defined?

would be considered creative, because the puzzle includes a novel and appropriate representation of herself (see Figure 9.5).

Because the creativity of a work of art or a solution to a problem is defined by the culture in which it occurs (Csikszentmihalyi, 1988), it is difficult to assess creativity. The most commonly used assessments, designed by E. P. Torrance (1966), involve verbal and graphic tests. In the verbal section, the student is asked to think of as many uses as possible for objects like a tin can or paperclip. In the graphic section, the student is presented with a page covered with thirty lines and asked to create different drawings from these lines. Responses are scored for three aspects: how many answers are given (which measures fluency), unusualness of answers (which assesses originality), and number of categories of responses (which assesses flexibility) (Sattler, 1992). Research shows that children who score well on these tests are more likely to have creative achievements later in life, although the relationship is not strong (Torrance, 1988).

Some researchers who have studied creativity think that anyone can be creative in the right situation (Hennessey & Amabile, 1988; Mellou, 1996). Four components appear to be needed for creativity:

✦ **Domain skills.** Creativity requires a solid background and ability in the particular domain of interest. For example, a scientist is unlikely to make a creative breakthrough in understanding cellular functioning without an extensive knowledge of biology.

✦ **Creative working style.** A creative working style is characterized by a dedication to working well, ability to concentrate, willingness to work hard, and persistence when roadblocks occur in thinking.

✦ **Creative thinking style.** Creative thinking includes "breaking set"—that is, being willing to drop old ways of thinking to try new ways. Creative thinking also involves perceiving things freshly, or taking a different perspective on the problem than most people would take (Russ, 1996).

✦ **Intrinsic motivation.** Creativity is facilitated when people are internally interested in and challenged by the problem (Hennessey & Amabile, 1988).

HOW DO OLDER CHILDREN UNDERSTAND THE SOCIAL WORLD?

Children use their cognitive skills to solve a wide array of problems, ranging from conservation tasks to arithmetic problems, but they also use cognitive skills to help them understand people and their actions. As children progress through later childhood, their knowledge about people and social situations becomes increasingly sophisticated. This increased understanding of the social world contributes to their more mature and responsible behavior and improved interactions with others.

SOCIAL PERSPECTIVE TAKING: COMMUNICATING WITH OTHERS

Imagine 3-year-old Shannon trying to communicate to 3-year-old Michael that he should pick a particular stuffed toy rabbit out of a group of toys. Shannon might say, "Pick up the one I like the most," not considering that Michael would not know which one was her favorite. To be able to effectively communicate with others, children (and adults) must be skilled in **social perspective taking**—the ability to move away from one's own perspective and recognize what others perceive.

In contrast to the preoperational child, concrete operational children are better able to view a wide variety of problems from another person's perspective. Concrete operational children are less egocentric because they have the ability to both consider their own view and recognize that others see things from different vantage points. Children's understanding of others' perspectives extends into many domains; they now can communicate effectively with others because they can better imagine what others are thinking and seeing.

Similar to how they think about themselves (see Chapter 8), preschool children tend to think about others by focusing on external characteristics and temporary situations. School-age children show a more sophisticated understanding of people (Hala, 1997; Yuille, 1997). Preschoolers tend to refer to other people in very concrete terms (focusing on age, appearance, and possessions), seldom using abstract characteristics to describe others (Miller & Aloise, 1989). Around the age of 8, children's thinking about others becomes more refined, and they are more likely to think about others in abstract and internal psychological terms. For instance, an 8-year-old child will describe her friend as shy rather than simply saying that she is a girl.

Because of their focus on external characteristics and behavior, preschoolers tend to think that people change frequently; they do not observe the stability in personality that older children notice. A 10-year-old child is likely to believe that a girl in his class who shared her lunch with another child would probably help someone who was hurt, inferring from this one behavior that the girl is helpful in many situations (Rholes & Ruble, 1984).

Just as preschoolers cannot easily view a scene from another person's perspective, they generally cannot view social events from any perspective but their own. By late childhood, children come to recognize that two different people involved in a social interaction may have differing views and attitudes about the event. They still, however, may not use both points of view to understand the event the way an adolescent or adult might (Flavell & Miller, 1998).

CHILDREN'S UNDERSTANDING OF OTHERS' BELIEFS AND FEELINGS

As you learned in Chapter 7, a key feature of developing social skills is coming to understand that others have thoughts, feelings, and beliefs of their own. By school age, children have learned to "read minds"—that is, they are aware of others' thoughts, beliefs, knowledge, desires, and intentions (Hala & Carpendale, 1997).

Imagine a situation in which 9-year-old Iris watches her friend Lisa walk into the room and then turn around and walk out of the room. Iris, like most older children, can consider the existence of mental events, so she might guess that Lisa was looking for something she thought was in the room or that Lisa heard a noise in the room and was looking for the source. In either case, Iris is considering mentalistic explanations for the actions that Lisa took. Mentalistic explanations are those that involve consideration of other people's mental states—their beliefs and thoughts. Not all children have the ability to consider mentalistic explanations. Some children, such as autistic children, are *mindblind*—they have no mentalistic explanations to help them understand others' actions. A mindblind person would have no explanation for Lisa's actions other than the suggestion that Lisa might carry out this action every day, and this explanation is likely to be proven wrong. Imagine how difficult it would be for a mindblind person to interpret other social events, especially a complex interaction involving several people. Most children, however, develop more sophisticated mentalistic concepts as they grow older and can readily understand that others experience feelings, emotions, and beliefs.

social perspective taking the ability to move away from one's own perspective and recognize what others perceive

CHILDREN'S UNDERSTANDING OF RACE AND PREJUDICE

The images that come to mind when we think of prejudice tend to be of adults or adolescents. For instance, we might visualize neo-Nazi groups or members of the Ku Klux Klan. When people encounter prejudicial or racist attitudes in children, they are quick to attribute them to children's imitation of adults rather than to the children's own personal preferences. This attribution, however, has been questioned by current research on race and prejudice, which indicates that the level of prejudice in children has not declined in the past fifty years as it has in adults (Aboud, 1988).

Prejudice refers to having preconceived ideas about a person or group of people, often having to do with physical characteristics, ethnicity, or race. Some people respond to their prejudices with **discrimination**—acting in an unfavorable manner toward people because of their affiliation with a group. Awareness of ethnic and racial groups is considered to be a prerequisite for some types of prejudice and discrimination (Carter & Rice, 1997). When do children consciously recognize ethnicity in individuals?

By 6 months of age, many infants can perceptually categorize people on the basis of physical appearance (Walsh, Katz, & Downey, 1991). Simply recognizing that some people look different does not indicate that a child understands ethnicity, however. But children show strong same-race peer preferences by 2 years of age, and these preferences become more clearly established in early grade school (Katz, 1992). By 4 years of age, children have considerable knowledge about racial stereotypes of African Americans and Caucasians (Levy & Katz, 1993). Although children distinguish between Caucasian and African American people by age 4, their recognition of other ethnic groups, such as Native Americans, Chinese Americans, or Mexican Americans, is delayed for a few years, probably because the distinctive physical features of members of these groups can be less obvious (Aboud, 1988).

Perception of differences among other ethnic groups arises between the ages of 6 and 8 years. At this time, children begin to use ethnicity to group people together and to understand and make guesses about what people are like. For instance, they assume that people of the same race are similar in many ways despite the fact that they have different facial features or different shades of color, and they assume that people of different races are different in many ways even when they have many features in common (Ramsey, 1987). By age 11, children have incorporated more flexibility into their beliefs. No longer do children always perceive people to be different because they are of different races; children often find similarities based on individual features such as emotional expressions or abilities.

Awareness that different ethnic groups exist plays a role in the development of prejudice, but ethnic awareness does not determine prejudice (Carter & Rice, 1997). Children may hold stereotypes about and be prejudiced against groups that they cannot identify. Also, most people are aware of stereotypes, yet not all people apply this knowledge or act in prejudicial ways.

The most widely held theory about the formation of prejudice is that children adopt their parents' prejudicial attitudes and behaviors. According to this theory, children learn prejudice from their parents either by direct instruction, as when a parent tells a child not to play with children of another race because they are not "good," or by observation of the parents' words or actions toward people of different races. The scientific evidence, however, suggests that children do not always adopt the prejudicial attitudes of their parents, and if they do, it is usually after 7 years of age (Branch & Newcombe, 1986). In addition, cases have been found in which children held prejudicial attitudes when their parents did not (Davey, 1983). For these reasons, it is unlikely that children's prejudice can be explained solely on the basis of learning from parents, other adults, or peers (Aboud & Doyle, 1996).

Theories of the development of prejudice also must account for the age-related changes observed in the development of children's prejudice (Black-Gutman & Hickson, 1996). There is an important shift in prejudice at about 7 years of age. After 7 years of age, Caucasian American children often show a decline in prejudice and minority children show a more widespread preference for their own group (Bigler & Liben, 1993).

prejudice preconceived ideas about a person or group of people, often based on physical characteristics, ethnicity, or race

discrimination acting in an unfavorable manner toward people because of their affiliation with a group

Reducing Prejudice in Children

What can be done to reduce prejudice in children? The answer to this question depends upon the age of the child. For children 4 to 7 years of age, the following suggestions may be helpful (Aboud, 1988; Katz, 1992):

- Help children develop perspective-taking skills. Prejudice at this age is based on the egocentric belief that there is only one way of experiencing the world.
- Help children develop a concern and compassion for others. Foster an ethic of caring rather than prejudice.

- Increase children's exposure to people of other races. Children's preferences for people of their own race and their negative attitudes toward people of other races will decrease. These effects generally are stronger for Caucasian American children than for minority children, although interracial exposure has been found to decrease African American children's lack of trust in and suspicion of Caucasians.

For children 7 to 12 years of age, a different set of principles should be followed to reduce prejudice:

- Encourage children to judge others on the basis of internal qualities rather than external attributes.
- Help children attend to similarities in different groups. Pointing out the ways that children are similar, even though they may look or act different, helps children identify qualities they can relate to and should reduce prejudice.
- Help children recognize that their perspective may differ from those of others and that two different perspectives can both be valid. Children's acceptance of ethnic differences will be enhanced.

A social-cognitive theory has been proposed to account for the development of prejudice. According to this theory, the ways in which children think about the social world around them are influenced by the level of cognitive development they have attained (Aboud, 1988). Early on, children's thinking is dominated by their emotions and preferences. Later, children begin to consider how similar or dissimilar other people are to themselves. Prejudice is related to the perceived degree of dissimilarity. People with different skin color, language, and/or clothing are noticeably different, and these perceptions dominate children's reactions. Finally, children begin to understand the difference between categories and individual qualities and learn to attend to more than one quality of a person at the same time (they realize that a person can have a different skin color but similar interests). Then, they can use categories as the basis for determining ethnicity and individual qualities as the basis for forming preferences.

Thus, as children acquire more advanced modes of thinking, their views of others become less extreme and polarized. They become aware of individuals' internal qualities, understand that ethnicity is permanent and unchangeable, and realize that ethnic differences are reconcilable. In other words, because of changes in cognitive development, older children's prejudice is reduced (Aboud, 1988; Black-Gutman & Hickson, 1996).

HOW DOES SCHOOLING INFLUENCE CHILDREN'S COGNITIVE DEVELOPMENT?

As children enter late childhood, schooling becomes a more and more important aspect of their intellectual (and social) life. Literally thousands of hours of a child's life are spent in the classroom. In addition to being influenced by what they do in the classroom, children are influenced by their schools' philosophies of education. Beliefs about the goals of education have varied; a strong emphasis on the basics in the early 1950s gave way to open classrooms, in which children explored and learned independently, in the 1960s. Although the debate over teaching the basics versus encouraging thinking skills continues, some broad patterns can be identified. Trends in education today include an emphasis on making the child an active participant in the learning process and using child-relevant situations to teach thinking skills.

Opportunities for Active Learning

Some teachers today, trained in the cognitive developmental theories of Piaget and Vygotsky, have adopted **constructivist theories of learning,** in which students are encouraged to actively participate in their own education. These teachers think of themselves as mentors for their students, encouraging them to discover and transform complex information for themselves (Steffe & Gale, 1995). Research shows that constructivist approaches have been used effectively for teaching many different topics, including science (Neale, Smith, & Johnson, 1990) and reading (Rosenshine & Meister, 1997). The variety of techniques teachers use to encourage students to become actively involved with the material include the following (Slavin, 1997):

+ In **cooperative learning,** students work together in groups to solve problems.
+ In **discovery learning,** students are encouraged to discover principles for themselves.
+ In **generative learning,** students are taught how to use specific methods of problem solving to integrate new information with pre-existing information.

Multicultural and Multilingual Education

Schools are facing new challenges as they try to provide optimal educational experiences for the increasingly diverse students who are entering schools today. Educating children from various backgrounds will become an even more central issue in the future.

What is the best way to balance the educational issues of minority cultures with those of the larger culture? Some people believe that a focus on diversity may cause divisions among groups at a national level, whereas others assert that an emphasis on minority cultures will strengthen the national culture. The practices of educators mirror these different beliefs. Educational practices in the schools range from emphasizing minority cultures to focusing on human relationship skills.

The many definitions of **multicultural education** reflect the lack of agreement about how best to deal with a diverse population of students. Some definitions describe multicultural education as a curriculum that includes non-European perspectives—for instance, discussions of Hispanic authors and their works in an English class. Other, broader definitions suggest that multicultural education refers to policies and practices that improve educational outcomes for students from a wide spectrum of ethnic, religious, gender, and disability backgrounds (Banks, 1995; Banks & Banks, 1993).

Some children have limited English proficiency (Hakuta & McLaughlin, 1996). By 2026, about 25 percent of children will come from families in which the primary language is not English (US Department of Education, 1998). What is the best way to help these children succeed in school? The issue of how to best educate students from diverse backgrounds with various language skills is especially a concern in the large US cities of Los Angeles, New York, Miami, and Atlanta. Consider, for instance, the quesiton of whether immigrant children should take their classes in English or in their native language (see At Issue).

Teachers' Bias in Achievement Expectations

Children differ from one another in many ways—in their sex, ethnicity, abilities, social class, and religion. Although in the ideal situation each child would receive equal attention and opportunities in school, this is not always the case.

constructivist theories of learning educational approach in which students are encouraged to actively participate in their education

cooperative learning educational approach in which students work together in groups to solve problems

discovery learning educational approach in which students are encouraged to discover principles for themselves

generative learning educational approach in which students are taught how to use specific methods of problem solving to integrate new information with pre-existing information

multicultural education educational practices and curricula that present non-European perspectives or improve educational outcomes for students from a wide spectrum of backgrounds

How Successful Is Bilingual Education?

Bilingual education consists of programs designed to teach English-language skills to children who have only limited proficiency in English. Educators agree about the need for bilingual education but do not agree on how to best accomplish it (Brisk, 1998). One group of educators recommends that children be given training in English at an early age, usually by removing them from the classroom for special instruction (Lampert, 1984). These children then spend the reminder of their school day in regular classrooms, learning math and science in their non-native language (English). The advantage of this approach is that children receive early exposure to English, but the disadvantage is that children spend hours a day in classes in which they have difficulty understanding the language being used.

Another group of educators advocates conducting children's primary education in their native language—teaching them to read, write, and communicate effectively in that language before introducing them to English (Willig, 1985). These educators believe that the skills children develop for thinking critically in their own language will easily translate into their new language (English). The advantage of this approach is that children do not fall behind in school, because they receive instruction in all topics in their native language. The disadvantage is that these children are separated from other children for their schooling.

Research has demonstrated that high-quality bilingual education programs are effective (Brisk, 1998) and enhance self-esteem in children (Wright & Taylor, 1995). Canadian studies suggest that bilingualism increases students' achievement in areas other than language (Bain & Yu, 1980). The type of program that is most beneficial to students remains unclear, however (Hakuta & McLaughlin, 1996). Some evidence suggests that children show good short-term gains from being trained early in English, but longer-term gains in academic ability seem to be promoted more by providing children with education in their native language (Willig, 1985). Furthermore, it is clear that it takes children five to seven years to become competent English speakers, but most programs involve only two to three years of training (Hakuta & McLaughlin, 1996).

A complicating factor in bilingual education is the many different native languages that are represented in some school districts. For instance, 58 percent of California's school-age children are non-native English speakers. The large majority of these children are Spanish speaking, but more than thirty-five other languages also are represented, including (in order of their occurrence) Vietnamese, Filipino, Cantonese, Korean, Cambodian, Hmong, Mandarin, Lao, Armenian, Japanese, and Farsi. There are not enough teachers available to teach this variety of languages in the California

school system. Only in school districts with a large concentration of students from one or two language backgrounds is it possible to develop high-quality bilingual educational programs.

Bilingual education recently has come under attack. Critics contend that children are damaged by bilingual education because of their inability to learn English well enough (Rothstein, 1998). In response to these attacks, California has passed a proposition that practically bans bilingual education in state schools. California will scrap bilingual programs and replace them with intensive one-year immersion courses (Cornwell, 1998). Whether or not other states follow California's lead depends in part on how much current bilingual programs are improved.

Thinking It Through:

1. What are the advantages and disadvantages to children of being educated in their native language? What difficulties do schools face in trying to accomplish this?
2. Do you think that, as the US population becomes more diverse, concerns about the effectiveness of bilingual education will increase?
3. Should all children in the United States learn to speak more than one language, as children in Europe do?

Children's classroom performance is influenced by the expectations teachers hold about their capabilities. Many studies have demonstrated that teachers have different expectations for and act differently toward students whom they believe to be high and low achievers. For example, children who are expected to be high achievers are given more

Do Teachers' Expectations Influence Children's School Performance?

In 1968, Robert Rosenthal and Leonard Jacobson published a book that had far-reaching implications for the understanding of how teachers' expectations could affect children's development. In *Pygmalion in the Classroom*, the two social psychologists examined how teachers' beliefs about children's abilities influence the ways they treat their students. The psychologists also were interested in showing that the expectations held by teachers have direct effects on children's behaviors. They referred to this phenomenon as the *self-fulfilling prophecy*, alluding to the idea that people act in accordance with what is expected of them.

Elementary school teachers in California were told that Rosenthal and Jacobson would test their students and select for them the 20 percent of the children who would "bloom," or "spurt," during the coming school year. The teachers were led to believe that these children would improve more than the rest of the children. In fact, however, the researchers selected the 20 percent entirely at random. There was no reason to believe that these children would perform any differently than any of the other children, unless the teachers' expectations brought this about.

Eight months after the teachers had been supplied with the information about the "bloomers," the children were tested again. Children identified as bloomers showed significantly greater increases in performance than did nonbloomers, and teachers believed that bloomers were better behaved and more mature than nonbloomers. These effects have been attributed to teachers' expectations: children who were expected by teachers to bloom were treated in ways that encouraged their development. The effect, however, was not consistent in every classroom; it did not occur for children in grades three through six.

Although the *Pygmalion in the Classroom* studies have been sharply criticized, later research supports the original findings. Teachers' expectations influence younger children's behavior more than older children's, especially if the teachers are unfamiliar with the children's actual performance (Raudenbush, 1984). The importance of teachers' actions also has been documented. When teachers act in ways that are counter to their expectations (such as when they focus a lot of attention on those they think will not be high achievers), their actions often have more influence than their expectations (Goldenberg, 1992). Of course, teachers' actions can be strongly influenced by the expectations they hold for students.

Thinking It Through:

1. What type of research design did Rosenthal and Jacobson use in their classic research on the Pygmalion effect?

2. How did they ensure that the effects were due to teachers' expectations and not to the qualities of the students?

3. Were you surprised by the results of the study? Why or why not? Do you think the same results would be found today?

4. What personal observations or experiences can you report about the effects of teachers' expectations on academic performance and achievement?

opportunities to participate in class and more time to respond. They also receive more praise for giving right answers and less criticism for giving wrong answers. Children who are not expected to perform well are given less opportunity to participate (Jussim, Madon, & Chatman, 1994; Kolb & Jussim, 1994).

Many teachers are not even aware of the preferential treatment they give to some children. This lack of awareness makes training in diversity and multicultural issues particularly important, to ensure that all children have equal opportunities for education. Unfortunately, few educators have become sensitized to the unequal treatment that children receive in the classroom (American Association of University Women [AAUW], 1994).

TABLE 9.3

The Numbers and Percentages of 6- to 21-Year-Olds with Disabilities, 1995

DISABILITY	NUMBER	PERCENTAGE OF ALL DISABLED CHILDREN AND ADOLESCENTS	PERCENT INCREASE IN INCIDENCE FROM 1990
Specific learning disabilities	2,513,977	51.1	17.3
Speech or language impairment	1,023,665	20.8	3.6
Mental retardation	570,855	11.6	3.5
Serious emotional disturbance	428,168	8.7	9.6
Multiple disabilities	89,646	1.8	−8.2
Hearing impairments	65,568	1.3	10.7
Orthopedic impairments	60,604	1.2	22.8
Other health impairments	106,509	2.2	89.0
Visual impairments	24,877	0.5	5.0
Autism*	22,780	0.5	321.0
Deaf-blindness	1,331	0.01	−12.7
Traumatic brain injury*	7,188	0.1	2834.0
All disabilities	4,915,168	100.0	12.7

*Data from 1990 were unavailable; data from 1991 were used instead.
SOURCE: US Department of Education, 1996.

HOW DO SCHOOLS ADDRESS STUDENTS' SPECIAL NEEDS?

About 10 percent of the children in the educational system have special needs due to physical disabilities, emotional disturbances, or mental retardation (see Table 9.3). Most children with special needs are between the ages of 6 and 11 (46.3 percent) or 12 and 17 (39.6 percent) (US Department of Education, 1996). Another 5 percent have special needs because they are gifted or particularly talented. The educational needs of children vary depending on their abilities.

Dramatic changes have occurred in the education of special needs children over the last twenty years. These changes are largely due to the passage of Public Law 94–142, the Education for All Handicapped Children Act of 1975, and its extension, the Individuals with Disabilities Education Acts of 1990 and 1994. These bills state that every disabled child is entitled to a public education appropriate to the child's needs, at public expense.

One feature of these bills that has had particular impact on educational practices is the mandate that children be educated in the least restrictive environment possible. Efforts to ensure that children spend as much time as possible in the "normal" academic environment have led to **mainstreaming**—including children with all sorts of disabilities in regular classrooms. For instance, a disabled student might spend most of the day in a special class but attend one or two regular classes. Most schools do not integrate severely disabled students into regular classrooms, although there is a debate about the advantages and disadvantages of full inclusion of these students in regular classes. The advantages of full inclusion are that it provides a less restrictive learning environment for disabled children

mainstreaming including children with all sorts of disabilities in regular classrooms

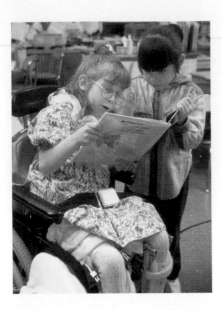

How does inclusion, or mainstreaming, in public school classrooms influence children's development? How do the issues of culture-fair and gender-fair education relate to the education of children with special needs?

and that it allows all children to have opportunities to interact and become friends with children of varied abilities (Marks, 1997). The disadvantages are that the special needs of the disabled child may not receive adequate attention in the general education classroom, that these children may become socially isolated, and that teachers may not be prepared to work with these students (Kelly, 1992; Keogh & MacMillan, 1996).

CHILDREN WITH PHYSICAL DISABILITIES

Education for the physically disabled child must be tailored to meet the specific needs of the child. Some children require spaces accessible to wheelchairs but need no other assistance. Other children, such as those with cerebral palsy, may need someone to guide their fingers over a computer keyboard so that they can communicate, because they have difficulties speaking.

Children who are blind or deaf also have specific educational requirements. Until the 1970s, most blind and deaf children were educated in residential centers, but today, most are educated in regular classrooms. Most commonly, blind children are provided with Braille reading materials. However, many blind children can read print if it is enlarged sufficiently, in which case they can be educated more flexibly in regular classrooms than when only Braille books can be used.

CHILDREN WITH ATTENTION-DEFICIT HYPERACTIVITY DISORDERS

Eight-year-old Reese lives in a fast-moving world where sounds, images, and thoughts are constantly changing. He is easily bored and has difficulty keeping his mind on the tasks he needs to complete. He often is unable to sit still, plan ahead, or finish a task he has started, and sometimes he does not seem fully aware of what is going on around him. He tends to overreact, sometimes fighting with others who accidentally bump into him, and this has gotten him into trouble several times. Reese often loses things, and he seems to be careless and sloppy in his work and play.

The world that Reese lives in is shared by many other children. Reese has been diagnosed as having **attention-deficit hyperactivity disorder (ADHD),** which is the most common mental disorder among children, affecting as many as 2 million American children. ADHD is marked by an inappropriately low level of attention and inappropriately high levels of impulsivity and activity. On the average, at least one child in every US classroom needs help for ADHD (Taylor, 1995). ADHD is diagnosed six times more often in boys than in girls (Arcia & Conners, 1998; Safer & Krager, 1994). Some children have attention deficit disorder without hyperactivity (ADD). These disorders can continue into adolescence and adulthood, causing a lifetime of frustration and pain.

In approximately half of the cases, onset of ADHD appears before age 4. During the preschool years, caregivers notice that the child is very active and energetic (Taylor, 1995). Caregivers' complaints about a child's hyperactivity at age 3 are predictive of later childhood problems (Biederman et al., 1998).

In late childhood, the demands of school make prolonged attention more important. Some children cope with the transition well and meet the demands of school, even if they are still highly active and uncontrolled at home (Taylor, 1995). Other children, like Reese, who are inattentive and highly active, are at risk for failing to learn and for developing poor peer relationships. Because ADHD children are likely to have problems in school, the disorder is frequently recognized when the child enters school.

As Reese's case shows, children with ADHD have difficulty staying on task and organizing and completing work. Written work is often sloppy and is characterized by impulsive, careless errors that are a result of not following directions or of guessing without considering all the alternatives. ADHD children frequently do not seem to be listening to adults' instructions. Group situations and those that require sustained attention are the most difficult for ADHD children (Jacobs, 1998).

attention-deficit hyperactivity disorder (ADHD) a disorder marked by an inappropriately low level of attention and inappropriately high levels of impulsivity and activity

Many children outgrow their hyperactivity after adolescence and escape later adjustment problems, but about one-third continue to show attention problems into adulthood (Klein & Mannuzza, 1991). Those who continue to have problems with ADHD are also likely to have an explosive or immature personality (Barkley, Fischer, Edelbrock, & Smallish, 1990; Hechtman & Weiss, 1986).

ADHD can be difficult to accurately diagnose. Even pediatricians who treat ADHD children find the diagnosis problematic (Kwasman, Tinsley, & Lepper, 1995). For ADHD to be diagnosed, a disturbance of at least six months' duration must occur prior to the age of 7 and at least eight of the following symptoms must be present (APA, 1994):

- often fidgets with hands or feet or squirms in seat
- has difficulty remaining seated when required to do so
- is easily distracted by extraneous stimuli
- has difficulty awaiting a turn in game or group situations
- often blurts out answers to questions before they have been completed
- has difficulty following through on instructions from others
- has difficulty sustaining attention in tasks or play activities
- often shifts from one uncompleted activity to another
- has difficulty playing quietly
- often talks excessively
- often interrupts or intrudes on others
- often does not seem to listen to what is being said to him or her
- often loses things necessary for tasks or activities at school or home (toys, books, assignments, etc.)
- often engages in physically dangerous activities without considering the possible consequences

The challenge for pediatricians is to distinguish these characteristics from normal, age-appropriate attentional and active behaviors.

Scientists believe that biological factors influence ADHD. For example, brain imaging studies show that parts of the frontal lobe of the brain function at lower levels in children with ADHD, which in turn decreases their ability to inhibit their behavior and focus their attention (Castellanos, 1997). As a result, ADHD children are less able to regulate their activity in response to the demands of the situation (Barkley, 1997).

Evidence from several studies suggests a genetically inherited component to ADHD (Hewett et al., 1997). Consistent with the pattern expected in genetic disorders, if one monozygotic twin has ADHD, the other is likely to be hyperactive too; the same is not true of dizygotic twins (Nadder, Silberg, Eaves, Maes, & Meyer, 1998). Children who have ADHD usually have at least one close relative who also has ADHD. At least one-third of all fathers who had ADHD as a child have children who have ADHD (Taylor, 1995).

Environmental factors involved in ADHD include poor maternal health during pregnancy, postmaturity (but not prematurity), long duration of labor, maternal use of alcohol and cigarettes, malnutrition during the first year of life, and chronic lead poisoning (Dulcan, 1989). These organic environmental factors affect the child's nervous system directly. Researchers also have identified various nonorganic environmental factors. For example, ADHD children are more common in families in which there is a considerable amount of hostility, either between parents or between parents and children (Lorys et al., 1993). ADHD is associated with overstimulating, anxious, and intrusive styles of mothering, as well as with single-parent families (Carlson, Jacobvitz, & Sroufe, 1995; Jacobvitz & Sroufe, 1987). Furthermore, ADHD children are more likely to come from families with low socioeconomic status (Pellegrini & Landers-Pott, 1996).

The most common way to treat many of the symptoms of ADHD is to use medications such as Ritalin. Although medications can be effective (Swanson, McBurnett, Wigal, & Pfiffner, 1993), their use with children remains controversial. Behavior management strategies, such as rewarding appropriate behavior and ignoring inappropriate behavior, can be effective, but they require the cooperation of parents and teachers (Dulcan, 1989).

Should ADHD Children Be Treated with Stimulants?

The most popular treatment for ADHD in children and adults has been medications in the class of drugs known as stimulants. Ritalin remains the treatment of choice, although other drugs (such as Aderall) have been developed that are easier to control and have fewer side effects (Pelham et al., 1999). Over 90 percent of pediatricians report using stimulants like Ritalin or Aderall to treat ADHD children, with over 55 percent recommending that children take the medication daily (Kwasman et al., 1995).

Parents naturally are concerned when their young children take such strong medication. Many children begin treatment with Ritalin very early in life (Bowen, Fenton, & Rappaport, 1991), and parents often complain about the side effects (Pelham et al., 1999): insomnia, headaches, decreased appetite, nervousness, and sadness (Kwasman et al., 1995). Critics argue that many children who do not have true ADHD are medicated with Ritalin as a way to control their disruptive or simply active behavior (Taylor, 1995). Given these concerns, it becomes particularly important to consider what the research evidence shows about the effectiveness and the drawbacks of treating ADHD children with medication.

When taking medication, ADHD children become less negative and more responsive to parents; they also are less disruptive and impulsive in the classroom and when interacting with peers (Pelham, Bender, Caddell, Booth, & Moorer, 1985). In turn, ADHD children's interactions with parents, teachers, and peers improve (Whalen & Henker, 1991; Whalen et al., 1989). Medication also helps school performance; the children show improved attentional, writing, and learning skills (Dulcan, 1986; Pelham, Milich, & Walker, 1986). Many studies indicate that there is a dosage effect: higher dosages of medication produce greater effects on social and academic behavior (Rapport, Stoner, DuPaul, Birmingham, & Tucker, 1985).

These drugs, when properly supervised, are generally considered to be safe. Although they can be addictive to adolescents and adults if misused, these medications are not addictive to children and do not lead to later addiction. In fact, by preventing the negative experiences ADHD children have with others in their environments, these drugs may actually help prevent later addictions (Taylor, 1995). These drugs do not make children "high," nor do they sedate children. Rather, they appear to help children control their hyperactivity, impulsiveness, and inattention.

There are drawbacks to these medications, however. It is difficult to predict how an individual child will respond to stimulants, so careful monitoring is required (Dulcan, 1989). Additionally, these medications appear to produce undesirable negative emotions such as sadness, depression, nervousness, and withdrawal in some children (Buhrmester, Whalen, Henker, MacDonald, & Hinshaw, 1992). Because the medication alleviates the symptoms but does not cure ADHD, it is likely to be needed for a long time; about 80 percent of those who need medication as children also need it as adolescents, and about 50 percent continue to need it as adults (Taylor, 1995).

Like children on any medication, children on stimulants need to be monitored by a physician, and parents need to be informed about possible side effects. Generally speaking, the benefits of medication appear to outweigh the drawbacks. Side effects that do occur often can be handled by reducing the dosage (Taylor, 1995).

Thinking It Through:

1. What are the most popular treatments of attention-deficit hyperactivity disorder?
2. Why is the use of stimulants with children controversial? What are potential long-term effects of drug use on children?
3. What criteria would you use in deciding whether to seek treatment for a child with symptoms of ADHD?

Diet therapies, such as restricting children's intake of food additives, have become popular, although the scientific evidence for their effectiveness is limited and complex (Breakey, 1997). Dietary treatments are most effective if there is direct evidence of an allergic disorder and changes in behavior associated with specific foods (Scahill & deGraft, 1997). For most ADHD children, neither medication nor behavioral strategies alone are sufficient to normalize behavior and improve academic performance. Most professionals therefore use a combination of treatments for children with ADHD.

TABLE 9.4

Characteristics of Individuals with Various Degrees of Mental Retardation

DEGREE OF MENTAL RETARDATION	APPROXIMATE PERCENTAGE OF THE MENTALLY RETARDED	IQ SCORE	CHARACTERISTICS
Mild	85%	50–70	Acquire academic skills up to approximately sixth-grade level May become self-sufficient Can live successfully in the community
Moderate	10%	35–55	Acquire academic skills up to approximately second-grade level May be able to perform jobs, under supervision Adapt well to life in the community, but usually in supervised group homes
Severe	3–4%	20–40	Have limited academic skills May perform simple tasks, with close supervision Adapt well to life in the community, usually in group homes or with families
Profound	1–2%	Below 20 or 25	Require a highly structured environment with constant aid for optimal development Can perform simple tasks under close supervision May live in the community, in group homes, or with families

SOURCE: American Psychiatric Association, 1994.

CHILDREN WITH MENTAL RETARDATION

Even prior to the advent of IQ testing, many children were identified by their parents or teachers as having low levels of intellectual functioning, often because they did not adapt well to life's circumstances. IQ tests provide a means of classifying people according to degree of intellectual functioning. Used alone, however, IQ scores are not always highly predictive of adult functioning. For instance, some children with very low IQ scores have been quite successful in their daily living, usually because they have "street smarts" and a supportive environment (Kasari & Bauminger, 1998). Today, **mental retardation** is defined broadly to include subaverage general intellectual functioning and impaired adaptive functioning, with onset during childhood (APA, 1994).

Four degrees of severity of intellectual impairment have been identified (see Table 9.4). A total of about 1 percent of the population falls into these categories, with more males than females being labeled as mentally retarded (APA, 1994). Mental retardation should not be considered a permanent feature of a person. Research has shown that many children labeled as mildly retarded "lose" their mental retardation as adults (Koegel & Edgerton, 1984). Some research suggests that even profoundly and severely retarded individuals can learn to live semi-independently, can maintain employment, and are able to develop social relationships (Mest, 1988).

A leading known cause of mental retardation is very early prenatal events (30 percent), including exposure to teratogens (as through maternal alcohol consumption). Environmental influences (such as lack of nurturance or cognitive stimulation) and other mental disorders (such as the onset of schizophrenia) account for many of the milder cases of mental retardation. About 10 percent of cases are due to genetic factors, such as

mental retardation condition characterized by subaverage general intellectual functioning and impaired adaptive functioning, with onset in childhood

Down syndrome, and health problems of childhood, such as lead poisoning and infections (Burack, Hodapp, & Zigler, 1998). The causes are unknown in about one-third of the cases of mental retardation.

Today, mentally retarded children are often integrated into general education classrooms, where they may receive specific step-by-step skill training, but these practices may not be the most effective. Research shows that it is more effective to teach these children cognitive skills, such as general problem-solving strategies and self-monitoring skills. Mentally retarded children have been taught, for instance, to use a specific strategy, to apply it appropriately, and to recognize the effort necessary to apply it. From these experiences, children learn how to behave in certain situations, as well as learning the importance of planning (Gordon, Saklofske, & Hildebrand, 1998). Other successful approaches are prevention-directed, helping younger children who are at risk for being labeled mentally retarded. If these children learn adaptive strategies early, they may adapt more easily to school.

GIFTED AND TALENTED CHILDREN

Just as it is difficult to define *intelligence*, it is difficult to define *giftedness*. The federal guidelines defining *giftedness* suggest that gifted children have outstanding abilities and need to have special programs and services beyond those that most children receive. Gifted children may have a single ability or many, including general intellectual ability, specific academic aptitude, creative thinking, leadership ability, talents in the visual and performing arts, and motor skills (Keogh & MacMillan, 1996).

Because teachers often identify children as gifted based on their school performance, they miss children who do not perform well in school or who are gifted in athletics, music, or performing arts. Some indication of these problems can be seen in Table 9.5, which compares the percentages of children from diverse backgrounds who are enrolled in gifted programs. Minority children are not included in gifted programs as often as Caucasian American children because of their tendency to come from disadvantaged backgrounds.

Gifted children are often bored and unchallenged by their school experiences. In some school districts, 60 percent of elementary school children scored above 80 percent on a test of the content of their math textbook *before* they had begun to use the book (Reis, 1989). If books present little or no challenge to the majority of students, it is clear that they will pose no challenge at all to gifted students.

Some gifted children attend special schools that focus on math and science or on the arts. Other gifted children attend special classes in regular schools. Whether in special classes or in special schools, the question is, What kind of program should gifted chil-

TABLE 9.5
Students Enrolled in Regular Educational Programs and Gifted Programs

GROUP	PERCENTAGE OF GENERAL ENROLLMENT	PERCENTAGE OF ENROLLMENT IN GIFTED PROGRAMS
Caucasian Americans	71.2 %	81.4 %
African Americans	16.2 %	8.4 %
Hispanics	9.1 %	4.7 %
Asian Americans	2.5 %	5.0 %

SOURCE: L. M. Cohen, 1996.

dren receive? **Acceleration programs** encourage children to move rapidly through the usual coursework, compressing the time usually spent in each course. For instance, the Study of Mathematically Precocious Youth program speeds up the pace at which children learn mathematics so that they are taking advanced college-level math courses before they complete eighth grade (Stanley & Benbow, 1983). Acceleration programs have been very successful in increasing students' achievement and academic abilities.

In contrast, **enrichment programs** encourage problem solving and creative activities, often through independent study or programs with individualized instruction and mentoring (Renzulli, 1986). Children might be asked to conduct an extensive science project or to write a newspaper. The effects of these programs are less clear because the skills that children develop are difficult to assess (Keogh & MacMillan, 1996).

HOW DO FAMILY AND CULTURE INFLUENCE CHILDREN'S INTELLECTUAL DEVELOPMENT?

Children's intelligence and achievement are influenced by the kind of family and community in which they grow up. Some children grow up in a home with many disadvantages. These children may have a difficult time developing their full intellectual potential. Other children have the advantages of good housing, health care, and nutrition and supportive caregivers, which increase their chances for optimal intellectual development.

IMPACT OF POVERTY ON CHILDREN'S INTELLECTUAL DEVELOPMENT

The incidence of mental retardation is about six times higher among children who are raised in chronic poverty than among children who are raised in middle- and upper-income families (Baumeister & Baumeister, 1989). Children raised in poverty also are likely to be undernourished, have substandard housing, be ill more often, receive less health care, and come from more disorganized families than children from wealthier backgrounds (Huston, 1991). Thus, poverty has the potential to adversely affect children's intellectual development and performance in school. Racial and ethnic differences in IQ and school achievement all but disappear once adjustments are made for economic and social differences (Brooks-Gunn, Klebanov, & Duncan, 1996).

The problems of poverty are intergenerational, complex, and enduring. For example, women living in poverty receive less prenatal care and have more difficulties with their pregnancies. Not surprisingly, they are more likely to give birth to premature and unhealthy babies, who then face high rates of illness and all the other debilitating conditions associated with poverty (McLoyd, 1998). The cumulative effects of poverty on many aspects of development make it all the more important to find ways to keep families out of the poverty cycle.

ROLE OF THE FAMILY IN CHILDREN'S GIFTEDNESS

Families and communities play a role in the development of gifted children. Studies of the early lives of remarkably accomplished young adults showed that these young people shared many family characteristics, even though they had diverse talents, as they ranged from concert pianists and neurologists to Olympic swimmers. In most cases, the family was intact and parents went to enormous lengths to help their children succeed at whatever task they undertook. Below are some of the characteristics that are commonly found in families of successful and talented children (Feldman, 1994; Howe, 1990):

◆ Parents value success and encourage children to do their best.
◆ Parents supervise practice sessions and training.

acceleration programs educational programs that encourage children to move rapidly through the usual coursework, compressing the time usually spent in each course

enrichment programs educational programs that encourage problem solving and creative activities through independent study or individualized instruction and mentoring

✦ Parents encourage active pursuits; they do not encourage television viewing or other passive pursuits.

✦ Parents devote time and energy to their children by reading to them, playing games with them, teaching them, checking homework, and supervising practice sessions.

✦ Family life is firmly structured, and children are required to share in responsibilities at home.

It is the parents who first introduce many children to the area in which they eventually excel, and often the parent is talented in this area as well. With parental encouragement and informal teaching, children can develop a high level of skill at home. The parents of gifted children realize the importance of practice and are sensitive to the need to support and encourage their children's practice (Strom, Strom, Strom, & Collinsworth, 1994). Although the families involved in these studies differed from one another in many ways, the one constant factor was the encouragement and support the parents gave their children.

In a longitudinal study, information was obtained about the lives of children from 1 to 8 years of age. At age 8, some of the children were identified as being gifted. When the early lives of the gifted children were compared with those of the other children, surprisingly few differences were found. Gifted and nongifted children had similar personalities, similar rates of behavioral and emotional problems, and similar social relationships. However, gifted and nongifted children's families differed. Gifted children's parents were more highly educated, and their families showed healthier functioning. Gifted children had more learning opportunities, more educational stimulation, more exposure to books, and more trips to libraries than children who were not gifted (Gottfried, Gottfried, Bathurst, & Guerin, 1994).

ROLES OF PARENTAL INVOLVEMENT AND CULTURAL BELIEFS IN ACADEMIC ACHIEVEMENT

For many years, American children have not performed as well as Chinese and Japanese children in most academic areas. Several factors, including classroom strategies and cultural beliefs and ceremonies, contribute to these differences (DeCorte, Greer, & Verschaffel, 1996; Stevenson, 1998a). Families also contribute to the differences found in the performance levels of children in different cultures. In an extensive research program, Harold Stevenson and his colleagues investigated mathematics achievement among first- and third-grade children in three large cities—Sendai, Japan; Minneapolis, Minnesota; and Taipei, Taiwan (Stevenson & Lee, 1990).

Although the children's performance did not differ much in the first grade, by the third grade, the Asian children were far outperforming the American children. The researchers found dramatic differences between the Asian and the American families. Parents in Japan and Taiwan mobilized their resources to help their children as soon as the children entered school. For instance, the percentage of parents who bought their children mathematics workbooks varied from 58 percent in Japan and 56 percent in Taiwan to only 28 percent in the United States. Almost all of the Japanese (98 percent) and Taiwanese (95 percent) children had their own desk and work space at home, compared to only 28 percent of the American children. The Asian parents monitored their children's homework more than the American parents did. And, although the Asian children were performing quite well overall, their parents expressed more concerns with the school system than American parents did. Another clue to the success of the Asian students may be the interpretation parents placed on good mathematics performance. Asian parents were likely to attribute good mathematics skills to hard work, whereas American parents were more likely to attribute these skills to natural ability (Stevenson, 1998b).

Research suggests that families' attitudes toward and encouragement of education are important factors in the lives of children from diverse ethnic groups within the United States as well (Stevenson, Chen, & Lee, 1993). In a large-scale study of African American, Caucasian American, and Hispanic children in Chicago schools, mothers' and children's attitudes toward school were investigated, as well as children's school achievement in reading and mathematics (Stevenson, Chen, & Uttal, 1990). In early elementary grades, African American and Hispanic children had lower school achievement scores than Caucasian American children did; by fifth grade, these differences had disappeared for mathematics but not for reading. Differences in children's mathematics achievement in fifth grade related to the mother's educational level, rather than the child's ethnicity. Children whose mothers had lower levels of education did not perform as well in mathematics as children whose mothers had higher levels of education. Overall, minority children were more positive in some of their attitudes about school. For instance, African American children tended to like homework more than Caucasian American children did, and in fifth grade, Hispanic children liked school more than Caucasian American children did.

Hispanic and African American children and their mothers were very positive about education, and the mothers held high expectations about their children's future prospects for education (Stevenson et al., 1990). Compared to Caucasian American mothers and teachers, minority mothers and teachers were more positive about the value of homework, competency testing, and lengthening school days to improve educational opportunities for children (see Figure 9.6).

Given the positive attitudes that children and their mothers have about schooling in the elementary grades, it seems surprising that so many minority children experience school failure during junior high and high school. An important goal for future research is to discover what factors have a destructive effect on older minority children's school achievement.

FIGURE 9.6
African American, Hispanic, and Caucasian American Mothers' Attitudes About Improving Children's Educational Performance

SOURCE: Stevenson, Chen, and Uttal, 1990 (p. 517).
Notice how the data contradict the stereotyped belief that minority parents do not emphasize academic achievement and hold high standards. How do parents' attitudes influence children's school performance?

CHAPTER SUMMARY

How do children develop physically during late childhood?

• Compared to preschoolers, older children have slower growth rates, which enable their coordination abilities to "catch up" to their body size.

• During the school years, children show marked improvements in motor development. Older children are stronger and more agile and have better balance than young children.

• Sports participation among older children has increased significantly since the 1970s. Children who participate in sports benefit from regular exercise and may learn to cooperate with others.

• Children's nutritional needs may not be met adequately because of parents' misconceptions about nutrition for children.

• Although children generally are healthy during the school years, health issues include poor physical fitness, sports injuries, and obesity.

How do older children think and solve problems?

• During the school years, for the first time, children's thinking and problem solving show the same type of logic—the use of operations—that is evident in adult thinking.

• Children no longer are likely to be fooled by appearances in problem solving; they can mentally represent actions and focus on multiple dimensions to solve conservation tasks.

• Children's understanding of seriation and number becomes increasingly sophisticated during these years.

• Children's thinking is influenced by their family, their culture, and their everyday life experiences.

How do language and literacy develop during the school years?

• Children's vocabulary continues to expand at a rapid rate, and children begin to master idiomatic expressions, which cannot be interpreted literally.

• Older children come to understand the pragmatics of language better, developing the ability to maintain a topic in a conversation and the ability to "repair" a conversation so that others understand what they are saying.

• Major accomplishments for most children during the school years include learning to read and write. Methods of teaching children to read have varied over the years, and many educators now recommend using a combination of approaches.

What characteristics define children's intelligence and creativity?

• The defining and measuring of intelligence are complex and controversial issues. The most common IQ test for children is the Wechsler Intelligence Scale for Children—III (WISC-III), which measures verbal and performance intelligence.

• Among the many controversial issues surrounding intelligence testing is the possibility that cultural biases may decrease IQ scores for some ethnic groups.

• Several alternative conceptions of intelligence have been proposed. Sternberg's triarchic theory describes three components involved in information processing that influence intelligence. Gardner's view of multiple intelligences suggests that there are many domains in which people may be intelligent.

• Creativity is difficult to assess. The most common tests use verbal and graphic components to measure fluency, flexibility, and originality. Educational efforts are focused on finding ways to foster creativity in all children by encouraging them to use specific thinking strategies and working styles.

How do older children understand the social world?

• Older children are more likely than young children to think of other people as having internal and stable personalities. As they grow older, children focus less on external appearances and more on other sources of information when making predictions about other people's actions.

• As children progress through the school years, they experience changes in their understanding of ethnic groups. Children move from a focus on appearances to consideration of more subtle sources of information about people, such as their talents and abilities or interests.

• Prejudice and discrimination may decrease as children apply more advanced cognitive skills to their understanding of people.

How does schooling influence children's cognitive development?

• Believing that children should take an active role in their own education, many educators use student-centered activities to encourage children to think and solve problems rationally and creatively.

• Children's educational needs are changing because of the increasingly diverse population of students. Part of the educational challenge is to provide better opportunities for all children and to provide for the special needs of some children.

• Teachers' expectations for students influence the students' performance. Because teachers may not be aware of their biases, workshops and training programs have been developed to provide methods for recognizing and overcoming biases.

How do schools address students' special needs?

• Children with special needs are guaranteed a free public education that is suitable to their needs. Schools are obliged to place these children in the least restricted environment possible, which provides a broad range of opportunities for them.

• The most common mental disorder among children is attention-deficit hyperactivity disorder, affecting approximately 2 million American children. Children with ADHD have an inappropriately low level of attention and are hyperactive and impulsive. The demands of school often bring these children to the attention of their teachers.

• Genetic and environmental factors influence the development of ADHD. Behavioral, nutritional, and drug-based treatments have been tried. Many children with ADHD are treated with stimulants, although the increasing use of these drugs has been very controversial.

• Children who are mentally retarded have subaverage intellectual functioning and impaired adaptive functioning. Four levels of retardation have been identified, but these labels do not always predict later functioning.

• Early prenatal events are the leading known cause of mental retardation, but environmental events may cause many cases of milder retardation.

• Children who are mentally retarded are less likely to be placed in special education classes today than previously. They are likely to be integrated into general classrooms.

• Gifted children may be difficult to identify, especially if they are underachievers or minority students. Gifted children may be bored and unchallenged in the typical classroom.

• Gifted children may be encouraged to enter special schools or classes that focus on their areas of talent. Debate continues about whether the best education involves an accelerated program or an enrichment program, although more scientific evidence supports the use of accelerated programs.

How do family and culture influence children's intellectual development?

• Children raised in poverty are less likely to achieve their full potential for intellectual development because of inadequate nutrition, health care, and housing.

• Families can provide important support for their children's intellectual and talent development through encouragement, supervision of practice sessions, and educational and intellectual stimulation.

• Cross-cultural studies illustrate the importance of families and their cultural values to children's achievements.

KEY TERMS & CONCEPTS

acceleration programs *(337)*
attention-deficit hyperactivity disorder
   (ADHD) *(332)*
compensation *(311)*
constructivist theories of learning *(328)*
cooperative learning *(328)*
creativity *(323)*
discovery learning *(328)*

discrimination *(326)*
emergent literacy *(319)*
enrichment programs *(337)*
generative learning *(328)*
mainstreaming *(331)*
mental retardation *(335)*
minimal distance principle **(MDP)** *(315)*
multicultural education *(328)*

obese *(310)*
phonics approach *(318)*
prejudice *(326)*
prodigies *(323)*
reversible thinking *(311)*
savants *(323)*
social perspective taking *(325)*
whole language approach *(318)*

ACTIVITIES & APPLICATIONS
Relating to Older Children

1. Watch children play an organized sport such as soccer or softball. What benefits do you think the children are deriving from their participation in the sport? What kinds of cognitive and social skills are encouraged by participation in this sport? Is it likely that different sports encourage different sorts of cognitive and social skills in children?

2. Try some of the Piagetian tasks in Figure 9.1 with an elementary-school child. Does the child exhibit an understanding of conservation of liquid quantities but not more difficult types of conservation? Does the child show evidence of understanding seriation (see Figure 9.3)?

3. Visit an elementary school during an art or music class. By simply watching or listening, can you identify children who appear to be particularly talented or creative? Ask the teacher for his or her definition of *creativity* in children, and find out what cues he or she uses to determine whether a child is particularly creative.

4. Talk to a child in elementary school about what she or he does in school, and try to determine the extent to which the child's teachers are using active thinking strategies. Does the child engage in projects that encompass several domains of learning (such as mathematics, language skills, and musical instruction)? What kind of reading instruction is stressed?

CHAPTER 10

Social & Emotional Development in LATE CHILDHOOD

CHAPTER OUTLINE

Eight-year-old Janet is a bright second-grader who is having problems. She cries every morning before going off to school, but if she is late for class, she also cries. She often is anxious, and she worries about what will happen to her at school. When she is called on in her class, she gets nervous, stutters, and starts to cry. If the teacher marks something wrong on her math problems, she cries. Her peers pick on her often, and when they do, she becomes sullen and withdrawn. She is afraid to talk to anyone or say anything during class. she feels as if she has no friends and that she cannot cope with the stress of school and the demands it makes on her. she is becoming more and more despondent and often is overwhelmed by sadness.

Late childhood marks a distinctive period of development. Children assume new roles and acquire new capabilities that launch them into more complex and diverse environments, with increased expectations from adults. Many of these expectations revolve around children's behavior and adherence to social and moral standards.

Late childhood also is the time when most children enter school, making new contacts with both older and younger children and a widening array of adults. The new environments and expanded interactions have major effects on children's social and emotional development. Most children meet these challenges with excitement and success. But some children, like Janet, are overwhelmed by these demands and changes.

HOW DO EMOTIONS DEVELOP DURING LATE CHILDHOOD?

During late childhood, children's emotional lives, as well as the environments that affect their emotional responses, become more complex and demanding. Older children have enhanced competencies and resources that they can call on to help them respond to these increased demands. Unfortunately, some children find themselves overwhelmed by their emotions and the demands made on them, which leads to behavior problems, depression, fear, and anxiety.

STRESS AND COPING

As children grow and change, their vulnerability to stress and the situations that produce it also changes. Events that cause stress in young children often appear innocuous to older children, and the situations that create stress in older children often leave young children unaffected. For example, young children may find being left alone overwhelmingly stressful, whereas older children generally do not. Older children, however, may become stressed about an upcoming exam at school, whereas young children usually do not confront this kind of situation.

The ways that older and younger children cope with stress also differ. Infants who are distressed by a loud noise may cope by crying out to elicit comfort and assistance from caregivers. Toddlers may cope with the fear of a stranger by clinging to their

TABLE 10.1

Rank Order of Common Stressors for Older Children in Six Countries

STRESSFUL EVENT	US	EGYPT	CANADA	AUSTRALIA	JAPAN	PHILIPPINES
Losing a parent	1	1	1	1	1	1
Going blind	2	2	2	2	6	2
Flunking a class	3	3	3	7	2	5
Wetting pants in class	4	5	4	3	3	8
Parental fights	5	4	7	4	9	3
Caught in theft	6	7	5	5	4	10
Suspected of lying	7	8	6	6	5	6
Poor grades	8	6	8	8	7	7
Sent to principal	9	9	9	10	8	*
Having an operation	10	12	10	13	12	11
Ridiculed in class	12	10	11	11	10	4
Scary dream	14	11	14	12	14	9
Test performance	15	15	*	15	15	*
Picked last on team	*	*	13	*	11	13
Losing a game	*	*	*	*	*	14

*Stressful event was not ranked among the top 15.

SOURCE: Yamamoto, Soliman, Parsons, and Davies, 1987.

mother's skirt. Preschoolers may cope with a frightening scene on television by covering their eyes. And elementary school children may cope with the fear of performing in front of others during a recital by distracting themselves with thoughts of something pleasant.

Changes in Contexts That Cause Stress

Developmental changes in children's relations to their environments contribute to changes in the contexts that cause stress. Because infants rely on caregivers, it is not surprising that early forms of stress relate to issues of caregiver presence or absence (Gunnar & Brodersen, 1992). During the early preschool years, stress is more likely to be caused by caregivers' efforts to exercise discipline in order to get their children to obey and comply. During the late preschool years, children are more likely to come into contact with stressors that involve other children (Eisenberg, Fabes, & Guthrie, 1997).

Table 10.1 ranks common sources of stress for school-age children from six different countries. Although there are some differences in the events that children from different countries rank as being stressful, the children's responses are quite similar. Their perceptions of the upsetting and stressful events of life reveal that children have much in common, regardless of where they grow up (Yamamoto, Soliman, Parsons, & Davies, 1987).

Note how many of the stressors in Table 10.1 are related to school. Children in different countries perceive school as a source of trying and stressful experiences. The increased focus on intellectual skills, evaluation, and achievement elicits stressors—in the form of homework, tests, grades, and comparisons with classmates—that do not face younger children (Skinner & Wellborn, 1997). School also is associated with increased stress related to peer relationships. Thus, the school context brings about changes in children's conceptions of themselves, in their relationships with peers and adults, and in the social situations in which they find themselves. Sometimes these changes disrupt the child's sense of well-being and consequently cause stress (Bryant, 1998).

Stress also may be produced when people change the culture in which they live (Gonzales & Kim, 1997). The type of stress that is associated with making a transition from one culture to another is referred to as **acculturative stress** (Moyerman & Forman, 1992). When families immigrate to the United States, they often must learn a new language, as well as adapt to new foods, traditions, and laws. Acculturation is a complex process of cultural adjustment that changes the conditions of one's life (Negy & Woods, 1992). Because children have spent less time in their original culture, they acculturate faster than do their parents (Szapocznik & Kurtines, 1993). Although highly acculturated parents are likely to follow the parenting practices of their new culture (Dumka, Roosa, & Jackson, 1997), differences in rates of acculturation can lead to conflict within immigrant families, as parents and children develop conflicting cultural values and behaviors. Highly acculturated children may be critical of their less acculturated parents, seeing them as old fashioned, traditional, and embarrassing (Gil, Vega, & Dimas, 1994). Thus, in addition to the demands placed on families and children when adapting to a new culture, familial differences in the degree of acculturation may represent a source of stress and conflict (Gil & Vega, 1996).

Changes in Coping Skills

Older children's responses to stress are different from those of young children. For example, older children are more likely to use **emotion-focused coping strategies**—efforts to manage or reduce the emotional distress (frustration, fear) that is aroused in stressful situations—than are younger children (Band & Weisz, 1988; Compas & Phares, 1991). Thinking of happy things and telling oneself that good things will come from the situation are examples of the emotion-focused coping strategies that increase over the elementary-school years. Because of their more advanced cognitive development, older children have a better understanding of stressful situations than young children do and can better use cognitive strategies (such as thinking of something pleasant) to cope with emotional distress (Eisenberg et al., 1997).

During late childhood, children also become more skilled in using **problem-focused coping strategies**—efforts to manage or modify the source of the stressful situation, such as finding a solution to the problem. As children develop better motor, communication, cognitive, and social skills, they are better able to effectively address and solve problems.

To cope effectively in situations involving other people, children need to understand the intentions of those involved. Understanding others' intentions is critical for developing a plan of action and interacting successfully with others (Kliewer, Fearnow, & Walton, 1998). Children who do not accurately interpret the intentions of others may cope ineffectively or inappropriately.

Research on aggressive children supports the importance of accurate interpretations of others' intentions. A child who interprets another's behavior as threatening and hostile is likely to respond aggressively, even when the other person's intentions are unclear (Dodge, 1991; Dodge, & Coie, 1987). Suppose 9-year-olds Ian and Mason are playing on the school playground. Ian bumps into Mason, but Ian's intentions are unclear. Mason must decide whether or not Ian meant to hurt him. Mason concludes that Ian bumped into him on purpose, so he responds by pushing and hitting Ian. If Mason consistently makes this kind of interpretation, he will continue to respond to others in harmful ways. Some children are more likely than other children to make inaccurate or inappropriate interpretations. Generally, however, their advanced cognitive development and social experience permit older children to more accurately interpret the intentions and behaviors of other people.

acculturative stress stress associated with making a transition from one culture to another

emotion-focused coping strategies efforts to manage or reduce the emotional distress that is aroused in a stressful situation

problem-focused coping strategies efforts to manage or modify the source of a stressful situation

Older children also cope better because they are more likely than young children to understand which situations they have some control over and which they do not (Harris, 1989). As discussed in Chapter 8, young children overestimate their capabilities, including their ability to control situations. They often use problem-focused strategies in situations where these are not going to have much effect. These attempts can cause frustration; it is difficult to address the source of the problem when the source is uncontrollable. Older children are more likely to use coping strategies that accurately reflect the actual control they have in the situation.

In situations where children have little control, emotion-focused coping strategies seem the most effective (Blount, Landolf-Fritsche, Powers, & Sturges, 1991; Compas, Malcarne, & Banez, 1992). For example, in coping with the frustration of having a trip to the amusement park canceled because of bad weather, children cannot address the source of the problem—namely, the weather. In this situation, an emotion-focused coping strategy, such as overcoming disappointment by distracting oneself, might be a more effective response. In stressful situations that children have some control over, problem-focused coping strategies are more effective (Altshuler & Ruble, 1989). Attempting to fix it might be an effective strategy for coping with the frustration of trying to play with a toy that is not working properly.

Individual Differences in Resilience

In any stressful situation, some children will come out relatively unscathed whereas other children will be adversely affected. Several studies (Masten, Morrison, Pellegrini, & Tellegen, 1990; Nuechterlein, Phipps-Yonas, Driscoll, & Garmezy, 1990) have shown that children whose mothers had mental disorders (schizophrenia or depression) were at risk for problems with cognitive and social functioning. But equally important were the large numbers of children who showed little, if any, signs of problem behavior. These children were resistant to stress despite their mothers' mental disorders.

Findings such as these tell us that some children are more stress resistant than others. Stress-resistant children seem to have **resilience**—the capacity to bounce back or recover from stressful situations. Resilience reflects healthy functioning despite exposure to stressful events (Masten & Coatsworth, 1998; Reynolds, 1998).

Marian Radke-Yarrow and her colleagues (Radke-Yarrow & Sherman, 1990) studied children who cope well despite having been reared in chaotic and threatening conditions by a parent who was emotionally ill. Let's consider one of these resilient children.

Dominique is the second daughter in a family of four daughters. Her mother, who suffers from severe depression, supports her family through prostitution and welfare. Dominique's father is intermittently in her life. He too suffers from depression and serious drug abuse. Dominique's mother, when not ill, is tough with her children. She yells at them much of the time and gets what she wants, even if she has to resort to physical violence. Dominique is healthy and sturdy and has been since birth. Her mother is proud of Dominique's health and appearance, spending hours keeping Dominique's hair stylishly braided.

Life in Dominique's family is very disorganized, with frequent moves, changes in caregivers, and limited opportunities to attend school. Despite these conditions, Dominique is curious, creative, outgoing, and charming. She also is doing well in school, and reports being happy and unafraid. In essence, Dominique is surviving despite the chaotic environment in which she finds herself.

In Dominique's case, there are several factors that protect her from the stressful and risky conditions in which she lives. Despite her mother's illness, Dominique has a warm relationship with her. Dominique's health and attractiveness are qualities that her mother values. Her mother prides herself on taking good care of her. Dominique also feels proud of her appearance and the fact that she can take care of herself when she needs to. Thus, Dominique has developed a positive self-concept and feelings of positive self-esteem.

resilience the capacity to bounce back or recover from stressful situations

Dominique is popular with other children, and her teachers view her as independent and competent. This positive regard feeds back to her family life. It is a source of great joy to her mother, and Dominique receives praise for bringing home good school reports.

Resilient children like Dominique possess certain qualities that protect them and help them adapt to their stressful and demanding environments. These qualities also are valued by others. Other children possess qualities that lower their resilience. Recall from Chapter 6 that children who react more intensely and who are more temperamentally difficult, unpredictable, and moody also are less adaptable to stress than other children (Carson & Bittner, 1994). In addition to being more vulnerable to stress, these children are viewed less positively by others than are children like Dominique.

Based on case studies like the one of Dominique, researchers have identified common characteristics of resilient children. Such children have above-average intelligence, possess attractive qualities that elicit positive responses in others, and have a positive place in the family (Masten & Coatsworth, 1998; Radke-Yarrow & Sherman, 1990).

What kinds of stress are associated with poverty? How do children cope with these stressors? What factors make some children more resilient than others?

CHILDREN'S RESPONSES TO COMMUNITY VIOLENCE

Community violence is a major source of stress for many children (Gorman-Smith & Tolan, 1998). In his book *There Are No Children Here*, Alex Kotlowitz (1991) tells the story of two boys growing up in an inner-city low-income housing project in Chicago. Lafeyette and Pharoah were 7 and 10 years of age when Kotlowitz began documenting their lives in a community filled with crime and violence. Kotlowitz describes how Lafeyette and Pharoah often had to huddle on the floor of their tiny apartment as gun shots rang out nearby:

> *Pharoah shook with each gun pop, his eyes darting nervously from one end of the long hallway to the other. He clutched a garbage bag filled with aluminum cans he'd collected; his small body was curled up against the security of the cool concrete wall.*
>
> —A. KOTLOWITZ (1991, P. 6)

Children like Lafeyette and Pharoah face constant violence and danger in their neighborhoods. By some estimates (Bell, 1991), one-third of the children in high-crime neighborhoods in US cities witness a homicide and more than two-thirds witness a serious assault. Mothers in a housing project in Chicago identified shootings as their major safety concern for their children (Dubrow & Garbarino, 1989).

In war-torn countries like Bosnia and Lebanon, children face traumatizing violence on a regular basis (Kocijan-Hercigonja, Rijavec, Marusic, & Hercigonja, 1998). For example, in Sarajevo, where almost 25 percent of all children were wounded in the war, 97 percent of the children interviewed said they had experienced being shelled with bombs, 55 percent said they had been shot at by snipers, and 66 percent said they had been in situations where they thought they would die (UNICEF, 1993). In response to these conditions, 29 percent of the children in Sarajevo said they felt "unbearable sorrow" and 20 percent said they had constant terrifying dreams. In addition to the physical dangers, these children were confronted with other extremely adverse conditions—schools were destroyed, teachers were attacked and killed, food and water became scarce, and families were torn apart. Because of the violence, these children face both physical and psychological risks.

What Can We Learn about Resilience from Children Who Survived the Holocaust?

Many studies of children's stress focus on how they cope with the everyday life events they experience. But how do children react to extremely stressful situations?

In trying to answer this question, researchers have looked at extreme situations in which children faced the most dire and dangerous of circumstances (Garbarino et al., 1992). Certainly, the concentration camps of Nazi Germany during World War II fit that description. In these camps, over 1 million children under the age of 16 died. The Russian soldiers who liberated Auschwitz in January of 1945 found 300 surviving children. The physical condition of these children was desperate. They were feeble, wasted, starving, and riddled with tuberculosis. The stresses they were subjected to were harsh, severe, and chronic. Hunger, cold, hard labor, and mistreatment by the guards were daily sources of stress in these children's lives. They witnessed or experienced unspeakable acts of violence and cruelty (Garmezy & Rutter, 1985).

When these children were returned to "normal" environments, short-term ob-servations of their adaptation showed developmental lags in physical growth and development, in physical hygiene, in social play, and in social interactions. Their behaviors were marked by destruc-tiveness, aggression, irritability, and aim-lessness. They mistrusted adults, and adult-child relationships were disturbed (Garmezy & Masten, 1990).

As time passed, many of the camp victims adjusted to their new surround-ings. Moral and social behaviors im-proved, and few children showed signs of serious mental disorders. However, the children continued to have problems coping with stress; even minor stresses led to breakdowns in coping. Impor-tantly, the quality of family life influ-enced children's coping. Children who were reared in stable families showed greater resilience. In contrast, children who lived in unstable families developed more severe disturbances (Garmezy & Masten, 1990).

What were these children like as adults? Moskovitz (1983) tried to answer this question by interviewing child sur-vivors of the Holocaust in their adult-hood. He found that many survivors pos-sessed strikingly positive qualities—a strong commitment to life and family, powerful religious beliefs, and a sense of love and purpose. These were survivors who were raised by strong and loving caregivers. Moskovitz concluded that emotional devastation does not automat-ically follow from early severe or pro-longed traumas; what happens to children after they experience such trauma matters enormously.

Thinking It Through:

1. What were the survivors' short-term adjustment problems? What aspects of concentration camp life most likely influenced the development of these problems?
2. What kinds of problems tended to persist in the long term, even in re-silient children? Why?
3. What proved to be the most impor-tant factors in survivors' successful long-term adjustment? How do fami-lies influence children's adjustment to early traumatic events?

How children respond to community violence depends on their developmental level (Straussner & Straussner, 1997). Because children's ability to control their environment is limited, safety is especially important to them (Garbarino, Dubrow, Kostelny, & Pardo, 1992). The younger the child, the more likely it is that safety issues are critical to her or his well-being. Children who experience traumatic violence prior to age 11 are three times more likely to have psychological problems (such as depression) than are children who experience such events after age 12 (Davidson & Smith, 1990). Children who ex-perience traumatic violence and have been separated from their families (as is often the case for children in war-torn countries) are particularly susceptible to psychological im-pairment (Macksoud & Aber, 1996).

Young children often respond to violence with passivity, displaying behaviors typi-cal of younger children. For example, they may become clingy, wet their bed, and show little desire to talk to or be with others. Young children's responses to community violence also may include increased aggression. In one study (Farver & Frosch, 1996), the play behavior of 4-year-old children who lived in the neighborhoods of south-central Los Angeles where the 1992 riots occurred was compared to the behavior of another group of 4-year-olds who were not exposed to the riots. The play behavior of the children exposed to the riots contained more aggressive and unfriendly themes, words, and outcomes than did the play behavior of those children who were not exposed to the riots.

Older children also are vulnerable to community violence, but they respond to it differently than do younger children. Because of their increased ability to understand the dangerous situations they encounter, older children are more likely to recognize the significance of the events that take place around them. School-age children may become aggressive, as well as depressed, and may develop physical complaints, distortions in thought, and learning difficulties as a result of the violence they are exposed to (Garbarino et al., 1992). They also may become increasingly distrustful of others. In Kotlowitz's (1991) description of Lafeyette's response to the violent death of his friend, nicknamed Bird Leg, we see evidence of these kinds of responses:

> Bird Leg's funeral haunted him. He believed he had seen Bird Leg's spirit at a friend's apartment. "He was trying to tell us something," he told his mother. . . . His face masked his troubles. It was a face without affect, without emotion . . . in Lafeyette it conveyed wariness . . . . "I don't have friends," he told his mother. "Just associates. Friends you trust."
>
> —A. KOTLOWITZ (1991, P. 55)

In the United States, exposure to community violence is greater for low-income children, who include a disproportionate number of minority children. According to one estimate (Gladstein, Slater-Rusonis, & Heald, 1992), 42 percent of inner-city African American children had seen someone shot, 25 percent had seen someone stabbed, and 23 percent had seen someone murdered. Hispanic and Native American children in the United States also are exposed to high rates of violence (Soriano, 1994; Yung & Hammond, 1994). For nonminority children, the percentages were half of those above.

One way to feel safe in a violent community is to identify with those who behave violently (Garbarino et al., 1992). Children growing up in violent communities often model themselves and their behavior on those individuals who cause the violence. In these communities, guns and knives are symbols of status, and their use often is positively reinforced (Bell, 1991). Exposure to violence puts children at risk of becoming violent

This picture depicts a funeral for a child. How does community violence undermine a child's sense of well-being? How might the responses of children exposed to urban violence relate to those of children in countries at war?

themselves (Gorman-Smith & Tolan, 1998), feeding back into the cycle of community violence, victimization, and fear.

As discussed earlier, children can be quite resilient in the face of what appears to be overwhelming stress. But children's resilience is not unlimited. For many children, community violence may be "the last straw." Community violence can undermine children's development by providing constant reminders of their vulnerability and of the inability of their families and communities to protect them (Milgram, 1998).

WHAT EMOTIONAL AND PSYCHOLOGICAL DISTURBANCES AFFECT CHILDREN IN LATE CHILDHOOD?

Late childhood is a time when emotional and psychological problems often surface, especially in children who lack the skills necessary to cope with their increasingly demanding environments. For example, referrals for mental health services rise rapidly after the age of 5 (Verhulst & Koot, 1995). Older children's emotional and psychological problems become closely intertwined with their functioning in school, often interfering with their general educational development. The problems of older children are more difficult to manage and extend to the world outside the family, often limiting their integration into age-appropriate social networks. Many of the emotional and psychological problems of adolescents and adults are direct outgrowths of disorders that appear during late childhood (Violato & LeRoy, 1995). Some of these problems may be self-correcting and need little intervention beyond that provided by parents or teachers. Others require professional help. Although a wide variety of emotional and psychological disturbances may occur, our discussion will focus on some of the more common problems: antisocial behavior, depression, and fear and anxiety.

ANTISOCIAL BEHAVIOR

A pattern of behavior that is aggressive, defiant, uncooperative, irresponsible, and/or dishonest defines **antisocial behavior** (APA, 1994). This pattern of behavior is disruptive to the individual, to his or her relationships, and to the community at large. Antisocial children often fail at school and are disliked by peers, teachers, and sometimes even their parents (Frick, 1998). Nearly half of all children referred to clinics for treatment are referred for antisocial behavior (Kazdin, 1989). A history of antisocial behavior as a child is related to a wide array of adult mental health problems, including troubled marriages, failure at work, and crime (Dishion, French, & Patterson, 1995). Antisocial adults tend to rear antisocial children, thus perpetuating the cycle across generations (Patterson & Dishion, 1988; Steinhausen, Meier, & Angst, 1998).

Boys are much more likely than girls to be referred for treatment for antisocial behavior (Dishion et al., 1995; Patterson, Reid, & Dishion, 1998). This phenomenon may be due to higher rates of antisocial behavior in boys, or it may be due to biased perceptions—that is, these kinds of behaviors are expected to occur more often in boys than in girls and therefore may be noticed more often in boys. Gender differences in antisocial behavior become even more apparent during late childhood, in settings that involve peer and school interactions (Sprague, Sugai, & Walker, 1998). For example, teachers generally find boys to be more antisocial than girls, although parents seldom report similar gender differences (Dishion & Andrews, 1996).

Children who are antisocial at early ages are likely to be so in later years (Cairns, Cairns, & Neckerman, 1989; Patterson & Yoerger, 1993). For instance, boys who were identified as aggressive and hostile at age 8 were more likely to be antisocial at age 30 (Huesmann, Eron, Lefkowitz, & Walder, 1984). The evidence of stability for girls is more limited but still considerable.

antisocial behavior a pattern of behavior that is aggressive, defiant, uncooperative, irresponsible, and/or dishonest

A Case Study of an Antisocial Child

Mitch is a 9-year-old boy from a single-parent household. His mother works part-time but relies on welfare supplements to get by. She feels overwhelmed and often is depressed. Mitch has two brothers with whom he constantly fights. The ferocity of this sibling fighting is intense; on one occasion Mitch stabbed his younger brother in the chest and emergency treatment was required. Mitch also fights with other children, and this too tends to be extreme. For example, Mitch attacked a child in his class with a baseball bat, breaking the child's arm. Mitch is disobedient, defies authority, and destroys others' property when he is angry. He argues frequently with his mother. He leaves home for hours at a time and has even stayed out all night.

Mitch has been suspended from school several times. While Mitch is home serving out his suspension, he and his mother argue even more often and more intensely. Mitch's mother no longer feels she can manage him and is even afraid of him. His behavior has become too dangerous for her and her other children.

At school, Mitch's performance and grades are consistently low. He has been placed in a special class for emotionally disturbed children because of his disruptive and aggressive behavior. He has a high activity level and has been labeled hyperactive. He has normal intelligence, but his performance in class is often below normal. He misses school frequently and has difficulty completing his work. He is not liked by his peers and is teased and picked on by them.

Mitch's case underscores some important points regarding antisocial behavior. First, antisocial behavior is not the rough play and aggression that sometimes is typical of 9-year-old boys. Instead, it is extreme, severe, persistent, and sometimes dangerous. Second, Mitch is a child who is out of control. Mitch's mother, his siblings, and his teachers cannot manage or tolerate his behavior. Third, Mitch's mother finds her life situation difficult and stressful. She is a single parent on welfare, is sometimes depressed, and cares for two other children. These family factors contribute to Mitch's antisocial behavior.

(Adapted from Kazdin, 1989.)

Antisocial children show a progression of coercive and aversive behaviors across childhood. As toddlers, antisocial children tend to be noncompliant, have frequent temper tantrums, and use physical aggression. As preschoolers, they continue to use these behaviors to coerce parents into letting them have their own way (Patterson, 1982). When children use coercive behaviors to get their way and are successful, the antisocial behavior pattern is reinforced and maintained. School-age children extend their antisocial behavior into the school setting. Teachers report that these children often fight and steal and are disobedient (Patterson et al., 1998). Thus, over the course of a lifetime, antisocial behavior begins in the form of noncompliance with parental requests and frequent temper tantrums; progresses to fighting, stealing, and lying in late childhood; and culminates in noncompliance with authority and law in adolescence and adulthood (Dishion et al., 1995).

Factors Affecting the Development of Antisocial Behavior

Diverse factors influence the development of antisocial behavior. The important influences can be grouped into four categories:

+ **Biological factors.** Antisocial behavior is partially influenced by biological factors. Studies of identical twins reveal similar life-course patterns of antisocial behavior (Moffitt, 1993). However, the genetic component of antisocial behavior is demonstrated more clearly in adolescents and adults than in children (Plomin, Nitz, & Rowe, 1990). Studies also show that ADHD (see Chapter 9) and certain traits associated with a difficult temperament, such as impulsivity and irritability (see Chapter 6), are related to antisocial behavior patterns (Barkley, 1989; Schwartz, Snidman, & Kagan, 1996). Underlying these characteristics may be biochemical factors such as enzymes or neurotransmitters. Some researchers have proposed that antisocial children have an overactive reward system and an underactive inhibition system, resulting in impulsive and reward-seeking behavior. Overactive reward systems and underactive inhibitory systems have been linked to the production of certain biochemicals, such as dopamine (Quay, 1988). However, in almost all of these studies, environmental factors such as the family have been identified as significant influences too (Dishion et al., 1995).

✦ **Family factors.**   Families contribute to children's antisocial behavior. Children who receive little parental supervision are more prone to antisocial behavior than are more closely supervised children, especially in high-risk urban neighborhoods (Shaw & Winslow, 1997). Antisocial behavior also is likely to be found in children who have few opportunities to engage in positive social interactions with parents (Snyder, Schrepferman, & St. Peter, 1997) and in children who observe physical spouse abuse (Jouriles et al., 1998). Having a parent who suffers from a mental illness is related to antisocial behavior too (Patterson et al., 1998); parents who are stressed, depressed, or antisocial generally use ineffective or inappropriate parenting practices, which contribute to antisocial behavior in their children (Belsky, Woodworth, & Crnic, 1996; Brenner & Fox, 1998). Finally, children identified as insecurely attached (see Chapter 6) are more prone to be antisocial if they come from high-risk backgrounds (Greenberg, Speltz, & DeKlyen, 1993).

✦ **Peer relationships.**   Experiences with peers promote antisocial behavior in three ways. First, children who have poor peer relationships are at risk for antisocial behavior because they lack positive experiences that help them learn how to control their antisocial impulses. Second, peers act as models and reinforcers for antisocial behavior. Third, antisocial children sometimes attract one another and form their own groups that then promote antisocial behavior (Dishion et al., 1995).

✦ **Social milieu.**   The degree to which children engage in antisocial behavior depends on their social environment. For example, antisocial behavior is more prevalent in urban than suburban areas and in low-income than middle-class neighborhoods (Crane, 1991). Moreover, the relationship between antisocial behavior and living in a stressful neighborhood increases over time because the stressful effects of such neighborhoods accumulate (Aber, Jones, Brown, Chaudry, & Samples, 1998). Elevated rates of antisocial behavior are found among minority children in the United States (Yung & Hammond, 1997), probably because they most often live in low-income urban areas (McLloyd, 1998).

Treatments for Antisocial Behavior

Several forms of treatment have been developed for antisocial behavior. Some treatments focus solely on the antisocial children, others on the family, and still others focus on the community. This diversity in emphasis reflects the fact that the treatment of antisocial children often requires the involvement of many people, including parents, peers, teachers, social workers, law enforcement officers, and judges. At present, no single treatment has been found to effectively address antisocial behavior problems (Kazdin, 1989). The difficulty of identifying a single effective treatment is due to the multiple causes of

How Do Families Contribute to Children's Antisocial Behavior?

Family interactions contribute to children's extreme aggression and antisocial behavior. Gerald Patterson (1982) proposed a model of family interaction to explain how children acquire these types of behaviors. Based on social learning theory, Patterson concluded that the family interactions of antisocial children are different from those of typical children. He found that antisocial children are at least three times more likely than normal children to act aversively. Patterson determined that the problem is not just the child but also the way family members, particularly the parents, respond to the child. Using these observations, Patterson described a model in which a cycle of coercive interactions takes place between parents and antisocial children.

In this cycle, aversive behavior is a characteristic of the whole family. Parents often respond to the aversive acts of the child with their own aversive acts, setting up an escalating cycle of retaliation and coercion. For example, a defiant boy may refuse to do his homework. In response to this defiance, the mother may scold and argue with the boy. In turn, the anti-

social boy argues back and becomes increasingly brazen in his defiance. If the mother backs down at this point, the boy is negatively reinforced for such acts—that is, his behavior is rewarded when his mother backs down and the aversive situation ends. This negative reinforcement increases the chances that the boy will use similar tactics in the future. When the mother backs down from the argument, the aversive interaction ceases for her too. Thus, she also is negatively reinforced for giving in, which increases the chances that she will give in to her son's coercive attempts in the future, thereby setting the stage for the continuation of the cycle.

When this scenario is repeated hundreds or thousands of times, children learn to use coercive behaviors to gain control over situations, and they eventually extend these behaviors to other people and other settings (Dishion et al., 1995). At the hub of this coercive cycle are the parents' inconsistent, harsh, and erratic attempts to set limits for their child. Often, families are not aware of this insidious cycle.

The coercive cycle in families can be changed. Patterson (1982) believes that intervention must include training to improve parents' skills at managing children's behavior. Parents are taught to recognize their role in the cycle and to respond more positively to children's good behavior. Although this approach can be effective (Dishion & Andrews, 1996), retraining is not easy and must involve the whole family.

Thinking It Through:

1. According to Patterson's research, what pattern of behavior tends to develop between parents and their antisocial children? Describe this pattern using a concrete example.
2. What role does reinforcement play in Patterson's model?
3. Based on Patterson's model, draw a diagram or flow chart that visually represents the coercive cycle by which children learn to use antisocial behaviors. At what points on your diagram could parents intervene to break the cycle?

antisocial behaviors, representing a complex interplay of individual, family, peer, and societal factors (Reid & Eddy, 1997).

Treatment may include counseling and psychotherapy, behavior modification, family therapy, and, sometimes, medication. Treatment is more successful with children and families who are motivated to receive help. In many cases, however, the motivation is not there. The long-term treatment outcome for children with antisocial behavior problems also depends on the severity of the antisocial behavior. Children whose antisocial behavior is limited to minor or isolated antisocial acts respond reasonably well to treatment. In contrast, children with severe and chronic antisocial problems do not respond positively to treatment (Graham, 1986). These findings highlight the importance of identifying ways to prevent antisocial behavior problems from developing (Olds et al., 1998).

CHILDHOOD DEPRESSION

Childhood depression is a serious mental health problem; about 1 in 6 children experiences a depressive disorder at some time during childhood (Lewinsohn, Hops, Roberts, Seeley, & Andrews, 1993). Among young children, roughly equal numbers of boys and girls are classified as depressed. By the end of late childhood, however, girls outnumber boys 3 or 4 to 1 (Graham, 1986). In the last thirty years, more children than ever before have been identified as depressed, and it is likely that there will be even more in the future as our ability to identify such children increases. To make matters worse, most depressed children do not receive treatment (Mufson & Moreau, 1997).

Childhood depressive disorders are conditions in which children display persistent negative moods and lack of pleasure in life. To be identified as clinically depressed, a child must exhibit four of the following eight symptoms on an almost daily basis (APA, 1994):

+ significant weight loss or weight gain
+ insomnia (inability to sleep) or hypersomnia (oversleeping)
+ motor agitation or retardation
+ loss of interest or pleasure in usual activities
+ fatigue or loss of energy
+ feelings of worthlessness or excessive guilt
+ impairment in thinking or concentrating
+ reoccurring thoughts of suicide

Symptoms of depression vary with age. Because young children have difficulty verbally expressing their feelings of depression, depression is more often inferred from their behavior. Depressed infants and preschoolers may spend much of their time crying or rocking. They may refuse food and sleep poorly. Although no physical abnormalities can be found, these young children may fail to thrive and are fretful, insecure, and clearly unhappy (Kaslow, Morris, & Rehm, 1998). Before age 6, children express their depression almost entirely through sadness without the guilt or loss of self-esteem that typically accompanies older children's depression (Bemporad, 1994).

By the age of 6 or 7 years, children begin to describe their emotional state somewhat as adults do—they refer to themselves as being sad or miserable. By 7 or 8 years, depressed children experience a devalued view of themselves. Additionally, they may believe that their future holds little to be positive about—something young children have difficulty doing because of their focus on the here-and-now.

Although older children describe feelings of depression better than young children do, they may not admit to such feelings readily. Instead, they may display psychosomatic symptoms, especially headaches or stomachaches that result from emotional distress. They may complain of being bored or uninterested in activities. All children complain sometimes about being bored, but nondepressed children do so only when they have nothing to do. In contrast, depressed children are likely to say they are bored most of the time. Additionally, depressed children generally are not well engaged with school or with learning and thus have lower grades and academic achievement (Barrett & Waterfield, 1997). Depressed children may be irritable, withdrawn, and unable to cope with even minor frustrations. As a result, depression tends to be more prolonged and enduring in older children than in young children (Kashani, Rosenberg, & Reid, 1989).

Factors Affecting the Development of Childhood Depression

The causes of depression in children are not well understood, partly because childhood depression is not well defined and partly because we are just beginning to grasp its complexity. Despite these problems, the causes of depression can be grouped into three categories relating to biology, temperament, and social relationships.

The child in this picture suffers from depression. Notice the sad and blank look on his face. What are some of the other signs of childhood depression? Can you identify some of the factors that contribute to the development of childhood depression?

✦ **Genetic and biological factors.** Several kinds of scientific evidence suggest that there is a genetic component to depression. Depressive symptoms are more common in children who have a history of depression in the family (Puig-Antich et al., 1989). Additionally, the chance that a depressive disorder diagnosed in one twin was shared by the other was found to be about 50 percent for identical twins, compared to only about 25 percent for fraternal twins (Nurcombe, 1994). Other evidence points to the role of neurochemistry—the chemistry of the brain. Neurochemicals such as serotonin and norepinephrine have powerful effects on emotional states in adults and adolescents and are implicated in some types of childhood depression (Emslie, Weinberg, Kennard, & Kowatch, 1994).

✦ **Temperament.** In the discussion of temperament in Chapter 6, you learned that some children are predisposed to react more intensely and with greater negative moods than others. Thus, some children possess temperamental qualities that may predispose them to depression. Children who are quiet and avoidant, slow to adapt to new situations, and prone to negative moods are likely to become depressed if they are stressed (Thomas, Chess, & Birch, 1968). Children with difficult temperaments also are prone to feelings of hopelessness and low self-esteem (Bemporad, 1994).

✦ **Family and social factors.** Children who are depressed often live in circumstances where they are undervalued or rejected. Parents who are emotionally unavailable to their children (perhaps because they themselves are depressed) or are critical and rejecting put their children at risk for depression (Nilzon & Palmerus, 1997). Children who are suffering abuse also are at risk for depression; however, children with a history of past abuse are no more likely to be depressed than are nonabused children (Kazdin, Moser, Colbus, & Bell, 1985). Children who have poor social skills and difficulty establishing meaningful relationships with others are prone to depression (Parker & Asher, 1987). Childhood depression also is associated with stressful life events, such as the loss of a parent (Goodyear, Kolvin, & Gatzanis, 1985). These findings suggest that depression in children is often dependent on the social situations in which they find themselves (Boyce et al., 1998).

Treatments for Childhood Depression

Most children with depression (about two-thirds) improve substantially following treatment (Stark, Rouse, & Kurowski, 1994). Unfortunately, a significant number remain depressed for a considerable period of time. Treatment of childhood depression takes many forms, depending on the specific symptoms, the age of the child, and the cause of the depression. Reducing stressors that affect children can relieve their depression. Children who are depressed because of repeated failure at school may benefit from individualized instruction, tutoring, positive feedback, activities that promote peer acceptance and self-esteem, and counseling. Although these measures may not be sufficient on their own, they are worth pursuing (Graham, 1986).

Intervention provided by counselors or therapists can help children and their families cope with depression (Schwartz, Kaslow, Racusin, & Carton, 1998). For children who have little prior experience with or knowledge of events that cause depression (such as the loss of a family member), facilitating communication within the family can help. Once children understand that other family members too are affected by the loss, they can identify with them and share the burden of the loss. Also, helping children develop a better self-concept and more self-esteem can be useful in treating depression (Stark et al., 1994).

Antidepressant medications generally are used only for seriously depressed children. These medications were not developed for children, and there are few studies on their safe use with children. Many of these drugs have negative side effects such as nausea, dizziness, headache, or insomnia (Johnston & Fruehling, 1994). Children's use of anti-depressants should be closely monitored by doctors and caregivers.

CHILDREN'S FEARS AND ANXIETIES

The emotions of fear and anxiety evolved as warning signals and a way of mobilizing thought and action in response to psychological or physical dangers. Some causes of fear and anxiety are common to us all. Gray (1971) classified these as **innate fears**—fears that are inborn and reflexive. Innate fears are caused by intense stimuli (loud noises or severe pain), novelty (strange places and people), signals of danger (high places or darkness), and threatening or aggressive social interactions. People also instinctually fear being alone and being approached suddenly (Bowlby, 1973). Many day-to-day fears are extensions of these innate fears. Children's fear of ghosts or monsters, for example, may be an extension of the natural fear of darkness. Some fears are learned from others. For instance, children may come to fear snakes if their parents react fearfully toward snakes.

In early childhood, fears and anxieties that were common in infancy—such as fear of strangers and separation anxiety—decrease, while other fears and anxieties increase. Classic studies of children's fear have shown that fear of animals, imaginary creatures, the dark, being left alone, death, and robbers all increase during the preschool years (Jersild & Holmes, 1935; Macfarlane, Allen, & Honzik, 1954). Older children are less likely to fear imaginary things that look scary, but they are more likely to fear real life events such as being attacked, being injured in an airplane crash, or going on a roller coaster (Bauer, 1976). Early experience with diminished control fosters a vulnerability to anxiety and fear (Chorpita & Barlow, 1998).

Between 7 and 8 years of age, as children master the concept of causality, they begin to fear things that might harm them. In addition, as children realize the importance of achievement and begin comparing themselves to others, they come to fear or worry about performing poorly or failing. This is part of the problem that Janet is facing in the opening story. Because school-age children like Janet tend to internalize negative experiences and information, their self-concept is more easily threatened than that of a younger child, leading to increased anxiety about their abilities (Thompson, 1990).

Young children express fear and anxiety by crying or looking sad or uncomfortable. During later childhood, children resist crying when they are scared or anxious (Izard, 1977). Throughout childhood, girls are more likely to express fear and anxiety than boys are (Silverman, La Greca, & Wasserstein, 1995).

Children's Phobias

Although most children fear something specific, some children develop extreme fears, or **phobias**—persistent and irrational fears that significantly affect their social functioning (APA, 1994). Only about 3 to 5 percent of children have phobias, although girls consistently report more extreme fears than boys do (Strauss & Francis, 1989). It is not clear, however, if the higher rate of fear and phobic reactions for girls reflects greater fearfulness among girls or simply a greater willingness of girls and their parents to express such fears.

One of the most common phobias of late childhood is **school phobia,** an extreme fear associated with school environments. Because children with this extreme fear typically refuse to attend school, school phobias cause considerable disruption to their academic and social functioning (Jenni, 1997). The frequent absenteeism of children with school phobia can cause them to fall behind in their coursework and then to lose contact with their peers if they have to repeat a grade. Thus, such fears can have long-term consequences. Compared to their nonphobic peers, children with school phobias have poorer psychological functioning as adults (Flakierska-Praquin, Lindstroem, & Gillberg, 1997).

innate fears fears that are inborn and reflexive

phobias persistent and irrational fears that significantly affect social functioning

school phobia an extreme fear associated with school environments

Children with school phobias need to be distinguished from nonphobic children who simply do not like school and want to avoid it for that reason. School-age children often express a lack of interest in school or a dislike for school, but they do not have the extreme and dysfunctional anxiety that children with school phobias have. Children with temporary fear or anxiety because of a change or transition in schooling, such as going to a new school for the first time, are not considered school phobic. Refusal to go to school because of separation anxiety is not considered a part of school phobia. In separation anxiety responses, children avoid school out of fear of being separated from a caregiver or from home rather than fear of the school environment itself. Children who refuse to go to school because of separation anxiety also usually show distress in other situations where they must be separated from the caregiver, such as visiting a friend's house without the caregiver (Strauss & Francis, 1989).

Treatments for Children's Phobias

Several effective techniques have been developed to treat children's phobic responses. The most widely used treatment method is modeling, in which the fearful child first observes someone else approaching a feared object or situation and then attempts that same approach. Modeling is particularly effective if the approach to the feared object or situation is gradual (Morris & Kratcochwill, 1998).

For older children, who have more advanced cognitive skills, cognitive techniques for treating childhood phobias may be effective (Last, Hansen, & Franco, 1998). Enhancing children's perceptions of control and competence—for example, training them to tell themselves "I am a brave boy" or "I am a brave girl"—helps them cope with fear-inducing events (Cortez & Bugental, 1995; Kanfer, Karoly, & Newman, 1975).

The age of the child when the phobia began is important both in selecting treatment and in predicting outcomes. For young children who experience an abrupt onset of school phobia, the most effective treatment approach is to get the child to return to school as quickly as possible. In contrast, for older children with a lengthy history of school phobia, the most effective treatment approach is a gradual one (Strauss & Francis, 1989).

HOW DO CHILDREN'S FAMILY RELATIONSHIPS CHANGE DURING LATE CHILDHOOD?

Although the family continues to play a significant role in older children's development, important changes take place that modify the nature of that role. The new abilities and competencies that develop during late childhood affect how children respond to their parents and how their parents respond to them. When 7- and 10-year-old children were asked to identify the ten most important individuals in their lives, 80 percent included their mother and 79 percent included their father (Bryant, 1985). Siblings and other relatives also were important. Nonrelated peers appeared in the top 10 list 72 percent of the time, and 23 percent of the children identified at least one nonrelated adult in their top 10 list.

REDUCED PARENT-CHILD INTERACTION

As children enter late childhood, there is a decline in the amount of time they spend with their parents and in the amount of time their parents devote to them. Compared to parents of preschool-aged children, parents of school-age children spend less than half

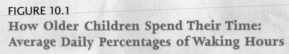

FIGURE 10.1
How Older Children Spend Their Time:
Average Daily Percentages of Waking Hours

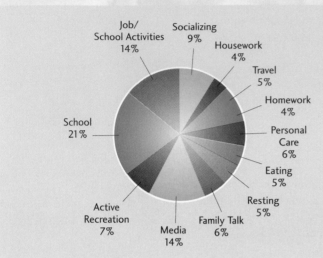

SOURCE: Larson and Richards, 1994. Copyright © 1994 by Reed Larson and Maryse Richards. Reprinted by permission of Basic Books, a subsidiary of Perseus Books Group, LLC.

According to this figure, school, jobs, media, and socializing account for a large part of older children's daily activities. How do the ways children spend their time change as they grow older? What factors account for these trends?

Many children return from school to an empty home. What do these children do while they wait for their parents to return home? In what ways do parents try to overcome the problems associated with lack of supervision and stimulation for these children?

as much time caring for, teaching, reading to, talking with, and playing with their children (Hill & Stafford, 1980). The drop in amount of interaction is greater among parents with less education (Maccoby, 1984).

Children's social interactions also change over the course of late childhood, becoming centered on activities that are beyond the context of the family. Figure 10.1 displays the percentages of their time that older children devote to different activities. As you can see in this figure, children spend a considerable amount of time (44 percent) involved in activities outside of the family—school, job/school activities, and socializing. Direct family interaction accounts for only 6 percent of their daily activities (Larson & Richards, 1994). How the time is spent at home also changes. Older children spend more time studying, watching television, and performing chores or housework, whereas young children spend more time playing (Bryant, 1985).

The concerns that parents have about their children alter as their children move into late childhood. During the preschool years, parental concerns revolve around safety, protection of personal property, respect for others, manners, and self-care (Gralinski & Kopp, 1993). Although some of these issues carry over into the school years, there are important changes in the issues that parents and their school-aged children deal with in their day-to-day interactions. In particular, parents become concerned about older children's involvement in household work, their performance in school, the friends they choose, and the values they hold.

These changes and concerns reflect issues relevant to American and other Western cultures. In contrast, in many non-Western societies, the period of late childhood is when children enter the work force and begin contributing to the necessary functions of the family by assuming tasks such as caring for younger children or tending animals or crops. For example, in Kumasi, one of the leading market cities in central Ghana, it is common for 8- or 9-year-old children to participate in the local trade, selling goods on their own and contributing the proceeds to family needs (Clark, 1994). In societies like that of Kumasi, most of the issues that occupy Western parents and children are of little relevance.

REDUCED PARENTAL SUPERVISION

Today's parents supervise their children less than parents did in the past. The decreased amount of supervision provided by parents comes at a cost. School-age children who are not well supervised by their parents are more likely to engage in antisocial and delinquent behaviors than are children who are well supervised (Dishion et al., 1995). Adequate parental supervision deters such behaviors.

Economic conditions have contributed to the change in parental roles. Parental supervision has been reduced in part because of the increased participation of mothers in the paid work force. Figure 10.2 illustrates how the number of women in the work force grew between 1950 and 1996. As you can see in this figure, labor force participation by women is greatest among mothers of school-age children and has risen steadily since 1950. Although many families prefer to have a parent available to supervise children, few families can afford to forgo the additional income brought in when both parents work outside the home. Also, more women are now single mothers who must earn income to provide for their children. And fewer families than in the past have access to extended family members who can provide after-school supervision. For these reasons, school-age children are increasingly likely to come home from school to a household where the mother and father are still at work. According to one estimate (Hafer, 1995), nearly 5 million school-age children spend time after school without adult supervision during a typical week.

The phrase **latchkey children** is used to describe children who are left unsupervised during the day or return home to an empty house after school. Each day, about 1.6 million school-age children in the United States are latchkey children (Casper, Hawkins, & O'Connell, 1994).

Age is an important predictor of whether children are left to care for themselves. As you can see in Figure 10.3, as children get older, they are more likely to come home to an empty house. By the time a child reaches the teenage years, he or she is two to three times more likely to be a latchkey child than is a younger child (US Census, 1996). Suburban children are about twice as likely to be latchkey children as are children living either in a city or in a rural area. This may be because suburban parents feel safer in their neighborhoods or because they can rely on their neighbors to a greater extent than can people who live in cities or rural areas (Casper et al., 1994).

Latchkey children are more likely than well-supervised children to be truant from school, feel stressed, receive poor grades, engage in risky behaviors, and use alcohol or tobacco (Dwyer et al., 1990). Such problems are particularly likely to arise when children are unsupervised and their parents do not know their whereabouts (Shulman, Kedem, Kaplan, Sever, & Braja, 1998; Steinberg, 1986). In contrast, enrollment in after-school care programs is associated with good grades and good peer relationships (Posner & Vandell, 1994). Thus, formal after-school care and supervision for children whose parents are not at home when they get out of school has the potential to protect children from possibly detrimental environments (Garbarino et al., 1992), particularly if the program is of high quality (Rosenthal & Vandell, 1996).

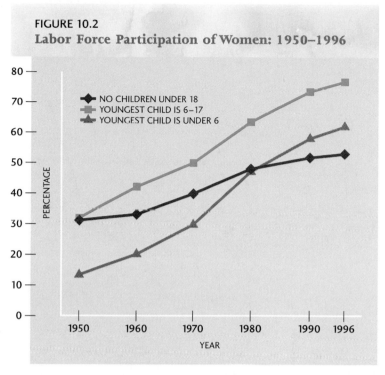

FIGURE 10.2
Labor Force Participation of Women: 1950–1996

- ◆ NO CHILDREN UNDER 18
- ■ YOUNGEST CHILD IS 6–17
- ▲ YOUNGEST CHILD IS UNDER 6

SOURCE: Hayghe, 1997; US Census Bureau, 1996.
This figure illustrates the increase over time in the number of women who work. Notice the trends in the graphs for those women who are parents —the increase is more significant than it is for women who do not have children under 18. What changes in US society have led to this increase? What impact has it had on families and children?

INCREASED IMPORTANCE OF SIBLING RELATIONSHIPS

Sibling relationships change during late childhood. By the time children enter school, those who have siblings spend considerably more time with them than they spend with their parents (Brody, 1998). According to one estimate, one-third of siblings share a room, 25 percent share chores, and 50 percent report that playing with their siblings is a central activity (Bryant, 1982). During late childhood, siblings increasingly compare themselves to one another, and it is through these comparisons that siblings learn how they are different from one another. An age gap of 2 to 4 years heightens the differences between siblings (Dunn, 1983). Thus, sibling relationships provide children with opportunities to learn about themselves (Updegraff & Obeidallah, 1999).

Older siblings often take on some of the functions that parents serve, sometimes providing caretaking, comforting, and support. But does sibling caretaking substitute for parental caretaking? At least in the United States, the answer appears to be no. Sibling caretaking lacks the richness and complexity of the care provided by parents (Bryant, 1992). For instance, when children go to parents and to siblings to discuss emotionally stressful experiences, parents suggest more coping strategies than do siblings.

latchkey children children who are left unsupervised during the day or return home to an empty house after school

FIGURE 10.3

Percentage of Children Who Are Latchkey Children, by Age

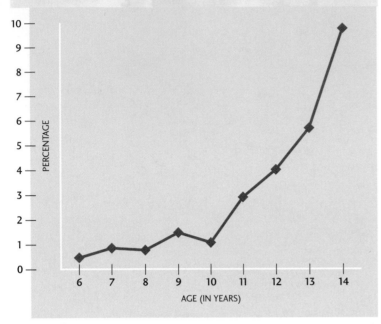

SOURCE: US Census Bureau, 1996.

Notice the dramatic increase in the number of children older than 10 who are left alone after school. What developmental changes might contribute to parents' willingness to allow older children to take care of themselves after school? How does lack of supervision relate to children's behavior problems?

Siblings may provide support or comfort, but it is not comparable to that provided by parents or other adult caregivers.

ONLY CHILDREN

Early in the twentieth century, the famous developmental psychologist G. Stanley Hall (see Chapter 2) was quoted as saying, "Being an only child is a disease in itself" (Fenton, 1928, p. 547). At that time, not having siblings was thought to be a type of social deprivation for children and was considered to have detrimental effects on their social development. The popular stereotype calls for an only child to be spoiled, insensitive, socially awkward, and egocentric. The research evidence, however, suggests that this belief is more popular myth than scientific fact (Richards & Goodman, 1996).

When findings from many studies were summarized, only children and children with siblings differed in just two out of sixteen ways (Polit & Falbo, 1987). Only children scored higher than children with siblings on motivation to achieve and on self-esteem. Only children were just as likely as children with siblings to be resourceful, popular, self-reliant, and successful in their relationships as children and adults (Blake, 1989; Dawson, 1991). Despite G. Stanley Hall's concern about the detrimental effects of being an only child, there appear to be few differences between only children and those who have siblings (Falbo, 1992).

WHAT FACTORS INFLUENCE OLDER CHILDREN'S PEER RELATIONSHIPS?

With the increase in recent years in the numbers of working mothers and single-parent families, children today enter into peer groups earlier and for longer periods of time than their predecessors did. Peer relationships may therefore play a more important role today than they did in earlier times (Asher, 1990). The period of late childhood is a critical time for the development of these peer relationships. As you learned in Chapter 8, friendships become more stable and significant during late childhood, and children spend more time with their peers and friends. Most of this time is spent playing or socializing with peers. As older children develop more advanced social, emotional, and cognitive skills, they become more adept at communicating with peers, understanding peers' behaviors and intentions, and coordinating their actions with those of others. Peer relationships also are important for children with disabilities, because peer relationships offer a context in which these children become valued members of a social circle (Salisbury & Palombaro, 1998). Thus, peer relationships represent important resources for children's successful adjustment (Ladd & Kochenderfer, 1998).

During late childhood, stable social groups emerge. By age 10 or 11, children report that most of their peer interactions take place in the context of these groups (Parker, Rubin, Price, & De Rosier, 1995). Although most children report being a member of a group, some do not, and those children who do not have good peer relationships are at risk for a variety of problem behaviors (Bagwell, Newcomb, & Bukowski, 1998; Rubin, Bukowski, & Parker, 1998).

How Can Public Policy Affect Children and Families?
The Case of China

In mainland China, overpopulation is a concern. In 1998, China's population was over 1.25 billion, making up almost 21 percent of the world's population. As a result, family planning has been proclaimed a fundamental state policy—one that is necessary if China is to progress in social and economic development. China has established a goal of reducing its population to under 1.2 billion by the year 2000 and plans to reach this goal by restricting families to having only one child.

Begun in the 1970s, the one-child policy has had mixed results. The birth rate has dropped from a high of 40.6 births per 1000 people in 1964 to less than 20 (van der Heijden, 1996). In addition, the average number of births to Chinese women of child-bearing age has dropped from four in 1970 to two (Heinemann, 1995). One-child couples account for about 70 percent of the total married populations of the larger cities and provinces. The policy has been less successful, however, in the rural areas. The reality for the Chinese people is that if they want to reach their goal by the end of this century, the average yearly increase in population must remain under 1 percent

(Jiao, Ji, & Jing, 1986). As of 1998, population growth in China was right at this critical rate (United Nations, 1998).

The policy has led to an increase in female infanticide and adoptions (as many rural couples still prefer boys) and between 5 and 10 million unregistered births per year. In addition, the policy may be contributing to a change in the culture's attitudes about children and childbearing (Heinemann, 1995).

Since the 1970s, urban Chinese couples who have become parents have known from the beginning of their child's life that she or he will be their only child. Knowing this, do Chinese parents treat their only child differently than American parents do? For example, do they indulge or protect their only child more than American parents do?

The limited evidence from China is inconsistent. There is some evidence that Chinese children with siblings are more cooperative and popular than are only children (Jiao et al., 1986) and have fewer behavior problems (Wang, Oakland, & Liu, 1992). Still other evidence fails to find any differences between Chinese only children and those who have siblings (Falbo & Poston, 1993). Findings also

vary across provinces and for urban and rural children (Falbo, 1992). Even when differences are found, it is difficult to know exactly what the reasons for the differences are. For example, in one study, only children were physically larger than those with siblings (Polit & Falbo, 1987). This finding may suggest that only children in China have better diets than children with siblings, who may have to share and who do not enjoy the rewards parents receive for having only one child. Additionally, findings reveal that the value Chinese parents place on the only-child policy influences their adherence to it and the possible effects it may have on their children (Jing & Wan, 1997).

Thinking It Through:

1. What are the demographic and cultural contexts that encouraged the adoption of China's one-child policy?
2. What are some consequences of this policy for Chinese children's development?
3. Based on your own or another's personal experiences, what do you think are some disadvantages and advantages of being an only child?

PEER REJECTION

Most children find interacting with peers rewarding and satisfying. Unfortunately, though, for some children, peer relationships are difficult, painful, and unsatisfying. Consider the following story told by the mother of an 8-year-old girl:

> I just found out that my daughter does not get along with her classmates at school. Her teachers are worried because her peers ignore and sometimes tease her. One teacher told me that she usually sits alone during her lunch or sits with the teachers. She sometimes does not want to go to school and often comes home dejected. It breaks my heart and leaves me sad and hurt.

By the end of her story, this mother was in tears over the pain she felt for her daughter. Her story shows how poor peer relationships are anguishing and painful, not only for the children themselves but also for their parents and teachers.

The number of children who have serious peer relationship problems during the school years varies depending on the group that is assessed. In general, however, among average-achieving elementary school children, about 10 to 15 percent do not have any friends (Parker et al., 1995). But not all children who lack friends are the same. Two types of unpopular children have been identified. The first type is referred to as **rejected children**—those who are overtly disliked by their peers, like Janet in the opening story of this chapter. The second type is referred to as **neglected children**—those who are reasonably well liked even though they lack friends. When children are asked to rate how much they like to play with other children, they like neglected children as much as they like most other children but do not like or want to play with rejected children (Rubin et al., 1998). Rejected children are unpopular for long periods of time, and their status rarely changes. In contrast, neglected children's popularity and status may change from time to time or from situation to situation (Asher, 1990). Thus, rejected children have enduring difficulties in their peer relationships, whereas neglected children usually do not.

Additionally, rejected and neglected children have different emotional experiences with peers. Rejected children are more likely than neglected children to be lonely and feel victimized (Coie, Dodge, & Kupersmidt, 1990). When rejected and neglected children were asked if they would like to learn how to get along better with their peers, 48 percent of the rejected children said they would but only 16 percent of the neglected said they would (Asher, Zelis, Parker, & Bruene, 1991). Rejected children are more isolated than neglected children and therefore more emotionally distressed by poor peer relationships.

The research evidence suggests that certain behavioral, personality, and cognitive tendencies contribute to children's being rejected or neglected (Parker et al., 1995). For instance, rejected children are likely to be aggressive (Coie, Dodge, Terry, & Wright, 1991) or depressed (Little & Garber, 1995). Neglected children have poor social skills and may be shy or withdrawn.

These findings suggest that different strategies are needed to improve rejected and neglected children's peer relationships. For rejected children, an important aim of intervention is to reduce the aggressive and disruptive nature of their peer interactions (Waas & Graczyk, 1998). Roughly half of all rejected children are characterized as behaving in ways that interfere with the smooth functioning of the peer group (French, 1988). Altering the consequences for aggressive and disruptive behavior (such as removing any reinforcement received for such behaviors) and teaching self-control strategies (such as recognizing anger cues) can help rejected children generate more adaptive solutions to anger-arousing situations (Coie & Koeppl, 1990). For neglected children, helping them develop social skills that enhance the initiation and maintenance of peer interactions (such as teaching them effective skills for communicating) can improve their status among their peers (Mize & Ladd, 1990).

DEVELOPMENT OF SOCIAL COMPETENCE

The discussion of rejected and neglected children points out that some children are more skilled at making friends than others are. Popular children find it easy to make friends and influence playmates, manage conflicts, and make peers want to be with them. Other children lack these skills and, as a result, are isolated or excluded from peer relationships.

The term **social competence** refers to a child's ability to use age-appropriate social behaviors to enhance peer relationships without harming anyone (Schneider, 1993). Notice that this definition emphasizes that social competence is a developmental concept; what is socially competent at one stage of development may not be socially competent

rejected children children who are overtly disliked by their peers

neglected children children who are reasonably well liked by their peers but lack friends

social competence the ability to use age-appropriate social behaviors to enhance peer relationships without harming anyone at another. Social competence is measured by the degree to which a child is accepted by his or her peers and the degree to which this acceptance is based on social behaviors that do not harm anyone. Teasing another child to gain the admiration of peers, for example, would not be considered a socially competent behavior because of the harm that is done to the child who is teased.

Social competence requires skills that foster smooth and satisfying interactions. Existing research demonstrates that socially competent children are skilled in at least four areas in which their less competent peers are not:

◆ **Initiating social interactions.**   Socially competent children initiate new relationships more gracefully than less competent children. For example, socially competent children are adept at gaining entry into an existing peer group without being rejected (Rydell, Hagekull, & Bohlin, 1997). They integrate themselves into a group in ways that do not disrupt the ongoing activity (Dodge, Pettit, McClaskey, & Brown, 1986). Socially competent children also are more confident of their social skills and keep trying to make friends, even if they do not always succeed (Putallaz & Wasserman, 1990).

◆ **Maintaining social interactions.**   Once they form relationships, socially competent children are successful at maintaining them (Creasey, Jarvis, & Berk, 1998). They smile at, attend to, and comply with others more than do children who have less social competence. They also are more helpful and less aggressive than children with less social competence (Parker et al., 1995).

◆ **Managing conflicts.**   Socially competent children settle disputes effectively, without damaging their relationships. They are assertive but also recognize the importance of sharing and taking turns. In contrast, children low in social competence attempt to resolve conflicts with behaviors such as fighting, throwing a temper tantrum, or sulking and are less likely to suggest alternative ways of dealing with conflicts (Murphy & Eisenberg, 1996).

◆ **Communicating for social purposes.**   Socially competent children have well-developed communication skills (Farmer, 1997). They express themselves effectively and are good listeners. Because speech and language are important prerequisites of social competence, children with speech or language deficiencies or impairments often have low social competence (Rice, Hadley, & Alexander, 1993) and poor peer relations (Guralnick, Connor, Hammond, Gottman, & Kinnish, 1996). Basic conversation and communication skills are necessary for initiating and maintaining positive social interactions with peers (Black & Hazen, 1990; Hadley & Schuele, 1995).

Children's social competence is influenced by a variety of factors. Children who are adaptable and positive and have well-regulated temperaments are more socially skilled than are children who are more temperamentally difficult (Eisenberg & Fabes, 1992). Children who have secure attachments with caregivers are more likely to form friendships and be popular with other children (Elicker, Englund, & Sroufe, 1992). In contrast, children whose parents are uninvolved and use harsh and inconsistent discipline tend to be low in social competence (Travillion & Snyder, 1993).

Children who violate common expectations may be at risk for low popularity and low social competence. As you learned in Chapter 8, children generally play with same-sex peers, and violations of this pattern may have serious consequences for children. During late childhood, elaborate rules and rituals surround other-sex interaction. In general, contact with members of the other sex in public settings evokes negative reactions (Thorne & Luria, 1986). Children often claim to be infected by the "germs" of the opposite sex (sometimes called cooties) and are teased for playing with someone of the other sex. Research shows that children who frequently cross gender boundaries in inappropriate ways have relatively low levels of social competence and are unpopular with peers (Sroufe, Bennett, Englund, & Urban, 1993).

During late childhood, peers play an increasingly important role in social and emotional development. Notice the exuberance of emotions displayed by the child in this picture. What factors contribute to positive peer relationships at this stage?

TABLE 10.2

Rejection by Peers as a Function of Family Background and Recent Life Event Factors

FACTOR	PERCENTAGE OF REJECTED CHILDREN AMONG WHOM FACTOR WAS NOT PRESENT	PERCENTAGE OF REJECTED CHILDREN AMONG WHOM FACTOR WAS PRESENT
Family Background		
Biological mother not in home	14%	26%
Biological father not in home	12%	19%
Lack of educational stimulation in home	11%	31%
Low-income home	10%	22%
Recent Life Events		
Illness in family	14%	23%
Death of family member	14%	27%
Child transferred school	13%	25%
Separation or divorce of parents	13%	36%

SOURCE: Patterson, Vaden, and Kupersmidt, 1991.

The living conditions children experience influence their level of social competence. Children who are low in social competence are likely to experience adverse living conditions or to have experienced a negative life event recently (Patterson, Griesler, Vaden, & Kupersmidt, 1992). In support of this conclusion, Table 10.2 lists, as a function of family background and recent life event factors, the percentages of children in one study who were rejected by their peers (Patterson, Vaden, & Kupersmidt, 1991). As you can see, rejected children were likely to come from single-parent, low-income, unstimulating homes and were likely to have experienced stressful events in their families and schools. The more of these factors children experienced, the greater the chances that their social competence was adversely affected. The percentage of children who were rejected rose from 18 percent of children who had none of the factors listed in Table 10.2 to almost 75 percent of those who had experienced at least five of the factors listed. These findings point out that the stress of certain conditions and events can undermine children's social competence and their ability to form positive peer relationships.

HOW DOES SCHOOL AFFECT OLDER CHILDREN'S SOCIAL AND EMOTIONAL DEVELOPMENT?

The most widely recognized function of school is to provide children with basic intellectual skills such as the abilities to read, write, and do arithmetic. A less frequently discussed, but equally important, function is to further children's social and emotional development. Children must learn to cooperate with teachers and other children and to deal with a diverse population of peers (Ryan, Adams, Gullotta, Weissberg, & Hampton, 1995).

INFLUENCE OF THE SCHOOL ENVIRONMENT

About 98 percent of children between the ages of 5 and 17 are enrolled in school, and this rate has held steady since the 1960s (US Department of Education, 1998). Classes generally are organized with a single teacher, usually female, in charge of 20 to 30 same-aged students. The total enrollment for many schools often exceeds several hundred children.

As indicated in Figure 10.4, the proportion of the school enrollment made up of ethnic minority students has increased. Thus, when children enter school today, they face an ethnically diverse environment, which provides both opportunities and challenges. Exposure to other children's personalities, values, behaviors, and customs requires new coping and interactional skills (Eisenberg et al., 1997). Because classmates tend to stay together from year to year, acceptance into the peer group becomes important, and not being accepted by one's schoolmates has negative consequences that can last for years (Parker et al., 1995).

The functioning and structure of the classroom affect children's emotional and social development. The classroom generally is task-oriented—daily classroom activities revolve around specific objectives. Preset performance standards are in place, and children's abilities to meet these standards vary. This structure focuses the attention of both the teacher and the students on differences in abilities and motivation, making competition and comparisons more likely than they were before children began school (Carlo, Fabes, Laible, & Kupanoff, 1999). As you learned earlier in this chapter, the increased competition and focus on school performance sometimes cause fear and anxiety in children. But these pressures also produce feelings of pride and satisfaction when a school task is done well.

Children's responses to the increased demands of the school environment vary. Some children underestimate their school abilities, and they may undermine their own

FIGURE 10.4
School Enrollments of Children 5 to 17 Years Old, by Ethnicity: 1976–1996

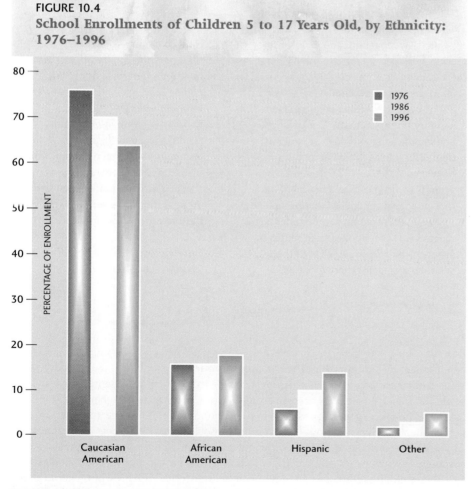

SOURCE: US Department of Education, 1998.

Notice the increase in the school enrollments of ethnic minorities. What changes account for these increases? What impact might these increases have on schools?

Are Schools Safe?

Most Americans agree that schools should provide a safe environment for students. Feeling secure and safe enhances children's social and academic competence and increases their motivation to go to school. After the tragic events in 1999 at Columbine High School in Littleton, Colorado, it is clear that crime and victimization in the schools pose serious threats to students' and teachers' well-being. In the United States, an estimated 2.7 million violent crimes take place annually at or near schools (National Center for Education Statistics, 1995). A large majority (71 percent) of students report having knowledge of someone's being bullied, physically attacked, or robbed at school, and more than half (56 percent) indicate that they witnessed such victimization (National Center for Education Statistics, 1995). In addition, most students (approximately 70 percent) report that drugs are easy to obtain at school (National Center for Education Statistics, 1998). In response to these kinds of statistics, most adults favor a zero-tolerance weapon and drug policy in schools (Gallup, 1997).

As children get older, their chances of witnessing violence or being victimized increase. Students at large schools and public schools are more likely to be victimized than are students at small or private schools. Teachers, too, believe that student behavior problems represent serious threats. Junior and senior high school teachers are three times more likely than are early elementary school teachers to believe that student behavior problems are serious (National Center for Education Statistics, 1993).

Attending school in an environment where disturbing and fearful events happen has an impact on students' sense of security. In one survey (National Center for Education Statistics, 1993), worries about becoming a victim at school were found to be more common among elementary school students (29 percent) and middle and junior high school students (34 percent) than among senior high school students (20 percent). Threats of victimization and crime had motivated many students to develop strategies for avoiding harm. Students indicated that they took special routes to school, avoided certain parts of the school building or school grounds,

stayed away from school-related events, stayed in groups while at school, or skipped school because they worried that someone might hurt or bother them. Minority children were more likely than non-minority children to indicate that they would stay away from school or school events to avoid being victimized. Although students develop coping strategies for dealing with victimization in school, this diverts energy that they could be using to play and learn.

Thinking It Through:

1. How do children's concerns about their personal safety affect their motivation to attend school? What coping strategies do children develop to feel safe?

2. Did you feel safe in elementary school and junior high school? Recall events in which you were threatened or victimized by peers. How did these experiences affect you and your relationships with others? How did the experiences interfere with your schooling?

3. What do you think can be done to improve school safety?

achievement by limiting their efforts in school, avoiding schoolwork, and spending extra time in other activities (such as music or sports). Focusing on nonacademic activities helps some children maintain a positive sense of self-worth (Paris & Cunningham, 1996). Other students, however, generalize their low perceptions of competence to other areas of achievement and may drop out or engage in antisocial behavior. Parents and teachers can unwittingly contribute to children's low perceptions of competence by overemphasizing grades, achievement, and social comparisons as a basis for self-worth (Covington, 1992).

Other children form a different kinds of school-related misperception about themselves: despite low or merely average school achievement, they have an extremely positive view of their school competence. This pattern appears in some inner-city minority

Maintaining High Expectations for All Children

Because children may suffer negative consequences when adults hold low expectations for them, it is important to avoid negative biases when dealing with children. Based on the research, here are some practical recommendations for concerned adults, teachers, and educators on maintaining high and positive expectations for all children (Banks, 1996; Persell, 1993; and Winter, 1995):

- Be aware of your attitudes toward people of different races, cultures, sexes, and socioeconomic backgrounds, and make a conscious commitment not to discriminate among children on the basis of these characteristics. Be alert for bias.
- Identify individual strengths in children, and set expectations that allow them to use these strengths to best advantage.
- Set expectations that are developmentally appropriate, realistic, and challenging.
- Expect and demand a lot from all children in the way of effort, thought, and work.

- Explicitly model and explain the criteria or benchmarks that will be used to evaluate children's ability to meet expectations successfully.
- Let children participate in setting expectations and goals.
- Interact with children equally. Give each child or group equal time, access, attention, consideration, and feedback.
- Gradually raise expectations appropriately as expectations are met.

students who have positive views of their competence and achievement even though they make low test grades (Stevenson, Chen, & Uttal, 1990). Such "illusions of competence" may result from unchallenging curricula or inflated praise by teachers and parents. Children with optimistic illusions may reduce their efforts and thereby lower their future achievement. Students who have an excessively pessimistic or optimistic view of their own competence, as a result of their experiences in school, may not invest appropriate effort in academic work and may have difficulty dealing with feedback that is not consistent with their perceptions of themselves (Paris & Cunningham, 1996).

With age, children's understanding of school becomes more complex and complete (Buchanan-Barrow & Barrett, 1998). As they acquire a better understanding of school and its demands, they also learn a great deal about self-control. To become effective students, children must plan, evaluate, monitor, and revise their actions as they adapt to the demands of the school environment. Children who cannot or do not make these adjustments are at risk for poor school outcomes (Nicholls, 1992).

INFLUENCE OF TEACHER–CHILD RELATIONSHIPS

Teachers act as role models, caregivers, and mentors for children. Relationships between teachers and children have important effects on children's social and emotional development and their adaptation to the school environment. For example, children who have warm, secure, and positive relationships with teachers are more cognitively and socially competent (Howes, Matheson, & Hamilton, 1994; Pianta & Nimetz, 1991). Sometimes, the quality of teacher-child relationships is more predictive of a child's behavior than is the quality of the child's relationships with his or her parents (Howes et al., 1994).

Teachers can have a significant influence on children's social development. This influence can be quite positive, encouraging feelings of competence and well-being. For example, teachers have been found to enhance positive outcomes for students if they (1) reduce the tendency of students to compare themselves with one another, (2) use cooperative interaction strategies in the classroom, (3) promote beliefs about students' competencies rather than their deficiencies, (4) increase chances for students to be successful, and (5) are warm, encouraging, and supportive (Shuell, 1996; Stipek, 1997). Other teachers are less successful at positively influencing their students' social development. How teachers respond to and influence their students depends on many factors:

- ✦ **Children's behaviors.**   Teachers generally respond more positively to students who achieve, conform, and are agreeable and compliant. They give attention to students who make demands that are appropriate to classroom activities, but they are indifferent to students who are silent or withdrawn. Teachers also may reject children who make many demands they consider illegitimate or who present behavior problems (Minuchin & Shapiro, 1983; Zimmerman, 1998).
- ✦ **Children's racial, ethnic, and socioeconomic backgrounds.**   Teachers sometimes stereotype children on the basis of race, culture, and social class. For example, teachers may attribute failure in school to a child's class or ethnic background (Persell, 1993; Weinstein, 1998). Some teachers expect less from lower-class and minority children, even when these children have abilities similar to those of other children. Teachers act more positively toward students they hold in high esteem, and they spend more time interacting with students whom they expect to work hard and achieve more (Demaray & Elliot, 1998). Because teachers' expectations are influenced more by negative than by positive information about their students (Persell, 1993) and because stereotypes about children from lower-class and/or ethnic families are more likely to be negative than positive, children from these socially vulnerable backgrounds are more susceptible than other children to teachers' expectations and behaviors (Ferguson, 1998; Tom & Cooper, 1986).
- ✦ **Children's gender.**   The available research supports the view that teachers treat boys and girls differently. Teachers generally give boys more attention than they give girls and more freedom (Sadker & Sadker, 1994). Teachers believe that boys possess greater school-related skills than girls do (Shepardson & Pizzini, 1992), so boys receive more approval, instruction, and time from their teachers (Bailey, 1993). Teachers believe that being nice and obedient is related to intellectual skills in girls but not in boys, although no research supports this argument (Gold, Crombie, & Noble, 1987). Thus, teacher-child relationships differ for boys and girls and are based on different qualities (Ruble & Martin, 1998).

WHAT CHANGES TAKE PLACE IN MORAL DEVELOPMENT DURING LATE CHILDHOOD?

A critical aspect of social and emotional development is the acquisition of moral values, intentions, and behaviors (Turiel, 1998). **Morality** is a set of principles or values that helps individuals distinguish right from wrong (Damon, 1988). Morality becomes a fundamental and important part of children's lives as soon as they start to develop relationships with others. Very early in life, children are aware of moral issues. As you learned in Chapter 8, young children and infants sometimes express concern about others' well-being and sometimes act prosocially. Young children also respond intensely

morality a set of principles or values that helps individuals distinguish right from wrong when they feel their rights have been violated. Older children have an even more advanced understanding of fairness and justice, and they know that they are supposed to be responsible, honest, fair, kind, and cooperative to parents, siblings, teachers, friends, and strangers.

Piaget's Theory of Moral Development

Although many theories address the issue of moral development (such as Freud's psychoanalytic concept of the superego; see Chapter 2), in recent years the cognitive developmental theories of Piaget and Kohlberg have been perhaps the most influential. Moral development provides an important example of the interconnectedness of developmental domains; advances in cognitive development and reasoning bring about important changes in how children interact with others and engage in moral behavior.

Piaget (1932/1965) based much of his theory of moral development on his observation and questioning of children playing marbles. He believed that the essence of morality lies in respect for rules. While playing marbles, children must deal with issues of fairness, turn taking, reciprocity, and justice. By studying how children thought about and followed the rules of the marble game, Piaget believed he could discover the principles of moral development.

Piaget theorized that it is through interactions with peers rather than interactions with parents that children make important advances in moral development. He argued that parents encourage immature levels of moral thinking because the parent-child relationship, which often depends on the rewards and punishments handed out by parents, promotes the belief that morality is dependent on authority. In contrast, peer relationships foster reciprocity and perspective taking as children try to find mutually satisfying ways of maintaining social interactions.

Piaget believed he could study the development of morality by observing children play games. How does children's game playing reflect their level of moral development?

Piaget's Stages of Moral Development

When preschoolers play a game, the point of the game is to have fun. They do not play systematically and do not have the intention to win. They make up their own rules and play the game according to whatever rules they like at the moment. Piaget labeled this stage of moral development the **premoral period**—the stage of moral development in which young children do not yet understand cooperative rules and goals associated with playing a game. Table 10.3 summarizes Piaget's stages of moral development and shows how children in these stages differ in terms of how they view rules, intentions, and punishment.

After age 5, children become concerned about playing by the rules and playing to win. During the period of concrete operations (between 6 and 10 years of age), children strictly adhere to rules—a stage of moral development that Piaget referred to as the **heteronomous morality stage.** Their moral decisions are based on the authority of others. Rules must be obeyed because they are sacred and unalterable. Any act that conforms to a rule is "good"; any act that does not conform is "bad." At this age, children have a sense of **moral realism**—judgments about morality are based on conforming to established rules set by powerful adults. Children between the ages of 6 and 10 react strongly to rule violations. Have you ever broken a rule in front of a child this age, perhaps by jaywalking or parking in a no-parking zone? Even if you have a good reason for doing so, children in this stage often consider these actions to be wrong and react strongly.

In contrast to adolescents and adults, children between the ages of 6 and 10 years believe that right and wrong are determined by the consequences associated with an action. When an action results in positive consequences, it is "good"; when an action results in

premoral period Piagetian stage of moral development in which young children do not yet understand cooperative rules and goals

heteronomous morality stage Piagetian stage of moral development in which children adhere strictly to rules and base moral decisions on the authority of others

moral realism the belief that morality is based on conforming to established rules set by powerful adults

TABLE 10.3
Outline of Piaget's Stages of Moral Development

CONCEPT	PREMORAL PERIOD (BEFORE AGE 6)	HETERONOMOUS MORALITY STAGE (AGES 6 TO 10)	AUTONOMOUS MORALITY STAGE (AFTER AGE 10)
Adherence to rules	Have little concern for or awareness of rules Do not understand that rules are a cooperative agreement about how a game should be played	Obey rules because they are sacred and unchangeable Believe that being "right" means always following the rules Believe that rules are made by those who have absolute authority	Understand that rules are arbitrary social agreements that can be challenged or changed Understand that rules can be violated in the service of human needs
Intentionality	Are too egocentric to take others' intentions into account	Judge acts of goodness or badness in terms of the physical consequences and not the motivation behind them	Believe that morality is determined by one's intentions rather than the consequences of an act
Punishment	Act to avoid punishment and maximize rewards	Favor severe punishment regardless of the misdeed—punishment does not fit the crime Base judgments of good or bad on whether the act elicits punishment and how much punishment it elicits Think that misdeeds inevitably lead to punishment—immanent justice	Favor milder punishment if it helps the person see that her or his action was wrong Believe that punishment should fit the crime

SOURCE: Hoffman, 1970.

negative consequences, it is "bad," regardless of the intentions behind the action. Consider the following exchange between a kindergarten child and her teacher:

> Katie: *I told my dad the truth. I was fighting with my brother, and my dad came and said, "Who started this?" I said it happened by accident.*
>
> Teacher: *Did your father believe you?*
>
> Katie: *He really did.*
>
> Teacher: *Was it an accident?*
>
> Katie: *Kind of.*
>
> Teacher: *Did you do it on purpose?*
>
> Katie: *Yeah, but I didn't get yelled at. See, I told you it was an accident.*

In this example, Katie's definition of acting morally depends on whether her father believes her and whether she is punished. Because her father believed her and because she did not get yelled at, Katie defines her actions and intentions as truthful and moral. This is not the case for older children.

In his work with children, Piaget (1932/1965) relied on children's reasoning for information about the development of morality. For example, he asked children of different ages questions about the following two stories:

(1) *A little boy who is called John is in his room. He is called to dinner. He goes into the dining room. But behind the door there is a chair and on this chair there is a tray with 15 cups on it. John couldn't have known that all this was behind the door. He goes in, the door knocks against the tray, and the 15 cups fall to the floor and break!*

(2) *Once there was a little boy named Henry. One day when his mother was out he tried to get some jam out of the cupboard. He climbed up on a chair and stretched out his arm. But the jam was too high up and he couldn't reach it. While he was trying to get it he knocked over a cup. The cup fell and broke on the floor!*

In the first story, the child accidentally breaks 15 cups; in the second, the child breaks one cup in an attempt to sneak some jam while his mother is out. Who is naughtier?

Children in the heteronomous morality stage of moral development (between 6 and 10 years of age) answer that John is naughtier because he broke more cups. Their beliefs about morality are based on the consequences of the act—John broke more cups than Henry did. They do not take intentions into account. They believe that because John broke more cups than Henry did, he is likely to be punished more severely than Henry. The act was "bad" because it was followed by more negative consequences, which will probably lead to more punishment. Piaget referred to this belief of children in the stage of moral realism—that breaking a rule always leads to punishment—as **immanent justice.**

From the age of 11 years on, coinciding with the end of the concrete operational period (see Chapter 9), children's ideas about rules are no longer as rigid and constrained as they had been. Older children's understanding of morality is based on the knowledge that rules can be changed if everybody agrees on the changes. Piaget refers to this stage of moral development, in which rules can be changed by the will of those involved in the game, as the **autonomous morality stage.**

Older children are likely to consider Henry to be the naughtier child because he was trying to sneak the jam. They take into account one's intentions and do not focus solely on the consequences of one's actions. Piaget argued that older children are more likely to believe that punishment should "fit the crime," whereas young children believe that punishment should always be severe no matter what the misdeed might be. This more realistic view reflects children's increased flexibility and perspective taking as they move beyond concrete operational thinking and into formal operational thinking.

Evaluation of Piaget's Theory of Moral Development

Piaget was among the first to suggest that children's morality develops in stages. His work stimulated great interest in morality and its development, but were his observations accurate?

The findings of several studies suggest that Piaget may have exaggerated young children's tendency to focus on *consequences* and overlook the *intentions* behind another's actions (Nelson-Le Gall, 1985; Schultz, Wright, & Schleifer, 1986). For example, even preschoolers evaluate a child who lied about a misdeed and got away with it more negatively than they do a child who told the truth and was punished for the misdeed (Bussey, 1992). Preschool children also judge a child who lied about a misdeed more negatively than they do a child who merely committed the misdeed. These findings are inconsistent with Piaget's belief that young children are moral realists. Because Piaget presented children with stories in which the information about the consequences of the actions was more obvious than the information about the children's intentions, young children tended to focus their attention on the information that was most obvious (Nelson, 1980). Young children have difficulty using subtle information about others' intentions, but when the intentions of another are made clear, they can and do use such information. By age 5, children understand that intentions and consequences are different kinds of information (Suber, 1982).

immanent justice the belief that breaking a rule always leads to punishment

autonomous morality stage Piagetian stage of moral development in which one believes that rules can be changed by the will of those involved

Although Piaget may have underestimated young children's ability to take into account the intentions of others, there is some support for his theory. For example, younger children's moral judgments depend on whether or not the misbehavior led to punishment. Children who were punished, regardless of whether they lied or told the truth, are more likely to be judged as bad than are children who behaved similarly but were not punished. In contrast, older children's judgments of goodness or badness are not influenced by whether the child was punished (Bussey, 1992). Additionally, young children develop rigidly defined moral rules. For young children, integrity means always keeping one's word regardless of the circumstances. Only around the age of 9 or 10 years do children come to understand that people can change their mind and that "being bad" occurs only when someone disappoints another person who was relying on him or her (Mant & Perner, 1988; Perner, 1989).

KOHLBERG'S THEORY OF MORAL DEVELOPMENT

One theorist who was greatly influenced by Piaget and who contributed many new and important insights into the development of morality was Lawrence Kohlberg (1969, 1984). Kohlberg identified six stages of moral development, based on his interviews with children, adolescents, and adults. In these interviews, he presented moral dilemmas in which the respondent was required to choose between obeying a rule or law and taking some action that conflicted with the rule or law but served a need. Consider the following moral dilemma:

> Judy was a 12-year-old girl. Her mother promised her that she could go to a special concert coming to their town if she saved up from baby-sitting and lunch money for a long time so she would have enough money to buy a ticket to the concert. She managed to save up the $5 the ticket cost plus another $3. But then her mother changed her mind and told Judy that she had to spend the money on new clothes for school. Judy was disappointed and decided to go to the concert anyway. She bought a ticket and told her mother that she had only been able to save $3. That Saturday she went to the performance and told her mother that she was spending the day with a friend. A week passed without her mother finding out. Judy then told her older sister, Louise, that she had gone to the performance and had lied to her mother about it. Louise wonders whether to tell their mother what Judy did. Should Louise, the older sister, tell her mother that Judy had lied about the money or should she keep quiet?
>
> —KOHLBERG, COLBY, GIBBS, AND SPEICHER-DUBIN (1978, P. 9)

Kohlberg was not interested in the specific answers respondents gave to the question—should Louise tell or not—but instead focused on the reasons they gave to justify their answers. From his analysis of the reasons they provided for their responses to this moral dilemma, Kohlberg identified three broad levels of moral development, with two stages at each level. These six stages are listed in Table 10.4, along with qualities that characterize each stage.

Kohlberg's Stages of Moral Development

At the first broad level of moral development, the **Preconventional Level,** morality is based on external forces. Children conform to rules to avoid punishment or to obtain personal rewards, and their reasoning reflects a belief that goodness or badness is determined by consequences. At the first stage within this level, *Punishment-and-Obedience Orientation,* obedience is valued for its own sake and the motivation for acting morally is to avoid punishment. Children have difficulty considering others' points of view. Actions are evaluated in terms of their physical consequences, such as the amount of damage done. Here is an example of a stage 1 answer to the moral dilemma:

> Louise should tell her mother about Judy's lie because if she doesn't, Louise is a liar.

Preconventional Level first level of Kohlberg's theory of moral development, in which morality is based on external forces

TABLE 10.4
Kohlberg's Levels and Stages of Moral Development

STAGE	CONTENT OF STAGE		SOCIAL PERSPECTIVE OF STAGE
	WHAT IS RIGHT	REASONS FOR DOING RIGHT	
Preconventional Level			
Stage 1: Punishment-and-Obedience Orientation	Definitions of right and wrong are based on consequences. Rules should not be broken. Obedience is important for its own sake. Physical damage to persons and property should be avoided.	To avoid punishment Belief in the superiority of authority figures	Fails to consider others' points of view Cannot consider two points of view Considers actions in terms of their physical consequences
Stage 2: Instrumental-Purpose Orientation	Rules should be followed only when it is in one's immediate interest. Pragmatic reciprocity is the underlying principle: "You scratch my back; I'll scratch yours."	To serve one's own needs or interests	Is aware that others have interests they pursue and that these conflict Believes that being right is relative to one's needs
Conventional Level			
Stage 3: Interpersonal Orientation ("Good boy–Good girl" orientation)	Doing right is what pleases others. Being good means having good motives and showing concern about others. Being loyal, trustworthy, and respectful to others is important.	To be seen as a nice person by others To maintain rules and authority Belief in the Golden Rule	Is aware of shared feelings and expectations, which are more important than individual interests
Stage 4: Social-Order-Maintenance Orientation	One should conform to social rules in order to avoid disapproval by authorities. Doing good is fulfilling what one has agreed to do.	Belief that rules and law maintain the social order and are worth following To avoid breakdown in the system if rules are not followed	Takes the point of view of the larger social system Considers individual relations in terms of their place in the larger social system
Postconventional Level			
Stage 5: Social-Contract Orientation	Moral actions are usually those that reflect the will of the majority. Rules must be determined by democratic procedures and must be impartial. Some values must be upheld in any society, regardless of the majority opinion.	A sense of obligation to laws To uphold the social contract that protects all people's rights To do the greatest good for the greatest number of people	Is aware of values and rights prior to social contracts Recognizes that moral and legal points of view may conflict
Stage 6: Universal-Ethical-Principle Orientation*	Right and wrong are based on self-chosen ethical principles. Laws and social agreements are valid because they rest on such principles. When laws violate these principles, one should act in accordance with the principles rather than the laws. Principles are universal principles of justice: the equality of human rights and respect for others as individuals.	Belief in the validity of universal moral principles and a sense of personal commitment to them	Gives equal consideration to the rights of all human beings Has respect for the value and dignity of all people

*In later work, Kohlberg (1984) proposed that Stage 6 is not distinguishable from Stage 5 and suggested that the two be combined.
SOURCE: Kohlberg, 1969; Rest, 1983.

At this stage, Louise's telling her mother is justified based on the simple, or absolute, standard that not telling her mother would be a lie and Louise would be a liar if she did not tell. No reason is needed beyond the fact that it would be considered wrong not to do so. Children under 10 typically are at this stage of moral development.

In stage 2 of this first level of moral development, *Instrumental-Purpose Orientation*, children believe that rules should be followed when it is in one's best interest to do so. Morality is based on serving one's own needs or interests. Children in stage 2 have some awareness of others' interests, but being right is considered only in relation to one's own needs. Here is a typical stage 2 answer to the moral dilemma:

> *Louise should keep quiet because if she does then Judy may keep quiet for Louise in the future.*

Louise's not telling is justified based on her self-interest and on an appreciation of the value of not telling their mom. Typically, stage 2 of moral development appears at age 10.

The next broad level of moral development is the **Conventional Level.** At this level, individuals strive to win praise and recognition for good conduct and for maintaining social order. Within this level, stage 3 morality—*Interpersonal Orientation*—reflects the belief that doing right is what pleases other people. Individuals are motivated to be seen by others as being nice and good. At this stage, individuals show more awareness of, and concern for, others' feelings and expectations than at earlier stages. Here is an example of stage 3 reasoning:

> *Louise should not tell her mother about Judy's lie because telling would destroy Judy's trust and betray her confidence in Louise.*

According to this stage of moral development, Louise should not tell her mother because it is important that she maintain her relationship with her sister. The desire to be seen as being loyal and trustworthy is imperative. Stage 3 of moral development begins to appear in early adolescence (ages 13–14).

Stage 4 of moral development, *Social-Order-Maintenance Orientation*, reflects a belief that rules maintain the social order and that the social system will break down if people do not follow rules. At this stage, doing good involves following through on what you have agreed to do, for the good of the larger social system. Here is an example of stage 4 reasoning:

> *Louise should not tell her mother because her mom promised Judy that she could use the money to go to the concert and her mom should keep her word. A promise should be sacred.*

This answer reflects concern about the promise that Judy's mother made to her. The mother is seen to have a duty, or obligation, to carry out her promise because society depends upon reliability and maintaining social contracts.

The third and highest broad level of moral development is the **Postconventional Level.** At this level, the individual is personally committed to a set of principles that are shared with others but go beyond particular authority figures. Moral standards are internalized and become part of the individual. In stage 5, *Social-Contract Orientation*, moral actions are defined as those that reflect the will of the majority. Morality reflects a sense of obligation to uphold social laws and contracts that protect all people's rights. At this stage, individuals have an awareness of many points of view and have a desire to do the greatest good for the greatest number of people. Here is an example of stage 5 reasoning:

> *Before you can say that Louise should tell her mother, you've got to consider the whole situation. Louise should respect her mother's point of view but parents' expectations and rules should not violate what one believes to be right.*

Judgments about morality are no longer seen as black or white. Moral judgments focus on the obligation of each person and the recognition that everyone involved has rights.

Conventional Level second level of Kohlberg's theory of moral development, in which moral reasoning is based on winning praise and recognition for good conduct and maintaining the social order

Postconventional Level third level of Kohlberg's theory of moral development, in which judgments about morality are based on principles that the individual is personally committed to and that are shared by others

The final stage of Kohlberg's theory of moral development is stage 6, *Universal-Ethical-Principle Orientation*. At this stage, right and wrong are based on self-chosen ethical principles. These are not concrete rules such as the Golden Rule, but rather are abstract moral principles of universal justice and respect for all individuals. When laws violate these moral principles, individuals should act in accordance with their principles rather than the law. At this stage, individuals consider the rights of all human beings. Here is an example of this level of reasoning:

> *One must always do what he or she thinks is right. If that means disobeying your parents, then so be it. Louise ought to do what she thinks a just person would do in this case, not do it just because of emotion or obligation.*

In this answer, the person recognizes that laws and social agreements are valid only because they rest on ethical principles. If a law violates these principles, one may disobey the law. Reasoning at this stage is based on universal principles and one's personal sense of commitment to these principles. Interestingly, none of Kohlberg's participants ever reached stage 6 (Kohlberg, 1981). Kohlberg described this stage as a "potential" stage and suggested that moral leaders such as Jesus, Gandhi, and Martin Luther King, Jr., exemplify this level of moral reasoning. In later work, Kohlberg (1984) proposed that stage 6 is not distinguishable from stage 5 and suggested that the two be combined.

Evaluation of Kohlberg's Theory of Moral Development

Several longitudinal studies provide support for Kohlberg's stages (Colby, Kohlberg, Gibbs, & Lieberman, 1983; Walker, 1989). As children grow older, their level of moral development becomes more abstract and advanced. Figure 10.5 illustrates some of these findings. This figure depicts the percentages of children and adults who display lower levels of moral development (focus on consequences) and higher levels of moral development (emphasis on dignity and autonomy). As you can see, the percentage of individuals using lower-level reasoning decreases with age, whereas the percentage of individuals using higher-level reasoning increases with age. Few people violated the stage sequence; of 233 participants, only 14 (or 6 percent) moved from a higher to a lower stage as they got older—and no one skipped a stage (Walker, 1989).

Kohlberg argued that higher moral reasoning is based on a decline in egocentrism and an increase in perspective taking and abstract reasoning. As indicated in Table 10.4, children at the Preconventional Level show only a limited awareness of others' thoughts, needs, and intentions. Morality at the Conventional Level is characterized by an increased recognition of others' points of view, and moral reasoning at the Postconventional Level is based on abstract principles and consideration of the rights of others. If Kohlberg was correct, there should be a correspondence between level of moral reasoning and cognitive development.

Formal tests of the relationship between level of moral reasoning and cognitive development generally support Kohlberg's theory—higher levels of cognitive

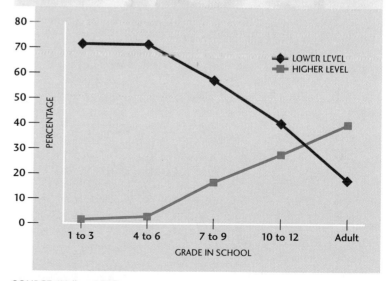

FIGURE 10.5

Percentages of Individuals at Lower and Higher Levels of Moral Reasoning Across Age Groups

SOURCE: Walker, 1989.

This figure shows that lower levels of moral reasoning decrease with age, whereas higher levels of moral reasoning increase with age. What factors might account for these changes? How do these data support Kohlberg's theory of moral development?

development and role taking are related to higher levels of moral reasoning (Rest, 1983; Walker, 1988). But people with higher levels of cognitive development do not necessarily act more morally than those with lower levels of cognitive development (Blasi, 1983; Walker & Henning, 1997). Although a person in stage 5 will often act differently in moral situations than a person in stage 3 or 2, it is difficult to predict how that person will act based simply on knowledge of his or her level of moral reasoning, because other factors influence actual moral behavior. Moreover, at each stage there is considerable variability within an individual in the use of moral reasoning—individuals use moral concepts differently as they cycle through developmental and personal changes (Thoma & Rest, 1999).

CULTURE AND MORALITY

According to Kohlberg, moral development was not learned by imitation or reinforcement. Nor did he believe that moral development was influenced by the specific content of the rules and laws of a culture. Rather, Kohlberg believed that morality was based on universal principles that developed in an invariant sequence, regardless of the culture in which a person was raised (Kohlberg, 1981).

Cross-cultural research provides evidence in support of Kohlberg's stages. Although stages 1 and 5 occur infrequently, stages 2, 3, and 4 can be found in many cultures (Eckensberger, 1994). Additionally, the sequence of stages is similar across different cultures (Snarey, 1985).

Moral themes, however, vary from culture to culture (Kahn, 1997). Table 10.5 lists some of the serious moral offenses identified by 8- to 10-year-old Hindu Brahman children (Shweder, Mahapatra, & Miller, 1987). People in India, like people in many non-Western cultures, treat moral rules as part of the natural world. Examination of Table 10.5 reveals that Indian children consider violations of food customs more important than uncharitable behavior or stealing (Schweder et al., 1987). Violations of customs are serious moral offenses because they are considered to be as much a breach of natural moral principles as is an intentional act that harms someone. In contrast, American children view morality as a contract between people (Damon, 1988). Thus, Indian and American

---

TABLE 10.5

Serious Moral Offenses Identified by Hindu Brahman Children, Ranked in Order of Seriousness

1. The day after his father's death, the eldest son had a haircut and ate chicken.
2. One of your family members eats beef regularly.
3. Six months after the death of her husband, the widow wore jewelry and bright-colored clothes.
4. A woman cooked rice and wanted to eat with her husband and his elder brother. Then she ate with them.
5. A beggar was begging from house to house with his wife and sick child. A home owner drove away without giving him anything.
6. In a family, a 25-year-old addresses his father by his first name.
7. A poor man went to the hospital after being seriously hurt in an accident. At the hospital they refused to treat him because he could not afford to pay.
8. A father told his son to steal flowers from his neighbor's garden. The boy did it.

SOURCE: Shweder et al., 1987. Copyright © 1987 University of Chicago Press.

Are There Gender Differences in Moral Reasoning?

Do males and females think about moral issues in similar ways? This question has been hotly debated, both in the scientific literature and in popular media. Carol Gilligan (1982) argues that, just as people from some cultures vary in their ideas about morality, females differ from males in their moral judgments. According to Gilligan, females rely on a morality of *caring* rather than one of justice. The ethic of care is based on the assumption that people are not separate units with conflicting needs requiring arbitration but, rather, that people are connected to one another. Based on an ethic of care, females place more emphasis on the maintenance of relation-

ships, whereas males place more emphasis on law and order (Haste & Baddeley, 1991). These differences come from the sex-typed cultures in which males and females grow up (Gilligan & Wiggins, 1987). In Gilligan's (1982) words, the sexes *speak in a different voice*. Neither voice is louder or better; the two are just different.

The scientific evidence generally does not support Gilligan's belief that males and females have different moral voices (Turiel, 1998). Although a few studies show gender differences in moral reasoning, the majority of studies do not find such differences (Walker, 1984, 1991). It appears that the ethic of justice and care are not in opposition to each other and

that moral problems do not force a choice between them (Walker, 1991).

Thinking It Through:

1. Do you think Kohlberg's stages of moral development reflect a gender bias toward males? Why or why not?
2. According to Carol Gilligan, how would the moral reasoning of girls differ from that of boys? On the basis of your experience, do you agree or disagree with Gilligan's ideas? Explain.
3. Working with classmates, develop a research plan that you think might help resolve the issue of whether males and females differ in their moral reasoning.

children have very different views of morality, and these cultural differences serve as a basis for differences in judgments about what is right and wrong.

Within American culture, there are differences in the moral values and orientations of different groups. For example, Mexican American children have a group orientation in which sharing, affiliation, and cooperation are highly valued moral qualities (Kagan, Knight, Martinez, & Santa, 1981). African American children generally focus on finding solutions to moral problems.

These differences in orientation influence how children respond to situations calling for moral judgements. In one study (Rotheram-Borus & Phinney, 1990), Mexican American and African American children were asked to identify what a person should do in certain moral situations, such as when someone asks for a loan, when someone is scolded by a teacher who is disappointed in that person, or when others are fighting. As you can see in Table 10.6, Mexican American children favored sharing money more often than African American children did. African American children were more inclined to stop a fight than were Mexican American children, who tended to feel bad or not want to get involved. After being scolded by a teacher, African American children favored apologizing more frequently than did Mexican American children, who were inclined to feel bad or angry. These differences generally are greater with age, perhaps reflecting the increased exposure older children have to the norms of their ethnic group (Rotheram-Borus & Phinney, 1990). Thus, moral development occurs as the result of the joint, reciprocal, and simultaneous influences of individual development and cultural socialization (Navaez, Geta, Rest, & Thoma, 1999)

TABLE 10.6

Children's Ideas of What Should Be Done in Different Moral Scenarios, by Ethnicity and Age

MORAL SCENARIO	THIRD-GRADERS		SIXTH-GRADERS	
	AFRICAN AMERICAN	MEXICAN AMERICAN	AFRICAN AMERICAN	MEXICAN AMERICAN
Asked to share money				
Share	24%	50%	76%	100%
Do not share	76%	50%	24%	0%
Scolded by teacher				
Apologize	28%	9%	62%	10%
Do something to change things	28%	18%	24%	14%
Feel bad	28%	36%	14%	67%
Get angry	16%	36%	0%	10%
Peers fighting				
Stop fight	48%	18%	62%	38%
Encourage fight	20%	23%	24%	10%
Feel bad	24%	45%	5%	24%
Do not get involved	8%	14%	10%	29%

SOURCE: Rotheram-Borus and Phinney, 1990.

CHAPTER SUMMARY

How do emotions develop during late childhood?

• As children develop, their vulnerability to stress changes. The situations that produce stress and the ways they cope with stress also change.

• Older children are more likely to become stressed because of increased expectations and pressures to achieve at school, whereas young children's stress revolves primarily around parent-child relationships.

• Stress also may be experienced when people change cultural environments. Acculturative stress occurs when families and children must adapt to the new customs of a different culture.

• Older children's ways of coping with stress are more abstract and cognitive than those of younger children.

• Some children are resilient, or stress-resistant, and adapt well even in situations that seem overwhelmingly stressful. Having above-average intelligence, possessing attractive qualities, and having a positive place in the family are common characteristics of resilient children.

• Community violence can undermine children's sense of well-being and place them at risk. Because of their increased ability to understand dangerous situations, older children respond to community violence in more diverse ways than younger children do.

What emotional and psychological disturbances affect children in late childhood?

• Late childhood is a time when emotional and psychological disturbances often surface. These problems are relatively rare, but when they do occur, they often are serious and have powerful effects on both the children who experience these problems and those who interact with them.

• Antisocial behavior is a pattern of behavior that is aggressive, defiant, uncooperative, and disruptive to the individual, to his or her relationships, and to the community. Antisocial children—who are more likely to be boys—show a progression of aversive behaviors across childhood and into adolescence and adulthood.

• Biological, familial, peer, and social factors all contribute to antisocial behavior. At present, no single treatment has been found to effectively address antisocial problems. Instead, the best outcomes involve multiple interventions addressing the diverse factors that contribute to antisocial behavior.

• Childhood depression is a serious mental health problem. Older children experience symptoms of depression similar to those suffered by adults—sadness, disengagement, and self-deprecation.

• Genetic, biological, temperamental, familial, and social factors contribute to depressive disorders in children. Effective treatment begins with helping children communicate depressed feelings.

- Fears and anxieties that are common in infancy and early childhood usually disappear during late childhood. During late childhood, children are no longer afraid of things simply because of the way they look but now are fearful of threats to their physical and psychological well-being.

- Phobias are extreme, persistent, and irrational fears that significantly affect a child's functioning. One of the most common phobias of late childhood is school phobia—an extreme fear associated with school environments. Several effective techniques have been developed to treat children's phobic responses.

How do children's family relationships change during late childhood?

- During late childhood, children spend less time with their families and more time with peers and in school activities. In recent years, parental supervision of older children has decreased. Many school-age children are latchkey children, left to care for themselves when they come home from school.

- Sibling relationships also change during late childhood. Those children who have siblings near their own age spend more time with them than they spend with their parents. Children with younger siblings spend time caring for them.

- Children who have no siblings tend to grow up much like children with brothers and sisters.

What factors influence older children's peer relationships?

- During late childhood, peer relationships take on greater importance.

- Children who have poor peer relationships are not all the same. Rejected children are actively disliked, whereas neglected children are not disliked but overlooked and ignored by peers.

- Children's levels of social competence—how well they initiate, maintain, manage, and communicate in social relationships—determine their ability to form meaningful and positive peer relationships. Many factors influence children's social competence, including individual, familial, and social factors.

How does school affect older children's social and emotional development?

- Entry into school exposes children to a wide variety of personalities, values, behaviors, and customs.

- The increased focus on academic performance and achievement leads children to compare themselves to one another. These pressures produce feelings of fear and anxiety, as well as feelings of pride and satisfaction.

- Teachers can have a significant influence on children's social development. Teachers enhance outcomes for students when they minimize competition and promote cooperation and supportive relationships.

- Teachers' responses to children are influenced by children's behaviors; their racial, ethnic, and socioeconomic backgrounds; and their gender.

What changes take place in moral development during late childhood?

- Piaget based his theory of morality on his observations of children's understanding of rules and how it changes with age. Young children do not understand cooperative rules (premoral period), but begin to adhere to them strictly during the school years (heteronomous morality stage). Adolescents and adults focus more on the internal qualities of morality—such as one's intention—than its consequences, and they recognize that rules can be changed by the will of those involved (autonomous morality stage).

- Based on his interviews with children, Kohlberg identified six stages of moral development. Children begin at the Punishment-and-Obedience stage, in which morality is based on avoiding punishment and receiving rewards. Next, in the Instrumental-Purpose stage, they reason based on what serves their own needs and interests. The next stage of reasoning is the Interpersonal stage, which reflects reasoning based on an effort to win praise and recognition for good conduct. Reasoning at stage 4, Social-Order-Maintenance, involves the belief that rules maintain the social order. In the Social-Contract stage, morality reflects a sense of obligation to uphold social laws and contracts. The last stage, the Universal-Ethical-Principle stage, represents a belief that right and wrong are self-chosen ethical principles.

- Longitudinal evidence generally supports Kohlberg's stage theory, and higher levels of cognitive development are related to higher levels of moral reasoning.

- Some aspects of moral development are similar across different cultures. Variation in other aspects is associated with cultural norms.

KEY TERMS & CONCEPTS

acculturative stress *(345)*
antisocial behavior *(350)*
autonomous morality stage *(371)*
Conventional Level *(374)*

emotion-focused coping strategies *(345)*
heteronomous morality stage *(369)*
immanent justice *(371)*

innate fears *(356)*
latchkey children *(359)*
moral realism *(369)*
morality *(368)*

ACTIVITIES & APPLICATIONS

Relating to Older Children

1. Interview school-age children about their experiences in school. Have them discuss their relationships with classmates and teachers. Ask them if they have ever experienced any safety issues while at school (such as being threatened or seeing someone with a knife). Use the material in the chapter to draw some conclusions about the impact of these experiences and relationships on the children's development.

2. Reread the story of Janet at the beginning of this chapter, and describe how individual, familial, and social factors contribute to the problems Janet is facing. What kinds of interventions and treatments might be effective in helping Janet cope with her problems?

3. Look through newspapers, magazines, or the Internet for a story on heroism or extreme courage displayed by a school-age child. How do such actions relate to moral development? What factors lead to heroism and courage? Draw some conclusions about the relationship between these types of behaviors and moral reasoning.

PART 5 LATE CHILDHOOD DEVELOPMENT
Grasping the Whole

Benchmarks in Late Childhood

PHYSICAL/MOTOR DEVELOPMENT	COGNITIVE DEVELOPMENT	SOCIAL/EMOTIONAL DEVELOPMENT
Slower growth than in previous years	Development of concrete operational thinking; decreased egocentrism and increased ability to mentally represent actions and objects; increased understanding of multiple classification and seriation	Change in contexts and types of stressors, increased use of emotion-focused and cognitive coping responses
Continuing myelination of brain and development of neural pathways		Increased evidence of antisocial behavior, depression, and fears, phobias, and anxieties
Increasing coordination and physical strength and improved motor skills	Increasingly complex understanding of syntax and use of language; increasing vocabulary and understanding of idioms	Reduced interactions with parents and increased interest in siblings and peers
Increased participation in sports and athletics	Development of reading and writing	Increased emphasis on peer relationships and problems related to them
Increased risk for accidents, injuries, and obesity	Increased emphasis on IQ and creativity because of the focus on school performance and achievement	Increased emphasis on the social aspects of school
	Enhanced ability to think of other people in abstract and differentiated ways; increased understanding of others' perspectives	Change in moral development from a focus on the consequences of one's actions (heteronomous morality) to a focus on one's intentions (autonomous morality)
	Changing views of race and ethnic groups	Change in moral reasoning from the preconventional to the conventional level

Status Report on Late Childhood

Large differences exist in the amount of money countries spend on primary education. Highly developed countries generally spend more on education than less developed countries do, but there are considerable differences even among highly developed countries. What factors contribute to these differences? What impact does spending have on the quality of education received by school-age children, and how does this affect their development?

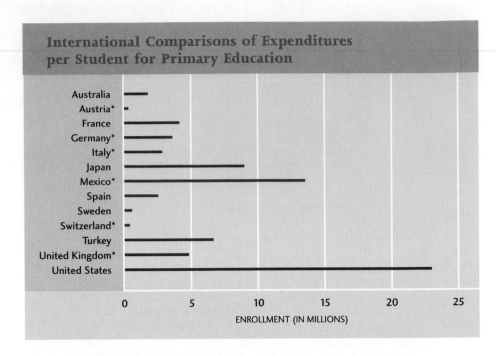

International Comparisons of Expenditures per Student for Primary Education

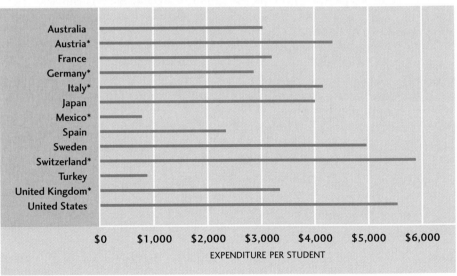

*Data are for public institutions only. (All other totals combine data from public and private institutions.)
SOURCE: US Department of Education, 1998.

SUGGESTED READINGS

Garbarino, J., Dubrow, N., Kostelny, K., & Pardo, C. (1992). *Children in danger: Coping with the consequences of community violence.* San Francisco: Jossey-Bass. A well-written book that offers valuable guidance on helping children cope with violence in their lives. These child-development specialists provide glimpses of the effects on children of living with chronic violence.

Kotlowitz, A. (1991). *There are no children here.* New York: Doubleday. In-depth, riveting account of children growing up in poverty. This powerful book paints an eloquently painful picture of two boys and their family as they struggle to cope with poverty, violence, and racism.

Salovey, P., & Sluyter, D. J. (1997). *Emotional development and emotional intelligence: Educational implications.* New York: Basic

Books. Cutting-edge research on emotions and emotional development presented in a manner useful to educators. This book, by experts in child development, links research and application by integrating scientific explanation with commentaries from educators on applications in the classroom.

Valdés, G. (1996). *Con respecto: Bridging the distance between culturally diverse families and schools.* New York: Teachers College, Columbia University. Rich and fascinating study of Mexican parents in border communities. Valdés describes how these families survive and learn to succeed in a new world and the problems associated with acclimating to our educational system.

RECOMMENDED WEBSITES

Kidshealth: This Website is devoted to the health of children and teens. Created by the medical experts at the Nemours Foundation, Kidshealth has accurate, up-to-date information about growth; food and fitness; childhood physical and mental health; and the latest treatments for medical and surgical conditions. Separate sections for children, parents, and professionals allow for individualized information. <http://kidshealth.org/>

National Alliance for Safe Schools: This Website was established to provide technical assistance, training, and research to parents, teachers, and school districts interested in reducing school-based crime and violence. It contains information pertaining to the latest research on school safety, anti-violence programs, and related issues. <http://www.safeschools.org/>

National Center for Education Statistics (NCES): NCES collects and reports statistics and information on the condition and progress of education in the United States and other nations, in order to promote and accelerate the improvement of American education. <http://nces.ed.gov/>

National Parents and Teachers Association: This is the Website of the oldest and largest volunteer association in the United States working exclusively on behalf of children and youth. Information on the site is designed to help governmental bodies and other organizations make decisions affecting children and to assist parents in developing the skills they need to raise and protect their children. <http://www.pta.org/>

Research Network on Successful Pathways Through Middle Childhood: The Network on Successful Pathways through Middle Childhood was established to study the influences and experiences that contribute to successful outcomes for children during the school years. The Website provides information and links about the network and its work, focusing on children from the time they enter school until early adolescence. <http://midchild.soe.umich.edu/>

Studies in Moral Development and Education: This homepage links educators, scholars, and citizens who want to share their work and learn more about research, practices, and activities in the area of moral development and education. It is maintained and developed by the Office for Studies in Moral Development and Character Formation in the College of Education at the University of Illinois, Chicago. <http://www.uic.edu/~lnucci/MoralEd/>

NATIONAL HOTLINES FOR SCHOOL-AGED CHILDREN

Mental Health Information Center: 800-969-6642

National Health Information Clearinghouse: 800-336-4797

National PTA Headquarters: 312-670-6782

Developmental Timeline

PRENATAL   NEONATAL DEVELOPMENT

CONCEPTION AND PRENATAL DEVELOPMENT	BIRTH	NEONATAL PERIOD (0–2 MONTHS)
GERMINAL STAGE • aligning of maternal and paternal chromosomes • genetic transmission of physical characteristics • sex determination • basic intelligence • basic personality and behavioral traits **EMBRYONIC STAGE** • development of nervous system and major organs • development of basic physical structures • cephalocaudal and proximodistal growth • serious teratogenic effects on growth and development **FETAL STAGE** • rapid growth in size and weight • rapid brain development • viability and preparation for birth • transfer of immunities from mother to child	• labor and dilation of cervix • crowning and molding of baby's head • delivery of baby • delivery of placenta • Apgar testing of health status • cultural and social expectations for birth	• adaptation to extrauterine environment • reflex responses • rapid brain development • short-term, context-bound memory • expression of basic emotions • states of arousal • ability to imitate • importance of caregiving

PERSONAL HISTORY

INFANCY & TODDLERHOOD

2–12 MONTHS	12–24 MONTHS	24–36 MONTHS
• critical brain development	• critical brain development	• critical brain development
• rapid growth in size	✓ • cruising, walking, and climbing	✓ • running
• voluntary reaching and grasping	✓ • stacking and sorting toys; scribbling	• negotiating stairs
• preference for hearing own language	• ability to search for hidden objects	✓ • throwing and catching a ball
• sensorimotor cognitive development: circular reactions and goal-directed behavior	• problem solving through active experimentation	• bowel and bladder control
• expression of temperament	• rapid language acquisition and growth of vocabulary	✓ • self-dressing and self-feeding
• development of attachment	• evidence of attachment	• development of self-concept and self-esteem
• color, pattern, face, motion, and depth perception	✓ • separation anxiety	✓ • pretend play, parallel play, and social play
• understanding of basic principles of objects and motions	✓ • self-recognition and self-reference	✓ • development of gender stereotypes and gender-typed preferences
• control of trunk; rolling over	• categorization of self and others on the basis of age and sex	• egocentrism, animism, and preoperational thinking
• crawling, sitting, and standing	✓ • gender-typed toy play	✓ • two- and three-word sentences
• imitation and deferred imitation	• development of self-conscious emotions	• development of multiple attachments
• memory for familiar people, places, and objects	• emergence of compliance and self-control	• beginning literacy and media exposure
• habituation	• ability to play turn-taking games	• development of empathy
• social smiling and laughter		
• stranger anxiety		
• use of gestures to communicate		
• cooing and babbling		
• first words; holophrases		

PERSONAL HISTORY

Developmental Timeline

EARLY CHILDHOOD

AGES 3–4	AGES 5–6
• improved coordination and balance	• improved memory
• "galloping," singing and dancing, tricycle riding	• identification of letters of the alphabet and development of phonemic awareness
• preoperational thought	• shoe tying and name writing
• egocentric and perceptually based reasoning	• improved ability to distinguish appearance from reality
• grasp of cause and effect	• greater use of self-discipline in directing attention
• classification of familiar objects	• basic ability to add and subtract
• use of private speech to guide behavior	• transition and adjustment to school
• ability to remember experiences using scripts	• continuing development of theory of mind
• ability to generalize information from one situation to another	• use of social cues to predict, interpret, and influence others' behavior
• understanding of false beliefs	• risk factors for the development of health problems, fears, and anxieties
• ability to count objects and grasp the principle of cardinality	• fast-mapping of new vocabulary; 10,000-word vocabulary
• overextension of grammatical rules	• understanding of gender consistency
• focus on parent-child interactions and discipline	• development of cooperation and aggression
• opportunities for preschool and peer experiences	
• increase in self-directed, interactive, and cooperative play	
• ability to distinguish moral rules from social conventions	
• preference for same-sex playmates	
• first friendships	

PERSONAL HISTORY

LATE CHILDHOOD

AGES 7–8	AGES 9–10
• marked skeletal growth	• start of growth spurt for girls
• permanent teeth	• improved coordination, balance, and reaction times
• increased nutritional, health, and safety risks	• cursive writing
• improvements in jumping, throwing, catching, kicking, and batting	• drawing three-dimensionally and in perspective
• participation in school life	• greater metacognitive awareness
• achievement of literacy and legible printing	• use of memory strategies in learning
• concrete operational thinking	• understanding of metaphors, double meanings, and humor
• knowledge of conservation and decentration	• interest in social comparisons of self with others
• development of logic and reversible thinking	• greater self-regulation
• increased skills in hierarchical classification and seriation	• ability to adapt conversations to needs of others
• appearance of heteronomous morality	• morality based on external qualities
• involvement in organized games and activities	
• peer group identification	
• increased prosocial behavior	
• higher-level development of friendships	
• academic, social, and physical self-esteem based on attributions of success and failure	

PERSONAL HISTORY

Photo Credits

Bibliography

Abbott, S. (1997). Gender, status, and values among Kikuyu and Appalachian adolescents. In T. S. Weisner & C. Bradley (Eds.), *African families and the crisis of social change* (pp. 86–105). Westport, CT: Bergin & Garvey/Greenwood Publishing Group.

Abel, E. L. (1996). Introduction. In E. Abel (Ed.), *Fetal alcohol syndrome.* Boca Raton, FL: CRC Press.

Aber, J. L., Jones, S. M., Brown, J. L., Chaudry, N., & Samples, F. (1998). Resolving conflict creatively: Evaluating the developmental effects of a school-based violence prevention program in neighborhood and classroom context. *Development and Psychopathology, 10,* 187–213.

Aboud, F. E. (1988). *Children and prejudice.* New York: Basil Blackwell.

Aboud, F. E., & Doyle, A. B. (1996). Parental and peer influences on children's racial attitudes. *International Journal of Intercultural Relations, 20,* 371–383.

Abrams, S. M., Field, T., Scafidi, F., & Prodromidis, M. (1995). Newborns of depressed mothers. *Infants Mental Health Journal, 16,* 233–239.

Achenbach, T. M., & Edelbrock, C. (1989). Diagnostic, taxonomic, and assessment issues. In T. H. Ollendick & M. Hersen (Eds.), *Handbook of child psychopathology* (pp. 53–69). New York: Plenum.

A. C. Nielsen. (1990). *Report on Sesame Street.* New York: A. C. Nielsen Company.

A. C. Nielsen. (1995). *Television use and ratings: 1995.* New York: Nielson Media Research Group.

Acredolo, L., & Goodwyn, S. (1988). Symbolic gesturing in normal infants. *Child Development, 59,* 450–466.

Acredolo, L., & Goodwyn, S. (1996). *Baby signs.* New York: Contemporary Books.

Adams, J. L. (1990). Conceptual blockbusting: A guide to better ideas. Reading, MA: Addison-Wesley.

Adams, M. J., Treiman, R., & Pressley, M. (1998). Reading, writing, and literacy. In W. Damon (Ed.), *Handbook of child psychology* (Vol. 4, pp. 275–356). New York: Wiley.

Adams, R. J. (1989). Newborn's discrimination among mid- and long-wave length stimuli. *Journal of Experimental Child Psychology, 47,* 130–141.

Adams, W. G., Geva, J., Coffman, J., Palfrey, S., & Bauchner, H. (1998). Anemia and elevated lead levels in underimmunized inner-city children. *Pediatrics, 101,* 1–7.

Adler, P. A., Kless, S. J., & Adler, P. (1992). Socialization to gender roles: Popularity among elementary school boys and girls. *Sociology of Education, 65,* 169–187.

Administration on Children, Youth, and Families. (1998). *Head Start 1998 fact sheet.* Washington, DC: Administration on Children, Youth, and Families.

Adolph, K. E. (1997). Learning in the development of infant locomotion. *Monographs of the Society for Research in Child Development 3,* Serial No. 251.

Ahmann, E. (1996). *Home care for the high-risk infant: A family-centered approach.* Gaithersburg, MD: Aspen.

Ainsworth, M. D. (1973). The development of infant-mother attachment. In B. M. Caldwell & H. N Ricciuti (Eds.), *Review of child development research* (Vol. 3, pp. 1–94). Chicago: University of Chicago Press.

Ainsworth, M. D., Blehar, M. C., Waters, E., & Wall, S. (1978). *Patterns of attachment: A psychological study of the strange situation.* Hillsdale, NJ: Erlbaum.

Akhtar, N., Carpenter, M., & Tomasello, M. (1996). The role of discourse novelty in early word learning. *Child Development, 67,* 635–645.

Alan Guttmacher Institute. (1994). *Sex and America's teenagers.* New York: Alan Guttmacher Institute.

Alan Guttmacher Institute. (1997). *The risk and realities of early childbearing worldwide, facts in brief.* New York: Alan Guttmacher Institute.

Alan Guttmacher Institute. (1998). *Teen sex and pregnancy.* New York: Alan Guttmacher Institute.

Alessandri, S. M., Sullivan, M. W., Imaizumi, S. & Lewis, M. (1993). Learning and emotional responsivity in cocaine-exposed infants. *Developmental Psychology, 29,* 989–997.

Alfieri, T., Ruble, D. N., & Higgins, E. T. (1996). Gender stereotypes during adolescence: Developmental changes and the transition to junior high school. *Developmental Psychology, 32,* 1129–1137.

Allen, L., & Mitchell, C. M. (1996). Poverty and adolescent health. In M. Kagawa-Singer & P. A. Katz (Eds.), *Health issues for minority adolescents* (pp. 1–35). Lincoln, NE: University of Nebraska Press.

Allen, M. C. (1993). The high-risk infant. *Pediatric Clinics of North America, 40,* 479–490.

Allen, M. C. (1996). The neonatal neurodevelopmental examination. In A. J. Capute, and P. J. Accardo (Eds.). *Developmental disabilities in infancy and childhood* (pp. 293–310). Baltimore, MD: Paul H. Brookes.

Allen, M. C., Donohue, P. K., & Dusman, A. E. (1993). The limit of viability—neonatal outcome of infants born at 22 to 25 weeks' gestation. *New England Journal of Medicine, 329,* 1597–1601.

Als, H. (1984). *Manual for the naturalistic observation of newborn behavior (preterm and full term infants).* Boston: The Children's Hospital.

Alsaker, F. D. (1992). Pubertal timing, overweight, and psychological adjustment. *Journal of Early Adolescence, 12,* 396–412.

Alsaker, F. D. (1995). Timing of puberty and reactions to pubertal changes. In M. Rutter (Ed.), *Psychosocial disturbances in young people: Challenges for prevention* (pp. 37–82). New York: Cambridge University Press.

Alsaker, F. D. (1996). Annotation: The impact of puberty. *Journal of Child Psychology and Psychiatry, 37,* 249–258.

Altarriba, J. (1993). The influence of culture on cognitive processes. In J. Altarriba (Ed.), *Cognition and culture* (pp. 379–385). Amsterdam: North-Holland.

Altshuler, J. L., & Ruble, D. N. (1989). Developmental changes in children's awareness of strategies for coping with uncontrollable stress. *Child Development, 60,* 1337–1349.

Amabile, T. M. (1993). What does a theory of creativity require? *Psychological Inquiry, 4,* 179–181.

Amato, M. (1997, April). Can this baby be soothed? *Child, 12,* 32–34.

Ambert, A. M. (1997). *Parents, children, and adolescents: Interactive relationships and development in context.* New York: Haworth Press.

American Academy of Pediatrics. (1987). Neonatal anesthesia. *Pediatrics, 80*(3), 446.

American Academy of Pediatrics. (1991). *Recommendations for preventive pediatric health care.* Elk Grove, IL: American Academy of Pediatrics.

American Academy of Pediatrics. (1996). *Smoking: Straight talk for teens.* Elk Grove, IL: American Academy of Pediatrics.

American Academy of Pediatrics. (1998). In-line skating injuries in children and adolescents. *Pediatrics, 101,* 720–722.

American Academy of Pediatrics. (1999a). *2 to 4 years: Safety for your child.* Elk Grove, IL: American Academy of Pediatrics.

American Academy of Pediatrics. (1999b). *Lead screening for children.* Elk Grove, IL: American Academy of Pediatrics.

American Academy of Pediatrics Committee on Sports Medicine. (1999). *A parent's guide to water safety.* Elk Grove, IL: American Academy of Pediatrics.

American Association of University Women. (1994). *Shortchanging girls, shortchanging America.* Washington, DC: Greenberg-Lake Analysis Group.

American College of Obstetricians and Gynecologists. (1990). *ACOG guide to planning for pregnancy, birth, and beyond.* Washington, DC: ACOG.

American College of Sports Medicine. (1987). Position statement on the use and abuse of anabolic-androgenic steroids in sports. *Medicine and Science in Sports, 9,* 11–13.

American Medical Association. (1996). *Physicians' guide to media violence.* Washington, DC: American Medical Association.

American Psychiatric Association. (1994). *Diagnostic and Statistical Manual of Mental Disorders* (Fourth Edition). Washington, DC: American Psychiatric Association.

American Psychological Association. (1993). *Violence and youth: Psychology's response. Volume I: Summary report of the American Psychological Association Commission on Violence and Youth.* Washington, DC: American Psychological Association.

Ames, N. L., & Miller, E. (1994). *Changing middle schools.* San Francisco: Jossey-Bass.

Anand, K. J. S., & Hickey, P. R. (1987). Pain and its effects in the human neonate and fetus. *New England Journal of Medicine, 137,* 1321–1329.

Anastasi, A. (1988). *Psychological testing.* New York: Macmillan.

Anderson, C. A., & Ford, C. M. (1986). Affect of the game player: Short-term effects of highly and mildly aggressive video games. *Personality and Social Psychology Bulletin, 12,* 390–402.

Anderson, G. C. (1984, April). *Crying in newborn infants: Physiology and developmental implications.* Paper presented at the International Conference on Infant Studies, New York.

Andersson, T., & Magnusson, D. (1990). Biological maturation in adolescence and the development of drinking habits and alcohol abuse among young males: A prospective longitudinal study. *Journal of Youth and Adolescence, 19,* 33–41.

Ando, K. (1987, July). *The development of empathy in prosocial behavior.* Paper presented to the International Society for the Study of Behavioral Development, Tokyo.

Andres, R. L., & Jones, K. L. (1994). Social and illicit drug use in pregnancy. In R. K. Creasy & R. Resnik (Eds.), *Maternal-fetal medicine: Principles and practice* (pp. 237–287). Philadelphia: W. B. Saunders.

Anglin, J. M. (1985). The child's expressible knowledge of word concepts. In K. E. Nelson (Ed.), *Children's language* (pp. 77–127). Hillsdale, NJ: Erlbaum.

Anglin, J. M. (1993). Vocabulary development. *Monographs of the Society for Research in Child Development 58,* (Whole No. 165).

Antill, J. K., Russell, G., Goodnow, J. J., & Cotton, S. (1993). Measures of children's sex typing in middle childhood. *Australian Journal of Psychology, 45,* 25–33.

Aoki, W. T., & Turk, A. A. (1997). Adolescent suicide: A review of risk factors and implications for practice. *Journal of Psychology and Christianity, 16,* 273–279.

Apgar, V. A. (1953). Proposal for a new method of evaluation of the newborn infant. *Anesthesia and Analgesia, Current Research, 22,* 260.

Appel, A. E., & Holden, G. W. (1998). The co-occurrence of spouse and physical child abuse: A review and appraisal. *Journal of Family Psychology, 12,* 578–599.

Apter, A. Galatzer, A., Beth-Halachmi, N., & Laron, A. (1981). Self-image in adolescents with delayed puberty and growth retardation. *Journal of Youth and Adolescence, 10,* 501–510.

Archer, S. L. (1989). Gender differences in identity development. *Journal of Adolescence, 12,* 117–138.

Archer, S. L. (1993). Identity in relational contexts. In J. Kroger (Ed.), *Discussions on ego identity* (pp. 75–99). Hillsdale, NJ: Erlbaum.

Arcia, E., & Conners, C. K. (1998). Gender differences in ADHD? *Journal of Developmental and Behavioral Pediatrics, 19,* 77–83.

Arditti, J. A. (1992). Investigating differences between joint custody and noncustodial fathers. *American Journal of Orthopsychiatry, 62,* 186–195.

Arditti, J. A., & Keith, T. Z. (1993). Visitation frequency, child support payment, and the father-child relationship postdivorce. *Journal of Marriage and the Family, 55,* 699–712.

Aries, E., & Moorehead, K. (1989). The importance of ethnicity in the development of identity in Black adolescents. *Psychological Reports, 65,* 75–82.

Aries, P. (1962). *Centuries of childhood.* New York: Vintage.

Arland, T. (1989). Changing attitudes towards family issues in the United States. *Journal of Marriage and the Family, 51,* 873–893.

Arms, K. G., Davidson, J. K., & Moore, N. B. (1992). *Cultural diversity and families.* Dubuque, IA: Brown.

Arnett, J. (1991). Adolescents and heavy metal music: From the mouths of metalheads. *Youth and Society, 23,* 76–98.

Arnett, J., & Balle-Jensen, L. (1993). Cultural bases of risk behavior: Danish adolescents. *Child Development, 64,* 1842–1855.

Asendorpf, J. B., & van Aken, M. A. G. (1994). Traits and relationship status: Stranger versus peer group inhibition and test intelligence versus peer group competence as early predictors of later self-esteem. *Child Development, 65,* 1786–1798.

Asher, S. R. (1990). Recent advances in the study of peer rejection. In S. R. Asher & J. D. Coie (Eds.), *Peer rejection in childhood* (pp. 3–16). Cambridge, England: Cambridge University Press.

Asher, S. R., Zelis, K. M., Parker, J. G., & Bruene, C. M. (1991, April). *Self-referral for peer relationship problems among aggressive and withdrawn low-accepted children.* Paper presented at the biennial meeting of the Society for Research in Child Development, Seattle.

Ashley, J., & Tomasello, M. (1998). Cooperative problem-solving and teaching in preschoolers. *Social Development, 7,* 143–163.

Aslin, R. N. (1987). Visual and auditory development in infancy. In J. D. Osofsky (Ed.), *Handbook of infant development* (pp. 5–97). New York: Wiley.

Aslin, R. N., Jusczyk, P. W., & Pisoni, D. B. (1998). Speech and auditory processing during infancy: Constraints on and precursors to language. In D. Kuhn & R. S. Siegler (Eds.), *Handbook of child psychology* (Vol. 2, pp. 147–198). New York: Wiley.

Atkin, C. (1983). Effects of realistic TV violence vs. fictional violence on aggression. *Journalism Quarterly, 60,* 615–621.

Atkin, L. C., Olvera, M. C., Givaudan, M., & Landeros, G. (1989). Neonatal and maternal perceptions of urban Mexican infants. In J. K. Nugent, B. M. Lester, & T. B. Brazelton (Eds.), The cultural context of the infant (Vol. 2, pp. 201–238). Norwood, NJ: Ablex.

Attie, I., & Brooks-Gunn, J. (1989). Development of eating problems in adolescent girls: A longitudinal study. Developmental Psychology, 25, 70–79.

Attie, I., Brooks-Gunn, J., & Petersen, A. C. (1990). A developmental perspective on eating disorders and eating problems. In M. Lewis & S. M. Miller (Eds.), Handbook of developmental psychopathology (pp. 409–420). New York: Plenum Press.

Auerbach, J., Greenbaum, C. W., Nowik, R., Guttman, R., Margolin, J., & Horwitz, F. D. (1989). Environment and early development: An Israeli cross-cultural comparison. In J. K. Nugent, B. M. Lester, & T. B. Brazelton (Eds.), The cultural context of infancy (Vol. 1, pp. 271–294). Norwood, NJ: Ablex.

Augoustinos, M. (1987). Developmental effects of child abuse. Child Abuse and Neglect, 11, 15–27.

Aylward, G. P. (1997). Conceptual issues in developmental screening and assessment. Journal of Developmental and Behavioral Pediatrics, 18, 340–349.

Azmitia, M., & Montgomery, R. (1993). Friendship, transactive dialogues, and the development of scientific reasoning. Social Development, 2, 202–221.

Azuma, H. (1986). Why study child development in Japan? In H. Sherman, H. Azuma, & K. Hakuta (Eds.), Child development and education in Japan (pp. 213–249). New York: W. H. Freeman.

Azuma, S. D., & Chasnoff, I. J. (1993). Outcome of children prenatally exposed to cocaine and other drugs; A path analysis of three-year data. Pediatrics, 92, 396–402.

Bachman, J. G., & Schulenberg, J. (1993). How part-time work intensity relates to drug use, problem behavior, time use, and satisfaction among high school seniors: Are these consequences or merely correlates? Developmental Psychology, 29, 220–235.

Bae, Y., & Smith, T. M. (1996). Women in mathematics and science. Washington, DC: U.S. Department of Education.

Bagwell, C. L., Newcomb, A. F., & Bukowski, W. M. (1998). Preadolescent friendship and peer rejection as predictors of adult adjustment. Child Development, 69, 140–153.

Bailey, S. M. (1993). The current status of gender equality research in American schools. Educational Psychologist, 28, 321–339.

Bailey, W. T. (1994). A longitudinal study of fathers' involvement with young children: Infancy to age 5 years. Journal of Genetic Psychology, 155, 331–339.

Baillargeon, R., & Graber, M. (1988). Evidence of location memory in 8-month-old infants in a nonsearch AB task. Developmental Psychology, 24, 502–511.

Baillargeon, R., Spelke, E. S., & Wasserman, S. (1985). Object permanence in five-month-old infants. Cognition, 20, 191–208.

Bain, B., & Yu, A. (1980). Cognitive consequences of raising children bilingually. Canadian Journal of Psychology 34, 304–313.

Balcazar, H., Peterson, G. W., & Krull, J. L. (1997). Acculturation and family cohesiveness in Mexican American pregnant women: Social and health implications. Family Community Health, 20, 16–31.

Bales, D. W., & Sera, M. D. (1995). Preschoolers' understanding of stable and changeable characteristics. Cognitive Development, 10, 69–107.

Baltes, M. M., & Silverberg, S. B. (1994). The dynamics between dependency and autonomy: Illustrations across the life span. In

D. L. Featherman & R. M. Lerner (Eds.), Life-span development and behavior (Vol. 12, pp. 41–90). Hillsdale, NJ: Erlbaum.

Bancroft, J. & Reinisch, J. (1990). Adolescence and puberty. New York: Oxford University Press.

Band, E. B., & Weisz, J. R. (1988). How to feel better when it feels bad: Children's perspectives on coping with everyday stress. Developmental Psychology, 24, 247–253.

Bandura, A. (1977). Social learning theory. Englewood Cliffs, NJ: Prentice-Hall.

Banks, J. A. (1995). Multicultural education and the modification of students' racial attitudes. In W. D. Hawley & A. W. Jackson (Eds.), Toward a common destiny: Improving race and ethnic relations in America (pp. 315–339). San Francisco: Jossey-Bass.

Banks, J. A. (1996). Approaches to multicultural curriculum reform. In J. A. Banks & C. A. M. Banks (Eds.), Multiculture education: Issues and perspectives (pp. 195–214). Boston: Allyn & Bacon.

Banks, J. A., & Banks, C. A. M. (1993). Multicultural education. Boston: Allyn & Bacon.

Banks, M. S. (1988). Visual recalibration and the development of contrast and optical flow. In A. Yonas (Ed.), Perceptual development in infancy (Vol. 20, pp. 145–196). Hillsdale, NJ: Erlbaum.

Barash, D. P. (1977). Sociobiology and behavior. New York: Elsevier/North-Holland.

Barbarin, O. A. (1993). Emotional and social development of African American children. Journal of Black Psychology, 19, 381–390.

Barber, B. K., Olsen, J. E., & Shagle, S. C. (1994). Associations between parental psychological and behavioral control and youth internalized and externalized behaviors. Child Development, 65, 1120–1136.

Bard, K. A. (1994). Evolutionary roots of intuitive parenting: Maternal competence in chimpanzees. Early Development and Parenting, 3, 19–28.

Bardin, C., Zelkowitz, P., & Papageorgious, A. (1997). Outcome for small-for-gestational age and appropriate-for-gestational age infants born before 27 weeks of gestation. Pediatrics, 100, 1–5.

Barkley, R. A. (1989). Attention deficit-hyperactivity disorder. In E. J. Mash & R. A. Barkley (Eds.), Treatment of childhood disorders (pp. 39–72). New York: Guilford.

Barkley, R. A. (1997). Attention-deficit/hyperactivity disorder, self-regulation, and time. Journal of Developmental and Behavioral Pediatrics, 18, 271–279.

Barkley, R. A., Fischer, M., Edelbrock, C. S., & Smallish, L. (1990). The adolescent outcome of hyperactive children diagnosed by research criteria: I. An 8-year prospective follow-up study. Journal of the American Academy of Child and Adolescent Psychiatry, 29, 546–557.

Barness, L. A., & Gilbert-Barness, E. (1992). Cause of death: SIDS or something else? Contemporary Pediatrics, 9, 13–31.

Barnett, S. W. (1998). Long-term cognitive and academic effects of early childhood education of children in poverty. Preventive Medicine, 27, 204–207.

Barr, H. M., Streissguth, A. P., Darby, B. L., & Sampson, P. D. (1990). Prenatal exposure to alcohol, caffeine, tobacco, and aspirin: Effects on fine and gross motor performance in 4-year-old children. Developmental Psychology, 26, 339–348.

Barrett, M., & Waterfield, J. (1997). The hidden factor: An educational perspective on depression in learning. In K. N. Dwivedi & V. P. Varma (Eds.), Depression in children and adolescents (pp. 106–123). London: Whurr Publishers.

Bartsch, K., & Wellman, H. M. (1995). *Children talk about the mind.* New York: Oxford University Press.

Bates, E., O'Connell, B., & Shore, C. (1987). Language and communication in infancy. In J. D. Osofsky (Ed.), *Handbook of infant development* (pp. 149–203). New York: Wiley.

Bates, J. E. (1987). Temperament in infancy. In J. D. Osofsky (Ed.), *Handbook of infant development* (pp. 1101–1149). New York: Wiley.

Bauer, D. H. (1976). An exploratory study of developmental changes in children's fears. *Journal of Child Psychology and Psychiatry, 17,* 69–74.

Bauer, P. J. (1993). Memory for gender-consistent and gender-inconsistent event sequences by twenty-five-month-old children. *Child Development, 64,* 285–297.

Baum, B. (1997, March 3). Scientists say cloning of monkeys aids medical research. *Seattle Times On-line,* 1–2.

Baumeister, A. A., & Baumeister, R. F. (1989). Mental retardation. In C. G. Last & M. Hersen (Eds.), *Handbook of child psychiatric diagnosis* (pp. 61–94). New York: Wiley.

Baumeister, R. F. (1993). *Self-esteem: The puzzle of low self-regard.* New York: Plenum.

Baumrind, D. (1967). Child care practices anteceding three patterns of preschool behavior. *Genetic Psychology Monographs, 75,* 43–88.

Baumrind, D. (1971). Current patterns of parental authority. *Developmental Psychology Monographs, 4* (1, Part 2).

Baumrind, D. (1989). Rearing competent children. In W. Damon (Ed.), *Child development today and tomorrow* (pp. 349–378). San Francisco: Jossey-Bass.

Beal, C. R. (1994). *Boys and girls: The development of gender roles.* New York: McGraw-Hill.

Beard, J. (1995). One person's view of iron deficiency, development, and cognitive function. *American Journal of Clinical Nutrition, 62,* 709–710.

Beckman, D. A., & Brent, R. L. (1986). Mechanisms of known environmental teratogens: Drugs and chemicals. *Clinical Perinatology, 13,* 649–689.

Begley, S. (1996, February 19). Your child's brain. *Newsweek.*

Beitel, A. H., & Parke, R. D. (1998). Parental involvement in infancy: The role of maternal and paternal attitudes. *Journal of Family Psychology, 12,* 268–288.

Bell, C. (1991). Traumatic stress and child in danger. *Journal of Health Care for the Poor and Underserved, 2,* 175–188.

Bell, S. M., & Ainsworth, M. D. S. (1972). Infant crying and maternal responsiveness. *Child Development 43,* 1171–1190.

Belsky, J. (1980). Child maltreatment: An ecological integration. *American Psychologist, 35,* 320–335.

Belsky, J. (1988). The "effects" of infant day care reconsidered. *Early Childhood Research Quarterly, 3,* 235–272.

Belsky, J. (1990). Parental and nonparental child care and children's socioemotional development: A decade in review. *Journal of Marriage and the Family, 52,* 885–903.

Belsky, J. (1993). Etiology of child maltreatment: A developmental-ecological analysis. *Psychological Bulletin, 114,* 413–434.

Belsky, J. (1996). Parent, infant, and social-contextual antecedents of father-son attachment security. *Developmental Psychology, 32,* 905–913.

Belsky, J., & Cassidy, J. (1994). Attachment: Theory and evidence. In M. Rutter & D. Hay (Eds.), *Development through life* (pp. 373–402). Oxford, England: Blackwell.

Belsky, J., Spritz, B., & Crnic, K. (1996). Infant attachment security and affective-cognitive information processing at age 3. *Psychological Science, 7,* 111–114.

Belsky, J., Steinberg, L., & Draper, P. (1991). Childhood experience, interpersonal development, and reproductive strategy: An evolutionary theory of socialization. *Child Development, 62,* 647–670.

Belsky, J., Woodworth, S., & Crnic, K. (1996a). Trouble in the second year: Three questions about family interactions. *Child Development, 67,* 556–578.

Belsky, J., Woodworth, S., & Crnic, K. (1996b). Troubled family interaction during toddlerhood. *Development and Psychopathology, 8,* 477–495.

Bem, S. L. (1981). Gender schema theory: A cognitive account of sex typing. *Psychological Review, 88,* 354–364.

Bem, S. L. (1983). Gender schema theory and its implications for child development: Raising gender-aschematic children in a gender-schematic society. *Signs, 8,* 598–616.

Bemporad, J. R. (1994). Dynamic and interpersonal theories of depression. In W. M. Reynolds & H. F. Johnston (Eds.), *Handbook of depression in children and adolescents* (pp. 81–95). New York: Plenum.

Ben-David, J. (1983). The kibbutz and the moshav. In E. Krausz (Ed.), *The sociology of the kibbutz* (pp. 37–50). New Brunswick, CT: Transaction Books.

Benedek, E. P., & Brown, C. F. (1995). *How to help your child overcome your divorce.* Washington, DC: American Psychiatric Press.

Bennett, V. R., & Brown, L. K. (1993). The fetus. In V. R. Bennett & L. K. Brown (Eds.), *Myles textbook for midwives* (pp. 365–376). London: Churchill Livingstone.

Bennett, W. (1993, April 7). Is our culture in decline? *Education Week, 12,* 32.

Benson, P. (1993). *The troubled journal: A portrait of 6th-12th grade youth.* Minneapolis: The Search Institute.

Benson, P. L., Donahue, M. J., & Erickson, J. A. (1989). Adolescence and religion. In M. L. Lynn & D. O. Moberg (Eds.), *Research in the social scientific study of religion* (pp. 153–181). Greenwich, CT: JAI Press.

Berenbaum, S. A., Korman, K., & Leveroni, C. (1995). Early hormones and sex differences in cognitive abilities. *Learning and Individual Differences, 7,* 303–321.

Berenbaum, S. A., & Snyder, E. (1995). Early hormonal influences on childhood sex-typed activity and playmate preferences: Implications for the development of sexual orientation. *Developmental Psychology, 31,* 31–42.

Berg, W. K., & Berg, K. M. (1987). Psychophysiological development in infancy: State, startle, and attention. In J. D. Osofsky (Ed.), *Handbook of infant development* (pp. 238–317). New York: Wiley.

Berk, L. E. (1994). Why children talk to themselves. *Scientific American, 272,* 78–83.

Berko, J. (1958). The child's learning of English morphology. *Word, 14,* 150–177.

Berkowitz, M. W. (1997). *The education of the complete moral person.* Champaign: University of Illinois Press.

Berliner, L., & Elliot, D. M. (1996). Sexual abuse of children. In J. Briere, L. Berliner, J. A. Bulkley, C. Jenny, & T. Reid (Eds.), *The APSAC handbook on child maltreatment* (pp. 51–71). Thousand Oaks, CA: Sage.

Berman, C. M., Rasmussen, K. L. R., & Suomi, S. J. (1994). Responses of free-ranging rhesus monkeys to a natural form of social separation. I. Parallels with mother-infant separation in captivity. *Child Development, 65,* 1028–1041.

Bernal, M. E., & Knight, G. P. (1997). Ethnic identity of Latino children. In J. G. Garcia & M. C. Zea (Eds.), *Psychological interventions and research with Latino populations* (pp. 15–38). Boston: Allyn & Bacon.

Berndt, T. J., & Perry, T. B. (1990). Distinctive features and effects of early adolescent friendships. In R. Montemayor, G. R. Adams, &

T. Gullotta (Eds.), *From childhood to adolescence* (pp. 269–287). Newbury Park, CA: Sage.

Berndt, T. J., & Savin-Williams, R. C. (1993). Peer relationships and friendships. In P. H. Tolan & B. J. Cohler (Eds.), *Handbook of clinical research and practice with adolescents* (203–219). New York: Wiley.

Bertenthal, B. I. (1996). Origins and early development of perception, action, and representation. *Annual Review of Psychology, 47,* 431–459.

Bertenthal, B. I., & Campos, J. J. (1984). A reexamination of fear and its determinants on the visual cliff. *Psychophysiology, 21,* 413–417.

Bertenthal, B. I., & Clifton, R. K. (1998). Perception and action. In W. Damon (Ed.), *Handbook of child psychology* (Vol. 2, pp. 51–102). New York: Wiley.

Bertenthal, B. I., Proffitt, D. R., Kramer, S. J., & Spetner, N. B. (1987). Infants' encoding of kinetic displays varying in relative coherence. *Developmental Psychology, 23,* 171–178.

Best, C. T. (1995). Learning to perceive the sound patterns of English. In C. Rovee-Collier & L. P. Lipsitt (Eds.), *Advances in infancy research* (pp. 122–156). Norwood, NJ: ABLEX.

Bettes, B. A. (1988). Maternal depression and motherese: Temporal and intonational features. *Child Development, 59,* 1089–1096.

Biddle, S. (1995). Exercise and psychosocial health. *Research Quarterly for Exercise and Sport, 66,* 292–297.

Biederman, J., Faraone, S. V., Taylor, A., Sienna, M., Williamson, S., & Fine, C. (1998). Diagnostic continuity between child and adolescent ADHD: Findings from a longitudinal clinical sample. *Journal of the American Academy of Child and Adolescent Psychiatry, 37,* 305–313.

Bier, J. A. B., Ferguson, A. E., Morales, Y., Liebling, J. A., Oh, W., & Vohr, B. R. (1997). Breastfeeding infants who were extremely low birth weight. *Pediatrics, 100,* 1–4.

Bigler, R. S., & Liben, L. S. (1993). A cognitive-developmental approach to racial stereotyping and reconstructive memory in Euro-American children. *Child Development, 64,* 1507–1518.

Bijur, P. E., Trumble, A., Harel, Y., Overpeck, M. D., Jones, D., & Scheidt, P. C. (1995). Sports and recreation injuries in U.S. children and adolescents. *Archives of Pediatric and Adolescent Medicine, 149,* 1009–1016.

Biller, H. B. (1993). *Fathers and families.* Westport, CT: Greenwood Publishing

Bingol, N., Fuchs, M., Diaz, V., Stone, R. K., & Gromisch, D. S. (1987). Teratogenicity of cocaine in humans. *Journal of Pediatrics, 110,* 93–96.

Bithoney, W. G. & Newberger, E. H. (1987). Child and family attributes of failure to thrive. *Journal of Developmental and Behavioral Pediatrics, 8,* 32.

Bjorklund, D. F. (1995). *Children's thinking.* Pacific Grove, CA: Brooks/Cole.

Bjorklund, D. F., & Green, B. L. (1992). The adaptive nature of cognitive immaturity. *American Psychologist, 47,* 46–54.

Black, B., & Hazen, N. L. (1990). Social status and patterns of communication in acquainted and unacquainted preschool children. *Developmental Psychology, 26,* 379–387.

Black, J. E. (1998). How a child builds its brain: Some lessons from animal studies of neural plasticity. *Preventative Medicine, 27,* 168–171.

Black, M. M., Nair, P., Kight, C., Wachtel, R., Roby, P., & Schuler, M. (1994). Parenting and early development among children of drug-abusing women. *Pediatrics, 94,* 440–448.

Black-Gutman, D., & Hickson, F. (1996). The relationship between racial attitudes and social-cognitive development in children. *Developmental Psychology, 32,* 448–456.

Blake, J. (1989). *Family size and achievement.* Berkeley: University of California Press.

Bland, K. (1997, March 9). Infant abuse leaves lasting repercussions. *Arizona Republic,* pp. B1, B4.

Blasi, A. (1983). Moral cognition and moral action: A theoretical perspective. *Developmental Review, 3,* 178–210.

Blass, E. M., Ganchrow, J. R., & Steiner, J. E. (1984). Classical conditioning in newborn humans 2–48 hours of age. *Infant Behavior and Development, 7,* 223–235.

Bloom, B. S. (1985). *Developing talent in young people.* New York: Ballantine.

Bloom, L. (1994). Meaning and expression. In W. Overton & D. Palermo (Eds.), *The ontogenesis of meaning* (pp. 215–235). Hillsdale, NJ: Erlbaum.

Bloom, L. (1998). Language acquisition in its developmental context. In W. Damon (Ed.), *Handbook of child psychology* (Vol. 2, pp. 309–370). New York: Wiley.

Bloom, L., Margulis, C., Tinker, E., & Fujita, N. (1996). Early conversations and word learning: Contributions from child and adult. *Child Development, 67,* 3154–3175.

Bloom, L., Rocissano, L., & Hood, L. (1976). Adult-child discourse. *Cognitive Psychology, 8,* 521–552.

Blount, R. L., Landolf-Fritsche, B., Powers, S. W., & Sturges, J. W. (1991). Differences between high and low coping children and between parent and staff behaviors during painful medical procedures. *Journal of Pediatric Psychology, 16,* 795–809.

Blum, L. (1998). Language acquisition in its developmental context. In W. Damon (Ed.), *Handbook of child psychology* (Vol. 2, pp. 309–370). New York: Wiley.

Blum, N. J., Taubman, B., & Osborne, M. L. (1997). Behavioral characteristics of children with stool toileting refusal. *Pediatrics, 99,* 50–53.

Blum, R. W. (1998). Healthy youth development as a model for youth health promotion. *Journal of Adolescent Health, 22,* 368–375.

Blumenfeld, W. J., & Raymond, D. (1993). *Looking at gay and lesbian life.* Boston: Beacon Press.

Boeck, M. A. (1992a). Bulimia nervosa. In S. B. Friedman, M. Fisher, & S. K. Schonberg (Eds.), *Comprehensive adolescent health care* (pp. 232–237). St. Louis, MO: Quality Medical Publishing.

Boeck, M. A. (1992b). Obesity. In S. B. Friedman, M. Fisher, & S. K. Schonberg (Eds.), *Comprehensive adolescent health care* (pp. 238–249). St. Louis, MO: Quality Medical Publishing.

Boer, F. (1990). *Sibling relationships in middle childhood.* Leiden, Germany: DSWO University of Leiden Press.

Boer, F., Goedhart, T., & Treffers, P. D. A. (1992). Siblings and their parents. In F. Boer & J. Dunn (Eds.), *Children's sibling relationships* (pp. 41–54). Hillsdale, NJ: Erlbaum.

Bohannon, J. N., & Warren-Leubecker, A. (1989). Theoretical approaches to language acquisition. In J. Berko-Gleason (Ed.), *The development of language* (pp. 167–223). Columbus, OH: Merrill.

Bon-De-Matte, L. (1998). Anorexic syndrome in adolescence and anorexia. In P. Bria & A. Ciocca (Eds.), *Psychotherapeutic issues in eating disorders* (pp. 41–48). Rome: Abramowicz.

Booth, D. A. (1994). *Psychology of nutrition.* London: Taylor and Francis.

Borke, H. (1975). Piaget's mountains revisited: Changes in the egocentric landscape. *Developmental Psychology, 11,* 240–243.

Borman, K., & Schneider, B. (1998). *The adolescent years.* Chicago: The National Society for the Study of Education.

Bornstein, M. H. (1985). Habituation of attention as a measure of visual information processing in human infants: Summary, systematization, and synthesis. In G. Gottlieb & N. A. Krasnegor (Eds.), *Measurement of audition and vision in the first year of postnatal life: A methodological overview* (pp. 253–300). Norwood, NJ: Ablex.

Bornstein, M. H. (1989). Sensitive periods in development. *Psychological Bulletin, 105,* 179–197.

Bornstein, M. H., & Lamb, M. E. (1992). *Development in infancy,* 3rd ed. New York: McGraw Hill.

Bornstein, M. H., & Ludemann, P. M. (1989). Habituation at home. *Infant Behavior and Development, 12,* 525–529.

Bornstein, M. H., Tal, J., & Tamis-LeMonda, C. S. (1991). Parenting in cross-cultural perspective: The United States, France, and Japan. In M. H. Bornstein (Ed.), *Cultural approaches to parenting* (pp. 69–90). Hillsdale, NJ: Erlbaum.

Bornstein, M. H., & Tamis-LeMonda, C. S. (1990). Activities and interactions of mothers and their firstborn infants in the first six months of life: Covariation, stability, continuity, correspondence, and prediction. *Child Development, 61,* 1206–1217.

Bornstein, M. H., & Tamis-LeMonda, C. S. (1997). Maternal responsiveness and infant mental abilities. *Infant Behavior and Development, 20,* 283–296.

Borstelmann, L. J. (1983). Children before psychology: Ideas about children from antiquity to the late 1800s. In P. H. Mussen (Ed.), *Handbook of child psychology* (Vol. 1, pp. 1–40). New York: Wiley.

Borsting, E. (1994). Overview of vision and visual processing development. In M. Scheiman & M. Rouse (Eds.), *Optimetric measure of learning-related vision problems* (pp. 131–145). St. Louis, MO: Mosby.

Boston, M. B., & Levy, G. D. (1991). Changes and differences in preschoolers' understanding of gender scripts. *Cognitive Development, 6,* 412–417.

Bosworth, P. (1985, February). Diane Sawyer. *Ladies' Home Journal,* 28–34.

Bowen, J., Fenton, T., & Rappaport, L. (1991). Stimulant medication and attention deficit-hyperactivity disorder: The child's perspective. *AJDC, 145,* 291–295.

Bower, J. (1982). *Development in infancy.* San Francisco: Freeman.

Bower, M. (1995). *Thalidomide.* San Francisco: Project Inform.

Bower, R. T. (1985). *The changing television audience in America.* New York: Columbia University Press.

Bowers, W. A., Evans, K., & Van-Cleve, L. (1996). Treatment of adolescent eating disorders. In M. A. Reinecke & F. M. Daggilio (Eds.), *Cognitive therapy with children and adolescents* (pp. 227–250). New York: Guilford.

Bowes, A., Church, H. N., & Pennington, J. A. (1994). *Food values of portions commonly used.* Philadelphia: Lippincott.

Bowlby, J. (1969). *Attachment and loss, Vol. 1.* New York: Basic Books.

Bowlby, J. (1973). *Attachment and loss, Vol. 2: Separation.* New York: Basic Books.

Bowman, P. J., & Howard, C. (1985). Race-related socialization, motivation, and academic achievement: A study of Black youths in three-generation families. *Journal of the American Academy of Child Psychiatry, 24,* 134–141.

Boxer, A. M., Cohler, J. J., Herdt, G., & Irvin, F. (1993). Gay and lesbian youth. In P. H. Tolan & J. J. Cohler (Eds.), *Handbook of clinical research and practice with adolescents* (pp. 249–280). New York: Wiley.

Boyce, W. T., Frank, E., Jensen, P. S., Kessler, R. C., Nelson, C. A., Steinberg, L., & The MacArthur Foundation Research Network on Psychopathology and Development. (1998). Social context in developmental psychopathology. *Development and Psychopathology, 10,* 143–164.

Boyer, D., & Fine, D. (1992). Sexual abuse as a factor in adolescent pregnancy and maltreatment. *Family Planning Perspectives, 24,* 4–11, 19.

Brackbill, Y., McManus, K., & Woodward, L. (1985). *Medication in maternity: Infant exposure and maternal information.* Ann Arbor: University of Michigan Press.

Bradbard, M. R., Martin, C. L., Endsley, R. C., & Halverson, C. F. (1986). Influence of sex stereotypes on children's exploration and memory: A competence versus performance distinction. *Developmental Psychology, 22,* 481–486.

Bradley, R. H., & Caldwell, B. M. (1976). The relation of infants' home environments to mental test performance at fifty-four months: A follow-up study. *Child Development, 47,* 1172–1174.

Bradley, R. H., & Caldwell, B. M. (1981). The HOME Inventory: A validation of the preschool scale for Black children. *Child Development, 52,* 708–710.

Bradley, R. H., Caldwell, B. M., Rock, S. L., Ramey, C. T., Barnard, K. E., Gray, C., Hammond, M. A., Mitchell, S., Gottfried, A. W., Siegel. L., & Johnson, D. L. (1989). Home environment and cognitive development in the first three years of life: A collaborative study involving six sites and three ethnic groups in North America. *Developmental Psychology, 25,* 217–235.

Bradley, R. H., Whiteside, L., Mundfrom, D. J., Casey, P. H., Kelleher, K. J., & Pope, S. K. (1994). Early indications of resilience and their relation to experiences in the home environments of low birthweight, premature children living in poverty. *Child Development, 65,* 346–360.

Braine, M. (1963). On learning the grammatical order of words. *Psychological Review, 70,* 323–348.

Bramadat, I. J. (1994). Induction of labor: An integrated review. *Health Care for Women International, 15,* 135–148.

Branch, C. (1998). *Adolescent gangs: Old issues, new approaches.* Philadelphia: Brunner/Mazel.

Branch, C. W., & Newcombe, N. (1986). Racial attitude development among young Black children as a function of parental attitudes: A longitudinal and cross-sectional study. *Child Development, 57,* 712–721.

Braungart-Rieker, J. M., & Stifter, C. A. (1996). Infants' responses to frustrating situations: Continuity and change in reactivity and regulation. *Child Development, 67,* 1767–1779.

Braverman, P. K., & Strasburger, V. C. (1993). Adolescent sexual activity. *Clinical Pediatrics, 32,* 658–668.

Braza, F., Braza, P., Carreras, M. R., & Munoz, J. M. (1997). Development of sex difference in preschool children: Social behavior during an academic year. *Psychological Reports, 80,* 179–188.

Brazelton, T. B. (1991). *Touchpoints: Your child's emotional and behavioral development.* Reading, MA: Addison-Wesley.

Brazelton, T. B., Nugent, K. J., & Lester, B. M. (1987). Neonatal behavioral assessment scale. In J. D. Osofsky (Ed.), *Handbook of infant development* (pp. 780–817). New York: Wiley.

Breakey, J. (1997). The role of diet and behavior in childhood. *Journal of Pediatric Child Health, 33,* 190–194.

Brederode, M. E. (1990). Research on Rua Sesamo, the Portuguese coproduction. In Children's Television Workshop (Ed.), *Sesame Street Research* (pp. 63–67). New York: Children's Television Workshop.

Bremer, J., & Rauch, P. K. (1998). Children and computers: Risks and benefits. *Journal of the American Academy of Child and Adolescent Psychiatry, 37,* 559–560.

Brendgen, M., Bowen, F., Rondeau, N., & Vitaro, F. (1999). Effect of friends' charactristics on children's social cognitions. *Social Development, 8,* 41–51.

Brenner, V., & Fox, R. A. (1998). Parental discipline and behavior problems in young children. *Journal of Genetic Psychology, 159,* 251–256.

Brent, D., May, D. C., & Kundert, D. K. (1996). The incidence of delayed school entry. *Early Education & Development, 7,* 121–135.

Bridges, A. (1986). Actions and things: What adults talk about to 1-year-olds. In S. Kuczaj & M. Barrett (Eds.), *The development of word meaning* (pp. 225–255). New York: Springer.

Bridges, K. (1932). Emotional development in early infancy. *Child Development, 3,* 324–341.

Bridges, L. J., Connell, J. P., & Belsky, J. (1988). Similarities and differences in mother-infant and father-infant interaction in the strange situation. *Developmental Psychology, 24,* 92–100.

Brisk, M. E. (1998). *Bilingual education.* Mahwah, NJ: Erlbaum.

Britner, P., & Reppucci, N. D. (1997). Prevention of child maltreatment: Evaluation of a parent education program for teen mothers. *Journal of Child and Family Studies, 6,* 165–175.

Britt, D. (1996). For teens, a revolution gone haywire. In F. C. Leeming, W. Dwyer, & D. P. Oliver (Eds.), *Adolescent sexuality* (pp. 3–5). Needham Heights, MA: Allyn & Bacon.

Broberg, A., Hwang, C., Lamb, M., & Ketterlinus, R. D. (1989). Child care effects on socioemotional and intellectual competence in Swedish preschoolers. In J. S. Lande, S. Scarr, & N. Gunzenhauser (Eds.), *Caring for children: Challenge to America* (pp. 49–76). Hillsdale, NJ: Erlbaum.

Brody, G. H. (1998). Sibling relationship quality: Its causes and consequences. *Annual Review of Psychology, 49,* 1–24.

Brody, G. H., Stoneman, Z., MacKinnon, C. E., & MacKinnon, R. (1985). Role relationships and behavior between preschool-aged and school-aged sibling pairs. *Developmental Psychology, 21,* 124–129.

Brody, G. H., Stoneman, Z., & McCoy, J. K. (1992). Associations of maternal and paternal direct and differential behavior with sibling relationships: Contemporaneous and longitudinal analyses. *Child Development, 63,* 82–92.

Brodzinsky, D. M., Lang, R., & Smith, D. W. (1995). Parenting adopted children. Fathers and families. In M. H. Bornstein (Ed.), *Handbook of parenting* (Vol. 3, pp. 233–254). Mahwah, NJ: Erlbaum.

Bronfenbrenner, U. (1979). *The ecology of human development: Experiments by nature and design.* Cambridge, MA: Harvard University Press.

Bronfenbrenner, U. (1986). Ecology of the family as a context for human development: Research perspectives. *Developmental Psychology, 22,* 723–742.

Bronfenbrenner, U., & Ceci, S. J. (1994). Nature-nurture reconceptualized in developmental perspective: A bioecological model. *Psychological Review, 101,* 568–586.

Bronfenbrenner, U., & Morris, P. A. (1998). The ecology of developmental processes. In W. Damon (Ed.), *Handbook of child psychology* (Vol. 1, pp. 993–1029). New York: Wiley.

Bronstein, P., Duncan, P., D'Air, A., Pieniadz, J., Fitzgerald, M., Abrams, C. L., Frankowski, B., Franco, O., Hunt, C., & Oh-Cha, S. Y. (1996). Family and parenting behaviors predicting middle school adjustment: A longitudinal study. *Family Relations, 45,* 415–426.

Brooks, J. B. (1998). *Parenting.* Mountain View, CA: Mayfield Publishing.

Brooks-Gunn, J. (Ed.), *Encyclopedia of adolescence* (pp. 454–458). New York: Garland.

Brooks-Gunn, J. (1988). Antecedents and consequences of variations in girls' maturational timing. *Journal of Adolescent Health Care, 9,* 365–373.

Brooks-Gunn, J. (1995). Children in families in communities: Risk and intervention in the Bronfenbrenner tradition. In P. Moen, G. H. Elder, & K. Luscher (Eds.), *Examining lives in context: Perspectives on the ecology of human development* (pp. 467–519). Washington, DC: American Psychological Association.

Brooks-Gunn, J., & Duncan, G. J. (1997). The effects of poverty on children. *The Future of Children, 7,* 55–71.

Brooks-Gunn, J., Duncan, G. J., Klebanov, P. K., & Sealand, N. (1993). Do neighborhoods influence child and adolescent development? *American Journal of Sociology, 99,* 353–395.

Brooks-Gunn, J., & Furstenberg, F. F. (1989). Adolescent sexual behavior. *American Psychologist, 44,* 249–257.

Brooks-Gunn, J., Klebanov, P. K., & Duncan, G. J. (1996). Ethnic differences in children's intelligence test scores: Role of economic deprivation, home environment, and maternal characteristics. *Child Development, 67,* 396–408.

Brooks-Gunn, J., & Paikoff, R. (1997). Sexuality and developmental transitions during adolescence. In J. Schulenberg & J. Maggs (Eds.), *Health risks and developmental transitions during adolescence* (pp. 190–219). New York: Cambridge University Press.

Brooks-Gunn, J., & Ruble, D. (1982). The development of menstrual-related beliefs and behaviors during early adolescence. *Child Development, 53,* 1567–1577.

Brooks-Gunn, J., & Warren, M. P. (1989). Biological and social contributions to negative affect in young adolescent girls. *Child Development, 60,* 40–55.

Brown, B. B., & Lohr, M. J. (1987). Peer-group affiliation and adolescent self-esteem: An integration of ego-identity and symbolic-interaction theories. *Journal of Personality and Social Psychology, 52,* 47–55.

Brown, B. B., Mory, M. S., & Kinney, D. (1994). Casting adolescent crowds in a relational perspective. In R. Montemayor & G. R. Adams (Eds.), *Personal relationships during adolescence* (pp. 123–167). Thousand Oaks, CA: Sage.

Brown, J., & Pollitt, E., (1996). Malnutrition, poverty and intellectual development. *Scientific American, 274,* 38–43.

Brown, J. D., & Lawton, M. (1986). Stress and well-being in adolescence: The moderating role of physical exercise. *Journal of Human Stress, 12,* 125–131.

Brown, J. R., & Dunn, J. (1992). Talk with your mother or your sibling? Developmental changes in early family conversations about feelings. *Child Development, 63,* 336–349.

Brown, K. H., Robertson, A. D., & Akhtar, N. A. (1986). Lactational capacity of marginally nourished mothers: Infants' milk nutrient consumption and patterns of growth. *Pediatrics, 78,* 920–927.

Bruck, M., (1992). Persistence of dyslexics' phonological deficits. *Developmental Psychology, 28,* 874–886.

Bruner, J. S. (1983). *Child's talk: Learning to use language.* New York: Norton.

Bryan, J. H., & Walbek, N. H. (1970). The impact of words and deeds concerning altruism upon children. *Child Development, 41,* 747–757.

Bryant, B. K. (1982). Sibling relationships in middle childhood. In M E. Lamb & B. Sutton-Smith (Eds.), *Sibling relationships* (pp. 87–122). Hillsdale, NJ: Erlbaum.

Bryant, B. K. (1985). The neighborhood walk. *Monographs of the Society for Research in Child Development* (Serial No. 210, Whole Number 3). Chicago: Society for Research in Child Development.

Bryant, B. K. (1992). Sibling caretaking: Providing emotional support during middle childhood. In F. Boer & J. Dunn (Eds.), *Children's* sibling relationships: *Developmental and clinical issues* (pp. 55–70). Hillsdale, NJ: Erlbaum.

Bryant, B. K. (1998). Children's coping at school. In L. H. Meyer & H. Park (Eds.), *Making friends: The influence of culture and development* (Vol. 3, pp. 353–367). Baltimore, MD: Brookes Publishing.

Bryk, A. S., & Driscoll, M. E. (1988). *The school as community.* Madison: University of Wisconsin Press.

Bryk, A. S., Lee, V. E., & Smith, J. B. (1990). High school organization and its effects on teachers and students: An interpretive summary of the research. In J. Witte & W. Clure (Eds.), *Choice and control in American education* (pp. 135–226). London: Falmer Press.

Buchanan-Barrow, B., & Barrett, M. (1998). Individual differences in children's understanding of the school. *Social Development, 7,* 250–268.

Buckley, S., & Wilgoren, D. (1994, April 24). Young and experienced: Area's teenagers are having sex earlier and with little concern for safety. *Washington Post,* 1.

Bugental, D. B., & Goodnow, J. J. (1998). Socialization processes. In W. Damon (Ed.), *Handbook of child psychology* (Vol. 3, 389–462). New York: Wiley.

Buhrmester, D. (1992). The developmental courses of sibling and peer relationships. In F. Boer & J. Dunn (Eds.), *Children's sibling relationships* (pp. 19–40). Hillsdale, NJ: Erlbaum.

Buhrmester, D., Goldfarb, J., & Cantrell, D. (1992). Self-presentation when sharing with friends and nonfriends. *Journal of Early Adolescence, 12,* 61–79.

Buhrmester, D., Whalen, C. K., Henker, B., MacDonald, V., & Hinshaw, S. P. (1992). Prosocial behavior in hyperactive boys: Effects of stimulant medication and comparison with normal boys. *Journal of Abnormal Child Psychology, 20,* 103–121.

Buis, J. M., & Thompson, D. N. (1989). Imaginary audience and personal fable: A brief review. *Adolescence, 24, 773–781.*

Bukoski, W. J. (1997). *Meta-analysis of drug abuse prevention programs.* Washington, DC: U.S. Department of Health and Human Services.

Bukowski, W. M., Gauze, C., Horz, B., & Newcomb, A. F. (1993). Differences and consistency between same-sex and other-sex peer relationships during early adolescence. *Developmental Psychology, 29,* 255–263.

Bullock, M. (1984). Preschool children's understanding of causal connections. *British Journal of Developmental Psychology, 2,* 139–142.

Bullock, M., & Gelman, R. (1979). Preschool children's assumptions about cause and effect: Temporal ordering. *Child Development, 50,* 89–96.

Bullock, M., Gelman, R., & Baillargeon, R. (1982). The development of causal reasoning. In W. F. Friedman (Ed.), *The developmental psychology of time* (pp. 209–253). New York: Academic Press.

Burack, J. A., Hodapp, R. M., & Zigler, E. (1998). *Handbook of mental retardation and development.* New York: Cambridge University Press.

Burchinal M., Lee, M., & Ramey, C. (1989). Type of day-care and preschool intellectual development in disadvantaged children. *Child Development, 60,* 128–137.

Burd, B. (1986). Infant swimming classes: Immersed in controversy. *The Physician and Sports Medicine, 14*(3), 239–244.

Burnett, J. W., Anderson, W. P., & Heppner, P. P. (1995). Gender roles and self-esteem: A consideration of environmental factors. *Journal of Counseling and Development, 73,* 323–326.

Burns, A., & Homel, R. (1989). Gender division of tasks by parents and their children. *Psychology of Women Quarterly, 13,* 113–125.

Burt, M. R., Resnick, G., & Novick, E. R. (1998). *Building supportive communitites for at-risk adolescents.* Washington, DC: American Psychological Assocation.

Burton, L. M. (1990). Teenage childbearing as an alternative life course strategy in multigeneration African American families. *Human Nature, 1,* 123–143.

Buss, A., & Plomin, R. (1984). *Temperament: Early developing personality traits.* Hillsdale, NJ: Erlbaum.

Buss, D. (1998). *Evolutionary psychology.* Boston: Allyn & Bacon.

Buss, K., & Goldsmith, H. H. (1998). Fear and anger regulation in infancy: Effects on the temporary dynamics of affective expression. *Child Development, 69,* 359–374.

Bussey, K. (1992). Lying and truthfulness: Children's definitions, standards, and evaluative reactions. *Child Development, 63,* 129–137.

Bussey, K., & Bandura, A. (1984). Influence of gender constancy and social power on sex-linked modeling. *Journal of Personality and Social Psychology, 47,* 1292–1302.

Bussey, K., & Bandura, A. (1992). Self-regulatory mechanisms governing gender development. *Child Development, 63,* 1236–1250.

Bussey, K., & Perry, D. G. (1982). Same-sex imitation: The avoidance of cross-sex models or the acceptance of same-sex models? *Sex Roles, 8,*773–785.

Butler, J., & Rovee-Collier, C. (1989). Contextual gating of memory retrieval. *Developmental Psychobiology, 22,* 533–552.

Byers, J. (1989). AIDS in children. Effects of neurological development and implications for the future. *Journal of Special Education, 23,* 5–16.

Byrne, B., & Fielding-Barnsley, B. R. (1995). Evaluation of a program to teach phonemic awareness to young children: A 2- and 3-year follow-up and a new preschool trial. *Journal of Educational Psychology, 87,* 488–503.

Byrne, D. (1983). Sex without contraception. In D. Byrne & W. A. Fisher (Eds.), *Adolescents, sex, and contraception* (pp. 3–31). Hillsdale, NJ: Erlbaum.

Byrnes, J. P. (1988). Formal operations: A systematic reformulation. *Developmental Review, 8,* 66–87.

Cairns, R. B. (1998). The making of developmental psychology. In W. Damon (Ed.), *Handbook of child psychology* (Vol. 1, pp. 25–107). New York: Wiley.

Cairns, R. B., Cadwallader, T. W., Estell, D., & Neckerman, H. J. (1997). Groups to gangs: Developmental and criminological perspectives and relevance for prevention. In D. M. Stoff & J. Breiling (Eds.), *Handbook of antisocial behavior* (pp. 194–204). New York: Wiley.

Cairns, R. B., Cairns, D. B., & Neckerman, H. J. (1989). Early school dropout: Configurations and determinants. *Child Development, 60,* 1437–1452.

Caissy, G. A. (1994). *Early adolescence.* New York: Insight Books.

Callanan, M. A. (1989). Development of object categories and inclusion relations: Preschoolers' hypotheses about word meanings. *Developmental Psychology, 25,* 207–216.

Campaign for Our Children (1997). *National teen pregnancy clock.* Baltimore, MD: Campaign for Our Children.

Campbell, K. H. S., McWhir, J., Ritchie, W. A., & Wilmut, I. (1996). Sheep cloned by nuclear transfer from a culture cell line. *Nature, 30,* 64–66.

Campos, F. (1996). *Latino, Hispanic, both, neither?* Austin: University of Texas Press.

Campos, J. J., Kermoian, R., & Zumbahlen, M. R. (1992). Socio-emotional transformations in the family system following infant crawling onset. In N. Eisenberg & R. A. Fabes (Eds.), *Emotion and its regulation in early development* (pp. 25–40). San Francisco: Jossey-Bass.

Campos, M. M. (1992). Child care in Brazil. In M. E. Lamb, K. J. Sternberg, C. Hwang, & A. G. Broberg (Eds.), *Child care in context* (pp. 479–508). Hillsdale, NJ: Erlbaum.

Caplan, N., Whitmore, J. K., & Choy, M. H. (1989). *The Boat People and achievement in American: A study of family life, hard work, and cultural values.* Ann Arbor: University of Michigan Press.

Capon, N., & Kuhn, D. (1979). Logical reasoning in the supermarket: Adult females' use of proportional reasoning strategy in an everyday context. *Developmental Psychology, 15,* 450–452.

Carlo, G., Fabes, R. A., Laible, D., & Kupanoff, K. (1999). Prosocial/moral development in early adolescence II: Social processes. *Journal of Early Adolescence, 14,* 1–8.

Carlo, G., Koller, S., Eisenberg, N., Pacheco, P., & Loguercio, A. (in press). Prosocial cognitions, emotions, and behaviors: A cross-cultural study of adolescents from Brazil and the United States. *Developmental Psychology.*

Carlson, E. A. (1998). A prospective longitudinal study of attachment disorganization/disorientation. *Child Development, 69,* 1107–1128.

Carlson, E. A., Jacobvitz, D., & Sroufe, L. A. (1995). A developmental investigation of inattentiveness and hyperactivity. *Child Development, 66,* 37–54.

Carnegie Council on Adolescent Development. (1989). *Turning points: Preparing American youth for the 21st century.* New York: Carnegie Foundation.

Carro, M. G., Grant, K. E., Gotlib, I. H., & Compas, B. E. (1993). Postpartum depression and child development: An investigation of mothers and fathers as sources of risk and resilience. *Development and Psychopathology, 5,* 567–579.

Carskadon, M. A. (1990). Patterns of sleep and sleepiness in adolescents. *Pediatrician, 17,* 5–12.

Carson, D. K., & Bittner, M. T. (1994). Temperament and school-aged children's coping abilities and responses to stress. *Journal of Genetic Psychology, 155,* 289–302.

Carter, B., & McGoldrick, M. (1988). The changing family life cycle. In B. Carter & M. McGoldrick (Eds.), *The changing family life cycle* (pp. 3–28). New York: Gardner Press.

Carter, C., & Rice, C. L. (1997). Acquisition and manifestation of prejudice in children. *Journal of Multicultural Counseling and Development, 25,* 185–194.

Carter, D. B., & Middlemiss, W. A. (1992). The socialization of instrumental competence in families in the United States. In J. L. Roopnarine & D. B. Carter (Eds.), *Parent-child socialization in diverse cultures* (pp. 107–120). Norwood, NJ: Ablex.

Cartwright, T., & Brent, M. R. (1997). Syntactic categorization in early language acquisition: Formalizing the role of distributional analysis. *Cognition, 63,* 121–170.

Case, R. (1992). Neo-Piagetian theories of child development. In R. Sternberg & C. Berg (Eds.), *Intellectual development* (pp. 161–196). New York: Cambridge University Press.

Case, R. (1998). The development of conceptual structures. In W. Damon (Ed.), *Handbook of child psychology* (Vol. 2, pp. 851–898). New York: Wiley.

Case, R., & Edelstein, W. (1993). The new structuralism in cognitive development. *Contributions to Human Development, 23.*

Case, R., & Okamoto, Y. (1996). Modeling the process of conceptual change in a continuously evolving hierarchical system. *Monographs of the Society for Research in Child Development, 61,* 283–295.

Casey, M. B., Nuttall, R. L., & Pezaris, E. (1997). Mediators of gender differences in mathematics college entrance test scores: A comparison of spatial skills with internalized beliefs and anxiety. *Developmental Psychology, 33,* 669–680.

Casey, P. H. (1992). Failure to thrive. In M. D. Levine, W. B. Carey, & A. C. Crocker (Eds.), *Developmental-behavioral pediatrics* (pp. 375–383). Philadelphia: W. B. Saunders.

Casper, L. B. (1990). Does family interaction prevent adolescent pregnancy? *Family Planning Perspectives, 30,* 54–61.

Casper, L. M., Hawkins, M., & O'Connell, M. (1994). *Who's minding the kids?* Washington, DC: US Census.

Caspi, A., Henry, B., McGee, R. O., Moffitt, T. E., & Silva, P. A. (1995). Temperamental origins of child and adolescent behavior problems: From age three to age fifteen. *Child Development, 66,* 55–68.

Caspi, A., & Moffitt, T. E. (1991). Individual differences are accentuated during periods of social change: The sample case of girls at puberty. *Journal of Personality and Social Psychology, 61,* 157–168.

Caspi, A., & Silva, P. A. (1995). Temperamental qualities at age three predict personality traits in young adulthood: Longitudinal evidence from a birth cohort. *Child Development, 66,* 486–498.

Cassidy, J., Kirsh, S. J., Scolton, K. L., & Parke, R. D. (1996). Attachment and representations of peer relationships. *Developmental Psychology, 32,* 892–904.

Cassidy, K. W. (1998). Preschoolers' use of desires to solve theory of mind problems in a pretense context. *Developmental Psychology, 34,* 503–511.

Cassidy, P. (1993). The first stage of labor: Physiology and early care. In V. R. Bennett & L. K. Brown (Eds.), *Myles textbook for midwives* (pp. 149–167). London: Churchill Livingstone.

Castellanos, F. X. (1997a). Neuroimaging of attention-deficit hyperactivity disorder. *Child and Adolescent Psychiatric Clinics of North America, 6,* 383–411.

Castellanos, F. X. (1997b). Toward a pathophysiology of attention-deficit/hyperactivity disorder. *Clinical Pediatrics, 36,* 381–393.

Castex, G. M. (1997). Immigrant children in the United States. In N. K. Phillips, & S. L. A. Straussner (Eds.), *Children in the urban environment* (pp. 43–60). Springfield, IL: Thomas Publishing.

Cauffman, E., & Steinberg, L. (1996). Interactive effects of menarcheal status and dating on dieting and disordered eating among adolescent girls. *Developmental Psychology, 32,* 631–635.

Ceci, S. J., & Bruck, M. (1995). *Jeopardy in the courtroom.* Washington, DC: American Psychological Association.

Ceci, S. J., & Bruck, M. (1998). Children's testimony: Applied and basic issues. In W. Damon (Ed.), *Handbook of child psychology* (Vol. 4, pp. 713–774). New York: Wiley.

Center for Applied Research and Educational Improvement. (1997). *School start time study.* Minneapolis: University of Minnesota Press.

Center for Media and Public Affairs. (1994). *A day in the life of television: 1992 versus 1994.* New York: Center for Media and Public Affairs.

Center for Media Education. (1998). *Computer and telephone access in the home.* Washington, DC: Center for Media Education.

Center for the Future of Children. (1996). *Financing child care.* Los Altos, CA: Center for the Future of Children.

Centers for Disease Control. (1994). *Preventing tobacco use among young people.* Washington, DC: Centers for Disease Control.

Centers for Disease Control. (1995a). Annual summary of births, marriages, divorces, and deaths: United States, 1994. *Monthly Vital Statistics Report, 43* (No. 13).

Centers for Disease Control. (1995b). Advance report of final divorce statistics, 1989 and 1990. *Monthly Vital Statistics Report, 43* (No. 9).

Centers for Disease Control (1995c). Births and deaths: United States, 1995. *Monthly Vital Statistics Report, 45* (No. 3, Supplement 2).

Centers for Disease Control. (1996). *HIV/AIDS Surveillance Report* (Vol. 8). Atlanta: Centers for Disease Control.

Centers for Disease Control. (1997a). *Fertility, family planning, and women's health*. Washington, DC: Centers for Disease Control.

Centers for Disease Control. (1997b). *Immunization and infectious diseases*. Washington, DC: Centers for Disease Control.

Centers for Disease Control. (1997c). *Triple births and trends and outcomes*. Washington, DC: Centers for Disease Control.

Centers for Disease Control. (1998a). *Youth risk behavior surveillance—United States, 1997*. Atlanta: Centers for Disease Control.

Centers for Disease Control. (1998b). *Teenage births in the U.S.: State trends, 1991–1996*. Washington, DC: Centers for Disease Control.

Cernoch, J. M., & Porter, R. H. (1985). Recognition of maternal axillary odors by infants. *Child Development, 56,* 1593–1598.

Chall, J. S., Jacobs, V. A., & Baldwin, L. E. (1990). *The reading crisis*. Cambridge, MA: Harvard University Press.

Chalmers, I., Enkin, M., & Keirse, M. (1989). *Effective care in pregnancy and childbirth*. New York: Oxford University Press.

Chan, R. W., Raboy, B., & Patterson, C. J. (1998). Psychosocial adjustment among children conceived via insemination by lesbian and heterosexual mothers. *Child Development, 69,* 443–457.

Chance, R. (1992). *Probation: Technical assistance manual*. Rockville, MD: Juvenile Justice Clearinghouse.

Chandler, M., Fritz, A. S., & Hala, Suzanne (1989). Small-scale deceit: Deception as a marker of two-, three-, and four-year-olds' early theories of mind. *Child Development, 60,* 1263–1277.

Channiah, D. (1997). *The Ryan White story*. Charlottesville: University of Virgina Press.

Charlesworth, R. (1989). "Behind" before they start? *Young Children, 44,* 5–13.

Chase, W. G., & Simon, H. A. (1973). Perception in chess. *Cognitive Psychology, 4,* 55–81.

Chase-Linsdale, P. L., & Hetherington, E. M. (1990). The impact of divorce on life-span development: Short- and long-term effects. In D. L. Featherman & R. M. Lerner (Eds.), *Life span development and behavior* (Vol. 10, pp. 105–151). Hillsdale, NJ: Erlbaum.

Chasnoff, I. J., Burns, W. J., Schnoll, S. H., & Burns, K. A. (1985). Cocaine use in pregnancy. *New England Journal of Medicine, 313,* 666–669.

Chasnoff, I. J., Chisum, G. M., & Kaplan, W. E. (1988). Maternal cocaine use and genitourinary tract malformations. *Teratology, 37,* 201–204.

Chassin, L., Presson, C. C., & Sherman, S. J. (1987). Applications of social developmental psychology to adolescent health behaviors. In N. Eisenberg (Ed.), *Contemporary topics in developmental psychology* (pp. 353–374). New York: Wiley.

Chen, C., & Stevenson, H. W. (1995). Culture and academic achievement. In M. L. Maher & P. R. Pintrich (Eds.), *Advances in motivation and achievement* (Vol. 9, 119–151). Greenwich, CT: JAI Press.

Chen, Z. Y., & Dornbusch, S. M. (1998). Relating aspects of adolescent emotional autonomy to academic achievement and deviant behavior. *Journal of Adolescent Research, 13,* 293–319.

Cherukuri, R., Minkoff, H., Feldman, J., Parekh, A., & Glass, L. (1988). A cohort study of alkaloidal cocaine in pregnancy. *Obstetrics and Gynecology, 72,* 147–151.

Cherukuri, R., Minkoff, H., Feldman, J., Parekh. A., & Glass, L. (1988). A cohort study of alkaloidal cocaine ("crack") in pregnancy. *Obstetrics and Gynecology, 72,* 147–151.

Chi, M. T. H. (1978). Knowledge structures and memory development. In R. S. Siegler (Ed.), *Children's thinking: What develops?* (pp. 73–96). Hillsdale, NJ: Erlbaum.

Chi, M. T. H., & Koeske, R. D. (1983). Network representation of a child's dinosaur knowledge. *Developmental Psychology, 19,* 29–39.

Child Care Action Campaign. (1996). *A child care primer for parents.* New York: Child Care Action Campaign.

Children's Defense Fund. (1992). *The state of America's children.* Washington, DC: Children's Defense Fund.

Children's Television Workshop. (1991). *What research indicates about the educational effects of Sesame Street.* New York: Children's Television Workshop.

Chilman, C. S. (1993). Hispanic families in the United States. In H. P. McAdoo (Ed.), *Family ethnicity* (pp. 141–163). Newbury Park, CA: Sage.

Chisholm, J. S. (1989). Biology, culture, and the development of temperament: A Navajo example. In J. K. Nugent, B. M. Lester, & T. B. Brazelton (Eds.), *The cultural context of the infant* (Vol. 1, pp. 341–366). Norwood, NJ: Ablex.

Chisholm, K. (1998). A three year follow-up of attachment and indiscriminate friendliness in children adopted from Romanian orphanages. *Child Development, 69,* 1092–1106.

Choi, S., & Gopnik, A. (1995). Early acquisition of verbs in Korean: A cross-linguistic study. *Journal of Child Language, 22,* 497–529.

Chomsky, N. (1965). *Aspects of the theory of syntax.* Cambridge, MA: MIT Press.

Chomsky, N. (1986). *Knowledge of language: Its nature, origin and use.* New York: Praeger.

Chorpita, B. F., & Barlow, D. H. (1998). The development of anxiety: The role of control in the early environment. *Psychological Bulletin, 124,* 3–21.

Christopher, F. S. (1996). Adolescent sexuality. In N. Vanzetti & S. Duck (Eds.), *A lifetime of relationships* (pp. 231–243). Pacific Grove, CA: Brooks/Cole.

Cicchetti, D., Rogosch, F. A., & Toth, S. L. (1998). Maternal depressive disorder and contextual risk: Contributions to the development of attachment insecurity and behavior problems in toddlerhood. *Development and Psychopathology, 10,* 283–300.

Cicchetti. D., & Toth, S. L. (1998). The development of depression in children and adolescents. *American Psychologist, 53,* 221–241.

Clancy, S. M., & Dollinger, S. J. (1993). Photographic depictions of the self: Gender and age differences in social connectedness. *Sex Roles, 29,* 477–495.

Clark, E. V. (1981). Lexical innovations: How children learn to create new words. In W. Deutsch (Ed.), *The child's construction of language* (pp. 299–328). London: Academic Press.

Clark, E. V. (1993). *The lexicon in acquisition.* Cambridge, England: Cambridge University Press.

Clark, E. V. (1997). Conceptual perspective and lexical choice in acquisition. *Cognition, 64,* 1–37.

Clark, G. (1994). *Onions are my husband: Survival and accumulation by West African market women.* Chicago: University of Chicago Press.

Clark, M. L., & Ayers, M. (1993). Friendship expectations and friendship evaluations. *Youth and Society,* 24, 299–313.

Clarke, A. T., & Kutz-Costes, B. (1997). Television viewing, educational quality of the home, and school readiness. *Journal of Educational Research,* 90, 279–285.

Clarke-Stewart, K. A. (1984). Day care: A new context for research and development. In M. Perlmutter (Ed.), *Parent-child interactions and parent-child relations in children's development* (Vol. 17, pp. 61–100). Hillsdale, NJ: Erlbaum.

Clarke-Stewart, K. A. (1992). Consequences of child care for children's development. In A. Booth (Ed.), *Child care in the 1990s: Trends and consequences* (pp. 63–82). Hillsdale, NJ: Erlbaum.

Clarke-Stewart, K. A., Allhusen, V. D., & Clements, D. C. (1995). Nonparental caregiving. Fathers and families. In M. H. Bornstein (Ed.), *Handbook of parenting* (Vol. 3, pp. 151–176). Mahwah, NJ: Erlbaum.

Clausen, J. (1975). The social meaning of differential physical and sexual maturation. In S. E. Dragastin & G. H. Elder, Jr. (Eds.), *Adolescence in the life cycle.* New York: Halsted.

Clausen, J. (1991). Adolescent competence and the shaping of the life course. *American Journal of Sociology,* 96, 805–842.

Clingempeel, W. G., Shuwall, M. A., & Heiss, E. (1988). Divorce and remarriage: Perspectives on the effects of custody arrangements on children. In S. A. Wolchik & P. Karoly (Eds.), *Children of divorce* (pp. 145–184). New York: Gardner Press.

Clinton, J. F. (1986). Expectant fathers at risk for couvade. *Nursing Research,* 35, 290–295.

Clubb, R. (1991). Chronic sorrow: Adaptation of parents with chronically ill children. *Pediatric Nursing,* 17, 461–466.

Cnattingius, S., Bergstrom, R., Lipworth, L., & Kramer, M. S. (1998). Prepregnancy weight and the risk of adverse pregnancy outcomes. *New England Journal of Medicine,* 388, 147–152.

Cohen, L. M. (1996). *Meeting the needs of gifted and talented minority language students.* ERIC Digest #E480.

Cohen, M. A. (1998). The monetary value of saving a high-risk youth. *Journal of Quantitative Criminology,* 14, 5–53.

Cohen, Y., Spirito, A., & Brown, L. K. (1996). Suicide and suicidal behavior. In R. DiClemente & W. B. Hansen (Eds.), *Handbook of adolescent health risk behavior* (pp. 193–224). New York: Plenum.

Cohn, A. H., & Daro, D. (1987). Is treatment too late: What ten years of evaluative research tells us. *Child Abuse and Neglect,* 11, 433–442.

Cohn, D. A., Lohrmann, B. C., & Patterson, C. (1985, April). *Loneliness and peer relations in young children.* Paper presented at the biennial meeting of the Society for Research in Child Development, Kansas City.

Cohn, J. E., Campbell, S. B., Matias, R., & Hopkins, J. (1990). Face-to-face interactions of postpartum depressed and nondepressed mother-infant pairs at 2 months. *Developmental Psychology,* 26, 15–23.

Coie, J. D., & Dodge, K. A. (1998). Aggression and antisocial behavior. In W. Damon (Ed.), *Handbook of child psychology* (Vol. 3, 778–862). New York: Wiley.

Coie, J. D., Dodge, K. A., & Kupersmidt, J. B. (1990). Peer group behavior and social status. In S. R. Asher & J. D. Coie (Eds.), *Peer rejection in childhood* (pp. 17–59). Cambridge, England: Cambridge University Press.

Coie, J. D., Dodge, K., Terry, R., & Wright, V. (1991). The role of aggression in peer relations: An analysis of aggression episodes in boys' play groups. *Child Development,* 62, 812–826.

Coie, J. D., & Koeppl, G. K. (1990). Adapting intervention to the problems of aggressive and disruptive rejected children. In S. R. Asher & J. D. Coie (Eds.), *Peer rejection in childhood* (pp. 309–337). Cambridge, England: Cambridge University Press.

Colby, A., Kohlberg, L., Gibbs, J., & Lieberman, M. (1983). A longitudinal study of moral judgment. *Monographs of the Society for Research in Child Development,* 48 (Nos. 1–2, Serial No. 200).

Cole, E. B. (1992). *Learning and talking: A guide to promoting spoken language in hearing-impaired children.* Washington, DC: Alexander Graham Bell Association for the Deaf.

Cole, M. (1990). Cognitive development and formal schooling: The evidence from cross-cultural reseach. In L. C. Moll (Ed.), *Vygotsky and education* (pp. 89–110). New York: Cambridge University Press.

Cole, M. (1997). Cultural mechanisms of cognitive development. In E. Amsel & K. A. Renninger (Eds.), *Change and development* (pp. 245–263). Hillsdale, NJ: Erlbaum.

Coles, C. (1994). Critical periods for prenatal alcohol exposure. *Alcohol Health and Research World,* 18, 22–29.

Coles, R. (1990). *The spiritual life of children.* Boston: Houghton Mifflin.

Coles, R., & Stokes, G. (1985). *Sex and the American teenager.* New York: Harper & Row.

Coley, R. L., & Chase-Linsdale, P. L. (1998). Adolescent pregnancy and parenthood. *American Psychologist,* 53, 152–166.

Colin, V. L. (1996). *Human attachment.* New York: McGraw-Hill.

Collaer, M. L., & Hines, M. (1995). Human behavioral sex differences: A role for gonadal hormone during early development? *Psychological Bulletin,* 118(1), 55–107.

Collier, J., Jr. (1988). Survival at Rough Rock: A historical overview of Rough Rock demonstration school. *Anthropology and Education Quarterly,* 19, 253–269.

Collins, W. A. (1990). Parent-child relationships in the transition to adolescence. In R. Montemayor, G. R. Adams, & T. Gullotta (Eds.), *From childhood to adolescence* (Vol. 2, pp. 85–106). Newbury Park, CA: Sage.

Collins, W. A., & Repinski, D. J. (1994). Relationships during adolescence: Continuity and change in interpersonal perspective. In R. Montemayor & G. R. Adams (Eds.), *Personal relationships during adolescence* (pp. 7–36). Thousand Oaks, CA: Sage.

Coltrane, S. (1995). *Family man.* New York: Oxford University Press.

Committee on Pediatric AIDS. (1998). Surveillance of pediatric HIV infection. *Pediatrics,* 101, 315–319.

Compas, B. E., Malcarne, V. L., & Banez, G. A. (1992). Coping with psychological stress: A developmental perspective. In B. Carpenter (Ed.), *Personal coping: Theory, research, and application* (pp. 47–63). New York: Praeger.

Compas, B. E., & Phares, V. (1991). Stress during childhood and adolescence: Sources of risk and vulnerability. In E. M. Cummings, A. L. Greene, & K. H. Karraker (Eds.), *Life-span developmental psychology: Perspectives on stress and coping* (pp. 111–130). Hillsdale, NJ: Erlbaum.

Comstock, G., & Paik, H. (1991). *Television and the American child.* New York: Academic Press.

Condry, J. (1989). *The psychology of television.* Hillsdale, NJ: Erlbaum.

Conger, R. D., Ge, X., Elder, G. H., Lorenz, F. O., & Simons, R. L. (1994). Economic stress, coercive family process, and developmental problems of adolescents. *Child Development,* 65, 541–561.

Connolly, J. A., & Johnson, A. M. (1996). Adolescents' romantic relationships and the structure and quality of their close interpersonal ties. *Personal Relationships,* 3, 185–195.

Connolly, S. D., Paikoff, R. L., & Buchanan, C. M. (1996). Puberty: The interplay of biological and psychosocial processes in adolescence.

In G. R. Adams & R. Montemayor (Eds.), *Psychosocial development during adolescence* (Vol. 8, pp. 259–299). Thousand Oaks, CA: Sage.

Connor, D. B., Knight, D. K., & Cross, D. R. (1997). Mothers' and fathers' scaffolding of their 2-year-olds during problem-solving and literacy interactions. *British Journal of Developmental Psychology, 15*, 323–338.

Consortium for Longitudinal Studies. (1983). *As the twig is bent . . . Lasting effects of preschool programs.* Hillsdale, NJ: Erlbaum.

Consumer Product Safety Commission. (1996). *Baseball safety.* Washington, DC: Consumer Product Safety Commission.

Cook, T. D., Appleton, H., Conner, R. F., Shaffer, A., Tamkin, G., & Weber, S. (1975). *Sesame Street revisited.* New York: Russell Sage Foundation.

Cooksey, E. C., & Fondell, M. M. (1996). Spending time with his kids: Effects of family structure on fathers' and children's lives. *Journal of Marriage and the Family, 58*, 693–707.

Cooper, H., & Hedges, L. V. (1994). *The handbook of research synthesis.* New York: Russell Sage Foundation.

Coopersmith, S. (1967). *The antecedents of self-esteem.* San Francisco: W. H. Freeman.

Coplan, R. J., & Rubin, K. H. (1998). Exploring and assessing nonsocial play in the preschool. *Social Development, 7*, 72–91.

Coplan, R. J., Rubin, K. H., Fox, N. A., Calkins, S. D., & Stewart, S. L. (1994). Being alone, playing alone, and acting alone: Distinguishing among reticence and passive and active solitude in young children. *Child Development, 65*, 129–137.

Copstick, S. M., Taylor, K. E., Hayes, R., & Morris, N. (1986). Partner support and the use of coping technique in labour. *Journal of Psychosomatic Research, 30*, 497–503.

Corcoran, J. (1998). Consequences of adolescent pregnancy/parents: A review of the literature. *Social Work and Health Care, 27*, 49–67.

Coren, S. (1993). *The left-hander syndrome.* New York: Vintage Books.

Coren, S., & Porac, C. (1977). Fifty centuries of right-handedness. *Science, 198*, 631–632.

Corkum, V., & Moore, C. (1998). The origins of joint visual attention in infants. *Developmental Psychology, 34*, 28–38.

Cornwell, T. (1998, June 12). California votes for English alone. *Times Educational Supplement*, 25.

Cortez, V. L., & Bugental, D. B. (1995). Priming of perceived control in young children as a buffer against fear-inducing events. *Child Development, 66*, 687–696.

Costa, P. T., & VandenBos, G. R. (1996). *Psychological aspects of serious illness.* Washington, DC: American Psychological Assocation.

Cote, J. F. (1996). Sociological perspectives on identity formation. *Journal of Adolescence, 19*, 417–428.

Counts, C. R., Jones, C., Frame, C. L., & Jarvie, G. J. (1986). The perception of obesity by normal-weight versus obese school-age children. *Child Psychiatry and Human Development, 17*, 113–120.

Coupey, S. M. (1992). Anorexia nervosa. In S. B. Friedman & M. Fisher (Eds.), *Nutrition and eating disorders* (pp. 206–249). St. Louis, MO: Quality Medical Publishing.

Covington, M. C. (1992). *Making the grade.* Cambridge, England: Cambridge University Press.

Cowden, J. E., Sayers, L. K., & Torrey, C. C. (1998). *Pediatric adapted motor development and exercise: An innovative, multisystem approach for professionals and families.* Springfield, IL: Charles C. Thomas.

Cozby, P. C., Worden, P. E., & Kee, D. W. (1989). *Research methods in human development.* Mountain View, CA: Mayfield.

Crain, W. (1992). *Theories of development: Concepts and applications.* Englewood Cliffs: Prentice-Hall.

Crandall, C. S. (1988). Social contagion of binge eating. *Journal of Personality and Social Psychology, 55*, 588–598.

Crane, J. (1991). The epidemic theory of ghettos and neighborhood effects on dropping out and teenage childbearing. *American Journal of Sociology, 100*, 1226–1259.

Crane, J. P., LeFevre, M. L., Winborn, R. C., Evans, J. K., Ewigman, B. G., Bain, R. P., Frigoletto, F. D., & McNellis, D. (1994). A randomized trial of prenatal ultrasonographic screening: Impact on the detection, management, and outcome of anomalous fetuses. *American Journal of Obstetrics and Gynecology, 171*, 392–399.

Cratty, B. J. (1986). *Perceptual and motor development in infants and children.* Englewood Cliffs, NJ: Prentice-Hall.

Cratty, B. J. (1999). *Movement behavior and motor learning.* Ann Arbor, MI: Books on Demand.

Creasey, G. L., Jarvis, P. A., & Berk, L. E. (1998). Play and social competence. In O. N. Saracho & B. Spodek (Eds.), *Multiple perspectives on play in early childhood education* (pp. 116–143). Albany: State University of New York Press.

Crick, N. R., & Grotpeter, J. K. (1995). Relational aggression, gender, and social-psychological adjustment, *Child Development, 66*, 710–722.

Crispell, D. (1995). Why working teens get into trouble. *American Demographics*, 19–20.

Crittenden, P. M. (1988). Distorted patterns of relationship in maltreating families. *Journal of Reproductive and Infant Psychology, 6*, 183–199.

Crittenden, P. M., & Ainsworth, M. D. (1989). Child maltreatment and attachment theory. In D. Cicchetti & V. Carlson (Eds.), *Child maltreatment* (pp. 432–463). Cambridge, England: Cambridge University Press.

Csikszentmihalyi, M. (1988). Society, culture, and person: A systems view of creativity. In R. J. Sternberg (Ed.), *The nature of creativity* (pp. 325–339). New York: Cambridge University Press.

Csikszentmihalyi, M., & Larson, R. (1984). *Being adolescent.* New York: Basic Books.

Culp, A. M., Osofsky, J. D., & O'Brien, M. (1996). Language patterns of adolescent and older mothers and their one-year-old children: A comparison study. *First Language, 16*, 61–75.

Culp, R. E., Watkins, R. V., Lawrence, H., Letts, D., Kelly, D. J., & Rice, M. L. (1991). Maltreated children's language and speech development: Abused, neglected, and abused and neglected. *First Language, 11*, 377–389.

Cummings, E. M., & Davies, P. (1996). Emotional security as a regulatory process in normal development and the development of psychopathology. *Development and Psychopathology, 8*, 123–139.

Cunningham, F. G., MacDonald, P. C., & Gant, N. F. (1993). *Williams obstetrics.* Norwalk, CT: Appleton & Lange.

Cunningham, M. R. (1985/1986). Levites and brother's keepers: A sociobiological perspective on prosocial behavior. *Humboldt Journal of Social Relations, 13*, 35–67.

Curran, D. J., & Renzetti, C. M. (1996). *Social problems.* Boston: Allyn & Bacon.

Curtiss, S. (1977). *Genie: A psycholinguistic study of a modern-day "wild child."* New York: Academic Press.

Cutler, G. B., Jr. (1988). Precocious puberty. In J. W. Hurst (Ed.), *Medicine for the practicing physician* (pp. 526–530). Boston: Butterworths.

Cutler, G. B., Jr. (1993). Treatment of precocious puberty. In R. M. Lerner, A. C. Petersen, & J. Brooks-Gunn (Eds.), *Encyclopedia of adolescence* (Vol. 2, pp. 903–907). New York: Garland.

Dacey, J., & Kenny, M. (1997). *Adolescent development*. Dubuque, IA: Brown and Benchmark.

Dainton, M. (1993). The myths and misperceptions of the stepmother identity: Descriptions and prescriptions for identity management. *Family Relations, 42*, 93–98.

Daly, K. (1993). Reshaping fatherhood: Finding the models. *Journal of Family Issues, 14*, 510–530.

Damasio, A. R., & Damasio, H. (1992). Brain and language. *Scientific American, 14*, 597–611.

Damon, W. (1988). *The moral child*. New York: Free Press.

Damon, W. (1995). *Greater expectations: Overcoming the culture of indulgence in America's homes and schools*. New York: Free Press.

Daniels, D. H. (1998). Age differences in concepts of self-esteem. *Merrill-Palmer Quarterly, 44*, 234–258.

Danish, S., Kleiber, D., & Hall, H. (1987). Enhancing motivation in the context of sport. In M. Maehr & D. Kleiber (Eds.), *Enhancing motivation* (pp. 211–238).Greenwich, CT: JAI Press.

Dannemiller, J. L., & Stephens, B. R. (1988). A critical test of infant pattern preference models. *Child Development, 59*, 210–216.

Daro, D. (1996). Preventing child abuse and neglect. In J. Briere, L. Berliner, J. A. Bulkley, C. Jenny, & T. Reid (Eds.), *The APSAC handbook on child maltreatment* (pp. 343–358). Thousand Oaks, CA: Sage.

Darwin, C. (1859). *On the origin of species*. London: J. Murray.

Darwin, C. (1877). Biographical sketch of an infant. *Mind, 2*, 285–294.

Dasen, P. R. (1994). Culture and cognitive development from a Piagetian perspective. In W. J. Lonner & R. S. Malpass (Eds.), *Psychology and culture* (p. 145–149). Boston: Allyn & Bacon.

Datta, L. E. (1985). Benefits without gains: The paradox of the cognitive effects of early childhood programs and implications for policy. *Special Services in the Schools, 3*, 103–126.

Davey, A. G. (1983). *Learning to be prejudiced*. London: Edward Arnold.

Davidson, J., & Smith, R. (1990). Traumatic experiences in psychiatric outpatients. *Journal of Traumatic Stress Studies, 3*, 459–475.

Davidson, J. E., & Sternberg, R. J. (1984). The role of insight in intellectual giftedness. *Gifted Child Quarterly, 28*, 58–64.

Davies, G., Lloyd-Bostock, S., McMurran, M., & Wilson, C. (Eds.). *Psychology, law, and criminal justice* (pp. 248–263). Berlin, Germany: Walter De Gruyter.

Davis, B. T., Hops, H., Alpert, A., & Sheeber, L. (1998). Child responses to parental conflict and their effect on adjustment. *Journal of Family Psychology, 12*, 163–177.

Davis, J. F. (1990/1991). Five important ideas to teach your kids about television. *Media & Values, 52/53*, 16–19.

Dawson, D. A. (1991). Family structure and children's mental health and well-being. *Journal of Marriage and the Family, 53*, 573–584.

Day, R. D., & Peterson, G. W. (in press). Predictors of the frequency of spanking of younger and older children. *Pediatrics*.

Deak, G. O., & Maratsos, M. (1998). On having complex representations of things: Preschoolers use multiple words for objects and people. *Developmental Psychology, 34*, 224–240.

Deal, J. E., Halverson, C. F., & Wampler, K. S. (1989). Parental agreement on child-rearing orientations: Relations to parental, marital, and child characteristics. *Child Development, 60*, 1025–1034.

Deater-Deckard, K., Scarr, S., McCartney, K., & Eisenberg, M. (1994). Paternal separation anxiety: Relationships with parenting stress, child-rearing attitudes, and maternal anxieties. *Psychological Science, 6*, 341–346.

DeCasper, A. J., & Fifer, W. P. (1980). Of human bonding: Newborns prefer their mother's voices. *Science, 208*, 174–176.

DeCasper, A. J., & Fifer, W. P. (1987). Of human bonding: Newborns prefer their mothers' voices. In J. Oates & S. Sheldon (Eds.), *Cognitive development in infancy* (pp. 111–118). Hove, England: Erlbaum.

DeCasper, A. J., & Spence, M. J. (1986). Prenatal maternal speech influences newborn's perception of speech sounds. *Infant Behavior and Development, 9*, 133–150.

Deci, E. L., & Ryan, R. M. (1995). Human autonomy: The basis for true self-esteem. In M. H. Kernis (Ed.), *Efficacy, agency, and self-esteem* (pp. 31–46). New York: Plenum.

Decker, M. D., Dewey, M. J., Hutcheson, R. H., & Schaffner, W. (1984). The use and efficacy of child restraint devices. *Journal of the American Medical Association, 252*, 2571–2575.

De Corte, E., Greer, B., & Verschaffel, L. (1996). Mathematics teaching and learning. In D. C. Berliner & R. C. Calfee (Eds.), *Handbook of educational psychology* (pp. 491–549). New York: Macmillan.

Deford, F. (1986). *Alex: The life of a child*. New York: Signet/New American Library.

deHass, I., Harlow, B. L., & Cramer, D. W. (1991). Spontaneous preterm birth: A case-control study. *American Journal of Obstetrics and Gynecology, 165*, 1290–1296.

Dekovic, M., & Janssens, J. M. (1992). Parents' child-rearing style and child's sociometric status. *Developmental Psychology, 28*, 925–932.

Della Corte, M., Benedict, H., & Klein, D. (1983). The relationship of pragmatic dimensions of mothers' speech to the referential-expressive distinction. *Journal of Child Language, 10*, 35–43.

DeLoache, J. S., Cassidy, D. J., & Brown, A. L. (1985). Precursors of mnemonic strategies in very young children's memory. *Child Development, 56*, 125–137.

Demaray, M. K., & Elliot, S. N. (1998). Teachers' judgments of students' academic functioning: A comparison of actual and predicted performance. *School Psychology Quarterly, 13*, 8–24.

DeMarie-Dreblow, D., & Miller, P. H. (1988). The development of children's strategies for selective attention: Evidence for a transitional period. *Child Development, 59*, 1504–1513.

Demuth, K. (1990). Maturation and the acquisition of the Sesotho passive. *Language, 65*, 56–81.

Denham, S. A., Renwick-DeBardi, S., & Hughes, S. (1994). Emotional communication between mothers and preschoolers: Relations with emotional competence. *Merrill Palmer Quarterly, 40*, 488–508.

Denham, S. A., Zoller, D., & Couchoud, E. A. (1994). Socialization of preschoolers' emotion understanding. *Developmental Psychology, 30*, 928–936.

Deregowski, J. B. (1980). *Illusions, patterns, and pictures: A cross-cultural perspective*. London: Academic Press.

de Roiste, A., & Bushnell, I. W. R. (1996). Tactile stimulation: Short- and long-term benefits for pre-term infants. *British Journal of Developmental Psychology, 14*, 41–53.

Deslandes, R., & Royer, E. (1997). Family-related variables and school disciplinary events at the secondary level. *Behavioral Disorders, 23*, 18–28.

Devereux, E. C., Shouval, R., Bronfenbrenner, U., Rodgers, R. R., Kav-Venaki, S., Kiely, E., & Karson, E. (1983). Socialization practices of parents, teachers, and peers in Israel: The kibbutz versus the city. In E. Krausz (Ed.), *The sociology of the kibbutz* (pp. 305–319). New Brunswick, CT: Transaction Books.

de Villiers, P., & de Villiers, J. (1992). Language development. In M. H. Bornstein & M. E. Lamb (Eds.), *Developmental psychology: An advanced textbook* (pp. 255–290). Hillsdale, NJ: Erlbaum.

Devlin, B., Daniels, M., & Roeder, K. (1997). The heritability of IQ. *Nature, 338,* 468–471.

DeVries, M. (1984). Temperament and infant mortality among the Masai of East Africa. *American Journal of Psychiatry, 141,* 1189–1994.

DeVries, M., & Sameroff, A. J. (1984). Culture and temperament: Influences on temperament in three East African societies. *American Journal of Orthopsychiatry, 54,* 83–96.

De Wolff, M. S., & van IJzendoorn, M. H. (1997). Sensitivity and attachment: A meta-analysis of parental antecedents of infant attachment. *Child Development, 68,* 571–591.

Diamond, A. (1991). Frontal lobe involvement in cognitive changes during the first year of life. In K. R. Gibson & A. C. Petersen (Eds.), *Brain maturation and cognitive development: Comparative and cross-cultural perspectives* (pp. 127–180). New York: Aldine de Gruyter.

Diamond, J. (1990, December). War babies. *Discover,* 70–75.

Diamond, M., & Sigmundson, K. (1997). Sex reassignment at birth: Long-term review and clinical implications. *Archives of Pediatric Adolescent Medicine, 151,* 298–304.

Diehl, S. F., Moffitt, K. A., & Wade, S. M. (1991). Focus group interview with parents of children with medically complex needs: An intimate look at their perceptions and feelings. *Children's Health Care, 20,* 170–178.

Dietz, T. L. (1998). An examination of violence and gender role portrayals in video games. *Sex Roles, 38,* 423–444.

Dietz, W. H., & Gormaker, S. L. (1984). Factors within the physical environment associated with childhood obesity. *American Journal of Clinical Nutrition, 39,* 704–708.

Dietz, W. H., & Gortmaker, S. L. (1985). Do we fatten our children at the television set? Obesity and television viewing in children and adolescents. *Pediatrics, 75,* 807–812.

DiGirolamo, A. M., Geis, H. K., & Walker, C. E. (1998). Developmental issues. In R. T. Ammerman & J. V. Campo (Eds.), *Handbook of pediatric psychology and psychiatry* (pp. 1–22). Boston: Allyn & Bacon.

DiLalla, L. F., & Watson, M. W. (1988). Differentiation of fantasy and reality: Preschoolers' reactions to interruptions in their play. *Developmental Psychology, 24,* 286–291.

DiMaggio, P. (1997). Culture and cognition. *Annual Review of Sociology, 23,* 263–267.

DiPietro, J. A., Hodgson, D. M., Costigan, K. A., & Johnson, T. R. B. (1996). Fetal antecedents of infant temperament. *Child Development, 67,* 2568–2583.

DiPietro, J. A., Larson, S. K., & Porges, S. W. (1987). Behavioral and heartrate pattern differences between breast-fed and bottle-fed neonates. *Developmental Psychology, 23,* 467–474.

Dishion, T. J. (1990). The peer context of troublesome child and adolescent behavior. In P. E. Leone (Ed.), *Understanding troubled and troubling youth* (pp. 128–153). Newbury Park, CA: Sage.

Dishion, T. J., & Andrews, D. W. (1996). A multicomponent intervention for families of young adolescents at risk: An analysis of short-term outcomes. *Journal of Consulting and Clinical Psychology, 63,* 538–548.

Dishion, T. J., French, D. C., & Patterson, G. R. (1995). The development and ecology of antisocial behavior. In D. Cicchetti & D. J. Cohen (Eds.), *Developmental psychopathology* (Vol. 2, pp. 421–471). New York: Wiley.

Dodge, K. A. (1991). Emotion and social information processing. In J. Garber & K. A. Dodge (Eds.), *The development of emotion: Regulation and dysregulation* (pp. 159–181). Cambridge, England: Cambridge University Press.

Dodge, K. A., Bates, J. E., & Pettit, G. S. (1990). Mechanisms in the cycle of violence. *Science, 250,* 1678–1683.

Dodge, K. A., & Coie, J. D. (1987). Social-information-processing factors in reactive and proactive aggression in children's peer groups. *Journal of Personality and Social Psychology, 53,* 1146–1158.

Dodge, K. A., Pettit, G. S., McClaskey, C. L., & Brown, M. M. (1986). Social competence in children. *Monographs of the Society for Research in Child Development* (Vol. 51, No. 2). Chicago: University of Chicago Press.

Doherty, W. J. (1997). The best of times and the worst of times: Fathering as a contested arena of academic discourse. In A. J. Hawkins & D. C. Dollahite (Eds.), *Generative fathering: Beyond deficit perspectives* (pp. 217–227). Newbury Park, CA: Sage.

Dollaghan, C., (1985). Child meet word: "Fast mapping" in preschool children. *Journal of Speech and Hearing Research, 28,* 449–454.

Donahue, M. J. (1995). Religion and the well-being of adolescents. *Journal of Social Issues, 51,* 145–160.

Donaldson, M. (1978). *Children's minds.* New York: W. W. Norton.

Dornbusch, S. M., Mont-Reynaud, R., Ritter, P. L., Chen, Z. Y., & Steinberg, L. (1991). Stressful events and their correlates among adolescents of diverse backgrounds. In M. E. Colten & S. Gore (Eds.), *Adolescent stress: Causes and consequences* (pp. 111–130). New York: Aldine de Gruyter.

Dotta, L. E. (1977). The research and development program of the National Institute of Education. *International Review of Applied Psychology, 26,* 127–131.

Doussard-Roosevelt, J. A., Porges, S. W., Scanlon, J. W., Alemmi, B., & Scanlon, K. B. (1997). Vagal regulation of heart rate in the prediction of development outcome for very low birth weight preterm infants. *Child Development, 68,* 173–186.

Doyle, L. W., Rickards, A. L., Kelly, E. A., Ford, G. W., & Callanan, C. (1992). Breastfeeding and intelligence. *Lancet, 339,* 744–745.

Drewett, R. F. (1993). The infant's regulation of nutritional intake. In I. St. James-Roberts, G. Harris, & D. Messer (Eds.), *Infant crying, feeding, and sleeping: Development, problems, and treatments* (pp. 83–98). New York: Harvester Wheatsheaf.

Druian, G., & Butler, J. A. (1987). Effective schooling practices and at-risk youth: What the research shows. *School Improvement Research Series, 1,* 1–13.

Dryfoos, J. G. (1990). *Adolescents at risk: Prevalence and prevention.* New York: Oxford University Press.

Dubas, J. S., Crockett, L. J., & Petersen, A. C. (in press). A longitudinal study of sex differences in cognitive abilities in early adolescence. *Child Development.*

DuBois-Reymond, M., & Ravesloot, J. (1996). The roles of parents and peers in the sexual and relational development of adolescents. In K. Hurrelmann & S. F. Hamilton (Eds.), *Social problems and social contexts in adolescence* (pp. 175–197). New York: Aldine de Gruyter.

Dubowitz, H. (1989). Prevention of child maltreatment: What is known. *Pediatrics, 83,* 570–577.

Dubrow, N. F., & Garbarino, J. (1989). Living in the war zone: Mothers and young children in a public housing development. *Child Welfare, 68,* 3–20.

Duda, J. (1988). The relationship between goal perspectives, persistence and behavioral intensity among male and female recreational sport participants. *Leisure Sciences, 10,* 95–106.

Dulcan, M. K. (1986). Comprehensive treatment of children and adolescents with attention deficit disorders: The state of the art. *Clinical Psychology Review, 6,* 539–569.

Dulcan, M. K. (1989). Attention deficit disorders. In C. G. Last & M. Hersen (Eds.), *Handbook of child psychiatric diagnosis* (pp. 95–128). New York: Wiley.

Dumka, L. E., Roosa, M. W., & Jackson, K. M. (1997). Risk, conflict, mothers' parenting, and children's adjustment in low-income, Mexican immigrant and Mexican American families. *Journal of Marriage and the Family, 59,* 309–323.

Dunbar, K., & Klahr, D. (1989). Developmental differences in scientific discovery processes. In D. Klahr & K. Kotovsky (Eds.), *Complex informaiton processing: The impact of Herbert A. Simon* (pp. 109–143). Hillsdale, NJ: Erlbaum.

Duncan, P., Ritter, P., Dornbusch, S., Gross, R., & Carlsmith, J. (1985). The effects of pubertal timing on body image, school behavior, and deviance. *Journal of Youth and Adolescence, 14,* 227–236.

Duncan, R. M., & Pratt, M. W. (1997). Microgenetic change in the quantity and quality of preschoolers' private speech. *International Journal of Behavioral Development, 20,* 367–383.

Dunn, J. (1983). Sibling relationships in early childhood. *Child Development, 54,* 787–811.

Dunn, J. (1988). *The beginnings of social understanding.* Cambridge, MA: Harvard University Press.

Dunn, J. (1992). Sisters and brothers: Current issues in developmental research. In F. Boer & J. Dunn (Eds.), *Children's sibling relationships* (pp. 1–18). Hillsdale, NJ: Erlbaum.

Dunn, J., & Munn, P. (1987). The development of justification in disputes. *Developmental Psychology, 23,* 791–798.

Dunn, J., & Slomkowski, C. (1992). Conflict and the development of social understanding. In C. U. Shantz & W. W. Hartup (Eds.), *Conflict in child and adolescent development* (pp. 70–92). Cambridge, England: Cambridge University Press.

Dusck, J. B. (1996). *Adolescent development and behavior.* Saddle River, NJ: Prentice Hall.

Dweck, C. S., & Leggett, E. L. (1988). A social-cognitive approach to motivation and personality. *Psychological Review, 95,* 256–273.

Dwyer, K. M., Richardson, J. L., Danley, K. L., Hansen, W. B., Sussman, S. Y., Brannon, B., Dent, C. W., Johnson, C. A., & Flay, B. R. (1990). Characteristics of eighth-grade students who initiate self-care in elementary and junior high school. *Pediatrics, 86,* 448–454.

Eaton, W. O., & Enns, L. R. (1986). Sex differences in human motor activity level. *Psychological Bulletin, 100,* 19–28.

Ebata, A. T., Petersen, A. C., & Conger, J. (1990). The development of psychopathology in adolescence. In J. Rolf, A. S. Masten, D. Cicchetti, K. H. Nuechterlein, & S. Weintraub (Eds.), *Risk and protective factors in the development of psychopathology* (pp. 308–333). Cambridge, England: Cambridge University Press.

Eccles, J. S., & Jacobs, J. E. (1986). Social forces shape math attitudes and performance. *Signs, 11,* 367–380.

Eccles, J. S., & Midgley, C. (1989). Stage-environment fit: Developmentally appropriate classrooms for young adolescents. In C. Ames & R. Ames (Eds.), *Research on motivation in education* (Vol. 3, pp. 139–186). Greenwich, CT: JAI Press.

Eccles, J. S., Wigfield, A., Flanagan, C. A., & Miller, C. (1989). Self-concepts, domain values, and self-esteem: Relations and changes at early adolescence. *Journal of Personality, 57,* 282–310.

Eccles, J. S., Wigfield, A., Midgley, C. H., Reuman, D., MacIver, D., & Feldlaufer, H. (1993). Negative effects of traditional middle schools on students' motivation. *Elementary School Journal, 93,* 553–574.

Eckenrode, J., Laird, M., & Doris, J. (1993). School performance and disciplinary problems among abused and neglected children. *Developmental Psychology, 29,* 53–62.

Eckensberger, L. H. (1994). Moral development and its measurement across cultures. In W. J. Lonner & R. S. Malpass (Eds.), *Psychology and culture* (pp. 75–79). Boston: Allyn & Bacon.

EDK Associates. (1997). *Alcohol advertisers' influence on teen drinking prompts a need for change in alcohol advertising.* New York: EDK Associates.

Egan, S. K., & Perry, D. G. (1998). Does low self-regard invite victimization? *Developmental Psychology, 34,* 299–309.

Egeland, B., & Hiester, M. (1995). The long-term consequences of infant day-care and mother-infant attachment. *Child Development, 66,* 474–485.

Egeland, B., & Sroufe, L. A. (1983). Developmental sequelae of maltreatment in infancy. In R. Rizley & D. Cicchetti (Eds.), *New directions for child development* (Vol. 11, pp. 77–72). San Francisco: Jossey-Bass.

Eisenberg, A., Murkoff, H. E., & Hathaway, S. E. (1991). *What to expect when you're expecting.* New York: Workman.

Eisenberg, N. (1992). *The caring child.* Cambridge, MA: Harvard University Press.

Eisenberg, N., & Fabes, R. A. (1991). Prosocial behavior and empathy: A multimethod, developmental perspective. In P. Clark (Ed.), *Review of personality and social psychology* (Vol. 12, pp. 24–61). Newbury Park, CA: Sage.

Eisenberg, N., & Fabes, R. A. (1992). Emotion regulation and the development of social competence. In P. Clark (Ed.), *Emotion and social behavior* (Vol. 14, pp. 119–150). Newbury Park, CA: Sage.

Eisenberg, N., & Fabes, R. A. (1998). Prosocial development. In W. Damon (Ed.), *Handbook of child psychology* (Vol. 3, pp. 701–778). New York: Wiley.

Eisenberg, N., Fabes, R. A., & Guthrie, I. K. (1997). Coping with stress: The roles of regulation and development. In S. A. Wolchik & I. N. Sandler (Eds.), *Handbook of children's coping* (pp. 41–72). New York: Plenum.

Eisenberg, N., Martin, C. L., & Fabes, R. A. (1996). Gender development and gender effects. In D. Berliner & R. Calfee (Eds.), *Handbook of educational psychology* (pp. 358–398). New York: Macmillan.

Eisenberg, N., & Miller, P. (1987). The relation of empathy to prosocial and related behaviors. *Psychological Bulletin, 101,* 91–119.

Eisenberg, N., & Strayer, J. (Eds.) (1987). *Empathy and its development.* Cambridge, England: Cambridge University Press.

Elardo, R. & Bradley, R. H. (1981). The Home Observation for Measurement of the Environment (HOME) Scale: A review of research. *Developmental Review, 1,* 113–145.

Elardo, R., Bradley, R. H., & Caldwell, B. M. (1975). The relation of infants' home environments to mental test performance from six to thirty-six months: A longitudinal analysis. *Child Development, 46,* 71–76.

Elder, G. H., Conger, R. D., Foster, E. M., & Ardelt, M. (1992). Families under economic pressure. *Journal of Family Issues, 13,* 5–37.

Elicker, J., Englund, M., & Sroufe, L. A. (1992). Predicting peer competence and peer relationships in childhood from early parent-child relationships. In R. D. Parke & G. W. Ladd (Eds.), *Family-peer relationships: Modes of linkage* (pp. 77–106). Hillsdale, NJ: Erlbaum.

Elkind, D. (1967). Egocentrism in adolescence. *Child Development, 38,* 1025–1033.

Elkind, D. (1987). *Miseducation: Preschoolers at risk.* New York: Knopf.

Elkind, D. (1988, January). Educating the very young: A call for clear thinking. *NEA Today,* 22–27.

Elkind, D., & Bowen, R. (1979). Imaginary audience behavior in children and adolescents. *Developmental Psychology, 15*, 38–44.

Elliott, D. S. (1994). Serious violent offenders: Onset, developmental course, and termination. *Criminology, 32*, 1–21.

Elo, I. T., King, R. B., & Furstenberg, F. F. (1999). Adolescent females: Their sexual partners and the fathers of their children. *Journal of Marriage and the Family, 61*, 74–84.

Emery, R. E. (1988). *Marriage, divorce, and children's adjustment.* Beverly Hills, CA: Sage.

Emery, R. E., & Laumann-Billings, L. (1998). An overview of the nature, causes, and consequences of abusive family relationships. *American Psychologist, 53*, 121–135.

Emes, C. E. (1997). Is Mr. Pac Man eating our children? *Canadian Journal of Psychiatry, 42*, 409–414.

Emslie, G. J., Weinberg, W. A., Kennard, B. D., & Kowatch, R. A. (1994). Neurobiological aspects of depression in children and adolescents. In W. M. Reynolds, & H. F. Johnston (Eds.), *Handbook of depression in children and adolescents* (pp. 143–165). New York: Plenum.

Ensminger, A. H., Ensminger, M. E., Konlande, J. E., & Robson, J. R. K. (1986). *Food for health: A nutritional encyclopedia.* Clovis, CA: Peguis Press.

Entwisle, D. R. (1990). Schooling and the adolescent. In S. S. Feldman & G. R. Elliott (Eds.), *At the threshold: The developing adolescent* (pp. 197–224). Cambridge, MA: Harvard University Press.

Epstein, J. L. (1986). Friend selection: Developmental and environmental influences. In E. Mueller & C. Cooper (Eds.), *Process and outcome in peer relationships* (pp. 171–192). New York: Academic Press.

Epstein, L. G., Sharer, L. R., Oleske, J. M., Connor, E. M., Goudsmit, J., Bagdon, L, Robert-Guroff, M., & Koenigsberger, M. R. (1986). Neurologic manifestations of human immunodeficiency virus infection in children. *Pediatrics, 78*, 678–687.

Erel, O., Margolin, G., & John, R. S. (1998). Observed sibling interaction: Links with marital and the mother-child relationship. *Developmental Psychology, 34*, 288–298.

Ericsson, R. J., & Beernink, F. (1987). Sex chromosome ratios in human sperm. *Fertility and Sterility, 47*, 531–532.

Erikson, E. H. (1959). *Identity and the life cycle in psychological issues* (Vol. 1). New York: International Universities Press.

Erikson, E. H. (1963). *Childhood and society.* New York: Norton.

Erikson, E. H. (1968). *Identity: Youth and crisis.* New York: Norton.

Erikson, E. H. (1969). *Gandhi's truth on the origins of militant nonviolence.* New York: Norton.

Erikson, E. H. (1980). *Identity and the life cycle.* New York: Norton.

Eron, L. D. (1982). Parent-child interaction, television violence, and aggression of children. *American Psychologist, 37*, 197–211.

Eron, L. D., Huesmann, L. R., Lefkowitz, M. M., & Walder, L. O. (1996). Does television violence cause aggression? In D. F. Greenberg (Ed.), *Criminal careers* (Vol. 2, pp. 311–321). Aldershot, England: Dartmouth Publishing.

Escarce, M. E. W. (1989). A cross-cultural study of Nepalese neonatal behavior. In J. K. Nugent, B. M. Lester, & T. B. Brazelton (Eds.), *The cultural context of infancy* (Vol. 1, pp. 65–86). Norwood, NJ: Ablex Publishing.

Espinoza, R. L., & Ehrlich, A. (1989). Personality, family relationships, and moral development in Chicano and Black adolescent gang members. *Adolescent Psychiatry, 16*, 216–227.

Eveleth, P. B., & Tanner, J. M. (1990). *Worldwide variation in human growth.* Cambridge, England: Cambridge University Press.

Ezzaki, A. (1990). Research on Iftah Ya Simsim, the Arabic coproduction. In Children's Television Workshop (Ed.)., *Sesame Street Research* (pp. 60–62). New York: Children's Television Workshop.

Fabes, R. A., Carlo, G., Kupanoff, K., & Laible, D. (1999). Transition to adolescence and prosocial/moral development I: Individual processes. *Journal of Early Adolescence, 14*, 1–14.

Fabes, R. A., & Eisenberg, N. (1992). Young children's coping with interpersonal anger. *Child Development, 63*, 116–128.

Fabes, R. A., & Eisenberg, N. (1998). Age differences in prosocial behavior: A meta-analysis. In W. Damon (Ed.), *Handbook of child psychology* (pp. 701–778). New York: Wiley.

Fabes, R. A., Eisenberg, N., Smith, M. C., & Murphy, B. C. (1996). Getting angry at peers: Associations with liking of the provocateur. *Child Development, 67*, 942–956.

Fabes, R. A., & Filsinger, E. E. (1988). Odor communication and parent-child interaction. In E. E. Filsinger (Ed.), *Biosocial perspectives on the family* (pp. 93–118). Newbury Park, CA: Sage.

Fabes, R. A., Fultz, J., Eisenberg, N., Plumlee, T. M., & Christopher, F. S. (1989). The effects of rewards on children's prosocial motivation: A socialization study. *Developmental Psychology, 25*, 509–515.

Fabes, R. A., Martin, C. L., & Smith, M. (1994). Further perspectives on child development research: A reconsideration and a recall; Invited response to McKinney and Lerner's paper. *Family Sciences Research Journal, 23*, 43–56.

Fabes, R. A., Wilson, P., & Christopher, F. S. (1989). A time to reexamine the role of television in family life. *Family Relations, 38*, 337–341.

Falbo, T. (1992). Social norms and the one-child family: Clinical and policy implications. In F. Boer & J. Dunn (Eds.), *Children's sibling relationships: Developmental and clinical issues* (pp. 71–82). Hillsdale, NJ: Erlbaum.

Falbo, T., & Poston, D. L. (1993). The academic, personality, and physical outcomes of only children in China. *Child Development, 64*, 18–35.

Falk, P. J. (1989). Lesbian mothers: Psychosocial assumptions in family law. *American Psychologist, 44*, 941–947.

Fanaroff, A. A., Martin, R. J., & Miller, M. J. (1994). Identification and management of high-risk problems in the neonate. In R. K. Creasy & R. Resnik (Eds.), *Maternal-fetal medicine: Principles and practice* (pp. 390–443). Philadelphia: W. B. Saunders.

Fang, J., Madhavan, S., & Alderman, M. H. (1999). Low birth weight: Race and maternal nativity—impact of community income. *Pediatrics, 103*, 1–6.

Farber, N. (1994). Perceptions of pregnancy risk: A comparison by class and race. *American Journal of Orthopsychiatry, 64*, 479–484.

Farmer, M. (1997). Exploring the links between communication skills and social competence. *Educational and Child Psychology, 14*, 38–44.

Farrar, M. J. (1990). Discourse and the acquisition of grammatical morphemes. *Journal of Child Language, 17*, 607–624.

Farrar, M. J., & Goodman, G. S. (1992). Developmental changes in event memory. *Child Development, 63*, 173–187.

Farrington, D. P. (1998). Youth crime and antisocial behavior. In A. Campbell & S. Muncer (Eds.), *The social child* (pp. 353–392). Hove, England: Psychology Press.

Farver, J. A. M., & Frosch, D. L. (1996). L. A. stories: Aggression in preschoolers' spontaneous narratives after the riots of 1992. *Child Development, 67*, 19–32.

Federal Bureau of Investigation. (1996). *Uniform crime reports, 1996.* Washington, DC: Federal Bureau of Investigation.

Federal Bureau of Investigation. (1997). *Uniform crime reports, 1997.* Washington, DC: Federal Bureau of Investigation.

Federal Bureau of Investigation. (1998). *A parent's guide to Internet safety.* Washington, DC: Federal Bureau of Investigation.

Federal Interagency Forum on Child and Family Statistics. (1997). *America's children: Key national indicators of well-being.* Washington, DC: Federal Interagency Forum on Child and Family Statistics.

Feingold, A. (1992). Good-looking people are not what we think. *Psychological Bulletin, 111,* 304–341.

Feiring, C. (1996). Concept of romance in 15-year-old adolescents. *Journal of Research on Adolescence, 6,* 181–200.

Feldman, D. H. (1994). Cultural organisms. In D. H. Feldman (Ed.), *Beyond universals in cognitive development* (pp. 122–145). New York: Wiley.

Feldman, S. S., & Rosenthal, D. A. (1994). Culture makes a difference . . . or does it? A comparison of adolescents in Hong Kong, Australia, and the United States. In R. K. Silbereisen & T. Eberhard (Eds.), *Adolescence in context* (pp. 99–124). New York: Springer-Verlag.

Fenson, L., Dale, P. S., Reznick, J. S., Bates, E., Thal, D. J., & Pethick, S. J. (1994). Variability in early communicative development. *Monographs of the Society for Research in Child Development* (Vol. 59, Serial number 242). Chicago: Chicago University Press.

Fenton, N. (1928). The only child. *Journal of Genetic Psychology, 35,* 546–556.

Ferber, R. (1986). *Solve your child's sleep problems.* New York: Simon and Schuster.

Ferguson, R. E. (1998). Teachers' perceptions and expectations and the Black-White test score gap. In C. Jenks & M. Phillips (Eds.), *The Black-White test score gap* (pp. 273–317). Washington, DC: Brookings Institution.

Fergusson, D. M., Beautrais, A. L., & Silva, P. A. (1982). Breast-feeding and cognitive development in the first seven years of life. *Social Science Medicine, 16,* 1705–1708.

Fergusson, D. M., Horwood, L. J., & Lynskey, M. T. (1993). Maternal smoking before and after pregnancy: Effects on behavioral outcomes in middle childhood. *Pediatrics, 92,* 815–822.

Fernald, A. (1985). Four-month-old infants prefer to listen to motherese. *Infant Behavior and Development, 8,* 181–195.

Fernald, A. (1989). Intonation and communicative intent in mothers' speech to infants: Is the melody the message? *Child Development, 60,* 1497–1510.

Feynman, R. P. (1985). *"Surely you're joking, Mr. Feynman!"* Toronto: Bantam Books.

Field, D. (1981). Can preschool children really learn to conserve? *Child Development, 52,* 326–334.

Field, T. M. (1991). Quality of infant day-care and grade school behavior and performance. *Child Development, 62,* 863–870.

Fincham, F. D. (1998). Child development and marital relationships. *Child Development, 69,* 543–574.

Fincham, F. D., & Cain, K. M. (1986). Learned helplessness in humans: A developmental analysis. *Developmental Review, 6,* 301–333.

Finders, M. J. (1997). *Just girls.* New York: Teachers College Press.

Fine, G. A., Mortimer, J. T., & Roberts, D. F. (1990). Leisure, work, and the mass media. In S. S. Feldman & G. R. Elliot (Eds.), *At the threshold: The developing adolescent* (pp. 225–252). Cambridge, MA: Harvard University Press.

Finkelman, B. (1995). *Physical and emotional abuse and neglect.* New York: Garland.

Finn, J. D. (1989). Withdrawing from school. *Harvard Educational Research, 59,* 117–142.

Fiscella, K., Kitzman, H. J., Cole, R. E., Sidora, K. J., & Olds, D. (1998). Does child abuse predict adolescent pregnancy? *Pediatrics, 101,* 620–624.

Fischer, J. L., Munsch, J., & Greene, S. M. (1996). Adolescence in intimacy. In G. R. Adams & R. Montemayor (Eds.), *Psychosocial development during adolescence* (Vol. 8, pp. 95–129). Thousand Oaks, CA: Sage.

Fischer, K. W., & Bidell, T. K. (1998). Dynamic relationship of psychological structures in action and thought. In W. Damon (Ed.), *Handbook of child psychology* (Vol. 1, pp. 467–562). New York: Wiley.

Fischer, K. W., & Rose, S. P. (1994). Dynamic development of coordination components in brain and behavior: A framework for theory and research. In G. Dawson & K. W. Fischer (Eds.), *Human behavior and the developing brain* (pp. 3–66). New York: Guilford.

Fisher, C. B., & Brone, R. J. (1991). Eating disorders in adolescence. In R. M. Lerner, A. C. Petersen, & J. Brooks-Gunn (Eds.), *Encyclopedia of adolescence* (Vol. 1, pp. 272–277). New York: Garland.

Fisher, M., Trieller, K., & Napolitano, B. (1989). Premenstrual symptoms in adolescents. *Journal of Adolescent Health Care, 10,* 369–375.

Fitzgerald, H. E., Davies, W. H., Zucker, R. A., & Klinger, M. (1994). Developmental systems theory and substance abuse. In L. L'Abate (Ed.), *Handbook of developmental family psychology and psychopathology* (pp. 350–372). New York: Wiley.

Fix, M., & Passell, J. S. (1994). *Immigration and immigrants: Setting the record straight.* Washington, DC: Urban Institute.

Flake, A. W., Roncarolo, M., Puck, J. M., Almeida-Porada, G., Evans, M. I., Johnson, M. P., Abella, E. M., Harrison, D. D., & Zanjani, E. D. (1996). Treatment of X-linked severe combined immunodeficiency by in utero transplantation of paternal bone marrow. *New England Journal of Medicine, 335,* 1806–1810.

Flakierska-Praquin, N., Lindstroem, M., & Gillberg, C. (1997). School phobia with separation anxiety: A comparative 20- to 29-year follow-up study of 35 school refusers. *Comprehensive Psychiatry, 38,* 17–22.

Flaks, D. K., Ficher, I., Masterpasqua, F. & Joseph, G. (1995). Lesbians choosing motherhood: A comparative study of lesbian and heterosexual parents and their children. *Developmental Psychology, 31,* 105–114.

Flanagan, C. A. (1990). Families and schools in hard times. In V. C. McCloyd & C. A. Flanagan (Eds.), *Economic stress: Effects on family life and child development* (pp. 7–26). San Francisco: Jossey-Bass.

Flanagan, P. (1998). Teen mothers: Countering the myths of dysfunction and developmental disruption. In C. G. Coll & J. L Surrey (Eds.), *Mothering against odds* (pp. 238–254). New York: Guilford Press.

Flannery, D. J., Huff, C. R., & Manos, M. (1998). Youth gangs: A developmental perspective. In T. P. Gullotta & G. R. Adams (Eds.), *Delinquent violent youth* (pp. 175–204). Thousand Oaks, CA: Sage.

Flannery, D. J., Montemayor, R., & Eberly, M. B. (1994). The influence of parents' negative emotional expression on adolescents' perceptions of their relationships with their parents. *Personal Relationships, 1,* 259–274.

Flavell, J. H. (1982). On cognitive development. *Child Development, 53,* 1–10.

Flavell, J. H. (1985). *Cognitive development.* Englewood Cliffs, NJ: Prentice-Hall.

Flavell, J. H. (1986). The development of children's knowledge about the appearance-reality distinction. *American Psychologist, 41,* 418–425.

Flavell, J. H. (1988). From cognitive connections to mental representations. In J. Astington, P. Harris, & D. Olson (Eds.), *Developing theories of mind* (pp. 244–267). New York: Cambridge University Press.

Flavell, J. H., Beach, D. R., & Chinsky, J. M. (1966). Spontaneous verbal rehearsal in a memory task as a function of age. *Child Development, 53,* 1–10.

Flavell, J. H., Friedrichs, A. G., & Hoyt, J. D. (1970). Developmental changes in memorization processes. *Cognitive Psychology, 1,* 324–340.

Flavell, J. H., Green, F. L., & Flavell, E. R. (1987). Development of knowledge about the appearance-reality distinction. *Monographs of the Society for Research in Child Development* (51, Serial No. 212). Chicago: University of Chicago Press.

Flavell, J. H., & Miller, P. H. (1998). Social cognition. In W. Damon (Ed.), *Handbook of child psychology* (pp. 851–898). New York: Wiley.

Fleming, J., Challela, M., Eland, J., Hornick, R., Johnson, P., Martinson, I., Nativio, D., Nokes, K., Riddle, I., Steele, N., Sudela, K., Thomas, R., Turner, Q., Wheeler, B., & Young, A. (1994). Impact on the family of children who are technology dependent and cared for in the home. *Pediatric Nursing, 20,* 379–388.

Fletcher, A., & Steinberg, L. (1994, February). *Generational status and country of origin as influences on the psychology of Asian-American adolescents.* Paper presented at the biennial meeting of the Society for Research in Adolescence, San Diego, CA.

Fletcher, J. L., & Gordon, R. C. (1990). Perinatal transmission of bacterial sexually transmitted diseases: Part I. Syphilis and gonorrhea. *Journal of Family Practice, 30,* 448–456.

Floyd, R. L., Zahniser, S. C., Gunter, E. P., & Kendrick, J. S. (1991). Smoking during pregnancy: Prevalence, effects, and intervention strategies. *Birth, 18,* 48–53.

Focus on the Family. (1992). Oppressed minority or counterfeits? *Focus on the Family Citizen, 6,* 1–5.

Fogel, A. (1997). *Infancy.* Minneapolis: West.

Fogel, A., & Thelen, E. (1987). Development of early expressive and communicative action: Reinterpreting the evidence from a dynamic systems perspective. *Developmental Psychology, 23,* 747–761.

Foltz, C., Overton, W. F., & Ricco, R. B. (1995). Proof construction: Adolescent development from inductive to deductive problem-solving strategies. *Journal of Experimental Child Psychology, 59,* 179–195.

Fombonne, E. (1995). Eating disorders: Time trends and possible explanatory mechanisms. In M. Rutter & D. J. Smith (Eds.), *Psychosocial disorders in young people: Time trends and their causes* (pp. 616–685). New York: Wiley.

Foorman, B. R., Francis, D. J., Fletcher, J. M., Schatschneider, C., & Mehta, P. (1998). The role of instruction in learning to read: Preventing reading failure in at-risk children. *Journal of Educational Psychology, 90,* 37–55.

Forbes, G. B. (1986). Body composition in adolescence. In F. Faulkner & J. M. Tanner (Eds.), *Human growth: A comprehensive treatise* (Vol. 2, pp. 119–145). New York: Plenum.

Fowler, A. E., Gelman, R., & Gleitman, L. R. (1994). The course of language learning in children with disabilities. In H. Tager-Flusberg (Ed.), *Constraints on language acquisition: Studies of atypical children* (pp. 91–140). Hillsdale, NJ: Erlbaum.

Fowler, F. J. (1993). *Survey research methods.* Thousand Oaks, CA: Sage.

Fowler, W. (1986). Early experiences of great men and women mathematicians. *New Directions in Child Development, 32,* 87–109.

Fox, L., Long, S. H., & Langlois, A. (1988). Patterns of language comprehension deficit in abused and neglected children. *Journal of Speech and Hearing Disorders, 53,* 239–244.

Fox, N. A., Kimmerly, N. L., & Schafer, W. D. (1991). Attachment to mother/attachment to father: A meta-analysis. *Child Development, 62,* 210–225.

Fox, R. A., & Solis-Camera, P. (1997). Parenting of young children by fathers in Mexico and the United States. *Journal of Social Psychology, 137,* 489–495.

Frable, D. S. (1997). Gender, racial, sexual, and class identities. *Annual Review of Psychology, 48,* 139–162.

Fracasso, M. P., Lamb, M. E., Scholmerich, A., & Leyendecker, B. (1997). The ecology of mother-infant interaction in Euro-American and immigrant Central American families living in the United States. *International Journal of Behavioral Development, 20,* 207–217.

Frankenberg, W. K., Dodds, J., Archer, P., Shapiro, H., & Bresnick, B. (1992). The Denver II: A major revision and restandardization of the Denver Developmental Screening Test. *Pediatrics, 89,* 91–97.

Fredrickson, B. L., Roberts, T. A., Noll, S. M., Quinn, M., & Twenge, J. M. (1998). That swimsuit becomes you: Sex differences in self-objectification, restrained eating, and math performance. *Journal of Personality and Social Psychology, 75,* 269–284.

Freeman, M., Csikszentmihalyi, M., & Larson, R. (1986). Adolescence and its recollection. *Merrill Palmer Quarterly, 32,* 167–185.

French, D. C. (1988). Heterogeneity of peer rejected boys: Aggressive and non-aggressive subtypes. *Child Development, 59,* 976–985.

Freppon, P. A., & Dahl, K. L. (1998). Balanced instruction: Insights and considerations. *Reading Research Quarterly, 33,* 240–251.

Freud, S. (1960). *The ego and the id* (J. Riviere, Trans.). New York: W. W. Norton. (Original work published 1923)

Freud, S. (1965). *A general introduction to psychoanalysis* (J. Riviere, Trans.). New York: Washington Square Books. (Original work published 1920)

Freund, L. S., Baker, L., & Sonnenschein, S. (1990). Developmental changes in strategic approaches to classification. *Journal of Experimental Child Psychology, 49,* 343–362.

Frick, P. J. (1998). *Conduct disorders and severe antisocial behavior.* New York: Plenum.

Friedman, S. B., Fisher, M., & Schonberg, S. K. (Eds.). (1992). *Comprehensive adolescent care.* St. Louis, MO: Quality Medical Publishing.

Friedrich, L. K., & Stein, A. H. (1975). Prosocial television and young children: The effects of verbal labeling and role playing on learning and behavior. *Child Development, 46,* 27–38.

Friedrich-Cofer, L. K., Huston, A., Kipnis, D. M., Susman, E. J., & Clewett, A. S. (1979). Environmental enhancement of prosocial television content: Effects on interpersonal behavior, imaginative play, and self-regulation in a natural setting. *Developmental Psychology, 15,* 637–646.

Frisch, R. E. (1991). Puberty and body fat. In R. M. Lerner, A. C. Petersen, & J. Brooks-Gunn (Eds.), *Encyclopedia of adolescence* (Vol. 2). New York: Garland.

Frisch, R. E., Wyshak, G., Albright, N. L., Albright, T. E., Schiff, I., Jones, K. P., Witschi, J., Shiang, E., Koff, E., & Marguglio, M. (1985). Lower prevalence of breast cancer and cancers of the reproductive system among former college athletes compared to non-athletes. *British Journal of Cancer, 52,* 885–891.

Frith, U. (1989). *Autism.* Oxford, England: Oxford University Press.

Frolund, L. (1997). Early shame and mirroring. *Scandinavian Psychoanalytic Review, 20,* 35–57.

Frome, P. M., & Eccles, J. S. (1998). Parents' influence on children's achievement-related perceptions. *Journal of Personality and Social Psychology, 74,* 435–452.

Frost, J. L., Shin, D., & Jacobs, P. J. (1998). Physical environments and children's play. In O. N. Saracho & B. Spodek (Eds.), *Multiple perspectives on play in early childhood education* (pp. 255–294). Albany: State University of New York Press.

Fuligni, A. J. (1997). The academic achievement of adolescents from immigrant families: The roles of family background, attitudes, and behavior. *Child Development, 68,* 351–363.

Fuligni, A. J. (1998). Authority, autonomy, and parent-adolescent conflict and cohesion: A study of adolescents from Mexican, Chinese, Filipino, and European backgrounds. *Developmental Psychology, 34,* 782–792.

Fuligni, A. J., & Eccles, J. S. (1993). Perceived parent-child relationships and early adolescents' orientation toward peers. *Developmental Psychology, 29,* 622–632.

Funnell, D. J., Frankel, S. J., Nanchahal, K., Peters, T. J., & Davey-Smith, G. (1998). Childhood obesity and adult cardiovascular mortality: A 57-year follow-up study based on the Boyd Orr cohort. *American Journal of Clinical Nutrition, 67,* 1111–1118.

Furman, W. (1996). The measurement of friendship perceptions: Conceptual and methodological issues. In W. M. Bukowski, A. F. Newcomb, & W. W. Hartup (Eds.), *The company they keep: Friendships in childhood and adolescence* (pp. 41–65). Cambridge, England: Cambridge University Press.

Furman, W., & Wehner, E. A. (1997). Adolescent romantic relationships: A developmental perspective. In S. Shulman & W. A. Collins (Eds.), *Romantic relationships in adolescence* (pp. 21–36). San Francisco: Jossey-Bass.

Furnham, A., & Alibhai, M. (1983). Cross-cultural differences in the perception of female body shape. *Psychological Medicine, 13,* 829–837.

Furstenberg, F. F., & Cherlin, A. J. (1991). *Divided families.* Cambridge, MA: Harvard University Press.

Futterman, D., & Hein, K. (1992). AIDS and HIV infection. In S. B. Friedman, M. Fisher, & S. K. Schonberg (Eds.), *Comprehensive adolescent health care* (pp. 521–531). St. Louis, MO: Quality Medical Publishing.

Future of Children. (1995a). *Critical issues for children and youths.* Los Altos, CA: Packard Foundation.

Future of Children. (1995b). *Long-term outcomes of early childhood programs.* Los Altos, CA: Future of Children.

Gaddis, A., & Brooks-Gunn, J. (1985). The male experience of pubertal change. *Journal of Youth and Adolescence, 14,* 61–70.

Gagnon, J. H. (1990). The explicit and implicit use of the scripting perspective in sex research. *Annual Review of Sex Research, 1,* 1–43.

Galambos, N. L., Almeida, D. M., & Petersen, A. C. (1991). Masculinity, femininity, and sex role attitudes in early adolescence. *Annual Progress in Child Psychiatry and Child Development, 5,* 77–91.

Gallahue, D. L., & Ozmun, J. C. (1995). *Understanding motor development.* Madison, WI: Brown & Benchmark.

Gallant, S. J., & Derry, P. S. (1995). Menarche, menstruation, and menopause: Psychosocial research and future directions. In A. L. Stanton & S. J. Gallant (Eds.), *The psychology of women's health* (pp. 199–259). Washington, DC: American Psychological Association.

Gallup Organization. (1997). *Public attitudes toward the public schools.* New York: Gallup Organization.

Gamble, T. J., & Zigler, E. (1989). The Head Start Synthesis Project. *Journal of Applied Developmental Psychology, 10,* 267–274.

Garbarino, J., Dubrow, N., Kostelny, K., & Pardo, C. (1992). *Children in danger.* San Francisco: Jossey-Bass.

Garbarino, J., & Stott, F. M. (1992). *What children can tell us.* San Francisco: Jossey-Bass.

Garber, J., Weiss, B., & Shanley, N. (1993). Cognitions, depressive symptoms, and development in adolescence. *Journal of Abnormal Psychology, 102,* 47–57.

Garcia Coll, C. T. (1990). Developmental outcome of minority infants: A process-oriented look into our beginnings. *Child Development, 61,* 270–289.

Garcia Coll, C. T., Lamberty, G., Jenkins, R., McAdoo, H. P., Crnic, K., Wasik, B. H., & Garcia, H. V. (1996). An integrative model for the study of developmental competencies in minority children. *Child Development, 67,* 1891–1914.

Gardner, H. (1980). *Artful scribbles.* New York: Basic Books.

Gardner, H. (1983). *Frames of mind.* London: Heinemann.

Garmezy, N., & Masten, A. (1990). The adaptation of children to a stressful world: Mastery of fear. In L. Eugene Arnold (Ed.), *Childhood stress* (pp. 459–474). New York: Wiley.

Garmezy, N., & Rutter, M. (1985). Acute reactions to stress. In M. Rutter & L. Hersov (Eds.), *Child psychiatry: Modern approaches* (pp. 152–176). Oxford: Blackwell Scientific.

Garner, P. W., Jones, D. C., & Palmer, D. (1994). Social cognitive correlates of preschool children's sibling caregiving behavior. *Developmental Psychology, 30,* 905–911.

Garrison, W. T., & McQuiston, S. (1989). *Chronic illness during childhood and adolescence.* Newbury Park, CA: Sage.

Garrod, A., Smulyan, L., Powers, S. I., & Kilkenny, R. (1995). *Adolescent portraits.* Boston: Allyn & Bacon.

Gauvain, M. (1998). Culture, development, and theory of mind: Comment on Lillard (1998). *Psychological Bulletin, 123,* 37–42.

Ge, X., Conger, R. D., & Elder, G. H. (1996). Coming of age too early: Pubertal influences on girls' vulnerability to psychological distress. *Child Development, 67,* 3386–3400.

Ge, X., Lorenz, F. O., Conger, R. D., Elder, G. H., & Simon, R. L. (1994). Trajectories of stressful life events and depressive symptoms during adolescence. *Developmental Psychology, 30,* 467–483.

Geary, D. C. (1989). A model for representing gender differences in the pattern of cognitive abilities. *American Psychologist, 102,* 1155–1156.

Gecas, V., & Seff, M. A. (1990). Social class and self-esteem. *Social Psychological Quarterly, 53,* 165–173.

Gelles, R. J. (1987). The family and its role in the abuse of children. *Psychiatric Annals, 17,* 229–232.

Gelman, R., & Baillargeon, R. (1983). A review of some Piagetian concepts. In P. Mussen (Ed.), *Handbook of child psychology* (Vol. 3, pp. 167–230). New York: Wiley.

Gelman, S. A., & Taylor, M. (1984). How two-year-old children interpret proper and common names for unfamiliar objects. *Child Development, 55,* 1535–1540.

Geraldson, B., & Hopkins, W. D. (1997). Children's lateralization on a finger-localization task. *Perceptual and Motor Skills, 84,* 1259–1264.

Gershenson, H. P., Musick, J. S., Ruch-Ross, H. S., Magee, V., Rubino, K. K., & Rosenberg, D. (1989). The prevalence of coercive sexual experience among teenage mothers. *Journal of Interpersonal Violence, 4,* 204–219.

Gershman, H. (1997). Sexual permissiveness and its consequences. In L. B. Schlesinger & E. Revitch (Eds.), *Sexual dynamics of anti-social behavior* (pp. 76–87). Springfield, IL: Charles C. Thomas.

Gerwitz, J. L., & Boyd, E. F. (1977). Does maternal responding imply reduced infant crying? A critique of the 1972 Bell and Ainsworth report, *Child Development, 48,* 1200–1207.

Geschwind, N., & Galaburda, A. M. (1987). *Cerebral lateralization: Biological mechanisms, associations, and pathology.* Cambridge, MA: MIT Press.

Gest, T., & Pope, V. (1996, March 25). Crime time bomb. *U.S. News and World Report,* (pp. 28–36).

Gibbs, R. S., & Sweet, R. L. (1994). Clinical disorders. In R. K. Creasy & R. Resnik (Eds.), *Maternal-fetal medicine: Principles and practice* (pp. 355–411). Philadelphia: W. B. Saunders.

Gil, A. G., & Vega, W. A. (1996). Two different worlds: Acculturation stress and adaptation among Cuban and Nicaraguan families. *Journal of Social and Personal Relationships, 13,* 435–456.

Gil, A. G., Vega, W. A., & Dimas, J. M. (1994). Acculturative stress and personal adjustment among Hispanic adolescent boys. *Journal of Community Psychology, 22,* 43–54.

Gilligan, C. (1982). *In a different voice: Psychological theory and women's development.* Cambridge, MA: Harvard University Press.

Gilligan, C., & Wiggins, G. (1987). The origins of morality in early childhood relationships. In J. Kagan & S. Lamb (Eds.), *The emergence of morality in young children* (pp. 277–305). Chicago: Chicago University Press.

Gilmore, M. R., Lewis, S. M., Lohr, M. J., Spencer, M. S., & White, R. D. (1997). Repeat pregnancies among adolescent mothers. *Journal of Marriage and the Family, 59,* 536–550.

Ginsburg, H. J., & Miller, S. M. (1982). Sex differences in children's risk-taking behavior. *Child Development, 53,* 426–428.

Giordano, P. C., Cernkovich, S. A., Groat, H. T., Pugh, M. D., & Swinford, S. P. (1998). The quality of adolescent friendships: Long-term effects. *Journal of Health and Social Behavior, 39,* 55–71.

Gladstein, J., Slater-Rusonis, E., & Heald, F. (1992). A comparison of inner-city and upper-middle class youths' exposure to violence. *Journal of Adolescent Health, 13,* 275–280.

Glass, R. H. (1994). Gamete transport, fertilization, and implantation. In R. K. Creasy & R. Resnik (Eds.), *Maternal-fetal medicine* (pp. 89–95). Philadelphia: W. B. Saunders.

Glastris, P. (1997, May 26). The alien payoff. *U.S. News & World Report,* pp. 20–22.

Gleason, J. B. (1993). *The development of language.* New York: Macmillan.

Gleason, J. B., Ely, R., Perlmann, R. Y., & Narasimhan, B. (1996). Patterns of prohibition in parent-child discourse. In D. I. Slobin & J. Gerhardt (Eds.), *Social interaction, social context, and language* (pp. 205–217). Mahwah, NJ: Erlbaum.

Gleitman, L. R., Newport, E. L., & Gleitman, H. (1984). The current status of the motherese hypothesis. *Journal of Child Language, 11,* 43–79.

Glover, V. (1997). Maternal stress or anxiety in pregnancy and emotional development of the child. *British Journal of Psychiatry, 171,* 105–106.

Golan, M., Weizman, A., Apter, A., & Fainaru, M. (1998). Parents as exclusive agents of change in the treatment of childhood obesity. *American Journal of Clinical Nutrition, 67,* 1130–1135.

Gold, D., Crombie, G., & Noble, S. (1987). Relations between teachers' judgments of girls' and boys' compliance and intellectual competence. *Sex Roles, 16,* 351–358.

Goldberg, S. (1983). Parent-to-infant bonding: Another look. *Child Development, 54,* 1355–1382.

Goldberg, S., & DiVitto, B. (1995). Parenting children born preterm. In M. Bornstein (Ed.), *Handbook of parenting* (Vol. 1, pp. 209–231). Mahwah, NJ: Erlbaum.

Goldenberg, C. (1992). The limits of expectations. *American Educational Research Journal, 29,* 517–544.

Goldfield, B. (1987). The contributions of child and caregiver to referential and expressive language. *Applied Psycholinguistics, 8,* 267–280.

Goldfield, B., & Reznick, J. S. (1990). Early lexical acquisition: Rate, content, and the vocabulary spurt. *Journal of Child Language, 17,* 171–183.

Goldstein, A. P., Glick, B., Carthan, W., & Blancero, D. A. (1994). *The prosocial gang.* Thousand Oaks, CA: Sage.

Golombok, S., & Tasker, F. (1996). Do parents influence the sexual orientation of their children? Findings from a longitudinal study of lesbian families. *Developmental Psychology, 32,* 3–11.

Goncalves, M. (1990). *A representaca da escola feita pela crianca de baixa renda em sua primeira exper^ncia discente.* Paper presented at the 13th annual congress of ANPED, Belo Horizonte, Brazil.

Goncu, A. (1993). Development of intersubjectivity in social pretend play. *Human Development, 36,* 185–198.

Gonzales, N. A., & Kim, L. A. (1997). Stress and coping in an ethnic minority context. In S. A. Wolchik & I. N. Sandler (Eds.), *Handbook of children's coping* (pp. 481–514). New York: Plenum.

Gonzalez-Mena, J., & Eyer, D. W. (1993). *Infants, toddlers, and caregivers.* Mountain View, CA: Mayfield Publishing.

Goodman, G. S., Emery, R. E., & Haugaard, J. J. (1998). Developmental psychology and law: Divorce, child maltreatment, foster care, and adoption. In W. Damon (Ed.), *Handbook of child psychology* (Vol. 4, pp. 775–874). New York: Wiley.

Goodman, R. A., & Whitaker, H. A. (1985). Hemispherectomy: A review (1928–1981) with special reference to the linguistic abilities and disabilities of the residual right hemisphere. In C. T. Best (Ed.), *Hemispheric function and collaboration in the child* (pp. 121–156). Orlando, FL: Harcourt Brace Jovanovich.

Goodyear, I., Kolvin, I., & Gatzanis, S. (1985). Recent undesirable life events and psychiatric disorders in childhood and adolescence. *British Journal of Psychiatry, 147,* 517–533.

Goosens, L., Seiffge-Krenke, I., & Marcoen, A. (1992). The many faces of adolescent egocentrism. Two European replications. *Journal of Adolescent Research, 7,* 43–48.

Gopnik, A. (1988). Three types of early words. *First Language, 8,* 49–70.

Gopnik, A., & Meltzoff, A. (1986). Relations between semantic and cognitive developments in the one-word stage: The specificity hypothesis. *Child Development, 57,* 1040–1053.

Gordon, B., Saklofske, D. H., & Hildebrand, D. K. (1998). Assessing children with mental retardation. In V. H. Booney (Ed.), *Psychological assessment of children* (pp. 454–481). New York: Wiley.

Gorman-Smith, D., & Tolan, P. H. (1998). The role of exposure to community violence and developmental problems among inner-city youth. *Development and Psychopathology, 10,* 101–116.

Gorman-Smith, D., Tolan, P. H., Zelli, A., & Huesmann, L. R. (1996). The relation of family functioning to violence among inner-city minority youths. *Journal of Family Psychology, 10,* 115–129.

Goswami, U. (1998). *Cognition in children*. Hove, England: Psychology Press.

Gottesman, I. I. (1991). *Schizophrenia genesis: The origins of madness*. New York: Freeman.

Gottfredson, D. C., Sealock, M. D., & Koper, C. S. (1996). Delinquency. In R. J. DiClemente & W. B. Hansen (Eds.), *Handbook of adolescent health risk behavior* (pp. 259–288). New York: Plenum.

Gottfredson, M. R., & Hirschi, T. (1995). A general theory of adolescent problem behavior: Problems and prospects. In R. D. Ketterlinus & M. E. Lamb (Eds.), *Adolescent problem behaviors* (pp. 41–56). Hillsdale, NJ: Erlbaum.

Gottfried, A. W. (1985). Environment of newborns in special care units. In A. W. Gottfried & J. L. Gaiter (Eds.), *Infant stress under intensive care: Environmental neonatology* (pp. 251–257). Baltimore, MD: University Park Press.

Gottfried, A. W., Gottfried, A. E., Bathurst, K., & Guerin, D. W. (1994). *Gifted IQ: Early developmental perspectives*. New York: Plenum Press.

Gottlieb, G. (1997). *Synthesizing nature-nurture: Prenatal roots of instinctive behavior*. Mahwah, NJ: Erlbaum.

Gottman, J. M. (1983). How children become friends. *Monographs of the Society for Research in Child Development* (48, Whole no. 201). Chicago: University of Chicago Press.

Gottwald, S. R., & Thurman, S. K. (1990). Parent-infant interaction in neonatal intensive care units: Implications for research and service delivery. *Infants and Young Children, 2*, 1–10.

Goubet, N., & Clifton, R. K. (1998). Object and event representation in 6½-month-old infants. *Developmental Psychology, 34*, 63–76.

Graber, J. A., Brooks-Gunn, J., & Warren, M. P. (1995). The antecedents of menarcheal age: Heredity, family environment, and stressful life events. *Child Development, 66*, 346–359.

Graber, J. A., Lewinsohn, P. M., Seeley, J. R., & Brooks-Gunn, J. (1997). Is psychopathology associated with the timing of puberty? *Journal of the American Academy of Child and Adolescent Psychiatry, 36*, 1768–1776.

Graham, P. (1986). *Child psychiatry: A developmental approach*. Oxford, England: Oxford University Press.

Graham, S. (1994). Motivation in African Americans. *Review of Educational Research, 64*, 55–117.

Gralinski, J. H., & Kopp, C. B. (1993). Everyday rules for behavior: Mothers' requests to young children. *Developmental Psychology, 29*, 573–584.

Grant, B. (1993). Multiple pregnancy. In V. R. Bennett & L. K. Brown (Eds.), *Myles textbook for midwives* (pp. 365–376). London: Churchill Livingstone.

Gray, J. A. (1971). *The psychology of fear and stress*. New York: McGraw-Hill.

Gray, W. M., & Hudson, L. M. (1984). Formal operations and the imaginary audience. *Developmental Psychology, 20*, 619–627.

Gredler, G. R. (1997). Issues in early childhood screening and assessment. *Psychology in the Schools, 34*, 98–106.

Green, E. H. (1933). Friendships and quarrels among preschool children. *Child Development, 4*, 236–252.

Green, J. A., Gustafson, G., & McGhie, A. C. (1998). Changes in infants' cries as a function of time in a cry bout. *Child Development, 69*, 271–279.

Green, M. (1989). *Theories of human development*. New York: Prentice-Hall.

Greenberg, B. S., Brown, J. D., & Buerkel-Rothfuss, N. (1993). *Media, sex, and the adolescent*. Cresskill, NJ: Hampton Press.

Greenberg, B. S., Edison, N., Korzenny, F., Fernandez-Collado, C., & Atkin, C. K. (1980). Antisocial and prosocial behaviors on television. In B. S. Greenberg (Ed.), *Life on television: Content analysis of U.S. television drama* (pp. 99–128). Norwood, NJ: Ablex Publishing.

Greenberg, B. S., Stanley, C., Siemicki, M., Heeter, C., Soderman, A., & Linsangan, R. (1986). *Sex content on soaps and primetime television series most viewed by adolescents*. East Lansing: Michigan State University Press.

Greenberg, M. T., Speltz, M. L., & DeKlyen, M. (1993). The role of attachment in early development of disruptive behavior problems. *Development and Psychopathology, 5*, 191–213.

Greenberger, E., & Chen, C. (1996). Perceived family relationships and depressed mood in early and late adolescence: A comparison of European and Asian Americans. *Developmental Psychology, 32*, 707–716.

Greenberger, E., & Steinberg, L. (1986). *When teenagers work: The psychological and social costs of adolescent employment*. New York: Basic Books.

Greene, B. (1984). *Good morning, merry sunshine*. New York: Penguin Books.

Greene, K., Rubin, D. L., Hale, J. L., & Walters, L. H. (1996). The utility of understanding adolescent egocentrism in designing health promotion messages. *Health Communication, 8*, 131–152.

Greenough, W. T., Black, J. E., & Wallace, C. S. (1987). Experience and brain development. *Science, 58*, 539–560.

Greenspan, S. I., & Greenspan, N. T. (1985). *First feelings: Milestones in the emotional development of your baby and child*. New York: Viking.

Greenwald, R. L., Bank, L., Reid, J. B., & Knutson, J. F. (1997). A discipline-mediated model of excessively punitive parenting. *Aggressive Behavior, 23*, 259–280.

Griffin, A., & Fein, G. (1996). *Infant day care: The critical issues*. Urbana, IL: ERIC Clearinghouse.

Griffin, R. S. (1998). *Sports in the lives of children and adolescents*. Westport, CT: Praeger.

Griffith, D. R., Azuma, S. D., & Chasnoff, I. J. (1994). Three-year outcome of children exposed prenatally to drugs. *Journal of the American Academy of Child and Adolescent Psychiatry, 33*, 20–27.

Griffiths, M. D. (1991). Amusement machine playing in childhood and adolescence: A comparative analysis of video games and fruit machines. *Journal of Adolescence, 14*, 53–73.

Groome, L. J., Swiber, M. J., Atterbury, J. L., Bentz, L. S., & Holland, S. B. (1997). Similarities and differences in behavioral state organization during sleep periods in the infant before and after birth. *Child Development, 68*, 1–11.

Gross, L., Aurand, S., & Adessa, R. (1988). *Violence and discrimination against lesbian and gay people in Philadelphia and the Commonwealth of Pennsylvania*. Philadelphia: Philadelphia Lesbian and Gay Task Force.

Grotevant, H. D. (1998). Adolescent development in family contexts. In W. Damon (Ed.), *Handbook of child psychology* (Vol. 3, pp. 1097–1150). New York: Wiley.

Gruber, H. E., & Voneche, J. J. (1977). *The essential Piaget*. New York: Basic Books.

Grunseit, A., Kippax, S., Aggleton, P., Baldo, M., & Slutkin, G. (1997). Sexuality education and young people's sexual behavior: A review of studies. *Journal of Adolescent Research, 12*, 421–453.

Grusec, J. E., Dix, T., & Mills, R. (1982). The effects of type, severity, and victim of children's transgressions on maternal discipline. *Canadian Journal of Behavioural Sciences, 14*, 276–289.

Grusec, J. E., & Goodnow, J. J. (1994). Impact of parental discipline methods on the child's internalization of values: A reconceptualization of current points of view. *Developmental Psychology, 30*, 4–19.

Grusec, J. E., & Lytton, H. (1988). *Social development: History, theory, and research*. New York: Springer-Verlag.

Guerin, D. W., Gottfried, A. W., & Thomas, C. W. (1997). Difficult temperament and behavior problems: A longitudinal study from 1.5 to 12 years. *International Journal of Behavioral Development, 21,* 71–90.

Guidubaldi, J. (1988). Differences in children's divorce adjustment across grade level and gender: A report from the NASP-Kent State Nationwide Project. In S. A. Wolchik & P. Karoly (Eds.), *Children of divorce* (pp. 185–232). New York: Gardner Press.

Gunnar, M. R. (1980). Contingent stimulation: A review of its role in early development. In S. Levine & H. Ursin (Eds.), *Coping and health* (pp. 316–345). New York: Plenum.

Gunnar, M. R. (1989). Studies of the human infant's adrenocortical response to potentially stressful events. *New Directions for Child Development, 45,* 3–18.

Gunnar, M. R., & Brodersen, L. (1992). Infant stress reactions to brief maternal separations in human and nonhuman primates. In T. M. Field, P. M. McCabe, & N. Schneiderman (Eds.), *Stress and coping in infancy and childhood* (pp. 1–18). Hillsdale, NJ: Erlbaum.

Gunnar, M. R., Fisch, R., Korsvik, S., & Donhowe, J. (1981). The effects of circumcision on serum cortisol and behavior. *Psychoneuroendocrinology, 6,* 269–275.

Gunnell, D. J., Frankel, S. J., Nanchahal, K., Peters, T. J., & Davey, S. G. (1998). Childhood obesity and adult cardiovascular mortality. *American Journal of Clinical Nutrition, 67,* 1111–1118.

Guralnick, M. J., Connor, R. T., Hammond, M. A., Gottman, J. M., & Kinnish, K. (1996). The peer relations of preschool children with communication disorders. *Child Development, 67,* 471–489.

Gustafson, G., & Harris, K. L. (1990). Women's responses to young infants' cries. *Developmental Psychology, 26,* 144–152.

Hack, M., Klein, N. K., & Taylor, H. G. (1995). Long-term developmental outcomes of low birth weight infants. *The Future of Children, 5,* 176–196.

Hack, M., Taylor, H. G., Klein, N., & Eiben, R. (1994). Outcome of < 750 gm birthweight children at school age. *New England Journal of Medicine, 331,* 753–759.

Hadley, P. A., & Schuele, C. M. (1995). Verbal interactions with peers in a preschool language intervention classroom. In M. Rice & K. Wilcox (Eds.), *Building a language-focused curriculum for the preschool classroom* (pp. 105–125). Baltimore, MD: Brookes.

Hafer, S. (1995). *Facts on school-age children.* Boston: Wellesley College Press.

Haith, M. M., & Benson, J. B. (1998). Infant cognition. In W. Damon (Ed.), *Handbook of child psychology* (Vol. 2, pp. 199–254). New York: Wiley.

Haka-Ikse, K. (1997). Female adolescent sexuality: The risks and management. In G. Creatsas & G. Mastorakos (Eds.), *Adolescent gynecology and endocrinology* (Vol. 816, pp. 446–470). New York: Academy of Sciences.

Hakanen, E. A. (1995). Emotional use of music by African American adolescents. *Howard Journal of Communication, 5,* 214–222.

Hakuta, K., & McLaughlin, B. (1996). Bilingualism and second language learning. In D. C. Berliner & R. C. Calfee (Eds.), *Handbook of educational psychology* (pp. 603–621). New York: Macmillan.

Hala, S. (1997). Theoretical and conceptual issues. In S. Hala (Ed.), *The development of social cognition* (pp. 3–34). East Sussex, England: Psychology Press.

Hala, S., & Carpendale, J. (1997). All in the mind: Children's understanding of mental life. In S. Hala (Ed.), *The development of social cognition* (pp. 189–240). East Sussex, England: Psychology Press.

Hall, D. G., & Graham, S. A. (1998). Beyond mutual exclusivity: Children use lexical form class information to constrain word-referent mapping. In E. V. Clark (Ed.), *The Proceedings of the 29th Annual Child Language Research Forum* (pp. 181–190). Stanford, CA: Center for the Study of Language and Information.

Hall, J. A. (1984). *Nonverbal sex differences: Communication accuracy and expressive style.* Hillsdale, NJ: Erlbaum.

Hall, N., & Schmidt, P. (1996 August). Why saying goodbye is hard to do. *Child,* 46–51.

Halpern, D. F. (1992). *Sex differences in cognitive abilities.* Mahwah, NJ: Erlbaum.

Halpern, D. F. (1997). Sex differences in intelligence: Implications for education. *American Psychologist, 52,* 1091–1102.

Hardy, J. B., Shapiro, S., Astone, N. M., Miller, T. L., Brooks-Gunn, J., & Hilton, S. C. (1997). Adolescent childbearing revisited: The age of inner-city mothers at delivery is a determinant of their children's self-sufficiency at age 27 to 33. *Pediatrics, 100,* 802–809.

Harkness, S., & Super, C. M. (1983). *The cultural structuring of children's play in a rural African community.* Paper presented at the annual meeting of the Association for the Anthropological Study of Play, Baton Rouge, LA.

Harpin, V., Chellappah, G., & Rutter, N. (1983). Responses of the newborn infant to overheating. *Biology and the Neonate, 44,* 65–75.

Harrington, R. (1996). Family-genetic findings in child and adolescent depressive disorders. *International Review of Psychiatry, 8,* 355–368.

Harris, D. V. (1991). Exercise and fitness during adolescence. In R. M. Lerner, A. C. Petersen, & J. Brooks-Gunn (Eds.), *Encyclopedia of Adolescence* (pp. 324–327). New York: Garland.

Harris, J. F., Durso, F. T., Mergler, N. L., & Jones, S. K. (1990). Knowledge base influences on judgments of frequency of occurrence. *Cognitive Development, 5,* 223–233.

Harris, J. R. (1995). Where is the child's environment? A group socialization theory of development. *Psychological Review, 102,* 458–489.

Harris, L. J. (1992). Left-handedness. In I. Rapid & S. J. Segalowitz (Eds.), *Handbook of neuropsychology* (Vol. 6, pp. 145–208). Amsterdam: Elsvier.

Harris, P. L. (1989). *Children and emotion.* Cambridge, MA: Basil Blackwell Ltd.

Harris, P. L., & Kavanaugh, R. D. (1993). Young children's understanding of pretense. *Monographs of the Society for Research in Child Development* (58, Serial No. 231). Chicago: University of Chicago Press.

Hart, B., & Risely, T. R. (1995). *Meaningful differences in the everyday experiences of young American children.* Baltimore, MD: Paul H. Brookes.

Hart, C. H., DeWolf, D. M., Wozniak, P., & Burts, D. C. (1992). Maternal and paternal disciplinary styles: Relations with preschoolers' playgroup behavior orientations and peer status. *Child Development, 63,* 879–892.

Hart, S. N., Brassard, M. R., & Karlson, H. C. (1996). Psychological maltreatment. In J. Briere, L. Berliner, J. A. Bulkley, C. Jenny, & T. Reid (Eds.), *The APSAC handbook on child maltreatment* (pp. 72–89). Thousand Oaks, CA: Sage.

Harter, S. (1990). Self and identity development. In S. S. Feldman & G. R. Elliot (Eds.), *At the threshold* (pp. 352–387). Cambridge, MA: Harvard University Press.

Harter, S. (1993). Causes and consequences of low self-esteem in children and adolescents. In R. F. Baumeister (Ed.), *Self-esteem: The puzzle of low self-regard* (pp. 87–116). New York: Plenum.

Harter, S. (1998). The development of self-representations. In W. Damon (Ed.), *Handbook of child psychology* (Vol. 3, pp. 553–618). New York: Wiley.

Harter, S., & Monsour, A. (1992). Developmental analysis of conflict caused by opposing attributes in the adolescent self-portrait. *Developmental Psychology, 28,* 251–260.

Hartup, W. W. (1993). Adolescents and their friends. In B. Laursen (Ed.), *Close friendships in adolescence* (Vol. 60, pp. 3–22). San Francisco: Jossey-Bass.

Hartup, W. W. (1996). The company they keep: Friendships and their developmental significance. *Child Development, 67,* 1–13.

Harwood, R. L., Miller, J. G., & Irizarry, N. L. (1995). *Culture and attachment.* New York: Guilford Press.

Harwood, R. L., Schoelmerich, A., Ventura-Cook, E., Schulze, P. A., & Wilson, S. A. (1996). Culture and class influences on Anglo and Puerto Rican mothers' beliefs regarding long-term socialization goals and child behavior. *Child Development, 67,* 2446–2461.

Hashima, P. Y., & Amato, P. R. (1994). Poverty, social support, and parental behavior. *Child Development, 65,* 394–403.

Hassold, T. J., & Patterson, D. (1998). *Down syndrome.* New York: Wiley.

Haste, H., & Baddeley, J. (1991). Moral theory and culture: The case of gender. In W. Kurtines & J. L. Gewirtz (Eds.), *Handbook of moral behavior and development* (Vol 1, pp. 223–250). Hillsdale, NJ: Erlbaum.

Hatton, D. D., Bailey, D. B., Jr., Burchinal, M. R., & Ferrell, K. A. (1997). Development growth curves of preschool children with vision impairments. *Child Development, 68,* 788–806.

Hauser, S. T., Borman, E. H., Bowlds, M. K., Powers, S. L., Jacobson, A. M., Noam, G. I., & Knoebber, K. (1991). Understanding coping within adolescence. In E. M. Cummings & A. Greene (Eds.), *Life-span developmental psychology: Perspectives on stress and coping* (pp. 177–194). Hillsdale, NJ: Erlbaum.

Hausfather, A., Toharia, A., LaRoche, C., & Engelsmann, F. (1997). Effects of age of entry, day-care quality, and family characteristics on preschool behavior. *Journal of Child Psychology and Psychiatry, 38,* 441–448.

Haveman, R., & Wolfe, B. (1994). *Succeeding generations.* New York: Russell Sage Foundation.

Hawkins, A. J., Christiansen, S. L., Sargent, K. P., & Hill, E. J. (1995). Rethinking fathers' involvement in child care: A developmental perspective. In W. Marsiglio (Ed.), *Fatherhood: Contemporary theory, research, and social policy* (pp. 41–56). Thousand Oaks, CA: Sage.

Hawkins, J. D., Catalano, R. F., & Miller, J. Y. (1992). Risk and protective factors for alcohol and other drug problems in adolescence and early adulthood: Implications for substance abuse prevention. *Psychological Bulletin, 112,* 64–105.

Hayes, D. N., & Hemenway, D. (1999). Age within school class and adolescent gun-carrying. *Pediatrics, 103,* 1–6.

Hayes, D. S., & Casey, D. M. (1992). Young children and television: The retention of emotional reactions. *Child Development, 63,* 1423–1436.

Hayghe, H. V. (1997, September). Developments in women's labor force participation. *Monthly Labor Review,* 41–47.

Hayne, H., Rovee-Collier, C., & Perris, E. E. (1987). Categorization and memory retrieval by three-month-olds. *Child Development, 58,* 750–767.

Haynes de Reght, H. L., Minkoff, H. L., Feldman, J., & Schwartz, R. H. (1986). Relation of private or clinic care to cesarean birth rate. *New England Journal of Medicine, 315,* 619–624.

Hayward, C., Killen, J. D., Wilson, D. M., & Hammer, L. D. (1997). Psychiatric risk associated with early puberty in adolescent girls. *Journal of the American Academy of Child and Adolescent Psychiatry, 36,* 255–262.

Hearold, S. (1986). A synthesis of 1043 effects of television on social behavior. In G. Comstock (Ed.), *Public communications and behavior: Volume I* (pp. 65–133). New York: Academic Press.

Hechtman, L., & Weiss, G. (1986). Controlled prospective fifteen-year follow-up of hyperactives as adults. *Canadian Journal of Psychiatry, 31,* 557–567.

Hedges, L. V., & Nowell, A. (1995). Sex differences in mental test scores, variability, and numbers of high scoring individuals. *Science, 269,* 41–45.

Hegyi, T., Carbone, T., Anwar, M., Ostfeld, B., Hiatt, M., Koons, A., Pinto-Martin, J., & Paneth, N. (1998). The Apgar score and its components in the preterm infant. *Pediatrics, 101,* 77–81.

Heinemann, R. (1995). [Population tables]. Unpublished data.

Helm, P., & Grolund, J. (1998). A halt in the secular trend toward earlier menarche in Denmark. *Acta Obstectrics and Gynecology Scandanavia, 77,* 198–200.

Henderson-King, E., & Henderson-King, D. (1997). Media effects on women's body esteem: Social and individual difference factors. *Journal of Applied Social Psychology, 27,* 399–417.

Hendrick, S. S., & Hendrick, C. (1995). Gender differences and similarities in sex and love. *Personal Relationships, 2,* 55–65.

Hennessey, B. A., & Amabile, T. M. (1988). The conditions of creativity. In R. Sternberg (Ed.), *The nature of creativity: Contemporary psychological perspectives.* (pp. 11–38). New York: Cambridge University Press.

Henry, C. S., & Peterson, G. W. (1995). Adolescent social competence, parental qualities, and parental satisfaction. *American Journal of Orthopsychiatry, 65,* 249–262.

Henry, C. S., Peterson, G. W., & Wilson, S. M. (1997). Adolescent social competence and parental satisfaction. *Journal of Adolescent Research, 12,* 389–409.

Herman, C. P., & Polivy, J. (1980). Restrained eating. In A. Stunkard (Ed.), *Obesity.* Philadelphia: Saunders.

Herman-Giddens, M. E., Slora, E. J., Wasserman, R. C., Bourdony, C. J., Bhapkar, M. V., Koch, G. G., & Hasemeier, C. M. (1997). Secondary sexual characteristics and menses in young girls seen in office practice: A study from the Pediatric Research in Office Settings Network. *Pediatrics, 99,* 505–512.

Herold, E. S., & Marshall, S. K. (1996). Adolescent sexual development. In G. R. Adams & R. Montemayor (Eds.), *Psychosocial development during adolescence* (Vol. 8, pp. 62–94). Thousand Oaks, CA: Sage.

Herrmann, D. J. (1998). The relationship between basic research and applied research in memory and cognition. In C. P. Thompson & D. J. Herrmann (Eds.), *Autobiographical memory* (pp. 13–27). Mahwah, NJ: Erlbaum.

Hershberger, S. L., & D'Augelli, A. R. (1995). The impact of victimization on the mental health and suicidality of lesbian, gay, and bisexual youths. *Developmental Psychology, 31,* 65–74.

Hertzler, A. A., & Frary, R. B. (1989). Food behavior of college students. *Adolescence, 24,* 349–356.

Hetherington, E. M., Arnett, J. D., & Hollier, E. A. (1988). Adjustment of parents and children to remarriage. In S. A. Wolchik & P. Karoly (Eds.), *Children of divorce* (pp. 67–107). New York: Gardner Press.

Hetherington, E. M., Bridges, M., & Insabella, G. M. (1998). What matters? What does not? Five perspectives on the association between martial transitions and children's adjustment. *American Psychologist, 53,* 167–184.

Hetherington, E. M., & Clingempeel, W. G. (1992). Coping with marital transitions. *Monographs of the Society for Research in Child Development* (Vol. 57, Serial No. 227).

Hetherington, E. M., Hagan, M. S., & Anderson, E. R. (1989). Marital transitions: A child's perspective. *American Psychologist, 44,* 303–312.

Hewett, J. K., Silberg, J. L., Rutter, M., Simonoff, E., Meyer, J. M., Maes, H., Pickles, A., Neale, M. C., Loeber, R., Erickson, M. T., Kendler, K. S., Heath, A. C., Turett, K. R., Reynolds, C. A., & Eaves, L. J. (1997). Genetics and developmental psychopathology. *Journal of Child Psychology and Psychiatry and Allied Disciplines, 38,* 943–963.

Hewitt, M. P. (1998). *The myth of self-esteem.* New York: St. Martin's Press.

Hewlett, B. S. (1992). The parent-infant relationship and social-emotional development among Aka Pygmies. In J. L. Roopnarine & D. B. Carter (Eds.), *Parent-child socialization in diverse cultures* (pp. 223–244). Norwood, NJ: Ablex.

Hieberg, E. H., & Raphael, T. E. (1996). Psychological perspectives on literacy and extensions to educational practice. In D. C. Berliner & R. C. Calfee (Eds.), *Handbook of educational psychology* (pp. 550–602). New York: Macmillan.

Hill, C. R., & Stafford, F. P. (1980). Parental care of children: Time diary estimates of quantity, predictability, and variety. *Journal of Human Resources, 15,* 219–239.

Hill, J. P. (1987). Research on adolescents and their families. In C. E. Irwin (Ed.), *Adolescent social behavior and health* (Vol. 13, pp. 13–31). San Francisco: Jossey-Bass.

Hill, J. P., Holmbeck, G. N., Marlow, L., Green, T., & Lunch, M. E. (1985). Menarchal status of parent-child relations in families of seventh-grade girls. *Journal of Youth and Adolescence, 14,* 301–316.

Hill, J. P., & Lynch, M. E. (1983). The intensification of gender-related role expectations during early adolescence. In J. Brooks-Gunn & A. C. Petersen (Eds.), *Girls at puberty* (pp. 201–228). New York: Plenum.

Hines, M. (1990). Gonadal hormones and human cognitive development. In J. Balthazart (Ed.), *Hormones, brain and behavior in vertebrates. 1. Sexual differentiation, neuroanatomical aspects, neurotransmitters and neuropeptides* (pp. 51–63). Basel, Switzerland: Barger.

Hinshaw, S. P., Zupan, B. A., Simmel, C., Nigg, J. T., et al. (1997). Peer status in boys with and without attention-deficit hyperactivity disorder. *Child Development, 68,* 880–896.

Hobar, J. D., & Lucey, J. F. (1995). Evaluation of neonatal intensive care technologies. *The Future of Children, 5,* 139–161.

Hochschild, A. R. (1989). *The second shift.* New York: Avon Books.

Hodnett, E. D., & Osborn, R. W. (1989). Effects of continuous intrapartum professional support on childbirth outcomes. *Research in Nursing and Health, 12,* 289–297.

Hoff-Ginsberg, E. (1985). Some contributions of mothers' speech to their children's syntactic growth. *Journal of Child Language, 12,* 367–385.

Hoff-Ginsberg, E. (1986). Function and structure in maternal speech: Their relation to the child's development of syntax. *Developmental Psychology, 22,* 155–163.

Hoff-Ginsberg, E. (1997). *Language development.* Pacific Grove, CA: Brooks/Cole.

Hoffman, M. L. (1970). Conscience, personality, and socialization techniques. *Human Development, 13,* 90–126.

Hoffman, M. L. (1982). Development of prosocial motivation: Empathy and guilt. In N. Eisenberg (Ed.), *The development of prosocial behavior* (pp. 281–313). New York: Academic Press.

Hoffman, M. L. (1994). Discipline and internalization. *Developmental Psychology, 30,* 26–28.

Hoffmann, B., & Dukas, H. (1972). *Albert Einstein: Creator and rebel.* New York: Viking Press.

Holditch-David, D., Black, B. P., Harris, B. G., Sandelowski, M., & Edwards, L. (1994). *Health Care Women International, 15,* 537–548.

Holland, A., & Andre, T. (1994). Athletic participation and the social status of adoelscent males and females. *Youth and Society, 25,* 388–407.

Holliday, M. A. (1986). Body composition and energy needs during growth. In F. Faulkner & J. M. Tanner (Eds.), *Human growth: A comprehensive treatise* (Vol. 2, pp. 101–117). New York: Plenum.

Holmbeck, G. N., Paikoff, R. L., & Brooks-Gunn, J. (1995). Parenting adolescents. In M. H. Bornstein (Ed.), *Handbook of parenting* (Vol. 1, pp. 91–118). Mahwah, NJ: Erlbaum.

Holzman, C., & Paneth, N. (1994). Maternal cocaine use during pregnancy and perinatal outcomes. *Epidemiology Review, 16,* 215–334.

Holzman, L. H. (1996). Pragmatism and dialectical materialism in language development. In H. Daniels (Ed.), *An introduction to Vygotsky* (pp. 75–98). London: Routledge.

Hoover, K. R., Marcia, J. E., & Parris, K. D. (1997). *The power of identity.* Chatham, NJ: Chatham House.

Hopkins, B. (1991). Facilitating early motor development: An intracultural study of West Indian mothers and their infants living in Britain. In J. Nugent, B. Lester, & T. Brazelton (Eds.), *The cultural context of infancy: Multicultural and interdisciplinary approaches to parent-infant relations* (pp. 93–143). Norwood, NJ: Ablex.

Hoppenbrouwers, T., Hodgman, J. E., Arawaka, K., Geidel, S. A., & Sterman, M. B. (1988). Sleep and waking states in infancy: Normative studies. *Sleep, 11,* 387–402.

Hopwood, N. J., Kelch, R. P., Hale, P. M., Mendes, T. M., Foster, C. M., & Beitins, I. Z. (1990). The onset of human puberty: biological and environmental factors. In J. Bancroft, & J. Reinisch (Eds.), *Adolescence and puberty* (pp. 29–49). New York: Oxford University Press.

Horn, J. L., & Trickett, P. K. (1998). Community violence and child development: A review of research. In P. K. Trickett & C. J. Schellenbach (Eds.), *Violence against children in the family and the community* (pp. 103–138). Washington, DC: American Psychological Association.

Horney, K. (1967). *Feminine psychology.* New York: Norton.

Horwood, L. J., & Fergusson, D. M. (1998, January). Breastfeeding and later cognitive and academic outcome. *Pediatrics, 101,* 1–7.

Howe, M. J. A. (1990). *The origins of exceptional abilities.* Oxford: Basil Blackwell.

Howe, M. J. A. (1997). *IQ in question: The truth about intelligence.* London: Sage.

Howes, C. (1988a). Peer interaction in young children. *Monographs of the Society for Research in Child Development* (Vol. 53, Serial No. 217). Chicago: University of Chicago Press.

Howes, C. (1988b). Relations between early child care and schooling. *Developmental Psychology, 24,* 53–57.

Howes, C. (1989). Friendships in very young children: Definition and functions. In B. H. Schneider, G. Attili, J. Nadel, & R. P. Weissberg (Eds.), *Social competence in developmental perspective* (pp. 127–130). Boston: Kluwer Academic Publishers.

Howes, C. (1990). Can the age of entry into child care and the quality of child care predict adjustment in kindergarten? *Developmental Psychology, 26,* 292–303.

Howes, C., Hamilton, C. E., & Matheson, C. C. (1994). Children's relationships with peers: Differential associations with aspects of the teacher/child relationship. *Child Development, 65,* 253–263.

Howes, C., & Matheson, C. C. (1992). Sequences in the development of competent play with peers: Social and pretend play. *Developmental Psychology, 28,* 961–974.

Howes, C., Matheson, C. C., & Hamilton, C. E. (1994). Maternal, teacher, and child care history correlates of children's relationships with peers. *Child Development, 65,* 264–273.

Hoyenga, K. B., & Hoyenga, K. T. (1993). *Gender related differences: Origins and outcomes.* Needham Heights, MA: Allyn & Bacon.

Hoyt, C. (1996, April). Debunking the myth of the terrible toddler. *Child,* 50–52.

Hsu, L. K. G., & Sobkiewicz, T. A. (1991). Body image disturbance: Time to abandon the concept of eating disorders? *International Journal of Eating Disorders, 10,* 15–30.

Hubbard, F. O. A., & van IJzendoorn, M. H. (1991). Maternal unresponsiveness and infant crying across the first 9 months: A naturalistic longitudinal study. *Infant Behavior and Development, 14,* 299–312.

Hudson, J. A. (1990). The emergence of autobiographical memory in mother-child conversation. In R. Fivush & J. A. Hudson (Eds.), *Knowing and remembering in young children* (pp. 166–196). Cambridge, England: Cambridge University Press.

Hudson, J. A., & Fivush, R. (1991). Planning in the preschool years: The emergence of plans from general event knowledge. *Cognitive Development, 6,* 393–415.

Hudson, J. A., & Sheffield, E. G. (1998). Deja vu all over again: Effects of reenactment on toddlers' event memory. *Child Development, 69,* 51–67.

Hudson, J. A., Shapiro, L. R., & Sosa, B. B. (1995). Planning in the real world: Preschool children's scripts and plans for familiar events. *Child Development, 66,* 984–998.

Huesmann, L. R., & Eron, L. D. (Eds.). (1986). *Television and the aggressive child: A cross national comparison.* Hillsdale, NJ: Erlbaum.

Huesmann, L. R., Eron, L. D., Lefkowitz, M. M., & Walder, L. O. (1984). Stability of aggression over time and generations. *Developmental Psychology, 20,* 1120–1134.

Huff, C. R. (1993). Gangs in the United States. In A. P. Goldstein & C. R. Huff (Eds.), *The gang intervention handbook* (pp. 3–20). Champaign, IL: Research Press.

Huff, C. R. (1996). The criminal behavior of gang members and non-gang at-risk youth. In C. R. Huff (Ed.), *Gangs in America* (pp. 75–102). Thousand Oaks, CA: Sage.

Hughes, F. P. (1995). *Children, play, and development.* Boston: Allyn & Bacon.

Huheey, J. E. (1977). Concerning the origin of handedness in humans. *Behavioral Genetics, 7,* 29–32.

Hunter, F. T., McCarthy, M. E., MacTurk, R. H., & Vietze, P. M. (1987). Infants' social-constructive interactions with mothers and fathers. *Developmental Psychology, 23,* 249–254.

Hunter, J. (1990). Violence against lesbian and gay youths. *Journal of Interpersonal Violence, 5,* 295–300.

Hurt, H., Brodsky, N. L., Betancourt, L, Braitman, L. E., Malmud, E., & Giannetta, J. (1995). Cocaine-exposed children: Follow-up through 30 months. *Journal of Developmental and Behavioral Pediatrics, 16,* 29–35.

Hurtado, A. (1995). Variations, combinations, and evolutions. In R. E. Zambrana (Ed.), *Understanding Latino families* (pp. 40–61). Thousand Oaks, CA: Sage.

Hussey, B. (1988). *Understanding my signals: Help for parents of premature infants.* Palo Alto, CA: VORT Corporation.

Huston, A. C. (1983). Sex-typing. In E. M. Hetherington (Ed.), *Handbook of child psychology: Socialization, personality, and social development* (Vol. 4, pp. 388–467). New York: Wiley.

Huston, A. C. (1991). Children in poverty: Developmental and policy issues. In A. C. Huston (Ed.), *Children in poverty* (pp. 1–22). Cambridge, England: Cambridge University Press.

Huston, A. C. (1994). *Children in poverty.* New York: Cambridge University Press.

Huston, A. C., & Alvarez, M. M. (1990). The socialization context of gender role development in early adolescence. In R. Montemayor & G. R. Adams (Eds.), *From childhood to adolescence* (pp. 156–179). Newbury Park, CA: Sage.

Huston, A. C., Donnerstein, E., Fairchild, H., Feshbach, N. D., Katz, P. A., Murray, J. P., Rubinstein, E. A., Wilcox, B., & Zuckerman, D. (1992). *Big world, small screen: The role of television in American society.* Lincoln: University of Nebraska Press.

Huston, A. C., & Wright, J. C. (1998). Mass media and children's development. In W. Damon (Ed.), *Handbook of child psychology* (Vol. 4, pp. 999–1058). New York: Wiley.

Hutchings, D. E., & Fifer, W. P. (1986). Neurobehavioral effects in human and animal offspring following prenatal exposure to methadone. In E. P. Riley and C. V. Vorhees (Eds.), *Handbook of behavioral teratology* (pp. 47–102). New York: Plenum.

Hutchinson, R. L., & Spangler-Hirsch, S. L. (1989). Family well-being, development, and disruption: An introduction. In C. A. Everett (Ed.), *Children of divorce* (pp. 5–24). New York: Haworth Press.

Huttenlocher, J. (1998). Language input and language growth. *Preventive Medicine, 27,* 195–199.

Huttenlocher, P. R. (1990). Morphometric study of human cerebral cortex development. *Neuropsychologia, 28,* 517–527.

Huttenlocher, P. R. (1994). Synaptogenesis in human cerebral cortex. In G. Dawson & K. W. Fischer (Eds.), *Human behavior and the developing brain* (pp. 35–54). New York: Guilford.

Hyde, J. S. (1984). How large are gender differences in aggression? A developmental meta-analysis. *Developmental Psychology, 20,* 722–736.

Hyde, J. S., Fennema, E., & Lamon, S. J. (1990). Gender differences in mathematics performance. *Psychological Bulletin, 107,* 139–155.

Hymel, S., Bowker, A., & Woody, E. (1993). Aggressive versus withdrawn unpopular children. *Child Development, 64,* 879–896.

Imperato-McGinley, J., Peterson, R. E., Gautier, T., & Sturla, E. (1979). Androgens and the evolution of male gender identity among male pseudohermaphrodites with 5-alpha-reductase deficiency. *New England Journal of Medicine, 300,* 123–127.

Ingram, D. (1989). *First language acquisition.* New York: Cambridge University Press.

Inhelder, B., & Piaget, J. (1958). *The growth of logical thinking from childhood to adolescence.* New York: Basic Books.

Inhelder, B., & Piaget, J. (1964). *The growth of logical thinking in the child.* New York: Harper & Row.

Institute of Medicine. (1990). *Science and babies: Private decisions, public dilemmas.* Washington, DC: National Academy Press.

International Association for the Evaluation of Educational Achievement. (1996). *IEA's third international mathematics and science study.* Washington, DC: U.S. Department of Education.

Intons-Peterson, M. J. (1988). *Children's concepts of gender.* Norwood, NJ: ABLEX.

Isabella, R. A. (1993). Origins of attachment: Maternal interactive behavior across the first year. *Child Development, 64,* 605–621.

Itard, J. (1972a). *Of the first developments of the young savage of Aveyron.* New York: Monthly Review Press. (Original work published 1801)

Itard, J. (1972b). *Report of the progress of Victor of Aveyron.* New York: Monthly Review Press. (Original work published 1806)

Itzkoff, S. W. (1996). *Children learning to read.* New York: Praeger.

Izard, C. E. (1977). *Human emotions.* New York: Plenum.

Izard, C. E., & Malatesta, C. Z. (1987). Perspective on emotional development I: Differential emotions theory of early emotional development. In J. D. Osofsky (Ed.), *Handbook of infant development* (pp. 419–494). New York: Wiley.

Jacobs, E. H. (1998). *Fathering the ADHD child.* Northvale, NJ: Jason Aronson, Inc.

Jacobs, J. E. (1991). Influence of gender stereotypes on parent and child mathematics attitudes. *Journal of Educational Psychology, 83,* 518–527.

Jacobs, J. E., & Eccles, J. S. (1985). Gender differences in math ability: The impact of media reports on parents. *Educational Researcher, 14,* 20–25.

Jacobs, R. A. (1997). Nature, nurture, and the development of functional specializations. *Psychonomic Bulletin and Review, 4,* 299–309.

Jacobvitz, D., & Sroufe, L. A. (1987). The early caregiver-child relationship and attention-deficit disorder with hyperactivity in kindergarten: A prospective study. *Child Development, 58,* 1496–1504.

Jaffe, M. L. (1997). *Understanding parenting.* Boston: Allyn & Bacon.

Jahoda, G. (1988). *Acquiring culture: Cross cultural studies of child development* (pp. 193–222). London: Croom Helm.

Jahoda, G. (1983). European "lag" in the development of an economic concept: A study in Zimbabwe. *British Journal of Developmental Psychology, 1,* 113–120.

Jain, A., Belsky, J., & Crnic, K. (1996). Beyond father behaviors: Types of dads. *Journal of Family Psychology, 10,* 432–442.

Janowsky, J. S., Oviatt, S. K., & Orwoll, E. S. (1994). Testosterone influences spatial cognition in older men. *Behavioral Neuroscience, 108,* 325–332.

Jelalian, E., & Lloyd, E. E (1997). Adolescent obesity: Assessment and treatment. *Medical Health, 80,* 367–369.

Jellinek, M. B., & Snyder J. B. (1998). Depression and suicide in children and adolescents. *Pediatric Review, 19,* 255–264.

Jenni, C. B. (1997). School phobia: How home-school collaborations can tame this frightful dragon. *School Counselor, 44,* 206–217.

Jersild, A., & Holmes, F. (1935). Children's fears. *Child Development Monographs* (Vol. 20). Chicago: University of Chicago Press.

Jessor, R. (1992). Risk behavior in adolescence: A psychosocial framework for understanding and action. In D. E. Rogers & E. Ginzberg (Eds.), *Adolescents at risk: Medical and social perspectives* (pp. 19–34). Boulder, CO: Westview Press.

Jiao, S., Ji, G., & Jing, Q. (1986). Comparative study of behavioral qualities of only children and sibling children. *Child Development, 57,* 357–361.

Jing, Q., & Wan, C. (1997). Socialization of Chinese children. In H. S. R. Kao & D. Sinha (Eds.), *Asian perspectives on psychology* (pp. 59–73). New Delhi: Sage.

Johnson, J. S., & Newport, E. L. (1989). Critical period effects in second language learning: The influence of maturational state on the acquisition of English as a second language. *Cognitive Psychology, 21,* 60–99.

Johnson, S. (1987). Early-developed sex differences in science and mathematics in the United Kingdom. *Journal of Early Adolescence, 7,* 21–33.

Johnson, T. R. B., Walker, M. A., & Niebyl, J. R. (1991). Preconception and prenatal care. In S. G. Gabbe, J. R. Niebyl, & J. L. Simpson (Eds.), *Obstetrics* (pp. 203–232). New York: Churchill Livingstone.

Johnson Institute. (1993). *Drugs mean alcohol too.* Minneapolis, MN: Johnson Institute.

Johnston, H. F., & Fruehling, J. J. (1994). Pharmacotherapy for depression in children and adolescents. In W. M. Reynolds & H. F. Johnston (Eds.), *Handbook of depression in children and adolescents* (pp. 365–397). New York: Plenum.

Johnston, J. R., Breunig, K., Garrity, C., & Baris, M. A. (1997). *Through the eyes of children.* New York: Free Press.

Jones, C. P., & Adamson, L. B. (1987). Language use in mother-child and mother-child-sibling interactions. *Child Development, 58,* 356–366.

Jones, G. (1989). Gender bias in classroom interaction. *Contemporary Education, 60,* 216–222.

Jones, M. C. (1965). Psychological correlates of somatic development. *Child Development, 36,* 899–911.

Jones, M. C., & Mussen, P. H. (1958). Self-conceptions, motivations and interpersonal attitudes of early and late maturing girls. *Child Development, 29,* 491–501.

Jones, O. W., & Cahill, T. C. (1994). Basic genetics and patterns of inheritance. In R. K. Creasy & R. Resnik (Eds.), *Maternal-fetal medicine: Principles and practice* (pp. 103–189). Philadelphia: W. B. Saunders.

Jones, R. E. (1997). *Human reproductive biology.* New York: Academic Press.

Jones, S. S., Collins, K., & Hong, H. (1991). An audience effect on smile production in 10-month-old infants. *Psychological Science, 2,* 45–49.

Jorgensen, S. R. (1993). Adolescent pregnancy and parenting. In T. P. Gullotta & G. R. Adams (Eds.), *Adolescent sexuality* (Vol. 5, pp. 103–140). Newbury Park, CA: Sage.

Josephson, W. L. (1995). *Television violence: A review of the effects on children of different ages.* Montreal: Department of Canadian Heritage.

Jouriles, E. N., McDonald, R., Norwood, W. D., Ware, H. S., Spiller, L. C., & Swank, P. R. (1998). Knives, guns, and interparent violence: Relations with child behavior problems. *Journal of Family Psychology, 12,* 178–194.

Jovanovic, J., & Dreves, C. (1995). *Math, science, and girls: Can we close the gender gap?* Urbana: University of Illinois Cooperative Extension Service.

Jovanovic, J., Lerner, R., & Lerner, J. V. (1989). Objective and subjective attractiveness and early adolescent adjustment. *Journal of Adolescence, 12,* 225–229.

Juffer, F., & Rosenboom, L. G. (1997). Infant-mother attachment of internationally adopted children in the Netherlands. *International Journal of Behavioral Development, 20,* 93–107.

Jusczyk, P. W. (1997). *The discovery of spoken language.* Cambridge, MA: Bradford.

Jussim, L., Madon, S., & Chatman, C. (1994). Teacher expectations and student achievement. In L. Heath & T. R. Scott (Eds.), *Applications of heuristics and biases to social issues* (Vol. 3, pp. 303–334). New York: Plenum.

Kachur, S. P., Stennies, G. M., Powell, K. E., Modzeleski, W., Stephens, R., Murphy, R., Kresnow, M., Sleet, D., & Lowry, R. (1996). School-associated violent deaths in the United States, 1992 to 1994. *Journal of the American Medical Association, 275*(22), 1729–1733.

Kagan, J. (1976). Emergent themes in human development. *American Scientist, 64,* 196.

Kagan, J. (1989). Temperamental contributions to social behavior. *American Psychologist, 44,* 668–674.

Kagan, J., Snidman, N., & Arcus, D. (1993). On the temperamental categories of inhibited and uninhibited children. In K. H. Rubin & J. B. Asendorpf (Eds.), *Social withdrawal, inhibition, and shyness in childhood* (pp. 19–30). Hillsdale, NJ: Erlbaum.

Kagan, S., Knight, G., Martinez, S., & Santa, P. (1981). Conflict resolution style among Mexican children. *Journal of Cross-Cultural Psychology, 12,* 222–232.

Kagan, S. L., & Neuman, M. J. (1998). Lessons from three decades of transition research. *Elementary School Journal, 87,* 365–379.

Kahn, P. H. (1997). Bayous and jungle rivers: Cross-cultural perspectives on children's environmental moral reasoning. In H. D. Saltztein (Ed.), *Culture as a context for moral development* (pp. 23–37). San Francisco: Jossey-Bass.

Kalamas, A. D., & Gruber, M. L. (1998). Electrodermal responses to implied versus actual violence on television. *Journal of General Psychology, 125,* 31–37.

Kanfer, F., Karoly, P., & Newman, A. (1975). Reduction of children's fear of the dark by competence-related and situational threat-related verbal cries. *Journal of Consulting and Clinical Psychology, 43,* 251–258.

Kantrowitz, B., Hager, M., Cowley, G., Beachy, L., Rossi, M., Craffey, B., Annin, P., & Crandall, R. (1992, August 3). Teenagers and AIDS. *Newsweek.*

Kao, G., & Tienda, M. (1995). Optimism and achievement: The educational performance of immigrant youth. *Science Quarterly, 76,* 1–19.

Kaplan, K. M., Cochi, S. L., Edmonds, L. D., Zell, E. R., & Preblud, S. R. (1990). A profile of mothers giving birth to infants with congenital rubella syndrome: An assessment of risk factors. *American Journal of Diseases of Children, 144,* 118–123.

Karpov, Y. V., & Haywood, H. C. (1998). Two ways to elaborate Vygotsky's concept of mediation. *American Psychologist, 53,* 27–36.

Kasari, C., & Bauminger, N. (1998). Social and emotional development in children with mental retardation. In J. A. Burack & R. M. Hodapp (Eds.), *Handbook of mental retardation and development* (pp. 411–433). New York: Cambridge University Press.

Kashani, J. H., Rosenberg, T. K., & Reid, J. C. (1989). Developmental perspectives in child and adolescent depressive symptoms in a community sample. *American Journal of Psychiatry, 146,* 871–876.

Kaslow, N. J., Morris, M. K., & Rehm, L. P. (1998). Childhood depression. In R. J. Morris & T. R. Kratochwill (Eds.), *The practice of child therapy* (pp. 48–90). Boston: Allyn & Bacon.

Kassianos, G. C. (1998). *Immunization: Childhood and travel health.* Malden, MA: Blackwell Scientific.

Katchadourian, H. (1977). *The biology of adolescence.* San Francisco: W. H. Freeman.

Katchadourian, H. (1990). Sexuality. In S. S. Feldman & G. R. Elliot (Eds.), *At the threshold: The developing adolescent* (pp. 330–351). Cambridge, MA: Harvard University Press.

Katz, L., & Gottman, J. M. (1997). Buffering children from marital conflict and dissolution. *Journal of Child Clinical Psychology, 26,* 157–171.

Katz, P. (1992). *Progress report to NIMH.* Unpublished manuscript.

Katzman, D. K. (1996). Adolescent eating disorders. In R. H. A. Haslam & P. J. Valletutti (Eds.), *Medical problems in the classroom* (pp. 491–513). Austin, TX: Pro-Ed, Inc.

Kaufman, J., & Cicchetti, D. (1995). The effect of maltreatment on school age children's socioemotional development. *Developmental Psychology, 25,* 516–524.

Kaufman, N. L. (1980). Review of reversal errors. *Perceptual and Motor Skills, 51,* 55–79.

Kavrell, S. M., & Petersen, A. C. (1984). Patterns of achievement in early adolescence. In M. L. Maehr (Ed.), *Advances in motivation and achievement* (Vol. 4, pp. 1–35). Greenwich, CT: JAI Press.

Kazdin, A. E. (1989). Conduct and oppositional disorders. In C. G. Last & M. Hersen (Eds.), *Handbook of child psychiatric diagnosis* (pp. 129–155). New York: Wiley.

Kazdin, A. E., & Marciano, P. L. (1998). Childhood and adolescent depression. In E. J. Mash & R. A. Barkley (Eds.), *Treatment of childhood disorders* (pp. 211–248). New York: Guilford Press.

Kazdin, A. E., Moser, J., Colbus, D., & Bell, R. (1985). Depressive symptoms among physically abused and psychiatrically disturbed children. *Journal of Abnormal Psychology, 94,* 298–307.

Keating, D. P., & Sasse, D. K. (1996). Cognitive socialization in adolescence: Critical period for a critical habit of mind. In G. R. Adams & R. Montemayor (Eds.), *Psychosocial development during adolescence* (Vol. 8, pp. 232–258). Thousand Oaks, CA: Sage.

Kehoe, E. J., & Macrae, M. (1998). Classical conditioning. In W. T. O'Donohue (Ed.), *Learning and behavior therapy* (pp. 36–58). Boston: Allyn & Bacon.

Keil, F. C. (1989). *Concepts, kinds, and cognitive development.* Cambridge, MA: MIT Press.

Keil, F. C. (1998). Cognitive science and the origins of thought and knowledge. In W. Damon (Ed.), *Handbook of child psychology* (Vol. 1, pp. 341–414). New York: Wiley.

Kelder, S. H., Perry, C. L., Klepp, K. I., & Lytle, L. L. (1994). Longitudinal tracking of adolescent smoking, physical activity, and food choice behaviors. *American Journal of Public Health, 84,* 1121–1126.

Keller, H. (1988). *The story of my life.* New York: Signet.

Keller, M. L., Duerst, B. L., & Zimmerman, J. (1996). Adolescents' views of sexual decision-making. *Journal of Nursing Scholarship, 28,* 125–130.

Kelley, K. (1991). Contraceptive behavior as a process. In R. M. Lerner, A. C. Petersen, & J. Brooks-Gunn (Eds.), *Encyclopedia of adolescence* (pp. 175–180). New York: Garland.

Kelley, M. L., Sanchez-Hucles, J., & Walker, R. R. (1993). Correlates of disciplinary practices in working- to middle-class African-American mothers. *Merrill-Palmer Quarterly, 39,* 252–264.

Kellman, P. J., & Banks, M. S. (1998). Infant visual perception. In W. Damon (Ed.), *Handbook of child psychology* (Vol. 2, 103–146). New York: Wiley.

Kelly, D. P. (1992). Hearing impairment. In M. D. Levine, W. B. Carey, & A. C. Crocker (Eds.), *Developmental-behavioral pediatrics* (pp. 510–518). Philadelphia: W. B. Saunders.

Kelly, J. B. (1994). The determination of child custody. *The Future of Children, 4,* 121–142.

Kelly, M. (1977). Papua New Guinea and Piaget: An eight-year study. In P. R. Dasen (Ed.), *Piagetian psychology: Cross-cultural contributions*. New York: Gardner.

Kendall-Tackett, K. A., & Eckenrode, J. (1997). The effects of neglect on academic achievement and disciplinary problems. In G. K. Kantor & J. L. Jasinski (Eds.), *Out of darkness: Contemporary perspectives on family violence* (pp. 105–112). Thousand Oaks, CA: Sage.

Keogh, B. K., & MacMillan, D. L. (1996). Exceptionality. In D. C. Berliner & R. C. Calfee (Eds.), *Handbook of educational psychology* (pp. 311–330). New York: Macmillan.

Kernis, M. H. (1993). The role of stability and level of self-esteem in psychological functioning. In R. F. Baumeister (Ed.), *Self-esteem: The puzzle of low self-regard* (pp. 167–180). New York: Plenum.

Kerns, K., Don, A., Mateer, C. A., & Streissguth, A. P. (1997). Cognitive deficits in nonretarded adults with fetal alcohol syndrome. *Journal of Learning Disabilities, 30*, 685–693.

Kerpelman, J. L., Pittman, J. F., & Lamke, L. K. (1997). Revisiting the identity control theory. *Journal of Adolescence Research, 12*, 363–371.

Kestenbaum, R., Farber, E. A., & Sroufe, L. A. (1989). Individual differences in empathy among preschoolers: Relation to attachment history. In N. Eisenberg (Ed.), *New directions for child development: Empathy and related emotional responses* (Vol. 44, pp. 51–64). San Francisco: Jossey-Bass.

Ketterlinus, R. D., Lamb, M. E., & Nitz, K. A. (1995). Adolescent nonsexual and sex-related problem behaviors: Their prevalence, consequences, and co-occurence. In R. D. Ketterlinus & M. E. Lamb (Eds.), *Adolescent problem behaviors* (pp. 17–40). Hillsdale, NJ: Erlbaum.

Kilbourne, J. (1994). Still killing us softly: Advertising and the obsession with thinness. In P. Fallon, M. Katzman, & S. Wooley (Eds.), *Feminist perspectives on eating disorders* (pp. 395–418). New York: Guilford Press.

Kilbride, P. L. (1980). Sensorimotor behavior of Baganda and Somia infants: A controlled comparison. *Journal of Cross-Cultural Psychology, 11*, 131–149.

Kimball, M. M. (1989). A new perspective on women' math achievement. *Psychological Bulletin, 105*, 198–214.

Kimura, D. (1993). Sex differences in the brain. *Mind and brain: Readings from Scientific American* (pp. 79–89). New York: W. H. Freeman.

King, M., & Yuille, J. (1987). Suggestibility and the child witness. In S. J. Ceci, D. Ross, & M. Toglia (Eds.), *Children's eyewitness memory* (pp. 24–35). New York: Springer-Verlag.

Kirby, D. (1997). *No easy answers: Research findings on programs to reduce teen pregnancy*. Washington, DC: The National Campaign to Prevent Teen Pregnancy.

Kirsh, S. J. (1998). Seeing the world through Mortal Kombat-colored glasses. *Childhood, 5*, 177–184.

Kiselica, M. S. (1995). *Multicultural counseling with teenage fathers*. Thousand Oaks, CA: Sage.

Kiser, L. J., Ostoja, E., & Pruitt, D. B. (1998). Dealing with stress and trauma in families. *Child and Adolescent Psychiatric Clinics of North America, 7*, 87–103.

Kittler, P. G., & Sucher, K. P. (1998). *Food and culture in America: A nutrition handbook*. Belmont, CA: West/Wadsworth.

Klaus, M. H., & Kennell, J. H. (1982). *Parent-infant bonding*. St. Louis, MO: Mosby.

Klaus, M. H., Kennell, J. H., Plumb, N., & Zeuhlke, S. (1970). Human maternal behavior at the first contact with her young. *Pediatrics, 46*, 187–192.

Klein, H. (1991). Couvade syndrome: Male counterpart to pregnancy. *International Journal of Psychiatry and Medicine, 21*, 57–69.

Klein, M. H. (1984). The bite of Pac-Man. *Journal of Psychohistory, 11*, 395–401.

Klein, R. G., & Mannuzza, S. (1991). Long-term outcome of hyperactive children: A review. *Journal of the American Academy of Child and Adolescent Psychiatry, 30*, 383–387.

Kliewer, W., Fearnow, M. D., & Walton, M. N. (1998). Dispositional, environmental, and context-specific predictors of children's threat perceptions in everyday stressful situations. *Journal of Youth and Adolescence, 27*, 83–100.

Klumph, L. F. (1985). Anorexia nervosa and other eating disorders. *Editorial Research Reports, 2*, 659–672.

Knight, G., Fabes, R. A., & Higgins, D. (1996). Concerns about drawing causal inferences from meta-analyses of gender differences: An example in the study of aggression. *Psychological Bulletin, 119*, 410–421.

Kochanska, G., & Askan, N. (1995). Mother-child mutually positive affect, the quality of child compliance to requests and prohibitions, and maternal control as correlates of early internalization. *Child Development, 66*, 236–254.

Kochanska, G., Coy, K. C., Tjebkes, T. L., & Husarek, S. J. (1998). Individual differences in emotionality in infancy. *Child Development, 69*, 375–390.

Kocijan-Hercigonja, D., Rijavec, M., Marusic, A., & Hercigonja, V. (1998). Coping strategies of refugee, displaced, and non-displaced children in a war area. *Nordic Journal of Psychiatry, 52*, 45–50.

Koegel, P., & Edgerton, R. B. (1984). Black "six-hour retarded children" as young adults. In R. B. Edgerton (Ed.), *Lives in process: Mildly retarded adults in a large city* (pp. 145–171). Washington, DC: American Association on Mental Deficiency.

Koff, E., & Rierdan, J. (1991). Menarche and body image. In R. M. Lerner, A. C. Petersen, & J. Brooks-Gunn (Eds.), *Encyclopedia of adolescence* (Vol. 2, pp. 631–636). New York: Garland.

Koff, E., & Rierdan, J. (1993). Advanced pubertal development and eating disturbance in early adolescent girls. *Journal of Adolescent Health, 14*, 433–439.

Kohlberg, L. (1966). A cognitive-developmental analysis of children's sex role concepts and attitudes. In E. E. Maccoby (Ed.), *The development of sex differences* (pp. 82–173). Stanford, CA: Stanford University Press.

Kohlberg, L. (1969). Stage and sequence: The cognitive-developmental approach to socialization. In D. A. Goslin (Ed.), *Handbook of socialization theory and research* (pp. 347–480). Chicago: Rand McNally.

Kohlberg, L. (1973). Stages and aging in moral development. *Gerontologist, 13*, 497–502.

Kohlberg, L. (1981). *Essays on moral development: Volume 1*. New York: Harper & Row.

Kohlberg, L. (1984). *Essays on moral development: Volume 2*. New York: Harper & Row.

Kohlberg, L., Colby, A., Gibbs, J., & Speicher-Dubin, B. (1978). *Standard form scoring manual*. Cambridge, MA: Harvard University Center for Moral Education.

Kohlberg, L., & Kramer, R. (1969). Continuities and discontinuities in childhood and adult moral development. *Human Development, 12*, 3–120.

Kohn, A. (1993). *Punished by rewards*. Boston: Houghton Mifflin.

Kolb, K. J., & Jussim, L. (1994). Teacher expectations and underachieving gifted children. *Roeper Review, 17*, 26–30.

Kolko, D. J. (1996). Child physical abuse. In J. Briere, L. Berliner, J. A. Bulkley, C. Jenny, & T. Reid (Eds.), *The APSAC handbook on child maltreatment* (pp. 21–50). Thousand Oaks, CA: Sage.

Koller, H., Lawson, K., Rose, S. A., Wallace, I., & McCarton, C. (1997). Patterns of cognitive development in very low birth weight children during the first six years of life. *Pediatrics, 99,* 383–389.

Konner, M. (1991). Universals of behavioral development in relation to brain myelination. In K. R. Gibson & A. C. Petersen (Eds.), *Brain maturation and cognitive development: Comparative and cross-cultural perspectives* (pp. 181–224). New York: Aldine de Gruyter.

Koolstra, C. M., van der Voort, T. H. A., & van der Kamp, L. J. T. (1997). Television's impact on children's reading comprehension and decoding skills: A 3-year panel study. *Reading Research Quarterly, 32,* 128–152.

Kopp, C. B. (1992). Emotional distress and control in young children. In N. Eisenberg & R. A. Fabes (Eds.), *Emotion and its regulation in early development* (Vol. 55, pp. 41–57). San Francisco: Jossey-Bass.

Korbin, J. E., Coulton, C. J., Chard, S., Platt-Houston, C., & Su, M. (1998). Impoverishment and child maltreatment in African American and European American neighborhoods. *Development and Psychopathology, 10,* 215–233.

Korkman, M., Liikanen, A., & Fellman, V. (1996). Neurophysiological consequences of very low birth weight and asphyxia at term: Follow-up until school-age. *Journal of Clinical and Experimental Neuropsychology, 18,* 220–233.

Korte, D., & Scaer, R. (1992). *A good birth, a safe birth.* Boston: Harvard Common Press.

Kotlowitz, A. (1991). *There are no children here.* New York: Doubleday.

Kovacs, M., & Paulaustkas, S. L. (1984). Developmental stage and the expression of depressive disorders in children. In D. Cicchetti & K. Schneider-Rosen (Eds.), *Childhood depression* (pp. 59–80). San Francisco: Jossey Bass.

Kovar, M. G. (1991). Health of adolescents in the United States: An overview. In R. M. Lerner, A. C. Petersen, & J. Brooks-Gunn (Eds.), *Encyclopedia of adolescence* (pp. 454–458). New York: Garland.

Kowal, A., & Kramer, L. (1997). Children's understanding of parental differential treatment. *Child Development, 68,* 113–126.

Kozol, J. (1988). *Rachel and her children.* New York: Fawcett.

Krahenbuhl, G. S., Skinner, J. S., & Korht, W. M. (1985). Developmental aspects of maximal aerobic power in children. *Exercise and Sport Science Review, 13,* 503.

Krajeski, M. A. (1996). *Is a birth center for you?* New York: iVillage.

Kramer, C. (1995, September 19). Former dropout makes new life at Yale. *Yale Daily News.*

Kroger, J. (1993). On the nature of structural transition in the identity formation process. In J. Kroger (Ed.), *Discussions on ego identity* (pp. 205–234). Hillsdale, NJ: Erlbaum.

Kuchuk, A., Vibbert, M., & Bornstein, M. H. (1986). The perception of smiling and its experiential correlates in three-month-old infants. *Child Development, 57,* 1054–1061.

Kuczynski, L., Kochanska, G., Radke-Yarrow, M., & Girnius-Brown, O. (1987). A developmental interpretation of young children's noncompliance. *Developmental Psychology, 23,* 799–806.

Kuhn, D. (1989). Children and adults as intuitive scientists. *Psychological Review, 96,* 674–689.

Kuhn, D., Amsel, E., O'Loughlin, M., Schauble, L., Leadbeater, B., & Yotive, W. (1988). *The development of scientific reasoning skills.* San Diego, CA: Academic Press.

Kuhn, D., Nash, S. C., & Brucken, L. (1978). Sex role concepts of two- and three-year-old children. *Child Development, 49,* 445–451.

Kumra, S., Wiggins, E., Krasnewich, D., Meck, J., Smith, A. C. M., Bedwell, J., Fernandez, T., Jacobsen, L. K., Lenane, M., & Rapoport, J. L. (1998). Association of sex chromosome anomalies with childhood-onset psychotic disorders. *Journal of the American Academy of Child and Adolescent Psychiatry, 37,* 292–296.

Kurdek, L. A. (1988). Cognitive mediators of children's adjustment to divorce. In S. A. Wolchik & P. Karoly (Eds.), *Children of divorce* (pp. 233–266). New York: Gardner Press.

Kwasman, A., Tinsley, B. J., & Lepper, H. S. (1995). Pediatricians' knowledge and attitudes concerning diagnosis and treatment of attention deficit and hyperactivity disorders. *Archives of Pediatric and Adolescent Medicine, 149,* 1211–1216.

Laboratory of Comparative Human Cognition. (1983). Culture and cognitive development. In P. Mussen (Ed.), *Handbook of child psychology* (Vol. 1, pp. 295–356). New York: Wiley.

Ladd, G. W., & Kochenderfer, B. J. (1998). Linkages between friendship and adjustment during early school transition. In W. M. Bukowski & A. F. Newcomb (Eds.), *The company they keep: Friendship in childhood and adolescence* (pp. 322–345). New York: Cambridge University Press.

Lage, E. (1991). Boys, girls, and microcomputing. *European Journal of Psychology of Education, 6,* 29–44.

Lagercrantz, H., & Slotkin, T. A. (1986). The "stress" of being born. *Scientific American, 254,* 100–107.

Lamb, M. E. (1982a). The bonding phenomenon: Misinterpretations and their implications. *Journal of Pediatrics, 101,* 555–557.

Lamb, M. E. (1982b). Early contact and mother-infant bonding: One decade later. *Pediatrics, 70,* 763–768.

Lamb, M. E. (1998). Nonparental child care: Context, quality, correlates, and consequences. In W. Damon (Ed.), *Handbook of child psychology* (Vol. 4, pp. 73–134). New York: Wiley.

Lamb, M. E., Sternberg, K. J., & Ketterlinus, R. D. (1992). Child care in the United States: The modern era. In M. E. Lamb, K. J. Sternberg, C. Hwang, & A. G. Broberg (Eds.), *Child care in context* (pp. 207–222). Hillsdale, NJ: Erlbaum.

Lampert, W. E. (1984). An overview of issues in immersion education. In Office of Bilingual and Bicultural Education (Ed.), *Studies in immersion education* (pp. 8–30). Sacramento, CA: California Department of Education.

Landau, R. (1982). Infant crying and fussing. *Journal of Cross Cultural Psychology, 13,* 427–444.

Landers, D. M., & Petruzzello, S. J. (1994). Physical activity, fitness and anxiety. In C. Bouchard, R. J. Shephard, & T. Stephens (Eds.), *Physical activity, fitness and health* (pp. 868–882). Champaign, IL: Human Kinetics Publishers.

Landry, D. J., & Forrest, J. D. (1995). How much older are U.S. fathers? *Family Planning Perspectives, 27,* 159–165.

Langendorfer, S. (1987). Separating fact from fiction in preschool aquatics. *National Aquatics Journal, 3,* 2–4.

Langer, J., & Killen, M. (1998). *Piaget, evolution, and development.* Mahwah, NJ: Erlbaum.

Langlois, J. H. (1981). Beauty and the beast: The role of physical attractiveness in the development of peer relations and social behavior. In S. S. Brehm, S. S. Kassin, & F. X. Gibbons (Eds.), *Developmental social psychology* (pp. 47–63). New York: Oxford University Press.

Langlois, J. H., & Downs, A. C. (1980). Mothers, fathers and peers as socialization agents of sex-typed play behaviors in young children. *Child Development, 51,* 1237–1247.

Langlois, J. H., Ritter, J. M., Roggman, L. A., & Vaughn, L. S. (1991). Facial diversity and infant preferences for attractive faces. *Developmental Psychology, 27,* 79–84.

Langlois, J. H., Roggman, L. A., Casey, R. J., Ritter, J. M., Rieser-Danner, L. A., & Jenkins, V. Y. (1987). Infant preferences for attractive faces: Rudiments of a stereotype? *Developmental Psychology, 23,* 363–369.

LaPorte, D. J. (1997). Gender differences in perceptions and consequences of an eating binge. *Sex Roles, 36,* 479–489.

Lapsley, D. K. (1993). Toward an integrated theory of adolescent ego development. *American Journal of Orthopsychiatry, 63,* 562–571.

Lapsley, D. K., FitzGerald, D. P., Rice, K. G., & Jackson, S. (1989). Separation-individuation and the "new look" at the imaginary audience and personal fable: A test of an integrative model. *Journal of Adolescent Research, 4,* 483–505.

Lapsley, D. K., & Murphy, M. N. (1985). Another look at the theoretical assumptions of adolescent egocentrism. *Developmental Review, 5,* 201–217.

Larson, R. (1994). Youth organizations, hobbies, and sports as developmental contexts. In R. Silbereisen & E. Todt (Eds.), *Adolescence in context: The interplay of family, school, peers, and work in adjustment* (pp. 46–65). New York: Springer-Verlag.

Larson, R., Kubey, R., & Colletti, J. (1989). Changing channels: Early adolescent media choices and shifting investments in family and friends. *Journal of Youth and Adolescence, 18,* 583–599.

Larson, R., & Richards, M. H. (1994). *Divergent realities: The emotional lives of mothers, fathers, and adolescents.* New York: Basic Books.

Larson, R. L., & McMahon, R. O. (1966). The epiphysis and the child athlete. *Journal of the American Medical Association, 196,* 607–612.

Last, C. G., Hansen, C., & Franco, N. (1998). Cognitive-behavioral treatment of school phobia. *Journal of the American Academy of Child and Adolescent Psychiatry, 37,* 404–411.

Latour, B. (1987). *Science in action.* Cambridge, MA: Harvard University Press.

Laughlin, C. D. (1991). Pre- and perinatal brain development and enculturation: A biogenetic structural approach. *Human Nature, 2,* 171–213.

Laursen, B., & Collins, W. A. (1994). Interpersonal conflict during adolescence. *Psychological Bulletin, 115,* 197–209.

Laursen, B., Coy, K. C., & Collins, W. A. (1998). Reconsidering changes in parent-child conflict across adolescence. *Child Development, 69,* 817–832.

Laursen, B., Hartup, W. W., & Koplas, A. L. (1996). Towards understanding peer conflict. *Merrill-Palmer Quarterly, 42,* 76–102.

Laursen, B., & Williams, V. A. (1997). Perceptions of interdependence and closeness in family and peer relationships among adolescents with and without romantic partners. In S. Shulman & W. A. Collins (Eds.), *Romantic relationships in adolescence* (pp. 3–20). San Francisco: Jossey-Bass.

Leach, P. (1997). *Your baby and child.* New York: Alfred A. Knopf.

Leaper, C. (1994). Exploring the consequences of gender segregation on social relationships. In C. Leaper (Ed.), *Childhood gender segregation* (pp. 67–86). San Francisco: Jossey-Bass.

Leaper, C., & Anderson, K. J. (1997). Gender development and heterosexual romantic relationships during adolescence. In S. Shulman & W. A. Collins (Eds.), *Romantic relationships in adolescence* (pp. 85–104). San Francisco: Jossey-Bass.

Lee, C. M., & Gotlib, I. H. (1995). Mental illness and the family. In L. L'Abate (Ed.), *Handbook of developmental family psychology and psychopathology* (pp. 243–264). New York: Wiley.

Lee, L. C. (1992). Day care in the People's Republic of China. In M. E. Lamb, K. J. Sternberg, C. Hwang, & A. G. Broberg (Eds.), *Child care in context* (pp. 355–392). Hillsdale, NJ: Erlbaum.

Leger, D. W., Thompson, R. A., Merritt, J. A., & Benz, J. J. (1996). Adult perception of emotion intensity in human infant cries: Effects of infant age and cry acoustics. *Child Development, 67,* 3238–3249.

Legerstee, M., Anderson, D., & Schaffer, A. (1998). Five- and eight-month-old infants recognize their faces and voices as familiar and social stimuli. *Child Development, 69,* 37–50.

Leinbach, M. D., & Fagot, B. I. (1993). Categorical habituation to male and female faces: Gender schematic processing in infancy. *Infant Behavior and Development, 16,* 317–332.

Leinbach, M. D., Hort, B. E., & Fagot, B. I. (1997). Bears are for boys: Metaphorical associations in young children's gender stereotypes. *Cognitive Development, 12,* 107–130.

Leiter, J., & Johnsen, M. C. (1997). Child maltreatment and school performance declines: An event-history analysis. *American Educational Research Journal, 34,* 563–589.

Lemery, K. S., Goldsmith, H. H, Klinnert, M. D., & Mrazek, D. A. (1999). Developmental models of infant and childhood temperament. *Developmental Psychology, 35,* 189–204.

Lenneberg, E. (1967). *Biological foundations of language.* New York: Wiley.

Lerner, R. M. (1993). Early adolescence: Toward an agenda for the integration of research, policy, and intervention. In R. M. Lerner (Ed.), *Early adolescence: Perspectives on research, policy, and intervention* (pp. 1–16). Hillsdale, NJ: Erlbaum.

Lerner, R. M., Delaney, M., Hess, L. I., Jovanovic, J., & von Eye, A. (1990). Early adolescent physical attractiveness and academic competence. *Journal of Early Adolescence, 10,* 4–20.

Lerner, R. M., & Foch, T. T. (1987). *Biological and psychosocial interactions in early adolescence.* Hillsdale, NJ: Erlbaum.

Lerner, R. M., & Olson, C. K. (1994, February). "Don't talk back!" *Parents,* 97–98.

Leslie, A. M. (1987). Pretense and representation: The origins of "theory of mind." *Psychological Review, 94,* 412–426.

Lester, B. M. (1985). There's more to crying than meets the ear. In B. M. Lester & C. F. Z. Boukydis (Eds.), *Infant crying* (pp. 1–28). New York: Plenum.

Lester, B. M., Freier, K., & LaGasse, L. (1995). Prenatal cocaine exposure and child outcome: What do we really know? In M. Lewis and M. Bendersky (Eds.), *Mothers, babies, and cocaine: The role of toxins in development* (pp. 19–39). Hillsdale, NJ: Erlbaum.

Leve, L. D., & Fagot, B. I. (1997). Gender-role socialization and discipline processes in one- and two-parent families. *Sex Roles, 36,* 1–21.

Leventhal, E. A., Leventhal, H., Shacham, S., & Easterling, D. V. (1989). Active coping reduces reports of pain from childbirth. *Journal of Consulting and Clinical Psychology, 57,* 365–371.

Leventhal, J. M., Forsyth, B. W. C., Qi, K., Johnson, L., Schroeder, D., & Votto, N. (1997). Maltreatment of children born to women who used cocaine during pregnancy. *Pediatrics, 100,* 1–6.

Levin, B. B., & Barry, S. M. (1997). Children's views of technology: The role of age, gender, and school setting. *Journal of Computing in Childhood Education, 8,* 267–290.

Levin, D. S., Smith, E. A., Caldwell, L. L., & Kimbrough, J. (1995). Violence and high school sports participation. *Pediatric Exercise Science, 7,* 379–388.

Levine, M. P., & Smolak, L. (1992). Toward a model of the developmental psychopathology of eating disorders: The example of early adolescence. In J. H. Crowther, D. L. Tennenbaum, S. E. Hobfoll, & M. A. P. Stephens (Eds.), *The etiology of bulimia nervosa: The individual and familial context* (pp. 59–80). Washington, DC: Hemisphere Publishing Corporation.

Levine, M. P., Smolak, L., Moodey, A. F., Shuman, M. D., & Hessen, L. D. (1994). Normative developmental challenges and dieting and eating disturbances in middle school girls. *International Journal of Eating Disorders, 15,* 11–20.

LeVine, R. A., Dixon, S., LeVine, S., Richman, A., Leiderman, P. H., Keefer, C. H., & Brazelton, T. B. (1994). *Child care and culture: Lessons from Africa.* Cambridge, England: Cambridge University Press.

Levinson, R. A. (1995). Reproductive and contraceptive knowledge, contraceptive self-efficacy, and contraceptive behavior among teenage women. *Adolescence, 30,* 65–85.

Levy, G. D., & Katz, P. A. (1993, March). *Differences in preschoolers' race schemas.* Paper presented at the biennial meeting of the Society for Research in Child Development, New Orleans, LA.

Levy, J., & Heller, W. (1992). Gender differences in human neuropsychological function. In A. A. Gerall & H. Moltz (Ed.), *Sexual differentiation* (Vol. 11, pp. 245–274). New York: Plenum.

Lewinsohn, P. M., Hops, H., Roberts, R. E., Seeley, J. R., & Andrews, J. A. (1993). Adolescent psychopathology. I. Prevalence and incidence of depression and other DSM-III-R disorders in high school students. *Journal of Abnormal Psychology, 102,* 133–144.

Lewis, G. M., Woods, N. F., Hough, E. E., & Bensley, L. S. (1989). The family's functioning with chronic illness in the mother: The spouse's perspective. *Social Science and Medicine, 29,* 1261–1269.

Lewis, H. B. (1987a). The role of shame in depression in women. In R. Formanck & A. Gurian (Eds.), *Women and depression* (pp. 182–199). New York: Springer.

Lewis, H. B. (1987b). *The role of shame in symptom formation.* Cambridge, MA: Harvard University Press.

Lewis, M. (1993). Self-conscious emotions: Embarrassment, pride, shame, and guilt. In M. Lewis & J. M. Haviland (Eds.), *Handbook of emotions* (pp. 563–573). New York: Guilford.

Lewis, M., Alessandri, S. M., & Sullivan, M. W. (1992). Differences in shame and pride as a function of children's gender and task difficulty. *Child Development, 63,* 630–638.

Lewit, E. M., & Baker, L. S. (1995). School readiness. *Future of Children, 5,* 128–139.

Liberman, A. M. (1996). *Speech: A special code.* Cambridge, MA: MIT Press.

Lickona, T., Schaps, E., & Lewis, C. (1997). *Eleven principles of effective character education.* Washington, DC: The Character Education Partnership.

Lieberman, P. (1984). *The biology and evolution of language.* Cambridge, MA: Harvard University Press.

Liebert, R. M., & Sprafkin, J. (1988). *The early window: Effects of television on children and youth.* New York: Pergamon Press.

Life Sciences Research Office. (1995). *Third report on nutrition monitoring in the United States.* Washington, DC: U.S. Government Printing Office.

Lifshitz, F., Finch, N. M., & Lifshitz, J. Z. (1991). *Children's nutrition.* Boston: Jones and Bartlett.

Lifshitz, F., & Moses, N. (1988). Nutritional dwarfing: Growth, dieting, and fear of obesity. *Journal of the American College of Nutrition, 7,* 367–376.

Lightfoot, C., & Valsiner, J. (1992). Parental belief systems under the influence: Social guidance of the construction of personal cultures. In I. E. Sigel, A. V. McGillicuddy-DeLisi, & J. J. Goodnow (Eds.), *Parental belief systems* (pp. 393–414). Hillsdale, NJ: Erlbaum.

Lil, S. R. (1993). *Handbook on gangs in schools.* Newbury Park, CA: Corwin Press.

Lillard, A. (1998). Ethnopsychologies: Cultural variations in theories of mind. *Psychological Bulletin, 123,* 3–32.

Lind, G. (1997). *The optimal age of moral education.* Constance, Germany: Unversity of Constance.

Lindberg, L. D., Sonenstein, F. L., Ku, L., & Martinez, G. (1997). Age differences between minors who give birth and their adult partners. *Family Planning Perspectives, 29,* 61–66.

Lingenfelter, S. G. (1993). Courtship and marriage on Yap. In R. A. Marksbury (Ed.), *The business of marriage* (pp. 149–174). Pittsburgh: University of Pittsburgh Press.

Linn, M. C., de Benedictis, T., & Delucchi, K. (1982). Adolescent reasoning about advertisements: Preliminary investigations. *Child Development, 53,* 1599–1613.

Linn, M. C., & Petersen, A. C. (1986). A meta-analysis of gender differences in spatial ability: Implications for mathematics and science achievement. In J. S. Hyde & M. C. Linn, (Eds.), *The psychology of gender: Advances through meta-analysis* (pp. 67–101). Baltimore, MD: The Johns Hopkins University Press.

Lipsey, M. W. (1994). Juvenile delinquency treatment: A meta-analytic inquiry into the variability of effects. In T. D. Cook, H. Cooper, D. S. Cordray, H. Hartmann, L. V. Hedges, R. J. Light, T. A. Louis, & F. Mosteller (Eds.), *Meta-analysis for explanation* (pp. 83–128). New York: Russell Sage.

Lipsitt, L. P., Engen, T., & Kaye, H. (1963). Developmental changes in the olfactory threshold of the neonate. *Child Development, 34,* 371–376.

Little, S., & Garber, J. (1995). Aggression, depression, and stressful life events predicting peer rejection in children. *Development and Psychopathology, 7,* 845–856.

Liu, X., Kaplan, H. B., & Risser, W. (1992). Decomposing the reciprocal relationships between academic achievement and general self-esteem. *Youth and Society, 24,* 123–148.

Livesley, W. J., & Bromley, D. B. (1973). *Person perception in childhood and adolescence.* London: John Wiley.

Locke, J. (1964). *Some thoughts concerning education.* Woodbury, NH: Barron's Educational Series. (Original work published 1690)

Lockwood, P., & Kunda, Z. (1997). Superstars and me: Predicting the impact of role models on the self. *Journal of Personality and Social Psychology, 73,* 91–103.

Loeber, R., Farrington, D. P., Stouthamer-Loeber, M., & Van-Kammen, W. B. (1998). *Antisocial behavior and mental health problems.* Mahwah, NJ: Erlbaum.

Lorys, V. A. R., Hynd, G. W., Lyytinen, H., & Hern, K. (1993). Etiology of attention deficit hyperactivity disorder. In J. L. Matson (Ed.), *Handbook of hyperactivity in children* (pp. 47–65). Boston: Allyn & Bacon.

Loucks, A. B. (1988). Osteoporosis prevention begins in childhood. In E. W. Brown & C. F. Branta (Eds.), *Competitive sports for children and youth* (pp. 213–223). Champaign, IL: Human Kinetics Books.

Lounsbury, J. H. (1996). Characteristics of middle level schools. *ERIC Digest* (No. ED 401 050).

Lovelace, V. O., & Huston, A. C. (1983). Can television teach prosocial behavior? *Prevention in Human Services, 2,* 93–106.

Lozoff, B., Klein, N. K., Nelson, E. C., McClish, D. K., Manuel, M., & Chacon, M. E. (1998). Behavior of infants with iron-deficiency anemia. *Child Development, 69,* 24–36.

Lubeck, S., DeVries, M., Nicholson, J., & Post, J. (1997). Head Start in transition. *Early Education and Development, 8,* 219–244.

Lucas, A., Morely, R., Cole, T. J., Lister, G. & Leeson-Payne, C. (1992). Breast milk and subsequent intelligence quotient in children born before preterm. *Lancet, 339,* 261–264.

Lutzker, J. R. (1998). *Handbook of child abuse research and treatment.* New York: Plenum.

Lynch, M. D. (1981). Self-concept development in childhood. In M. D. Lynch, A. A. Norem-Hebeisen, & K. Gergen (Eds.), *Self-concept: Advances in theory and research* (pp. 110–143). Cambridge, MA: Ballinger.

Lyon, G. R. (1998). Why reading is not a natural process. *Educational Leadership, 55,* 14–18.

Lysne, M., & Levy, G. D. (1997). Differences in ethnic identity in Native American adolescents as a function of school context. *Journal of Adolescent Research, 12,* 372–388.

Lytton, H., & Romney, D. M. (1991). Parents' differential socialization of boys and girls: A meta-analysis. *Psychological Bulletin, 109,* 267–296.

Lyytinen, P., Poikkeus, A. M., & Laakso, M. L. (1997). Language and symbolic play in toddlers. *International Journal of Behavioral Development, 21,* 289–302.

Maas, J. (1995, November). *Asleep in the fast lane.* Paper presented at the Master's Forum, Minneapolis, MN.

MacArthur, C., & Knox, E. G. (1988). Smoking and pregnancy: Effects of stopping at different stages. *British Journal of Obstetrics and Gynecology, 95,* 551–555.

Maccoby, E. E. (1980). *Social development.* San Diego, CA: Harcourt Brace Jovanovich.

Maccoby, E. E. (1984). Middle childhood in the context of the family. In W. A. Collins (Ed.), *Development during middle childhood* (pp. 184–239). Washington, DC: National Academy Press.

Maccoby, E. E. (1987). The varied meanings of "masculine" and "feminine." In J. M. Reinsch, L. A. Rosenblum, & S. A. Sanders (Eds.), *Masculinity/femininity* (pp. 227–239). New York: Oxford University Press.

Maccoby, E. E. (1988). Gender as a social category. *Developmental Psychology, 24,* 755–765.

Maccoby, E. E. (1990). Gender and relationships. *American Psychologist, 45,* 513–520.

Maccoby, E. E., Depner, C. E., & Mnookin, R. H. (1990). Coparenting in the second year after divorce. *Journal of Marriage and the Family, 52,* 141–155.

Maccoby, E. E., & Jacklin, C. N. (1974). *The psychology of sex differences.* Stanford, CA: Stanford University Press.

Maccoby, E. E., & Jacklin, C. N. (1980). Sex differences in aggression: A rejoinder and reprise. *Child Development, 51,* 964–980.

Maccoby, E. E., & Jacklin, C. N. (1987). Gender segregation in childhood. In H. W. Reese (Ed.), *Advances in child development and behavior* (Vol. 20, pp. 239–287). Orlando, FL: Academic Press.

Maccoby, E. E., & Martin, J. A. (1983). Socialization in the context of the family. In E. M. Hetherington (Ed.), *Handbook of child psychology: Vol. 4. Socialization, personality, and social development* (pp. 1–101). New York: Wiley.

Maccoby, E. E., & Mnookin, R. H. (1992). *Dividing the child: Social and legal dilemmas of custody.* Cambridge, MA: Harvard University Press.

MacFarlane, A. (1975). Olfaction in the development of social preferences in the human neonate. *Ciba Foundation Symposium, 33,* 103–117.

Macfarlane, J. W., Allen, L., & Honzik, M. P. (1954). *A developmental study of the behavior problems of normal children between twenty-one months and fourteen years.* Berkeley: University of California Press.

MacIver, D. J., & Epstein, J. L. (1991). *How equal are opportunities for learning in disadvantaged and advantaged middle grade schools?* Baltimore, MD: Johns Hopkins University.

Mackey, M. C. (1990). Women's preparation for the childbirth experience. *Maternal and Child Nursing Journal, 19,* 143–173.

MacKinnon, C. E. (1989). Sibling interactions in married and divorced families: Influence of ordinal position, socioeconomic status, and play context. In C. A. Everett (Ed.), *Children of divorce* (pp. 221–234). New York: Haworth Press.

Macksoud, M. S., & Aber, J. L. (1996). The war experiences and psychosocial development of children in Lebanon. *Child Development, 67,* 70–88.

MacKune-Karrer, B. (1992). Unifying diverse parameters: The multicultural framework. In D. Breunlin, R. C. Schwartz, & B. MacKune-Karrer (Eds.), *Metaframeworks* (pp. 193–236). San Francisco: Jossey-Bass.

MacLean, P. D. (1985). Brain evolution relating to family, play, and the separation call. *Archives of General Psychiatry, 42,* 405–417.

MacWhinney, B. (1989). Competition and lexical categorization. In R. Corrigan, F. Eckman, & M. Noonam (Eds.), *Linguistic categorization* (pp. 195–241). Amsterdam: John Benjamin.

Magid, L. J. (1993). *The little PC book.* New York: Peachpit Press.

Magnusson, D. (1988). *Individual development from an interactional perspective: A longitudinal study.* Hillsdale, NJ: Erlbaum.

Magnusson, D. (1995). Individual development: A holistic, integrated model. In P. Moen, G. H. Elder, & K. Luscher (Eds.), *Examining lives in context* (pp. 19–60). Washington, DC: American Psychological Association.

Magnusson, D., Sattin, H., & Allen, V. (1986). Differential maturation among girls and its relation to social adjustment in a longitudinal perspective. In P. Baltes, D. Featherman, & R. Lerner (Eds.), *Life-span development and behavior* (Vol. 7, pp. 156–189). Hillsdale, NJ: Erlbaum.

Maier, S. E., Chen, W. A., & West, J. R. (1996). The effects of timing and duration of alcohol exposure on development of the fetal brain. In E. Abel (Ed.), *Fetal alcohol syndrome* (pp. 27–50). Boca Raton, FL: CRC Press.

Main, M., & Solomon, J. (1990). Procedures for identifying infants as disorganized/disoriented during the Ainsworth Strange Situation. In M. Greenberg, D. Cicchetti, & M. Cummings (Eds.), *Attachment in the preschool years* (pp. 121–160). Chicago: Chicago University Press.

Malatesta, C. Z. (1990). The role of emotions in the development and organization of personality. In R. A. Thompson (Ed.), *Socioemotional development* (Vol. 36, pp. 1–56). Lincoln: University of Nebraska Press.

Malina, R. M. (1986). Growth of muscle tissue and muscle mass. In F. Faulkner & J. M. Tanner (Eds.), *Human growth: A comprehensive treatise* (Vol. 2, pp. 77–99). New York: Plenum.

Malina, R. M., & Bouchard, C. (1991). *Growth, maturation, and physical activity.* Champaign, IL: Human Kinetics.

Maloney, M. J., McGuire, J., Daniels, S. R., & Specker, B. (1989). Dieting behavior and eating attitudes in children. *Pediatrics, 84,* 482–489.

Malson, L. (1972). *Wolf children and the problem of human nature.* New York: Monthly Review Press.

Mandler, J. M. (1990). A new perspective on cognitive development in infancy. *American Scientist, 78,* 236–243.

Mandler, J. M. (1992). The foundations of conceptual thought in infancy. *Cognitive Development, 7,* 273–285.

Mandler, J. M. (1993). On concepts. *Cognitive Development, 8,* 141–148.

Mandler, J. M., Bauer, P. J., & McDonough, L.(1991). Separating the sheep from the goats: Differentiating global categories. *Cognitive Psychology, 23,* 263–298.

Mange, E. J., & Mange, A. P. (1994). *Basic human genetics.* Sunderland, MA: Sinauer.

Mangelsdorf, S. C., Plunkett, J. W., Dedrick, C. F., Berlin, M., Meisels, S. J., McHale, J. L., & Dichtellmiller, M. (1996). Attachment security in very low birth weight infants. *Developmental Psychology, 32,* 914–920.

Manlove, J. (1998). The influence of high school dropout and school disengagement on the risk of school-age pregnancy. *Journal of Research on Adolescence, 8,* 187–220.

Mant, C. M., & Perner, J. (1988). The child's understanding of commitment. *Developmental Psychology, 24,* 343–351.

Maratsos, M. (1998). The acquisition of grammar. In W. Damon (Ed.), *Handbook of child psychology* (Vol. 2, pp. 421–467). New York: Wiley.

March of Dimes. (1998). *Leading categories of birth defects.* White Plains, NY: March of Dimes.

Marcia, J. E. (1987). The identity status approach to the study of ego identity development. In T. Honess & K. Yardley (Eds.), *Self and identity* (pp. 161–171). Boston: Routledge & Kegan Paul.

Marcia, J. E. (1993). The relational roots of identity. In J. Kroger (Ed.), *Discussions on ego identity* (pp. 101–120). Hillsdale, NJ: Erlbaum.

Marcus, G. F., Pinker, S., Ullman, M., Hollander, M., Rosen, T. J., & Xu, F. (1992). Overregularization in language acquisition. *Monographs of the Society for Research in Child Development* (57, Serial No. 228). Chicago: University of Chicago Press.

Marin, G. (1994). The experience of being a Hispanic in the United States. In W. J. Lonner & R. S. Malpas (Eds.), *Psychology and culture* (pp. 23–28). Boston: Allyn & Bacon.

Markel, K. S., & Frone, M. R. (1998). Job characteristics, work-school conflict, and school outcomes among adolescents. *Journal of Applied Psychology, 83,* 277–287.

Marks, S. B. (1997). Reducing prejudice against children with disabilities in inclusive settings. *International Journal of Disability, Development, and Education, 44,* 117–131.

Markson, L., & Bloom, P. (1997). Evidence against a dedicated system for word learning in children. *Nature, 385,* 813–815.

Markus, H. R., & Kitayama, S. (1991). Culture and the self: Implications for cognition, emotion, and motivation. *Psychological Review, 98,* 224–253.

Marques-Bruna, P., & Grimshaw, P. N. (1997). 3-dimensional kinematics of overarm throwing action of children age 15 to 30 months. *Perceptual and Motor Skills, 84,* 1267–1283.

Marshall, S. P., & Smith, J. D. (1987). Sex differences in learning mathematics: A longitudinal study with item and error analyses. *Journal of Educational Psychology, 79,* 372–383.

Marshall, W. A., & Tanner, J. M. (1970). Variations in the pattern of pubertal change in boys. *Archives of Disease in Childhood, 45,* 13–23.

Marshall, W. A., & Tanner, J. M. (1986). Puberty. In F. Faulkner & J. M. Tanner (Eds.), *Human growth: A comprehensive treatise* (pp. 171–210). New York: Plenum.

Marsiglio, W., & Cohan, M. (1997). Young fathers and child development. In M. E. Lamb (Ed.), *The role of the father in child development* (pp. 227–244). New York: Wiley.

Martin, C. A., Hill, K. K., & Welsh, R. (1998). Adolescent pregnancy, a stressful life event. In T. W. Miller (Ed.), *Children of trauma* (pp. 141–160). Madison, CT: International Universities Press.

Martin, C. L. (1989). Children's use of gender-related information in making social judgments. *Developmental Psychology, 25,* 80–88.

Martin, C. L. (1991). The role of cognition in understanding gender effects. In H. Reese (Ed.), *Advances in child development and behavior* (Vol. 23, pp. 113–149). San Diego, CA: Academic Press.

Martin, C. L. (1994). Cognitive influences on the development and maintenance of gender segregation. In C. Leaper (Ed.), *Childhood gender segregation* (pp. 35–52). San Francisco: Jossey-Bass.

Martin, C. L., Eisenbud, L., & Rose, H. (1995). Children's gender-based reasoning about toys. *Child Development, 66,* 1453–1471.

Martin, C. L., & Halverson, C. F. (1981). A schematic processing model of sex typing and stereotyping in children. *Child Development, 52,* 1119–1134.

Martin, C. L., & Halverson, C. F. (1983). Gender constancy: A methodological and theoretical analysis. *Sex Roles, 9,* 775–790.

Martin, C. L., Woods, C. H., & Little, J. K. (1990). The development of gender stereotype components. *Child Development, 61,* 1891–1904.

Martin, D. L., & Hoover, H. D. (1987). Sex differences in educational achievement: A longitudinal study. Special issues: Sex differences in early adolescents. *Journal of Early Adolescence, 7,* 65–83.

Martin, K. (1996). *Puberty, sexuality, and the self: Boys and girls at adolescence.* New York: Routledge.

Martinez, R. O., & Dukes, R. L. (1997). The effects of ethnic identity, ethnicity, and gender on adolescent well being. *Journal of Youth and Adolescence, 26,* 503–516.

Martini, M. (1994). Peer interaction in Polynesia: A view from the Marquesas. In J. L. Roopnarine, J. E. Johnson, & F. H. Hooper (Eds.), *Children's play in diverse cultures* (pp. 73–103). New York: State University of New York Press.

Martorano, S. C. (1977). A developmental analysis of performance on Piaget's formal operations task. *Developmental Psychology, 13,* 666–672.

Marzano, R. J., & Hutchins, C. L. (1987). *Thinking skills: A conceptual framework.* ERIC Document Reproduction Service (No. ED 266 436).

Masataka, N. (1992). Motherese in a signed language. *Infant Behavior and Development, 15,* 453–460.

Masataka, N. (1996). Perception of motherese in a signed language by 6-month-old deaf infants. *Developmental Psychology, 32,* 874–879.

Masataka, N. (1998). Perception of motherese in Japanese sign language by 6-month-old hearing infants. *Developmental Psychology, 34,* 241–246.

Massey, C. M., & Gelman, R. (1988). Preschoolers' ability to decide whether a photographed unfamiliar object can move itself. *Developmental Psychology, 24,* 307–317.

Masten, A. S., & Coatsworth, J. D. (1998). The development of competence in favorable and unfavorable environments. *American Psychologist, 53,* 205–220.

Masten, A. S., Morrison, P., Pellegrini, D., & Tellegen, A. (1990). Competence under stress. In J. E. Role & A. S. Masten (Ed.), *Risk and protective factors in the development of psychopathology* (236–256). New York: Cambridge University Press.

Mastrogiannis, D. S., Decavalas, G. O., Verma, U., & Tejani, N. (1990). Perinatal outcome after recent cocaine usage. *Obstetrics and Gynecology, 76,* 8–11.

Maughan, B., & Rutter, M. (1998). Continuities and discontinuities in social behavior from childhood to adult life. *Advances in Child Clinical Psychology, 20,* 1–47.

Maurer, D., & Barrerra, M. E. (1981). Infants' perception of natural and distorted arrangements of a schematic face. *Child Development, 52,* 196–202.

Maxfield, M., & Widom, C. (1996). The cycle of violence: Revisited 6 years later. *Archives of Pediatric Adolescent Medicine, 150,* 390–395.

May, D. C., & Kundert, D. K. (1997). School readiness practices and children at-risk. *Psychology in the Schools, 34,* 73–84.

Mayes, L. C., Granger, R. H., Bornstein, M. H., & Zuckerman, B. (1992). The problem of prenatal cocaine exposure: A rush to judgment. *Journal of the American Medical Association, 267,* 406–408.

Mazur, E. (1993). Developmental differences in children's understanding of marriage, divorce, and remarriage. *Journal of Applied Developmental Psychology, 14,* 191–212.

McAdoo, H. P. (1993). *Family ethnicity.* Newbury Park, CA: Sage.

McBride-Chang, C. (1995). What is phonological awareness? *Journal of Educational Psychology, 87,* 179–192.

McCauley, E., Kay, T., Ito, J., & Treder, R. (1987). The Turner syndrome: Cognitive deficits, affective discrimination, and behavior problems. *Child Development, 58,* 464–473.

McClelland, D. C. (1993). Intelligence is not the best predictor of job performance. *Current Directions in Psychological Science, 2,* 5–6.

McCloskey, L. A., Figueredo, A. J., & Koss, M. P. (1995). The effects of systemic family violence on children's mental health. *Child Development, 66,* 1239–1261.

McClurg, P. A., & Chaille, C. (1987). Computer games: Environments for developing spatial cognition? *Journal of Educational Computing Research, 3,* 95–111.

McCormick, M. C., Gortmaker, S. L., & Sobol, A. M. (1990). Very low birth weight children: Behavior problems and school difficulty in a national sample. *Journal of Pediatrics, 117,* 687–693.

McDonnell, L. M., & Hill, P. T. (1993). *Newcomers in American schools: Meeting the educational needs of immigrant youth.* Santa Monica, CA: Rand.

McGrath, M. P., Wilson, S. R., & Franssetto, S. (1995). Why some forms of induction are better than others at encouraging prosocial behavior. *Merrill-Palmer Quarterly, 41,* 347–360.

McGrory, A. (1990). Menarche: Responses of early adolescent females. *Adolescence, 25,* 265–270.

McHale, S. M., Crouter, A. C., McGuire, S., & Updegraff, K. A. (1995). Congruence between mothers' and fathers' differential treatment of siblings: Links with family relations and children's well-being. *Child Development, 66,* 116–128.

McKenna, J., Mosko, S., Richard, C., Drummond, S., Hunt, L., Cetel, M. B., & Arpaia, J. (1994). Experimental studies of infant-parent co-sleeping: Mutual physiological and behavior influences and their relevance to SIDS. *Early Human Development, 38,* 187–201.

McLoyd, V. C. (1998). Children in poverty. In W. Damon (Ed.), *Handbook of child psychology* (Vol. 4, pp. 135–208). New York: Wiley.

McLoyd, V. C., & Wilson, L. (1991). The strain of living poor: Parenting, social support, and child mental health. In A. Huston (Ed.), *Children in poverty* (pp. 105–135). Cambridge, England: Cambridge University Press.

McManus, I. C., & Bryden, M. P. (1992). The genetics of handedness, cerebral dominance, and lateralization. In I. Rapin & S. J. Segalowitz (Eds.), *Handbook of neuropsychology* (Vol. 6., pp. 115–144). Amsterdam: Elsevier.

Meadow-Orlans, K. P. (1995). Parenting with a sensory or physical disability. In M. H. Bornstein (Ed.), *Handbook of parenting* (Vol. 4, pp. 57–84). Mahwah, NJ: Erlbaum.

Meaney, M. J. (1988). The sexual differentiation of social play. *Trends in Neuroscience, 7,* 54–58.

Measelle, J. R., Ablow, J. C., Cowan, P. A., & Cowan, C. P. (1998). Assessing young children's views of their academic, social, and emotional lives. *Child Development, 69,* 1556–1576.

Mediascope. (1996, June). *Interactive video games.* Los Angeles, CA: EBS International.

Meece, J. L. (1987). The influence of school experiences on the development of gender schemata. In L. S. Liben & M. L. Signorella (Eds.), *Children's gender schemata* (pp. 57–73). San Francisco: Jossey-Bass.

Meehan, A. M. (1984). A meta-analysis of sex differences in formal operational thought. *Child Development, 55,* 1110–1124.

Meehan, A. M., & Astor-Stetson, E. (1997). *Annual editions of adolescent psychology.* Guilford, CT: Dushkin.

Mehta, P., & Bentrup, K. L. (1996). Women and HIV infection. *Journal of the Florida Medical Association, 83,* 473–478.

Mellou, E. (1996). Can creativity be nurtured in young children? *Early Child Development and Care, 119,* 119–130.

Melnick, M. J., Vanfossen, B. E., & Sabo, D. F. (1988). Developmental effects of athletic participation among high school girls. *Sociology of Sport Journal, 5,* 22–36.

Meltzer, D. (1981). *Birth: An anthology of ancient texts, songs, prayers, and stories.* San Francisco: North Point Press.

Meltzoff, A. N. (1995). What infant memory tells us about infantile amnesia: Long-term recall and deferred imitation. *Journal of Experimental Child Psychology, 59,* 497–515.

Meltzoff, A. N., & Moore, M. K. (1994). Imitation, memory, and the representation of persons. *Infant Behavior and Development, 17,* 83–99.

Melzak, S. (1992). The secret life of children who have experienced physical aggression and violence. In V. P. Varma (Ed.), *The secret life of vulnerable children* (pp. 101–129). New York: Routledge.

Mena-Gonzalez, J., & Eyer, D. W. (1989). *Infants, toddlers, and caregivers.* Mountain View, CA: Mayfield.

Mendelsohn, A. L., Dreyer, B. P., Fierman, A. H., Rosen, C. M., Legano, L. A., Kruger, H. A., Lim, S. W., & Courtlandt, C. D. (1998). Low-level lead exposure and behavior in early childhood. *Pediatrics, 101,* 1–6.

Menyuk, P. (1988). *Language development: Knowledge and use.* New York: Harper Collins.

Menyuk, P., Liebergott, J. W., & Schultz, M. C. (1995). *Early language development in full-term and premature infants.* Hillsdale, NJ: Lawrence Erlbaum.

Mercer, R. T., Ferketich, S., May, K., DeJoseph, J., & Sollid, D. (1988). Further exploration of maternal and paternal fetal attachment. *Research in Nursing and Health, 11,* 83–95.

Merriman, W. E., & Bowman, L. L. (1989). The mutual exclusivity bias in children's word learning. *Monographs of the Society for Research in Child Development* (54, Whole no. 130).

Mest, G. M., (1988). With a little help from their friends: Use of social support by persons with retardation. *Journal of Social Issues, 44,* 117–125.

Metha, A., Chen, E., Mulvenon, S., & Dode, I. (1998). A theoretical model of adolescent suicide risk. *Archives of Suicide Research, 4,* 115–133.

Midgley, C. M. (1989). Change in teacher efficacy and student self- and task-related beliefs during the transition to junior high school. *Journal of Educational Psychology, 81,* 247–258.

Midgley, C. M. (1993). Motivation and middle level schools. In M. L. Maehr & P. R. Pintrich (Eds.), *Advances in motivation and achievement* (Vol. 8, pp. 217–274). Greenwich, CT: JAI Press.

Midgley, C. M., Feldlaufer, H., & Eccles, J. S. (1988). The transition to junior high school. *Journal of Youth and Adolescence, 17,* 543–562.

Milgram, N. A. (1998). Children under stress. In T. H. Ollendick & M. Hersen (Eds.), *Handbook of child psychopathology* (pp. 505–553). New York: Plenum.

Miller, B. C. (1998). *Family matters: A research synthesis of family influences on adolescent pregnancy.* Washington, DC: The National Campaign to Prevent Teen Pregnancy.

Miller, B. C., Norton, M. C., Curtis, T., Hill, E. J., Schvaneveldt, P., & Young, M. H. (1997). The timing of sexual intercourse among adolescents: Family, peer, and other antecedents. *Youth and Society, 29,* 54–83.

Miller, C. L., Eccles, J. S., Flanagan, C., Midgley, C. M., Feldlaufer, H., & Goldsmith, R. (1990). Parents' and teachers' beliefs about adolescence: Effects of sex and experience. *Journal of Youth and Adolescence, 19,* 363–394.

Miller, J. G. (1984). Culture and development of everyday social explanation. *Journal of Personality and Social Psychology, 46,* 961–978.

Miller, J. G. (1986). Early cross-cultural commonalities in social explanation. *Developmental Psychology, 22,* 514–520.

Miller, K. S., Forehand, R., & Kotchick, B. A. (1999). Adolescent sexual behavior in two ethnic minority samples. *Journal of Marriage and the Family, 61,* 85–98.

Miller, N. B., Cowan, P. A., Cowan, C. P., Hetherington, E. M., & Clingempeel, W. G. (1993). Externalizing in preschoolers and early adolescents: A cross-study replication of a family model. *Developmental Psychology, 29,* 4–18.

Miller, P. H. (1993). *Theories of developmental psychology.* New York: W. H. Freeman.

Miller, P. H., & Aloise, P. A. (1989). Young children's understanding of the psychological causes of behavior: A review. *Child Development, 60,* 257–285.

Millstein, S. G. (1990). Risk factors for AIDS among adolescents. In W. Gardner, S. G. Millstein, & B. L. Wilcox (Eds.), *Adolescents in the AIDS epidemic: New directions for child development* (pp. 3–15). San Francisco: Jossey-Bass.

Milner, J. S., & Chilamkurti, C. (1991). Physical child abuse: Perpetrator characteristics. *Journal of Interpersonal Violence, 6,* 345–366.

Minkoff, H. L. (1994). Human immunodeficiency virus. In R. K. Creasy & R. Resnik (Eds.), *Maternal-fetal medicine: Principles and practice* (466–505). Philadelphia: W. B. Saunders.

Minton, C., Kagan, J., & Levine, J. A. (1971). Maternal control and obedience in the two-year-old. *Child Development, 42,* 1873–1894.

Mintz, J. (1995). Self in relation to other: Preschoolers' verbal social comparisons within narrative discourse. In L. L. Sperry & P. A. Smiley (Eds.), *Exploring young children's concepts of self and other through conversation* (pp. 61–74). San Francisco: Jossey-Bass.

Minuchin, P. P., & Shapiro, E. K. (1983). The school as a context for social development. In P. Mussen (Ed.), *Handbook of child psychology* (Vol. IV, pp. 197–274). New York: Wiley.

Mischel, W. (1966). A social-learning view of sex differences in behavior. In E. E. Maccoby (Ed.), *The development of sex differences* (pp. 57–81). Stanford, CA: Stanford University Press.

Miyake, K., Chen, S., & Campos, J. J. (1985). Infant temperament, mother's mode of interaction, and attachment in Japan: An interim report. In I. Bretherton & E. Waters (Eds.), *Growing points of attachment theory and research* (pp. 276–297). Chicago: Society for Research in Child Development.

Mize, J., & Ladd, G. W. (1990). Toward the development of successful social skills training for preschool children. In S. R. Asher & J. D. Coie (Eds.), *Peer rejection in childhood* (pp. 338–364). Cambridge, England: Cambridge University Press.

Modell, J., & Goodman, M. (1990). Historical perspectives. In S. S. Feldman & G. R. Elliot (Eds.), *At the threshold: The developing adolescent* (pp. 93–122). Cambridge, MA: Harvard University Press.

Moerk, E. L. (1989). The LAD was a lady and the tasks were ill-defined. *Developmental Review, 9,* 21–57.

Moffitt, T. E. (1993). Adolescence-limited and life course persistent antisocial behavior: Developmental taxonomy. *Psychological Review, 100,* 674–701.

Monahan, S. C., Buchanan, C. N., Maccoby, E. E., & Dornbusch, S. M. (1993). Sibling differences in divorced families. *Child Development, 63,* 152–168.

Money, J., & Ehrhardt, A. A. (1972). *Man and woman. Boy and girl.* Baltimore, MD: Johns Hopkins University Press.

Monheit, A. C., & Cunningham, P. J. (1992). Children without health insurance. *The Future of Children, 2*(2), 154–170.

Montemayor, R., Adams, G. R., & Gullotta, T. P. (1990). *From childhood to adolescence: A transitional period?* Newbury Park, CA: Sage.

Montemayor, R., Adams, G. R., & Gullotta, T. P. (1994). *Personal relationships during adolescence.* Thousand Oaks, CA: Sage.

Moon, C., Cooper, R. P., & Fifer, W. P. (1993). Two-day-olds prefer their native language. *Infant Behavior and Development, 16,* 495–500.

Moore, J. P., & Terrett, C. P. (1999). *National Youth Gang Survey, 1996.* Washington, DC: U.S. Department of Justice.

Moore, K. A., & Driscoll, A. (1997). *Partners, predators, peers, protectors: Males and teen pregnancy.* Washington, DC: Child Trends Inc.

Moore, K. L. (1998). *The developing human. Clinically oriented embryology,* 6th ed. Philadelphia: W. B. Saunders.

Moore, S., & Rosenthal, D. (1993). *Sexuality in adolescence.* London: Routledge.

Moore, S. M., & Gullone, E. (1995). Fear of weight gain: Its correlates among school-aged adolescents. *Psychological Reports, 76,* 1305–1306.

Moore, T. R., Origel, W., Key, T. C., & Resnik, R. (1986). The perinatal and economic impact of prenatal care in a low socio-economic population. *American Journal of Obstetrics and Gynecology, 154,* 29–33.

Moreau, G. F., Ferron, C., Jeannin, A., & Dubois, A. F. (1996). Adolescent sexuality: The gender gap. *AIDS Care, 8,* 641–653.

Morelli, G. A., Rogoff, B., Oppenheim, D., & Goldsmith, D. (1992). Cultural variation in infants' sleeping arrangements. *Developmental Psychology, 28,* 604–613.

Morgan, W. P. (1994). Physical activity, fitness and depression. In C. Bouchard, R. J. Shephard, & T. Stephens (Eds.), *Physical activity, fitness and health* (pp. 851–867). Champaign, IL: Human Kinetics Publishers.

Morris, K. (1998). Short course of AZT halves HIV-1 perinatal transmission. *Lancet, 351,* 651.

Morris, R. J., & Kratochwill, T. R. (1998). Childhood fears and phobias. In R. J. Morris & T. R. Kratochwill (Eds.), *The practice of child therapy* (pp. 91–131). Boston: Allyn & Bacon.

Morris, T. W., & Levinson, E. M. (1995). Relationship between intelligence and occupational adjustment and functioning. *Journal of Counseling and Development, 73,* 503–514.

Morrison, F. J., Alberts, D. M., & Griffith, E. M. (1997). Nature-nurture in the classroom: Entrance age, school readiness, and learning in children. *Developmental Psychology, 33,* 254–262.

Morrison, G. S. (1997). *Teaching in America.* Needham Heights, MA: Allyn & Bacon.

Mortimer, J. T., & Finch, M. D. (1996). *Adolescents, work, and family.* Thousand Oaks, CA: Sage.

Moskovitz, S. (1983). *Love despite hate: Child survivors of the Holocaust and their adult lives.* New York: Schocken Books.

Moyerman, D. R., & Forman, B. D. (1992). Acculturation and adjustment: A metaanalytic study. *Hispanic Journal of Behavioral Sciences, 14,* 163–200.

Mruk, C. (1995). *Self-esteem research, theory, and practice.* New York: Springer Publishing.

Mufson, L., & Moreau, D. (1997). Depressive disorders. In R. T. Ammerman & M. Hersen (Eds.), *Handbook of prevention and treatment with children and adolescents* (pp. 403–430). New York: Wiley.

Muller, T., & Espenshade, T. J. (1985). *The fourth wave: California's newest immigrants.* Washington, DC: Urban Institute Press.

Munakata, Y., McClelland, J. L., Johnson, M. H., & Siegler, R. S. (1997). Rethinking infant knowledge: Toward an adaptive process account of successes and failures in object permanence tasks. *Psychological Review, 104,* 686–713.

Munn, P., & Dunn, J. (1988). Temperament and the developing relationship between siblings. *International Journal of Behavioral Development, 12,* 433–451.

Muret-Wagstaff, S., & Moore, S. G. (1989). The Hmong in America: Infant behavior and rearing practices. In J. K. Nugent, B. M. Lester, & T. B. Brazelton (Eds.). *The cultural context of infancy* (Vol. 1, pp. 319–340). Norwood, NJ: Ablex Publishing.

Murphy, B. C., & Eisenberg, N. (1996). Provoked by a peer: Children's anger-related responses and their relations to social functioning. *Merrill-Palmer Quarterly, 42,* 103–124.

Murphy, W. D., & Smith, T. A. (1996). Sex offenders against children. In J. Briere, L. Berliner, J. A. Bulkley, C. Jenny, & T. Reid (Eds.), *The APSAC handbook on child maltreatment* (pp. 175–191). Thousand Oaks, CA: Sage.

Murray, J. P. (1995). Children and television violence. *Kansas Journal of Law & Public Policy, 4,* 7–14.

Murray, L., & Trevarthen, C. (1986). The infant's role in mother-infant communication. *Journal of Child Language, 13,* 15–29.

Mussen, P. H., & Jones, M. C. (1957). Self-concepts, motivations, and interpersonal attitudes of late and early maturing boys. *Child Development, 28,* 243–256.

Muuss, R. E. (1998). Marcia's expansion of Erikson's theory of identity formation. In R. E. Muuss & H. D. Porton (Eds.), *Adolescent behavior and society* (pp. 260–270). New York: McGraw-Hill.

Myers, B. J. (1984). Mother-infant bonding: The status of this critical-period hypothesis. *Developmental Review, 4,* 240–274.

Nadder, T. S., Silberg, J. L., Eaves, L. J., Maes, L. J., & Meyer, J. M. (1998). Genetic effects on ADHD symptomatology in 7- to 13-year-old twins. *Behavioral Genetics, 28,* 83–99.

Nagy, W. E., Anderson, R. C., & Herman, P. A. (1987). Learning word meanings from context during normal reading. *American Educational Research Journal, 24,* 237–270.

Nash, J. M. (1997, February 3). Fertile minds. *Time,* pp. 49–62.

Nathanieisz, P. W. (1995). The role of basic science in preventing low birth weight. *The Future of Children, 5,* 57–70.

National Academy of Sciences. (1989). *Recommended dietary allowances.* Washington, DC: National Academy Press.

National Association for the Education of Young Children. (1995a). *How to choose a good early childhood program.* Washington, DC: NAEYC.

National Association for the Education of Young Children. (1995b). *What parents should know about school readiness.* Washington, DC: NAEYC.

National Association for the Education of Young Children. (1997). *Developmentally appropriate practice in early childhood programs.* Washington, DC: NAEYC.

National Association for the Education of Young Children. (1998). *Learning to read and write. Young Children, 53,* 30–46.

National Center for Education Statistics. (1993a). *Early childhood: School readiness.* Washington, DC: U.S. Department of Education.

National Center for Education Statistics. (1993b). *National household education survey.* Washington, DC: U.S. Department of Education.

National Center for Education Statistics. (1995). *Student victimization at school.* Washington, DC: U.S. Department of Education.

National Center for Education Statistics. (1996a). *Parent and family involvement in education.* Washington, DC: U.S. Department of Education.

National Center for Education Statistics. (1996b). *Youth indicators, 1996.* Washington, DC: U.S. Department of Education.

National Center for Education Statistics. (1997). *Dropout rates in the United States.* Washington, DC: U.S. Department of Education.

National Center for Education Statistics. (1998). *Condition of education.* Washington, DC: U.S. Department of Education.

National Center for Health Statistics. (1976). *Growth charts.* Washington, DC: National Center for Health Statistics.

National Center for Health Statistics. (1994). *Health, United States, 1993.* Washington, DC: National Center for Health Statistics.

National Center for Health Statistics. (1995a). Advance report of final divorce statistics. *Monthly Vital Statistics Report, 43,* 1–32.

National Center for Health Statistics. (1995b). *Live births and infant deaths by weight at birth.* Washington, DC: National Center for Health Statistics.

National Center for Health Statistics. (1996). *Health, United States, 1995.* Hyattsville, MD: Public Health Service.

National Center for Health Statistics. (1997a). *Cesarean delivery in the United States.* Washington, DC: National Center for Health Statistics.

National Center for Health Statistics. (1997b). *Health, United States, 1996.* Washington, DC: National Center for Health Statistics.

National Center for Health Statistics. (1997c). *Injury chartbook: Health United States, 1996–1997.* Washington, DC: National Center for Health Statistics.

National Center for Health Statistics. (1997d). *Report of final mortality statistics, 1995.* Washington, DC: National Center for Health Statistics.

National Center for Health Statistics. (1998a). *Birth and death: 1997.* Washington, DC: National Center for Health Statistics.

National Center for Health Statistics. (1998b). *Smoking during pregnancy.* Washington, DC: National Center for Health Statistics.

National Center for Injury Prevention and Control. (1996). *Ten leading causes of death, 1994.* Atlanta, GA: NCIPC.

National Center for Missing and Exploited Children. (1994). *Child safety on the information highway and teen safety.* Arlington, VA: National Center for Missing and Exploited Children.

National Center on Addiction and Substance Abuse. (1996). *National survey of American attitudes and substance abuse II*. New York: Columbia University Press.

National Clearinghouse on Child Abuse and Neglect. (1999). *Child abuse and neglect fact sheet*. Washington, DC: NCCAN.

National Diffusion Network. (1993). *Eucational programs that work*. Longmont, CO: Sopris West.

National Down Syndrome Society. (1997). *Down syndrome: General information*. New York: National Down Syndrome Society.

National Highway Traffic Safety Administration. (1995). *Traffic safety facts*. Washington, DC: National Highway Traffic Safety Administration.

National Institute of Mental Health. (1994). *Eating disorders*. Washington, DC: National Institute of Mental Health.

National Institute on Drug Abuse. (1991). *National household survey on drug abuse for 1990*. Bethesda, MD: National Institute on Drug Abuse.

National Institute on Drug Abuse. (1995). *Monitoring the future, 1975–1995* (Vol. I). Washington, DC: National Institute on Drug Abuse.

National Institute on Drug Abuse. (1997). *Preventing drug use among children and adolescents*. Washington, DC: U.S. Government Printing Office.

National Issues Forum. (1989). *The day care dilemma*. Dubuque, IA: Kendall/Hunt Publishing.

National Middle School Association. (1995). *Developmentally responsive middle level schools*. Columbus, OH: National Middle School Association.

National Parents' Resource Institute for Drug Education. (1995). *PRIDE survey*. Bowling Green, KY: National Parents' Resource Institute for Drug Education.

National Parents' Resource Institute for Drug Education. (1997). *PRIDE survey*. Bowling Green, KY: National Parents' Resource Institute for Drug Education.

National Research Council. (1993). *Understanding child abuse and neglect*. Washington, DC: National Academy Press.

National Research Council. (1998). *The new Americans: Economic, demographic, and fiscal effects of immigration*. Washington, DC: National Research Council.

National Telecommunications and Information Administration. (1998). *Falling through the Net II*. Washington, DC: National Telecommunications and Information Administration

Navaez, D., Getz, I., Rest, J. R., & Thoma, S. J. (1999). Individual moral judgment and cultural ideologies, *Developmental Psychology, 35*, 478–488.

Neale, D. C., Smith, D., & Johnson, V. G. (1990). Implementing conceptual change teaching in primary science. *Elementary School Journal, 91*, 109–131.

Negy, C., & Woods, D. J. (1992). The importance of acculturation in understanding research with Hispanic-Americans. *Hispanic Journal of Behavioral Sciences, 14*, 224–227.

Neher, L. S., & Short, J. L. (1998). Risk and protective factors for children's substance use and antisocial behavior following parental divorce. *American Journal of Orthopsychiatry, 68*, 154–161.

Neisser, V. (1979). The concept of intelligence. *Intelligence, 3*, 217–227.

Nelson, C. A., & Bloom, F. E. (1997). Child development and neuroscience. *Child Development, 68*, 970–987.

Nelson, K. (1973). Structure and strategy in learning to talk. *Monographs of the Society for Research in Child Development, 38*, Whole No. 149.

Nelson, K. (1986). *Event knowledge: Structure and function in development*. Hillsdale, NJ: Erlbaum.

Nelson, K. (1993). The psychological and social origins of autobiographical memory. *Psychological Science, 4*, 1–8.

Nelson, K. E. (1981). Individual differences in language development. *Developmental Psychology, 17*, 170–187.

Nelson, S. A. (1980). Factors influencing young children's use of motives and outcomes as moral criteria. *Child Development, 51*, 823–829.

Nelson-Le Gall, S. A. (1985). Motive-outcome matching and outcome foreseeability: Effects on attribution of intentionality and moral judgments. *Developmental Psychology, 21*, 332–337.

Neuman, D. (1991). Technology and equity. *ERIC Digest* (#339400).

Newcomb, A. F., & Bagwell, C. L. (1995). Children's friendship relations: A meta-analytic review. *Psychological Bulletin, 117*, 306–347.

Newcomb, A. F., & Bagwell, C. L. (1998). The developmental significance of children's friendship relations. In W. M. Bukowski, A. F. Newcomb, & W. W. Hartup (Eds.), *The company they keep: Friendships in childhood and adolescence* (pp. 289–312). New York: Cambridge University Press.

Newcomb, A. F., Bukowski, W. M., & Pattee, L. (1993). Children's peer relations: A meta-analytic review of popular, rejected, neglected, controversial, and average sociometric status. *Psychological Bulletin, 113*, 99–128.

Newman, L. F., & Buka, S. L. (1991). Every child a learner. *American Educator, 42*, 27–33.

Newman, L. S. (1991). Why are traits inferred spontaneously? A developmental approach. *Social Cognition, 9*, 221–253.

Newport, E. L. (1990). Maturational constraints on language learning. *Cognitive Science, 14*, 543–560.

Newport, E. L. (1991). Contrasting concepts of the critical period for language. In S. Carey & R. Gelman (Eds.), *The epigenesis of mind: Essays on biology and cognition* (pp. 111–130). Hillsdale, NJ: Erlbaum.

Niaz, M. (1997). How early can children understand some form of "scientific reasoning"? *Perceptual and Motor Skills, 85*, 1272–1274.

NICHD Early Child Care Research Network. (1996, April). *Infant child care and attachment security*. Symposium presented at the NICHD Early Child Care Research Network meeting, Providence, RI.

NICHD Early Child Care Research Network. (1997). Familial factors associated with the characteristics of nonmaternal care for infants. *Journal of Marriage and the Family, 59*, 389–408.

NICHD Early Child Care Research Network. (1998). Early child care and self control, compliance, and problem behavior at twenty-four and thirty-six months. *Child Development, 69*, 1145–1170.

Nicholls, J. G. (1992). Students as educational theorists. In D. Schunk & J. Meece (Eds.), *Student perceptions in the classroom* (pp. 267–286). Hillsdale, NJ: Erlbaum.

Nicolaisen, I. (1988). Concepts and learning among the Punan Bah of Sarawak. In G. Johoda (Ed.), *Acquiring culture: Cross cultural studies of child development* (pp. 193–222). London: Croom Helm.

Nieman, R. H., & Gaithright, J. F. (1981). *The long-term effects of ESEA Title I preschool and all-day kindergarten*. Cincinnati, OH: Cincinnati Public Schools.

Nilzon, K. R., & Palmerus, K. (1997). The influence of familial factors on anxiety and depression in childhood and early adolescence. *Adolescence, 32*, 935–943.

Ninio, A., & Snow, C. E. (1996). *Pragmatic development*. Boulder, CO: Westview Press.

Noller, P. (1994). Relationships with parents in adolescence: Process and outcome. In R. Montemayor & G. R. Adams (Eds.), *Personal relationships during adolescence* (Vol. 6, pp. 37–77). Thousand Oaks, CA: Sage.

Nosphitz, J. D., & King, R. A. (1991). *Pathways of growth: Essentials of child psychiatry.* New York: Wiley.

Nottelmann, E. D., Susman, E. J., Blue, J. H., Inoff-Germain, G. D., Dorn, L. D., Loriaux, D. B., Cutler, G. P., & Chrousos, G. P. (1987). Gonadal and adrenal hormone correlates of adjustment in early adolescence. In R. Lerner & T. Foch (Eds.), *Biological-psychological interactions in early adolescence* (pp. 303–321). Hillsdale, NJ: Erlbaum.

Nozza, R. J. (1995). Estimating the contribution of nonsensory factors to infant-adult differences in behavioral thresholds. *Hearing Research, 91,* 72–77.

Nsamenang, A. B. (1987). A West African perspective. In M. E. Lamb (Ed.), *The father's role: Cross-cultural perspectives* (pp. 273–293). Hillsdale, NJ: Erlbaum.

Nsamenang, A. B. (1992). *Human development in cultural context: A third world perspective.* Newbury Park, CA: Sage.

Nsamenang, A. B., & Laosebikan, S. (1981, April). *Father-child relationship and the development of psychopathology.* Paper presented to the Nigerian Psychological Society Conference, Jos, Nigeria.

Nuechterlein, K. H., Phipps-Yonas, S., Driscoll, R., & Garmezy, N. (1990). Vulnerability factors in children at risk: Anomalies in attentional functioning and social behavior. In J. E. Role & A. S. Masten (Eds.), *Risk and protective factors in the development of psychopathology* (pp. 445–479). New York: Cambridge University Press.

Nurcombe, B. (1994). The validity of the diagnosis of major depression in childhood and adolescence. In W. M. Reynolds & H. F. Johnston (Eds.), *Handbook of depression in children and adolescents* (pp. 61–77). New York: Plenum.

Nyiti, R. M. (1982). The validity of "cultural differences" explanations for cross-cultural variation in the rate of Piagetian cognitive development. In D. Wagner & H. Stevenson (Eds.), *Cultural perspectives on child development* (pp. 167–202). New York: W. H. Freeman.

Oates, R. K., Peacock, A., & Forrest, D. (1985). Long-term effects of nonorganic failure to thrive. *Pediatrics, 75,* 36–40.

Offer, D., Ostrov, E., Howard, K. I., & Atkinson, R. (1988). *The teenage world: Adolescents' self image in ten countries.* New York: Plenum.

Office of Management and Budget. (1995). Standards for the classification of federal data on race and ethnicity. *Federal Register, 60,* 44673–44693.

Ogbu, J. U. (1991). Immigrant and involuntary minorities in comparative perspective. In M. G. Gibson & J. U. Ogbu (Eds.), *Minority status and schooling* (pp. 131–156). New York: Garland.

Ogbu, J. U. (1994). From cultural differences to differences in cultural frame of reference. In P. Greenfield & R. Cocking (Eds.), *Cross-cultural roots of minority child development* (p. 365–391). Hillsdale, NJ: Erlbaum.

Olds, D., Pettitt, L. M., Robinson, J., Henderson, C., Eckenrode, J., Kitzman, H., Cole, B., & Powers, J. (1998). Reducing risks for antisocial behavior with a program of prenatal and early childhood home visitation. *Journal of Community Psychology, 26,* 65–83.

Olweus, D. (1995). Bullying or peer abuse in school: Intervention and prevention. In G. Davies, S. Lloyd-Bostock, M. McMurran, & C. Wilson (Eds.), *Psychology, law, and criminal justice.* Berlin, Germany: Walter De Gruyter.

O'Neill, D. B., & Micheli, L. J. (1988). Overuse injuries in the young athlete. *Clinical Sports Medicine, 7,* 591–610.

Opler, M. E. (1981). "Water has been put on top of his head." In D. Meltzer (Ed.), *Birth* (pp. 189–191). San Francisco: North Point Press.

Orenstein, P. (1994). *School girls.* New York: Anchor Books.

Orr, D. P., Weller, S. C., Satterwhite, B., & Pless, I. B. (1984). Psychosocial implications of chronic illness in adolescents. *Journal of Pediatrics, 104,* 152.

Ortiz, V. (1995). The diversity of Latino families. In R. E. Zambrana (Ed.), *Understanding Latino families* (pp. 18–29). Thousand Oaks, CA: Sage.

Otake, M., & Schull, W. J. (1984). In utero exposure to A-bomb radiation and mental retardation. *British Journal of Radiology, 57,* 409–414.

Overton, W. F. (1998). Developmental psychology: Philosophy, concepts, and methodology. In W. Damon (Ed.), *Handbook of child psychology* (Vol. 1, pp. 107–188). New York: Wiley.

Overton, W. F., & Byrnes, J. P. (1991). Cognitive development. In R. M. Lerner, A. C. Petersen, & J. Brooks-Gunn (Eds.), *Encyclopedia of adolescence* (Vol. 1, pp. 151–156). New York: Garland.

Owens, R. E. (1996). *Language development: An introduction.* Boston: Allyn & Bacon.

Padilla, M. T. (1997, May 14). Tiger Woods helps bring multiracial issue to fore. *Arizona Republic,* pp. 1, 2.

Page, R. M., & Allen, O. (1995). Adolescent perceptions of body weight and weight satisfaction. *Perceptual and Motor Skills, 81,* 81–82.

Paik, H. & Comstock, G. (1994). The effects of television violence on antisocial behavior: A meta-analysis. *Communication Research, 21,* 516–546.

Paikoff, D. F., Luster, T., Villarruel, F. A., & Small, S. (1998). An ecological risk-factor examination of adolescents' sexual activity in three ethnic groups. *Journal of Marriage and the Family, 60,* 660–673.

Paikoff, R. L., & Brooks-Gunn, J. (1991). Do parent-child relationships change during puberty? *Psychological Bulletin, 110,* 47–66.

Paikoff, R. L., Brooks-Gunn, J., & Warren, M. P. (1991). Effects of girls' hormonal status on depressive and aggressive symptoms over the course of one year. *Journal of Youth and Adolescence, 20,* 191–215.

Paikoff, R. L., Collins, W. A., & Laursen, B. (1988). Perceptions of efficacy and legitimacy of parental influence techniques by children and early adolescents. *Journal of Early Adolescence, 8,* 37–52.

Palardy, N., Greening, L., Ott, J., Holderby, A., & Atchinson, J. (1998). Adolescents' health attitudes and adherence to treatment for insulin-dependent diabetes mellitus. *Journal of Developmental and Behavioral Pediatrics, 19,* 31–37.

Paley, V. G. (1987). *Wally's stories: Conversations in the kindergarten.* Cambridge, MA: Harvard University Press

Panneton, R. K., & DeCasper, A. J. (1986, April). *Newborns' postnatal preference for a prenatally experienced melody.* Paper presented at the International Conference on Infant Studies, Los Angeles.

Papini, D. R., & Roggman, L. A. (1992). Adolescent perceived attachment to parents in relation to competence, depression, and anxiety: A longitudinal study. *Journal of Early Adolescence, 12,* 420–440.

Papini, D. R., & Sebby, R. A. (1987). Adolescent pubertal status and affective family relationships: A multivariate assessment. *Journal of Youth and Adolescence, 16,* 1–15.

Paris, S. G., & Cunningham, A. E. (1996). Children becoming students. In D. C. Berliner & R. C. Calfee (Eds.), *Handbook of educational psychology* (pp. 117–147). New York: MacMillan.

Parke, R. D. (1995). Fathers and families. In M. H. Bornstein (Ed.), *Handbook of parenting* (Vol. 3, pp. 27–64). Mahwah, NJ: Erlbaum.

Parke, R. D., & Buriel, R. (1998). Socialization in the family. In W. Damon (Ed.), *Handbook of child psychology* (Vol. 3, 463–552). New York: Wiley.

Parker, B., McFarlane, J., & Socken, K. (1994). Abuse during pregnancy: Effects on maternal complications and birth weight in adult and teenage women. *Obstetrics and Gynecology, 84,* 323–328.

Parker, J. G., & Asher, S. R. (1987). Peer relations and later personal adjustment: Are low-accepted children at risk? *Psychological Bulletin, 102,* 357–389.

Parker, J. G., & Gottman, J. M. (1989). Social and emotional development in a relational context: Friendship interaction from early childhood to adolescence. In T. J. Berndt & G. W. Ladd (Eds.), *Peer relationships in child development* (pp. 95–131). New York: Wiley.

Parker, J. G., Rubin, K. H., Price, J., & De Rosier, M. E. (1995). Peer relationships, child development, and adjustment: A developmental psychopathology perspective. In D. Cicchetti & D. J. Cohen, (Eds.), *Developmental psychopathology* (Vol. 2, pp 96–161). New York: Wiley.

Parker, S., Nichter, M., Vuckovic, N., Sims, C., & Ritenbaugh, C. (1995). Body image and weight concerns among African American and White adolescent females: Differences that make a difference. *Human Organization, 54,* 103–114.

Parkhurst, J. T., & Asher, S. R. (1992). Peer rejection in middle school. *Developmental Psychology, 28,* 231–241.

Parten, M. (1933). Social play among preschool children. *Journal of Abnormal and Social Psychology, 28,* 136–147.

Patterson, C. J. (1992). Children of lesbian and gay parents. *Child Development, 63,* 1025–1042.

Patterson, C. J. (1995). Lesbian mothers, gay fathers, and their children. In A. R. D'Augelli & C. J. Patterson (Eds.), *Lesbian, gay, and bisexual identities over the lifespan* (pp. 262–290). New York: Oxford University Press.

Patterson, C. J., Griesler, P. C., Vaden, N. A., & Kupersmidt, J. B. (1992). Family economic circumstances, life transitions, and children's peer relations. In R. D. Parke & G. W. Ladd (Eds.), *Family-peer relationships: Modes of linkage* (pp. 385–424). Hillsdale, NJ: Erlbaum.

Patterson, C. J., Vaden, N. A., & Kupersmidt, J. B. (1991). Family background, recent life events, and peer rejection during childhood. *Journal of Social and Personal Relationships, 8,* 347–361.

Patterson, G. R. (1982). *Coercive family process.* Eugene, OR: Castalia.

Patterson, G. R., & Dishion, T. J. (1988). Multilevel modes of family process: Traits, interactions, and relationships. In R. Hinde & J. Stevenson-Hinde (Eds.), *Relationships and families: Mutual influences* (pp. 283–310). Oxford, England: Clarendon Press.

Patterson, G. R., Reid, J. B., & Dishion, T. J. (1998). *Antisocial boys.* Eugene, OR: Castalia.

Patterson, G. R., & Stoolmiller, M. (1991). Replications of a dual failure model for boys' depressed mood. *Journal of Consulting and Clinical Psychology, 59,* 491–498.

Patterson, G. R., & Yoerger, K. (1993). Developmental models for delinquent behavior. In S. Hodgins (Ed.), *Crime and mental disorder* (pp. 140–172). Newbury Park, CA: Sage.

Paulson, J. A. (1988). The epidemiology of injuries in adolescents. *Pediatric Annals, 17,* 84–96.

Pearson, J. L., & Ferguson, L. R. (1989). Gender differences in patterns of spatial ability, environmental cognition, and math and English achievement in late adolescence. *Adolescence, 24,* 421–431.

Pelham, W. E., Aronoff, H. R., Midlam, J. K., Shapiro, C. J., Gnagy, E. M., Chronis, A. M., Onyango, A. N., Forehand, G., Nguyen, A., & Waxmonsky, J. (1999). A comparison of Ritalin and Aderall: Efficacy and time-course in children with ADHD. *Pediatrics, 103,* 1–14.

Pelham, W. E., Bender, M. E., Caddell, J., Booth, S., & Moorer, S. H. (1985). Methylphenidate and children with attention deficit disorder: Dose effects on classroom academic and social behavior. *Archives of General Psychiatry, 42,* 948–952.

Pelham, W. E., Milich, R., & Walker, J. L. (1986). Effects of continuous and partial reinforcement and methylphenidate on learning in children with attention deficit disorder. *Journal of Abnormal Psychology, 95,* 319–325.

Pellegrini, A. D., & Landers-Pott, M. (1996). Children, classroom context and activity and attention to tasks. *Emotional and Behavioral Difficulties, 1,* 29–35.

Pellegrini, A. D., & Smith, P. K. (1998). Physical activity play: The nature and function of a neglected aspect of play. *Child Development, 69,* 577–598.

Peracchio, L. A. (1993). Young children's processing of a televised narrative: Is a picture really worth a thousand words? *Journal of Consumer Research, 20,* 281–293.

Perez-Granados, D. R., & Callanan, M. A. (1997). Parents and siblings as early resources for young children's learning in Mexican-descent families. *Hispanic Journal of Behavioral Sciences, 19,* 3–33.

Perner, J. (1989). Higher-order beliefs and intentions in children's understanding of social interaction. In J. W. Astington, P. L. Harris, & D. R. Olson (Eds.), *Developing theories of mind* (pp. 271–294). Cambridge, England: Cambridge University Press.

Perrin, J., Guyer, B., & Lawrence, J. M. (1992). Health care services for children and adolescents. *The Future of Children, 2,* 58–77.

Perrin, J. M., Shayne, M. W., & Bloom, S. R. (1993). *Home and community care for chronically ill children.* New York: Oxford University Press.

Perris, E. E., Myers, N. A., & Clifton, R. K. (1990). Long-term memory for a single infancy experience. *Child Development, 61,* 1796–1807.

Perry, D. G., Perry, L. C., & Rasmussen, P. (1986). Cognitive social learning mediators of aggression. *Child Development, 57,* 700–711.

Persell, C. H. (1993). Social class and educational equality. In J. A. Banks & C. A. M. Banks (Eds.), *Multiculture education: Issues and perspectives* (pp. 71–89). Boston: Allyn & Bacon.

Perusse, D., Neale, M. C., Heath, A. C., & Eaves, L. J. (1994). Human parental behavior: Evidence for genetic influence and potential implication for gene-culture transmission. *Behavioral Genetics, 24,* 327–335.

Peskin, H. (1973). Influence of the developmental schedule of puberty on learning and ego development. *Journal of Youth and Adolescence, 2,* 273–290.

Peters, H. E., Argys, L. M., Maccoby, E. E., & Mnookin, R. H. (1993). Enforcing divorce settlements: Evidence from child support compliance and award modifications. *Demography, 30,* 719–735.

Petersen, A. C. (1987). The nature of biological-psychosocial interactions: The sample case of early adolescence. In R. M. Lerner & T. T. Foch (Eds.), *Biological-psychological interactions in early adolescence* (pp. 35–61). Hillsdale, NJ: Erlbaum.

Petersen, A. C. (1988). Adolescent development. *Annual Review of Psychology, 39,* 583–607.

Petersen, A. C., & Taylor, B. (1980). The biological approach to adolescence: Biological change and psychological adaptation. In J. Adelson (Ed.), *Handbook of adolescent psychology.* New York: Wiley.

Peterson, G. W. (1986). Parent-youth power dimensions and the behavior autonomy of adolescents. *Journal of Adolescent Research, 1,* 231–249.

Peterson, G. W. (1995). The need for common principles in prevention programs for children, adolescents, and families. *Journal of Adolescent Research, 10,* 470–485.

Peterson, G. W., & Haan, D. (1999). Socializing children and parents in families. In M. Sussman, S. Steinmetz, & G. W. Peterson (Eds.), *Handbook of marriage and the family* (pp. 455–501). New York: Plenum.

Peterson, G. W., & Leigh, G. K. (1990). The family and social competence in adolescence. In T. P. Gullotta & G. R. Adams (Eds.), *Developing social competency in adolescence* (Vol. 3, pp. 97–138). Newbury Park, CA: Sage.

Peterson, J., Moore, K. A., & Furstenburg, F. F. (1984, August). *Media preferences of sexually active teens: A preliminary analysis.* Paper presented at the meeting of the American Psychological Association, Toronto, Canada.

Peterson, J. L., & Zill, N. (1986). Parent-child relationships and behavior problems in children. *Journal of Marriage and the Family, 48,* 295–307.

Pettegrew, J., Lewis, L. A., Brown, J. D., Schulze, L., Zook, K. B., Perry, I., Rose, T., & Ledbetter, J. (1995). Music videos and rap music: Cultural conflict and control in the age of the image. In G. Dines & J. M. Humez (Eds.), *Gender, race, and class in media* (pp. 479–544). Thousand Oaks, CA: Sage.

Pettit, G. S., Bates, J. E., & Dodge, K. A. (1997). Supportive parenting, ecological context, and children's adjustment. *Child Development, 68,* 908–923.

Phelps, L. A., Johnston, L. S., Jimenesez, D. P., Wilczenski, F. L., Andrea, R. K., & Healy, R. W. (1993). Figure preference, body dissatisfaction, and body distortion in adolescence. *Journal of Adolescent Research, 8,* 297–310.

Phillips, D., & Howes, C. (1987). Indicators of quality in child care. In D. Phillips (Ed.), *Quality in child care: What does research tell us?* (pp. 1–20). Washington, DC: NAEYC.

Phillips, D., Lande, J., & Goldberg, M. (1990). The state of childcare regulation: A comparative analysis. *Early Childhood Research Quarterly, 5,* 151–179.

Phillips, D., McCartney, K., & Scarr, S. (1987). Child-care quality and children's social development. *Developmental Psychology, 23,* 537–543.

Phinney, J. S. (1996). Understanding ethnic diversity: The role of ethnic identity. *American Behavioral Scientist, 40,* 143–152.

Phinney, J. S., Cantu, C. L., & Kurtz, D. A. (1997). Ethnic and American identity as predictors of self esteem among African American, Latino, and White adolescents. *Journal of Youth and Adolescence, 26,* 165–185.

Phinney, J. S., & Devich-Navarro, M. (1997). Variations in bicultural identification among African Americans and Mexican Americans. *Journal of Research on Adolescence, 7,* 3–32.

Phinney, J. S., DuPont, S., Espinosa, C., Revill, J., & Sanders, K. (1994). Ethnic identity and American identification among ethnic minority youths. In A. M. Bouvy & F. J. R. van de Vijver (Eds.), *Journeys into cross-cultural psychology* (pp. 167–183). Amsterdam: Swets & Zeitlinger.

Phinney, J. S., & Rosenthal, D. A. (1992). Ethnic identity in adolescence. In G. R. Adams & T. P. Gullotta (Eds.), *Adolescent identity formation* (Vol. 4, pp. 145–172). Newbury Park, CA: Sage.

Piaget, J. (1952). *The origins of intelligence in children.* New York: International Universities Press.

Piaget, J. (1963). *The origins of intelligence in children* (M. Cook, Trans.). New York: W. W. Norton. (Original work published 1936)

Piaget, J. (1965). *The moral judgment of the child.* New York: Free Press. (Original work published 1932)

Piaget, J. (1969). *The child's conception of time* (A. J. Pomerans, Trans.). London: Routledge and Kegan Paul. (Original work published 1946)

Piaget, J. (1971). *Biology and knowledge.* Chicago: University of Chicago Press.

Piaget, J. (1972). Intellectual evolution from adolescence to adulthood. *Human Development, 15,* 1–12.

Piaget, J. (1977). *The development of thought.* New York: Viking.

Piaget, J., & Inhelder, B. (1958). *The growth of logical thinking from childhood to adolescence.* New York: Basic Books.

Pianta, R. C., & Nimetz, S. L. (1991). Relationships between children and teachers: Associations with classroom and home behavior. *Journal of Applied Developmental Psychology, 12,* 379–393.

Pipher, M. (1994). *Reviving Ophelia.* New York: Grosset/Putnam.

Plimpton, C. E., & Regimbal, C. (1992). Differences in motor proficiency according to gender and race. *Perceptual and Motor Skills, 74,* 399–402.

Plomin, R. (1994). *Genetics and experience: The interplay between nature and nurture.* Thousand Oaks, CA: Sage.

Plomin, R., DeFries, J. C., & McClearn, G. E. (1990). *Behavioral genetics: A primer.* New York: W. H. Freeman.

Plomin, R., DeFries, J. C., McClearn, G. E., & Rutter, M. (1997). *Behavioral genetics.* New York: W. H. Freeman & Co.

Plomin, R., Fulker, D. W., Corley, R., & DeFries, J. C. (1997). Nature, nurture, and cognitive development from 1 to 16 years: A parent-offspring adoption study. *Psychological Science, 8,* 442–447.

Plomin, R., Nitz, K., & Rowe, D. C. (1990). Behavior genetics and aggressive behavior in childhood. In M. Lewis & S. Miller (Eds.), *Handbook of development psychology* (pp. 119–133). New York: Plenum.

Plumb, P., & Cowan, G. (1984). A developmental study of stereotyping and androgynous activity preference of tomboys, nontomboys, and males. *Sex Roles, 10,* 703–712.

Plunkett, J. W., Meisels, S. J., Stiefel, G. S., Pasick, P. L., & Roloff, D. W. (1986). Patterns of attachment among preterm infants of varying biological risk. *Journal of the American Academy of Child Psychiatry, 25,* 794–800.

Polit, D. F., & Falbo, T. (1987). Only children and personality development: A quantitative review. *Journal of Marriage and the Family, 49,* 309–325.

Pollitt, E., Golub, M., Gorman, K., Grantham-McGregor, S., Levitsky, D., Schurch, B., Strupp, B., & Wachs, T. (1996). A recommendation of the effects of undernutrition on children's biological, psychosocial, and behavioral development. *Society for Research in Child Development Social Policy Report, 10,* 1–23.

Pomerantz, E. M., Ruble, D. N., Frey, K. S., & Greulich, F. (1995). Meeting goals and confronting conflict: Children's changing perceptions of social comparison. *Child Development, 66,* 723–738.

Pooler, W. S. (1991). Sex of child preferences among college students. *Sex Roles, 25,* 569–576.

Pope, A. W., & Bierman, K. L. (1999). Predicting adolescent peer problems and antisocial activities: The relative roles of aggression and dysregulation. *Developmental Psychology, 35,* 335–346.

Popenoe, D. (1993). American family decline, 1960–1990: A review and appraisal. *Journal of Marriage and the Family, 55,* 527–542.

Popkin, B. M., & Udry, J. R. (1998). Adolescent obesity increases significantly in second and third generation U.S. immigrants. *Journal of Nutrition, 128,* 701–706.

Porac, C., Coren, S., & Searleman, A. (1986). Environmental factors in hand preference formation. *Behavior Genetics, 16,* 251–261.

Porter, R. H., Cernoch, J. M., & McLaughlin, F. J. (1983). Maternal recognition of neonates through olfactory cues. *Physiology and Behavior, 30,* 151–154.

Porter, R. H., Makin, J. W., Davis, L. B., & Christensen, K. M. (1992). Breast-fed infants respond to olfactory cues from their own mother and unfamiliar lactating females. *Infant Behavior and Development, 15,* 85–93.

Posada, G., Gao, Y., Wu, F., Posada, R., Tascon, M., Schoelmerich, A., Sagi, A., Kondo-Ikemura, K., Haaland, W., & Synnevaag, B. (1995). The secure-base phenomenon across cultures: Children's behavior, mothers' preferences, and experts' concepts. In E. Waters, B. Vaughan, G. Posada, & K. Kondo-Ikemura (Eds.), *Caregiving, cultural, and cognitive perspectives on secure-base behavior and working models* (pp. 27–48). Chicago: Society for Research in Child Development.

Posner, J. K., & Vandell, D. L. (1994). Low-income children's after-school care: Are there beneficial effects of after-school programs? *Child Development, 65,* 440–456.

Potts, R., Doppler, M., & Hernandez, M. (1994). Effects of television content on physical risk-taking in children. *Journal of Experimental Child Psychology, 58,* 321–331.

Poulin, F., Cillessen, A. H. N., Hubbard, J. A., Coie, J. D., et al. (1997). Children's friends and behavioral similarity in two social contexts. *Social Development, 6,* 224–236.

Powell, G. F., Low, J. F., & Speers, M. A. (1987). Behavior as a diagnostic aid in failure to thrive. *Journal of Developmental Behavioral Pediatrics, 8,* 18–24.

Power, A. R., & Power, F. C. (1992). A raft of hope: Democratic education and the challenge of pluralism. *Journal of Moral Education, 21,* 193–205.

Power, F. C., Higgins, A., & Kohlberg, L. (1989). *Lawrence Kohlberg's approach to moral education.* New York: Columbia University Press.

Power, F. C., & Makogon, T. A. (1995). *The just community approach to care.* South Bend, IN: Notre Dame University Press.

Power, T. G., McGrath, M. P., Hughes, S. O., & Manire, S. H. (1994). Compliance and self-assertion: Young children's responses to mothers versus fathers. *Developmental Psychology, 30,* 980–989.

Pransky, J. (1991). *Prevention: The critical need.* Springfield, MO: Burrell Foundation.

Prectl, H. F. R., & Beintema, D. (1965). *The neurological examination of the full-term newborn infant.* London: William Heinemann Medical Books.

President's Council on Physical Fitness and Sports. (1997). *Physical activity and sport in the lives of young girls: Physical and mental health dimensions from an interdisciplinary approach.* Washington, DC: U.S. Department of Health and Human Services.

Pressley, M. (1998). *Reading instruction that works: The case for balanced teaching.* New York: Guilford.

Price, D. W. W., & Goodman, G. S. (1990). Visiting the wizard: Children's memory for a recurring event. *Child Development, 61,* 664–680.

Prugh, D. G., Staub, E. M., Sands, H. H., Kirschbaum, R. M., & Lenihan, E. A. (1953). A study of the emotional reactions of children in families to hospitalization and illness. *American Journal of Orthopsychiatry, 23,* 70–106.

Prysak, M., & Castronova, F. C. (1998). Elective induction versus spontaneous labor. *Obstetrics and Gynecology, 92,* 47–52.

Public Health Service. (1995). *Precocious puberty.* Washington, DC: Public Health Service.

Public Health Service. (1996a). *Health United States, 1995.* Washington, DC: Public Health Service.

Public Health Service (1996b). *Sexually transmitted disease surveillance, 1995.* Washington, DC: Public Health Service.

Puig-Antich, J., Geotz, D., Davies, M., Kaplan, T., Davies, S., Ostrow, L., Asnis, L., Toomey, J., Iyengar, S., & Ryan, N. (1989). A controlled family history study of prepubertal major depressive disorder. *Archives of General Psychiatry, 46,* 406–418.

Pulos, S., & Linn, M. C. (1981). Generality of the controlling variables scheme in early adolescence. *Journal of Early Adolescence, 1,* 26–37.

Putallaz, M., & Wasserman, A. (1990). Children's entry behavior. In S. R. Asher & J. D. Coie (Eds.), *Peer rejection in childhood* (pp. 60–89). Cambridge, England: Cambridge University Press.

Quay, H. C. (1988). The behavioral reward and inhibition system in childhood behavior disorder. In L. M. Bloomingdale (Ed.), *Attention deficit disorder* (Vol. 3, pp. 176–186). Oxford, England: Pergamon.

Radke-Yarrow, M., & Sherman, T. (1990). Hard growing: Children who survive. In J. Rolf, A. S. Masten, D. Cicchetti, K. H. Nuechterlein, & S. Weintraub (Eds.), *Risk and protective factors in the development of psychopathology* (pp. 97–119). Cambridge, England: Cambridge University Press.

Raeff, C. (1997). Cultural values, children's social interactions, and the development of an American individualistic self. *Developmental Review, 17,* 205–238.

Raffaelli, M., Bogenschneider, K., & Flood, M. F. (1998). Parent-teen communication about sexual topics. *Journal of Family Issues, 19,* 315–333.

Ramsey, P. G. (1987). Young children's thinking about ethnic differences. In J. S. Phinney & M. J. Rotheram (Eds.), *Children's ethnic socialization* (pp. 56–72). Beverly Hills, CA: Sage.

Rapport, M. D., Stoner, G., DuPaul, G. J., Birmingham, B. K., & Tucker, S. (1985). Methylphenidate in hyperactive children: Differential effects of dose on academic learning and social behavior. *Journal of Abnormal Child Psychology, 13,* 227–244.

Rastam, M., & Gillberg, C. (1991). The family background in anorexia nervosa: A population-based study. *Journal of the American Academy of Child and Adolescent Psychiatry, 30,* 283–289.

Rathus, S. A., Nevid, J. S., & Fichner-Rathus, L. (1993). *Human sexuality in a world of diversity.* Boston: Allyn & Bacon.

Raudenbush, S. W. (1984). Magnitude of teacher expectancy effects on pupil IQ as a function of the credibility of expectancy induction. *Journal of Educational Psychology, 76,* 85–97.

Raver, C. C., & Zigler, E. F. (1997). New perspectives on Head Start. *Early Childhood Research Quarterly, 12,* 363–385.

Reichman, N. E., & Pagnini, D. L. (1997). Maternal age and birth outcomes. *Family Planning Perspectives, 29,* 268–272.

Reid, J. B., & Eddy, J. M. (1997). The prevention of antisocial behavior: Some considerations in the search for effective interventions. In D. M. Stoff & J. Breiling (Eds.), *Handbook of antisocial behavior* (pp. 343–356). New York: Wiley.

Reinisch, J. M. (1990). *The Kinsey Institute new report on sex: What you must know to be sexually literate.* New York: St. Martin's Press.

Reis, S. M. (1989). Reflections on policy affecting the education of gifted and talented students. *American Psychologist, 44,* 399–408.

Reisman, J. E. (1987). Touch, motion, and proprioception. In P. Salapatek & L. Cohen (Eds.), *Handbook of infant perception* (Vol. 1, pp. 265–303). New York: Academic Press.

Reissland, N. (1988). Neonatal imitation in the first hour of life: Observations in rural Nepal. *Developmental Psychology, 24,* 464–469.

Remafedi, G. (1991). Adolescent homosexuality. In R. M. Lerner, A. C. Petersen, & J. Brooks-Gunn (Eds.), *Encyclopedia of adolescence* (pp. 504–507). New York: Garland.

Renzulli, J. S. (1984). The Triad/Revolving Door system: A research-based approach to identification and programming for the gifted and talented. *Gifted Child Quarterly, 28,* 163–171.

Renzulli, J. S., & McGreevy, A. M. (1986). Twins included and not included in special programs for the gifted. *Roeper Review, 9,* 120–127.

Repacholi, B. M., & Gropnik, A. (1997). Early reasoning about desires: Evidence from 14- and 18-month-olds. *Developmental Psychology, 33,* 12–21.

Resnick, M. D. (1997). *Adolescents and work.* Unpublished data, University of Minnesota.

Resnick, S. M., Berenbaum, S. A., Gottesman, I. I., & Bouchard, T. J., Jr. (1986). Early hormonal influences on cognitive functioning in congenital adrenal hyperplasia. *Developmental Psychology, 22,* 191–198.

Rest, J. R. (1983). Morality. In J. H. Flavell & E. M. Markman (Eds.), *Handbook of child psychology* (Vol. III, pp. 556–629). New York: Wiley.

Reuter, M. A., Conger, R. D., & Ramisetty-Mikler, S. (1999). Assessing the benefits of a parenting skills training program: A theoretical approach to predicting direct and moderating effects. *Family Relations, 48,* 67–77.

Reynolds, A. J. (1998). Resilience among Black urban youth: Prevalence, intervention effects, and mechanisms of influence. *American Journal of Orthopsychiatry, 68,* 84–100.

Reynolds, C. A., Hewitt, J. K., Erickson, M. T., & Silberg, J. L. (1996). The genetics of children's oral reading performance. *Journal of Child Psychology and Psychiatry and Allied Disciplines, 37,* 425–434.

Rheingold, H. L. (1982). Little children's participation in the work of adults: A nascent prosocial behavior. *Child Development, 53,* 114–125.

Rhode, M. (1997). *Sexual orientation.* Seattle: Friends Project.

Rholes, W. S., & Ruble, D. N. (1984). Children's understanding of dispositional characteristics of others. *Child Development, 33,* 550–560.

Rice, C., Koinis, D., Sullivan, K., Tagar-Flusberg, H., & Winner, E. (1997). When 3-year olds pass the appearance-reality test. *Developmental Psychology, 33,* 54–61.

Rice, E. P. (1996). *The adolescent: Development, relationships, and culture.* Boston: Allyn & Bacon.

Rice, M. L. (1990). Preschoolers QUIL: Quick incidental learning of words. In G. ContiRamsden & C. Snow (Eds.), *Children's language* (Vol. 7, pp. 171–195). Hillsdale, NJ: Erlbaum.

Rice, M. L., Hadley, P. A., & Alexander, A. (1993). Social biases toward children with specific language impairment: A correlative causal model of language limitations. *Applied Psycholinguistics, 14,* 445–471.

Rice, M. L., Huston, A. C., Truglio, R. T., & Wright, J. C. (1990). Words from Sesame Street: Learning vocabulary while viewing. *Developmental Psychology, 26,* 421–428.

Richards, H., & Goodman, R. (1996). Are only children different? A study of psychiatric referrals. *Journal of Child Psychology and Psychiatry, 37,* 753–757.

Richards, M. H., Casper, R. C., & Larson, R. (1990). Weight and eating concerns among pre- and young adolescent boys and girls. *Journal of Adolescent Health, 11,* 203–209.

Richards, M. H., Crowe, P. A., Larson, R., & Swarr, A. (1998). Developmental patterns and gender differences in the experience of peer companionship during adolescence. *Child Development, 69,* 154–163.

Richardson, J. G., & Simpson, C. H. (1982). Children, gender, and social structure: An analysis of the contents of letters to Santa Claus. *Child Development, 53,* 429–436.

Richman, N., Stevenson, J. E., & Graham, P. (1982). *Preschool to school: A behavioral study.* London: Academic.

Rieber, R. W., & Hall, M. J. (1998). *The collected works of L. S. Vygotsky.* New York: Plenum.

Robbins, C., & Ehri, L. C. (1994). Reading storybooks to kindergartners helps them learn new vocabulary words. *Journal of Educational Psychology, 86,* 54–64.

Roberts, L. R., Sarigiani, P. A., Petersen, A. C., & Newman, J. L. (1993). Gender differences in the relationship between achievement and self-image during early adolescence. In R. A. Pierce & M. A. Black (Eds.), *Life span development* (pp. 126–139). Dubuque, IA: Kendall/Hunt.

Roberts, W., & Strayer, J. (1996). Empathy, emotional expressiveness, and prosocial behavior. *Child Development, 67,* 449–470.

Robertson, J. A. (1996). Legal uncertainties in human egg donation. In C. B. Cohen (Ed.), *New ways of making babies* (pp. 175–187). Bloomington: Indiana University Press.

Robinson, A., Goodman, S., & O'Brien, D. (1984). Genetic and chromosomal disorders, including inborn errors of metabolism. In C. H. Kempe, H. K. Silver, & D. O'Brien (Eds.), *Current pediatric diagnosis and treatment* (pp. 322–367). Los Altos, CA: Lange Medical.

Robinson, D. L. (1996). *Brain, mind, and behavior: A new perspective on human nature.* Westport, CT: Praeger.

Robinson, J. P. (1981). Television and leisure time. *Journal of Communication, 31,* 120–130.

Roche, A. F. (1979). Secular trends in human growth, malnutrition, and development. *Monographs of the Society for Research in Child Development* (44, Serial no. 179).

Roche, A. M. (1998). Alcohol and drug education: A review of key issues. *Drugs: Education, Prevention, and Policy, 5,* 85–99.

Rodgers, B. R. (1999). Parenting processes related to sexual risk-taking behaviors of adolescent males and females. *Journal of Marriage and the Family, 61,* 99–109.

Rodgers, J. L., Rowe, D. C., & Buster, M. (1998). Social contagion, adolescent sexual behavior, and pregnancy. *Developmental Psychology, 34,* 1096–1113.

Roffey, S., Majors, K., & Tarrant, T. (1997). Friends—who needs them? *Educational and Child Psychology, 14,* 51–56.

Rogoff, B. (1990). *Apprenticeship in thinking: Cognitive development in social context.* New York: Oxford University Press.

Rogoff, B. (1998). Cognition as a collaborative process. In D. Kuhn & R. S. Siegler (Eds.), *Handbook of child psychology* (Vol. 2, pp. 679–744). New York: Wiley.

Rogoff, B., Mistry, J., Goncu, A., & Mosier, C. (1993). Guided participation in cultural activity by toddlers and caregivers. *Monographs of the Society for Research in Child Development* (58, Whole no. 179).

Rohner, R. P. (1986). *The warmth dimension: Foundations of parental acceptance-rejection theory.* Beverly Hills, CA: Sage.

Roopnarine, J. L., Lasker, J., Sacks, M., & Stores, M. (1998). The cultural contexts of children's play. In O. N. Saracho & B. Spodek (Eds.), *Multiple perspectives on play in early childhood education* (pp. 194–219). Albany: State University of New York Press.

Roosa, M. W., & Christopher, F. S. (1990). Evaluation of an abstinence-only adolescent pregnancy prevention program. *Family Relations, 39,* 363–367.

Roosa, M. W., Tein, J., Reinholtz, C., & Angelini, P. J. (1997). The relationship of sexual abuse to teenage pregnancy. *Journal of Marriage and the Family, 59*, 119–130.

Roper Organization. (1993). Survey of March 13–27, 1993. *Roper Reports, 93.* New York: Roper Organization.

Rose, K. J. (1988). *The body in time.* New York: Wiley.

Rose, S. A., & Blank, M. (1974). The potency of context in children's cognition. *Child Development, 45,* 499–502.

Rosenbaum, M. B. (1993). The changing image of the adolescent girl. In M. Sugar (Ed.), *Female adolescent development* (pp. 62–80). New York: Brunner/Mazel Inc.

Rosenblith, J. F. (1992). *In the beginning: Development from conception to age two.* Newbury Park, CA: Sage.

Rosenshine, B., & Meister, C. (1997). Cognitive strategy instruction in reading. In S. A. Stahl & D. A. Hayes (Eds.), *Instructional models in reading* (pp. 85–107). Mahwah, NJ: Erlbaum.

Rosenstein, D., & Oster, H. (1988). Differential facial responses to four basic tastes in newborns. *Child Development, 59,* 1555–1568.

Rosenthal, B. S. (1998). Non-school correlates of dropout: An integrative review of the literature. *Child and Youth Services Review, 20,* 413–433.

Rosenthal, M. K. (1991). Daily experiences of toddlers in three child care settings in Israel. *Child and Youth Care Forum, 20,* 37–58.

Rosenthal, R., & Jacobson, L. (1969). *Pygmalion in the classroom: Teacher expectation and pupils' intellectual development.* New York, Holt, Rinehart and Winston.

Rosenthal, R., & Vandell, D. L. (1996). Quality of care at school-aged child-care programs: Regulatable features, observed experiences, child perspectives, and parent perspectives. *Child Development, 67,* 2434–2445.

Ross, H. S., & Conant, C. L. (1992). The social structure of early conflict: Interaction, relationships, and alliances. In C. U. Shantz & W. W. Hartup (Eds.), *Conflict in child and adolescent development* (pp. 153–186). Cambridge, England: Cambridge University Press.

Rosser, P. L., & Randolph, S. M. (1989). Black American infants: The Howard University normative study. In J. K. Nugent, B. M. Lester, & T. B. Brazelton (Eds.), *The cultural context of infancy* (Vol. 1, pp. 133–165). Norwood, NJ: Ablex.

Rossner, S. (1998). Childhood obesity and adulthood consequences. *Acta Pediatrics, 87,* 1–5.

Rothbart, M. K. (1989). Temperament and development. In G. Kohnstamm, J. Bates, & M. K. Rothbart (Eds.), *Temperament in childhood* (pp. 187–247). Chichester, England: Wiley.

Rotheram-Borus, M. J., & Phinney, J. S. (1990). Patterns of social expectations among Black and Mexican-American children. *Child Development, 61,* 542–556.

Rothstein, R. (1998). Bilingual education: The controversy. *Phi Delta Kappan, 79,* 672.

Roucheleau, B. (1995). Computer use by school-age children. *Journal of Educational Computing Research, 12,* 1–17.

Rousseau, J. J. (1911). *Emile* (B. Foxley, Trans.). London: Dent. (Original work published 1762)

Rovee-Collier, C. K., Enright, M., Lucas, D., Fagan, J., & Gekoski, M. J. (1981). The forgetting of newly acquired and reactivated memories of 3-month-old infants. *Infant Behavior and Development, 4,* 317–331.

Rovee-Collier, C. K., & Fagen, J. W. (1981). The retrieval of memory in early infancy. *Advances in Infancy Research, 1,* 225–254.

Rovee-Collier, C. K., & Shyi, C. W. G. (1992). A functional and cognitive analysis of infant long-term retention. In M. L. Howe, C. J. Brainerd, & V. F. Reyna (Eds.), *Development of long-term retention* (pp. 456–494). New York: Springer-Verlag.

Rovet, J., Netley, C., Keenan, M., Bailey, J., & Stewart, D. (1996). The psychoeducational profile of boys with Klinefelter syndrome. *Journal of Learning Disabilities, 29,* 180–196.

Rowe, D. C. (1995). Genetic and cultural explanations of adolescent risk taking and problem behavior. In R. D. Ketterlinus & M. E. Lamb (Eds.), *Adolescent problem behaviors* (pp. 109–126). Hillsdale, NJ: Erlbaum.

Rowland, T. W. (1991). Effects of obesity on aerobic fitness in adolescent females. *American Journal of Diseases of Children, 145,* 764–768.

Royce, L. (1996, June 19). Grad's degree late, but sweet. *Danbury News-Times.*

Rubin, K. H., & Asendorpf, J. B. (1993). Social withdrawal, inhibition, and shyness in childhood: Conceptual and definitional issues. In K. H. Rubin & J. B. Asendorpf (Eds.), *Social withdrawal, inhibition, and shyness in childhood* (pp. 3–18). Hillsdale, NJ: Erlbaum.

Rubin, K. H., Bukowski, W., & Parker, J. G. (1998). Peer interactions, relationships, and groups. In W. Damon (Ed.), *Handbook of child psychology* (Vol. 3, pp. 619–700). New York: Wiley.

Rubin, K. H., LeMare, L. J., & Lollis, S. (1990). Social withdrawal in childhood: Developmental pathways to peer rejection. In S. R. Asher & J. D. Coie (Eds.), *Peer rejection in childhood* (pp. 217–249). New York: Cambridge University Press.

Ruble, D. N. (1977). Premenstrual symptoms: A reinterpretation. *Science, 197,* 291–292.

Ruble, D. N., & Brooks-Gunn, J. (1982). The experience of menarche. *Child Development, 53,* 1557–1566.

Ruble, D. N., & Dweck, C. S. (1995). Self-perceptions, person conceptions, and their development. In N. Eisenberg (Ed.), *Social development* (Vol. 15, pp. 109–139). Thousand Oaks, CA: Sage.

Ruble, D. N., & Martin, C. L. (1998). Gender development. In W. Damon (Ed.), *Handbook of child psychology* (Vol. 3, pp. 933–1016). New York: Wiley.

Ruff, H. A. (1986). Components of attention during infants' manipulative exploration. *Child Development, 57,* 105–114.

Ruffman, T., Perner, J., Olson, D. R., & Doherty, M. (1993). Reflecting on scientific thinking: Children's understanding of the hypothesis-evidence relation. *Child Development, 64,* 1617–1636.

Rumbaut, R. G. (1994). The crucible within: Ethnic identity, self-esteem and segmented assimilation among children of immigrants. *International Migration Review, 28,* 748–794.

Russ, S. W. (1996). Development of creative process in children. In M. Runco (Ed.), *Creativity from childhood through adulthood: The developmental issues. New Directions for Child Development,* pp. 31–42. San Francisco: Jossey-Bass.

Russell, M., Czarnecki, D. M., Cowan, R., & McPherson, E. (1991). Measures of maternal alcohol use as predictors of development in early childhood. *Alcoholism, 15,* 991–1000.

Rutter, M., Dunn, J., Plomin, R., Simonoff, E., Pickles, A., Maughan, B., Ormel, J., Meyer, J., & Eaves, L. (1997). Integrating nature and nurture: Implications of person-environment correlations and interactions for developmental psychopathology. *Development and Psychopathology, 9,* 335–364.

Ruusuvaara, L. (1997). Adolescent sexuality. In G. Creatsas & G. Mastorakos (Eds.), *Adolescent gynecology and endocrinology* (Vol. 816, pp. 411–413). New York: Academy of Sciences Press.

Ryan, A. S. (1997). The resurgence of breastfeeding in the United States. *Pediatrics, 99,* 1–6.

Ryan, B. A., Adams, G. R., Gullotta, T. P., Weissberg, R. P., & Hampton, R. L. (1995). *The family-school connection.* Thousand Oaks, CA: Sage.

Ryan, K. (1996). Character education in the United States. *Journal for a Just and Caring Education, 2,* 75–84.

Ryan, S. A., Millstein, S. G., & Irwin, C. E. (1996). Puberty questions asked by early adolescents. *Journal of Adolescent Health, 19,* 145–152.

Rydell, A. M., Hagekull, B., & Bohlin, G. (1997). Measurement of two social competence aspects in middle childhood. *Developmental Psychology, 33,* 824–833.

Rymer, R. (1993). *Genie.* New York: HarperPerennial.

Saarni, C., Mumme, D. L., & Campos, J. J. (1998). Emotional development: Action, communication, and understanding. In W. Damon (Ed.), *Handbook of child psychology* (Vol. 3, 237–310). New York: Wiley.

Sabogal, F., Marin, G., & Otero-Sabogal, R. (1987). Hispanic familism and acculturation: What changes and what doesn't? *Hispanic Journal of Behavioral Sciences, 9,* 397–412.

Sacks, C. H., & Mergendoller, J. R. (1997). The relationship between teachers' theoretical orientation toward reading and student outcomes in kindergarten children with different initial reading abilities. *American Educational Research Journal, 34,* 721–739.

Sacks, J. J., Smith, J. D., Kaplan, K. M., Lambert, D. A., Sattin, W., & Sikes, K. (1989). The epidemiology of injuries in Atlanta day-care centers. *Journal of the American Medical Association, 262,* 1641–1645.

Sacks, O. (1970). *The man who mistook his wife for a hat.* New York: Harper & Row.

Sadker, M., & Sadker, D. (1985). Sexism in the schoolroom in the 80's. *Psychology Today, 19,* 54–57.

Sadker, M., & Sadker, D. (1994). *Failing at fairness: How America's schools cheat girls.* New York: Charles Scribner's Sons.

Safer, D. J., & Krager, J. M. (1994). The increased rate of stimulant treatment for hyperactive/inattentive students in secondary schools. *Pediatrics, 94,* 462–464.

Saffran, J. R., Aslin, R. N., & Newport, E. L. (1996). Statistical learning by 8-month-old infants. *Science, 274,* 1926–1928.

Saffron, L. (1996). *What about the children?* New York: Wellington House.

Sagi, A., & Hoffman, H. L. (1976). Empathic distress in the newborn. *Developmental Psychology, 12,* 15–176.

Sagi, A., Van IJzendoorn, M. H., Aviezer, O., Donnell, F., & Mayseless, O. (1994). Sleeping out of home in a kibbutz communal arrangement: It makes a difference for infant-mother attachment. *Child Development, 65,* 992–1004.

Sagi, A., Van IJzendoorn, M. H., Scharf, M., Joels, T., Koren-Karie, N., & Aviezer, O. M. O. (1997). Ecological constraints for intergenerational transmission of attachment. *International Journal of Behavioral Development, 20,* 287–299.

Sahin, N. (1990). Research on Susam Sokagi, the Turkish coproduction. In Children's Television Workshop (Ed.)., *Sesame Street Research* (pp. 68–72). New York: Children's Television Workshop.

St. James-Roberts, I. (1993). Infant crying: Normal development and persistent crying. In I. St. James-Roberts, G. Harris, & D. Messer (Eds.), *Infant crying, feeding, and sleeping* (pp. 7–25). London: Harvester Wheatsheaf.

St. James-Roberts, I., & Halil, T. (1991). Infant crying patterns in the first year: Normative and clinical findings. *Journal of Child Psychology and Psychiatry, 32,* 951–968.

St. James-Roberts, I., & Plewis, I. (1996). Individual differences, daily fluctuations, and developmental changes in amounts of infant waking, fussing, crying, feeding, and sleeping. *Child Development, 67,* 2527–2540.

Salihu, H. M., Boos, R., & Schmidt, W. (1997). A report on 158 cases of transcervical chorionic villus sampling. *Archives of Gynecology and Obstetrics, 259,* 91–95.

Salisbury, C. L., & Palombaro, M. M. (1998). Friends and acquaintances: Evolving relationships in an inclusive elementary school. In L. H. Meyer & H. Park (Eds.), *Making friends: The influence of culture and development* (Vol. 3, pp. 81–104). Baltimore, MD: Brookes Publishing.

Salovey, P., & Sluyter, D. J. (1997). *Emotional development and emotional intelligence.* New York: Basic Books.

Sameroff, A. J. (1987). The social context of development. In N. Eisenberg (Ed.), *Contemporary topics in developmental psychology* (pp. 273–291). New York: Wiley.

Sameroff, A. J. (1989). Principles of development and psychopathology. In A. J. Sameroff & R. N. Emde (Eds.), *Relationship disturbances in early childhood* (pp. 17–32). New York: Basic Books.

Sameroff, A. J., Seifer, R., & Bartko, W. T. (1997). Environmental perspectives on adaptation during childhood and adolescence. In S. S. Luthar & J. A. Burack (Eds.), *Developmental psychopathology* (pp. 507–526). New York: Cambridge University Press.

Sampson, E. E. (1989). The challenge of social change for psychology. Globalization and psychology's theory of the person. *American Psychologist, 44,* 914–921.

Sampson, R. J., & Laub, J. H. (1997). A life course theory of cumulative disadvantage and the stability of delinquency. In T. P. Thronberry (Ed.), *Developmental theories of crime and behavior* (Vol. 7, pp. 133–161). New Brunswick, NJ: Transaction Publishers.

Samuels, C. A., & Ewy, R. (1985). Aesthetic perception of faces during infancy. *British Journal of Developmental Psychology, 3,* 221–228.

Samuels, H. R. (1980). The effect of an older sibling on infant locomotor exploration of a new environment. *Child Development, 51,* 607–609.

Samuelson, L. K., & Smith, L. B. (1998). Memory and attention make smart word learning. *Child Development, 69,* 94–104.

Sander, L., Julia, H., Stechler, G., & Burns, P. (1972). Continuous 24-hour interactional monitoring in infants reared in two caretaking environments. *Psychosomatic Medicine, 34,* 270–282.

Santoli, A. (1988). *New Americans: An oral history.* New York: Ballantine Books.

Sattler, J. M. (1992). *Assessment of children: WISC-III and WPPSI-R supplement.* San Diego: Sattler.

Savin-Williams, R. C. (1991). Gay and lesbian youths. In R. M. Lerner, A. C. Petersen, & J. Brooks-Gunn (Eds.), *Encyclopedia of adolescence* (pp. 385–388). New York: Garland.

Savin-Williams, R. C. (1994). Verbal and physical abuse as stressors in the lives of lesbian, gay male, and bisexual youths: Associations with school problems, running away, substance abuse, prostitution, and suicide. *Journal of Consulting and Clinical Psychology, 62,* 261–269.

Savin-Williams, R. C. (1995). An exploratory study of pubertal maturation timing and self-esteem among gay and bisexual male youths. *Developmental Psychology, 31,* 56–64.

Savin-Williams, R. C., & Cohen, K. M. (1996). Psychosocial outcomes of verbal and physical abuse among lesbian, gay, and bisexual youths. In R. C. Savin-Williams & K. M. Cohen (Eds.), *The lives of lesbians, gays, and bisexuals: Children to adults* (pp. 181–200). Fort Worth, TX: Harcourt Brace College Publishers.

Scahill, L., & deGraft, J. A. (1997). Food allergies, asthma, and attention deficit hyperactivity disorder. *Journal of Child and Adolescent Psychiatric Nursing,* 10, 36–42.

Scardamalia, M. (1977). Information processing capacity and the problem of horizontal decalage: A demonstration using combinatorial reasoning tasks. *Child Development,* 48, 28–37.

Scarr, S. (1998). American child care today. *American Psychologist,* 53, 95–109.

Schaefer, C. E., & DiGeronimo, T. F. (1995, September). Understanding anger. *Child,* 48–55.

Schauble, L. (1990). Belief revision in children: The role of prior knowledge and strategies for generating evidence. *Journal of Experimental Child Psychology,* 49, 31–57.

Schebendach, J., & Shenker, I. R. (1992). Nutrition. In S. B. Friedman, M. Fisher, & S. K. Schonberg (Eds.), *Comprehensive adolescent health care* (pp. 206–212). St. Louis, MO: Quality Medical Publishing Inc.

Schepher-Hughes, N. (1987). Basic strangeness: Maternal estrangement and infant death. In C. Super (Ed.), *The role of culture in developmental disorders* (pp. 131–153). San Diego, CA: Academic Press.

Scherman, A., Goodrich, C., & Kelly, C. (1988). Grandparents as a support system for children. *Elementary School Guidance and Counseling,* 23, 16–22.

Schlottmann, A. (1999). Seeing it happen and knowing how it works: How children understand the relation between perceptual causality and underlying mechanisms. *Developmental Psychology,* 35, 303–317.

Schneider, B. (1993). *Children's social competence in context.* New York: Pergamon Press.

Schneider, W., & Bjorklund, D. F. (1998). Memory. In W. Damon (Ed.), *Handbook of child psychology* (Vol. 2, pp. 467–521). New York: Wiley.

Schothorst, P. F., & van Engeland, H. (1996). Long-term behavioral sequelae of prematurity. *Journal of the American Academy of Child and Adolescent Psychiatry,* 35, 175–183.

Schulenberg, J., Bachman, J. G., Johnston, L. D., & O'Malley, P. M. (1994). *Historical trends in attitudes and preferences regarding family, work, and the future among American adolescents: National data from 1976–1992.* Ann Arbor, MI: Institute for Social Research.

Schulman, C. (1997, January). High energy handful. *Child,* 52–57.

Schulman, M., & Mekler, E. (1985). *Bringing up a moral child.* Reading, MA: Addison-Wesley.

Schultz, R. T., Wright, K., & Schleifer, M. (1986). Assignment of moral responsibility and punishment. *Child Development,* 57, 177–184.

Schuster, B., Ruble, D. N., & Weinert, F. E. (1998). Causal inferences and the positivity bias in children: The role of the covariation principle. *Child Development,* 69, 1577–1596.

Schutte, N. S., Malouff, J. M., Post-Gordon, J. C., & Rodasta, A. L. (1988). Effects of playing video games on children's aggressive and other behaviors. *Journal of Applied Social Psychology,* 18, 103–109.

Schwartz, C. E., Snidman, N., & Kagan, J. (1996). Early childhood temperament as a determinant of externalizing behavior in adolescence. *Development and Psychology,* 8, 527–537.

Schwartz, J. A., Gladstone, T. R. G., & Kaslow, N. J. (1998). Depressive disorders. In T. H. Ollendick & M. Hersen (Eds.), *Handbook of child psychopathology* (pp. 269–289). New York: Plenum.

Schwartz, J. A., Kaslow, N. J., Racusin, G. R., & Carton, E. R. (1998). Interpersonal family therapy for childhood depression. In V. B. Van Hasselt & M. Hersen (Eds.), *Handbook of psychological treatment protocols for children and adolescents* (pp. 109–151). Mahwah, NJ: Erlbaum.

Schwartz, W. (1995). *School dropouts: New information about an old problem.* ERIC Document (No. ED 386 515).

Sebald, H. (1992). *Adolescence: A social psychological analysis.* Englewood Cliffs, NJ: Prentice-Hall.

Sedlak, A. J., & Broadhurst, D. D. (1996). *Executive summary of the Third National Incidence Study of Child Abuse and Neglect.* Washington, DC: U.S. Department of Health and Human Services.

Segall, M. H., Dasen, P. R., Berry, J. W., & Poortinga, Y. H. (1990). *Human behavior in global perspective: An introduction to cross-cultural psychology.* New York: Pergamon Press.

Seidenberg, M. S. (1997). Language acquisition and use: Learning and applying probabilistic constraints. *Science,* 275, 1599–1603.

Seifer, R., & Schiller, M. (1995). The role of parenting sensitivity, infant temperament, and dyadic interaction in attachment theory and assessment. *Monographs of the Society for Research in Child Development,* 60, 146–174.

Seifer, R., Schiller, M., Sameroff, A. J., Resnick, S., et al. (1996). Attachment, maternal sensitivity, and infant temperament during the first year of life. *Developmental Psychology,* 32, 12–25.

Seiffge-Krenke, I. (1993). Close friendship and imaginary companions in adolescence. *New Directions in Child Development,* 60, 73–87.

Seiffge-Krenke, I. (1997). The capacity to balance intimacy and conflict: Differences in romantic relationships between healthy and diabetic adolescents. In S. Shulman & W. A. Collins (Eds.), *Romantic relationships in adolescence* (pp. 53–68). San Francisco: Jossey-Bass.

Sells, C. W., & Blum, R. W. (1996). Morbidity and mortality among U.S. adolescents: An overview of data and trends. *American Journal of Public Health,* 86, 513–519.

Selman, R. L. (1980). *The growth of interpersonal understanding.* New York: Academic Press.

Selman, R. L., Beardslee, W., Schultz, L. H., Krupa, M., & Podorefsky, D. (1986). Assessing adolescent interpersonal negotiation strategies: Toward the integration of structural and functional models. *Developmental Psychology,* 22, 450–459.

Selman, R. L., Lavin, D. R., & Brion-Meisels, S. (1982). Troubled children's use of self-reflection. In F. C. Serafica (Ed.), *Social-cognitive development in context.* London: Methuen.

Serbin, L. A., Sprafkin, C., Elman, M., & Doyle, A. B. (1984). The early development of sex differentiated patterns and social influence *Canadian Journal of Social Science,* 14, 350–363.

Serketich, W. J., & Dumas, J. E. (1997). Adults' perceptions of the behavior of competent and dysfunctional children based on the children's physical appearance. *Behavior Modification,* 21, 457–469.

Sessa, F. M., & Steinberg, L. (1991). Family structure and the development of autonomy during adolescence. *Journal of Early Adolescence,* 11, 38–55.

Setterberg, S. R. (1992). Suicidal behavior and suicide. In S. B. Friedman, M. Fisher, & S. K. Schonberg (Eds.), *Comprehensive adolescent health care* (pp. 862–867). St. Louis, MO: Quality Medical Publishing.

Sex Information and Education Council of the United States. (1997). *Guidelines for comprehensive sexuality education.* New York: SIECUS.

Shavinina, L. (1997). Extremely early high abilities, sensitive periods, and development of giftedness. *High Ability Studies,* 8, 247–258.

Shaw, D., & Winslow, E. B. (1997). Precursors and correlates of antisocial behavior from infancy to preschool. In D. M. Stoff & J. Breiling (Eds.), *Handbook of antisocial behavior* (pp. 148–158). New York: Wiley.

Shedler, J., & Block, J. (1990). Adolescent drug use and psychological health: A longitudinal inquiry. *American Psychologist,* 45, 612–630.

Sheehan, P. W. (1983). Age trends and the correlates of children's television viewing. *Australian Journal of Psychology, 35,* 417–431.

Sheehy, G. (1995). *New passages: Mapping your life across time.* New York: Random House.

Shepard, L. A. (1997). Children are not ready to learn? The invalidity of school readiness testing. *Psychology in the Schools, 34,* 85–97.

Shepard, L. A., & Smith, M. L. (1988). Synthesis of research on school readiness and kindergarten retention. In J. P. Bauch (Ed.), *Early childhood education in the schools* (pp. 88–94). Washington, DC: National Education Association.

Shepardson, D. P., & Pizzini, E. L. (1992). Gender bias in female elementary teachers' perceptions of the scientific ability of students. *Science Education, 76,* 147–163.

Sherrod, L. R., Haggerty, R. J., & Featherman, D. L. (1993). Introduction: Late adolescence and the transition to adulthood. *Journal of Research on Adolescence, 3,* 216–226.

Shettles, L., & Rorvik, D. M. (1984). *How to choose the sex of your baby.* New York: Doubleday.

Shifflett, K., & Cummings, E. M. (1999). A program for educating parents about the effects of divorce and conflict on children. *Family Relations, 48,* 79–89.

Shrum, W., Cheek, N. H., & Hunter, S. M. (1988). Friendship in school: Gender and racial homophily. *Sociology of Education, 61,* 227–239.

Shucard, D. W., Shucard, L. L., & Thomas, D. G. (1987). Sex differences in electrophysiological activity in infancy: Possible implications for language development. In S. U. Philips, S. Steele, & C. Tanz (Eds.), *Language, gender, and sex in a comparative perspective* (pp. 278–295). Cambridge, England: Cambridge University Press.

Shuell, T. J. (1996). Teaching and learning in a classroom context. In D. C. Berliner & R. C. Calfee (Eds.), *Handbook of educational psychology* (pp. 726–764). New York: Simon & Schuster.

Shulman, S., Collins, W. A., & Knafo, D. (1997). Romantic relationships in adolescence—More than casual dating. In S. Shulman & W. A. Collins (Eds.), *Romantic relationships in adolescence* (pp. 105–110). San Francisco: Jossey-Bass.

Shulman, S., Kedem, P., Kaplan, K. J., Sever, I., & Braja, M. (1998). Latchkey children: Potential sources of support. *Journal of Community Psychology, 26,* 185–197.

Shure, M. R. (1982). Interpersonal problem solving: A cog in the wheel of social cognition. In F. C. Serafica (Ed.), *Social-cognitive development in context.* London: Methuen.

Shurkin, J. N. (1992). *Terman's kids.* Boston: Little, Brown.

Shute, N. (1997, November 10). No more hard labor. *U.S. News & World Report,* pp. 92–95.

Shwe, H., & Markman, E. M. (1997). Young children's appreciation of the mental impact of their communicative signals. *Developmental Psychology, 33,* 630–636.

Shweder, R. A., Mahapatra, M., & Miller, J. (1987). Culture and moral development. In J. Kagan & S. Lamb (Eds.), *The emergence of morality in young children* (pp. 130–204). Chicago: University of Chicago Press.

Siegler, R. S. (1998). *Children's thinking.* New York: Prentice Hall.

Sigman, M., Beckwith, L., Cohen, S. E., & Parmelee, A. H. (1989). Stability in the biosocial development of the child born preterm. In M. H. Bornstein & N. A. Krasnegor (Eds.), *Stability and continuity in mental development* (pp. 29–42). Hillsdale, NJ: Erlbaum.

Signorella, M. L., Bigler, R. S., & Liben, L. S. (1993). Developmental differences in children's gender schemata about others: A meta-analytic review. *Developmental Review, 13,* 147–183.

Signorella, M. L., Bigler, R. S., & Liben, L. S. (1998). A meta-analysis of children's memories for own-sex and other-sex information. *Journal of Applied Developmental Psychology, 18,* 429–445.

Signorella, M. L., & Liben, L. S. (1984). Recall and reconstruction of gender-related pictures: Effects of attitudes, task difficulty, and age. *Child Development, 55,* 393–405.

Silber, T. J. (1986). Anorexia nervosa in blacks and Hispanics. *International Journal of Eating Disorders, 5,* 121–128.

Silverberg, S. B., & Gondoli, D. M. (1996). Autonomy in adolescence: A contextual perspective. In G. R. Adams & R. Montemayor (Eds.), *Psychosocial development during adolescence* (Vol. 8, pp. 12–61). Thousand Oaks, CA: Sage.

Silverman, W. K., La Greca, A. M., & Wasserstein, S. (1995). What do children worry about? Worries and their relation to anxiety. *Child Development, 66,* 671–686.

Simeon, D. T., & Grantham-McGregor, S. (1990). Nutritional deficiencies and children's behavior and mental development. *Nutrition Research Reviews, 3,* 1–24.

Simmons, R. G., & Blyth D. A. (1987). *Moving into adolescence: The impact of pubertal change and school context.* New York: Aldine de Gruyter.

Simmons, R. G., Burgeson, R., Carlton-Ford, S., & Blyth, D. (1987). The impact of cumulative change in early adolescence. *Child Development, 58,* 1220–1234.

Simmons, R. G. & Zhou, Y. (1994). Parental supervision, family structure, and adolescent development. In D. J. Smith (Ed.), *Psychosocial development in children and youth* (pp. 233–269). New York: Wiley.

Simmons Marketing Research. (1998). *Simmons Teen Age Research Study.* New York: Simmons Marketing Research.

Simon, W., & Gagnon, J. H. (1986). Sexual scripts: Permanence and change. *Archives of Sexual Behavior, 15,* 97–120.

Simons, R. L., Johnson, C., & Conger, R. D. (1994). Harsh corporal punishment versus quality of parental involvement as an explanation of adolescent maladjustment. *Journal of Marriage and the Family, 56,* 591–607.

Simonton, D. K. (1994). *Greatness: Who makes history and why.* New York: Guilford Press.

Simpson, J. L., & Elias, S. (1994). Fetal cells in maternal blood: Overview and historical perspective. *Annals of the New York Academy of Sciences, 731,* 1–8.

Singer, J. L., & Singer, D. G. (1998). *Barney and Friends* as entertainment and education. In J. K. Asamen & G. L. Berry (Eds.), *Research paradigms, television, and social behavior* (pp. 305–367). Thousand Oaks, CA: Sage.

Singer, R. S. (1992). Physical activity and psychological benefits: A position statement of the International Society of Sport Psychology (ISSP). *The Sports Psychologist, 6,* 199–203.

Singer, S., & Hilgard, H. R. (1978). *The biology of people.* San Francisco: W. H. Freeman.

Sizer, F., & Whitney, E. (1997). *Nutrition: Concepts and controversies.* Belmont, CA: West.

Skinner, B. F. (1957). *Verbal behavior.* New York: Appleton-Century-Crofts.

Skinner, E. A., & Wellborn, J. G. (1997). Children's coping in the academic domain. In S. A. Wolchik & I. N. Sandler (Eds.), *Handbook of children's coping* (pp. 387–422). New York: Plenum.

Skuse, D., Wolke, D., & Reilly, S. (1992). Failure to thrive: Clinical and developmental aspects. In H. Remschmidt & M. H. Schmidt (Eds.), *Developmental psychopathology* (pp. 46–71). Goettingen, Germany: Hogrefe & Huber.

Slade, A., & Wolf, D. P. (1994). *Children at play: Clinical and developmental approaches to meaning and representation.* New York: Oxford University Press.

Slap, G. B. (1991). Injury during adolescence, risk factors for. In R. M. Lerner, A. C. Petersen, & J. Brooks-Gunn (Eds.), *Encyclopedia of adolescence* (pp. 549–556). New York: Garland.

Slater, A., Mattock, A., Brown, E., & Bremner, G. J. (1991). Form perception at birth: Cohen and Younger revisited. *Journal of Experimental Child Psychology, 51,* 395–406.

Slavin, R. E. (1997). When does cooperative learning increase student achievement? In E. Dubinsky & D. Mathews (Eds.), *Readings in cooperative learning for undergraduate mathematics* (pp. 71–84). Washington, DC: The Mathematical Association of America.

Sleep, J. (1993). Physiology and management of the second stage of labor. In V. R. Bennett & L. K. Brown (Eds.), *Myles textbook for midwives* (pp. 199–215). London: Churchill Livingstone.

Slotkin, T. A., Kudlacz, E. M., Hou, Q. C., & Seidler, F. J. (1990). Maturation of the sympathetic nervous system: Role in neonatal physiological adaptations and in cellular development of peripheral tissues. In J. M. Cuezva, A. M. Pascual-Leone, & M. S. Patel (Eds.), *Endocrine and biochemical development of the fetus and neonate* (pp. 67–75). New York: Plenum.

Slotkin, T. A., & Seidler, F. J. (1989). Catecholamines and stress in the newborn. In O. Zinder & S. Breznitz (Eds.), *Molecular biology of stress* (pp. 133–142). New York: A. R. Liss.

Small, M. Y. (1990). *Cognitive development.* San Diego, CA: Harcourt Brace Jovanovich.

Small, S. S., Eastman, G., & Cornelius, S. (1988). Adolescent autonomy and parental stress. *Journal of Personality and Social Psychology, 17,* 377–391

Smetana, J. G. (1988a). Adolescents' and parents' conceptions of parental authority. *Child Development, 59,* 321–335.

Smetana, J. G. (1988b). Concepts of self and social convention: Adolescents' and parents' reasoning about hypothetical and actual family conflicts. In M. R. Gunnar & W. A. Collins (Eds.), *Development during the transition to adolescence. Minnesota symposium on child psychology* (Vol. 21, 79–121). Hillsdale, NJ: Erlbaum.

Smith, B. A., & Blass, E. M. (1996). Taste-mediated calming in premature, preterm, and full-term human infants. *Developmental Psychology, 32,* 1084–1089.

Smith, F. (1992). Learning to read: The never-ending debate. *Phi Delta Kappan, 74,* 432–441.

Smith, G. A., Bowman, M. J., Luria, J. W., & Shields, B. J. (1997). Babywalker-related injuries continue despite warning labels and public education. *Pediatrics, 100,* 1–7.

Smith, G. A., & Shields, B. J. (1998). Trampoline-related injuries to children. *Archives of Pediatric and Adolescent Medicine, 152,* 694–699.

Smith, P. K., & Green, M. (1974). Aggressive behavior in English nurseries and playgroups. Sex differences and response of adults. *Child Development, 45,* 211–214.

Snarey, J. R. (1985). Cross-cultural universality of social-moral development: A critical review of Kohlbergian research. *Psychological Bulletin, 92,* 202–232.

Snow, C. E. (1990). Building memories: The ontogeny of autobiography. In D. Cicchetti & M. Beeghly (Eds.), *The self in transition* (pp. 213–242). Chicago: University of Chicago Press.

Snow, C. W. (1989). *Infant development.* Englewood Cliffs, NJ: Prentice Hall.

Snyder, J., Schrepferman, L., & St. Peter, C. (1997). Origins of antisocial behavior: Negative reinforcement and affect dysregulation of behavior as socialization mechanisms in family interaction. *Behavior Modification, 21,* 187–215.

Soberon, H. (1996). *Latino, Hispanic, both, neither?* Gainesville, FL: University of Florida.

Solis, J. (1995). The status of Latino children and youth: Challenges and prospects. In R. E. Zambrama (Ed.), *Understanding Latino families* (pp. 62–84). Thousand Oaks, CA: Sage.

Sonenstein, F. L., Ku, L., Lindberg, L. D., Turner, C. F., & Pleck, J. H. (1998). Changes in sexual behavior and condom use among teenaged males. *American Journal of Public Health, 88,* 956–959.

Sonis, W. A., Comite, F., Blue, J., Pescovitz, O. H., Rahn, C. W., Hench, K. D., Cutler, G. B., Jr., Loriaux, D. L., & Klein, R. P. (1985). Behavior problems and social competence in girls with precocious puberty. *Journal of Pediatrics, 106,* 156–160.

Soriano, F. I. (1993). Cultural sensitivity and gang intervention. In A. P. Goldstein & C. R. Huff (Eds.), *The gang intervention handbook* (pp. 421–462). Champaign, IL: Research Press.

Soriano, F. I. (1994). U.S. Latinos. In L. D. Eron, J. H. Gentry, & P. Schlegel (Eds.), *Reason to hope: A psychosocial perspective on violence and youth* (pp. 119–132). Washington, DC: American Psychological Association.

Sotos, J. F. (1997). Genetic-disorder with overgrowth. *Clinical Pediatrics, 36,* 37–49.

Spear-Swerling, L., & Sternberg, R. J. (1994). The road not taken: An integrative theoretical model of reading disability. *Journal of Learning Disability, 27,* 91–103.

Spelke, E. S., Breinlinger, K., Macomber, J., & Jacobson, K. (1992). Origins of knowledge. *Psychological Review, 99,* 605–632.

Spencer, M. B. (1990). Development of minority children: An introduction. *Child Development, 61,* 267–269.

Spencer, M. B., & Dornbusch, S. M. (1990). Challenges in studying minority youth. In S. S. Feldman & G. R. Elliott (Eds.), *At the threshold* (pp. 123–146). Cambridge, MA: Harvard University Press.

Spencer, M. B., & Markstrom-Adams, C. (1990). Identity processes among racial and ethnic minority children in America. *Child Development, 61,* 290–310.

Spergel, I. A. (1990). *Perceptions of former youth gang influentials.* Rockville, MD: Juvenile Justice Clearinghouse

Spergel, I. A., & Curry, G. D. (1993). The National Youth Gang Survey. In A. P. Goldstein & C. R. Huff (Eds.), *The gang intervention handbook* (pp. 359–400). Champaign, IL: Research Press.

Spergel, I. A., Ross, R. E., Curry, G. D., & Chance, R. (1989). *Youth gangs: Problems and response.* Washington, DC: Office of Juvenile Justice and Delinquency Prevention.

Sprafkin, J., Gadow, K. D., & Abelman, R. (1992). *Television and the exceptional child: A forgotten audience.* Hillsdale, NJ: Erlbaum.

Sprague, J., Sugai, G., & Walker, H. (1998). Antisocial behavior in schools. In T. S. Watson & F. M. Gresham (Eds.), *Handbook of child behavior therapy* (pp. 451–474). New York: Plenum.

Sprecher, S. (1989). Premarital sexual standards for different categories of individuals. *Journal of Sex Research, 26,* 232–248.

Squires, P. C. (1927). Wolf children of India. *American Journal of Psychology, 38,* 313–315.

Sroufe, L. A. (1977). *Knowing and enjoying your baby.* Englewood Cliffs, NJ: Prentice-Hall.

Sroufe, L. A. (1989). Relationships, self, and individual adaptation. In A. J. Sameroff & R. N. Emde (Eds.), *Relationship disturbances in early* childhood: *A developmental approach* (pp. 70–96). New York: Basic Books.

Sroufe, L. A. (1990). An organizational perspective on the self. In D. Cicchetti & M. Beeghly (Eds.), *The self in transition: Infancy to childhood* (pp. 281–307). Chicago: University of Chicago Press.

Sroufe, L. A. (1996). *Emotional development*. Cambridge, England: Cambridge University Press.

Sroufe, L. A., Bennett, C., Englund, M., & Urban, J. (1993). The significance of gender boundaries in preadolescence: Contemporary correlates and antecedents of boundary violation and maintenance. *Child Development, 64,* 455–466.

Sroufe, L. A., & Waters, E. (1976). The ontogenesis of smiling and laughing: A perspective on the organization of development in infancy. *Psychological Review, 83,* 173–189.

Stack, D. M., & LePage, D. E. (1996). Infants' sensitivity to manipulations of maternal touch during face-to-face interactions. *Social Development, 5,* 41–55.

Stafford, L., & Bayer, C. L. (1993). *Interaction between parents and children.* Newbury Park, CA: Sage.

Stager, J. M., Ritchie, B. A., & Robertshaw, D. (1984). Reversal of oligo/amenorrhea in collegiate distance runners. *New England Journal of Medicine, 310,* 51.

Stang, H. J., Snellman, L. W., Condon, L. M., Conroy, M. M., Liebo, R., Brodersen, L., & Gunnar, M. R. (1997). Beyond dorsal penile nerve block: A more humane circumcision. *Pediatrics, 100,* 1–6.

Stangor, C., & McMillan, D. (1992). Memory for expectancy-congruent and expectancy-incongruent information. *Psychological Bulletin, 111,* 42–61.

Stangor, C., & Ruble, D. N. (1987). Development of gender role knowledge and gender constancy. In L. S. Liben and M. L. Signorella (Eds.), *Children's gender schemata* (pp. 5–22). San Francisco: Jossey-Bass.

Stangor, C., & Ruble, D. N. (1989). Differential influences on gender schemata and gender constancy on children's information processing and behavior. *Social Cognition, 7,* 353–372.

Stanley, B. K., Weikel, W. J., & Wilson, J. (1986). The effects of father absence on interpersonal problem-solving skills of nursery school children. *Journal of Counseling and Development, 64,* 383–385.

Stanley, J. C., & Benbow, C. P. (1982). Huge sex ratios at upper end. *American Psychologist, 37,* 972.

Stanley, J. C., & Benbow, C. P. (1983). SMPY's first decade: Ten years of posing problems and solving them. *Journal of Special Education, 17,* 11–25.

Stark, K. D., Rouse, L. W., & Kurowski, C. (1994). Psychological treatment approaches for depression in children. In W. M. Reynolds & H. F. Johnston (Eds.), *Handbook of depression in children and adolescents* (pp. 275–307). New York: Plenum.

Starsen, M. (1991, February 25). A team spawns pride in a land of despair. *The New York Times,* A1, A16.

State v. Michaels, 136 N.J. 299, 642 A.2d 489 (New Jersey, 1994).

Stattin, H., & Magnusson, D. (1990). *Pubertal maturation in female development.* Hillsdale, NJ: Erlbaum.

Status of Women Council. (1994). *Girls and science.* Yellowknife, NWF: Status of Women Council.

Steele, C. M. (1997). A threat in the air: How stereotypes shape intellectual identity and performance. *American Psychologist, 52,* 613–629.

Steffe, L. P., & Gale, J. E. (1995). *Constructivism in education.* Hillsdale, NJ: Erlbaum.

Stein, D. M., & Reichert, P. (1990). Extreme dieting behaviors in early adolescence. *Journal of Early Adolescence, 10,* 108–121.

Stein, N. L., & Trabasso, T. (1989). Children's understanding of changing emotional states. In C. Saarni & P. L. Harris (Eds.), *Children's understanding of emotion* (pp. 50–77). New York: Cambridge University Press.

Steinberg, L. (1986). Latchkey children and susceptibility to peer pressure: An ecological analysis. *Developmental Psychology, 22,* 433–439.

Steinberg, L. (1987). Impact of puberty on family relations: Effects of pubertal status and pubertal timing. *Developmental Psychology, 23,* 451–460.

Steinberg, L. (1988). Reciprocal relation between parent-child distance and pubertal maturation. *Developmental Psychology, 24,* 122–128.

Steinberg, L. (1989). Pubertal maturation and parent-adolescent distance. In G. R. Adams & R. Montemayor (Eds.), *Biology of adolescent behavior and development* (pp. 71–97). Newbury Park, CA: Sage.

Steinberg, L. (1990). Autonomy, conflict, and harmony in the family relationship. In S. S. Feldman & G. R. Elliot (Eds.), *At the threshold* (pp. 255–276). Cambridge, MA: Harvard University Press.

Steinberg, L. (1996). *Adolescence.* New York: McGraw-Hill.

Steinberg, L., Darling, E., & Fletcher, A. C. (1995). Authoritative parenting and adolescent adjustment: An ecological journal. In P. Moen & G. H. Elder (Eds.), *Examining lives in context* (pp. 423–466). Washington, DC: American Psychological Association.

Steinberg, L., & Dornbusch, S. (1991). Negative correlates of part-time work in adolescence: Replication and elaboration. *Developmental Psychology, 17,* 304–313.

Steinberg, L., Fegley, S., & Dornbusch, S. M. (1993). Negative impact of part-time work on adolescent adjustment: Evidence from a longitudinal study. *Developmental Psychology, 29,* 171–180.

Steinberg, L., Lamborn, S. D., Darling, N., Mounts, N., & Dornbusch, S. M. (1994). Over-time change in adjustment and competence among adolescents from authoritative, authoritarian, indulgent, and neglectful families. *Child Development, 65,* 754–766.

Steinberg, L., & Levine, A. (1990). Enjoying your child's teenage years. *Temple Review,* 20–23.

Steinberg, L., Mounts, N. S., Lamborn, S. D., & Dornbusch, S. M. (1991). Authoritative parenting and adolescent adjustment across varied ecological niches. *Journal of Research on Adolescence, 1,* 19–36.

Steinhausen, H. C., Meier, M., & Angst, J. (1998). The Zurich long-term outcome study of child and adolescent psychiatric disorders in male. *Psychological Medicine, 28,* 275–383.

Stern, A. E., Lynch, D. L., Oates, R. K., O'Toole, B. I., & Cooney, G. (1995). Self esteem, depression, behaviour and family functioning in sexually abused children. *Journal of Child Psychology and Psychiatry, 36,* 1077–1089.

Stern, D. (1992). *Diary of a baby.* New York: Basic Books.

Sternberg, R. J. (1985). *Beyond IQ.* New York: Cambridge University Press.

Sternberg, R. J., & Wagner, R. K. (1993). The g-ocentric view of intelligence and job performance is wrong. *Current Directions in Psychological Science, 2,* 1–5.

Stevenson, H. W. (1998a). Cultural interpretations of giftedness: The case of East Asia. In R. C Friedman & K. B. Rogers (Eds.), *Talent in context* (pp. 61–77). Washington, DC: American Psychological Association.

Stevenson, H. W. (1998b). A study of three cultures: Germany, Japan, and the United States. *Phi Delta Kappan, 79,* 524–529.

Stevenson, H. W., Chen, C., & Lee, S. (1992). Chinese families. In J. L. Roopnarine & D. B. Carter (Eds.), *Parent-child socialization in diverse cultures* (pp. 17–34). Norwood, NJ: Ablex.

Stevenson, H. W., Chen, C., & Lee, S. (1993). Mathematics achievement in Chinese, Japanese, and American children. *Science, 259,* 53–58.

Stevenson, H. W., Chen, C., & Uttal, D. (1990). Beliefs and achievement: A study of black, white, and Hispanic children. *Child Development, 61,* 508–523.

Stevenson, H. W., & Lee, S. (1990). Contexts of achievement. *Monographs of the Society for Research in Child Development* (55, Whole no. 221). Chicago: University of Chicago Press.

Stevenson, H. W., & Stigler, J. W. (1992). *The learning gap.* New York: Summit Books.

Stevens-Simon, C., & McAnarney, E. R. (1996). Adolescent pregnancy. In R. J. DiClemente & W. B. Hansen (Eds.), *Handbook of adolescent health risk behavior* (pp. 313–332). New York: Plenum.

Stipek, D. J. (1981). Children's perceptions of their own and their classmates' ability. *Journal of Educational Psychology, 73,* 404–410.

Stipek, D. J. (1997). Success in school—for a head start in life. In L. S. Luthar & J. A. Burack (Eds.), *Developmental psychopathology: Perspectives on adjustment, risk, and disorder* (pp. 75–92). New York: Cambridge University Press.

Stipek, D. J., Recchia, S., & McClintic, S. (1992). Self-evaluation in young children. *Monographs of the Society for Research in Child Development* (57, Whole no. 226). Chicago: University of Chicago Press.

Straus, M. A., & Donnelly, D. A. (1994). *Beating the devil out of them: Corporal punishment in American families.* New York: Lexington Books.

Strauss, C. C., & Francis, G. (1989). Phobic disorders. In C. G. Last & M. Hersen (Eds.), *Handbook of child psychiatric diagnosis* (pp. 170–190). New York: Wiley.

Straussner, J. H., & Straussner, S. L. A. (1997). Impact of community and school violence on children. In N. K. Phillips & S. L. A. Straussner (Eds.), *Children in the urban environment* (pp. 61–77). Springfield, IL: Charles C. Thomas.

Streissguth, A. P. (1997). *Fetal alcohol syndrome.* Baltimore, MD: Brookes Publishing.

Streissguth, A. P., Barr, H. M., Sampson, P. D., Darby, B. L., & Martin, D. C. (1989). IQ at age 4 in relation to maternal alcohol use and smoking during pregnancy. *Developmental Psychology, 25,* 3–11.

Strelau, J. (1994). The concepts of arousal and arousability as used in temperament studies. In J. E. Bates & T. D. Wachs (Eds.), *Temperament: Individual differences at the interface of biology and behavior* (pp. 117–143). Washington, DC: American Psychological Association.

Striefel, S., Robinson, M. A., & Truhn, P. (1998). Dealing with child abuse and neglect within a comprehensive family-support program. In J. R. Lutzker (Ed.), *Handbook of child abuse and treatment* (pp. 267–289). New York: Plenum.

Stringer, P. (1998). One night Vygotsky had a dream: Implications for educational psychologists. *Educational and Child Psychology, 15,* 14–20.

Strober, M., McCracken, J., & Hanna, G. (1991). Affective disorders. In R. M. Lerner, A. C. Petersen, & J. Brooks-Gunn (Eds.), *Encyclopedia of adolescence* (pp. 18–25). New York: Garland.

Strom, R., Strom, S., Strom, P., & Collinsworth, P. (1994). Parent competence in families with gifted children. *Journal for the Education of the Gifted, 18,* 39–54.

Strouse, J. S., & Buerkel-Rothfuss, N. L. (1993). Media exposure and the sexual attitudes and behaviors of college students. In B. S. Greenberg, J. D. Brown, & N. L. Buerkel-Rothfuss (Eds.), *Media, sex, and the adolescent* (pp. 277–292). Cresskill, NJ: Hampton Press.

Strouse, J. S., & Fabes, R. A. (1987). A conceptualization of transition to nonvirginity in adolescent females. *Journal of Adolescent Research, 2,* 331–348.

Suarez-Orozco, C., & Suarez-Orozco, M. M. (1995). *Transformations: Immigration, family life, and achievement motivation among Latino adolescents.* Stanford, CA: Stanford University Press.

Suber, C. F. (1982). Separable effects of motives, consequences, and presentation order on children's moral judgments. *Developmental Psychology, 18,* 257–266.

Super, C. M., & Harkness, S. (1991). The development of affect in infancy and childhood. In M. Woodhead & R. Carr (Eds.), *Becoming a person: Child development in social context* (Vol. 1., pp. 56–73). London: Routledge.

Surgeon General. (1996). *Physical activity and health.* Washington, DC: U.S. Department of Health.

Susman, E. J., Dorn, L. D., & Chrousos, G. P. (1991). Negative affect and hormone levels in young adolescents. *Journal of Youth and Adolescence, 20,* 167–190.

Susman, E. J., Koch, P. B., Maney, D. W., & Finkelstein, J. W. (1993). Health promotion in adolescence: Developmental and theoretical considerations. In R. M. Lerner (Ed.), *Early adolescence: Perspectives on research, policy, and intervention* (pp. 247–260). Hillsdale, NJ: Erlbaum.

Susman-Stillman, A., Kalkose, M., Egeland, B., & Waldman, I. (1996). Infant temperament and maternal sensitivity as predictors of attachment security. *Infant Behavior and Development, 19,* 33–47.

Sutton, H. E. (1988). *An introduction to human genetics.* San Diego: Harcourt Brace Jovanovich.

Sutton-Smith, B. (1994). Does play prepare the future? In J. H. Goldstein (Ed.), *Toys, play, and child development* (pp. 130–146). Cambridge, England: Cambridge University Press

Sutton-Smith, B. (1998). *The ambiguity of play.* Cambridge, MA: Harvard University Press.

Swanson, J. M., McBurnett, K., Wigal, T., & Pfiffner, L. J. (1993). Effect of stimulant medication on children with attention deficit disorder. *Exceptional Children 60,* 154–161.

Swarr, A. E., & Richards, M. H. (1996). Longitudinal effects of adolescent girls' pubertal development, perceptions of pubertal timing, and parental relations on eating patterns. *Developmental Psychology, 32,* 636–646.

Synnott, A. (1988). Little angels, little devils: A sociology of children. In G. Handel (Ed.), *Childhood socialization* (pp. 25–43). Hawthorne, NY: Aldine de Gruyter.

Szagun, G. (1992). Children's understanding of the feeling experience and causes of sympathy. *Journal of Child Psychology and Psychiatry, 33,* 1183–1191.

Szapocznik, J., & Kurtines, W. (1993). Family psychology and cultural diversity: Opportunities for theory, research, and application. *American Psychologist, 48,* 400–407.

Taffel, S. M., Placek, P. J., & Moien, M. (1989). Cesarean section rate levels off in 1987. *Family Planning Perspective, 21,* 227–228.

Tager-Flusberg, H. (1994). *Constraints on language acquisition: Studies of atypical children.* Mahwah, NJ: Erlbaum.

Takahashi, K. (1990). Are the key assumptions of the "Strange Situation" procedure universal? A view from Japanese research. *Human Development, 30,* 23–30.

Tamis-LeMonda, C. S., Bornstein, M. H., Cyphers, L., Toda, S., & Ogino, M. (1992). Language and play at one year: A comparison of toddlers and mothers in the United States and Japan. *International Journal of Behavioral Development, 15,* 33–45.

Tangney, J. P. (1990). Sharing shame and guilt. *Contemporary Social Psychology, 14,* 83–88.

Tanner, J. M. (1975). Growth and endocrinology of the adolescent. In L. Gardner (Ed.), *Endocrine and genetic diseases of childhood* (pp. 77–121). Philadelphia: W. B. Saunders.

Tanner, J. M. (1989). *Fetus into man.* Cambridge, MA: Harvard University Press.

Tanner, J. M. (1991). Growth spurt, adolescent I. In R. M. Lerner, A. C. Petersen, & J. Brooks-Gunn (Eds.) *Encyclopedia of adolescence* (Vol. 1, pp. 277–303). New York: Garland.

Tanner, J. M., & Davies, P. S. (1985). Clinical longitudinal standards for height and height velocity for North American children. *Journal of Pediatrics, 107,* 317–329.

Tappan, M. B. (1998). Sociocultural psychology and caring pedagogy: Exploring Vygotsky's "hidden curriculum." *Educational Psychologist, 33,* 23–33.

Tasker, F. L., & Golombok, S. (1997). *Growing up in a lesbian family.* New York: Guilford Press.

Tatzer, E., Schubert, M. T., Timischl, W., & Simbruner, G. (1985). Discrimination of taste and preference for sweet in premature babies. *Early Human Development, 12,* 23–30.

Taubman, B. (1997). Toilet training and toileting refusal for stool only: A prospective study. *Pediatrics, 99,* 54–58.

Taylor, E. (1995). Dysfunctions of attention. In D. Cicchetti & D. J. Cohen (Eds.), *Developmental psychopathology* (Vol. 2, pp. 243–273). New York: Wiley.

Taylor, H. G., Klein, N., & Hack, M. (1994). Academic functioning in < 750 gm birthweight children who have normal cognitive abilities: Evidence for specific learning disabilities. *Pediatric Research, 35,* 289.

Taylor, J. A., & Sanderson, M. (1995). A reexamination of the risk factors for the sudden infant death syndrome. *Journal of Pediatrics, 126,* 887–891.

Taylor, M., & Carlson, S. M. (1997). The relation between individual differences in fantasy and theory of mind. *Child Development, 68,* 436–455.

Taylor, M., & Hort, B. C. (1990). Can children be trained to make the appearance-reality distinction? *Cognitive Development, 5,* 89–99.

Taylor, R. D. (1995). Social contextual influence on family relations: Adolescent adjustment and competence in African-American families. In M. L. Maher & P. R. Pintrich (Eds.), *Advances in motivation and achievement* (Vol. 9, 229–253). Greenwich, CT: JAI Press.

Teale, W. H., & Sulzby, E. (1985). *Emergent literacy: Writing and reading.* Exeter, NH: Heinemann Educational Books.

Telama, R., Yang, X., Laakso, L., & Viikari, J. (1997). Physical activity in childhood and adolescence as predictors of physical activity in young adulthood. *American Journal of Preventive Medicine, 13,* 317–323.

Tellegen, A. (1988). The analysis of consistency in personality assessment. *Journal of Personality, 56,* 621–663.

Terman, L. M. (1925). *Genetic studies of genius.* Stanford, CA: Stanford University Press.

Terman, L. M., & Oden, M. H. (1959). *The gifted group in midlife: Thirty-year follow-up of the superior child.* Stanford, CA: Stanford University Press.

Teti, D. M. (1992). Sibling interaction. In V. B. Van Hesselt & M. Hersen (Eds.), *Handbook of social development* (pp. 201–228). New York: Plenum.

Teti, D. M., Sakin, J. W., Kucera, K., Corns, K. M., & Eiden, R. D. (1996). And baby makes four: Predictors of attachment security among preschool-age firstborns during the transition to siblinghood. *Child Development, 67,* 579–596.

Thelen, E. (1989). Self-organization in developmental processes: Can systems approaches work? In M. Gunnar & E. Thelen (Eds.), *Systems in development* (Vol. 22, 77–117). Hillsdale, NJ: Erlbaum.

Thelen, E., & Smith, L. B. (1994). *A dynamic systems approach to the development of cognition and action.* Cambridge, MA: MIT Press.

Thelen, E., & Smith, L. B. (1998). Dynamic systems theories. In W. Damon (Ed.), *Handbook of child psychology* (Vol. 1, pp. 563–633). New York: Wiley.

Thoma, S. J., & Rest, J. R. (1999). The relationship between moral decision making and patterns of consolidation and transition in moral judgment development. *Developmental Psychology, 35,* 323–334.

Thoman, E. B. (1990). Sleeping and waking state in infants: A functional perspective. *Neuroscience and Biobehavioral Review, 14,* 93–107.

Thoman, E. B., Hammond, K., Affleck, G., & Desilva, H. (1995). The Breathing Bear with preterm infants: Effects on sleep, respiration, and affect. *Infant Mental Health Journal, 16,* 160–168.

Thoman, E. B., & Whitney, M. P. (1990). Behavior states in infants: Individual differences and individual analyses. In J. Colombo & J. Fagen, (Eds.), *Individual differences in infancy: Reliability, stability, prediction* (pp. 113–136). Hillsdale, NJ: Erlbaum.

Thomas, A., & Chess, S. (1970). The origins of personality. *Scientific American, 223,* 102–109.

Thomas, A., & Chess, S. (1977). *Temperament and development.* New York: Brunner/Mazel.

Thomas, A., & Chess, S. (1985). The behavioral study of temperament. In J. Strelau, F. Farley, & A. Gale (Eds.), *The biological bases of personality and behavior* (Vol. 1, pp. 213–225). Washington, DC: Hemisphere.

Thomas, A., Chess, S., & Birch, H. G. (1968). *Temperament and behavior disorders in childhood.* New York: New York University Press.

Thomas, J. R., & French, K. E. (1985). Gender differences across age in motor performance: A meta-analysis. *Psychological Bulletin, 98,* 260–282.

Thomas, R. M. (1996). *Comparing theories of child development.* Belmont, CA: Wadsworth.

Thompson, K. P. (1993). Media, music, and adolescents. In R. M. Lerner (Ed.), *Early adolescence: Perspectives on research, policy, and intervention* (pp. 407–418). Hillsdale, NJ: Erlbaum.

Thompson, R., & Zuroff, D. C. (1998). Dependent and self-critical mothers' responses to adolescent autonomy and competence. *Personality and Individual Differences, 24,* 311–324.

Thompson, R. A. (1990). Vulnerability in research: A developmental perspective on research risk. *Child Development, 61,* 1–16.

Thompson, R. A. (1991). Infant day care: Concerns, controversies, choices. In J. V. Lerner & N. L. Galambos (Eds.), *Employed mothers and their children* (pp. 9–36). New York: Garland Publishing.

Thompson, R. A. (1998). Early sociopersonality development. In W. Damon (Ed.), *Handbook of child psychology* (Vol. 3, pp. 25–104). New York: Wiley.

Thompson, S. C., Sobowlew-Shubin, A., Graham, M. A., & Janigan, A. S. (1989). Psychosocial adjustment following a stroke. *Social Science and Medicine, 28,* 239–247.

Thornberry, T. P., Smith, C. A., & Howard, G. J. (1997). Risk factors for teenage fatherhood. *Journal of Marriage and the Family, 59,* 505–520.

Thorne, B. (1993). *Gender play: Girls and boys in school.* New Brunswick, NJ: Rutgers University Press.

Thorne, B., & Luria, Z. (1986). Sexuality and gender in children's daily worlds. *Social Problems, 33*, 176–190.

Thornton, M. C., Chatters, L. M., Taylor, R. J., & Allen, W. R. (1990). Sociodemographic and environmental correlates of racial socialization by Black parents. *Child Development, 61*, 401–409.

Thorp, J. A., & Breedlove, G. (1996). Epidural analgesia in labor: An evaluation of risks and benefits. *Birth, 23*, 63–83.

Thorpe, K. J., Dragonas, T., & Golding, J. (1992). The effects of psychosocial factors on the mother's emotional well-being during early parenthood: A cross-cultural study of Britain and Greece. *Journal of Reproductive and Infant Psychology, 10*, 205–217.

Time. (1993, Fall). Special issue, September 8–9 poll. *Time, 10*.

Tobin-Richards, M. H., Boxer, A. M., & Petersen, A. C. (1983). The psychological significance of pubertal change: Sex differences in perceptions of self during early adolescence. In J. Brooks-Gunn & A. C. Petersen (Eds.), *Girls at puberty* (pp. 113–134). New York: Plenum Press.

Tolan, P. H., & Loeber, R. L. (1993). Antisocial behavior. In P. H. Tolan & B. J. Cohler (Eds.), *Handbook of clinical research and clinical practice with adolescents* (pp. 307–331). New York: Wiley.

Tom, D., & Cooper, H. (1986). The effect of student background on teacher performance attributions. *Basic and Applied Social Psychology, 7*, 53–62.

Tomasello, M. (1992). The social bases of language acquisition. *Social Development, 1*, 67–87.

Tomasello, M., & Akhtar, N. (1995). Two-year-olds use pragmatic cues to differentiate reference to objects and actions. *Cognitive Psychology, 10*, 201–224.

Tomasello, M., & Mannie, S. (1985). Pragmatics of sibling speech to one-year-olds. *Child Development, 56*, 911–917.

Tomasello, M., Strosberg, R., & Akhtar, N. (1996). Eighteen-month-old children learn words in non-ostensive context. *Journal of Child Language, 23*, 157–176.

Torney-Purta, J. (1992). Cognitive representations of the political system in adolescents: The continuum from pre-novice to expert. In H. Haste & J. Torney-Purta (Eds.), *The development of political understanding* (pp. 11–25). San Francisco: Jossey-Bass.

Torney-Purta, J. (1994). Dimensions of adolescents' reasoning about political and historical issues: Ontological switches, development processes, and situated learning. In M. Carretero & J. F. Voss (Eds.), *Cognitive and instructional processes in history and the social sciences* (pp. 103–122). Hillsdale, NJ: Erlbaum.

Torrance, E. P. (1966). Attitude patterns of creatively gifted high school seniors. *Gifted Child Quarterly, 10*, 48–52.

Torrance, E. P. (1988). The nature of creativity as manifest in its testing. In R. Sternberg, *The nature of creativity: Contemporary psychological perspectives* (pp. 43–75). New York: Cambridge University Press.

Travillion, K., & Snyder, J. (1993). The role of maternal discipline and involvement in peer rejection and neglect. *Journal of Applied Developmental Psychology, 14*, 37–57.

Treboux, D. A., & Bush-Rossnagel, N. A. (1991). Age differences in adolescent sexual behavior, sexual attitudes, and contraceptive use. In R. M. Lerner, A. C. Petersen, & J. Brooks-Gunn (Eds.), *Encyclopedia of adolescence* (pp. 1018–1021). New York: Garland.

Trent, K., & Crowder, K. (1997). Adolescent birth intentions, social disadvantage, and behavioral outcomes. *Journal of Marriage and the Family, 59*, 523–535.

Trice, A. D., & Rush, K. (1995). Sex-stereotyping in four-year-olds' occupational aspirations. *Perceptual and Motor Skills, 81*, 701–702.

Trickett, P. K., & Kuczynski, L. (1986). Children's misbehavior and parental discipline in abusive and non-abusive families. *Developmental Psychology, 57*, 115–123.

Trickett, P. K., & McBride-Chang, C. (1995). The developmental impact of different forms of child abuse and neglect. *Developmental Review, 15*, 331–337.

Troll, L. E. (1987). Mother-daughter relationships through the life span. In S. Oskamp (Ed.), *Family processes and problems: Social psychological aspects* (pp. 284–305). Newbury Park, CA: Sage.

Trommsdorff, G. (1995). Person-context relations as developmental conditions for empathy and prosocial action: A cross-cultural analysis. In T. A. Kindermann & J. Valsiner (Eds.), *Development of person-context relations* (pp. 113–146). Hillsdale, NJ: Erlbaum.

Tschann, J. M., Adler, N. E., Irwin, C. E., Millstein, S. G., Turner, R. A., & Kegeles, S. M. (1994). Initiation of substance use in early adolescence: The roles of pubertal timing and emotional distress. *Health Psychology, 13*, 326–333.

Tucker, J. S., Friedman, H. S., Schwartz, J. E., Criqui, M. H., et al. (1997). Parental divorce: Effects on individual behavior and longevity. *Journal of Personality and Social Psychology, 73*, 381–391.

Tulasiewcz, W., & Adams, A. (1989). *Teachers' expectations and teaching reality.* New York: Routledge.

Turecki, S., & Tonner, L. (1985). *The difficult child.* New York: Bantam.

Turiel, E. (1983). *The development of social knowledge.* Cambridge, England: Cambridge University Press.

Turiel, E. (1998). The development of morality. In W. Damon (Ed.), *Handbook of child psychology* (Vol. 3, pp. 863–932). New York: Wiley.

Turner, H. A., & Finkelhor, D. (1996). Corporal punishment as a stressor among youth. *Journal of Marriage and the Family, 58*, 155–166.

Udry, J. R. (1995). Integrating biological and sociological models of adolescent problem behaviors. In R. D. Ketterlinus & M. E. Lamb (Eds.), *Adolescent problem behaviors* (pp. 93–108). Hillsdale, NJ: Erlbaum.

Ungerer, J. A., Brody, L. R., & Zelazo, P. R. (1978). Long-term memory for speech in 2- to 4-week-old infants. *Infant Behavior and Development, 1*, 177–186.

UNICEF. (1993). *Psychosocial programme: Emergency in former Yugoslavia.* New York: UNICEF.

UNICEF. (1998). *The state of the world's children, 1998.* New York: UNICEF.

United Nations. (1998). *Population and development indicators for Asia and the Pacific, 1998.* Bangkok, Thailand: United Nations.

U.S. Census Bureau. (1993). *Children living with biological, step, and adoptive married-couple parents, by race and Hispanic origin of mother.* Washington, DC: U.S. Department of Commerce.

U.S. Census Bureau. (1996a). *Household and family characteristics: March 1995.* Washington, DC: U.S. Census Bureau.

U.S. Census Bureau. (1996b). *Population projections of the United States by age, sex, race, and Hispanic origin.* Washington, DC: U.S. Government Printing Office.

U.S. Census Bureau. (1997). *The foreign-born population, 1996.* Washington, DC: U.S. Government Printing Office.

U.S. Census Bureau. (1998). *School enrollment, 1996.* Washington, DC: U.S. Government Printing Office.

U.S. Department of Commerce. (1996, March). *Who's minding our preschoolers? Current Population Reports.* Washington, DC: U.S. Department of Commerce.

U.S. Department of Education. (1993). *Public school kindergarten teachers' views on children's readiness for school.* Washington, DC: U.S. Department of Education.

U.S. Department of Education. (1994). *High school completion.* Washington, DC: U.S. Department of Education.

U.S. Department of Education. (1995). *Reforming schools, transforming partnerships.* Washington, DC: U.S. Department of Education.

U.S. Department of Education. (1996a). *Achievement of U.S. students in science, 1969 to 1994; mathematics, 1973 to 1994; reading, 1971 to 1994; writing, 1984 to 1994.* Washington, DC: U.S. Department of Education.

U.S. Department of Education. (1996b). *The condition of education, indicator 6. National Center for Education Statistics, High School and Beyond (HS&B) study.* Washington, DC: U.S. Department of Education.

U.S. Department of Education. (1996c). *Number and disabilities of children and youth served under IDEA.* Washington, DC: U.S. Department of Education.

U.S. Department of Education. (1996d). *Youth indicators, 1996.* Washington, DC: Department of Education.

U.S. Department of Education. (1997a). *Advanced telecommunications in U.S. public elementary and secondary schools.* Washington, DC: U.S. Department of Education.

U.S. Department of Education. (1997b). *Dropout rates in the United States: 1995.* Washington, DC: U.S. Department of Education.

U.S. Department of Education. (1998). *The condition of education, 1997.* Washington, DC: U.S. Department of Education.

U.S. Department of Health and Human Services. (1998). *Child maltreatment 1996: Reports from the states to the National Child Abuse and Neglect Data System.* Washington, DC: U.S. DHHS.

U.S. Department of Justice. (1998). *Criminal behavior of gang members and at-risk youths.* Washington, DC: U.S. Department of Justice.

Upchurch, D. M., Levy-Storms, L., Sucoff, C. A., & Aneshensel, C. S. (1998). Gender and ethnic differences in the timing of first sexual intercourse. *Family Planning Perspectives, 30,* 121–127.

Updegraff, K. A., & Obeidallah, D. A. (1999). Young adolescents' patterns of involvement with siblings and friends. *Social Development, 8,* 52–69.

Valdez, E. O. (1996). Chicano families and urban poverty: Familial strategies of cultural retention. In R. M. De Anda (Ed.), *Chicanas and Chicanos in contemporary society* (pp. 63–74). Boston: Allyn & Bacon.

Valdez, J. (1994, September 18). Teen pregnancy: Interviews and statistics. *Arizona Republic.*

Vandell, D. L., & Corasaniti, M. A. (1990). Child care and the family: Complex contributors to child development. *New Directions for Child Development, 49,* 23–37.

van der Heijden, J. (1996). *World population.* Unpublished data.

van de Vijver, F. J. R., & Willemsen, M. E. (1993). Abstract thinking. In J. Altarriba (Ed.), *Cognition and culture* (pp. 317–342). Amsterdam: North-Holland.

Van-Evra, J. P. (1998). *Television and child development.* Mahwah, NJ: Erlbaum.

Van Griffin, K., & Haith, M. M. (1984). Infant visual response to gestalt geometric forms. *Infant Behavior and Development, 7,* 335–346.

van IJzendoorn, M. (1995). Adult attachment representations, parental responsiveness, and infant attachment. *Psychological Bulletin, 117,* 387–403.

Vanished Children's Alliance. (1995). *Vanished children.* San Jose, CA: Vanished Children's Alliance.

Vartanian, L. R. (1997). Separation-individuation, social support, and adolescent egocentrism. *Journal of Early Adolescence, 17,* 245–270.

Vartanian, L. R., & Powlishta, K. K. (1996). A longitudinal examination of the social-cognitive foundations of adolescent egocentrism. *Journal of Early Adolescence, 16,* 157–178.

Vaughn, L. S. (1991). Facial diversity and infant preferences for attractive faces. *Developmental Psychology, 27,* 79–84.

Vellutino, F. R. (1991). Introduction to three studies on reading acquisition: Convergent findings on theoretical foundations of code-oriented versus whole-language approaches to reading instruction. *Journal of Educational Psychology, 83,* 437–443.

Verhulst, F. C., & Koot, H. M. (1995). *The epidemiology of child and adolescent psychopathology.* Oxford, England: Oxford University Press.

Vigil, J. D. (1988). Group processes and street identity: Adolescent Chicano gang members. *Ethos, 16,* 421–445.

Violato, C., & LeRoy, T. (1995). *Advances in adolescent psychology.* Calgary, Alberta, Canada: Detselig Enterprises.

Vitaro, F., Tremblay, R. E., Kerr, M., Pagant, L., & Bukowski, W. M. (1997). Disruptives, friends' characteristics, and delinquency in early adolescence: A test of two competing models of development. *Child Development, 68,* 676–689.

Vogt, C. J. (1999). A model of risk factors involved in childhood and adolescent obesity. In A. J. Goreczny & M. Hersen (Eds.), *Handbook of pediatric and adolescent health psychology* (pp. 221–234). Boston: Allyn & Bacon.

Volling, B. L., & Elins, J. L. (1998). Family relationships and children's emotional adjustment as correlates of maternal and paternal differential treatment *Child Development, 69,* 1640–1656.

Volling, B. L., Youngblade, L. M., & Belsky, J. (1997). Young children's social relationships with siblings and friends. *American Journal of Orthopsychiatry, 67,* 102–111.

von Hofsten, C. (1983). Catching skills in infancy. *Journal of Experimental Psychology: Human Perception and Performance, 9,* 75–85.

Vorhees, C. V., & Mollnow, E. (1987). Behavioral teratogenesis: Long-term influences on behavior from early exposure to environmental agents. In J. D. Osofsky (Ed.), *Handbook of infant development* (pp. 913–971). New York: Wiley.

Vygotsky, L. S. (1978). *Mind in society.* Cambridge, MA: Harvard University Press.

Vygotsky, L. S. (1986). *Thought and language* (A. Kozulin, Trans.). Cambridge, MA: MIT Press. (Original work published 1934)

Waas, G. A., & Graczyk, P. A. (1998). Group intervention for the peer-rejected child. In. K. C. Stoiber & T. R. Kratochwill (Eds.), *Handbook of group intervention for children and families* (pp. 141–158). Boston: Allyn & Bacon.

Wachs, T. D. (1992). *The nature of nurture.* Newbury Park, CA: Sage.

Wachs, T. D. (1995). Relation of mild-to-moderate malnutrition to human development: Correlational studies. *Journal of Nutrition Supplement, 125,* 2245S-2254S.

Wachs, T. D., & King, B. (1994). Behavioral research in the brave new world of neuroscience and temperament: A guide to the biologically perplexed. In J. E. Bates & T. D. Wachs (Eds.), *Temperament: Individual differences at the interface of biology and behavior* (pp. 307–336). Washington, DC: American Psychological Association.

Waldman, S., & Springen, K. (1992). Too old, too fast? *Newsweek,* 80–88.

Walk, R. D., & Gibson, E. J. (1961). A comparative and analytical study of visual depth perception. *Psychological Monographs* (15, Whole No. 519).

Walker, K., Taylor, E., McElroy, A., & Phillip, D. (1995). Familial and ecological correlates of self-esteem in African American children. In M. N. Wilson (Ed.), *African American family life: Its structural and ecological aspects* (pp. 23–34). San Francisco: Jossey-Bass.

Walker, L. J. (1984). Sex differences in the development of moral reasoning: A critical review. *Child Development, 55,* 677–691.

Walker, L. J. (1988). The development of moral reasoning. *Annals of Child Development, 5,* 33–78.

Walker, L. J. (1989). A longitudinal study of moral reasoning. *Child Development, 60,* 157–166.

Walker, L. J. (1991). Sex differences in moral reasoning. In W. Kurtines & J. L. Gewirtz (Eds.), *Handbook of moral behavior and development* (Vol. 2, pp. 333–364). Hillsdale, NJ: Erlbaum.

Walker, L. J., & Henning, K. H. (1997). Moral development in the broader context of personality. In S. Hala (Ed.), *The development of social cognition* (pp. 297–327). Hove, England: Psychology Press.

Walker, L. J., & Pitts, R. C. (1998). Naturalistic conceptions of moral maturity. *Developmental Psychology, 34,* 403–419.

Walker, L. J., Pitts, R. C., Henning, K. H., & Matsuba, M. K. (1995). Reasoning about morality and real-life moral problems. In M. Killen & D. Hart (Eds.), *Morality in everyday life* (pp. 371–407). New York: Cambridge University Press.

Wallace-Broscious, A., Serafica, F. C., & Osipow, S. H. (1994). Adolescent career development. *Journal of Research on Adolescence, 4,* 127–149.

Wallerstein, J. S., & Kelly, J. B. (1975). The effects of parental divorce: Experiences of the preschool child. *Journal of the American Academy of Child Psychiatry, 14,* 600–616.

Wallerstein, J. S., & Kelly, J. B. (1976). The effects of parental experiences of the child in later latency. *American Journal of Orthopsychiatry, 46,* 256–269.

Wallerstein, J. S., & Kelly, J. B. (1980). *Surviving the breakup: How children and parents cope with divorce.* New York: Basic Books.

Wallerstein, R. S., & Goldberger, L. (1998). *Ideas and identities: The life and work of Erik Erikson.* Madison, CT: International Universities Press.

Walsh, P. E., & Stolberg, A. L. (1989). Parental and environmental determinants of children's behavioral, affective and cognitive adjustment to divorce. *Journal of Divorce, 12,* 265–282.

Walsh, P. V., Katz, P. A., & Downey, E. P. (1991, April). *A longitudinal perspective on race and gender socialization in infants and toddlers.* Paper presented at the biennial meeting of the Society for Research in Child Development, Seattle, WA.

Wanamaker, C. E., & Reznikoff, M. (1989). Effects of aggressive and nonaggressive rock songs on projective and structured tests. *Journal of Psychology, 123,* 561–570.

Wang, F., Oakland, T., & Liu, D. H. (1992). Behavior problems exhibited by Chinese children from single- and multiple-child families. *School Psychology International, 13,* 313–321.

Wanner, E. (1992). Foreword. In T. D. Cook, H. Cooper, D. S. Cordray, H. Hartmann, L. V. Hedges, R. J. Light, T. A. Louis, & F. Mosteller (Eds.), *Meta-analysis for explanation* (pp. vii-x). New York: Russell Sage.

Wapner, R. J. (1997). Chorionic villus sampling. *Obstetrics and Gynecology Clinics of North America, 24,* 83–110.

Wasz-Hockert, O., Michelsson, K., & Lind, J. (1985). Twenty-five years of Scandinavian cry research. In B. M. Lester & C. F. Z. Boukydis (Eds.), *Infant crying* (pp. 349–354). New York: Plenum.

Waterman, A. S. (1988). Identity status theory and Erikson's theory. *Developmental Review, 8,* 185–208.

Watkins, J., & Peabody, P. (1996). Sports injuries in children and adolescents treated at a sports injury clinic. *Journal of Sports Medicine and Physical Fitness, 36,* 43–48.

Watson, J. B., & Raynor, R. (1920). Conditioned emotional reactions. *Journal of Experimental Psychology, 3,* 1–14.

Wechsler, D. (1991). *Wechsler Intelligence Scale for Children-III.* San Antonio, TX: The Psychological Corporation.

Wedemeyer, N. V., Bickhard, N. H., & Cooper, R. G. (1989). The development of structural complexity in the child's concept of family: The effect of cognitive stage, sex, and intactness of family. *The Journal of Genetic Psychology, 150,* 342–357.

Wegener, D. H., & Aday, L. A. (1989). Home care for ventilator-assisted children: Predicting family stress. *Pediatric Nursing, 15,* 271–376.

Weinberg, R. A. (1989). Intelligence and IQ: Landmark issues and great debates. *American Psychologist, 44,* 98–104.

Weinstein, R. A. (1998). Promoting positive expectations in schooling. In N. M. Lambert & B. L. McCombs (Eds.), *How students learn* (pp. 81–111). Washington, DC: American Psychological Association.

Weiss, B., & Dodge, K. A. (1992). Some consequences of early harsh discipline: Child aggression and a maladaptive social information processing style. *Child Development, 63,* 1321–1335.

Weiss, M. R., & Hayashi, C. T. (1995). All in the family: Parent-child influences in competititve youth gymnastics. *Pediatric Exercise Science, 7,* 36–48.

Wellman, H. M., & Gellman, S. A. (1998). Knowledge acquisition in foundational domain. In W. Damon (Ed.), *Handbook of child psychology* (Vol. 2, pp. 523–574). New York: Wiley.

Wellman, H. M., & Woolley, J. D. (1990). From simple desires to ordinary beliefs: The early development of everyday psychology. *Cognition, 35,* 245–275.

Wentzel, K. R., & Erdley, C. A. (1993). Strategies for making friends: Relations to social behavior and peer acceptance in early adolescence. *Developmental Psychology, 29,* 819–826.

Werker, J. F., & Tees, R. C. (1984). Cross-language speech perception: Evidence for perceptual reorganization during the first year of life. *Infant Behavior and Development, 7,* 49–63.

Werner, E. E., & Smith, R. S. (1982). *Vulnerable but invincible: A longitudinal study of resilient children and youth.* New York: McGraw Hill.

Whalen, C. K., & Henker, B. (1991). Therapies for hyperactive children: Comparisons, combinations, and compromises. *Journal of Consulting and Clinical Psychology, 59,* 126–137.

Whalen, C. K., Henker, B., Buhrmester, D., Hinshaw, S. P., Huber, A., & Laski, K. (1989). Does stimulant medication improve the peer status of hyperactive children? *Journal of Consulting and Clinical Psychology, 57,* 545–549.

Wheeler, L., & Kim, Y. (1997). What is beautiful is culturally good: The physical attractiveness stereotype has different content in collectivistic cultures. *Personality and Social Psychology Bulletin, 23,* 795–800.

White, M., & LeVine, R. A. (1986). What is an Ii ko (good child)? In H. Stevenson, H. Azuma, & K. Hakuta, (Eds.), *Child development and education in Japan* (pp. 55–62). New York: Freeman.

White, S. D., & DeBlassie, R. R. (1992). Adolescent sexual behavior. *Adolescence, 27,* 183–191.

Whitebook, M., Howes, C., & Phillips, D. (1989). *Who cares? Childcare teachers and the quality of care in America.* Oakland, CA: Childcare Employee Project.

Whitehead, B. D. (1993, May/June). The new family values. *Utne Reader.*

Whiting, B. B., & Edwards, C. P. (1988). *Children of different worlds: The formation of social behavior.* Cambridge, MA: Harvard University Press.

Whiting, B. B., & Whiting, J. W. M. (1975). *Children of six cultures: A psychocultural analysis.* Cambridge, MA: Harvard University Press.

Widerstrom, A. H., Mowder, B. A., & Sandall, S. R. (1991). *At-risk and handicapped newborns and infants: Development, assessment, and intervention.* Englewood Cliffs, NJ: Prentice-Hall.

Wierson, M., Long, P. J., & Forehand, R. L. (1993). Toward a new understanding of early menarche: The role of environmental stress in pubertal timing. *Adolescence, 28,* 913–924.

Wiese, D., & Daro, D. (1996). *Current trends in child abuse reporting and fatalities.* Chicago: National Committee to Prevent Child Abuse.

Wietz, L. J., Bynum, T. W., Thomas, J. A., & Steger, J. A. (1973). Piaget's system of 16 binary operations: An empirical investigation. *Journal of Genetic Psychology, 123,* 279–284.

Wigfield, A. (1993). Why should I learn this? In M. L. Maehr & P. R. Pintrich (Eds.), *Advances in motivation and achievement* (Vol. 8, pp. 99–138). Greenwich, CT: JAI Press.

Wigfield, A., & Eccles, J. S. (1989). Test anxiety in elementary and secondary school students. *Educational Psychologist, 24,* 159–183.

Wigfield, A., Eccles, J. S., & Pintrich, P. R. (1996). Development between the ages of 11 and 25. In D. C. Berliner & R. C. Calfee (Eds.), *Handbook of educational psychology* (pp. 148–185). New York: MacMillan.

Wikander, B., & Helleday, A. (1996). The excessively crying infant: The mother-infant relationship. *Early Child Development and Care, 124,* 11–23.

Wilcox, M. J., Hadley, P. A., & Ashland, J. E. (1996). Communication and language development in infants and toddlers. In M. J. Hanson (Ed.), *Atypical infant development* (pp. 365–402). Austin, TX: Pro-Ed.

Wilcox, M. J., & Terrell, B. Y. (1985). Child language behavior: The acquisition of social communicative competence. In C. S. McLoughlin & D. F. Gullo (Eds.), *Young children in context* (pp. 40–65). Springfield, IL: Charles Thomas.

Willett, J. B., Singer, J. D., & Martin, N. C. (1998). The design and analysis of longitudinal studies of development and psychopathology in context. *Development and Psychopathology, 10,* 395–426.

Williams, S., & McGee, R. (1991). Adolescent self-perceptions of their strengths. *Journal of Youth and Adolescence, 20,* 325–337.

Williams, T. M. (1986). *The impact of television: A natural experiment in three communities.* New York: Academic Press.

Williamson, L. (1998). Eating disorders and the cultural forces behind the drive for thinness. *Social Work in Health Care, 28,* 61–73.

Willig, A. (1985). A meta-analysis of selected studies on the effectiveness of bilingual education. *Review of Educational Research, 55,* 269–317.

Wills, C. (1998, January). A sheep in sheep's clothing? *Discover,* 22–23.

Wilson, B. J., & Smith, S. L. (1998). Children's responses to emotional portrayals on television. In P. A. Andersen & L. K. Guerrero (Eds.), *Handbook of communication and emotion* (pp. 533–569). San Diego, CA: Academic Press.

Wilson, C., & Keye, W. (1989). A survey of adolescent dysmenorrhea and premenstrual symptom frequency. *Journal of Adolescent Health Care, 10,* 317–322.

Wilson, E. O. (1978). *On human nature.* Cambridge, MA: Harvard University Press.

Wilson, G. S. (1989). Clinical studies of infants and children exposed prenatally to heroin. *Annals of the New York Academy of Sciences, 562,* 183–194.

Windass, A. (1989). Classroom practices and organization. In C. Skelton (Ed.), *Whatever happens to little women?* (pp. 38–49). Milton Keynes, England: Open University Press.

Winsler, A., Diaz, R. M., & Montero, I. (1997). The role of private speech in the transition from collaborative to independent task performance in young children. *Early Childhood Research Quarterly, 12,* 59–79.

Winter, S. M. (1995). Diversity: A program for all children. *Childhood Education, 22,* 91–95.

Wisniewski, L., & Marcus, M. D. (1998). Childhood obesity. In V. B. Van Hasselt & M. Hersen (Eds.), *Handbook of psychological treatment protocols for children and adolescents* (pp. 179–201). Mahwah, NJ: Erlbaum.

Witkin, G. (1991, April 8). Kids who kill. *U.S. News and World Report.*

Witkin, G. (1996, March 25). Colorado has a new brand of tough love. *U.S. News and World Report,* 38–39.

Wolf, A. E. (1996, October). Tantrums. *Child,* 42–46.

Wolf, D. P. (1990). Being of several minds: Voices and versions of the self in early childhood. In D. Cicchetti & M. Beeghly (Eds.), *The self in transition* (pp. 183–212). Chicago: University of Chicago Press.

Wolf, F. M. (1986). *Meta-analysis.* Newbury Park, CA: Sage.

Wolfe, D. A. (1993). Prevention of child neglect: Emerging issues. *Criminal Justice and Behavior, 20,* 90–111.

Wolfe, D. A., Edwards, B., Manion, I., & Koverola, C. (1988). Early intervention for child abuse and neglect: A preliminary investigation. *Journal of Consulting and Clinical Psychology, 56,* 40–47.

Wolfe, L. A., Hall, P., Webb, K. A., Goodman, L., Monga, M., & McGrath, M. J. (1989). Prescription of aerobic exercise during pregnancy. *Sports Medicine, 8,* 273–301.

Wolff, P. H. (1963). Observations on the early development of smiling. In B. Foss (Ed.), *Determinants of infant behavior* (Vol. 2, pp. 113–138). London: Methuen.

Wolff, P. H. (1969). The natural history of crying and other vocalizations in early infancy. In B. M. Foss (Ed.), *Determinants of infant behavior* (Vol. 4, pp. 97–112). London: Methuen.

Wolfner, G. D., & Gelles, R. J. (1993). A profile of violence toward children: A national study. *Child Abuse & Neglect, 17,* 197–212.

Wolfson, A. R., & Carskadon, M. A. (1996). Early school start times affect sleep and daytime functioning in adolescents. *Sleep Research, 25,* 117.

Wolfson, A. R., & Carskadon, M. A. (1998). Sleep schedules and daytime functioning in adolescents. *Child Development, 69,* 875–887.

Wolfson, A. R., Tzischinsky, O., Brown, C., Darley, C., Acebo, C., & Carskadon, M. A. (1995). Sleep, behavior, and stress at the transition to senior high school. *Sleep Research, 24,* 5–20.

Wolke, D. (1993). The treatment of problem crying behavior. In I. St. James-Roberts, G. Harris, & D. Messer (Eds.), *Infant crying, feeding, and sleeping* (pp. 47–80). New York: Harvester Wheatsheaf.

Women's Sports Foundation. (1998). *Sport and teen pregnancy.* New York: Women's Sports Foundation.

Wong, D. L., & Perry, S. E. (1998). *Maternal child nursing care.* St. Louis, MO: Mosby.

Woods, E. G. (1995). Effective schooling practices and at-risk youth: What the research shows. *School Improvement Research Series, 17,* 1–21.

Woods, N. S., Eyler, F. D., Behnke, M., & Conlon, M. (1993). Cocaine use during pregnancy: Maternal depressive symptoms and infant neurobehavior over the first month. *Infant Behavior and Development,* 16, 83–98.

Woodward, A. L., & Markman, E. M. (1998). Early word learning. In W. Damon (Ed.), *Handbook of child psychology* (Vol. 2, pp. 371–420). New York: Wiley.

Woodworth, S., Belsky, J., & Crnic, K. (1996). The determinants of fathering during the child's second and third years of life: A developmental analysis. *Journal of Marriage and the Family,* 58, 679–692.

Woolley, J. D., & Wellman, H. M. (1990). Young children's understanding of realities, nonrealities, and appearances. *Child Development,* 61, 946–961.

Wright, S. C., & Taylor, D. M. (1995). Identity and the language of the classroom. *Journal of Educational Psychology,* 87, 241–252.

Wynn, K. (1992). Addition and subtraction by human infants. *Nature,* 358, 749–750.

Wynne, E. A. (1997). For character education. In A. Molnar (Ed.), *The construction of children's character* (pp. 63–76). Chicago: The National Society for the Study of Education.

Wyshak, G. (1983). Secular changes in age at menarche in a sample of U.S. women. *Annals of Human Biology,* 10, 75–78.

Wysocki, T., & Green, P. (1997). Self-management of childhood diabetes in family context. In D. S. Gochman (Ed.), *Handbook of health behavior research II: Provider determinants* (pp. 169–187). New York: Plenum.

Yagel, S., Anteby, E., Hochner-Celnikier, D., Ariel, I., Chaap, T., & Ben-Neriah, Z. (1998). The role of midtrimester target fetal organ screening combined with the "triple test" and maternal age in the diagnosis of trisomy 21. *American Journal of Obstetrics and Gynecology,* 178, 40–44.

Yamamoto, K., Soliman, A., Parsons, J., & Davies, O. L., Jr. (1987). Voices in unison: Stressful events in the lives of children in six countries. *Journal of Child Psychology and Psychiatry,* 28, 855–864.

Yankelovich, S., & White, C. (1989). *The role of Sesame Street among children in poverty.* New York: Children's Television Workshop.

Yee, D. K., & Eccles, J. S. (1988). Parents' perceptions and attributions for children's math achievement. *Sex Roles,* 19, 317–333.

Yetman, N. R. (1991). *Majority and minority.* Boston: Allyn & Bacon.

Yi, S. H., & Lee, S. E. (1997). Video game experiences and children's abilities of self-control and visual information processing. *Journal of Child Studies,* 18, 105–120.

Yin, R. K. (1994). Discovering the future of the case study method in evaluation research. *Evaluation Practice,* 15, 283–290.

YMCA Division of Aquatics. (1984). *YMCA Guidelines for Infant Swimming.* Chicago: YMCA of the USA.

Young, J. (1996). *Developmental care of the premature baby.* Philadelphia: Balliere Tindall.

Youniss, J. (1980). *Parents and peers in social development.* Chicago: University of Chicago Press.

Youniss, J., McLellen, J. A., & Strouse, D. (1994). "We're popular, but we're not snobs": Adolescents describe their crowds. In R. Montemayor, G. R. Adams, & T. P. Gullotta (Eds.), *Personal relationships during adolescence* (pp. 101–122). Thousand Oaks, CA: Sage.

Yuille, N. (1997). Children's understanding of traits. In S. Hala (Ed.), *The development of social cognition* (pp. 273–296). East Sussex, England: Psychology Press.

Yung, B. R., & Hammond, W. R. (1994). Native Americans. In L. D. Eron, J. H. Gentry, & P. Schlegel (Eds.), *Reason to hope: A psychosocial perspective on violence and youth* (pp. 133–144). Washington, DC: American Psychological Association.

Yung, B. R., & Hammond, W. R. (1997). Antisocial behavior in minority groups. In D. M. Stoff & J. Breiling (Eds.), *Handbook of antisocial behavior* (pp. 474–495). New York: Wiley.

Zabin, L. S., & Hayward, S. C. (1993). *Adolescent sexual behavior and childbearing.* Newbury Park, CA: Sage.

Zahn-Waxler, C., Radke-Yarrow, M., Wagner, E., & Chapman, M. (1992). The development of concern for others. *Developmental Psychology,* 28, 1038–1047.

Zaiwalla, Z., & Stein, A. (1993). The physiology of sleep in infants and young children. In I. St. James-Roberts, G. Harris, & D. Messer (Eds.), *Infant crying, feeding and sleeping: Development, problems, and treatment,* pp. 135–149. New York: Harvester Wheatsheaf.

Zebrowitz, L., Kendall-Tackett, K., & Fafel, J. (1991). The impact of children's facial maturity on parental expectations and punishments. *Journal of Experimental Child Psychology,* 52, 221–238.

Zebrowitz, L., & Montepare, J. M. (1992). Impressions of babyfaced individuals across the lifespan. *Developmental Psychology,* 28, 1143–1152.

Zeifman, D., Delany, S., & Blass, E. M. (1996). Sweet taste, looking, and calm in 2- and 4-week-old infants: The eyes have it. *Developmental Psychology,* 32, 1090–1099.

Zelasko, C. J., Van Huss, W. D., Evans, S. A., Wells, R. L., & Anderson, D. J. (1988). Body composition of young runners and young wrestlers. In E. W. Brown & C. F. Branta (Eds.), *Competitive sports for children and youth: An overview of research and issues* (pp. 17–25). Champaign, IL: Human Kinetics Books.

Zeskind, P. S. (1985). A developmental perspective on infant crying. In B. M. Lester & C. F. Z. Boukydis (Eds.), *Infant crying* (pp. 158–186). New York: Plenum.

Zhou, M. (1997). Growing up American: The challenge confronting immigrant children and children of immigrants. *Annual Review of Sociology,* 23, 63–95.

Zigler, E., & Gilman, E. (1998). *The legacy of Jean Piaget.* Mahwah, NJ: Erlbaum.

Zigler, E., & Styfco, S. J. (1998). Applying the findings of developmental psychology to improve early childhood intervention. In S. G. Paris & H. M. Wellman (Eds.), *Global prospects for education* (pp. 345–365). Washington, DC: American Psychological Association.

Zillmann, D. (1982). Television viewing and arousal. In D. Pearl, L. Bouthilet, & J. Lazar (Eds.), *Television and behavior* (Vol. 2, pp. 53–67). Washington, DC: U.S. Government Printing Office.

Zillmann, D., & Gan, S. L. (1997). Musical taste in adolescence. In D. J. Hargreaves (Ed.), *The social psychology of music* (pp. 161–187). New York: Oxford University Press.

Zimmerman, B. F. (1998). Classroom disruption: Educational theory as applied to perception and action in regular and special education. In A. Rotatori & J. Schwenn (Eds.), *Advances in special education* (Vol. 11, pp. 77–98). Greenwich, CT: Jai Press.

Zimmerman, M. A., Copeland, L. A., Shope, J. T., & Dielman, T. E. (1997). A longitudinal study of self esteem: Implications for adolescent development. *Journal of Youth and Adolescence,* 26, 117–141.

Glossary

acceleration programs educational programs that encourage children to move rapidly through the usual coursework, compressing the time usually spent in each course

accommodation changing a scheme to fit new information from the environment

acculturative stress stress associated with making a transition from one culture to another

actual self how adolescents see themselves

adolescence the developmental period between childhood and adulthood

adolescent egocentrism an adolescent's belief that his or her thoughts and ideas are unique and are not understood by others

age of viability the point at which postnatal survival is likely

ambivalent attachment pattern characterized by inconsistent behavior toward a caregiver

amniocentesis a procedure used to determine whether genetic defects are present, in which amniotic fluid is collected

amnion a membrane that grows over the embryo and becomes filled with amniotic fluid, which protects the embryo

animism attributing lifelike qualities to objects that are not alive

anorexia nervosa an eating disorder, occurring most often in young women, in which individuals eat very little but believe that they are overweight

A-not-B error infants' tendency to search in the first hiding spot (A) while ignoring the second (B)

antisocial behavior a pattern of behavior that is aggressive, defiant, uncooperative, irresponsible, and/or dishonest

Apgar Scale a method of diagnosing potential problems in full-term and preterm newborns, in which five vital signs are examined: respiration, reflex responsiveness, muscle tone, color, and heart rate

assimilated identifying with the majority culture and rejecting one's ethnic culture

assimilation directly processing information that fits a scheme

associational fluency ability to produce synonyms for a given word

associative play play in which various children engage, but with different goals

attachment an enduring emotional tie characterized by a tendency to seek and maintain closeness to a specific figure (the attachment figure), particularly under conditions of stress

attachment theory explanation of development that focuses on the quality of the early emotional relationships developed between children and their caregivers

attention-deficit hyperactivity disorder (ADHD) a disorder marked by an inappropriately low level of attention and inappropriately high levels of impulsivity and activity

authoritarian parenting a style of parenting in which parents try to shape, control, and judge the behaviors and attitudes of their children according to rigid standards of conduct

authoritative parenting a style of parenting in which parents encourage verbal give-and-take and share with their children the reasons behind discipline and household rules

autonomous morality stage Piagetian stage of moral development in which one believes that rules can be changed by the will of those involved

autonomy the ability to govern oneself and make independent decisions

autosomes the first twenty-two pairs of chromosomes, which account for most of the body cells

avoidant attachment pattern characterized by conspicuous avoidance of contact or interaction with the caregiver

axon long part of a neuron that is located at the cell base and sends messages to other neurons

babbling repeating consonant-vowel combinations two or more times

balanced polymorphism a kind of genetic diversity in which the genes that cause diseases provide certain genetic advantages as well as disadvantages

behavioral autonomy the capacity to make and follow through with decisions on regulating one's behavior

bicultural identifying with both the majority and the minority culture

blended family family structure formed when a widowed or divorced person remarries

Braxton-Hicks contractions mild, irregular contractions of the uterus experienced throughout pregnancy, especially during the last month or two

breech presentation fetal position in which the buttocks or feet lead the way

bulimia nervosa an eating disorder characterized by secret eating binges and purges

caesarean section procedure by which the fetus is delivered through an incision in the mother's abdomen

carriers people who are heterozygous for a recessive disorder

case study method in which the researcher collects information about aspects of a person's life

centration the tendency to focus attention on the most obvious and striking characteristic of an object while ignoring others

cephalocaudal development the principle that growth occurs from the head downwards

character education curriculum and instruction focused on students' conduct and models of traditional values and behaviors

child development changes in physical, social, emotional, and intellectual functioning over time, from conception through adolescence

child-directed speech a special version of language that caregivers use with their children; also called motherese

chorion a membrane that grows to surround the embryo after about one month of development and helps form the placenta

chorionic villus sampling (CVS) a procedure used to assess genetic material in fetal cells in which cells are removed from the projections on the chorionic membrane

chromosomes the structures on which genes reside

classical conditioning Pavlov's theory of how responses to neutral stimuli become conditioned

class inclusion part-whole relations of categories

clinical interview method in which the researcher asks detailed questions while interacting with the participant

cliques small groups of peers, usually of the same sex and age, who interact with one another on a regular basis

cognitive development involves development of mental processes used to process information, become aware, solve problems, and gain knowledge

cohort a group of individuals who are the same age or who experience similar events at the same time

cohort-sequential research design a cross-sectional study expanded so that data are collected from the same cohorts at different points in time

colostrum a pre-milk substance containing antibodies from the mother that protect the baby from infections

commitment the making of voluntary choices about life directions from among the many available options

compensation the understanding that one change can offset another

compliance obedience brought about by external pressures (such as the knowledge that one will be rewarded or punished for actions)

concrete operational stage Piaget's third stage of cognitive development (7 to 11 years), in which children begin to use logic to solve problems

conservation tasks tasks used to assess children's use of operations, in which children must decide whether a transformed object is the same as or different from what it was before

constructivist theories of learning educational approach in which students are encouraged to actively participate in their education

control group comparison group that is treated in the same way as the experimental group but does not receive the independent variable

control parameters the individual parts of a dynamic system

Conventional Level second level of Kohlberg's theory of moral development, in which moral reasoning is based on winning praise and recognition for good conduct and maintaining the social order

cooing making soft, repetitive vowel sounds such as "aah" and "ooh"

cooperative learning educational approach in which students work together in groups to solve problems

cooperative play play in which two or more children engage, with a common goal that requires social interaction

correlational study method in which researchers compare participants on two variables to determine whether the variables relate to each other

correlation coefficients calculated measures of the relations between variables

creativity novel and appropriate behavior that is different from what the person has done or seen before

crisis/exploration the process of making choices about life directions by considering options, values, and goals

critical periods periods during which specific biological or environmental events must occur if development is to proceed normally

cross-sectional study method in which individuals of different ages are tested at the same point in time and the results from each age group are compared

crowds peer groups defined by members' activities and social standing

crowning when the top of the baby's head becomes visible during childbirth

cruise in infant development, to move around while holding onto things for support

deferred imitation imitation of behaviors that occurred in the past

delinquency the legal term for antisocial acts committed by juveniles

demandingness the tendency of parents to exert firm control over children, requiring them to act in mature and appropriate ways

dendrites parts of a neuron that are located on the cell body and receive messages from other neurons

dependent variable the behavior thought to be affected by the independent variable

developmental domains the three categories established to provide a basis for focusing on the specific areas of physical, cognitive, and social-emotional development

discipline attempts by parents to alter children's behaviors or attitudes

discovery learning educational approach in which students are encouraged to discover principles for themselves

discrimination acting in an unfavorable manner toward people because of their affiliation with a group

dishabituation an increase in attention to a new stimulus after an infant has habituated to a previous stimulus

disorganized/disoriented attachment pattern characterized by lack of a coherent strategy for handling separations from and reunions with the caregiver

dizygotic (DZ) twins twins who develop from two separate eggs fertilized by two separate sperm cells; fraternal twins

dominant gene a gene whose code is expressed when only one copy of the gene is present

double standard the imposition of different social expectations for males' and females' sexual attitudes and behavior

dynamic systems theory a theory based on the idea that complex systems form from basic and simple conditions without requiring a master plan for development

dysmenorrhea menstrual cramps and discomfort

eating disturbances mild versions of eating disorders

ecological model Bronfenbrenner's model of the different spheres of influence on development

ectopic pregnancy a pregnancy that occurs outside the uterus

ego the part of the psyche that is the source of reason and operates within the conditions and demands of the real world

egocentric speech Piaget's term for speech directed toward the self

egocentrism the assumption, characteristic of most preschoolers, that their own perspective is shared by other people

elaboration memory strategy involving the forming of associations among objects

embryonic stage the second stage of prenatal development, which begins at implantation and lasts until about eight weeks

emergent literacy educational approach in which it is assumed that children will naturally develop the skills involved in written and oral language and gradually improve these skills as they grow older

emotional autonomy the ability to understand oneself as a person who is emotionally distinct from one's parents

emotion-focused coping strategies efforts to manage or reduce the emotional distress that is aroused in a stressful situation

empathy an emotional state that matches another person's emotional state—for instance, feeling bad because someone else is feeling bad

endogenous smile smile that is triggered by changes in nervous system activity and involves only the lower face muscles

enrichment programs educational programs that encourage problem solving and creative activities through independent study or individualized instruction and mentoring

epidural block a common method for controlling the pain of labor, in which a local anesthetic is delivered to block pain in the region from the waist to the feet

episiotomy a small incision made in the skin below the vagina to prevent tearing of the vaginal tissues as the baby emerges

ethnic identity the sense of belonging to an ethnic group

ethnicity a group whose members share a common cultural heritage and a sense of belonging

ethological theory explanation of development that focuses on the causes and adaptive value of behavior, considering both the evolutionary history of the species and the social context

evolutionary theories explanations of development that focus on how behaviors promote the survival of the individual and the species

exogenous smile smile that is triggered by external stimuli

exosystem the part of the ecological model that represents the linkages among settings, one of which does not include the child, and how these influence development

expansion taking young children's simplified language and adding complexity and completeness to it

experimental group group that receives the independent variable

experimental study method in which scientists bring people into a laboratory where the situation is manipulated and the effects of the manipulation are noted

expressive language children's ability to produce language

expressive language style language style focused on using words to regulate social interactions with adults

extended family family structure consisting of one or more parents, one or more of the parents' children, and one or more other relatives living together in one household

externalizing problems psychological difficulties that involve acting out against society

extinction reducing unwanted behavior by withholding all positive consequences

fact a statement, based on observation, with which many people would agree

failure to thrive (FTT) a term used to describe infants and children who do not grow at the expected rates

false labor moderately intense, rhythmic contractions late in the pregnancy

fast mapping associating the sound of a word with the concept the word stands for, sometimes in a single exposure

fetal alcohol effects (FAE) the effects, including mildly retarded physical development and learning disabilities, that may occur if a mother drinks moderately during pregnancy

fetal alcohol syndrome (FAS) a constellation of problems, including physical deformities and intellectual deficits, that may occur if a mother drinks heavily during pregnancy

fetal stage the third and final stage of prenatal development, which begins at about eight weeks and lasts until birth

foreclosure identity status of those adolescents who have not explored alternatives but nonetheless have made a definite commitment to a specific identity

formal operational stage Piaget's fourth stage of cognitive development (begins around the age of 11), in which individuals are capable of applying logical principles to hypothetical and abstract situations

fragile X syndrome a condition passed on by sex-linked transmission and characterized by protruding ears, prominent jaw, unusual speech, poor eye contact, and mild to moderate retardation

functional isolation the increased disengagement from one's social and physical environments that may result from a poor environment and inadequate nutrition

gender consistency understanding that gender does not change despite changes in appearance or activities

gender identity understanding and acceptance that one is a boy or a girl

gender labeling labeling oneself and others on the basis of gender group

gender schemas mental representations about the sexes

gender stability understanding that gender is stable over time

gender stereotypes beliefs people share about the typical characteristics of males and females

generation gap a conflict of basic interests, beliefs, and values between youth and their parents

generative learning educational approach in which students are taught how to use specific methods of problem solving to integrate new information with pre-existing information

genes the structures containing the code that provides the blueprint for development

genotype a person's genetic code

germinal stage the first stage of prenatal development, which begins at conception and lasts until the fertilized egg implants itself in the uterine wall

goal-corrected partnership an attachment relationship in which the child becomes a partner in planning how the relationship develops

gonadotropins chemical messengers that stimulate the production of hormones by the glands

habituation a decrease in attention to a stimulus that has been presented repeatedly

heritability an estimate of the degree to which variation of a characteristic in a population is influenced by genetic factors

heteronomous morality stage Piagetian stage of moral development in which children adhere strictly to rules and base moral decisions on the authority of others

heterosexual having a sexual attraction to members of the other sex

heterozygous describes a child's condition with respect to a trait when each parent has contributed a different copy of the gene for that trait to their child

heuristic a shortcut or rule of thumb used to help solve a problem

holophrases individual words that convey as much meaning as whole sentences

homosexual having a sexual attraction to members of the same sex

homozygous describes a child's condition with respect to a trait when both parents have contributed identical copies of the gene for that trait to their child

hostile aggression aggression directed against another person, generally in retaliation for his or her actions

hypothetico-deductive reasoning the type of reasoning used in science

id the part of the psyche that is primitive and instinctual

identity one's sense of who one is, where one has been, and where one is going in life

identity achieved identity status of those adolescents who have experienced a period of exploration, crisis, and commitment

identity concept the essential "sameness" of an object despite physical changes to it

identity confused identity status of those adolescents who have not explored or committed themselves to a specific identity choice

identity diffusion an incomplete sense of self

image schemas primitive notions, based on the visual appearance of objects, that lay a foundation for thinking about them

imaginary audience a characteristic of adolescents' self consciousness, involving the feeling that they are on stage with people watching their every move

immanent justice the belief that breaking a rule always leads to punishment

independent variable the condition that is assumed to be the cause of the behavior and is manipulated by the scientist

inductive reasoning disciplinary techniques in which parents use reasoning and verbal communication for the purpose of changing children's behavior

infantile amnesia inability to recall events that occurred very early in life

information processing theory explanations for development that are based on a model in which people have limited capacities for learning but can flexibly apply strategies to find ways around those limitations

innate fears fears that are inborn and reflexive

instrumental aggression aggression used for a specific purpose

internalization obedience based on internal controls and standards that children have incorporated into their own expectations of themselves

internalizing problems psychological difficulties, such as anxiety or depression, that involve a focus on or within the self

Internet a global network of computers

iron-deficiency anemia a nutrient deficiency common in infants and toddlers

just community schools schools in which students participate in a democratic community and decisions are made through consensus rather than by majority rule

juvenile an individual who is not yet an adult in the eyes of the law

karyotype a photograph of chromosomes, used by geneticists to align each chromosome with the other member of its pair

language acquisition device (LAD) in Chomsky's biological theory, a part of the brain that allows children to understand the properties of all human languages

latchkey children children who are left unsupervised during the day or return home to an empty house after school

learning changes that occur as the result of observation, experience, instruction, or practice

libido the source of action and sexual desire

lightening when the fetus drops into the pelvic cavity, decreasing pressure on the mother's diaphragm

longitudinal study method in which the same group of individuals is tested at different points in time

long-term memory the part of the information processing system that has an unlimited capacity for storing information over long periods of time

love withdrawal disciplinary techniques in which parents ignore, withhold affection from, or express lack of love for the child

low birthweight term describing infants born after 37 weeks' gestation but weighing less than 5 pounds

macrosystem the outermost sphere of the ecological model, which represents societal values and attitudes

mainstreaming including children with all sorts of disabilities in regular classrooms

manipulative tantrums tantrums children throw to manipulate others into giving them what they want

marginal living within the majority culture but feeling alienated or outcast

maturation changes brought about largely as a result of the unfolding of one's genetic code

meiosis the process of cell replication undergone by ova and sperm, involving one duplication of chromosomes and two cell divisions, resulting in twenty-three chromosomes

menarche the onset of the menstrual cycle

mental retardation condition characterized by subaverage general intellectual functioning and impaired adaptive functioning, with onset in childhood

mental rotation the ability to imagine how objects would appear if their positions were rotated

mesosystem the middle sphere of the ecological model, which encompasses the connections among settings including the child, and how these connections influence the child

metacognition awareness of memory and monitoring of memory performance

microsystem the inner sphere of the ecological model, which represents the immediate environment and includes influences such as physical objects, the structure of the environment, and the roles and relationships among family members

minimal distance principle (MDP) the assumption that the noun most closely preceding the verb is the subject of the sentence

mitosis the process of cell replication involving one duplication of chromosomes and one cell division, resulting in twenty-three pairs of chromosomes (forty-six total)

molding when the bones of the baby's skull, which are not yet fused, press together and even overlap to accommodate passage through the birth canal

monozygotic (MZ) twins twins who share the same genetic code because they developed from one fertilized egg, which divided into two separate individuals; identical twins

moral domain issues that concern universal principles reflecting concepts of harm, welfare, and fairness

morality a set of principles or values that helps individuals distinguish right from wrong

moral realism the belief that morality is based on conforming to established rules set by powerful adults

moratorium identity status of those adolescents who are actively exploring identity issues but have not yet made any firm commitments

multicultural education educational practices and curricula that present non-European perspectives or improve educational outcomes for students from a wide spectrum of backgrounds

multiparous women women who have previously given birth

multiracial a term used to describe people who are of two or more races

myelination the process in which a neuron is sheathed in a smooth layer of fatty proteins (myelin)

naturalistic study method in which researchers observe the behavior of people in their natural environments

natural selection the process in nature, whereby individuals who are best adapted to their surroundings survive and reproduce, and the adaptive characteristics of those individuals are passed on to the next generation

nature versus nurture debate controversy over the extent to which biological/genetic and environmental factors influence development

negative reinforcement removal of a negative or aversive stimulus that increases the likelihood that a behavior will recur

neglect failure to provide shelter, clothing, or protection for a child

neglected children children who are reasonably well liked by their peers but lack friends

Neonatal Behavioral Assessment Scale a measure commonly used to assess a newborn's responses to the environment

neonate an infant who is in the first one to two months of life

neurodevelopmental approaches explanations of development that focus on the relationship of brain development to behavior and thinking

neurons the nerve cells that make up the communication system of the brain

nuclear family family structure in which the biological mother and father and their children live together

obese weighing more than 20 percent over one's ideal weight (based on height, sex, and body composition)

object permanence the concept that people and objects have an independent existence beyond one's own perception of them

onlooker play play in which one child watches another child or children but does not directly participate

operant conditioning learning based on the principle that the consequences of a behavior affect the likelihood that the behavior will be repeated

operations actions internalized as symbols that can be reversed and coordinated

organization memory strategy involving the clustering of information into groups of similar objects or into meaningful categories

overextension the use of words to refer to objects or things that are outside the bounds of the category named by the word

overregularization application of language rules when they do not apply

ovum a human egg

parallel play　play in which two or more children engage in the same activity at the same time and place, but each child still plays separately

parity　the number and spacing of children a woman bears

permissive parenting　a style of parenting in which parents make few demands on their children—they are accepting and tolerant of their children's impulses and desires

personal domain　issues that reflect personal preference and taste and are not socially regulated

personal fable　a story adolescents tell themselves that emphasizes their uniqueness and invulnerability

personality　a person's unique behavioral, motivational, and mental styles of responding

phenotype　the outward expression of the genotype

phobias　persistent and irrational fears that significantly affect social functioning

phonemes　the sounds of a language that are the basis for word construction

phonemic awareness　knowledge of permissible and nonpermissible strings of sounds in one's native language

phonics approach　technique used to teach children to read, in which children are trained to translate letters and groups of letters into sounds

physical abuse　abuse that causes death, serious physical harm, or imminent risk of serious harm

physical development　involves growth and change in a person's body and bodily functions

physical fitness　a state of physical well-being that allows a person to function effectively without undue fatigue

placenta　the structure through which nutrients and waste products are exchanged between the mother and the developing embryo

placental barrier　a line of protection for the unborn child, created by blood vessel walls that separate the maternal and fetal circulatory systems

positive reinforcement　presentation of stimuli that increase the likelihood that a behavior will recur

possible self　how adolescents wish themselves to be in the future

Postconventional Level　third level of Kohlberg's theory of moral development, in which judgments about morality are based on principles that the individual is personally committed to and that are shared by others

postpartum depression　intense feelings of sadness, anxiety, or despair experienced by a mother after the birth of a child

power assertion　disciplinary techniques in which parents use physical force or threats of physical force to control children's behavior

pragmatics　the practical rules guiding the use of verbal and nonverbal communication in differing situations

precocious puberty　extremely early puberty, often caused by a genetic disorder

Preconventional Level　first level of Kohlberg's theory of moral development, in which morality is based on external forces

prejudice　preconceived ideas about a person or group of people, often based on physical characteristics, ethnicity, or race

premenstrual syndrome (PMS)　a whole constellation of emotional and physical symptoms, such as backaches, headaches, moodiness, and water retention, that occur before menstruation

premoral period　Piagetian stage of moral development in which young children do not yet understand cooperative rules and goals

preoperational stage　Piaget's second stage of cognitive development (2 to 7 years), in which children begin to think in symbols but are egocentric and perceptually bound in their thinking

pretend play　play in which children let objects or persons symbolize things or people they are not

preterm or **premature**　term describing infants born prior to 37 weeks' gestation

primary circular reactions　repetitive actions that are centered on an infant's own body and motions

primary prevention　efforts targeted at the population as a whole, to sensitize people to basic issues or to provide particular skills

primary sexual characteristics　physical features directly related to reproduction, such as the ovaries, penis, and testes

primiparous women　women who are having their first child

private speech　Vygotsky's term for speech directed toward the self, used when solving problems

problem-focused coping strategies　efforts to manage or modify the source of a stressful situation

prodigies　children who show exceptional abilities at a very young age in one domain of intelligence but not necessarily in others

prosocial behavior　voluntary actions intended to benefit another person

proximodistal development　the principle that body parts closer to the central axis of the body develop first, while those farther away from the center of the body develop later

psychoanalytic theories　explanations of development that focus on the unconscious drives and forces that develop within the mind

psychological maltreatment　emotional abuse caused by threatening harm or conveying to an individual that she or he is worthless, unloved, or unwanted

psychosexual development　Freud's stage theory of development, based on how the libido is transformed into different structures and modes of expression

psychosocial crises　In Erikson's lifespan theory, the struggles that occur at the various stages of development between two conflicting personality characteristics

psychosocial moratorium　a period during which youths are reasonably free of adult responsibilities that might prevent them from adequately addressing identity issues

puberty　developmental milestone reached when a person becomes sexually mature and capable of having children

pubescence　the period of time during which sexual maturation takes place

punishment　application of unpleasant consequences to decrease the likelihood that a behavior will be repeated

quickening fetal movements during pregnancy

race a group whose members share a genetic heritage

random assignment randomly assigning people to groups in a study so that the effects of uncontrolled variables will be the same for all groups in the study

random sampling selecting participants for a study at random

rate-limiting component the slowest, or last-developing, part of a dynamic system

receptive language children's understanding of language

recessive gene a gene whose code is not expressed in the presence of a dominant gene

referential language style language style focused on developing a vocabulary that includes many object names

reflective abstraction the ability to rearrange and rethink information already acquired

reflexes simple, coordinated, unlearned responses

rehearsal memory strategy involving the reviewing of information

rejected children children who are overtly disliked by their peers

relational aggression aggression designed to damage someone's relationships with others, by withdrawing friendship, excluding someone from a group, and so on

resilience the capacity to bounce back or recover from stressful situations

responsiveness the tendency of parents to be warm, accepting, and willing to take into account the wishes and feelings of the child

reversible thinking the understanding that actions can be undone or reversed

risk-taking behavior a syndrome of multiple behavior problems

rites of passage initiations that mark an adolescent's new status and roles within the community

savants people who show exceptional abilities in one domain of intelligence but have retarded mental development in some other domains

scaffolding informal teaching methods that guide children's participation in daily events

schematic consistency the tendency of children's behavior and thinking to match their schemas

scheme a cognitive guide or blueprint for processing information about the world

school phobia an extreme fear associated with school environments

scripts concepts that people form about routines involved in everyday interactions and events

secondary circular reactions repetitive actions focused on the qualities of objects, such as the noises they make or their shapes and colors

secondary prevention efforts targeted at a specific segment of the population thought to be at high risk

secondary sexual characteristics features that are outward manifestations of sexual development but are not directly involved in reproduction, such as breasts, facial and body hair, and an adult body shape

secure attachment pattern in which infants use their attachment figures as a secure base, obtaining comfort from their presence and becoming distressed by their absence

self-concept an individual's beliefs about the attributes and capacities she or he possesses

self-conscious emotions those emotions that involve injury to or enhancement of one's sense of self (such as pride and shame)

self-esteem the value an individual attaches to the mental picture of himself or herself

semantics the meanings associated with words

sensitive periods periods of time that are optimal for the development of certain behaviors or functions.

sensorimotor stage Piaget's first stage of cognitive development (0 to 2 years), in which the child relates to objects and people through his or her senses and motor skills

sensory register the part of the information processing system that allows people to very briefly retain information taken in through the senses

separated identifying only with one's own ethnic culture and rejecting the majority culture

separation anxiety a response in which negative protests accompany separation from attachment figures

sex chromosomes the twenty-third pair of chromosomes, which accounts for a person's sex

sexual abuse abuse that involves engaging in sexual activity

sexually transmitted diseases (STDs) diseases that may be transmitted from one person to another through sexual contact

sexual orientation characteristic determined by the sex of the sexual partners one is attracted to

shaping the process of rewarding behaviors that approximate the desired behavior

short-term memory the part of the information processing system that holds information long enough for the person to evaluate and selectively act on the input

single-parent family family structure in which children live with only their mother or their father

social cognition thinking about people and interpersonal relationships

social communicative competence the ability to effectively convey an intended message to others

social competence the ability to use age-appropriate social behaviors to enhance peer relationships without harming anyone

social-conventional domain issues and actions that are defined as right or wrong because of a social agreement that they are so

social-emotional development involves development of processes related to one's interactions with others

socialization the process by which children learn social roles and become members of groups

social learning theory Bandura's theory that individuals are greatly influenced by observing and imitating other people

social perspective taking the ability to move away from one's own perspective and recognize what others perceive

social smile smile that is triggered by social stimuli (such as the mother's face)

solitary play play in which a child is alone, even if surrounded by other children

spatial perception the ability to locate the horizontal or vertical while ignoring distracting information

spatial visualization the ability to find figures and shapes hidden within other figures

spatial-visual skills the cognitive abilities involved in orienting oneself in the environment

spermatids the result of the division of spermatocytes, each one containing twenty-three chromosomes and including either an X or a Y sex chromosome

spermatocytes sperm in the early stage of development, at which time each one contains forty-six chromosomes, including one X and one Y sex chromosome

spermatogenesis the process by which sperm develop

spermatozoa mature spermatids, which are fully functional and capable of fertilizing a human ovum

state of arousal the degree to which an infant is alert, attentive, and awake

static thinking the tendency to attend more to the outcome than to the changes that produced the outcome

status offenses acts that are illegal for juveniles but not for adults, such as running away from home

stepfamily family structure formed when a person who has children from a former marriage remarries

stranger anxiety a wary and fearful reaction to strangers

Strange Situation a procedure used to assess infants' attachment behavior under conditions of increasing stress due to separations from caregivers and strangers

superego the part of the psyche that represents one's conscience and morals and social conventions

survey study method in which a number of people respond to a set of structured questions

symbolic representations mental representations of objects and people that can be manipulated in the mind

sympathy feeling sorry or concerned for other people because of their emotional states or conditions

synapses small gaps, or spaces, between the cells through which information is transmitted from one neuron to the next

syntax the grammar, or rules, of a language

teenager a youth between 13 and 19 years of age

telegraphic speech early language in which only highly informative words are used and less informative words are neglected

temperament the predisposition to respond in certain enduring and characteristic ways to one's environment

temperamental tantrums anger response when some aspect of a child's style of interacting has been violated

teratogens agents that cross the placental barrier and cause or increase the incidence of physical malformations and behavioral and cognitive deficits

tertiary circular reactions subtle modifications infants make in their behavior so as to explore the effects of those modifications

tertiary prevention efforts directed at preventing or decreasing the reoccurrence of an event that has already occurred

theory a structured set of ideas that attempts to organize and explain facts

theory of mind the understanding of inner mental events—that people think, imagine, pretend, and wonder about the world around them

transactional perspective the view that development occurs as the result of the interplay between the diversity of qualities individuals bring to their environments and the diversity of environments individuals experience

transductive reasoning the inference that if two particular examples or events occur together, they must be causally related

transverse presentation fetal position in which the shoulders and arms lead the way

ultrasound a procedure used to identify some developmental problems, in which video images of the fetus and the fetus's internal organs are produced from the echoes of sound waves

umbilical cord the lifeline of the embryo, consisting of two arteries and one vein

underextension the use of words to refer to a smaller group than the word actually names

uninvolved parenting a style of parenting in which parents make few demands on their children and are unresponsive or rejecting

values autonomy the capacity to make judgments and choices about personal beliefs and principles

vernix caseosa a white, waxy covering that provides the infant with protection from bacteria

vicarious reinforcement learning by watching the consequences to others of their behaviors

visual cliff apparatus a checkerboard pattern covered with Plexiglas, used to create an illusion of depth

whole language approach technique used to teach children to read, in which learning to read is assumed to be a natural process that occurs most effectively in a print-rich environment

youth a broad, nonspecific term for the younger generation—children, adolescents, and young adults

zone of proximal development Vygotsky's term for the difference between what a child can do unaided and what a child can do through interaction with skilled helpers

zygote the fertilized ovum

Author Index

Subject Index